D0108476

American
Jewish
Year Book

With this volume, the American Jewish Committee becomes the sole publisher of the AMERICAN JEWISH YEAR BOOK. The Committee acknowledges with appreciation the foresight and wisdom of the founders of the Jewish Publication Society (of America) in the creation of the YEAR BOOK in 1899, a work committed to providing a continuous record of developments in the U.S. and world Jewish communities. For over a century JPS has occupied a special place in American Jewish life, publishing and disseminating important, enduring works of scholarship and general interest on Jewish subjects.

The American Jewish Committee assumed responsibility for the compilation and editing of the YEAR BOOK in 1908. The Society served as its publisher until 1949; from 1950 through 1993, the Committee and the Society were co-publishers.

American

Jewish

Year Book 1994

VOLUME 94

Editor
DAVID SINGER
Executive Editor
RUTH R. SELDIN

THE AMERICAN JEWISH COMMITTEE
NEW YORK

Fairleigh Dickinson
University Library

Teaneck, New Jersey

E
184
.J5
A6
V. 94

COPYRIGHT © 1994 BY THE AMERICAN JEWISH COMMITTEE

All rights reserved. No part of this book may be reproduced in any form without permission in writing from the publisher, except by a reviewer who may quote brief passages in a review to be printed in a magazine or newspaper.

ISBN 0-87495-105-4

Library of Congress Catalogue Number: 99-4040

PRINTED IN THE UNITED STATES OF AMERICA
BY THE HADDON CRAFTSMEN, INC., SCRANTON, PA.

Preface

The timely subject of Jewish migration and resettlement is the focus of the special articles in this year's volume. In "Soviet Jews in the United States," Steven J. Gold summarizes the developments leading to the arrival during the past 20 years of over a quarter of a million Jews from the USSR—the largest wave of Jewish immigration to this country since the 1920s. He describes the resettlement process, provides a sociodemographic profile of the new arrivals, and examines various facets of their integration into general American society and the Jewish community. The story of a second recent and historic migration, that of the Jews of Ethiopia to Israel over the last decade, is recounted by Israeli-American scholars Steven Kaplan and Chaim Rosen. In "Ethiopian Jews in Israel" they offer a profile of the people, analyze the special problems entailed in their absorption into Israeli society, and evaluate their progress and prospects.

This volume also includes an update on the situation of Jews in various countries of the Middle East and North Africa, by George E. Gruen.

Regular articles on Jewish life in the United States are "Intergroup Relations," by Jerome A. Chanes; "The United States, Israel, and the Middle East," by Kenneth Jacobson; and "Jewish Communal Affairs," by Lawrence Grossman.

Menachem Shalev provides extensive coverage of the year's events in Israel. Reports on Jewish communities around the world this year include Canada, Great Britain, France, the Netherlands, Italy, Germany, Austria, the former Soviet Union, Eastern Europe, Australia, and South Africa.

Updated estimates of Jewish population are provided: for the United States, by Barry Kosmin and Jeffrey Scheckner, of the North American Jewish Data Bank; and for the world, by U.O. Schmelz and Sergio DellaPergola, of the Hebrew University of Jerusalem.

Carefully compiled directories of national Jewish organizations, periodicals, and federations and welfare funds, as well as religious calendars and obituaries, round out the 1994 AMERICAN JEWISH YEAR BOOK.

We gratefully acknowledge the assistance of Terry Smith and of colleagues at the American Jewish Committee, especially Cyma M. Horowitz and Michele Anish of the Blaustein Library.

THE EDITORS

Contributors

HENRIETTE BOAS: Dutch correspondent, Jewish Telegraphic Agency and Israeli newspapers; Amsterdam, Holland.

JEROME A. CHANES: co-director for domestic concerns, National Jewish Community Relations Advisory Council.

SERGIO DELLAPERGOLA: head, Division of Jewish Demography and Statistics, A. Harman Institute of Contemporary Jewry, Hebrew University of Jerusalem, Israel; visiting scholar, University of California, Los Angeles, and University of Judaism.

ALLIE A. DUBB: Mendel Kaplan Professor of Jewish Civilization and director, Kaplan Centre for Jewish Studies and Research, University of Cape Town, South Africa.

ZVI GITELMAN: professor, political science, and Tisch Professor of Judaic Studies, University of Michigan.

STEVEN J. GOLD: associate professor, sociology, Michigan State University; senior fellow, Wilstein Institute of Jewish Policy Studies.

MURRAY GORDON: author and consultant on Eastern and Central European politics; adjunct professor, Austrian Diplomatic Academy, Vienna, Austria.

LAWRENCE GROSSMAN: director of publications, American Jewish Committee.

RUTH ELLEN GRUBER: veteran foreign correspondent and author, specialist in European and Jewish affairs; Morre, Italy.

GEORGE E. GRUEN: adjunct professor, international relations, and visiting scholar, Middle East Institute, Columbia University.

NELLY HANSSON: director, Foundation of French Judaism, Paris, France.

KENNETH JACOBSON: director, international affairs, Anti-Defamation League of B'nai B'rith.

STEVEN KAPLAN: associate professor, comparative religion and African studies, Hebrew University of Jerusalem; assistant director, Ben-Zvi Institute for the Study of Oriental Jewish Communities, Jerusalem, Israel.

LIONEL E. KOCHAN: historian; Oxford, England.

MIRIAM L. KOCHAN: writer, translator; Oxford, England.

BARRY A. KOSMIN: director, Mandell L. Berman Institute–North American Jewish Data Bank, City University of New York Graduate Center; director of research, Council of Jewish Federations.

ROBIN OSTOW: research associate, Center for Russian and East European Studies, University of Toronto, Canada.

CHAIM ROSEN: anthropologist, Government of Israel Ministry of Absorption, Department of Planning and Research, Jerusalem, Israel.

HILARY RUBINSTEIN: historian; Melbourne, Australia.

JEFFREY SCHECKNER: administrator, North American Jewish Data Bank, City University of New York Graduate Center; research consultant, Council of Jewish Federations.

U.O. SCHMELZ: professor emeritus, Jewish demography, A. Harman Institute of Contemporary Jewry, Hebrew University of Jerusalem, Israel.

MILTON SHAIN: senior lecturer, Hebrew and Jewish studies, University of Cape Town, South Africa.

MENACHEM SHALEV: diplomatic correspondent, *Ma'ariv* Hebrew daily; Jerusalem, Israel.

DAVID A.H. SMULIAN: technical writer and translator, EDP systems analyst; Tel Aviv, Israel.

RACHELE MEGHNAGI SMULIAN: instructor, Italian, Tel Aviv University and Italian Cultural Institute; translator and editor, Israel Foreign Ministry Italian-language publications; Tel Aviv, Israel.

HAROLD M. WALLER: acting dean (academic), Faculty of Arts, and professor, political science, McGill University; director, Canadian Centre for Jewish Community Studies; Montreal, Canada.

Contents

OTHER COUNTRIES

DIRECTORIES, LISTS, AND OBITUARIES

Special Articles

Soviet Jews in the United States

by STEVEN J. GOLD

SINCE THE MID-1960s, over 280,000 Jews from the former Soviet Union have settled in the United States.[1] They constitute the largest single group of Jewish immigrants to enter the United States since the 1920s. Although they share kinship ties with the many American Jews whose roots are also in the precommunist Russian empire, their lives have been shaped by different forces: the Bolshevik revolution, the suffering and losses of World War II, and the unique conditions of life in a communist state, including, for Jews, discrimination and persecution. Like American Jews, contemporary émigrés are distinguished by high levels of skill and education, are urban and disproportionately professionals. Unlike most American Jews, they have had minimal exposure to formal Jewish training and Jewish religious life, and no experience with a highly organized Jewish community.

In terms of settlement and absorption, their experience differs from that of earlier Russian immigrants in the extensive resettlement services they receive from both Jewish agencies and the government. These address the basics of housing, employment, and health, as well as language training and acculturation into both American and Jewish society.

Enormous resources have been invested in this immigration, by both the U.S. government and the organized Jewish community. The process began with the political struggle to win the right for Jews to emigrate and now includes the panoply of agencies and programs devoted to easing their way into new lives as Americans and as Jews. Approximately 20 years have passed since serious immigration began, time enough to begin to evaluate

---

Note: I wish to acknowledge the help of the following persons in preparing this article: Yoav Ben-Horin, Richard Bernard, Barry Chiswick, Linda Gordon, Pini Herman, Bethamie Horowitz, Ariela Keysar, Igor Kotler, Michael Lichter, Mark Littman, Fran Markowitz, Harvey Paretzky, Bruce Phillips, David Preddy, Miriam Prum Hess, Jeffrey Scheckner, Len Schneiderman, Gila Shabanow, Marcia Tabenken, Madeleine Tress, Mia Tuan, and Roger Waldinger.

[1]HIAS, Annual Statistics, 1965–1993. From 1988 to the present, persons from the former Soviet Union have been the largest refugee nationality to enter the U.S. For example, during fiscal year 1992, Kings County (Brooklyn), New York, home to the nation's biggest Soviet Jewish community, was the number one destination for refugees arriving in the United States. The nearly 15,000 refugees who settled there were approximately double the number opting for the second most popular county of destination—Los Angeles—home to another major Soviet refugee community. Mark Littman, *Office of Refugee Resettlement Monthly Data Report for September 1992* (Washington, D.C., Office of Refugee Resettlement).

how Soviet Jews have fared and are faring, how well they are integrating into American society, and to what extent the hopes and expectations of American Jews have been realized—to see their beleaguered co-religionists free to be Jews in ways that were denied them in the USSR.

SOURCES OF DATA

Relatively little research has been carried out on Soviet Jewish émigrés. The paucity of research is striking when compared to the burgeoning literature on earlier Jewish migrants as well as on contemporary immigrant and refugee groups such as Cubans, Koreans, Vietnamese, Mexicans, and Chinese. Further, given the enormous efforts expended by the American Jewish community over the last 25 years to rescue Soviet Jewry, it is surprising that so little energy has been devoted to investigating the fate of this sizable population whose very presence represents the culmination of years of heroic effort. The lack of federal research may reflect the government's view of Soviet Jews as a group that adjusts fairly rapidly, that has the benefit of Jewish community help in resettlement, that poses no serious social problems, and thus requires little special attention. On the Jewish side, it has been suggested that communal agencies have been wary of research because findings both negative and positive could present problems, e.g., criticism of the agencies or reduction in federal funds.[2] It seems equally likely that agencies pressured by the immediate demands of resettling new arrivals were unable or unwilling to use limited human and financial resources for this purpose. From a practical standpoint, research on Soviets is difficult because once émigrés leave the resettlement program, they are hard to follow up, especially if they move to another locale.

Still, a growing body of research on Soviet Jews does exist.[3] It consists of many small pieces that do not lend themselves to easy comparisons or synthesis. Studies were conducted at various times over the last 20 years, using different questions, with samples representing different locations. Research undertaken through different organizations reflects disparate interests. Studies supported by religious agencies, for example, address chiefly religious concerns. Reports funded by federal government agencies, such as the INS (U.S. Immigration and Naturalization Service), the Bureau of the Census, and the Office of Refugee Resettlement (ORR) downplay ethnic

---

[2]Barry R. Chiswick, "Soviet Jews in the United States: An Analysis of Their Linguistic and Economic Adjustment," *International Migration Review* 27, no. 102, Summer 1993, pp. 260–85.

[3]Although the Soviet Union no longer exists, the term "Soviet Jews" is used for convenience. The term "Russian Jews" is not used because it applies to only a portion.

and religious questions and may not even distinguish among Jews, Armenians, Pentecostalists, and other migrant groups from the former USSR.

Still another body of research on Soviet Jewish émigrés has been carried out by academics—historians, political scientists, anthropologists, sociologists, and others. Their studies reflect the particular theoretical and methodological concerns of the researcher's particular scholarly discipline. Statistical and quantitative studies are helpful for assessing the general trends of Soviet émigrés' status in the United States, their income, synagogue membership, age, and so forth,[4] but are less likely to capture the rich, complex, and often contradictory nature of the Soviet Jews' experience. Studies of this sort tend to suffer from small sample sizes and from the fact that those willing to cooperate with a researcher may not be representative of the entire community, a well-known phenomenon among recent immigrants. Finally, there is good reason to question the validity of former Soviets' responses to telephone surveys, since they are noted for their distrust and manipulation of bureaucrats.[5]

Other studies use qualitative methodology, whereby the researcher involves him or herself with émigrés over a period of time. Using this approach, the subtle and complex experience of Soviet Jews' lives is explored and recorded. Further, participant observation methods are well suited for observing émigrés over time as they adjust to life in the United States.[6] However, such techniques are limited in their ability to represent a broad cross-section of the population and may be especially subject to the researcher's personal biases and style of relating to subjects.

A third body of information on Soviet Jewish émigrés applies neither qualitative nor quantitative research methodologies, but rather conveys the

---

[4]The two nationwide studies of this type are Rita J. Simon, Julian Simon, and Jim Schwartz, *The Soviet Jews' Adjustment to the United States* (Council of Jewish Federations, 1982), also published in Rita J. Simon, ed., *New Lives: The Adjustment of Soviet Jewish Immigrants in the United States and Israel* (Lexington, Mass., 1985); and Barry A. Kosmin, *The Class of 1979: The "Acculturation" of Jewish Immigrants from the Soviet Union* (North American Jewish Data Bank, CUNY Graduate School and University Center, 1990).

[5]See Hesh Kestin, "Making Cheese from Snow," *Forbes*, July 29, 1985, pp. 90–95; Wayne Di Francisco and Zvi Gitelman, "Soviet Political Culture and Covert Participation in Policy Implementation," *American Political Science Review* 78, no. 3, 1984, pp. 603–21.

[6]See Fran Markowitz, "The Not Lost Generation: Family Dynamics and Ethnic Identity Among Soviet Adolescent Immigrants of the 1970s," paper presented at the Wilstein Institute for Jewish Policy Studies Conference, Soviet Jewish Acculturation—Beyond Resettlement, Palo Alto, June 1991; idem, *A Community in Spite of Itself: Soviet Jewish Emigres in New York* (Washington, D.C., 1993); Steven J. Gold, *Refugee Communities: A Comparative Field Study* (Newbury Park, Calif., 1992); Annalise Orleck, "The Soviet Jews: Life in Brighton Beach, Brooklyn," in *New Immigrants in New York*, ed. Nancy Foner (New York, 1987), pp. 273–304. The present author has conducted fieldwork with Soviet Jews in California from 1982 to the present. Several quotes and observations contained in this article have their origins in this research.

experience and outlook of persons who work with émigrés. A number of articles by religious and community service professionals published in the *Journal of Jewish Communal Service* fall into this category.

In addition to the above, the present study draws on two relatively recent data sources. One is the 1990 U.S. census, specifically the data on Soviet émigrés from the two largest locations of their settlement, New York City and Los Angeles County.[7] These two locations account for about 45 percent of post-1965 migrants in the 1990 census.[8] In addition, a comparison of descriptive statistics of these two populations shows a very high degree of similarity.

The question of the Jewish proportion of former Soviets in the census requires some clarification. According to the 1990 census, 336,889 persons born in the USSR reside in the United States. Although the census does not provide information on religion or ethnicity, HIAS, the Hebrew Immigrant Aid Society, the major Jewish resettlement agency, reported a figure of 173,535 Soviet Jews resettled by it from 1966 through 1990.[9] (The 1990 National Jewish Population Study found 160,000 USSR-born Jews in the United States.) Others entered the country under different auspices or programs, and still others came to this country prior to World War II. Thus, estimating conservatively, somewhat over half of the census's Soviet population nationwide is presumed to be Jewish, and some experts believe it is higher. Additionally, we have increased the likelihood that the tabulations for New York and Los Angeles represent a population with a high fraction of Jews by excluding Armenians (the other major group of post-1965 immigrants from the former USSR) from our analysis.[10]

The second data source is the 1991 New York Jewish Population Study, the data for which were released early in 1994. This is the most recent and most comprehensive survey of a sample of Jews from the former Soviet Union—who were interviewed by Russian-speaking interviewers—and is thus a primary source of information.[11]

---

[7]Data were drawn from the 1990 census (5 percent Public Use Microdata Sample).

[8]Office of Refugee Resettlement Program (hereafter ORR), *Report to Congress 1990*, p. 10.

[9]According to Linda Gordon, a demographer currently employed by the U.S. Immigration and Naturalization Service, with years of previous experience at the Office of Refugee Resettlement, HIAS data on Soviet Jews are an accurate and reliable source.

[10]According to the 1990 census, 41,995 persons born in the USSR migrated to L.A. County from 1965 to 1990. Of these, 28,267 (67 percent) were Armenians (i.e., they reported Armenian ancestry or spoke Armenian at home). In contrast, of the 60,044 post-1965 émigrés from the former USSR in New York City, only 543 (1 percent) were Armenian. After the late 1980s, the fraction of Armenians entering the U.S. as refugees declined.

[11]Many of the findings from this study have been published in Bethamie Horowitz, *The 1991 New York Jewish Population Study* (United Jewish Appeal-Federation of Jewish Philanthropies of New York, 1993). For the present study, computer runs were made from the data tape, made available by the North American Jewish Data Bank.

This article utilizes all the sources described to present what can be considered an interim report on Soviet Jews in the United States—who they are, how they are faring, and the nature of their relationship to the larger Jewish community.

MIGRATION AND RESETTLEMENT

The Migration Process

The exodus of Jews from the USSR has been shaped by a complex of factors involving developments within Soviet society, foreign relations— chiefly with the United States—and the impact of international public opinion.[12] Because of an official policy that discouraged emigration, few Jews left the country before 1970. In the 1970s and 1980s, Soviet policy on emigration loosened considerably, but remained unpredictable. Thus, from 1976 to 1979, the pace of emigration increased rapidly, then dropped steadily through 1986, then began to climb again, reaching its highest levels ever in the years 1989–1992. (See table 1.) Peak years of entry for these two periods were 1979, when 28,794 arrived, and 1992, when 45,888 Jews from the former Soviet Union entered the United States.[13]

One of the factors influencing emigration was the rise of a Soviet Jewry movement, within the USSR itself and in the worldwide Jewish community. Following the Six Day War in 1967, Soviet Jews—long isolated from their Jewish peers elsewhere—experienced a surge of Jewish self-consciousness and identification with Israel. Endemic anti-Semitism and growing discrimination in higher education, employment, and other areas contributed to the pressure to consider leaving. Among Jews in other countries, the prospect of "rescuing" Soviet Jewry ("Let my people go!") ignited a passionate and effective advocacy movement that succeeded in enlisting the support of most Western governments. On the Soviet side, a desire to develop trade and financial ties with the West, and the linkage by the U.S. Congress of trade and emigration produced greater openness to the idea of emigration.

Under Soviet law, emigration was at least theoretically permitted for reasons of family reunification or national repatriation; however, permission was not granted automatically, and restrictions could be imposed. By and large, those Jews pressing most insistently to leave sought to join family in Israel. Within the Soviet Jewry advocacy movement, the rescue of Soviet

---

[12]A number of specialists have analyzed the reasons for the fluctuations in Soviet policy. See, for example, Robert O. Freedman, ed., *Soviet Jewry in the 1980s: The Politics of Anti-Semitism and Emigration and the Dynamics of Resettlement* (Durham, N.C., 1989).

[13]ORR, *Report to Congress 1990*; HIAS, Annual Statistics, 1965–1993.

Jews was always viewed in Zionist terms, it being understood that the Jewish state would be their new home. In the early 1970s, Soviet Jews began requesting and receiving from relatives in Israel *vyzovs*, affidavits for exit visas, and growing numbers of applicants were approved. Up to 1974, nearly 100 percent of these emigrants went to Israel. By the late '70s, however, more and more emigrants were "dropping out" at the transit station in Vienna, opting to go to some other country instead, chiefly to the United States, which accorded most of them refugee status. By the late 1970s, the proportion going to Israel had fallen to one-third; by the late 1980s, less than 10 percent chose to settle in the Jewish state. However, by 1989–90, when the mass exodus of the current wave reached its peak, many more Soviets went to Israel (258,032) than to the United States (68,021). This trend has continued, although the proportion going to Israel has decreased. In 1993, roughly twice as many (69,132) went to Israel as to the United States (35,581).

Some authorities claim that Israel simply became a less attractive destination after the 1973 Yom Kippur War, and that reports of work and housing difficulties in Israel discouraged many. Another factor was the change in the composition of the emigration stream in the late '70s. Those choosing Israel were primarily from Georgia, Central Asia, and the Baltic states—areas in which Jews had retained more of Jewish life and culture and a commitment to return to Zion. By contrast, those from the heartland—Russia and Ukraine—were the most Russified and the most distant from Jewish life and identification and had no religious or Zionist motivation.[14]

The change in the direction of the emigration in the 1970s gave rise to conflict between the Zionist and Israeli factions, on one side, and those supporting freedom of choice for the emigrants, on the other. The tension eased in the early 1980s, as emigration virtually dried up. It could have become a problem again in the late '80s, when the Soviets opened the doors wide, and large numbers of Jews began to express an interest in leaving. However, the United States stopped accepting individuals with exit visas for Israel who were "dropping out," and instead established its own system for processing would-be immigrants. This system established an unofficial annual limit of 40,000 Jewish refugees from the Soviet Union and gave first priority to those applicants who already had close relatives living in the United States. Soviet Jews were required to apply from Moscow—thus eliminating the dropout option. (Jews also had the opportunity to enter with parole status, but this would deny them any refugee benefits.)[15]

---

[14]Zvi Gitelman, "The Quality of Life in Israel and the United States," in Simon, *New Lives*, p. 47.

[15]Elaine Woo, "Anticipated Reunion Turns into a Nightmare for Soviet Emigre," *Los Angeles Times*, Nov. 24, 1989, pp. B1, B12; *New York Times*, "Visa Applicants Deluge

When interviewed on the subject, Jews from the former Soviet Union cite several reasons for their preference for the United States over Israel, among them greater economic opportunity, a higher level of national security, and the fact that there is no compulsory military service. (For a group who paid a great human price in World War II, the latter considerations are of major significance.) Some émigrés assert that they feel more comfortable in the secular and pluralistic United States than they would in Israel, which they refer to as "an Orthodox country."[16] Finally, some Russian Jews say they are accustomed to being part of a big nation and prefer exchanging one superpower for another, as opposed to moving to a tiny country whose total population is less than that of their former city of residence.

The number of all Soviet refugees currently permitted to enter the United States (Jewish and non-Jewish) is limited to 50,000 a year. Priority is given to selected groups of former Soviets whom the U.S. Congress has identified as likely targets of persecution. These include Jews, Evangelical Christians, Ukrainian Catholics, and followers of the Ukrainian Autocephalous Orthodox Church. Eligible persons with close legal-resident relatives (parent, spouse, children, siblings, grandparents and grandchildren) in this country are granted priority for entry. Members of these denominations who have immediate relatives (parent, spouse, or unmarried minor child) who are U.S. citizens must apply as immigrants rather than refugees.[17]

The Resettlement Process

Since the mid-1970s, a number of programs have been adopted by Congress to encourage the smooth adjustment of refugees from several nations, including the former Soviet Union. The most important of these is the Refugee Act of 1980 (Public Law 96–212), reauthorized in 1991. This legislation was intended to provide "transitional assistance to refugees in the United States," to make "employment training and job placement available in order to achieve economic self-sufficiency among refugees as quickly as

---

Embassy in Moscow," Oct. 3, 1989, p. 4; Madeleine Tress, "United States Policy Toward Soviet Emigration," *Migration* 3/4, nos. 11/12, 1991, pp. 93–106.

[16]Gold, *Refugee Communities*. According to the 1991 Jewish population study of New York, the fraction of former Soviet Jews who have seriously considered living in Israel exceeds the rate of all Jewish New Yorkers by only 11 percent. (30 percent of post-1965 Jewish immigrants from the former Soviet Union have considered living in Israel, while 19 percent of the entire Jewish community have done so.)

[17]The number of former Soviets currently entering the U.S. as immigrants (not refugees) is rather small, accounting for only about 4 percent of all former Soviet arrivals in 1991. However, INS officials expect this number to grow in the future. Linda Gordon, INS statistician, personal communication, Sept. 1993; *New York Times*, "Visa Applicants Deluge Embassy in Moscow," Oct. 3, 1989, p. 4; Washington Processing Center (Instructions for application for refugee status), ND.

possible," to offer refugees English-language training, and to ensure "that cash assistance is made available to refugees in such a manner as to not discourage their economic self-sufficiency."[18]

The services enabled by the Refugee Act of 1980 as well as other legislation are delivered and administered by a diverse network of government, religious, nonprofit, and profit-making agencies and organizations. A major role in the resettlement of refugees is carried out by 13 voluntary agencies, or VOLAGS, which are funded by charitable contributions and by the federal government. Refugee cash assistance (RCA) is distributed by county welfare departments.

While the largest numbers of refugees in recent years have been resettled by the United States Catholic Conference (USCC), nearly all Soviet Jews as well as members of other groups have been resettled by the Hebrew Immigrant Aid Society (HIAS).[19] HIAS, in turn, works through a national resettlement network composed of local Jewish family service agencies and federations, and in New York with the New York Association for New Americans (NYANA), the largest Jewish resettlement agency in the country. The HIAS model of resettlement coordinates centralized policy-making, administration, and data collection with the provision of service at the local level, which allows each community the flexibility required to help clients according to local conditions and needs. For example, HIAS mandates certain program standards, such as reunion with relatives and "earliest appropriate job placement" in order to "avoid fostering reliance on public and private institutions." However, actual service provision is carried out by the professional staff members of local agencies in coordination with family members already residing here and community volunteers. "Consequently, the nature of programs developed within each community is often unique to that community's specific environment."[20]

FUNDING RESETTLEMENT

All resettlement agencies receive Reception and Placement Grant funds of roughly equivalent per capita amounts through the Department of State. In addition, agencies are eligible for Matching Grant funds through the Department of Health and Human Services, to cover expenses beyond the

---

[18]Section 311, quoted in Michael Murray and Associates, *A Report on Refugee Services in San Francisco* (Center for Southeast Asian Refugee Resettlement, San Francisco, 1981).

[19]See Timothy J. Eckles, Lawrence J. Lewin, David S. North, and Dangole J. Spakevicius, "A Portrait in Diversity: Voluntary Agencies and the Office of Refugee Resettlement Matching Grant Program" (Lewin and Associates, 1982), p. 42.

[20]ORR, *Report to Congress 1993*, pp. C-10, C-11.

initial basic services.[21] Because the agencies working with Soviet Jews are highly centralized and integrated, long established, and well funded, they tend to be in a better position than agencies devoted to other ethnic and nationality groups to raise funds needed to qualify for Matching Grants. As a result, a higher proportion of newcomers resettled by Jewish agencies benefit from Matching Grant funds (fewer, for example, being placed on welfare). In fiscal 1992, the Matching Grant Program (then administered by the Council of Jewish Federations, but since 1994 by HIAS) received almost $34 million to resettle almost 34,000 refugees, of whom 90 percent were Soviets. During the same year, four other agencies received a total of $5.2 million to resettle just over 5,000 refugees who were members of other ethnic and nationality groups.[22]

In addition to HIAS, resettlement of Soviet Jews is underwritten by local Jewish communities and agencies and by the social service departments of the states in which they settle. Finally, to help defray costs of resettlement, so-called anchor families—established relatives of recently arrived émigrés—are expected to contribute money or in-kind services to the resettlement agency. If families are unable to contribute, other community resources are utilized.

HIAS itself is funded by a combination of government funds, allocations from Jewish federations throughout the United States and Canada—especially New York UJA-Federation—and by other sources, such as memberships, contributions, and repayments of loans from migrants. In 1992, HIAS's total expenses were $10.3 million, while its income was $15.5 million. Income included $10 million from government, $2.3 million from Jewish federations, and $2.3 million from contributions and bequests.[23] More recently, because of difficult economic conditions in the United States, both public and private funds for refugee resettlement have become more scarce, resulting in cutbacks in many programs.[24]

As refugees, émigrés are entitled to a series of benefits including health care, housing assistance, job and language training, and public assistance. Local agencies may also offer supplementary services such as job placement, aid with social adjustment, assistance in opening small businesses, and a variety of cultural and religious activities. Because of the constitutional separation of church and state, resettlement activities with a religious con-

---

[21]Eckles et al., "Portrait in Diversity"; HIAS, *Financial Statement and Auditor's Report*, Dec. 31, 1991; HIAS, Annual Statistics, 1965–1993.

[22]ORR, *Report to Congress 1993*, p. 29.

[23]HIAS, *Financial Statement and Auditor's Report*, Dec. 31, 1992.

[24]Len Schneiderman, Jewish Federation Council of Greater Los Angeles, *FY 91–92 Actual Expenses and FY 92–93 Resettlement Projections*, Summer 1993.

tent may not be supported with governmental funds.

The period of eligibility for these benefits was 18 months in the early 1980s, but it has gradually been scaled back to 8 months. Support in the first month is provided to émigrés by the U.S. Department of State Reception and Placement Grant. For many refugees, resettlement activity in the second through fourth months is funded through the Matching Grant Program, as noted above, with funds furnished in equal parts by Jewish federations and the U.S. Department of Health and Human Services. The next four months of benefits are delivered by the social service departments of the states in which refugees reside. After eight months of residency in the United States, émigrés no longer have special entitlements. Their applications for governmental or Jewish community services are treated (and funded) in the same manner as would be the case for U.S. citizens.[25]

AGENCIES OFFERING SERVICES

Depending on the community, services to Soviet Jews are available from a number of coordinated agencies and may vary both in terms of benefits available and quality of services provided. Intake services, vocational and language training, and health care are often accessible from public agencies and community colleges or adult schools. The Jewish Family and Children's Service provides counseling, financial aid, and case management. The Jewish Vocational Service offers job placement and occasionally job training. Jewish community centers (JCCs) and YMHA/YWHAs deliver social and recreational activities, and the Bureau of Jewish Education contributes a variety of religious and cultural activities. Many synagogues, Jewish camps, and Jewish day schools have developed programs on their own or in concert with Jewish federations to welcome émigré families. For example, in Los Angeles, Chabad has used its own resources as well as those from the Jewish federation and the city of West Hollywood to support several Soviet émigré programs. Jewish agencies for the elderly extend services such as health care, transportation, housing, and social activities to the many aged Soviet refugees. Local families, communities, and synagogues provide émigrés with a whole variety of volunteer services including home visits, informal job and language training, transportation, invitations to religious services and Sabbath dinners, housing, furniture, and other benefits.

Just as the services available to Soviet émigrés vary according to the resources of the local Jewish agencies resettling them, benefits available through state and local sources also vary. For example, due to state regula-

---

[25]Miriam Prum Hess, Refugee Acculturation Coordinator, Jewish Federation Council of Los Angeles, personal communication, Sept. 1993; Schneiderman, Jewish Federation Council of Greater Los Angeles, Summer 1993.

tions, a refugee family of four living in California in 1989 was eligible for $734 monthly in AFDC (Aid to Families with Dependent Children) benefits. The same family living in Texas received a maximum of $221. Further, while two-parent, indigent families are eligible for AFDC in California, they are not in Texas.[26]

DEMOGRAPHIC PROFILE

Size: Through the end of 1993, HIAS resettled a total of 289,719 Soviet Jews in the United States. This figure refers only to Soviet Jews who have come to the United States over the last 28 years, not to the size of the current Soviet Jewish community, which is harder to estimate. For one thing, the number of émigrés has been diminished by mortality. Because former Soviets are an elderly population, their mortality rate is undoubtedly fairly high. At the same time, Jews from the former Soviet Union have given birth to an unknown number of American-born children, who are part of the Soviet émigré community and consequently contribute to its size. Finally, there is the question of whether all those resettled can be considered Jewish. For example, an extended family whose members include an intermarried couple and the non-Jewish spouse's parents contains at least three non-Jews, who nevertheless have been resettled and counted by HIAS as Jews.[27] In sum, while there is no definite figure for the size of the Soviet Jewish community, an accepted estimate is around a quarter of a million.

Origins: The greatest number of resettled Soviet Jews come from the Russian and Ukrainian republics of the Soviet Union, which also have the largest Jewish populations. However, while the Russian Republic has the largest number of Jews, Ukraine is the major source of émigrés. Of the 194,047 Soviet Jews who entered the United States between 1980 and May 1993, 42 percent (81,421) were from Ukraine, 24 percent (46,391) from the Russian Republic, 13 percent (24,437) from Belarus, 6 percent (12,591) from Uzbekistan, 6 percent (11,113) from Moldova, 2 percent (4,715) from Azerbaijan, and 2 percent (4,486) from Latvia. The remainder (4 percent) came from other Soviet republics or had unknown origins.[28] (See table 2.)

Age: Soviet Jews are consistently reported as being the oldest of refugee

---

[26]Ruben Rumbaut, "The Structure of Refuge: Southeast Asian Refugees in the United States, 1975–1985," *International Review of Comparative Public Policy* 1, 1989, p. 103.

[27]Bethamie Horowitz, "Where Do Jewish New Yorkers Come From?" New York UJA-Federation, 1993.

[28]Simon et al., "Soviet Jews' Adjustment"; Rita J. Simon and Melanie Brooks, "Soviet Jewish Immigrants' Adjustment in Four United States Cities," *Journal of Jewish Communal Service* 60, no. 1, 1983, pp. 56–64; Kosmin, *Class of 1979*; HIAS, Annual Statistics, 1965–1993.

groups entering the United States, and there is reason to believe that their average age has been slowly rising. Between 1983 and 1991, the average age of all Soviet refugees entering the United States was 31.[29] Allowing for about 20 percent non-Jews in this population—a generally younger group—the average for Soviet Jews was undoubtedly somewhat higher. According to HIAS, the median age of entering Soviet Jews in 1993 was 35.5; this compares to a median age for all entering refugees (from all countries) of 28 years. The Soviets' age distribution also differs significantly from that of the total refugee population. For example, the former includes 12.5 percent young children; the latter 20.2 percent. In the older age category (65 and over), the Soviet Jewish proportion is 17.5 percent, compared to 8 percent in the total refugee population.[30] Females tend to be older than males, due to greater life expectancy and the impact of World War II.

Male/female ratio: There have consistently been slightly more females than males in the Soviet Jewish émigré population, averaging around 53 percent, compared with a more equal distribution in the total refugee population.[31]

Family size: Family size for Soviet Jews tends to be small. Rounding statistics, three-person nuclear families are consistently reported. Based on anecdotal evidence, it appears that a fair number of émigré families are having more than one child in the United States.[32]

Family type: Soviet Jewish families are usually intact and often include three generations. Prior to the removal of migration restrictions in the late 1980s, Soviet emigration policy fostered the exit of multigenerational families. When a Soviet citizen applied to emigrate, "consent from both parents for permission to leave was also required regardless of the individual's age or nature of relationship to the parent. When parents provided consent, they too were viewed as 'traitors' and they too were harassed," thus increasing the likelihood that they themselves would emigrate.[33] Accordingly, a very high proportion of Soviet Jewish families are multigenerational and, as noted above, they include a very elderly population.

Intermarriage: Soviet survey data suggest that Soviet Jews value marital endogamy (marrying within one's own group) far more than other Soviet ethnic and nationality groups. Nevertheless, they display relatively high

---

[29]ORR, *Report to Congress 1992*, p. 48.

[30]HIAS, *Statistical Abstract FY 93*, Feb. 1994, p. 14.

[31]ORR, *Report to Congress 1987*; HIAS, ibid.

[32]Eckles et al., "Portrait in Diversity," p. 26; Rita J. Simon, "Refugee Families' Adjustment and Aspirations: A Comparison of Soviet Jewish and Vietnamese Immigrants," *Ethnic and Racial Studies* 6, no. 4, 1983, pp. 492–504; HIAS, *Annual Statistics 1979–1991*, 1991.

[33]Diane Drachman and Anna Halberstadt, "A Stage of Migration Framework as Applied to Recent Soviet Emigres," *Social Work with Immigrants and Refugees*, ed. Angela Shen Ryan (New York, 1992), p. 67.

rates of intermarriage.[34] The 1979 Soviet census "shows that an estimated 33 percent of the Jewish population of the RSFSR [Russian Republic], 19 percent of the Jews in the Ukraine and 14 percent of the Jews in Byelorussia live in mixed families." Most recently, Sergio DellaPergola has estimated the rate of outmarriage of Jews in the USSR as of the late 1980s to be between 45 and 54.9 percent, or approximately the same rate as in the United States.[35]

The data on Soviet Jews' marriage patterns in the United States are limited. In Kosmin's 1990 study of émigrés living in the United States at least eight years, 87 percent were currently married, and the reported rate of mixed marriages was somewhere between 8 and 12 percent. (This is considerably lower than the known rate for all Soviet Jews, and may simply reflect the small sample size or that this is a case of selective migration.) Finally, attitudinal data from the 1991 New York Jewish population study indicate that Jews from the former Soviet Union are much less tolerant of intermarriage (with non-Jews) than is the larger New York Jewish community. While 60 percent of all New York Jews report that they would accept, support, or strongly support their child's marriage to a non-Jew, only 33 percent of former Soviets would accept or support such a union, while 58 percent would oppose it. However, if the non-Jewish spouse were to convert to Judaism, acceptance or support of the marriage climbs to 70 percent. By comparison, 84 percent of all Jews polled in New York would then support the marriage.

PATTERNS OF RESETTLEMENT

Geographic Distribution

While we know the total number of Soviet Jews who have been resettled in the United States, we have less specific information about the size of populations in various localities. We do know that rates of secondary migration (émigrés who leave their initial place of settlement in the United States for another destination) are relatively high, especially for those initially settled in small communities in the Midwest and South. For example, as of 1990, according to the Jewish Community Federation of San Francisco,

---

[34]Rasma Karklins, "Determinants of Ethnic Identification in the USSR: The Soviet Jewish Case," *Ethnic and Racial Studies* 10, no. 1, 1987, pp. 27–47.

[35]Benjamin Pinkus, "National Identity and Emigration Patterns Among Soviet Jewry," *Soviet Jewish Affairs* 15, no. 3, 1985, p. 11; Sergio DellaPergola, "Israel and World Population: A Core-Periphery Perspective," in *Population and Social Change in Israel*, ed. C. Goldscheider (Boulder, 1992), p. 55. See also Sergio DellaPergola, "World Jewish Population," AJYB 1993, pp. 434–37.

about 10 percent of the Bay Area's Soviet Jewish population were secondary migrants. Similarly, the Jewish Federation of Chicago estimates that about 2,000 of its 16,500 émigrés are secondary migrants.[36]

Chiswick's analysis of 1980 census data determined that 36 percent of post-1965 Soviet immigrants resided in the New York Standard Metropolitan Statistical Area, 16 percent in Los Angeles/Long Beach, 7 percent in Chicago, 4 percent each in San Francisco/Oakland and Boston, and 3 percent in Miami. In all, these six SMSAs accounted for 70 percent of Soviet immigrants.[37]

State-level data from the 1990 census reveal that 30 percent of USSR-born American residents (Jews and non-Jews) live in New York, 23 percent in California, 6 percent each in New Jersey and Illinois, and 5 percent each in Florida, Pennsylvania, and Massachusetts. Hence, 80 percent of those born in the Soviet Union reside in seven states. (See table 3.) As noted above, there is no sure way of knowing what proportion of these are Jews. Los Angeles, for example, is the major point of settlement for Soviet Armenians. Analysis of the 1990 census reveals that only 33 percent of post-'65 former Soviet residents in Los Angeles county are *not* of Armenian ethnicity. In contrast, only about 500 of the more than 60,000 post-'65 former Soviets in New York City are of Armenian ethnicity.[38]

CHOICE OF LOCATION

The Jewish communal resettlement process is predicated on the assistance and participation of family members already resident in this country. Thus, the initial choice of settlement location for a new émigré is based primarily on the presence of "anchor" relatives in a given community. If there are no relatives, or if relatives are unwilling or unable to help out, newcomers are referred to other communities. There is some correlation between the size of a city's Jewish community and the number of émigrés resettled there. At the same time, the size of a given community's Soviet Jewish population is influenced by newcomers' decisions to leave the initial place of settlement for other locations through secondary migration. Apart from the presence of family or friends, secondary migrants generally select a given city because of preference for the climate or the availability of jobs or cultural amenities.

---

[36]Anita Friedman, "Status Report on Soviet Jewish Resettlement in the San Francisco Bay Area," Jewish Community Federation of San Francisco, the Peninsula, Marin and Sonoma Counties Emigre Program, 1990; Joel M. Carp, "Absorbing Jews Jewishly: Professional Responsibility for Jewishly Absorbing New Immigrants in Their New Communities," *Journal of Jewish Communal Service* 66, no. 4, 1990, pp. 366–74.

[37]Chiswick, "Soviet Jews in the United States," p. 275.

[38]ORR, *Report to Congress 1991,* and 1990 census.

Research reveals that certain émigré communities in the United States are disproportionately drawn from specific cities or regions of the USSR. For example, the North Shore of Massachusetts has a heavy representation of émigrés from the Russian Republic. Kosmin suggests that Odessans settle in Cleveland; those from Kiev move to Philadelphia; and Jews from Minsk and Azerbaijan migrate to Baltimore. Markowitz as well as Simon and Brooks found that Chicago has a heavy representation of émigrés from the heartland Ukrainian cities of Kiev and Kharkov, as well as Minsk in Belarus. Even neighborhoods within a single city may develop a regional focus. Barber discovered that, despite the existence of a lively (and largely Ukrainian) émigré community in Brooklyn, professionals from Moscow and Leningrad self-consciously created their own enclave, a lengthy subway ride away in Manhattan's Washington Heights.[39]

Regional differences reflect differences in cultural and other background factors as well as the ways in which émigrés view and relate to each other. In general, those from the former Russian Republic—Moscow and Leningrad (now St. Petersburg)—consider themselves to be culturally superior to other émigrés. Ukrainians have lower status. Odessans are seen as skilled in deal-making, and not as refined as Russians. Émigrés from the Baltic republics, which have been under Soviet hegemony only since the 1940s, are much more likely to know Yiddish, while those from the less cosmopolitan eastern regions of the USSR are less assimilated (to Russian culture) and accordingly are noted for their religiosity and stable family and community structures.[40]

While regional differences are often overcome in the United States, connections with communities of origin still hold some sway among Soviet Jews, especially among those of eastern and Sephardic origins.[41] Hence, regional differences, along with those based on social class, former occupa-

---

[39]Kosmin, *Class of 1979*, p. 16; Jewish Family Service of the North Shore, Mass., *Social Needs Survey of Immigrants to the North Shore from the Soviet Union*, 1990; Markowitz, "The Not Lost Generation," p. 47; Simon and Brooks, "Soviet Jewish Immigrants' Adjustment"; Jennifer Barber, "The Soviet Jews of Washington Heights," *New York Affairs* 10, no. 1, 1987, pp. 34–43.

[40]Barber, "Soviet Jews of Washington Heights"; Gold, *Refugee Communities*; Markowitz, *Community in Spite of Itself*; Zvi Gitelman, "Soviet Immigrants and American Absorption Efforts: A Case Study in Detroit," *Journal of Jewish Communal Service* 55, no. 1, 1978, pp. 77–82; Mitchell Serels, "The Soviet Sephardim in the United States," New York: Yeshiva University, 1990; Marilyn Halter, "Ethnicity and the Entrepreneur: Self-Employment Among Former Soviet Jewish Refugees," in *New Migrants in the Marketplace: Boston's Ethnic Entrepreneurs*, ed. Marilyn Halter (Amherst, Mass., in press).

[41]According to the 1991 Jewish population study of New York, 8 percent of post-1965 Jews born in the former Soviet Union are of Sephardic ethnicity, 70 percent are Ashkenazic, and 22 percent are unsure of their ethnicity. This distribution is nearly identical to that of the larger New York Jewish community.

tion, and educational level contribute significantly to the development of both connections and antipathies among Jews from the former Soviet Union. As Zvi Gitelman notes:

> If the unsophisticated American social worker can't tell the difference between the Leningrad accent of a scientist and the Latvian accent of a technician, the immigrants themselves certainly can. Thus, the immigrants themselves will resist attempts to get them to "cooperate," to associate with and help people with whom they feel they have little in common.[42]

OBTAINING U.S. CITIZENSHIP

Soviets show a higher propensity to naturalize and do so more rapidly than the other major refugee groups (Cubans and Southeast Asians) that have entered the United States in recent years. From 1980 through 1991, almost 60,000 persons born in the USSR became citizens. This represents about 57 percent of those who arrived in the country between 1975 and 1985 as refugees.[43] The former Soviets' rapid naturalization provides members of this group with opportunities for political participation, eligibility for jobs and scholarships, and a higher priority ranking when assisting relatives to gain entry into the United States.[44]

Employment and Economic Factors

As a group, Soviet Jews are highly educated and experienced in technical and professional fields. Simon and Brooks, in a nationwide sample, found the average educational level to be 13.5 years, and a study of émigrés in Massachusetts' North Shore found that 97 percent of adults had a bachelor's or higher degree and a professional occupation prior to migration. The average educational level of Soviet Jews exceeds that of the U.S. population by a year and is among the highest of all immigrant groups entering the country.[45] Data from the 1990 census are consistent with Simon and Brooks's estimate. Average education was above 13 years for Soviet-born persons in both New York City and Los Angeles, and 58 percent of former Soviets in New York City and 72 percent in Los Angeles County had one or more years of college. (See tables 4–5.)

Surveys indicate that Soviet Jewish émigrés generally experience rapid

---

[42]Gitelman, "Soviet Immigrants and American Absorption Efforts," pp. 74–75.

[43]ORR, *Report to Congress 1993*, p. 61.

[44]According to the 1991 Jewish population study of New York, 33 percent of post-1965 Jews born in the former Soviet Union are registered to vote.

[45]Simon and Brooks, "Soviet Jewish Immigrants' Adjustment"; Jewish Family Service of the North Shore, "Social Needs Survey"; Gold, *Refugee Communities*, p. 43.

economic adjustment. Average family income in 1989 for those in the United States 8 years or more was $34,000. In the North Shore of Massachusetts, 63 percent were making over $30,000.[46]

These findings appear to be supported by the 1990 census, which shows that, with the exception of recent arrivals (those in the country three or fewer years), the income of all Soviet émigrés was relatively high, particularly in Los Angeles. Employed Soviet men residing in New York City who arrived between 1975 and 1981 earned on average $32,000 annually in 1990—more than all foreign-born men ($25,871) but less than both native-born white men ($45,677) and all foreign-born white men ($36,224). In Los Angeles, Soviet men were making over $43,000 on average—more than both all foreign-born white men ($41,527) and all foreign-born men ($24,083) and only slightly less than the average for native-born white men ($46,285). Employed Soviet women who entered the United States between 1975 and 1981 made about $22,500 in New York—about the same as all foreign-born white women ($22,991) and more than all foreign-born women ($19,048), but less than native-born white women ($31,114). In Los Angeles, Soviet women earned approximately $26,000 on average, about the same as native-born white women ($26,473) and more than both foreign-born white women ($23,388) and all foreign-born women ($16,376). As might be expected, recently arrived Soviet men and women made much less in 1990 than those émigrés with longer tenure in the country. (See table 6.)

While the average income of Soviet immigrants suggests a generally successful merger into the American middle class, the economic profile of this population actually includes a wide range, from poverty to significant wealth. For example, in June 1991, about 30 percent of refugees (Jews and non-Jews) from the former USSR who had been in the United States for a year or less were receiving cash assistance. Among Soviet Jewish émigrés in the United States eight years or more in 1989: 42 percent of households in New York and 36 percent in Los Angeles were making less than $20,000 per household; 50 percent in New York and 48 percent in Los Angeles were earning $20,000–$60,000; 8 percent in New York and 16 percent in Los Angeles were earning over $60,000.[47] Soviet Jews in Los Angeles proudly describe the financial success of their community as they refer to the many emigrants who own homes in Mount Olympus, an affluent neighborhood adjacent to Beverly Hills.[48]

---

[46]Kosmin, *Class of 1979*; Jewish Family Service of the North Shore, "Social Needs Survey"; Chiswick, "Soviet Jews in the United States," p. 274.

[47]ORR, *Report to Congress 1992*, pp. A-18, A-19; Kosmin, *Class of 1979*, pp. 24–25.

[48]Si Frumkin, "Who Are the Russians?" *Jewish Journal* (Los Angeles), Nov. 19–25, 1993, p. 17.

LABOR-FORCE PARTICIPATION

Labor-force participation rates for Soviet Jews in the United States have generally been quite high. However, with the large numbers arriving since 1990 and the depressed economic conditions they encounter in many receiving communities, a sizable fraction of recent arrivals are underemployed.

The 1990 census determined that the labor-force participation rate for all Soviet immigrants in New York City (arriving since 1965) was 76 percent for men and 57 percent for women. Excluding recent arrivals, the labor-force participation rate was 89 percent for men and 68 percent for women. Roughly similar trends were evident in Los Angeles, where the labor-force participation rate for Soviet immigrant men was 79 percent and 63 percent for women. Excluding recent arrivals, the rate was 88 percent for men and 71 percent for women. Excluding those in the United States three years or less in 1990, unemployment rates were quite low, less than 7 percent for men or women in New York and Los Angeles. (See table 7.)

DEPENDENCE VS. SELF-SUFFICIENCY

Data from the 1990 census show that 14 percent of Soviet-born men and 13 percent of Soviet-born women (aged 24–65) in New York City and 7 percent of Soviet-born men and 11 percent of Soviet-born women in Los Angeles County were on SSI, AFDC, or General Relief in 1990. However, excluding recent arrivals, dependency rates decline to 5 percent for men and 10 percent for women in New York and 5 percent for men and 9 percent for women in Los Angeles. Clearly, once settled, refugees are able to reduce their rates of dependency. (One exception is the over-65 age group, a large fraction of which receives SSI.) (See table 8.) Data produced by the Council of Jewish Federations[49] show that the self-sufficiency rate for Soviet Jews after four months was 24.6 percent for those arriving in 1990, 23.8 percent for those entering in 1991, and 18.3 percent for those arriving in 1992. In general, it appears that émigrés arriving in smaller cities had a better chance of being self-supporting after four months than those who settled in larger cities. For example, Baltimore achieved an 80-percent-plus rate of self-sufficiency among Soviet Jews after four months in the years 1989–1992. By contrast, the four-month self-sufficiency rate for Los Angeles émigrés was between 22 percent and 12 percent for the same years; émigrés coming to New York achieved four-month self-sufficiency rates around 5 percent after 1989. The difference between smaller and larger community size may be related to the relative ease of placement when agency staff have more

---

[49]Harvey Paretzky, *An Employment Profile of Soviet Jewish Refugees in the United States* (Council of Jewish Federations, 1993).

manageable caseloads. In addition to community size, other factors, such as the state-determined availability of public assistance, may also influence self-sufficiency rates. The fact that New York and California have much more generous benefit programs than does Maryland may partly explain the higher rates of self-sufficiency evident in Baltimore as compared with Los Angeles and New York.[50] (See table 9.)

Although the combination of large numbers of émigrés entering the United States and the recession since 1990 have made initial job-finding difficult for former Soviets, their dependence on RCA (refugee cash assistance) actually declined between 1990 and 1991. To quote from the Office of Refugee Resettlement *Report to Congress 1993*: "The RCA utilization rate for the Soviets is the lowest of any large group (28 percent) and represents a dramatic decrease from the previous year (50 percent), when a surge of arrivals in the winter and early spring of 1991 contributed to heavy RCA utilization."[51] The high skill levels of émigrés, their motivation to find work, and the assistance provided them by agencies and community members can be credited for this impressive performance.

AREAS OF EMPLOYMENT

As the above statistics demonstrate, Soviet Jews in the United States appear to be successful in finding jobs and earning a good living within a relatively short period after arrival. One problem they confront, however, is an inability to meet their previous level of occupational prestige. For example, a study of New York's Soviet Jewish community found that, while 66 percent had professional, technical, and managerial occupations in the USSR, only half of these, 33 percent, found similar jobs in the United States.[52] Data from the 1990 census offer similar findings, tabulating professional, technical, and managerial employment rates at 34 percent for men and 37 percent for women in New York, and 47 percent for men and 41 percent for women in Los Angeles. (See table 10.)

Highly skilled Soviet Jews have problems finding appropriate American jobs because they lack job-related licenses and certification, have limited English-language skills, or because certain Soviet occupations are simply not in demand. For example, there are few American job opportunities for classical accordion players, coaches of sports seldom played in the United States, or engineers who designed tundra-friendly (and by U.S. standards, hopelessly outdated) structures for the Siberian oil industry. A large pro-

---

[50]Council of Jewish Federations, *Immigration Data*, 1993; Harvey Paretzky, personal communication, Sept. 14, 1993.

[51]ORR, *Report to Congress 1993*, p. 24.

[52]Paretzky, *Employment Profile*.

portion of recent Soviet Jews are able to adapt to the U.S. economy by finding jobs in the skilled trades, bookkeeping and accounting, computer programming, and engineering.[53] (See table 11.)

Self-employment is the traditional means by which many immigrant Jews have supported their families. This long-standing pattern characterized the German Jews of the 1850s and the Eastern Europeans of the 1880–1920 era, and applies to contemporary Israelis and Iranians. The literature on Soviet Jewish émigrés includes several descriptive accounts of émigré entrepreneurship. Former Soviets gravitate toward various types of enterprises, including engineering companies, restaurants and grocery stores, retail trade, and construction and real estate. In a study of Soviet émigré businesses in Boston, Halter determined that, while a relatively small fraction of Soviet Jews enter self-employment, they tend to be successful. In describing business owners, she noted a preponderance of women proprietors, an individualistic (rather than communal) entrepreneurial style, and a high degree of compatibility between entrepreneurship and their Soviet-based, secular Jewish identity.[54]

In the 1980s, taxi companies in New York and Los Angeles employed many Soviets, but émigrés often leave this risky occupation after only a few years. In Los Angeles, two taxi cooperatives enabled émigrés to develop the connections, skills, and capital sources that allowed their eventual movement into more extensive self-employment activities.[55] The Moscow-born vice-president of one cooperative described his experience as typical for a Soviet Jewish cab owner:

> When I got here first, I got a job in East L.A. in a garment factory. I worked very hard by the way, always sweating. Just moving around cloth—I sure wasn't satisfied. And then I found out about cab association. It's got 201 members, 94 are Russians. And I found out I can make a little more money driving a cab. I worked as a lease driver at first, and in 1978, I bought my own cab. Now I lease it at nights to other Russian driver.

> I'm not going to drive my cab for all my life. I'm planning for the future to go to some kind of different business—a shop or restaurant. My wife already has a beauty parlor.

> So that's why we have so many Russians. Most of them—like me—are business-minded people. Driving a cab is a start. In the future, a lot of them will go into

---

[53]Federation of Jewish Philanthropies of New York, *Jewish Identification and Affiliation of Soviet Jewish Immigrants in New York City—A Needs Assessment and Planning Study*, 1985.

[54]Kestin, "Making Cheese from Snow"; Nancy Lubin, "Small Business Owners," in *New Lives*, ed. Rita J. Simon, pp. 151–64; Orleck, "Soviet Jews: Life in Brighton Beach"; Steven J. Gold, "Refugees and Small Business: The Case of Soviet Jews and Vietnamese," *Ethnic and Racial Studies* 11, no. 4, 1988, pp. 411–38; Gold, *Refugee Communities*; Halter, "Ethnicity and the Entrepreneur"; Raymond Russell, *Sharing Ownership in the Workplace* (Albany, 1985).

[55]Russell, *Sharing Ownership*.

other businesses. A lot are already in businesses—stores, restaurants, body shops. They rely on partnerships.[56]

Through such business networks, Soviet émigrés obtain a variety of resources useful in opening and running a successful operation. Well-established entrepreneurs often give novices advice about contracts, licenses, and appropriate store locations.[57] Members also offer each other opportunities for investment. For example, in San Francisco, a Soviet Jewish realty company distributed information about available storefronts and supplied real-estate speculators with lists of homes that could be purchased and refurbished for resale. Soviet entrepreneurs also supplied one another with investment capital.[58]

For many members of the business subgroup, self-employment provides not only a source of income, but also a sense of personal and ethnic identity, a means of access to American society, and a social life. As such, ethnic identity and solidarity are reinforced through economic cooperation. Because these émigrés came from a secular society, their understanding of Jewish identity draws more from Jews' accomplishments than from religious teachings and practices. Many even see a predisposition toward business as a central component of Jewish ethnicity, priding themselves on an ability to survive under any and all conditions.

In Los Angeles, over 100 Soviet doctors formed a professional association. Because foreign medical graduates find it difficult to obtain certification in a specialty, they seldom obtain employment in hospitals or HMOs (health maintenance organizations). Instead, many enter private practice—a form of self-employment. Their offices are located adjacent to neighborhoods where Russian émigrés—who prefer to visit Russian-speaking physicians—live. Soviet émigré doctors happily accept their fellow refugees' government-provided health benefits. In turn, émigré doctors and dentists support self-employed Russian pharmacists, physical therapists, dentists, and the like. Finally, émigré doctors buy a large proportion of the advertising in the Russian-language print and broadcast media. For example, in 1991, 50 of the 108 advertisements in the 1991 Los Angeles Russian-language telephone directory offered various medical services.

Data from the 1990 census suggest that a sizable fraction of Soviets are self-employed. In New York, 15 percent are self-employed (21 percent of men and 8 percent of women), with higher rates in Los Angeles, where 25

---

[56]Gold, *Refugee Communities*, pp. 202–03.
[57]Lubin, "Small Business Owners"; Halter, "Ethnicity and the Entrepreneur."
[58]Gold, "Refugees and Small Business"; Steven J. Gold, "Patterns of Interaction and Adjustment Among Soviet Jewish Refugees," *Contemporary Jewry* 9, no. 2, 1988, pp. 87–105; idem, "Nascent Mobilization in a New Immigrant Community: The Case of Soviet Jews in California," *Research in Community Sociology* 2, 1991, pp. 185–208.

percent (33 percent of men and 17 percent of women) are self-employed. (See table 12.) When compared to 1980 census data about various migrant groups, the Los Angeles figure puts Soviet Jews among those groups with the highest rates of self-employment. This is an impressive finding, considering that, as refugees from a communist nation, Soviet Jews lack two of the most essential resources for entrepreneurship—business experience and investment capital. On the other hand, the rate of entrepreneurship among Jewish immigrants to the United States has always been high, since it was viewed as a viable adjustment strategy.[59]

WOMEN IN TECHNICAL FIELDS

One economic asset of the Soviet Jews over natives or other immigrant groups is the unusually high number of women with professional and technical skills: 67 percent of Soviet Jewish women in the United States were engineers, technicians, or other kinds of professionals prior to migration. In contrast, only 16.5 percent of American women work in these occupations.[60] (See table 13.)

According to the 1990 census, 29 percent of all Soviet émigré women in New York City and 26 percent of Soviet émigré women in Los Angeles County work as professionals in the United States. In New York, a smaller proportion of Soviet-born men are employed in these occupations; however, Soviet-born men in Los Angeles exceed Soviet-born women's professional employment by 2 percent. (See table 10.)

Simon et al., using 1981 data, report that, despite their high rates of education and professional experience, Soviet Jewish women were still making less than 60 percent of Soviet Jewish men's income in the United States. Results from the 1990 census suggest that the income gap has not closed a great deal, although women who arrived in the United States between 1975 and 1981 and live in New York City make about 70 percent of their male counterparts' incomes. (See table 6.) Simon et al. also found that Soviet women are generally less satisfied with their work situation in the United States than are Soviet men. About 30 percent of women said their work

---

[59]Gold, "Patterns of Interaction and Adjustment"; Boris Z. Gorbis, "Give Us Your Poor Homeless Organizations: A Review of California's Soviet-Jewish Organizations," in *New Voices: The Integration of Soviet Emigres and Their Organizations into the Jewish Communal World*, ed. Madeleine Tress and Deborah Bernick (Council of Jewish Federations, 1992), pp. 17–23.

[60]Simon, *New Lives*, p. 17; Rita J. Simon, Louise Shelly, and Paul Schneiderman, "Social and Economic Adjustment of Soviet Jewish Women in the United States," in *International Migration: The Female Experience*, ed. Rita James Simon and Caroline B. Brettell (Totowa, N.J., 1986), pp. 76–94; Eckles et al., "Portrait in Diversity," p. 29; *Statistical Abstract of the U.S. 1984*, p. 416.

situation was better than in the USSR, compared to 40 percent of men. In contrast, 49 percent of women called their work situation worse, while only 41 percent of men felt this way.[61]

Relations with Resettlement Agencies

Soviet Jews in the United States enjoy perhaps the best-funded and most professionally staffed resettlement system provided to any recent immigrants and refugees.[62] Soviet Jews generally have positive evaluations of the services they receive in resettlement. Gitelman found that 80.4 percent of émigrés to the United States rated their resettlement agencies as working "very well; well; or not badly" (versus 44.3 percent of Soviet Jews in Israel).[63] A New York-based study found that 71 percent of émigrés had a positive impression of NYANA (their major resettlement agency), while only 29 percent had a negative impression.[64]

Still, émigrés confront difficulties in adjusting to the United States, particularly in regard to what Simon et al. call "bread and butter issues": learning English, finding a job, earning enough money, and missing family and friends.

Unlike most immigrants, who have little experience in obtaining government services, former Soviets come from a society in which substantially more of life's necessities are distributed by government agencies than is the case here. Despite their experience in interacting with bureaucracies, however, former Soviets have to learn new ways of interacting with agencies in a dramatically different social context. A fairly large literature addresses Soviets' encounters with American-style bureaucracy in various areas of service provision, including cash assistance, physical and mental health, job placement, and community socialization.[65]

---

[61]Simon et al., "Social and Economic Adjustment," p. 89.

[62]Eckles et al., "Portrait in Diversity"; GAO (U.S. General Accounting Office), *Soviet Refugees: Processing and Admittance to the United States*, GAO/NSIAD-90–158, 1990, p. 25.

[63]Gitelman, "Quality of Life," p. 62.

[64]Federation of Jewish Philanthropies of New York, "Jewish Identification," p. 39.

[65]Steven J. Gold, "Dealing with Frustration: A Study of Interactions Between Resettlement Staff and Refugees," in *People in Upheaval*, ed. Scott Morgan and Elizabeth Colson (New York, 1987), pp. 108–28; idem, *Refugee Communities*; Fran Markowitz, "Jewish in the USSR, Russian in the USA," in *Persistence and Flexibility: Anthropological Perspectives on the American Jewish Experience*, ed. Walter P. Zenner (Albany, 1988), pp. 79–95; idem, *Community in Spite of Itself*; Meryl Brod and Suzanne Heurtin-Roberts, "Older Russian Emigres and Medical Care," *Western Journal of Medicine* 157, no. 3, 1992, pp. 333–36; Rochelle P. Stutz, "Resettling Soviet Emigres: How Caseworkers Coped," *Social Work*, Mar.-Apr. 1984, pp. 187–88; Dorsh de Voe, "Framing Refugees as Clients," *International Migration Review* 15, no. 1, 1981, pp. 88–94; Maria Coughlin and Regina Rosenberg, "Health Education and Beyond: A Soviet Women's Group Experience," *Journal of Jewish Communal Service* 60, no.

The difficulties involved in resettlement result from the near impossibility of the task at hand—delivering elusive elements of social membership on demand. No matter how well funded a resettlement agency nor how skillful its staff, the major goals of resettlement—economic self-sufficiency and cultural adjustment—are difficult to attain. Economic self-sufficiency is largely dependent on economic factors beyond any resettlement worker's control. Similarly, cultural adjustment, learning English, and coping with the mental trauma brought on by the refugee experience itself can only be achieved through the efforts of refugees themselves, expended over protracted periods of time.

Further complicating matters are the differences in cultural backgrounds of providers and recipients of services. For many refugees, resettlement staff are the first representatives of American society with whom they have any significant contact, and even the most basic interactions involve various forms of cultural conflict. Thus, to do their job at all, resettlement agencies, schools, and the like must socialize their clients in the ways of American society. In the words of one government resettlement report: "There are aspects of American life with which refugees must simply learn to cope."[66]

LANGUAGE

Soviet émigrés (with the exception of the elderly) tend to make excellent progress with language. Several studies found that, while about half spoke no English on arrival, within a few years upward of two-thirds or more rate themselves as "good" (or better) in the English language and a large proportion (50–70 percent) have taken English classes.[67]

JOB PLACEMENT

The development of economic self-sufficiency is one of the major responsibilities of the refugee resettlement system. Staff and clients alike agree that refugees should find jobs, but recently arrived refugees who lack compe-

1, 1983, pp. 65–69; Nina Dorf and Fay Katlin, "The Soviet Jewish Immigrant Client: Beyond Resettlement," *Journal of Jewish Communal Service* 60, no. 2, 1983, pp. 146–54; Drachman and Halberstadt, "A Stage of Migration Framework," pp. 63–78; Joann Ivry, "Paraprofessionals in Refugee Resettlement," in Ryan, ed., *Social Work with Immigrants and Refugees*, pp. 99–117.

[66]Donald J. Cichon, Elizabeta M. Gozdziak, and Jane G. Grover, *The Economic and Social Adjustment of Non-Southeast Asian Refugees*, vol. 1: *Analysis Across Cases* (Research Management Corp., Dover, N.H., 1986), p. 87; Lewin and Associates, *Assessment of the MAA Incentive Grant Initiative*; ORR, *Report to Congress 1986*.

[67]Kosmin, *Class of 1979*; Simon, *New Lives*; Federation of Jewish Philanthropies of New York, "Jewish Identification"; Jewish Family Service of the North Shore, "Social Needs Survey," table 6.

tence in English generally have little understanding of the American economy and the means of finding jobs within it. Adding to the difficulty, many Soviet Jewish refugees entered the U.S. job market during the early 1980s and a decade later, in the late 1980s and early 1990s—periods marked by recession and high unemployment rates—when jobs were often scarce.

All the relevant factors—the need for jobs, the scarcity of job opportunities, and refugees' lack of understanding of American job-finding practices—must be confronted during face-to-face interactions in the job-placement units of refugee resettlement agencies, most commonly the Jewish Vocational Service. Émigrés are heavy consumers of job-placement services. According to data from the 1990–91 Jewish population study of New York, one in four post-1965 Jewish immigrants from the former Soviet Union sought help in finding a job in the 12 months prior to the date of the survey. In contrast, only one in ten members of the larger Jewish community sought such services.

Because of the vast differences between Soviet and American procedures for finding employment, some recently arrived émigrés have particularly difficult interactions with American job-placement workers. Some émigrés interpret their interactions with the Jewish Vocational Service in light of past encounters with Raspredelenie, the Soviet state employment agency. Under this system, qualified workers simply showed their diplomas and credentials to the centralized placement office and were assigned appropriate jobs. Elements typical of the American job-search process, such as finding openings, dealing with employment services, preparing resumes, and selling one's self in interviews were nonexistent. Hence, émigrés are often overwhelmed by the complexity and uncertainty of the American process. Drawing upon their Soviet experience, in which desired services were often delivered by bureaucrats in exchange for favors, émigrés who are not referred to jobs of their liking sometimes assume that agency staff are holding out in order to receive a payoff.[68] Accordingly, émigrés have occasionally attempted to bribe staff or offer indirect payment in the form of contributions to the Jewish federation.

Émigrés have also tried to acquire jobs through Soviet-style political machinations involving *"blat"* (influence) and *"sviazy"* (connections). This quote from a job-finding class for émigré engineers at a California JCC illustrates a common émigré mind-set:

> All of this training, it's no good. This is what we should do. Do you know the director of the Jewish Federation? Does he make appointments with people like us? We will talk to him. He could go to the president of big engineering company, Jewish president, and tell him to hire some of us. There are only a few of us. He could hire one of us each week.[69]

---

[68] Di Francisco and Gitelman, "Soviet Political Culture."
[69] Gold, *Refugee Communities*, p. 147.

Émigrés like this see American institutions through the lens of their Soviet experience. Rather than following the suggestions of agency staff, they try to apply job-finding techniques that worked in the USSR.

The fact that many Soviet Jewish refugees are professionals only serves to intensify the conflicts with job-placement agencies. With university education and years of experience, they identify strongly with their previous occupations and are unhappy about accepting the lower-status positions to which they are often referred. Some Soviet Jews may be angered by their job-placement experience to the point of distancing themselves from the Jewish community. They may complain of inadequate guidance and career counseling, not enough personal involvement, and of being pushed to accept low-level jobs.

In the words of a Los Angeles Soviet Jewish activist, some of the complaints are justified, and some of the expectations are realistic. Yet for many, there is only a one- or two-time exposure to a counselor of family or vocational service. Those who are dissatisfied tend to view the whole Jewish community in America in a negative light.[70]

MENTAL HEALTH

Another area in which extensive cultural conflict and misunderstanding arise between resettlement staff and their Soviet Jewish clients is that of psychological therapy. When health assessments revealed that refugees suffer from a variety of mental-health problems, the government and resettlement agencies established mental-health programs specifically for this population. Unfortunately, Soviet Jews often lack the cultural prerequisites of a successful American-style therapy interaction, such as a willingness to confide in bureaucrats and a belief in the unconscious. Most refugees also do not see a connection between the process of therapy and the problems that, for them, are most pressing.

Social workers and therapists who work with Soviet refugees describe extensive conflicts based on mistrust, the stigmatized status of mental-health problems in the USSR, and the fact that mental illness was generally treated by medication rather than psychological therapy. "Depression, for example, is perceived in the Soviet Union as a biological entity and biochemical treatment is offered. A refugee client experiencing depression, therefore, expects to be treated with a pill. A service provider who attempts to deal with the depression through a commonly used method of talking therapy is not only perceived as strange but is also viewed as incompetent as the client doesn't receive what he/she thinks is needed."[71]

---

[70]Ibid., p. 149.
[71]Drachman and Halberstadt, "A Stage of Migration Framework," p. 73.

Despite their generally negative impression of American-style therapy interactions, immigrants apparently do consume such services at a fairly high rate. According to the 1990–91 Jewish population study of New York, 11 percent of post-1965 Jewish immigrants from the former Soviet Union sought personal, group, or family counseling in the previous year, compared with 17 percent of all New York Jews. However, former Soviets sought help with their children's emotional or behavioral problems at twice the rate of members of the Jewish community at large.

In sum, culture-based conflicts in several areas of service delivery are challenging to resettlement staff and clients alike. Moreover, since job placement, religious socialization, and mental-health services account for a significant portion of the encounters between Soviet Jews and American Jewish agencies, the images that the two communities often develop of each other in a hostile setting may overwhelm the mutual good will with which they began their relationship.

School and Social Adjustment

SCHOOL

School-aged émigrés are generally well educated and tend to excel in American schools. For example, in a 1991 comparison of the 12 largest immigrant groups in the New York City public schools, grades 3–12, who had been in the country three years or less, students from the former Soviet Union ranked first in reading scores, second in math, and fifth in English. Their reading and math scores were much higher than those of all students in New York schools, including the native-born. In addition, their mean increase in score over the previous year was the highest among all groups in both reading and English and among the highest in math.[72]

Despite their academic prowess, Soviet youth often experience frustration in American schools and may have difficulty working toward their own goals. Schools in the former USSR are generally more rigorous and accelerated than their American counterparts, with students attending a ten-year (most recently eleven) rather than a twelve-year system. Soviet students begin studying advanced subjects such as calculus and biology before Americans and consequently are years of ahead of Americans of the same age.[73]

Because of the lack of structural congruency between the two educational

---

[72]*Test Scores of Recent Immigrants and Other Students, New York City Public Schools, Grades 3–12* (New York City Public Schools, Office of Research, Evaluation and Assessment, 1991).

[73]Steven J. Gold and Mia Tuan, "Jews from the Former Soviet Union in the United States," *New Faces of Liberty*, 1993.

systems, Russian students are frequently required to repeat earlier work, which tends to erode the high levels of achievement motivation they come with initially. Students' frustration is compounded by the fact that their limited English ability prevents them from expressing themselves or demonstrating their advanced knowledge.[74]

A few young émigrés who experience their years in American high schools as an unwarranted delay that prevents them from achieving preset life goals choose to follow an alternative educational path. Having discovered that junior colleges will often accept students without a diploma, they drop out to pursue what they see as the fast track to a college education. Some follow the correct procedures for withdrawal, while others simply stop coming to school. If their plans to obtain the AA degree are thwarted, such students find themselves lacking even basic English skills and a high-school diploma and accordingly find few options for employment.

FAMILY PATTERNS

Unlike most immigrant and refugee groups, which are characterized by a youthful population, many Russian Jewish families contain elderly individuals. Refugee families experience problems because the elderly have difficulties learning English, finding employment, and making their way in the United States. Families that have successfully adapted to American life express concern over the relative isolation of elderly family members.

Generational conflict, which exists among all immigrant families, may be aggravated by the gaps in levels of adjustment between the generations. For example, Sasha, a 35-year-old Russian Jew, was making $30,000 a year as a computer programmer two years after his arrival in this country in 1982. His position contrasted dramatically with that of his parents, who knew almost no English, did not drive, and were unemployed. Consequently, Sasha had to support them financially, serve as their translator, and provide transportation in addition to managing his own career and family life. To offer the parents some independence, the family resided in a Russian-speaking neighborhood, but this was far from his job, requiring Sasha to make an 80-mile commute.[75]

Many patterns typical of Soviet émigré families, including small size, employment of both parents outside the home, and the high priority placed on children's education facilitate their adjustment to American society. At

---

[74]Gloria Zicht, "The Effects of Emigration on Soviet Jewish Children: Latency to Adolescence," *Journal of Jewish Communal Service*, Fall 1993, pp. 57–63.

[75]Gold, *Refugee Communities*. See S. N. Eisenstadt, *From Generation to Generation: Age Groups and Social Structure* (New York, 1956); and Carlos E. Sluzki, "Migration and Family Conflict," *Family Process* 18, no. 4, 1979, pp. 381–94.

the same time, certain family and cultural patterns pose difficulties in the new setting. In the former Soviet Union, parents tend to be highly involved in their children's lives. In contrast, the peer group, a central force in American adolescents' socialization, has relatively little influence. This is especially so among Jewish families, because parents feel their efforts are necessary to shield children from anti-Semitism and ensure chances for success. Carried over to the United States, this desire to protect children may foster excessive dependence and prevent émigré youth from dealing with American life on their own terms.[76] A San Francisco resettlement worker referred to this as she observed that many Soviet Jewish adolescents lack a life of their own:

> I have seen such cases of depressing loneliness in a 20-year-old boy or girl. It is easy if they live on the campus—that's a real chance to meet people. But many don't do it. They come and go to City College or a business school for a year.
>
> Then they go to work and they live with their parents. If they don't have friends among other immigrants, it's unbelievable. I know this one 22-year-old. She's beautiful, she's subtle. I think you would say she is a very intelligent young girl. She spends most of her time at work and then she spends time with her family. There is no outlet to go out because she doesn't know how to.[77]

In general, Soviets show a marked preference for social interaction with other émigrés, and this extends to the younger generation.[78] In a pilot study of dating behavior, for example, Fruchtbaum and Skager found that teenage émigré girls who had lived in the United States from 8 to 14 years (and so were quite acculturated) all "expressed their preference for Russian men as boyfriends and marriage partners," because they believed it would be easier to understand, trust, and become close with a young man with whom they shared a common background. The girls' parents openly encouraged them to date Russians. "The need for the boyfriend to be accepted by the parents and the family, and the importance of good communication between parents and the boyfriend were expressed by all of the participants."[79]

---

[76]Michael Aronowitz, "The Social and Emotional Adjustment of Immigrant Children: A Review of the Literature," *International Migration Review* 18, no. 2, 1984, pp. 237–57; Phillis Hulewat, "Dynamics of the Soviet Jewish Family: Its Impact on Clinical Practice for the Jewish Family Agency," *Journal of Jewish Communal Service* 58, no. 1, 1981, pp. 53–60.

[77]Gold, *Refugee Communities*, p. 85.

[78]Kosmin, *Class of 1979*, pp. 15–37; Markowitz, *Community in Spite of Itself.*

[79]Simcha R. Goldberg, "Jewish Acculturation and the Soviet Immigrant," *Journal of Jewish Communal Service* 57, no. 1, 1981, pp. 154–63; Steven J. Gold, "Differential Adjustment Among New Immigrant Family Members," *Journal of Contemporary Ethnography* 17, no. 4, 1989, pp. 408–34; Irene Fruchtbaum and Rodney Skager, "Influence of Parental Values on Dating Behavior of Young Russian Women: A Cross-Cultural Perspective," UCLA Department of Education, 1989, pp. 18–19.

COMMUNITY TIES

Soviet Jews have considerable social interaction with each other, but take part in few organized activities. They tend to live in geographically concentrated communities, which allows the many aged émigrés to mingle easily. Neighborhood networks of family and friends are important not only as sources of social connection but as resources for information and practical help.[80] The many ethnic small businesses in these areas direct their goods and services to émigrés. Various publications, especially *Novoye Russkoye Slovo* (New York) and *Panorama* (Los Angeles), are available as well as Russian-language TV and radio. Émigrés are also frequent consumers of American media.[81]

As already noted, the Soviet Jewish communities are marked by divisions based on region of origin, educational level, occupation, and other factors. At the same time, Jews from the former Soviet Union, especially the great majority from the European republics, have many social similarities. They tend to be educated, urbanized, and Russian-speaking, and to share many common values. Generally more conservative than the Jewish and non-Jewish Americans near whom they reside, émigrés often complain about gays, minority groups, graffiti, the crime rate, drug use, pornography, and lack of discipline in schools. While retaining a fear of anti-Semitism, they nevertheless have a strong identity as whites and sometimes make disparaging comments regarding blacks and Asians. They are especially incensed by liberals (heavily represented in the American Jewish community) who oppose nuclear power, distrust the military, and demand civil liberties for social misfits.[82]

These views separate them politically from many of their co-ethnic hosts. Jews from the former Soviet Union have been described as "a community that is staunchly conservative Republican and is quite puzzled by the left-leaning liberalism of American Jews." A Soviet Jewish journalist commented on Soviet Jews' differences with their American counterparts: "Most American Jews are used to being liberals. But Russian Jews, having very tough experience, know what socialism does mean. They are very close to the right wing, politically. We have gotten involved with the campaigns. I think that almost everybody voted for Republicans."[83]

---

[80]Kosmin, *Class of 1979*; Orleck, "Soviet Jews: Life in Brighton Beach"; Markowitz, *Community in Spite of Itself*.

[81]Gold, "Refugees and Small Business"; idem, "Patterns of Interaction and Adjustment"; Orleck, "Soviet Jews: Life in Brighton Beach"; Markowitz, *Community in Spite of Itself*.

[82]Gold, *Refugee Communities*; Leo Noonan, "Russians Go Republican," *Jewish Journal* (Los Angeles), Nov. 18–24, p. 31. Markowitz, in *Community in Spite of Itself*, describes how New York's Soviet Jews strongly supported Bernard Goetz, a white man who shot four black youths demanding money in the subway.

[83]Frumkin, "Who Are the Russians?" p. 17; Gold, *Refugee Communities*, p. 209.

RELATIONS WITH AMERICAN JEWS

It appears that Soviet Jews do not form many close relationships with American Jews or non-Jews. One reason is the cultural and linguistic gap between émigrés and American Jews, including the differences in social and political attitudes. Another, particularly in large metropolitan areas, is geographic separation—Soviet Jews tend to live in self-contained enclaves. A Soviet Jewish woman who had lived in the San Francisco Bay Area for ten years commented on the difficulty of developing friendships with Americans:

> From the beginning, everybody wants to be assimilated, to get out of this ghetto, and nobody wants to accept it that they are in a ghetto in the Richmond District, Sunset District. But after that, people get out and a lot of them probably didn't fill up their expectation and they had a problem socializing with Americans [Jews] and this is not their language. And after a while, they get back together and about 25 percent of the community still wanted to get out and 75 percent completely satisfied with what they have.[84]

Émigrés are also drawn together as they encounter the resentment that some American Jews harbor toward them. In interviews, émigrés bristled at American Jews' assertion that they should have settled in Israel or that because they lacked religious knowledge, they were not "real Jews."

> I remember, even when I didn't know the language so well, I could hear the question "How do you know you are a Jew if you didn't do this and you didn't know that." And "Why didn't they go to Israel?"

> I tell you, each family have some that died in the Ghetto. That's the kind of experience that you grow up with as a kid. Not long ago, we had a discussion on Jewish religious education with American Jews and we told them, "We are Jewish enough and sometimes more than enough."[85]

Soviet Jews who arrived prior to 1990 disliked being called "*noshrim*" (dropouts) for not settling in Israel. Whenever Jewish agencies discussed measures to force Soviets to settle in the Jewish state, émigrés expressed their displeasure, pointing out the hypocrisy of such statements, saying, "Let my people go, indeed!" In the words of a Los Angeles activist:

> This is a very sensitive problem, but we have to face it and be honest, because unfortunately, I have to say that I've heard a lot of statements on behalf of American Jews, okay, which I can only describe as a double standard. Why should they sit in Beverly Hills and accuse me of not going over to Israel and I left Russia with $120 and he has all the money in the world?[86]

The feeling of being rejected by American Jews provides Soviet Jews with yet another reason to turn toward fellow émigrés.

---

[84]Gold, *Refugee Communities*, p. 208.
[85]Ibid.
[86]Ibid., pp. 162–63.

RESISTANCE TO ORGANIZATION

Émigrés generally avoid formal organizations. This is both because they lack experience in creating voluntary associations, and also because in the USSR, such entities were imposed by government bureaucrats rather than voluntarily created by members. Consequently, émigrés assume that persons who take leadership roles in communal activities do so only in order to obtain some personal benefit. According to a report on Soviet Jewish émigré organizations, émigrés "developed a very strong negative attitude toward such organizations and activities," and "the figure of the social activist acquired a permanent negative classification in the minds of many new immigrants."[87] Studies on both coasts describe émigrés' difficulties in creating viable associations.[88]

Nevertheless, several types of formal organizations have come into being: broad-based groups that seek to unite all Russian Jews or "new Americans"; veterans' associations; networks of entrepreneurs (as described above); professional associations; and groups involved with leisure and cultural activities, such as sports and music. In the religious sphere, the Chabad-Lubavitch organization has organized synagogues for Russian speakers in several localities. In different ways, these entities seek to help newcomers adapt to the United States, retain Russian-language culture, and develop a Jewish identity. They vary widely in terms of their emphasis on a Russian or Jewish cultural orientation, their financial well-being, stability, and relations with American Jewish groups.

In considering the communal life of Soviet Jews, it has been noted that the high levels of skill they possess—together with the many benefits they receive from the Jewish community and the U.S. government—may actually reduce their need to create mutual-aid associations of the type common among other migrant communities, including earlier cohorts of Russian Jews.[89] Consequently, by their very existence, resettlement services may offer a disincentive to group formation.

JEWISH IDENTITY AND BEHAVIOR

Jewish identity is a complex issue for Soviet émigrés. Although most have had little formal Jewish education (Kosmin reported 4 percent having had

---

[87]Pavel Ilyin and Mikaella Kagan, "Finding a Niche in American Jewish Institutional Life—Soviet Jewish Emigre Organizations," paper presented at the Wilstein Institute for Jewish Policy Studies Conference, Soviet Jewish Acculturation—Beyond Resettlement, Palo Alto, 1991, p. 5.

[88]Gold, *Refugee Communities*; Markowitz, *Community in Spite of Itself*.

[89]Eckles et al., "Portrait in Diversity."

one year prior to migration), many appear to have deep feelings of connectedness and a strong sense of ethnic or national identification as Jews.[90]

The Soviet émigré population is marked by generational variation in religious background. Three generations of Soviet émigrés in the United States—the elderly, the middle-aged, and the young—have each had a different experience with Judaism.[91] The elderly are often familiar with the traditional Eastern European Judaism that they learned from their parents or before the Stalinist crackdowns of the 1930s. Middle-aged Soviet Jews grew up in an atheistic environment that encouraged them to assimilate and deprived them of any Jewish content in their lives. An engineer in his forties describes his lack of Jewish knowledge:

> No Jewish culture at all . . . you know our family lost it completely. It was a shame. When we went to Vienna [after leaving the USSR], they were kind of sorting people who the agencies would be taking care of. And they looked at our family—we didn't look like Jews to them. And they started to ask questions what we know about Jewish life. Do we know any holidays? And we were so ashamed— we didn't know any. Then I remembered. When I was a little kid, my grandfather gave us Hanukkah gold—Gelt. I recalled getting presents. And I told them about the Hanukkah Gelt—they started to laugh like crazy.[92]

Finally, émigré children who have spent a few years in the United States have by now had some exposure to contemporary Judaism, since numerous religious activities, scholarships to Jewish camps, schools, and the like are made available as part of their resettlement program.

In general, Jewish identification among émigrés is secular or nationalistic rather than religious. Kosmin found that over 60 percent of émigrés surveyed felt that the meaning of being Jewish in America was "Cultural" or "Nationality," while less than 30 percent felt it was "Religious." The New York Federation of Jewish Philanthropies found similar results, with 79 percent favoring "Nationality," 62 percent "Culture/History; Ethnic Group," and 24 percent "Religion" as definitions of Jewish identity in the United States.[93]

Emigrés from the former Soviet Union are in various ways more "ethnic" than many American Jews in their involvement with other Jews, networks, and outlooks. In this sense—following the analysis of sociologist Herbert Gans—the Soviet Jews are at an earlier stage in their group identity. According to Gans, assimilated, third-plus-generation American white ethnics

---

[90]Kosmin, *Class of 1979*; Markowitz, "Jewish in the USSR."

[91]Alexander Orbach, "The Jewish of Soviet-Jewish Culture: Historical Considerations," *Journal of Jewish Communal Service* 58, no. 3, 1980, pp. 145–53; Lionel Kochan, ed., *The Jews in Soviet Russia Since 1917* (London, 1978).

[92]Gold, *Refugee Communities*, p. 36.

[93]Federation of Jewish Philanthropies of New York, 1985, p. 21; Kosmin, *Class of 1979*, p. 35.

(notably Jews) maintain "symbolic ethnicity" through self-selected, identity-related expressive behaviors, whereas first-generation individuals rely extensively on their own ethnic communities and networks for the fulfillment of basic needs.[94]

Evidence of the Soviet émigrés' strong ethnic ties can be gleaned from their responses to several questions in the 1990–91 New York Jewish population study (table 14). For example, Jews from the former Soviet Union are more competent in Yiddish, more likely to be members of Jewish community centers (JCCs) or YMHAs, and read more Jewish publications than all New York Jews. They are much more likely than all New York Jews to have close friends or immediate family living in Israel, to have Jews as their closest friends, and to believe that when it comes to a crisis, Jews can only depend on other Jews. Finally, as noted above, Jews from the former USSR have more negative views of intermarriage, even when the non-Jewish spouse converts to Judaism, than do all New York Jews. These measures suggest that, despite Russian émigrés' lower rates of Jewish education and religiosity than American Jews, their Jewish identity is expressed in a variety of other ways.

Soviet Jews in Brighton Beach (Brooklyn), for example, have created their own rituals, such as bar mitzvahs and weddings, that take place in Russian restaurants and feature Russian-speaking American rabbis. Symbolically blending and reconciling Jewish and American identities in the context of a Russian nightclub/restaurant, they demonstrate that the bar mitzvah child, and by extension the family and all others present, are fully accepted as Jews in America, and also, that being Jewish is worthy and fun.[95]

The 1991 Jewish population study of New York found that post-1965 émigrés are especially likely to be involved in certain Jewish community celebrations. For example, their rates of attendance at "activities that support Israel or Soviet Jewry," Purim carnivals, Israel Independence Day, and Holocaust commemorations all exceed those of the greater New York Jewish community. The high rates of former Soviets' involvement in these may be the result of effective programming by Jewish community agencies. (See table 15.)

Yiddish

Different studies report different levels of Yiddish knowledge among émigrés, depending in part on what exactly was asked. A 1985 New York

---

[94]Herbert Gans, "Symbolic Ethnicity: The Future of Ethnic Groups and Cultures in America," *Ethnic and Racial Studies* 2, no. 1, 1979, pp. 1–20.
[95]Markowitz, *Community in Spite of Itself*, p. 161.

study reported that 68 percent of émigrés understand, and 43 percent speak, Yiddish; the 1990–91 New York Jewish population study found that 42 percent of post-1965 Soviet Jewish émigrés speak Yiddish, in contrast to 38 percent of all Jews in New York. However, the percentage that can read or write the language is smaller, 13 percent or less. As might be expected, the elderly tend to have much more Yiddish ability. Krautman's Los Angeles study found that 50 percent understand Yiddish. Kosmin reported that 43 percent speak Yiddish. According to the 1990 census, 2.3 percent of émigrés in New York and 0.3 percent of émigrés in Los Angeles speak Yiddish at home, while 1.4 percent in New York and 1.9 percent in Los Angeles speak Hebrew at home.[96] (See table 16.)

Religious and Communal Participation

A number of surveys have explored Soviet Jews' participation in specific Jewish rituals and behaviors and found it to be roughly similar to that of American Jews. Émigrés who have been in the United States longer and are financially better off tend to be more involved in Jewish life.[97] (See table 17.)

SYNAGOGUE MEMBERSHIP

Kosmin found that around 40 percent of Soviet Jews belong to synagogues, with Reform being the dominant affiliation. This finding is consistent with the 1990–91 Jewish population study of New York, which determined that 42 percent of post-1965 Jewish immigrants from the former Soviet Union are dues-paying members of a synagogue or temple, the same proportion as in the larger New York community. The rank order of their membership—Reform, Conservative, Orthodox, and Reconstructionist—is the same as that of the larger community. In the New York study, the Soviets' pattern of synagogue attendance differs somewhat from that of other Jews: roughly 40 percent of Soviets attend only on High Holy Days, compared with 16 percent of all Jews; but the proportions saying they attend once a month or more are about the same. (See table 18.)

Krautman's 1990 Los Angeles study found that 28 percent of Soviet émigrés had belonged to a synagogue at some point during their stay in the

---

[96]Jerry Allan Krautman, "A Study of the Acculturation and Jewish Identity of Soviet Jews Emigrating to Los Angeles Between 1972 and 1989" (MBA thesis, University of Judaism, 1990), p. 21; Kosmin, *Class of 1979*, p. 19; Federation of Jewish Philanthropies of New York, 1985, p. 11.

[97]Kosmin, *Class of 1979*, p. 53; Simon, *New Lives*, p. 36; Federation of Jewish Philanthropies of New York, 1985, pp. 28–29, 38. In comparing the figures, Simon found lower rates on most practices. This may be due to the fact that her data were collected at an earlier date. The higher rates may also reflect the interviewees' perception of desired response.

United States, with far higher membership (42 percent) among those who came prior to 1980. In Los Angeles, Chabad was the most commonly cited form of synagogue membership, followed by Reform. For example, nearly all Soviet Jews in Los Angeles can name the two Russian Chabad rabbis, while far fewer are familiar with American rabbis or synagogues.[98]

OTHER JEWISH ORGANIZATIONS

In addition to synagogues, Soviet Jews are most often involved with Jewish community centers. Kosmin, in a national sample, found about 20 percent with some JCC involvement. Krautman found that Los Angeles émigrés were most often involved with health and resettlement agencies, the Jewish Federation Council, and the JCC. The 1985 New York Federation study found the JCC and YM-YWHA were the most common Jewish affiliations, with 35 percent involved. In the 1991 New York study, 24 percent of post-1965 émigrés indicated participation in YM-YWHA activities, compared with 13 percent of all Jews. Asked whether they had heard of New York UJA-Federation, 89 percent of all Jews had, compared with 56 percent of Soviets.[99]

JEWISH EDUCATION FOR CHILDREN

Surveys reflect a strong interest on the part of émigré parents to promote their children's involvement in Jewish activities. When free or reduced day-school tuition is offered to recently arrived Soviet Jewish children, a large proportion accept. However, as fee waivers expire, many leave these schools. Émigré parents' desire to send their children to day school is motivated not only by religious goals but by concern about the lack of safety, attention, and discipline they associate with urban public schools. Barber asserts that Soviet Jews generally favor academic over religious training and often object to expending more than what they consider to be a minimal amount of time on Judaic studies.[100]

Kosmin found that 80 percent of 12-year-olds were being sent to some kind of Jewish education. He indicates that Jewish education is most directly associated with preparation for the bar or bat mitzvah, with participation falling off rapidly after age 13. Income is significantly correlated with

---

[98]Krautman, "Study of the Acculturation . . . Los Angeles"; Gorbis, "Give Us Your Poor Homeless Organizations"; Kosmin, *Class of 1979.*

[99]Kosmin, *Class of 1979;* Krautman, "Study of the Acculturation . . . Los Angeles"; Federation of Jewish Philanthropies of New York, 1985; 1991 New York Jewish Population Study.

[100]Federation of Jewish Philanthropies of New York, 1985; Barber, "Jews of Washington Heights."

children's receiving Jewish education. In Los Angeles, 20 percent of the young people surveyed were getting some kind of Jewish education.[101]

The 1991 New York study found that 28 percent of post-1965 adult Jewish immigrants from the former Soviet Union had received some formal Jewish education as children, compared to 77 percent for all members of the larger New York Jewish community. While members of the larger community most often received their Jewish education in afternoon schools, the most common form of Jewish education for Soviets was day school. Twenty-four percent of émigrés in the New York study report having had "a bar or bat mitzvah or confirmation" when they were young, in contrast to 55 percent of all New York Jews. The Soviet figures seem high in light of what is known about the absence of Jewish education under Communism, and we may assume that some of this Jewish education was acquired after arrival in this country. Also, since the late 1980s, more Jewish educational activities have been available in the former USSR. Finally, the New York study does not specify the amount of Jewish education, so that even a one-time study session might qualify as "Jewish education" (in contrast to the Kosmin study, which specified one year).

By and large, émigré parents encourage their children to get a Jewish education and to engage in Jewish activities. For example, Simon found that 79 percent would encourage or strongly encourage children to get a Jewish education; the 1985 New York study found that 97 percent feel it is important or very important to be educated about Jewish history and culture, while 76 percent of those surveyed want their children to get a Jewish religious education.[102] (See table 19.)

Jewish Socialization

The Jewish agencies involved in the resettlement of Soviet Jews see one of their primary functions as enhancing ethnic ties and integrating émigrés into the life of the American Jewish community. Accordingly, resettlement policy has been directed at including Soviet émigrés in American Jewish activities rather than encouraging the creation of Russian or Russian-Jewish activities. Conflicts involving the religious and cultural socialization of Soviet émigrés were most intense during the early years of resettlement (prior to the mid-1980s), when media exposure to the image of the pious refusenik led most American Jews to assume that Soviet Jews would be both religious and anti-Soviet. The executive director of Jewish Family Service of Akron exemplified this position when he described the "assimilation

---

[101]Kosmin, *Class of 1979*, p. 39; Krautman, "Study of the Acculturation . . . Los Angeles," p. 25.

[102]Simon, *New Lives*, p. 38; Federation of Jewish Philanthropies of New York, 1985.

task" for Soviet exiles in a 1980 article: "If our program succeeds in its goal of awakening Jewish consciousness, then these new Americans, in the near future, should become vital, responsible, and contributing members of our Jewish community."[103]

The arrival in the United States of Russian Jews who did not fit the preconceived notion of either Yiddish-speaking shtetl characters or of knowledgeable, committed Jews and Zionists caused consternation in many Jewish circles. David Harris, then Washington representative of the American Jewish Committee, pointed out that "it has become somewhat misleading to assert that the Soviet Jew, among other reasons, 'emigrates for a new life as a Jew'—at least, that is, if he is going to the United States. On the contrary, he emigrates to the United States (or Canada, etc.) to seek a new life as a freer individual, and, often, to have, at least in the beginning, a brief respite from being a Jew."[104]

A Soviet Jewish activist in San Francisco put it this way:

> First of all, we are not like your grandparents, people from Shalom Aleichem. We are educated, professional people. If you talk about the community in general, it's a non-religious community and that's it. Because we don't have religious ground. You have to form this ground first, but I don't think this will be an overnight thing. Right now, I try really to impress to American community, for us, Jewishness is non-religious.[105]

With time, some Soviet émigrés respond positively to the Jewish socialization component of resettlement, joining synagogues, sending their children to Jewish day schools and camps, participating in Jewish community activities, and raising funds for Jewish philanthropic activities. In the 1991 New York study, for example, 57 percent of émigrés reported giving to Jewish charities in the year prior to the survey, while 66 percent of all New York Jews did so. Not surprisingly, émigrés were the most likely to give $100 or less and the least likely to give $1,000 or more. (See table 17.)

Just as émigrés sometimes resist efforts at religious training, most also retain a strong Russian identity. While most Soviet Jews generally dislike communism, many retain a feeling of attachment to the culture, language, cuisine, literature, landscape, and way of life of their homeland and are unwilling to abandon their traditions in favor of American ways. When Americans approach former Soviets with strident criticism of Russia and clear expectations that they should forsake their background, émigrés are alienated. In this they surely resemble the earlier generations of Russian

---

[103]Larry R. Schwartz, "Soviet Jewish Resettlement: Operationalizing Jewish Consciousness Raising," *Journal of Jewish Communal Service* 57, no. 1, 1980, p. 55.

[104]David Harris, "A Note on the Problem of 'Noshrim,' " *Soviet Jewish Affairs* 6, no. 2, 1976, p. 108.

[105]Gold, *Refugee Communities*, p. 209.

Jews who resisted the Americanization programs of German Jews.[106]

While officially there has been a strong emphasis on the inculcation of religion in Soviet Jewish resettlement activities, in reality, many resettlement personnel distance themselves from this task. Social workers realize that émigrés' most immediate interests involve achieving economic stability and ensuring secure careers for their children, not studying Hebrew or going to temple.[107]

By the late 1980s, acknowledgment was finally given at the organizational level to the fact that most Soviet Jews were not religiously active. Initial hopes to "create a Jewish need" or "foster Jewish language skills" and make Soviet émigrés into "vital, responsible, and contributing members of our Jewish community" were replaced by a more realistic acknowledgment of Soviet émigrés' secular and ethnic rather than religious identification.[108] An American rabbi who works with Soviet Jews reflected this realization: "One of the disappointments that many rabbis felt was that most of the Soviet Jews did not find a need to express their Jewishness. We should have understood this, because they come from a secular, atheistic country, but it was difficult to accept."[109]

By the early 1990s, there were scattered reports of religious or communal involvement on the part of some former Soviets, suggesting that the picture was not entirely uniform. For example, the Reform Beth Shalom People's Temple in Bensonhurst (Brooklyn), New York, had attracted some 500 Soviet Jewish members with programs intended to welcome émigrés on their own terms. Similarly, in Los Angeles, Russian-born rabbis involved in the Chabad movement created a number of programs, including a synagogue, where some 1,400 émigrés attended services on Yom Kippur in 1993.[110]

---

[106]Markowitz, "Jewish in the USSR"; Bernard Farber, Charles H. Mindel, and Bernard Lazerwitz, "The Jewish American Family," in *Ethnic Families in America*, 3rd ed., ed. Charles H. Mindel, Robert Habenstein, and Roosevelt Wright, Jr. (New York, 1988), pp. 400–37.

[107]Gayle Zahler, "Jewish Identity and the Soviet Emigre Newcomer," paper presented at the National Conference of Jewish Communal Workers, Boca Raton, Fla., 1989.

[108]Simcha R. Goldberg, "Jewish Acculturation and the Soviet Immigrant," *Journal of Jewish Communal Service* 57, no. 3, 1981, pp. 154–63; Schwartz, "Soviet Jewish Resettlement"; Alvin I. Schiff, "Language, Culture and the Jewish Acculturation of Soviet Jewish Emigres," *Journal of Jewish Communal Service* 57, no. 1, 1980, pp. 44–49. See also Kosmin, *Class of 1979*; Zahler, "Jewish Identity"; and Carp, "Absorbing Jews Jewishly."

[109]Barber, "Soviet Jews of Washington Heights."

[110]Walter Ruby, "Russian Jews in America," *Long Island Jewish World*, Apr. 2–8, 1993, pp. 16–19; Naftoli Estulin, "Chabad Russian Immigrant Program and Synagogue," leaflet, Sept. 1993.

CONCLUSION

The patterns of economic and social adjustment and the political outlook of Soviet Jewish émigrés appear to be fairly clear. Highly skilled and educated, learning English fairly quickly, and taking advantage of excellent services, émigrés generally do well in their economic adaptation, if not always in the same high-status jobs they held in the USSR. Socially, most prefer the company of fellow émigrés, in an informal context that emphasizes their Russian culture and politically conservative views. It can be said that their general adaptation to American life appears to be following a predictable course.

What remains to be seen is the degree to which these émigrés will become involved in Jewish life in the future, either on their own terms or in consort with the American Jewish community. While identifying as Jews, most are not religious, but they maintain an ethnic attachment to their community that is more intense than that of American Jews. The general consensus regarding former Soviet Jews' communal and religious lives suggests that they are not drawn to formal organizations and are not religiously motivated; however, that image is beginning to be challenged. We have noted recent reports showing small groups of émigrés in various communities throughout the country creating organizations and becoming involved in Jewish life.

As today's émigrés often point out, the recently arrived Jews from the former Soviet Union are drastically different from the cohort of their *landsleit* who came to these shores from Russia almost a century ago. They want to be accepted on their own terms, as individuals and as Jews, and to win respect for their culture and background. They care deeply about the traditions of their European way of life and, while grateful to America for the opportunities and freedom it offers, strongly guard their independence from established Jews whom they see as over-zealously planning their American and Jewish acculturation. Like previous waves of immigrants before them, they will shape an identity that is uniquely their own—in their own way and in their own time.

TABLE 1. SOVIET JEWISH IMMIGRATION TO THE UNITED STATES[a]
(BY CALENDAR YEAR)

Year	Number	Year	Number
1965	12	1980	15,461
1966	36	1981	6,980
1967	72	1982	1,327
1968	92	1983	887
1969	156	1984	489
1970	135	1985	570
1971	214	1986	641
1972	453	1987	3,811
1973	1,449	1988	10,576
1974	3,490	1989	36,738
1975	5,250	1990	31,283
1976	5,512	1991	34,715
1977	6,842	1992	45,888
1978	12,265	1993	35,581
1979	28,794		
		Total	289,719

[a]HIAS-assisted émigrés, who account for most of the total Jewish immigration.
Source: HIAS.

TABLE 2.   ORIGINS OF SOVIET JEWISH EMIGRES IN THE U.S. BY YEAR
OF ARRIVAL

Republic	1980 to 1989		1980 through May 1993		1990 through May 1993	
Ukraine	43%	(32,850)	42%	(81,421)	41%	(48,571)
Russia	27	(20,237)	24	(46,391)	22	(26,154)
Belarus	14	(10,419)	13	(24,437)	12	(14,018)
Moldova	4	(3,376)	6	(11,113)	7	(7,737)
Latvia	3	(2,313)	2	(4,486)	2	(2,173)
Uzbekistan	4	(3,111)	6	(12,591)	8	(9,480)
Azerbaijan	2	(1,608)	2	(4,715)	3	(3,107)
Unknown		(10)	1	(2,856)	2	(2,846)
Other	3	(2,405)	3	(6,037)	3	(3,632)
Total	100%	(76,329)	100%[a]	(194,047)	100%	(117,718)

[a]Exceeds 100% due to rounding.
Sources: HIAS 1991; 1993.

TABLE 3.   LOCATION OF PERSONS BORN IN THE USSR CURRENTLY RESIDING IN
THE U.S., 1980 AND 1990

1980 (By Standard Metropolitan Statistical Areas)		1990 (By State)[a]	
New York SMSA	36%	New York	30%
Los Angeles/Long Beach	16	California	23
Chicago	7	Illinois	6
San Francisco/Oakland	4	New Jersey	6
Boston	4	Massachusetts	5
Miami	3	Florida	5
		Pennsylvania	5
Six SMSAs total = 70%		Seven states total = 80%	

[a]As of writing, SMSA data are unavailable.
Sources: 1980 data from Barry R. Chiswick, "Soviet Jews in the United States: An Analysis of Their Linguistic and Economic Adjustment," *International Migration Review* 27, no. 2, 1993; 1990 U.S. Census.

TABLE 4. EDUCATIONAL LEVEL, PERSONS BORN IN THE USSR, AGED 24–65, NEW YORK CITY AND LOS ANGELES COUNTY, 1990[a]

Educational Level	New York City			Los Angeles County		
	Men	Women	Total	Men	Women	Total
8th grade or less	7%	8%	8%	5%	6%	6%
Some high school	11	8	9	7	9	8
Finished high school	23	26	25	15	14	15
Some college	20	23	22	14	28	21
College grad or more	38	35	36	59	43	51
(One or more years college)	(58)	(58)	(58)	(73)	(71)	(72)

[a]Persons migrating to the U.S. since 1965. Anyone with Armenian ancestry or who reported speaking Armenian at home was excluded.
Source: 1990 Census.

TABLE 5. AVERAGE YEARS OF EDUCATION BY PERIOD OF ARRIVAL, PERSONS AGED 24–65, BORN IN THE USSR, NEW YORK CITY AND LOS ANGELES COUNTY, 1990[a]

Period of Arrival	New York City		Los Angeles County	
	Men	Women	Men	Women
1987–90	13.5	13.4	14.1	13.6
1980–81	13.4	12.9	14.3	13.6
1975–79	13.5	13.3	15.3	14.2

[a]Persons migrating to the U.S. since 1965. Anyone with Armenian ancestry or who reported speaking Armenian at home was excluded.
Source: 1990 Census.

TABLE 6. AVERAGE EARNINGS BY PERIOD OF ARRIVAL, EMPLOYED PERSONS BORN IN THE USSR, AGED 24–65, NEW YORK CITY AND LOS ANGELES COUNTY, 1990[a]

Period of Arrival	New York City			Los Angeles County		
	Men	Women	Ratio Women/Men	Men	Women	Ratio Women/Men
1987–90	$19,372	$ 8,187	42%	$19,672	$12,604	64%
1980–81	$31,748	$22,732	72	$44,619	$27,521	62
1975–79	$33,050	$22,495	68	$43,061	$25,031	58

[a]Persons migrating to the U.S. since 1965. Anyone with Armenian ancestry or who reported speaking Armenian at home was excluded.
Source: 1990 Census.

TABLE 7. LABOR-FORCE PARTICIPATION RATE BY PERIOD OF ARRIVAL FOR PERSONS BORN IN THE USSR, AGED 24–65, NEW YORK CITY AND LOS ANGELES COUNTY, 1990[a]

	New York City					
	Men			Women		
	1965–90	1965–86	1987–90	1965–90	1965–86	1987–90
In labor force	76%	89%	60%	57%	68%	41%
(Employed)	(65)	(86)	(35)	(48)	(63)	(25)
(Unemployed)	(12)	(3)	(24)	(9)	(4)	(16)
Not in labor force	24	11	41	43	32	59

	Los Angeles County					
	Men			Women		
	1965–90	1965–86	1987–90	1965–90	1965–86	1987–90
In labor force	79%	88%	53%	63%	71%	42%
(Employed)	(71)	(81)	(43)	(58)	(68)	(30)
(Unemployed)	(8)	(7)	(10)	(6)	(3)	(12)
Not in labor force	21	12	47	37	29	58

[a]Persons migrating to the U.S. since 1965. Anyone with Armenian ancestry or who reported speaking Armenian at home was excluded.
Source: 1990 Census.

TABLE 8. WELFARE USE[a] BY PERIOD OF ARRIVAL, PERSONS BORN IN THE USSR,
AGED 24–65, NEW YORK CITY AND LOS ANGELES COUNTY, 1990[b]

Period of Arrival	New York City		Los Angeles County	
	Men	Women	Men	Women
1965–90	14%	13%	7%	11%
1965–86	5	10	5	9
1987–90	26	18	12	15

[a]AFDC, SSI, General Relief.
[b]Persons migrating to the U.S. since 1965. Anyone with Armenian ancestry or who reported speaking Armenian at home was excluded.
Source: 1990 Census.

TABLE 9. LARGE-CITY REFUGEE TOTALS AND SELF-SUFFICIENCY RATES, 1989–1992[a]

City	Total Refugees at 4 Months[b]	No. Self-Sufficient	Self-Sufficiency Rate
Baltimore			
1989	239	191	80.0%
1990	893	721	80.7
1991	472	409	86.7
1992[c]	610	503	82.4
Boston			
1989	1,073	286	26.7%
1990	1,254	336	26.8
1991	572	47	8.2
1992	1,008	94	9.3
Chicago			
1989	1,381	169	12.2%
1990	3,000	403	13.4
1991	990	129	13.0
1992	2,333	293	12.5
Los Angeles			
1989	1,467	245	16.7%
1990	2,449	535	21.8
1991	1,370	198	14.4
1992	2,066	244	11.8
New York			
1989	10,162	1,220	12.0%
1990	19,973	969	4.9
1991	8,131	395	4.5
1992	16,760	905	5.4
Philadelphia			
1989	723	68	9.4%
1990	1,474	174	11.8
1991	558	103	18.5
1992[c]	745	162	21.7

TABLE 9.—*(Continued)*

City	Total Refugees at 4 Months[b]	No. Self-Sufficient	Self-Sufficiency Rate
San Francisco			
1989	726	129	17.7%
1990	1,665	566	34.0
1991	806	114	14.1
1992	1,572	109	6.9
Total for 7 cities			
1989	15,771	2,308	14.6%
1990	30,708	3,704	12.1
1991	12,899	1,395	10.8
1992	25,094	2,310	9.2
Total for whole CJF system			
1990	41,349	10,155	24.6%
1991	19,352	4,599	23.8
1992	33,620	6,151	18.3

[a]Years shown are Matching Grant Program Years: 1989 = 10/1/88–9/30/89; 1990 = 10/1/89–12/31/90; 1991 = 1/1/91–12/31/91; 1992 = 1/1/92–12/31/92.
[b]Total at 4 months is total number of Matching Grant refugees who completed 4 months of service during each year.
[c]Baltimore and Philadelphia's 1992 figures do not include data for final period of 1992.
Source: HIAS Matching Grant Department.

TABLE 10. OCCUPATIONS OF EMPLOYED PERSONS BORN IN THE USSR, AGED 24–65, NEW YORK CITY AND LOS ANGELES COUNTY, 1990[a]

	New York City			Los Angeles County		
	Men	Women	Total	Men	Women	Total
Manager/Administrator	12%	8%	10%	19%	15%	17%
Prof/Tech	22	29	25	28	26	27
Sales	11	6	9	11	16	13
Clerical	6	25	15	5	20	12
Craft	25	2	15	20	6	14
Operative	3	4	3	2	4	3
Transport	11	0.3	6	8	0	4
Laborer	2	1	2	1	0	1
Service	7	23	14	3	13	8
Farm				1	0	1

[a]Persons migrating to the U.S. since 1965. Anyone with Armenian ancestry or who reported speaking Armenian at home was excluded.
Source: 1990 Census.

TABLE 11. SOVIET REFUGEE EMPLOYMENT PATTERNS, 1992 (INDIVIDUALS)

Last Employment in USSR	First Employment in USA											
	Arch Engin	Math Science	Comput Progm	Soc Sci Educ	Medcl Health	Human Art/Mus	Manag Adm/Clr	Bkkp Acct	Sales Service	Barber Cosm	Skill Trds	Total
Arch/Engin	83	8	4	1	5	2	7	29	5	0	108	252
Math/Science	8	9	2	2	5	1	2	2	0	0	5	36
Computer Prog	4	0	75	2	1	0	2	5	0	0	1	90
Soc Sci/Educ	0	0	2	26	3	2	7	59	3	6	6	114
Medical/Health	0	0	0	1	18	1	0	4	3	4	5	36
Human/Art/Mus	0	0	0	1	0	25	2	2	5	1	21	57
Mng/Adm/Clerk	0	1	0	4	1	0	2	5	3	0	8	24
Bookkeep/Acct	0	0	1	2	0	1	1	57	3	3	3	71
Sales/Service	1	0	0	0	1	0	0	1	8	2	6	19
Barber/Cosmet	0	0	0	0	0	0	0	1	0	21	0	22
Skilled Trades	6	1	2	3	1	2	8	10	6	0	240	279
TOTAL	102	19	86	42	35	34	31	175	36	37	403	1,000

Note: Analysis based on 1,000 most recent job placements recorded in NYANA computer system as of May 21, 1992.
Source: Operations Analysis Dept., New York Association for New Americans.

TABLE 12. ECONOMIC SECTOR OF EMPLOYED PERSONS BORN IN THE USSR, AGED 24–65, NEW YORK CITY AND LOS ANGELES COUNTY, 1990[a]

Economic Sector	New York City			Los Angeles County		
	Men	Women	Total	Men	Women	Total
Private	70%	78%	74%	62%	78%	69%
Public	10	14	11	6	5	5
Self-employed	21	8	15	33	17	25

[a]Persons migrating to the U.S. since 1965. Anyone with Armenian ancestry or who reported speaking Armenian at home was excluded.
Source: 1990 Census.

TABLE 13. FORMER SOVIET JEWISH PROFESSIONALS & ENGINEERS[a] IN THE U.S., 1979–1992[B]

Sex	Men	Women	Total
	Professionals		
N	15,425	27,111	42,536
% of total labor force	15	27	41
	Engineers[a]		
N	12,475	6,557	19,032
% of total labor force	12	6	19
	Professionals & Engineers Combined		
N	27,900	33,668	61,568
% of total labor force	28	33	61
	All Occupations		
N	50,641	50,492	101,133
% of total labor force	50	50	100

[a]These two occupational categories for former occupation are tabulated separately. Engineer category also includes architects.
[b]Data for 1979–1991 are for calendar year; data for 1992 are fiscal year. 1990 data are not available.
Source: HIAS 1979–1993.

TABLE 14. ETHNIC TIES OF NEW YORK JEWS, 1991

Speak Yiddish:

	All Jews	Post '65 Soviets
Yes	38%	42%

Respondent or any member of household has been a dues-paying member of a YMHA or Jewish Community Center within the past 12 months:

	All Jews	Post '65 Soviets
Yes	15%	17%

Regularly read any Jewish publications:

	All Jews	Post '65 Soviets
Yes	41%	49%

Respondent or spouse has close friends or immediate family living in Israel:

	All Jews	Post '65 Soviets
Yes	46%	83%

Of the people respondent considers closest friends:

	All Jews	Post '65 Soviets
Few or none are Jewish	6%	0.2%
Most, almost all or all are Jewish	66%	96%

When it comes to a crisis, Jews can only depend on other Jews.

	All Jews	Post '65 Soviets
Disagree	47%	25%
Agree	50%	68%

Source: The 1991 New York Jewish Population Study.

TABLE 15. INVOLVEMENT IN COMMUNITY EVENTS OF NEW YORK JEWS, 1991

Participate in activities that support Israel or Soviet Jewry:

	All Jews	Post '65 Soviets
Yes	50%	56%

Attended a Purim carnival or celebration during the past year:

	All Jews	Post '65 Soviets
Yes	34%	67%

Celebrated Yom Ha'atzma'ut (Israel Independence Day) in any way during the past year:

	All Jews	Post '65 Soviets
Yes	19%	30%

Attended a Holocaust commemoration during the past year:

	All Jews	Post '65 Soviets
Yes	22%	34%

Source: The 1991 New York Jewish Population Study.

TABLE 16. LANGUAGE SPOKEN AT HOME, PERSONS BORN IN THE USSR, AGED 5+, NEW YORK CITY AND LOS ANGELES COUNTY, 1990[a]

	New York City		Los Angeles County	
	Number	Percent	Number	Percent
Russian	53,133	91.1	12,000	89.0
Yiddish	1,363	2.3	46	0.3
English	1,267	2.2	543	4.0
Hebrew	820	1.4	252	1.9
Hungarian			185	1.4
Syriac			144	1.3

[a]Persons migrating to the U.S. since 1965. Anyone with Armenian ancestry or who reported speaking Armenian at home was excluded.
Source: 1990 Census.

TABLE 17. COMPARATIVE JEWISH BEHAVIORS, SOVIET JEWS AND U.S. JEWS[a]

Study and Year Data Collected	Soviet Jews in U.S.		Soviet Jews in N.Y.		U.S. Jews[b]
	Simon 1981	Kosmin[c] 1989	N.Y. Fed. 1984	NYJPS[d] 1991	NJPS 1990
Fast on Yom Kippur	50%	84%	65%	78%	58%
Attend Passover seder	—	67	75	90[d]	89[e]
Light Hanukkah candles	58	68	70	94[d]	83[e]
Light Sabbath candles	22	27	41	64[d]	43[e]
Kosher meat	—	20	20	—	17[f]
Two sets of dishes	12	18	—	70[d]	—
Member of synagogue	—	41	—	42	41[f]
Give to Jewish charity	—	82	58	57	62[f]
UJA contribution	—	57	10	—	45[f]
Visited Israel	—	21	—	33	31
Avoid bread on Passover	53	—	41	—	—

[a]Questions are not always identical. These are approximations for comparative purposes. For actual questions, see original studies.
[b]Jewish by religion.
[c]Respondents in the U.S. at least 8 years.
[d]While many of these responses seem quite high, the rates for all Jewish New Yorkers in certain behaviors are the same or higher, e.g., seder attendance (93%), Hanukkah candles (93%), two sets of dishes (78%), and Jewish charity (66%).
[e]Sometimes, Usually, Always.
[f]Households, not individuals.
Sources: Rita J. Simon, ed., *New Lives: The Adjustment of Soviet Jewish Immigrants in the United States and Israel* (Lexington, Mass., 1985); Barry A. Kosmin, *The Class of 1979: The "Acculturation" of Jewish Immigrants from the Soviet Union,* North American Jewish Data Bank, CUNY Graduate School and University Center, 1990; Federation of Jewish Philanthropies of New York, *Jewish Identification and Affiliation of Soviet Jewish Immigrants in New York City—A Needs Assessment and Planning Study,* 1985; Bethamie Horowitz, *The 1991 New York Jewish Population Study,* United Jewish Appeal-Federation of Jewish Philanthropies of New York, 1993; Sidney Goldstein, "Profile of American Jewry: Insights from the 1990 National Jewish Population Survey," AJYB 1992 (fast, seder, candles); Barry A. Kosmin et al., *Highlights of the CJF 1990 National Jewish Population Survey,* Council of Jewish Federations, 1991.

TABLE 18.   SYNAGOGUE MEMBERSHIP, DENOMINATION, AND ATTENDANCE OF
            NEW YORK JEWS, 1990

Respondent or any member of household currently a dues-paying member of a
synagogue or temple:

	All Jews	Post '65 Soviets
	42%	42%

Jewish denomination of respondent:

	All Jews	Post '65 Soviets
Conservative	34%	20%
Orthodox	15	11
Reform	35	29
Reconstructionist	2	5
Something else	12	19

Frequency of attendance at any type of organized Jewish religious service:

	All Jews	Post '65 Soviets
Not at all	16%	8%
Once or twice a year	11	9
Only on special occasions	8	2
Only on High Holy Days	16	39
3+ times a year	19	11
About once a month	7	7
Several times a month	5	6
About once a week	6	10
Several times a week	6	7

Source: The 1991 New York Jewish Population Study.

TABLE 19.   IMPORTANCE OF JEWISH ACTIVITIES FOR CHILDREN AS RATED BY
SOVIET JEWISH PARENTS[a]

Study and Year Data Collected	Simon (U.S.) 1981	N.Y. Fed. 1984	Krautman (L.A.) 1990
Marry another Jew	87%	84%	90%
Observe Sabbath	45	69	—
Give to Jewish charities	87	—	89
Belong to Jewish orgs.	76	74	75
Have mostly Jewish friends	74	70	—
Visit Israel	—	80	90
Get a Jewish education	79	97–76[b]	—

[a]Questions are not always identical. These are approximations for comparative purposes. For actual questions, see original studies.
[b]97% Jewish history and culture; 76% Jewish religion.
Sources: Rita J. Simon, ed., *New Lives: The Adjustment of Soviet Jewish Immigrants in the United States and Israel* (Lexington, Mass., 1985); Federation of Jewish Philanthropies of New York, *Jewish Identification and Affiliation of Soviet Jewish Immigrants in New York City—A Needs Assessment and Planning Study,* 1985; Jerry Allan Krautman, *A Study of the Acculturation and Jewish Identity of Soviet Jews Emigrating to Los Angeles Between 1972 and 1989,* MBA thesis, University of Judaism, 1990.

Ethiopian Jews in Israel

by STEVEN KAPLAN and CHAIM ROSEN

OF THE MANY DIASPORA JEWISH communities, none has undergone more dramatic change in recent years than the Beta Israel (Falashas).[1] Prior to 1977 all but a handful of Beta Israel lived in Ethiopia. During the 1980s, almost half the community emigrated to Israel, and the center of Beta Israel life shifted from Ethiopia to Israel. In 1991, "Operation Solomon" put an end to the Beta Israel as an active and living Diaspora community, and by the end of 1993 virtually all Beta Israel were in Israel.

This article describes and analyzes the process of their immigration (*aliyah*) to, and absorption *(klitah)* in, Israel. Although every attempt has been made to provide as much quantitative statistical data as possible, significant gaps remain. Most of the research undertaken on the Ethiopians in Israel has been qualitative in nature. Even in those cases where attempts have been made to carry out precise surveys of immigrants, the results have not always been satisfactory.[2] Since Ethiopian immigrants usually arrived in Israel with few official documents, basic "facts" such as age and family status were often unverifiable, and immigrants were registered on the basis of their own or family members' testimony. Once they were settled in the country, the multiplicity of agencies dealing with the immigrants further complicated the process of compiling comprehensive and authoritative information.[3]

---

[1] In Ethiopia, the members of the group usually referred to themselves as Beta Israel (the House of Israel) or simply Israel. They were more widely known as "Falashas." Today, they prefer to be called Ethiopian Jews.

[2] The Israel Ministry of Absorption has, for example, released several sets of figures concerning the number of Ethiopian immigrants that have arrived in Israel. In some cases the number said to have arrived in a given year has varied by as much as 25 percent!

[3] The bibliographic references contained in this article have been prepared with a primarily English-reading audience in mind. Only the most essential sources in other languages have been cited. This has resulted in an unfortunate, but inevitable, neglect of the vast and growing Hebrew literature concerning Ethiopian Jews in Israel. Every attempt has been made to summarize the major findings of that literature in the appropriate sections. Two extremely useful bibliographies containing Hebrew material have been published in recent years. They can be obtained by contacting Betachin, R. Yafo 101, Jerusalem 94342, and the Henrietta Szold Institute, 9 Columbia St., Jerusalem 96583.

BACKGROUND

The history of the Beta Israel did not, of course, begin with their arrival in Israel. Long before their encounter with world Jewry, the Beta Israel worshiped and created, struggled and fought, all within the context of the wider stream of Ethiopian history. Although some aspects of this history, particularly the question of "Falasha origins," have provoked considerable controversy in recent years, events prior to the late 19th or early 20th century are of little relevance to our concerns in this article.[4]

More recent events form the starting point for our discussion. For almost a century and a half prior to their *aliyah*, the Beta Israel were exposed to outside influences that slowly altered their religious life, social norms, and self-image. While none of the changes from this period had as immediate and overwhelming an impact as emigration from Ethiopia and immigration to Israel, neither can they be ignored. It is only possible to report the effects of the move to Israel faithfully if we begin with an accurate picture of what existed before.[5]

The modern history of the Beta Israel began in 1859 with the establishment in their midst of a Protestant mission under the auspices of the London Society for Promoting Christianity Among the Jews. It was the mission's activities more than anything else in the period before the 20th century that made these isolated Jews aware of the existence of a more universal form of Jewish identity and brought them to the attention of world Jewry.[6]

In response to the missionary threat, a number of prominent Jewish leaders began to lobby for aid to be sent to the Beta Israel. In 1867, Joseph Halévy was sent to Ethiopia as the emissary of the Alliance Israélite Universelle.[7] Despite Halévy's unequivocal confirmation of the Beta Israel's Jewishness, and his enthusiastic support for the establishment of institutions to

---

[4]One of the central ironies of recent years is that only during the period of their emigration from Ethiopia has their history in that country begun to be clearly understood. See in particular Kay Kaufman Shelemay, *Music, Ritual and Falasha History* (East Lansing, Mich., 1989); James Arthur Quirin, *The Evolution of the Ethiopian Jews* (Philadelphia, 1992); and Steven Kaplan, *The Beta Israel (Falasha) in Ethiopia: From Earliest Times to the Twentieth Century* (New York, 1992).

[5]Steven Kaplan and Chaim Rosen, "Ethiopian Immigrants in Israel: Between Preservation of Culture and Invention of Tradition," *Jewish Journal of Sociology* 35, no. 1, June 1993, pp. 35–48.

[6]On the activities of this mission, see Kaplan, *Beta Israel*, pp. 116–42, and Quirin, *Ethiopian Jews*, pp. 179–91.

[7]On Halévy's visit and its significance, see Kaplan, *Beta Israel*, pp. 138–42. For Halévy's account of his journey, see Joseph Halévy, "Travels in Abyssinia," tr. James Picciotto, in A. Levy, *Miscellany of Hebrew Literature* (London, 1877).

assist them, no action was taken for almost 40 years, when Halévy's pupil Jacques (Ya'acov) Faitlovitch journeyed to Ethiopia in 1904. Faitlovitch, who dedicated his life to the cause of Ethiopian Jewry, was responsible more than any other single person for their entry into Jewish history and consciousness. The common thread that ran through all aspects of his program on their behalf was the attempt to bring them closer to other Jewish communities. To this end, he sought to raise their standards of education and created a Western-educated elite capable of interacting with their foreign Jewish counterparts. He also attempted to reform Beta Israel religion to bring it closer to "normative" Judaism. Among the innovations he introduced were the lighting of Sabbath candles, the recitation of Hebrew prayers, the use of the Star of David, and the observance of holidays such as Simhat Torah. Faitlovitch worked on behalf of Ethiopian Jewry until his death in 1955.[8]

During the years immediately following the establishment of the State of Israel, no attempt was made to bring the Beta Israel on *aliyah*. Lingering questions concerning their Jewishness, as well as social, medical, and political considerations, all convinced successive Israeli governments to defer any decisive action. Efforts were made, however, by the Jewish Agency and other organizations to strengthen their ties to world Jewry and Israel. From 1953 to 1958, representatives of the Jewish Agency's Department for Torah Education in the Diaspora were active in Ethiopia. Two groups totaling 27 Ethiopian youngsters were also brought to the Kfar Batya Youth Aliyah village in Israel to be trained as teachers and future leaders of their fellow Ethiopians. Eventually a network of schools was established throughout the Gondar region, which at its peak served hundreds of students. The impact of their efforts was not felt evenly among all sectors of the population. Some communities, particularly those in peripheral regions, remained largely unaffected. Others, in or near villages in which schools were established, underwent a more dramatic transformation as they were exposed to rabbinic Judaism, Zionism, and modernization.[9] Israel and Jerusalem, which had existed mainly as symbols of a lost biblical period, began to be perceived as living realities and for some a goal to be struggled toward. Not surpris-

---

[8]Unfortunately, we lack a detailed study of Faitlovitch's life and works. See, however, Simon D. Messing, *The Story of the Falashas: "Black Jews" of Ethiopia* (Brooklyn, 1982), pp. 62–79; Itzhak Grinfeld, "Jacques Faitlovitch—'Father' of the Falashas," in *The Jews of Ethiopia—A Community in Transition*, ed. Yossi Avner et al. (Tel Aviv, 1986), pp. 30–35; and especially Faitlovitch's article in AJYB 1920–21, vol. 22, pp. 80–100.

[9]The best discussion of these issues in English is G. Jan Abbink, "The Falashas in Ethiopia and Israel: The Problem of Ethnic Assimilation," in *Nijmegen Sociaal Anthropologische Cahiers*, vol. 15, 1984. This work also contains a useful, albeit dated, discussion of Ethiopian Jewish absorption in Israel.

ingly, youngsters tended to adopt new ideas more quickly than their elders, and in some cases generational tensions developed.[10]

Such intergenerational tensions were further exacerbated following the Ethiopian revolution of 1974, which led to the overthrow of Emperor Haile Selassie and the institution of a military Marxist regime.[11] Young people exposed to secular education and political indoctrination rejected the ways of their elders as old-fashioned. Contacts with non-Beta Israel increased significantly as young people joined political organizations, were conscripted into the security forces, or simply sought the professional and educational opportunities available in urban areas.

A Tale of Three Aliyot

While the significance of such changes should not be minimized, they pale in comparison to what happened from 1977 onward. At the beginning of 1977, fewer than 100 Ethiopian Jews had been grudgingly allowed—by either Ethiopian or Israeli authorities—to settle in Israel. By the end of 1993 the number of immigrants had risen to nearly 45,000! This mass migration took place over a relatively short period, not as a single event but rather in a series of waves, each of which had its own special characteristics.

Although it was generally not realized at the time, 1973 was a crucial year in the history of the Beta Israel. Early that year, Ovadia Yosef, the Sephardi chief rabbi of Israel, issued a religious ruling recognizing the Falashas as Jews. Citing rabbinic opinions from more than 400 years earlier, he stated that they were descendants of the lost tribe of Dan.[12] Rabbi Yosef's pronouncement brought no immediate change in the fortunes of Ethiopian Jewry. Indeed, the breaking off of diplomatic relations between Ethiopia and Israel in the wake of the Yom Kippur War in October 1973 if anything increased their isolation. His decision did, however, remove most doubts concerning the Jewishness of the Beta Israel, and thus made it possible for Jews in Israel and the Diaspora to agitate on their behalf. Slowly, their

---

[10]This was especially the case following the return of the Ethiopian youngsters who had studied at the Kfar Batya Youth Aliyah village.

[11]Galia Sabar Friedman, "Religion and the Marxist State of Ethiopia: The Case of the Ethiopian Jews," *Religion in Communist Lands* 17, no. 3, 1989, pp. 247–56.

[12]The best English discussion of the halakhic status of Ethiopian Jews is by (former Israeli Supreme Court justice) Menachem Elon, "The Ethiopian Jews: A Case Study in the Functioning of the Jewish Legal System," *New York University Journal of International Law and Politics* 19, 1986–87, pp. 535–63. Hebrew volumes include: (Rabbi) Menachem Waldman, *Beyond the Rivers of Ethiopia: The Jews of Ethiopia and the Jewish People* (Tel Aviv, 1989); idem, *From Ethiopia to Jerusalem: Ethiopian Jewry in the Modern Era* (Jerusalem, 1991); (Rabbi) David Chelouche, *The Exiles of Israel Will Be Gathered* (Jerusalem, 1988); and (Attorney) Michael Corinaldi, *Ethiopian Jewry: Identity and Tradition* (Jerusalem, 1989).

controversial and sometimes confrontational tactics bore fruit. The issue of Ethiopian Jewry began to appear on the agenda of more and more Jewish organizations, and pressure grew for Israel to act on their behalf.[13]

From 1977 onward, successive Israeli governments began to turn their attention to the issue of Ethiopian Jewry. In that year, 121 Ethiopian Jews were brought to Israel as part of an "arms for Jews" deal between the Israelis and the Ethiopians. Unfortunately, in February of 1978, Foreign Minister Moshe Dayan revealed the military side of the agreement, and an embarrassed Ethiopian government terminated the arrangement.

Although promises of land reform and freedom of worship led many to hope that Ethiopia's Marxist rulers would ameliorate the situation of the Beta Israel, this did not prove to be the case. While seldom victims of organized persecution, they suffered all the tribulations inflicted on the general population as well as those reserved for a particularly weak and vulnerable minority group. As conditions in Ethiopia deteriorated, their religious devotion to Jerusalem began to be transformed into an active desire to emigrate.

Rather surprisingly, the first significant wave of Beta Israel to leave Ethiopia did not include those who had had the most contact with foreign Jews and Israelis.[14] Starting in 1980, Jews from the relatively isolated regions of Tigre and Walqayit began to journey to the Sudan and to settle in refugee camps. Some were to wait there for as long as two or three years before being taken to Israel. Although Sudan was officially opposed to the emigration of these Jews, several Sudanese government officials agreed to allow their removal in exchange for large bribes and on condition of confidentiality. By the end of 1983, over 4,000 Beta Israel, virtually the entire Jewish population of Tigre and Walqayit, had reached Israel.

The Sudanese camps, however, far from emptying out, became home to an ever increasing number of refugees. Most were fleeing yet another famine in war-torn Ethiopia. A small number, Beta Israel from the Gondar region, were driven not by the search for food, but by their desire to reach Israel.

---

[13]Rabbi Yosef's decision also paved the way for the granting of citizenship to the handful of Ethiopian Jews already in the country. For a recent study focusing on the American efforts on behalf of Ethiopian Jewry, see Jeffery A. Kaye, "On the Wings of Eagles: A History and Analysis of the Movement to Rescue Ethiopian Jewry" (M.A. thesis, HUC-JIR, Cincinnati, 1993). Among the most significant groups active in these efforts were the American Association for Ethiopian Jews (AAEJ), the Canadian Association for Ethiopian Jews (CAEJ), the North American Conference on Ethiopian Jewry (NACOEJ), and in England the Falasha Welfare Association (FWA).

[14]This is not to say that these Tigrean Jews had been completely cut off from Jewish contacts. Cf. G.J. Abbink, "An Ethiopian Jewish 'Missionary' as Cultural Broker," in *Ethiopian Jews and Israel*, ed. Michael Ashkenazi and Alex Weingrod (New Brunswick, N.J., 1988), pp. 21–32.

Despite many obstacles, what had hitherto been a trickle of Jewish emigrants from Gondar became a flood in 1984, and by the middle of the year, close to 10,000 additional Ethiopian Jews had crossed the border into the Sudan. As the situation in the refugee camps deteriorated and the mortality rate rose, the Israeli government decided to abandon its policy of gradual immigration in favor of a more ambitious policy. During a period of less than two months, starting in mid-November 1984, more than 6,700 Ethiopian Jews were airlifted to Israel in what became known as Operation Moses.[15]

Almost from the start, Operation Moses was an open secret, as hundreds of Israelis struggled to accommodate the new arrivals. Although strict censorship was imposed in Israel, this did not prevent several foreign papers from carrying reports on the airlift accredited to reporters outside Israel. Despite the fears of Israeli authorities, the Sudanese government ignored these stories and allowed the operation to continue. On January 3, 1985, representatives of the Jewish Agency, the Foreign Ministry, and the Ministry of Immigrant Absorption, in an apparent attempt to divert media attention from the airlift and toward those Ethiopians already in Israel, gave a detailed briefing to the local and foreign press. On January 5, the Sudanese government suspended the airlift.

The untimely disruption of Operation Moses left several hundred Jews stranded in the Sudan. The U.S. and Israeli governments immediately formulated plans to rescue them. A few months later, a further 648 Beta Israel were removed from the Sudan in a CIA-sponsored airlift variously labeled Operation Sheba or Operation Joshua.

The trek to the Sudan and the ensuing sojourn in Sudanese refugee camps had a devastating effect on Ethiopian family life. Almost every Ethiopian who reached Israel during this period had both lost family members and left others behind in Ethiopia.[16] Scarcely a single family survived intact. For

---

[15]Although a number of books were published on Operation Moses, they were intended as popular, not scholarly, works. They include: Tudor Parfitt, *Operation Moses* (London, 1985); Louis Rapoport, *Redemption Song: The Story of Operation Moses* (New York, 1986); Claire Safran, *Secret Exodus* (New York, 1987); Ruth Gruber, *Rescue: The Exodus of the Ethiopian Jews* (New York, 1987). Vastly different in tone and more scholarly in intent are two recent articles: Ahmed Karadawi, "The Smuggling of the Ethiopian Falasha to Israel Through Sudan," *African Affairs* 90, no. 358, Jan. 1991, pp. 23–50; and Teshome Wagaw, "The International Political Ramifications of Falasha Emigration," *Journal of Modern African Studies* 29, no. 4, 1991, pp. 557–81. Only one book has been published to date about Operation Solomon: Ya'acov Friedmann, *Operation Solomon: One Year and Thirty-One Hours* (in Hebrew) (Jerusalem, 1992). Books are also being prepared by former Israeli ambassador to Ethiopia Asher Naim and by journalist Charles Hoffmann.

[16]Although no exact figures exist for the number of Ethiopian Jews who perished, community members often speak of 4,000. For some sample figures and the psychological impact of these difficulties, see our discussion of mental health below, especially note 90.

many, moreover, loss and separation were accompanied by uncertainty, as the fate of at least one family member remained unclear. Family reunification became the watchword of the Ethiopian community in Israel.

During the period from August 1985 until the end of 1989, about 2,500 additional immigrants managed to reach Israel—either directly from Addis Ababa or in small groups from the Sudan. The reestablishment of diplomatic relations between Ethiopia and Israel in the fall of 1989 opened the possibility of a renewal of the *aliyah* movement, this time openly and in a manner agreed upon by both sides. Although immigration from Ethiopia was limited at first, the Ethiopian government allowed small numbers of Beta Israel to leave on a regular basis. This fueled the expectations of others, who were encouraged by representatives of the American Association for Ethiopian Jews to migrate to the Ethiopian capital of Addis Ababa. By the summer of 1990, over 20,000 Ethiopian Jews had traveled to Addis Ababa in the hope of receiving exit visas. Jewish Agency and Israeli government officials, who had had no hand in the migration, were caught unprepared. Thus, the conditions initially encountered by the migrants were extremely difficult. Malnutrition, inadequate housing, and disease all threatened the Beta Israel.

Responding to the crisis, the combined efforts of the Israeli embassy, Jewish Agency, Jewish Joint Distribution Committee (JDC), and other organizations, most notably the North American Conference on Ethiopian Jewry, ensured that the basic needs of the refugees were met, thus avoiding the catastrophic mortality rates associated with Operation Moses.[17] The city, however, held dangers of a new and different kind. Traditional patterns of communal village life deteriorated as Jews settled in shantytowns throughout the urban sprawl of the Ethiopian capital. Families, customarily the ultimate refuge and source of security in times of crises, found themselves completely incapable of providing for their members' most basic needs. Removed from their traditional occupational setting, many settled into a pattern of lethargy and dependence, living off the stipends and other assistance provided by the Jewish organizations working in Addis.

Meanwhile, Ethiopia's Marxist regime continued its struggle against regionally based opposition groups. In the northern province of Eritrea, rebels seeking independence from Ethiopia had fought a bloody civil war for several decades. A little further south, in Tigre province, forces opposed to the regime hoped to defeat president Mengistu Haile Mariam and gain control of the entire country. In the early 1990s, rebels from both provinces joined forces and began marching south in the hope of conquering Addis Ababa and toppling the Mengistu regime.

---

[17]On the medical aspects of these efforts, see note 81 below.

Throughout the first months of 1991, as the internal political situation in Ethiopia continued to decline, Israeli negotiators laid the groundwork for a rescue operation; at the same time, American officials attempted to put together a deal that would both secure the safety of the Beta Israel and limit bloodshed. In the middle of May, as rebel forces closed in on Addis Ababa, President Mengistu fled to Zimbabwe. Fears grew that the Beta Israel would be trapped in what threatened to be a bitter struggle.

During a period of 36 hours spanning May 24 and 25, over 14,000 Beta Israel were airlifted to Israel in a mission code-named Operation Solomon. On the most basic level, this massive undertaking was vastly successful in ending the problem of family disintegration. With the *aliyah* of over 90 percent of all Beta Israel—almost 45,000 immigrants—only a relatively small number of family members remained in Ethiopia.

Still, the total number of immigrants must be considered incomplete. Small groups of Jews as well as individuals interested in making *aliyah* continue to be discovered in remote areas, or areas previously thought to be without Jews, such as Gojjam province. There is also the as yet unresolved issue of the Christianized Jewish population, specifically the group referred to as the Falas Mura. An estimated 4,000–5,000 are in Addis Ababa (including 2,800 who have been there since before Operation Solomon), expecting to emigrate. In addition, estimates have been made of anywhere from 25,000 to 250,000 more who are waiting to see the fate of their kinfolk before they, too, demand to emigrate in accordance with the Law of Return, as former Jews, or to achieve unification with family members who have already reached Israel during previous operations.

The Falas Mura Controversy

Supporters of Ethiopian *aliyah* both in Israel and abroad had always stressed the steadfastness with which the Beta Israel clung to their Judaism. At the time of the Ethiopians' initial confrontation with the rabbinate, moreover, it had been argued that anyone who had even passing contact with non-Jews risked exclusion from the Jewish community in Ethiopia. It came as something of a shock, therefore, when several thousand Falashas who had lived as Christians joined in the migration to Addis Ababa in 1991 and demanded to be taken to Israel. Known by a number of names, including *Maryam Wodet* (Lovers of Mary) or *Falas/Faras Mura*,[18] these Falasha Christians posed an unprecedented challenge to Israeli and Jewish organizations in Ethiopia.

---

[18]This name has been popularly interpreted as *falas* (Falasha), *Mura* (converts, from the Hebrew term: *hamarat dat*, conversion). There is no basis for this interpretation. Other no less problematic interpretations rely on the word *faras* (horse) and translate the term as a lone horse or part of the horse's digestive system.

So long as immigration from Ethiopia continued at a rate of several hundred or even a thousand a month, a final decision on the Falas Mura could be delayed. After consultation with members of the community, Israeli authorities decided that the Falas Mura would be taken to Israel only after those judged to be bona fide Jews had been removed. The events leading up to Operation Solomon upset this thinking, and it was decided to leave the known Falas Mura behind, while the airlift took place.

The government's decision to leave converts of Jewish descent in Ethiopia focused unprecedented public and media attention on these "Falasha Christians." As in most matters relating to the Beta Israel, strong positions have been taken on both sides of the issue. Those advocating *aliyah* for the Falas Mura claim that the converts constitute a clearly defined community, limited to 25,000 individuals, who have never married non-Falas Mura and who basically have never ceased to be Jewish. They also put forth various, sometimes contradictory, explanations of the group's origins, claiming that they are "Marranos" forced to convert during times of persecution, secularized Jews who had never converted to Christianity, or disappointed Zionists dismayed by Israel's refusal to rescue the Falashas for more than 30 years. The decision not to bring them to Israel, some charge, was based on racism and counter to all legal and humanitarian norms.

Many experts on Ethiopian history and society see the picture as far more complex.[19] On the subject of numbers, they claim that the Falas Mura now found in the vicinity of the Israeli embassy in Addis Ababa represent only a fraction of the possible descendants of Beta Israel, whose total number could reach tens of thousands of potential emigrants, and even, as some Ethiopian government officials have claimed, reach into the hundreds of thousands.[20]

Contrary to what is often suggested, this school of thought claims that neither coercion nor direct financial inducements appears to have played a major role in enticing Beta Israel to join the mission. Rather, the offer of educational opportunities, social advancement, and the possibility of gaining rights to own land were the crucial factors drawing Ethiopian Jews away from their villages and their ancestral religion. Over time there arose a broad spectrum of converted Falashas, ranging from active disciples of the missionaries, who sought to convert others as well, to ostensible Christians for whom a formal Christian identity was just another of the trappings of high office and elite status. While some identified with Protestant sects, the

---

[19]Steven Kaplan, "Falasha Christians: A Brief History," *Midstream*, Jan. 1993, pp. 20–21.
[20]In the summer of 1993, an Ethiopian political activist living in Switzerland requested that "the Semitic Tribes of the Gihon," who, he claimed, numbered several million, be recognized as Jews. This previously unheard-of group does not appear to have any chance of being recognized by Israeli authorities.

vast majority followed the Hebraic-biblical norms of the Ethiopian Orthodox Church.

However, the Falas Mura did not simply disappear into the larger society. For one thing, despite their willingness to be practicing Christians, many of these converts were only partially successful in changing their affiliation and achieving the goals they had set for themselves. In many cases, they retained their involvement in the low-status crafts, such as potting and smithing, that marked the Beta Israel as a despised semicaste within the broader Ethiopian society and often continued to be labeled as "Falasha" on an ethnic basis.[21] Perhaps most importantly, despite communal norms dictating that such converts be excluded from the *"Oritawi Falasha"* (Old Testament Falasha) community, many of them continued to retain contacts with family members and even to attend Jewish religious celebrations. Whatever their outward appearance or the attitude of the community at large, their relatives often remained convinced that "inside" they were still Jews.

So long as *aliyah* to Israel remained only a dream for the Jews of Ethiopia, the benefits in assuming and maintaining a Christian identity were usually quite obvious. Events from 1977 onward, however, dramatically changed this situation. Already today, the 45,000 figure for Ethiopian immigrants in Israel greatly exceeds the 28,000 identified as "practicing" in 1976. High birthrates and previously overlooked villages notwithstanding, this number undoubtedly reflects the presence of an estimated 5,000 Falas Mura or genuine Christians (spouses of Jews) already in the country.

An interministerial committee convened in the fall of 1992 by Absorption Minister Yair Tsaban heard testimony and recommendations from scholars, rabbis, jurists, diplomats, Ethiopian religious and political leaders, Falas Mura activists, and Falas Mura already in Israel. Early in 1993 the committee presented its recommendation that only a limited number of Falas Mura be allowed to come to Israel, as part of a family reunification program based on humanitarian considerations, rather than as immigrants under the Law of Return. Although the recommendations of the Tsaban committee were adopted by the Israeli cabinet, Falas Mura activists— among them a number of prominent figures from across the Israeli political and religious spectrum—have continued to oppose them.

Ethiopian immigrants in Israel are themselves divided as to the best way to handle the problem of the Falas Mura. While those with relatives still in Ethiopia obviously wish for them to be brought to Israel, and many are sympathetic to their plight, others are less enthusiastic and in some cases

---

[21]While their adherence to such biblically sanctioned observances as circumcision and abstinence from pork might lead those not familiar with Ethiopian culture to label them as Marranos, these customs are, in fact, an intrinsic part of Ethiopian Christianity.

even opposed to their *aliyah*. Only a handful of the 60–70 *qessotch* (religious leaders) in Israel, for example, agreed to sign a letter calling for the *aliyah* of the Falas Mura or have appeared in public on their behalf.

By the time the Tsaban committee concluded its hearings, more than 20 months had passed since Operation Solomon. Another half year was to pass before the first Falas Mura were brought to Israel under the family reunification plan. By the fall of 1993, many of those in Addis Ababa had been there, waiting to be taken to Israel, for more than two years. During this period, the approximately 3,000 under the direct care of the JDC and the North American Conference on Ethiopian Jewry (NACOEJ) were receiving instruction in Jewish and Israeli culture. This activity, too, sparked considerable controversy, with some charging that it was a calculated attempt to "Judaize" the Falas Mura and thus make it harder for the Israeli government to refuse to bring them to Israel. Ethiopian government officials, who had always viewed the Falas Mura campaign as an unwanted intervention in their internal matters, viewed such Jewish "missionary" activity with particular concern. In July of 1993, they expelled eight Jewish teachers brought to Ethiopia by NACOEJ, along with the organization's resident director.

As of this writing, no speedy end to the Falas Mura controversy appears in sight. Although the Ethiopian government will probably continue to allow small numbers of Falas Mura who meet the criteria set by the Israeli government to emigrate,[22] this will neither satisfy nor silence those who wish to see all Falas Mura brought to Israel.

THE DEMOGRAPHY OF THE ETHIOPIAN COMMUNITY

As noted above, nearly 45,000 Beta Israel came to Israel between 1972 and 1993 (table 1). During the period from 1977 to 1992, 8,200 Ethiopian children were born in Israel. Thus, even if the exact number born in 1993 is not known, it is clear that well over 50,000 Ethiopians were living in Israel by the end of 1993.[23]

---

[22]As of November 1993, 260 individuals from 50 families had been granted the right to emigrate.

[23]These figures are a composite of statistics compiled from monthly and yearly internal reports issued by the Ministry of Absorption and the Central Bureau of Statistics. The figure on births in Israel was contributed by Danny Budowski, who obtained them from the Israel Central Bureau of Statistics.

TABLE 1. ETHIOPIAN JEWISH IMMIGRATION
TO ISRAEL, 1972–1993

1972–1976	91
1977	125
1978	3
1979	30
1980	258
1981	601
1982	528
1983	2,192
1984	8,240
1985	1,763
1986	209
1987	252
1988	603
1989	1,334
1990	4,121
1991	20,026
1992	3,538
1993	700
Total	44,614

Gender and Age

It is notoriously difficult to compile accurate demographic data on Ethiopian immigrants, as virtually every category except gender is subject to cultural confusion and situational redefinition. According to figures from the Israel Ministry of Immigrant Absorption, from 1977 to 1993, 22,541 Ethiopian males and 22,996 females arrived in the country.[24] With regard to age (table 2), the Ethiopian immigrant population appears highly weighted toward youth, with almost 46 percent of the population aged 0–18, 36 percent aged 19–44, 11 percent aged 45–64, and 7 percent aged 65 and older.[25]

These figures must, however, be viewed with a certain degree of caution.

---

[24]No breakdown of immigrants who arrived before 1977 is available. They were, however, in the main, young men in their late teens or early twenties.

[25]These figures are based on data from the Ministry of Absorption. Among those who arrived (mainly through the Sudan) until mid-1985, 52.2 percent were 0–18 years of age, and only 5.9 percent were over age 60.

TABLE 2. AGE DISTRIBUTION

Age	Male	Female
0–2	338	316
3–5	1,628	2,490
6–9	2,490	2,254
10–14	3,734	3,338
15–18	2,505	2,389
19–24	2,789	2,767
25–34	3,010	3,244
35–44	1,968	2,237
45–49	804	784
50–59	1,122	1,135
60–64	421	641
65–74	1,189	1,006
75–84	439	306
85+	104	89

Since most immigrants had no independent documentation regarding their date of birth, officials have been forced to rely on oral testimony. The ages (and marital status) claimed have often been dependent on the immigrants' perceptions as to what ages or status will confer the most benefits in Israel. Requests to "correct" such information are common. For example, a young man in his twenties may claim to be only 15 in order to be assigned to a boarding school, rather than a job training program, while older immigrants may seek to add to their age in order to qualify as pensioners.

Family Structure

Similarly, differences between Ethiopian and Israeli concepts of "family" have created problems for demographers and absorption workers alike.

For the Beta Israel, social life was traditionally organized around the flexible and often overlapping concepts of the extended family (*zamad*) and the household (*beta sa'ab*). *Zamad* is a term whose precise meaning varies according to the circumstances and context. Thus, *zamad* is most frequently used to refer to an extended family (as opposed to strangers), but it may also be used to distinguish blood relations from in-laws.[26] In Ethiopia, within the borders of the *zamad*, little attention was paid to the "real"

---

[26]When searching for a spouse for a son or daughter, parents would automatically exclude anyone in their *zamad*, counting back seven generations.

relationships between members. Thus, according to the circumstances, grandparents, uncles, or older siblings might function like a child's "parents." A person's "children" might easily include nieces, nephews, stepchildren, and younger siblings.

In contrast to the geographically dispersed *zamad*, the *beta sa'ab* (household) was a residential unit whose membership changed over time. Although often composed around a core nuclear family, widowed parents, divorced siblings, elderly relatives, various children, and even servants were often vital parts of a single *beta sa'ab*. At any given moment, the precise configuration of the *beta sa'ab* was determined by an assortment of personal preferences and economic needs, and it would change as these changed.

In light of the above, it is often difficult to determine the precise biological relationships that exist among a group of Ethiopians sharing a residence.

TABLE 3.   HOUSEHOLD STRUCTURE

One-Parent	2,667
Single (Nonelderly)	3,945
Single (Elderly)	960
Couples (Nonelderly)	858
Couples (Elderly)	296
Couples with 1–3 children	2,845
Couples with 4 children or more	2,655
Other	162
Total households:	14,388

TABLE 4.   HOUSEHOLD SIZE

Single	4,905
2 persons	2,369
3 persons	1,665
4 persons	1,449
5 persons	1,161
6 persons	1,012
7 persons	784
8 persons	536
9 or more	544

These household units are, moreover, fluid and subject to frequent restructuring. The figures given in tables 3 and 4 are, therefore, a useful guide rather than a definitive picture.

No aspect of Ethiopian family life in Israel has aroused more comment among absorption workers and other professionals than the large number of one-parent families. Approximately a third of all Ethiopian children live in one-parent households. This compares with less than 9 percent among the rest of the Israeli population.

This relatively high figure can be attributed to several factors. Such families were created, for example, when couples made *aliyah* at different times, or when one of the partners died on the way to Israel. In Israel itself, the redefinition of gender roles, conflicts over personal goals, and sharp differences between husbands and wives in their rates of adjustment to new conditions contribute to the breakup of two-parent units. To this must be added such "universal" factors as disagreements over child rearing and tensions created by crowded housing and economic difficulties.

Although no precise statistics exist, many children in Ethiopia apparently lived with only one of their parents. However, the safety net provided by an extended family as well as the fluid character of household units meant that few children lived in one-*adult* households.[27]

THE ABSORPTION PROCESS: RELIGION AND COMMUNAL ORGANIZATION

The Ethiopians and the Rabbis

As noted above, Rabbi Ovadia Yosef's decision to recognize the Jewishness of the "Falashas" was a turning point in their history.[28] His pronouncement, however, not only opened the doors to a more active policy in favor of Ethiopian immigration, it also placed those Ethiopian Jews who did arrive—together with all other Jews in Israel—under the religious jurisdiction of the Chief Rabbinate. Although the chief rabbis had affirmed the *communal* status of the Ethiopians as Jews, they continued to express reservations concerning the *personal* status of individuals. In particular, they voiced their concern that the Ethiopians' ignorance of rabbinic law (Halakhah) had rendered divorces and conversions, performed by *qessotch*

---

[27]Shalva Weil, *Ethiopian One-Parent Families in Israel* (Hebrew with English abstract) (Jerusalem, Hebrew University, 1991); Ruth Westheimer and Steven Kaplan, *Surviving Salvation: The Ethiopian Jewish Family in Transition* (New York, 1992), pp. 105–09.

[28]See note 12 for a bibliography on the halakhic status of the Ethiopians.

("priests," the religious leaders of the Beta Israel in Ethiopia) for centuries in Ethiopia, invalid. According to the Chief Rabbinate, as a result of non-halakhic conversions, hundreds of individuals whose status as Jews was questionable had immigrated from Ethiopia. And nonhalakhic divorces, they claimed, had raised considerable questions about the danger of *mamzerut* (illegitimacy) among the Ethiopians.[29] In either case, grave difficulties existed with regard to a simple and immediate integration of the Ethiopians into the general Jewish population. Ethiopian immigrants strongly rejected both claims.

Throughout the 1970s and early 1980s, the Chief Rabbinate required Ethiopian immigrants to undergo a modified conversion ceremony consisting of ritual immersion, a declaration accepting rabbinic law, and, in the case of men, a symbolic recircumcision. Although initially applied to all Ethiopians, the requirement was eventually limited to those wishing to marry. Toward the end of 1984, the demand for recircumcision was dropped.[30]

During the period from 1972 to 1984, several thousand Ethiopian immigrants, from Tigre, Walqayit, and Gondar submitted to the demands of the rabbinate. From 1985 onward, however, organized resistance to what was labeled "forced conversion" became increasingly apparent. One particular group of young men, members of a newly formed organization called Beta Israel, organized a systematic campaign in all the absorption centers against any cooperation with rabbis. Recently arrived immigrants, acting on the advice of these more experienced Ethiopians, refused to cooperate with the rabbinate. Their resistance culminated in a month-long protest opposite the Chief Rabbinate headquarters in the fall of 1985.[31]

In April 1986, in an attempt to circumvent the rabbinate's marriage requirements, 15 Ethiopian couples were brought together in a Tel Aviv wedding hall to be married in a "traditional ceremony" conducted by four of the *qessotch* who had participated in the strike. Such marriages, which would have been completely valid in Ethiopia, had no legal status in Israel and were not accepted by Interior Ministry authorities. Couples married by

---

[29] According to Jewish law, the child of an adulterous sexual relationship is a *mamzer*. In the case of the Ethiopians, the rabbinate argued that if their divorces were indeed invalid according to Jewish law, subsequent remarriages were adulterous, producing offspring who were illegitimate, who in turn passed this status down to their offspring for centuries.

[30] Changes in rabbinic policies were the result of a number of factors, including a significant rise in the rate at which immigrants were arriving, pressure exerted by those already in the country, and an improved understanding on the part of the rabbinate of circumcision as practiced by the Ethiopians.

[31] Steven Kaplan, "The Beta Israel and the Rabbinate: Law, Politics and Ritual," *Social Science Information* 27, no. 3 (Sept. 1988), pp. 357–70.

qessotch could, however, by visiting a notary, gain recognition of their union as a common-law marriage. This assured them of being treated as a couple for certain civil purposes, such as public housing. From a religious point of view, such marriages created enormous halakhic problems. If, for instance, a woman had not been officially certified as divorced or widowed—which would be the case if she had been divorced in Ethiopia or if her husband had died in the Sudan, but she had no proof of his death—then all of her children born in Israel would automatically be considered *mamzerim* (illegitimate).

The number of "*qes* marriages" dropped significantly following the appointment of Rabbi David Chelouche of Netanya, a prominent supporter of the Ethiopians, as the sole official marriage registrar for the entire community. Under this compromise, sanctioned by the Israeli Supreme Court in June 1989, any Ethiopian in the country could travel to Rabbi Chelouche to register to be married.

While the appointment of Rabbi Chelouche provided a solution that preserved both the Ethiopians' dignity and the rabbinate's sovereignty, bitterness over the dispute lingered. Active protests concerning the issue seemed on the wane until, in early 1991, several months prior to Operation Solomon, a well-known elderly *qes*, *Qes* Menashe, was brought to Israel. He immediately aligned himself with the opponents of the Supreme Court decision, against Rabbi Chelouche and against any compromise with the Chief Rabbinate. These *qessotch* demanded full recognition of themselves as "rabbis," qualified without any additional training to perform all ceremonies for their community, just as they had done in Ethiopia.

Their pleas went largely unheeded until early in 1992. Then a newly formed group of activists seized upon the issue of the lack of respect given their *qessotch*. These young, mainly secular, men organized strikes and incited violent demonstrations (something that had not previously been part of Ethiopian protests), demanding that the *qessotch*, or rather those associated with *Qes* Menashe, be certified by the Chief Rabbinate to be the sole arbiters of religious ceremonies for their community. The *qessotch*'s case received widespread media coverage, especially when their ranks were swelled by almost 80 elderly men (most of whom had arrived in Operation Solomon), all clad in white turbans and black capes, the external signs of *qes* status.

Once again the chief rabbis reiterated their position that without training in those aspects of Jewish law required to perform a marriage ceremony or write a divorce writ, it would be impossible to permit the *qessotch* to do these things. They pointed out that, if they were to grant them the right to conduct marriage ceremonies, the result would be a Karaite-like status, in effect separating the Ethiopians from the rest of Jewry and prejudicing their full acceptance as equals among all other Jews.

In November 1992, a special interministerial committee recommended that all the *qessotch* be given paid positions on the religious councils that exist in every municipality. They urged the *qessotch* to attend special courses, so that they could serve, ultimately, as official rabbis (presumably for anyone who approached them, not just Ethiopians). Even though *qessotch* who had been among the demonstrators were members of the committee, and signed their names to the list of recommendations, their young activist supporters threatened to organize renewed demonstrations unless all of the original demands were met in full.

In the meantime, an attempt has been made by those *qessotch* who have been attending classes and learning the basics of Jewish law to bring about a reconciliation, first of all between the group supporting the Chief Rabbinate and that opposing it (both of whose members are from the Gondar region, the Tigrean *qessotch* having remained aloof from all such "political" frays), and then between all the *qessotch* and the Chief Rabbinate. Attempts have been made to include *qessotch* on religious councils in areas that have a sizable Ethiopian population. In some cases, the local councils have objected that the *qessotch* appointed lack sufficient knowledge; in others, Ethiopian activists have objected to the specific *qessotch* named to the council. Nevertheless, the number of *qessotch* on such councils continues to grow. As these Ethiopian religious leaders come into more regular contact with local rabbis and begin (albeit on a limited basis) to once again meet their community's religious needs, the tensions between them and the Israeli religious establishment may diminish.

During the past decade a number of *qessotch* have been studying at Makhon Meir, a yeshivah in Jerusalem. The same institution also runs a special program that prepares young Ethiopians for rabbinic ordination. The first graduates of this program, about a dozen in number, were expected to be ordained in 1994.[32] It is hoped that their presence will increase the awareness and understanding of rabbinic Judaism in the Ethiopian community and pave the way for a rapprochement between community elders and the Chief Rabbinate.

Other Religious Matters

The Ethiopians have been confronted with a number of other issues relating to Jewish observance. In Ethiopia, the Beta Israel had survived by

---

[32]There is, to date, only one Ethiopian rabbi in Israel, Rabbi Yosef Hadane. He, however, was trained and ordained prior to the start of large-scale immigration from Ethiopia.

clinging tenaciously to their Jewish identity and to distinctive practices including purity rituals and the isolation of women when menstruating and after giving birth.

The transition to Israeli observances and customs since *aliyah* has not been easy. For the Beta Israel, who had no fires on the Sabbath and hence no hot food, the custom of eating *cholent* and other dishes kept warm throughout the day appears to be a violation of strict observance. Although both Ethiopians and Israeli Orthodox Jews share a concern for ritual purity, the former believe that immersion must take place in a river or stream and have been reluctant to accept the *mikveh*, ritual bath, as a substitute.

In the past, immigrants to Israel have tended to establish their own synagogues, which preserve distinctive ethnic practices and forms. Thus far, however, the Ethiopians have only partially conformed to this pattern. Beersheba, for example, has long had an Ethiopian *minyan*, and there is soon to be an Ethiopian synagogue. There are thriving Ethiopian congregations in both Ashdod and Lod. In other cases, however, it has not proven easy to make the transition from one religious system to another. Prayers in Ge'ez recited by the *qes* in Ethiopia are not easily replaced by a Hebrew liturgy led by a rabbi. Indeed, many Ethiopians find little familiar in the worship of their local synagogues beside the use of "amen."

Efforts have been made to adapt some Beta Israel traditional practices to fit in with the conditions of their new homeland. They have, for instance, transformed one of their primary festivals, known as Sigd—a commemoration of the return from exile described in the Books of Ezra and Nchemiah—into a holiday which they can celebrate in Jerusalem. They have even sought to interest other Israelis in their unique holiday, so that the Sigd can, like well-known Moroccan and Kurdish festivals, be of more than just parochial interest.[33]

Communal Organization and Leadership

As indicated by the discussion of relations with the rabbinate, Ethiopian immigrants in Israel have shown considerable political initiative since their arrival in the country. No community in Israel has demonstrated as pronounced a proclivity to take to the streets in protest or to form organizations ostensibly intended to promote the interests of their members.

---

[33]G.J. Abbink, "*Seged* Celebration in Ethiopia and Israel: Continuity and Change of a Falasha Religious Holiday," *Anthropos* 78, 1983, pp. 789–810; S. Ben-Dor, "The Sigd of Beta-Israel: Testimony to a Community in Transition," in Ashkenazi and Weingrod, *Ethiopian Jews*, pp. 140–59; Emmanuel Grupper and Anita Nudelman, "Cross-Cultural Pluralism in Action: The Case of 'Seged' Celebration of Ethiopian Jews in Youth Aliyah Institutions," in *Between Africa and Zion: Proceedings of the First International Congress of the Society for the Study of Ethiopian Jewry* (Ben Zvi Institute, Jerusalem, forthcoming).

In part, at least, this decentralized form of organization can be seen as a continuation of patterns of communal organization found in Ethiopia. The Beta Israel "community" was actually a loosely connected network of villages and local communities linked by religious, cultural, and marital ties, but lacking any centralized political authority. Even on the local level, political authority was exercised by a variety of figures who acted through consensus building rather than the use of coercive power or through reliance on state institutions.[34]

This tendency to decentralization has been exacerbated by the increasing interaction with world Jewry, which has introduced a variety of external patrons to the community, enabling each faction to draw support from the wide range of Jewish and Israeli interest groups. Thus, the Reform and Conservative movements and secularist groups are prepared to support almost all demonstrations against the Chief Rabbinate, while several prominent members of Gush Emunim have taken up the cause of the Falas Mura.

The move to Israel has also disrupted traditional patterns of leadership. The deterioration in the position of the *qessotch* has been discussed above. Similarly, the community elders (*shmagilotch*), who were the main representatives of their people in nonreligious, official matters in Ethiopia, have not been able to function effectively as leaders in Israel. Their "wisdom" no longer captures anyone's attention and seems to be of no practical value, particularly when it relates to making one's way in Israel. By contrast, the youngsters, primarily due to their quicker grasp of Hebrew and of the Israeli mentality, have forged ahead of their parents and are less willing to ask for, let alone abide by, their parents' advice than they had been in the past.

This role diminution is to some extent inevitable, but it is felt particularly acutely by the Ethiopians. In contrast to the avowedly child- and youth-centered norms of Israeli society, the Beta Israel of Ethiopia respected and honored the elderly and aged. As a man grew older, his personal status grew. If he was well thought of and behaved honorably, he would be considered a *shmagile* (elder) by the time he reached his late thirties or early forties. People came to him with their problems and asked for his advice. Although the *shmagilotch* (elders) were exclusively men, older women also had an important role to play. A senior woman, known as a *baaltet*, would be consulted on issues relating to women, including childbirth, illness, and disputes between younger women.

Although the status of parents and elders in Ethiopia had begun to decline even before the revolution of 1974, they were able to retain a

---

[34]Steven Kaplan, "Leadership and Communal Organization Among the Beta Israel: An Historical Study," *Encyclopaedia Judaica Year Book 1986/1987* (Jerusalem, 1987), pp. 154–63; Shalva Weil, "Leadership Among Ethiopian Jews in Israel," in *Between Africa and Zion* (forthcoming).

modicum of authority so long as the Beta Israel remained in Ethiopia. Their experience in handling the day-to-day problems of village life remained a valuable commodity. Once they reached Israel, however, their situation deteriorated rapidly. Faced with unprecedented challenges in a strange new society, their years of accumulated wisdom suddenly seemed irrelevant. Settled haphazardly around the country, the reputation for sound judgment they had earned through years of shrewd arbitration on a village level appeared to evaporate. Immigration agencies, moreover, saw the elderly as neither a source of wisdom nor an object of veneration, but a problematic "generation of the wilderness" that could never be successfully integrated into their new society.

The peripheralization of the *shmagilotch* was significant, not only for its impact on the elders themselves but also for its effect on the community as a whole. At precisely the time when the Ethiopian community was experiencing some of its greatest difficulties, one of its most important institutions for dealing with crises was in ruins. Fortunately, attempts have been made by some organizations in recent years to consult and mobilize the *shmagilotch*.[35]

Successive waves of *aliyah* have produced divisions within the immigrant community between newcomers and oldtimers, veterans with establishment positions and young Turks. Since the early 1980s, the community has been rife with factions. The first serious conflict to emerge erupted between Tigreans and Gondaris in 1981. Although the site of this conflict was the absorption center in Beersheba,[36] its ramifications spread, so that even today relations between members of these two groups are often far from cordial.[37] Disagreements on how best to further the cause of immigration and the reunification of families have also led to altercations between individuals and within families. In the absence of any procedures for electing representatives, there has been a tendency for talented individuals to assert that they are leaders, whether or not they have any significant backing from anyone outside of their immediate families.

For a time, two secular groups composed predominantly of young people competed with each other as to which could best claim to be the legitimate

---

[35]In the most ambitious such project, *Betachin* (Amharic: Our House), an organization sponsored by the JDC, employs a number of Ethiopian staffers, including laymen and *qessotch* as mediators and counselors to help Ethiopian families resolve problems. They have also published a number of Hebrew pamphlets on issues of family life, mediation, and conflict.

[36]Abbink, "Falashas . . . Ethnic Assimilation," pp. 174–88, 293–314.

[37]Ibid., pp. 277–78. See also Michael Ashkenazi, "Political Organization and Resources Among Ethiopian Immigrants," *Social Science Information* 17, no. 3, 1988, pp. 371–89. On Tigrean and Gondari contrasts, see Chaim Rosen, "The Many Ways of Ethiopian Jews: Similarities and Differences Between Beta Israel from Gondar and Tigre" (in Hebrew), *Pe'amim* 33, 1988, pp. 93–108.

voice of the people. Both were composed exclusively of Gondaris and had little connection with the Tigrean and Walqayit segments of the community. The organizers of both groups acquired their basic political experience through involvement in opposition political groups in Ethiopia prior to their flight to Israel.

In 1987 an attempt was made to bring these two groups together around the issue of family reunification. When this proved impossible, a third group, known as the Rescue Committee, was formed. It captured public attention by organizing a six-week sit-in outside the Knesset to highlight the reunification issue. This was followed by a large rally in Jerusalem's Binyanei Ha-umah (Convention Center), which was attended by prominent Israeli politicians and international human-rights activists.

The unity displayed in the calls for family reunification was, however, only superficial, and new organizations sprang up in rapid succession. Several leaders of the Rescue Committee created yet another organization, which they named after the "father of Ethiopian Jewry," Jacques Faitlovitch. A short time later the Ethiopian Students' Organization, composed of students in institutions of higher education, was formed. The National Committee for Ethiopian Jewry, which had been dormant for some years, was also resuscitated.

In 1990, following a year or so of bickering and mutual recrimination, the leaders of seven organizations agreed to set their differences aside and unite in the Umbrella Organization of Ethiopian Jewish Organizations. This move was warmly applauded by top Jewish Agency figures, who promptly rewarded the leaders of the group with large sums of money to support their new venture. Despite the Israeli media's tendency to portray the Umbrella Organization as *the* representative of Ethiopian Jewry, one large Ethiopian organization refused to operate under its auspices, and various additional factions continued to emerge. The former, in particular, made constant attacks on the small group of individuals who, in addition to dominating the Umbrella Organization, controlled the Amharic radio program and published the only regular Ethiopian-language magazine in the country.[38]

In the aftermath of Operation Solomon, two additional groups emerged. The Zionist Movement for the Cause of Ethiopian Jewry has taken over the battle for the recognition of the *qessotch*; the South Wing to Zion lobbies for the immediate immigration to Israel of the Falas Mura.

As of this writing, the community is badly divided. *Qessotch* are at odds with one another. The group that is critical of the rabbinate refuses to eat meat slaughtered by the *qessotch* who have studied ritual slaughtering at Makhon Meir, a Jerusalem yeshivah. Young activists denounce each other,

---

[38]See *"Kesef Shahor"* (Black Money), *Ha'olam Ha'zeh*, Aug. 3, 1992, pp. 18–21.

passing out flyers at every public gathering, depicting their rivals as corrupt and incompetent. Such divisions have a clearly deleterious effect on the Ethiopians' overall integration. The political influence that they would normally have acquired as a rapidly growing ethnic group is being severely dissipated. Each group's leadership insists that it speaks for the majority of the community, yet the reality of mutual recriminations and accusations weakens all of them. It may well be that only the next generation will see the emergence of young leaders capable of forging a truly unified, community-oriented leadership, one that can become a significant factor in the Israeli political arena.[39]

THE ABSORPTION PROCESS: HOUSING, EDUCATION, EMPLOYMENT, HEALTH

Housing and Residential Distribution

Of all the challenges facing the Israeli immigration authorities, none has proven more complex and fraught with difficulties than settling the Ethiopians in permanent housing. Unlike language courses, job-training programs, health facilities, and many other services offered to new *olim* (immigrants), apartments cannot be easily produced in response to a sudden rise in demand. If vacancies exist, they are usually in less desirable areas, which are the least equipped to deal with a large influx of newcomers. Settling too many immigrants in a single location can lead to their being ghettoized; settling too few can leave them isolated and make it difficult for helping agencies to reach them. Housing decisions are among those with the broadest impact, for they affect educational opportunities, employment prospects, and social integration. Housing mistakes are also among the hardest to correct, for rebuilding is usually impractical, and repeated moves are almost always disruptive.

Throughout most of 1984 all Ethiopian immigrants were temporarily housed in absorption centers before being moved into permanent housing.[40] Such centers did not have sufficient space, however, to handle the large

[39]A discussion of problems facing the present activist leaders, plus a survey of the large number of major and minor organizations within the community, can be found in *Ha'aretz*, July 27, 1992, where an unpublished report written by Dr. Shalva Weil is extensively quoted.

[40]Absorption centers are designed to house immigrants temporarily and to ease their initial adjustment to their new surroundings. By concentrating immigrants in separate buildings or housing projects, absorption authorities are able to exercise better control over their access to government services, Hebrew instruction, job information, etc. Initially established in 1969 to assist Western immigrants during their first six months in Israel, they have since been used in the absorption of other immigrants. For a critical view of this process, see Michael Ashkenazi and Alex Weingrod, *Ethiopian Immigrants in Beersheba* (Highland Park, Ill., 1984);

influx of immigrants from Operation Moses. Accordingly, about one-third of the 6,700 immigrants who arrived at the end of 1984 were placed in ten hotels rented by the Jewish Agency. They lived for over a year in these hotels in what can best be described as a hothouse atmosphere; they were fed in dining halls and had almost all their needs met by outsiders. Hotel residents were, not surprisingly, relatively slow to develop even the minimum skills required for leading an independent life in Israel.

Only in 1986, after much wrangling between absorption agencies, were all Ethiopian immigrants removed from hotels. Since only a few were judged to be ready to live on their own in apartments, the majority were transferred to regular absorption centers, where they joined hundreds of other immigrants from various countries.

In general, the longer the Ethiopians were in the country, the more specific their housing preferences became, and the harder it was to move them out of the centers. Most wished to live close to family members already settled in permanent housing. Others were guided by their perceptions of employment opportunities in different regions. As a result, too, of interministerial squabbling over how to deal with them, the Ethiopians' temporary sojourn in absorption centers stretched on for years. At the end of 1987, almost 40 percent of those who arrived in Operation Moses had still not been resettled. In some cases, absorption officials, rather than moving the Ethiopians into permanent housing, left the immigrants in place and simply changed the status of absorption centers by removing the services they had provided. Nine absorption centers—former apartment complexes designed to accommodate people on a short-term basis—were decreed overnight to be permanent homes, whose residents had to pay rent, utilities, taxes, and so on. Ethiopian residents of these converted centers complained bitterly, feeling that they had been deprived of the opportunity to choose where to live.

On a larger scale, this decision resulted in the instant "ghettoization" of many immigrants. Despite explicit recommendations that no apartment building house more than 3–4 Ethiopian families, some blocks suddenly had over 50 and many others more than 15. Moreover, despite vague promises to the contrary, these families had almost no chance of moving into other apartments, since all available public housing was required for those still living in more cramped absorption centers.

Another housing problem developed when several hundred families were placed in previously abandoned mobile homes (*caravanim*) located at the edge of small towns and cities. In a short time, newspaper reports and even documentary films appeared showing the crumbling walls, unsanitary facili-

see also Esther Hertzog, "The Israeli Absorption Bureaucracy and the Ethiopian Immigrants," in *Between Africa and Zion* (forthcoming).

ties, and hazardous living conditions in these *caravanim*. Nevertheless, it took almost four years to find better housing for these immigrants. Even after Operation Solomon, at least 200 families from the time of Operation Moses were still living in absorption facilities of one type or another.

The lessons learned from the experience of housing the Operation Moses immigrants were quite clear and were reflected in the Ministry of Absorption's *Master Plan, Second Stage*, which was published in April 1991. Based on the assumption that Ethiopian immigrants would continue to arrive in Israel at a rate of 500–800 a month throughout 1991 and 1992, it focused on "direct absorption" in apartments made available when they immigrated. The arrival of more than 14,000 immigrants during Operation Solomon completely undermined these assumptions. In seeking an instant emergency solution for this large group, the Jewish Agency was forced to fill every available hotel, residence house, rest home, and established mobile-home site.[41]

Immediately after Operation Solomon, Minister of Housing Ariel Sharon promised that all Ethiopian immigrants would be in permanent apartments within one year. Despite his promises, not only did few families find permanent housing, new ones kept arriving to join those already in the various absorption facilities. By June 1992, a total of almost 24,000 Ethiopians were living in absorption facilities. Sharon's major response, which was immediately implemented by the Jewish Agency (which had to pay $13,500 a year for each Ethiopian living in a hotel), was to revive the previously failed policy of placing the Ethiopians "temporarily" in mobile homes.

Between June and September 1992, thousands of Ethiopians were transferred out of their hotels and other residential facilities into caravan sites scattered throughout the country. Despite the drawbacks of life in a tiny mobile home, this arrangement at least gave the Ethiopians more control over their lives than they had in the hotels. At a number of absorption centers and hotels the Ethiopians mounted protests demanding permanent apartments in public housing, rather than being transferred to yet another form of temporary residence. Sharon met with the Ethiopian protesters and once again promised that all Ethiopians would be in permanent housing within a year, by July 1993. A few weeks later, however, national elections were held, and Sharon was no longer in office. His successor, Binyamin Ben-Eliezer, immediately abrogated all commitments that had been made to the Ethiopians.

In November 1992, the government announced that it would take three to four years before all of the caravan sites could be evacuated. In order to achieve this target date, 6,000 apartments would have to be acquired for

---

[41]During 1991–92, only 150 families, as an experiment, were offered direct absorption, being placed in apartments in Ofakim, Arad, and Dimona.

Ethiopian immigrants. Starting in April 1993, Ethiopian immigrants were offered special conditions for purchasing an apartment; these include a direct grant of $80,000 as well as interest-free loans. Thus, a family with four or more children receives as much as $110,000 toward the purchase of an apartment in any of 52 authorized locations in the center of the country. These unprecedented terms, which may cover as much as 99 percent of the total cost of an apartment, are far better than those available to any other group of either immigrants or veteran Israelis.

Despite their initial skepticism, some 1,750 families out of 5,961 took advantage of this offer during the first six months of the campaign. Most Ethiopian immigrants, however, view the entire idea of home-purchase with suspicion. They fear that such large grants will carry hidden payments, or that the government will one day come to reclaim apartments. In order to alleviate such fears and to relieve the crush of the caravan camps, a carefully designed information campaign for the Ethiopians has been undertaken.

As noted above, the primary problem with the mobile homes at the time of Operation Moses was their physical deterioration. The problem today is their uncanny resemblance to the segregated tent camps (*ma'abarot*) that were used to house immigrants in the 1950s. Huge mobile-home towns have been erected, usually in isolated open areas where Ethiopians are segregated from the general Israeli population.[42]

As of December 1993, 21 caravan sites (in which some 16,000 Ethiopians were living) were operating under the supervision of the Ministry of Absorption. In addition, 6,200 Ethiopians were still living in 27 absorption centers and 3 hotels. Thus, by the end of 1993, about half of the entire Ethiopian immigrant population was still in temporary housing, receiving either government or Jewish Agency subsidies. As a result of the mortgage campaign, it was projected that, by the end of 1994, the majority of families would either have purchased apartments or be eligible for public housing.

PERMANENT HOUSING

At least in part, the Ethiopians' housing preferences are based on pragmatic considerations they share with most groups in the population: the availability of work, the suitability of the climate, and the centrality of the location. Thus, despite their age-old dream of living in Jerusalem, few Ethiopians have decided to do so, because the work opportunities are limited and the climate is too cold. Their aversion to living on the West Bank has stemmed not from political considerations but from its relative isolation.

---

[42]As of Sept. 1993, 70 percent of those living in mobile homes were Ethiopian immigrants. Most immigrants from the former Soviet Union refused to live in mobile homes, unless faced with homelessness.

TABLE 5. REGIONAL DISTRIBUTION OF ETHIOPIAN
HOUSEHOLDS AND INDIVIDUALS

Region	Households	Individuals
North	5,103	15,704
Tel Aviv	1,741	5,028
Negev	2,234	7,962
Jerusalem	2,522	7,733
Center	2,787	8,002

TABLE 6. MAJOR CENTERS OF ETHIOPIAN IMMIGRANT
RESIDENCE, OCTOBER 1993

Afikim	893
Afula	1,113
Ashdod	1,266
Ashkelon	2,531
Barutayim	786*
Beersheba	3,249
Beit Hatzor	1,012*
Gedera	763
Hadera	1,286
Haifa	1,723
Hatzrot Yesef	1,763*
Hulda	1,023*
Jerusalem	1,156
Kadourie	825*
Kiryat Gat	1,548
Kiryat Yam	1,203
Ma'agalim	765*
Mevo'im	839*
Nazareth	1,154
Netanya	2,259
Ramle	770
Safed	1,066
Tiberias	974

*Caravan sites; other settlements include both permanent and temporary housing.

In general, however, the primary factor influencing Ethiopians' choice of housing has been their desire to live near close relatives. Although most prefer not to live in a building occupied only by Ethiopians, they do favor neighborhoods that have many related families within easy walking distance. Since many of the first Ethiopians to find permanent housing were sent to towns around Tel Aviv such as Bat Yam, Holon, and Netanya, or neighborhoods in Beersheba, many subsequent immigrants expressed a preference for these locales. Thus, despite plans calling for a dispersion of the Ethiopians in order to avoid ghettoization, their own inclination was to live together in extended family groups.[43]

Another important factor shaping preferences in a manner not anticipated by absorption planners is the Ethiopians' perspective on the job market. Here, too, the greater Tel Aviv area enjoys a good reputation among Ethiopian immigrants. Not only did they find ready employment in the factories of the region, they also discovered that the salaries they received were better than those for comparable jobs in, for example, Jerusalem. The more the Ethiopians received apartments in towns like Bat Yam, Holon, Rishon LeZion, and Petah Tikvah, the greater the demand for apartments in these places among those remaining in absorption centers. As the supply of public apartments available for Ethiopian immigrants in these cities dwindled, a slow process began of redefining "close to Tel Aviv." From 1988 on, there was a growing interest in a second tier of towns, including Rehovot, Nes Ziona, Ramle, and, more recently, Yavneh, Lod, Ashdod, and Ashkelon.[44] (See tables 5 and 6.)

Education

Since approximately 60 percent of the Ethiopian immigrants were under age 24 at the time of their arrival in Israel, providing appropriate educational programs has been one of the greatest challenges facing absorption authorities.[45]

When Ethiopian immigrants first began arriving in Israel, it was decided

---

[43]This conflict between the Ethiopians' preferences and the government's desire to avoid concentrating too many in one place has led to some towns being "closed" to Ethiopians. An appeal challenging this policy was filed with the Supreme Court, but it was dismissed.

[44]For the distribution of Ethiopians in Israel in permanent housing in August 1985 and August 1988, see S. Kaplan, *Les Beta Israel (Falashas)* (Turnhout, Belgium, 1990), pp. 170–73.

[45]See V. Netzer, R. Elazar, and S. Ben-Dor, eds., *Saga of Aliyah: The Jews of Ethiopia. Aspects of Their Linguistic and Educational Absorption* (Jerusalem, 1990), for background on the approaches to education followed in Israel, and G. Ben-Ezer, *K'mo ohr be'kad* (Like Light in a Jug) (Jerusalem, 1992), for an account of the psychological aspects of Youth Aliyah's educational programs.

that all Ethiopian children would be sent to state religious schools during their first year in Israel.[46] This policy, based on the assumption that it would ease the transition for immigrants from a traditional religious background, was applied not only in elementary schools but in Youth Aliyah secondary-level boarding schools as well. Thus, all Ethiopian youngsters absorbed by Youth Aliyah were registered in religious schools. Although parents were permitted to transfer a child to any school after the first year, in practice this seldom occurred. A 1988 study revealed that of the 3,500 Ethiopian students then learning in elementary schools, only about 280, or 8 percent, were in secular schools.[47]

Whatever the political and social considerations behind the decision to send Ethiopians to religious schools, it significantly limited the options available to ministry officials. On the one hand, a large portion of the educational system was deprived of any contact with the Ethiopian students; on the other, certain schools and areas were called upon to assume a considerable burden. Schools of the right size, serving the right age groups, and with the necessary facilities were not always available in proximity to immigrant housing or absorption centers. In some cases, classes suddenly had a large percentage of Ethiopian students, and some schools found themselves with a student body that was 60–70 percent Ethiopian.[48]

Immediately after Operation Solomon, a major effort was made to find suitable schools for the Ethiopian children who had arrived. When arrangements were finally made for them, they were often placed in "special" classes with only Ethiopian children. In some cases they were taught by young women doing national service or other nonprofessional teachers who were unprepared for the challenge of handling so many newcomers who could not read or write their native Amharic, let alone Hebrew.

At the start of the 1993–94 school year, more than two years after Operation Solomon, some 4,000 Ethiopian children were registered in elementary schools. Although most Ethiopian children had been in school for over a year, and were thus no longer required to attend a religious school,

---

[46]According to the State Education Law of 1953, Israeli schools are divided into two trends: state (secular) education and state religious education. This law also allows for "recognized" schools, such as those run by the ultra-Orthodox, which are not state schools. Approximately 60 percent of Jewish children attend secular schools, 30 percent religious schools, and 10 percent independent recognized schools. Youth Aliyah is a department of the Jewish Agency that operates a network of secondary boarding schools as well as urban day centers. The boarding schools are also either religious or secular.

[47]Shalva Weil, *Emunot veminhagim dati'im shel yehudei etiyopia be-yisrael* (Beliefs and Religious Customs of Ethiopian Jews in Israel; Hebrew with English abstract) (Jerusalem, 1988), pp. 124–41.

[48]For a critique of the decision to send Ethiopian immigrants to religious schools, as well as a general discussion of their education in the mid-1980s, see Teshome G. Wagaw, *For Our Soul: Ethiopian Jews in Israel* (Detroit, 1993).

the community was not, as a whole, interested in placing its children in other schools. In fact, despite the efforts of the Ministry of Absorption, Ethiopian organizations, and other activists to promote secular schools, the percentage of students in nonreligious schools actually declined, from 8 percent in 1988 to 5 percent (approximately 200) in 1993.[49] In effect, most Ethiopian parents seem to be more concerned that their children receive a religious education than with the academic standards of the institutions in question.

Thus, there was still a great need to find religious schools capable of handling so large an influx of students. Since few religious schools were situated near caravan sites, young children were often being bused up to one or one-and-a-half hours in order to attend an appropriate elementary school. Needless to say, in such cases, even the most concerned parents could have little if any contact with their children's school or teachers. Although one early study found that about 20 percent of the Ethiopian children in the elementary schools were having learning problems, which was approximately the same percentage as for the general population,[50] more recent reports indicate that the situation has deteriorated.

PARENTS AND CHILDREN

The decision to send Ethiopian students to religious schools was actually one of the few educational policy decisions made during the period prior to and through Operation Moses. Indeed, as the Israel State Comptroller noted in his report of 1986, thousands of Ethiopian students had already entered the school system by the time planning began on appropriate educational programs. "[The Ministry of Education] began to prepare itself—with regard to preparing cadres of teachers, curricula, and syllabi, and drawing up an overall policy—very late, after the [Ethiopian] children were attending school. Even then, the pace was very slow."[51]

One direct consequence of this lapse was that most Ethiopian parents sent their children off to school with little sense of the norms or expectations of the school system. For their part, the teachers and school staff had little sense of what needed to be explained. Tardiness, inadequate dress, unkempt appearance, a lack of supplies (pencils, notebooks), and insufficient lunches were only a few of the problems that developed at the outset. Ultimately,

---

[49]This decline is evident even if one counts an additional 70 Ethiopian students placed in special programs for gifted students in secular schools.

[50]Penina Golan-Kook, Tamar Horowitz, and Leah Shaftiah, *Histaglut Hatalmidim Ha'olim Me'etiyopia Lemisgeret Beit-Hasefer* (The Adaptation of Ethiopian Immigrant Children to the School Framework) (Jerusalem, 1987).

[51]*Israel State Comptroller's Report* 36, 1986, pp. 693–94, quoted in Steven Kaplan, "Beta Israel," *Encyclopaedia Judaica Year Book 1986–87* (Jerusalem, 1988), pp. 214–16.

however, the "mechanical" aspects of school attendance were no harder to learn than the use of unfamiliar objects like refrigerators, flush toilets, and toasters. Such problems rarely persisted for long. Once in the classroom, Ethiopian students tended to be well behaved and highly motivated.

Other difficulties have been harder to resolve. Even when Ethiopian parents understand the purpose and organization of school work, few are capable of helping their children study or prepare assignments. Indeed, from the Ethiopian parents' perspective, formal education is noteworthy for the manner in which it reduces the child's link to his or her family. For the first time in living memory, children's daily lives no longer revolve around their household and kin. Much of their time is spent in school, in a world both physically and culturally distant from that of their parents.[52] Here they are exposed to models of behavior greatly at odds with those of Ethiopia and their parents. Frequently, this places them in a terrible bind: the more successfully they pursue their natural desire to integrate and become like their non-Ethiopian friends and classmates, the greater the distance between them and their parents. While some strive and even manage to achieve a precarious balance, acting Israeli in the street and Ethiopian at home, others find themselves torn between two sets of seemingly irreconcilable cultural norms.

Among Ethiopians in Israel, as among most immigrant groups, children tend to adapt more quickly and completely than their parents.[53] Accordingly, while young Ethiopians have generally learned Hebrew with alacrity and have quickly grasped the workings of Israeli society, their elders have often gained only the most minimal skills in the new language and remain mystified by the world around them.[54] In some cases, traditional roles are almost completely reversed as children assume the primary responsibility for representing the family to the outside world and serve as translators and mediators.

YOUTH ALIYAH

Youth Aliyah (*Aliyat Hanoar*), founded in 1932 by Henrietta Szold, accepted its first group of parentless children from Germany in 1933. Many others were to follow, and the organization established a network of boarding secondary schools (youth villages) that sought to provide a standard

---

[52]While this is the case for all school students, it is particularly true for those who live in Youth Aliyah villages (see below) and see their parents on an irregular basis.

[53]Tsili Doleve-Gandelman, *Ethiopian Jews in Israel, Family Portraits: A Multi-Faceted Approach* (Hebrew) (Jerusalem, 1989). See also Westheimer and Kaplan, *Surviving Salvation*, pp. 59–78.

[54]Tsili Doleve-Gandelman, " 'Ulpan Is Not Berlitz': Adult Education and the Ethiopian Jews in Israel," *Social Science Information* 28, no. 1, 1989, pp. 4–24.

education, as well as to offer emotional support and inculcate Jewish and Israeli culture. During the period of the massive *aliyah* from the Middle East and North Africa in the 1950s, most of the the immigrant children placed in Youth Aliyah institutions had parents in the country but were removed from their homes to speed their acculturation.

Although misgivings developed during the 1980s over policies that separated immigrant youths from their parents, over 96 percent of Ethiopian immigrants aged 13–18 were placed in youth villages.[55] What began as an effort to care for the many youngsters who had arrived without their parents in the early 1980s became the standard track for nearly every Ethiopian teenager. As a result, Ethiopians came to be a disproportionately large part of the villages' population. In 1993 Ethiopian students accounted for 37 percent of those learning throughout the entire system,[56] but they were 65 percent of the students in religious villages. The fact that some of the system's weakest schools are in religious institutions severely limits chances for widespread scholastic achievement and social integration. At the same time, Ethiopians' achievements at some of the system's stronger schools, such as Yemin Orde and Kfar Batya (both religious), have been quite impressive.

Recent studies of the educational record of Youth Aliyah graduates show that Ethiopian immigrants have overwhelmingly been sent to vocational, rather than academic, programs. Thus, in 1992–93 only 27 percent of those Ethiopians completing the 12th grade were prepared to take *bagrut* (university matriculation) exams; and only a small percentage of these achieved results that would have permitted them to pursue university or college studies.[57] For their part, according to press accounts, those in the vocational track often expressed dissatisfaction with the limited occupational choices available in most schools.

[55]See the special issues of *Alim*, a Youth Aliyah publication in Hebrew devoted to this subject: Summer 1983; Spring 1985; Tamar Dothan, "Diagnosing Ethiopian Immigrant Youth," in *The Integration of Immigrant Adolescents* (Youth Aliyah, Jerusalem, 1984), pp. 69–81; Nisan Kouri, "Vocational-Technological Training in Youth Aliyah," *Youth Aliyah Bulletin*, Summer 1987, pp. 65–72; Rivka Hanegbi and Sara Itziksohn Menuchin, "Problems of Cultural and Development Passages for Ethiopian-Jewish Adolescents in an Israeli Environment," in *Cultural Transition: The Case of Immigrant Youth* (Jerusalem, 1988), pp. 140–49; Anita Nudelman, "Understanding Immigrant Adolescents," *Practicing Anthropology* 15, no. 2 (Spring 1993), pp. 13–15.

[56]The percentage of Ethiopian youngsters in Youth Aliyah rose from 24 percent in 1991, to 35 percent in 1992, to 37 percent in 1993.

[57]Rachel Gindin, "Aliyat Hanoar Graduates of Ethiopian Origin 1992–93" (in Hebrew), Ministry of Immigrant Absorption, Oct. 1993. A total of 125 students (72 boys and 53 girls) completed the program designed to prepare them for matriculation exams. Even these students had particular problems with English and mathematics, and many of them did not take the matriculation exams in these subjects.

Even under the best of circumstances, the Youth Aliyah option remains problematic. While no one questions the short-term benefits for many children, the long-term implications of a policy that removes children from their families during their teens remains the subject of much controversy. In the light of past experiences with earlier immigrants from Asia and Africa, it seems likely that the widespread use of boarding schools may once again produce a generation of immigrant youth with few links to the local population and no family roots.

COLLEGES AND UNIVERSITIES

For those young people who managed to go to secondary school in Ethiopia, or even to college, the Student Administration, funded by both the Jewish Agency and the Ministry of Absorption, assisted in setting up special preparatory courses in which those who seem qualified for higher education can have a chance to prove their competence. Although this type of program, or *mekhinah*, is normally one year for Israelis and other immigrants, it has at times been extended to two years for Ethiopians, so that some of the difficulties they encounter can be better handled through special courses. For example, since almost every Ethiopian student had trouble passing the national psychometric tests, special instruction was provided.[58] Although not all passed, this did not bar them from further study, since certain programs, as well as certain universities, place less importance on the test scores than others. Also, it has been found that, with help, many Ethiopian students succeed in university, even if their psychometric results remain below standard.[59]

In order to assist those Ethiopians who seek to study beyond high school, special "affirmative" conditions have been created that are unavailable to any other immigrant group. Beside the right to a second year of *mekhinah*, the Ethiopian student has the formal right to free higher education for as long as it takes him or her to complete a bachelor's degree. In contrast, a Russian immigrant student has the right to free education for only a two-year period.[60]

---

[58]Psychometric exams are standardized tests designed to measure general academic ability and aptitude. Until recently, they were required of all Israeli high-school and *mekhinah* students who applied to a university. As in similar tests given in other countries, many of the questions are culturally bound. For Ethiopian students, moreover, the structure and form of the exam are also unfamiliar.

[59]Cf. the articles by Phyllis A. Rothman, "The Mathematics Program for Ethiopian Students," *Nitzanim*, Spring 1987, and Moshe Fasi and Debi Kohn, "Absorption of Students from Ethiopia in the Rothberg School," ibid.

[60]This was reported on in the newspaper *Ha'aretz* (July 27, 1992), under the heading "Positive Discrimination," in which it was also pointed out that from two-and-a-half to five

Despite these advantages, only 148 Ethiopian students attended university, college, or pre-academic *mekhinah* during the 1992–93 school year, a relatively modest figure. Included in this figure were 30 degree students at the Hebrew University, 3 of them working at the master's degree level; 18 at Bar-Ilan University, the majority in an ongoing special social-work program; 9 at Ben-Gurion University; 14 at Tel Aviv University; and 4 at the Haifa Technion. Thirty-five students were enrolled in the Technological College in Beersheba.

During the 1993–94 academic year, over 300 Ethiopians were studying in institutions of higher education. Of this number, 110 were registered in universities, colleges, and technical schools. In addition, over 200—including both those who had arrived in Operation Solomon and veterans who had attended Youth Aliyah schools without completing the necessary matriculation—were enrolled in a number of *mekhinot* and experimental programs. At the Hebrew University *mekhinah*, 20 students were registered; at Tel Aviv University, 31. A search that was made for newly arrived individuals who had had more than ten years of schooling in Ethiopia but were still not qualified for university or college-level programs produced 90 individuals. They were registered in technological and vocational training programs at the Western Galilee College, School of Technology, near Acre. Special courses have also been introduced to train Ethiopians to be teachers, dental technicians, and rabbis. A pretechnicians' course was established at the Hadassah Community College in Jerusalem for another 40. An experimental first-year program was set up at Haifa University for 60 Ethiopians who had arrived in Operation Solomon with 11–12 years of academic background. At the end of a year all but one had passed the course, and the majority were able to enter directly into academic or professional training programs. These and similar results in the *mekhinah* programs seem to indicate that policies that exclude Ethiopians from academic programs may be seriously underestimating their potential.

YOUTH PROJECT

Ethiopian immigrants between the ages of 18 and 28 who had either very limited prior schooling or none at all posed a special challenge for the educational system. Rather than ignore the needs of this age group, or simply push nearly 1,000 young people into unskilled work, the Ministry of Absorption, through its Student Administration, devised a special two-

---

times more money is invested in the absorption of each Ethiopian immigrant than in a comparable immigrant from the former Soviet Union.

year intensive education program known as the Youth Project, which was inaugurated in July 1985.[61]

Working in cooperation with the Ministries of Education, Labor, and Religious Affairs, with help from the Jewish Agency and the Joint Distribution Committee (JDC), the Student Administration contracted with some 20 institutions, including yeshivahs, vocational schools, and various comprehensive high schools. The Ethiopian students were taught half a day of academic subjects (primarily Hebrew, mathematics, civics, and Bible) and half a day of vocational courses (mainly welding, auto mechanics, carpentry, electricity, and printing for men; sewing, home economics, child care, and secretarial skills for women).

Thanks to generous funding, the Youth Project was able to mobilize the talents of highly qualified teachers and to bring young Ethiopians into some of the country's finest vocational schools. Unfortunately, the vocations offered were often of limited demand in the open job market. Nonetheless, it was evident after two years that the socialization experience alone, quite apart from actual skills learned, contributed to a marked improvement in most participants' ability to organize their time, plan their futures, and deal with the demands of Israeli society. Four years after the original Youth Project participants ended their study, a survey conducted by the JDC found that around 70 percent of project graduates were employed, although not necessarily in the area of their training.

In the meantime, the Youth Project was continued. All the young people between ages 18 and 28 who arrived in Operation Solomon with 0–9 years of previous education were placed in vocational training schools. As of October 1993, a thousand students were enrolled in this two-year program.

ARMY TRAINING

In the early years of the two-year Youth Project, all able-bodied men who completed it were placed in a specially designed pre-induction military training program. This intensive six-week course, called *Magen Tsion*, aimed at bridging the gap between the life experience of the Ethiopians and that of the Israeli youths with whom they were expected to serve in the Israel Defense Forces (IDF). Before this course was set up, the tendency was to excuse Ethiopians from any serious participation in military service and to direct them to courses in driving, mechanics, and cooking—something many youths did not want. The *Magen Tsion* program was subse-

---

[61]See Chaim Rosen's evaluation of this project: "*Proyekt Ha-Tse'irim: Olei Etiyopia Minekudat Mabat Tarbutit*" (The Youth Project: Ethiopian Immigrants from a Cultural Perspective), (Ministry of Absorption, Jerusalem, 1987).

quently discontinued in favor of more individual approaches. As many youths as possible are inducted and immediately integrated with other recruits. When deemed necessary, special preparatory courses that draw on the lessons learned in *Magen Tsion* are made available.

Often showing a flair for military endeavors and possessed of superb stamina, many young Ethiopians have deliberately chosen to serve in the ranks of the infantry, tank corps, paratroopers, and, when possible, in the elite combat units of the regular army. There is already a small but definitely growing cadre of Ethiopian officers, which is a clear indicator of their determination, as well as their ability to compete on an equal basis with other Israelis. As of 1993, more than 2,000 Ethiopian males had completed army training. In June 1993, 850 were in active service, including 17 officers and 16 career soldiers.[62]

Based on the numbers of graduates bound to come from Youth Aliyah in the years ahead, the contribution of Ethiopian Jews to the Israeli armed forces is likely to increase. Those who arrived in Operation Solomon have yet to be inducted (including 3,000 in Youth Aliyah and 1,000 in the Youth Project). Once they are eligible, they will swell the ranks of the Ethiopians doing military service.

Ethiopian women have been far slower than their male counterparts to enter the army. By 1992 only about two dozen women had entered the IDF. During the next year, however, their number doubled to about 50. In part, at least, this low figure is a natural result of the decision to send Ethiopians to religious boarding schools. Female students at such schools are often discouraged from entering the army, and in some cases are even asked to sign a document indicating that they will request a deferment on religious grounds. In addition, it must be said that most Ethiopian parents do not want their daughters to go into the army, where women are exposed to nontraditional behaviors and mores.

Employment

THE PROBLEM OF DEPENDENCE

For many Ethiopians, their sojourn in Israeli absorption centers and hotels continued a pattern of dependence that had begun either in the Sudan or Addis Ababa. For months or even years, they had lived as refugees and relied on the generosity of others for their survival. Although attempts were

---

[62]Malka Shabtay, "The Re-formation of Cultural Identity Among Ethiopian Immigrants to Israel," in *Between Africa and Zion* (forthcoming); idem, "Absorption of Ethiopians Through the Israeli Defense Forces," *Practicing Anthropology* 15, no. 2, Spring 1993, pp. 16–17.

made during the period prior to Operation Solomon to find meaningful work for as many Ethiopians as possible in Addis Ababa, both their numbers and the external conditions made this extremely difficult. In any event, such efforts came to an end as soon as they arrived in Israel and became involved in an absorption process designed to familiarize them as quickly as possible with the language, customs, and norms of their new homeland.

Many Ethiopians were, for a number of reasons, all too ready to accept the cocoon-like protection they were offered. In part, at least, their response to the assistance they were offered may have been modeled on common behavior patterns in Ethiopia, where the poor often fare better from charity than from striking out on their own.[63] In addition, not unlike refugees elsewhere in the world, Ethiopian immigrants arrived in Israel with a strong belief that, having found sanctuary, they would now be compensated for their suffering. As refugee expert Barry N. Stein has noted, refugees have a "strong belief that they are owed something by someone. Since their persecutors are unavailable, the refugees shift their demands to the government and helping agencies."[64] Moreover, as immigrants warmly welcomed and cared for by the Jewish state, they carried high expectations that all their needs would be met.

At first, this was indeed the case. Not only did the various absorption agencies provide the immigrants with housing, clothing, and food, but hundreds of Israelis came forward with gifts of clothing, toys, blankets, and anything else they could think of. This tremendous beneficence was, however, not without its darker side. In some instances, dramatic gestures of giving seemed designed more to satisfy the donor than to assist the recipient. While giving presents such as school supplies and toys directly to smiling Ethiopian children was immensely gratifying to both sides and provided excellent photo opportunities, it also reinforced the children's perception that, in their new home, outsiders, not parents, were the people to turn to for both satisfying needs and obtaining luxuries.

More generally, the longer the Ethiopians were helped because they were helpless, the more adept many of them became at displaying their need for charity.[65] Some grew quite accustomed to the role of indigent ward and came to view it as natural. Thus, they felt deeply wronged when immigrant benefits such as free housing and medical care were terminated after the end of the mandated period. They had been loyal and obedient, why were their

---

[63]John Iliffe, *The African Poor: A History* (Cambridge, Eng., 1987), pp. 16–17.

[64]Barry N. Stein, "The Refugee Experience," *International Migration Review* 15, nos. 1–2, 1981, p. 327.

[65]Michael Ashkenazi, "Studying the Students: Information Exchange, Ethiopian Immigrants, Social Workers, and Visitors," in *Ethiopian Jews and Israel*, ed. Ashkenazi and Weingrod, pp. 85–96.

benefactors "punishing" them? Even programs that called for only a symbolic financial contribution from the *olim* were often resisted. In some cases, immigrant parents went on strike when it was suggested that they contribute toward the cost of their children's clothing, rather than simply taking clothes from a box of donated items. Others seemed to view individual initiative as something to be hidden. Students often attempted to conceal the fact that they had paying jobs, assuming that scholarships were given only to the truly needy and that they might be penalized for their enterprise. Thus, while most Ethiopians in Israel struggle for independence, eking out a living any way possible, some devote their energies to winning the favors of the absorption agencies and seemingly endless flow of charitable bodies, measuring their success by how much they can get from outsiders.

VOCATIONAL TRAINING AND EMPLOYMENT

Unlike almost all other immigrants to Israel, who seek jobs in their fields or register for retraining courses, the majority of the Ethiopian men, and practically all of the women, arrived with neither a vocation nor any readily marketable skills. The majority lived in rural villages, where their work experience included ox-plow farming, simple metalworking, weaving, and, for women, pottery making.

In order to facilitate their integration into a technological society, the Ministry of Absorption, in cooperation with the Ministry of Labor and experts from the Joint Distribution Committee (JDC), has endeavored to create meaningful vocational training programs. These have included specially adapted courses to prepare Ethiopians for such occupations as the building trades for men and jewelry making for women.

A survey of 2,800 Operation Moses immigrants, conducted by the Brookdale Institute in the summer of 1992, found that 85 percent of the men and 39 percent of the women had participated in at least one training program.[66] Among the most popular courses for men were auto mechanics (343), metalworking (202), building trades (100), carpentry (97), and auto electronics (92). Significant numbers of women had studied sewing (129), geriatric care (96), practical nursing (91),[67] and infant care (69).

During the period prior to Operation Solomon, finding employment did not seem to have been a problem for the Ethiopians. It is generally estimated—official figures were never made available—that about 80 percent of those eligible for work did find jobs.[68] Although at first there were fears

---

[66]Gila Noam and Chen Lipschitz, "A Survey of Young Ethiopians from Ethiopia" (in Hebrew), unpublished manuscript (Brookdale Institute, Jerusalem, Aug. 1993).

[67]Forty-nine men also attended practical nursing courses. Once Russian immigrants began to arrive, among them an abundance of already trained people willing to work in this field, funds for training Ethiopians as nurses diminished.

[68]The Brookdale survey cited above found that 83 percent of the men and 43 percent of the

of the Ethiopian Jew being exploited to serve as unskilled "black labor," replacing Arab workers, this has not been common. The Ethiopians themselves have consistently refused menial work.[69] Once they left the protection of the absorption centers, most were quick to see the need to work hard in order to obtain an adequate income to cover all of the expenses of their new urban life. In Ethiopia, the Jews more than any other group had worked at a variety of occupations, usually simultaneously. A man would divide his day among two or three different activities, including farming, weaving, and blacksmithing. This model of multiple tasks has been translated by some industrious individuals into a willingness to work in factories that offer double shifts and the opportunity for overtime pay. This enables the Ethiopians to upgrade their salaries significantly and removes the stigma of having to apply every month to the National Insurance for supplementary salary payments.[70]

The employment situation for the latest arrivals has not been particularly impressive. In part the problem lies in where they are living: most of the caravan sites are far from the major employment centers. Then, too, the unemployment benefits they are eligible to receive are usually larger than whatever salaries they can earn. In addition, as noted above, their absorption situation has contributed to the feeling that there is no need to work hard, since the government will take care of them. A variety of new training programs have been established in which several thousand people have been involved. Job placement, so far, has been sporadic, and ongoing efforts are being made to integrate training with access to jobs.

WOMEN AT WORK

Ethiopian women in Israel are encouraged to assume a more important role in family life and to have greater autonomy in their dealings with the surrounding society. In Ethiopia, women traditionally deferred to men, who held all positions of authority. In Ethiopia, a woman's responsibilities were

---

women sampled were either employed, serving in the army, or studying. More specifically, 68 percent of the men and 41 percent of the women were working. The State Comptroller's Report, 38, 1988, p. 499, noted that in July 1987, 73.5 percent of eligible Ethiopians were not permanently employed. The difference in these figures reflects the fact that the survey was limited to those under age 40, and that the comptroller did not count either seasonal workers or those in vocational courses as employed. A large number of Ethiopians are in both these categories. For a still useful earlier study of employment in Ethiopia and Israel, see R. Best, "Wirtschaftsweisen der Beta Israel in Athiopien (Geschichte und Darstellung) und Aspekte ihrer okonomischen Integration in Israel" (M.A. Johann Wolfgang Goethe Universitat, February 1988).

[69]The Brookdale survey found that 55 percent of women, but only 23 percent of men, were employed as unskilled labor.

[70]This applies chiefly to those residing in the Tel Aviv area, where most such factories are located.

generally limited to the domestic realm, as part of a rigid, gender-based division of labor. Women's activities included cleaning, cooking, embroidery, caring for young children, bringing water, washing clothes, making clay vessels for eating and cooking, and weaving straw baskets for storage. Men were responsible for building the family house, farming, smithing, weaving cloth, and any endeavor associated with the outside world.[71] The division was usually strictly observed, and it would be unthinkable for a woman to perform most male tasks or for a man to perform "woman's work."

Although the feminist movement has had far less influence in Israel than in the United States or Western Europe, the average Israeli's expectations of a woman's role differ enormously from those of Beta Israel society. Ethiopians first encounter Western-style women in the absorption bureaucracy; Hebrew teachers, social workers, and house mothers are particularly prominent.[72] These Israeli women are significant not only because they represent the unprecedented phenomenon of female authority figures, but also for the simple reason that they are working outside the home.

Initially, Ethiopian women brought to Israel were relieved of some of their domestic responsibilities. Hotels, in particular, assumed most of the work associated with the preparation of food. Even when they moved to mobile homes or permanent housing, many of their former chores—including making dishes and pots, fetching water, and weaving baskets—were suddenly obsolete. Nevertheless, the basic ethos remained the same: whatever was done in the house was considered the responsibility of the woman.

But while the domestic realm remained restricted to women, women were no longer restricted to the domestic realm. Indeed, both ideological and practical pressures were brought to bear on Ethiopian women to explore the options for work outside the house. Although it has often been suggested that the woman's decision to work outside the house is itself the cause of considerable tension and strife, this may be a case of the chicken and the egg. In some instances at least, women who view themselves as trapped in unsatisfactory marriages may seek outside work and the income it brings in order to gain independence. In such cases, the woman's work is not the problem, but (at least in her eyes) the solution. What is undeniable is the fact that, in Israel, a woman's options are far broader than they were in

---

[71]Although the distinctions drawn by the Beta Israel were essentially the same as those observed by their neighbors, there were some slight differences. In contrast to their Christian counterparts, Beta Israel women were known for making clay pots that were sold to outsiders. Symbolically, however, this form of work was associated with the domestic realm and the home.

[72]On these female authority figures and on women in general, see Westheimer and Kaplan, *Surviving Salvation*, pp. 79–102. See also Eva Leitman, "The Cultural Adaptation of Three Generations of Ethiopian Women," in *Between Africa and Zion* (forthcoming).

Ethiopia, and that many take advantage of this either within the framework of marriage or outside it.

The tensions between women's traditional roles and the opportunities offered in Israel are most clearly seen when the wife goes out to work while the husband remains unemployed. Although the overall unemployment rate among Ethiopian women appears to be higher than among men (see above), the phenomenon of unemployed husband–employed wife is common, largely because of disparity in ages. In Ethiopia, the husband was generally several years older than his wife. However, in some circumstances, such as second marriages, he might be 10, 20, even 25 years her senior. A 35-year-old woman will be offered more training programs and probably adapt more quickly than her 50-year-old husband. Indeed, at that age, unless he is part of the tiny minority of educated immigrants, he is unlikely to be seriously considered as a candidate for the workforce. Once the wife is working, not only does her income make her more independent, but her exposure to the world around her greatly accelerates her adaptation. While she confronts the daily challenges of working life—Hebrew conversation, bus routes and schedules, work relations, pay slips, etc.—the husband remains behind: isolated, confused, frustrated.

PENSIONERS

The one age group that has been the least productive in Israel is that of people over age 50.[73] Whereas in Ethiopia a man of this age and older would be very active in his fields and at his hearth, in Israel he suddenly finds himself a "pensioner." At the time of their initial adjustment to life in Israel, many distinguished elders found themselves with nothing to do and often with no one to talk to except other "old people," as everyone else was either learning or working.[74] For a while the oldsters simply enjoyed the miraculous "gift" of money they received each month for doing nothing. Gradually, at least some of these people—who, given the vagueness of age reckoning in Ethiopia, could well be younger than the "65 or over" they were registered as—began to suffer from constantly being at home.

For some, the solution has been to draw on a typical Ethiopian inclination to wander. They leave their homes and families and set out to visit relatives or to attend weddings and funerals, whenever they have the chance to do so. Others have realized that they need to be productive, and so have become "working pensioners," doing weaving in their homes, working as guards or checkers at supermarkets, or finding work in greenhouses or even factories. Those who do this have no trouble continuing to receive their

---

[73]On the general decline in the position and authority of "elders," see the discussion above.
[74]About 7 percent of the Ethiopian population receive pensions.

pensions along with their salaries.[75] The existence of working pensioners contradicts the oft-repeated claim that every Ethiopian over 45 is "over the hill" and will have great difficulty in finding a place for himself, or in learning Hebrew to any great extent. They usually gain remarkable fluency in Hebrew and continue to be influential in their community's affairs. In contrast, the "wanderers" seldom if ever progress with Hebrew or adjust to their new environment.

Health Issues

The arrival of the Ethiopian Jews in Israel has confronted the Israeli medical establishment with a variety of unprecedented challenges. Not only did many immigrants arrive with medical problems that were unfamiliar to Israeli authorities, but each successive wave of *olim* presented a slightly different health profile. Almost without exception, moreover, Ethiopian immigrants were unfamiliar with the vocabulary, technology, and underlying principles of Western medical practice.[76]

As noted above, the vast majority of Ethiopian immigrants who arrived prior to 1986 were illegal migrants who journeyed to the Sudan and spent extended periods in refugee camps before being airlifted to Israel. Although no exact figures exist, somewhere between 2,000 and 4,000 Ethiopian Jews died in or on their way to the Sudan.[77] Those who survived and reached Israel were generally in poor physical condition.[78] Between 32 and 52 per-

---

[75]Since such working pensioners do not report that they are employed, they do not figure in government statistics, and it is impossible to determine their number.

[76]Two issues of the *Israel Journal of Medical Sciences* (*IJMS*), comprising a total of over 40 articles, have been devoted to health issues concerning Ethiopian immigrants: vol. 27, no. 5, May 1991, and vol. 29, nos. 6–7, June-July 1993. See below for references to specific articles.

[77]Tudor Parfitt, *Operation Moses*, p. 87. The Ethiopian community and Israeli officials consistently cite the higher figure in discussions of mortality during this period and at the annual memorial service held in Jerusalem.

[78]C. Hershko, G. Nesher, A.M. Yinnon, et al., "Medical Problems in Ethiopian Refugees Airlifted to Israel: Experiences of 131 Patients Admitted to a General Hospital," *Journal of Tropical Medicine and Hygiene* 89, 1986, pp. 107–11. This should not be confused, however, with certain positive elements in their health profile prior to their departure for the Sudan. Upon arrival in Israel, Ethiopian immigrants have low cholesterol levels and few dental caries. In Israel their diet tends to change and includes increased consumption of foods associated with higher blood pressure and heart disease. There is also evidence for an increase in dental cavities as a result of the consumption of sweets. Judith T. Shuval, *Social Dimensions of Health in Israel* (Westport, Conn., 1992), p. 127; U. Goldbourt, T. Rosenthal, and A. Rubinstein, "Trends in Weight and Blood Pressure in Ethiopian Immigrants During Their First Years in Israel . . . ," *IJMS* 27, no. 5, pp. 260–63; U. Goldbourt, M. Khoury, E. Landau, L.H. Reisin, and A. Rubinstein, "Blood Pressure in Ethiopian Immigrants . . . ," ibid., pp. 264–67; idem, "Blood Pressure and Body Mass Index in Ethiopian Immigrants: Comparisons of Operation Solomon and Moses," *IJMS* 29, nos. 6–7, pp. 360–63; S. Cohen, H. Sarnat, Z. Rakocs, and

cent of those who arrived during Operation Moses suffered from malnutrition, and over 80 percent tested positive for intestinal parasites.[79] A quarter of those who arrived between 1980 and 1988 were diagnosed as having malaria, while during the same period about 2 percent were identified as having tuberculosis.[80]

In contrast to this group, those who arrived in the 1990s, and particularly those who came after a clinic was established in Addis Ababa in July 1990 by the American Jewish Joint Distribution Committee, were far healthier on their arrival in Israel.[81] The average weight of males who arrived prior to Operation Solomon was, for example, only 47.5 kilograms (about 105 pounds), while for those who arrived in Operation Solomon it was 58 kilograms (about 128 pounds).[82] Few required immediate hospitalization. Having avoided the rigors of the Sudan and/or received treatment for existing conditions, only a small number tested positive for malaria.[83] These improvements notwithstanding, parasitic infections and evidence of exposure to hepatitis B virus continued to be common among the new arrivals, and the incidence of tuberculosis remained disturbingly high.[84]

E. Amir, "Increased Caries Prevalence in Adolescents Who Immigrated from Ethiopia to Israel," *IJMS* 27, no. 5, pp. 297–99.

[79]Jacov Nahmias, Zalman Greenberg, Leo Djerras, and Leumit Giladi, "Mass Treatment of Intestinal Parasites Among Ethiopian Immigrants," *IJMS* 27, no. 5, pp. 278–83; Jacov Nahmias, Zalman Greenberg, et al., "Health Profile of Ethiopian Immigrants in Israel: An Overview," ibid., p. 339.

[80]P.E. Slater, C. Costin, and Z. Greenberg, "Malaria in Israel: The Ethiopian Connection," *IJMS* 27, no. 5, pp. 284–87; S.A. Wartski, "Tuberculosis in Ethiopian Immigrants," ibid., pp. 288–92. The prevalence rate of 1.9/100 compares to 4.5/100,000 in the general Israeli public. During the period immediately after Operation Moses (1985), Ethiopian immigrants accounted for slightly more than half of all cases of tuberculosis in Israel. This trend continued and even increased following Operation Solomon.

[81]J. Lachter, "Medicine and the Ethiopian Jews: Report and Analysis from Addis Ababa," *IJMS* 28, no. 1, 1992, pp. 43–46; Theodore M. Myers, "A Medical Care Program for Ethiopian Jewish Migrants in Addis Ababa," *IJMS* 29, nos. 6–7, pp. 334–37. When this clinic was established in July 1990, Ethiopian Jews in Addis Ababa were dying at a rate of almost 40 a month (a figure still slightly lower than comparable rates among the local population). During the period March–May 1991, only 12 deaths were reported.

[82]Nahmias, "Profile," p. 339.

[83]Paul Slater, Zalman Greenberg, and Corina Costin, "Imported Malaria from Ethiopia—End of an Era?" *IJMS* 29, nos. 6–7, pp. 383–84. Between May 1990 and May 1991, only 33 cases were found among the 19,614 immigrants who arrived.

[84]E. Ben-Porath, L. Hornstein, J. Zeldis, J. Nahmias, "Hepatitis B Virus Infection and Liver Disease in Ethiopian Immigrants to Israel," *Hepatology* 6, 1986, pp. 662–66; L. Hornstein, E. Ben-Porath, A. Cuzin, Z. Baharir, N. Rimon, J. Nahmias, "Hepatitis B Virus Infection in Ethiopian Immigrants," *IJMS* 27, no. 5, pp. 268–72; E. Flateau, O. Segol, A. Shneour, H. Tabenkin, R. Ras, "Prevalence of Markers of Infection with Hepatitis B and C Viruses in Immigrants of Operation Solomon," *IJMS* 29, nos. 6–7, pp. 387–89; R. Edman and Z. Greenberg, "Intestinal Parasitic Infection in Operation Solomon Immigrants," ibid., pp. 374–76. During the period 1989–1991, the rate of tuberculosis among Ethiopian immigrants

In one respect, at least, immigrants who arrived via Addis Ababa were at greater risk than those who had come through the Sudan. While the latter were not exposed to HIV/AIDS, which had yet to become widespread in Ethiopia, the former were. By the early 1990s, Addis Ababa was one of the mostly highly infected cities in the world.[85] Beta Israel males, dislocated from their traditional residences and occupations, with time on their hands and money (from Jewish welfare organizations) in their pockets, were able to visit local prostitutes, 60 percent of whom were infected with the HIV virus. Unprotected blood supplies and nonsterile needles (used medically) put others at risk. Since no testing was done for HIV in Ethiopia prior to immigration, those carrying the virus simply brought it to Israel. Thus, while none of a group of 1,439 Operation Moses immigrants tested HIV positive, 226 of approximately 10,000 immigrants (over 10 years old) who arrived in 1991 were found to be carriers.[86]

HEALTH EDUCATION

The challenge posed by cases of HIV/AIDS is perhaps the most vivid example of the problems relating to the medical status of Ethiopian immigrants in Israel. Although rare or unfamiliar diseases brought by the immigrants may have initially baffled Israeli medical personnel, in most cases these have yielded to treatment. A more complex challenge is the interaction with a population that has little or no familiarity with the Western biomedical model of healing: its terminology, technology, or assumptions. Most Ethiopian immigrants continue to hold, in whole or in part, to their traditional system of medical explanation, healing, and healers. Both secular healers (midwives, herbalists, uvula cutters, and "surgeons") and more religiously oriented specialists (*dabtara*, *tonkway*, *balazar*) continue to operate in Israel.[87] Immigrants turn to such healers both when they are dissat-

---

declined from 1.9 percent to a still relatively high 1.3 percent. S.A. Wartski, "Tuberculosis Case Finding and Treatment in Ethiopian Immigrants to Israel, 1989–1991," ibid., pp. 376–80.

[85]Ethiopian Ministry of Health, "Report to W.H.O.: AIDS Control and Prevention Activities," Annual Report 1989.

[86]Shlomo Maayan, Nurit Vardinon, Rivka Yazkan, Erica Cohen, Flora Ben-Yshai, and Israeli Yust, "Lack of Exposure to HTLV1 Among Ethiopian Immigrants of Operation Solomon (1991) Arriving to the Jerusalem Area," *IJMS* 29, nos. 6–7, pp. 393–95. Among Ethiopian immigrants, the HIV virus appears to be most commonly transmitted by heterosexual contact, tattooing, bloodletting, and other traditional medical practices.

[87]On the traditional Ethiopian medical system in general, see Simon Messing, *The Target of Health in Ethiopia* (Information Corporation, New York, 1972). On Ethiopian immigrants in Israel, see Nudelman, "Immigrant Adolescents"; idem, "Health Behavior and Traditional Healing Among Ethiopian Immigrants in Israel," in *Between Africa and Zion* (forthcoming); and Richard M. Hodes and Befekade Teferedegne, "Traditional Ideas of Health and Disease Among Ethiopian Jews," in *Social Science and Medicine* (forthcoming). The term *tonkway* is often used as a generic term for all sorts of "sorcerers" or mystical healers. The *dabtara*

isfied with the treatment they have received from Western practitioners and as a supplement to ongoing treatment, which addresses social and spiritual aspects of illness usually ignored in the West.

Thus, medical interventions and health education inevitably involve a process of cultural translation for both health professionals and patients. How are apparently healthy individuals to be convinced that they need to refrain from certain behavior, subject themselves to a regimen of treatments, or regularly take specified medicine because "tests" reveal them to be infected with malaria, hepatitis, tuberculosis, or HIV? How are Israeli health professionals to interpret immigrants' descriptions of medical symptoms and to distinguish between different types of physical and psychological distress?

In response to these challenges, health educators, doctors, and anthropologists have trained Ethiopian immigrants to serve as cultural mediators between immigrant patients and Israeli medical personnel.[88] Innovative health education programs have been developed to bridge the gap between the different medical systems. These have included such subjects as nutrition, personal hygiene, the use of the health system, preventive medicine, sex education and birth control, sexually transmitted diseases, including HIV/AIDS, and first aid.[89]

MENTAL HEALTH

No aspect of medical care for Ethiopian immigrants has proven more complex than that of mental health care. No "wonder drug" exists to treat the many cases of posttraumatic stress disorder, depression, culture shock, somatization, and suicide that have emerged in Israel in recent years. In no area, moreover, is the contrast between the Ethiopian and Western medical systems more striking.

One does not have to look far to understand the etiology of many of these

---

is a learned man who makes use of books and writing to heal. The *balazar* heals through a cult associated with spirit (*zar*) possession. This cult will be discussed in greater detail below.

[88]Shabtay, "Defense Forces," p. 17; Nudelman, "Immigrant Adolescents," p. 14.

[89]Nudelman, "Immigrant Adolescents," p. 14; Diane Levin-Zamir, Dina Lipsky, Ellen Goldberg, and Zipora Melamed, "Health Education for Ethiopian Immigrants in Israel, 1991–2," *IJMS* 29, nos. 6–7, pp. 422–28; Tsipora Bental, Rina Gersten and Michael Alkan, "Health Education for the Ethiopian Community in the Negev," ibid., pp. 429–37; Michael Alkan, Tsipora Bental, and Rina Gersten, "Health Education in the Ethiopian Community in the Negev Region," *Family Physician* 18, 1990, pp. 159–62; Daniel Chemtov, Haim (Chaim) Rosen, Ronny Shtarkshall, and Varda Soskolne, "A Culturally Specific Educational Program to Reduce the Risk of HIV and HBV Transmission Among Ethiopian Immigrants to Israel: A Preliminary Report on Training Veteran Immigrants as Health Educators," ibid., pp. 437–42; Daniel Chemtov and Haim (Chaim) Rosen, *Be "Gobez" for the Sake of Your Health* (Jerusalem, Multiagency Committee for Education and Information on HIV Infection and Related Diseases, 1992).

problems. Almost every area discussed above carries with it immense psychological stress and the seeds of potential disorders. For some Ethiopians it is the trauma of the *aliyah* process itself, during which they were threatened by arrest, robbery, rape, illness, and starvation.[90] Those who survived often suffered the loss of loved ones and were usually separated from close family members still in Ethiopia.[91] Almost all experienced a sudden and dramatic change in lifestyle as they entered a highly urbanized Western country and confronted a strange language, new foods and clothing, a foreign economic system, and a sometimes hostile religious establishment. Changing gender roles and the removal of children from the home for educational purposes put additional strain on the family unit and added to the sense of extreme disorientation felt by many.

Many of the symptoms displayed by Ethiopian psychiatric patients, including anxiety, depression, sleep disturbances, and somatization are all too familiar to Israeli mental health officials. Trancelike states and dissociative disorders pose a more unusual challenge. Although such phenomena were not considered "normal" in Ethiopia, they were a familiar and widely understood part of life. They were understood, however, not as the result of internal conflicts and disturbances, but as the product of a type of spirit known as *zar*.[92] A woman, or much more rarely a man, who was possessed

---

[90]Gadi Ben-Ezer is currently completing a dissertation that examines psychosocial aspects of Ethiopian immigrants' accounts of their emigration and *aliyah*. Recent research has found a clear correlation between the seriousness of traumas suffered on the way to Israel and extent of psychological difficulties in Israel. See Ariel Arieli, "Persecutory Experience and Post-traumatic Stress Disorders Among Ethiopian Immigrants," in *Grief and Bereavement in Contemporary Society* III, ed. Emanuel Chigier (London, 1988), pp. 70–76; and Ariel Arieli and Seffefe Ayche, "Psychopathological Aspects of the Ethiopian Immigration," *IJMS* 29, nos. 6–7, pp. 411–18. For a study of children in Addis Ababa, see Gadi Ben-Ezer and Haim Peri, *Displaced Children: A Report of the Condition of Displaced Jewish Children in Addis Ababa* (Israel Section of Defence for Children International, Jerusalem, 1991).

[91]Ben-Ezer and Peri, *Displaced Children*, p. 415. Among 87 Ethiopian immigrants treated by a mental health center in Netanya, 35 percent had lost one family member, 30 percent had lost more than one member; 40 percent were forced to bury their dead without conducting religious ceremonies, and 56 percent had arrived in Israel without any other family member. See also Sara Minuchen Itziksohn and Rivka Hanegbi, "Loss and Mourning in the Ethiopian Community: An Anthropological-Psychological Approach," in *Grief and Bereavement in Contemporary Society* III, ed. Emanuel Chigier.

[92]On the *zar* in Ethiopia and Israel, see Yael Kahana, "The Zar Spirits: A Category of Magic in the System of Mental Health in Ethiopia," *International Journal of Social Psychiatry* 31, 1985, pp. 125–43; Alan Young, "Why Amhara Get *kurenya*: Sickness and Possession in an Ethiopian Zar Cult," *American Ethnologist* 14, 1975, pp. 245–65; G. Ratzoni, R. Blumensohn, A. Apter, and S. Tyano, "Psychopathology and Management of Hospitalized Suicidal Ethiopian Adolescents in Israel," *IJMS* 27, no. 5, pp. 293–96; G. Ratzoni, A. Apter, R. Blumensohn, and S. Tyano, "Psychopathology and Management of Hospitalized Ethiopian Immigrant Adolescents in Israel," *Journal of Adolescence* 11, no. 3, 1988, pp. 231–36; G. Ratzoni, Isabel Ben Amo, Tal Weizman, Ronit Weizman, Ilan Modai, and Alan Apter, "Psychiatric Diag-

by a *zar* would behave in a bizarre fashion until put under the care of a *balazar* (literally, the owner of a *zar*), a healer who had him/herself been possessed. Thereafter, she would belong to a cult group and would meet with others who had themselves been possessed by *zar* spirits.

Israeli health practitioners quickly discovered that diagnosis and treatment of patients in a dissociative state often required them to become familiar with the context of traditional healing. Often their patients had visited or were continuing to visit a *balazar* at the same time as they received Western treatment. In some cases, "second opinions" from and "referrals" to traditional healers were even initiated by the Israeli doctors.

By far the most troubling feature of the Ethiopians' psychological adjustment to Israel has been the comparatively large number of suicides. In 1985, the suicide rate among Ethiopian immigrants was six times that found among veteran Israelis.[93] Although the rate has declined somewhat over the years, it still remains significantly higher than that found among the bulk of the population.

Under the best of circumstances, it is difficult to state unequivocally why a particular person commits suicide and another in similar circumstances does not. In the case of Ethiopian immigrants in Israel the problem is complicated by recurrent attempts to politicize the phenomenon. Thus, painful personal and family tragedies are exploited to score points in ongoing political debates. During the conflict with the rabbinate, for example, suicides were said to have resulted from the inability of Ethiopians to marry legally, but in discussions concerning university studies, the same cases were attributed to having been refused admission. While the suicides following Operation Moses were often attributed to the trauma of *aliyah*, the guilt of "survivors' syndrome," and concern for relatives in Ethiopia, the massive family reunification of Operation Solomon, far from putting an end to such tragedies, produced a new wave of deaths.[94] An editorial published on December 20, 1991, in the *Jerusalem Post* argued (apparently on the basis of a single case) that Ethiopian suicides in Israel were not connected to difficulties in the absorption process, but were directly attributable to the failure to bring the Falas Mura, Beta Israel who had converted to Christianity, to Israel.

The attempts of the *Post* and others notwithstanding, any attempt to find a single cause and a simple solution to the problem of Ethiopian suicides in Israel appears doomed to failure. Suicide does not appear to have been

---

noses in Hospitalized Adolescent and Adult Ethiopian Immigrants in Israel," *IJMS* 29, nos. 6–7, pp. 419–21.

[93]Arieli and Ayche, "Psychopathological Aspects," p. 412; Ratzoni et al., "Psychopathology and Management . . . Suicidal"; Westheimer and Kaplan, *Surviving Salvation*, pp. 113–17.

[94]Arieli and Ayche, "Psychopathological Aspects," pp. 417–18.

common among the Beta Israel in Ethiopia. This does not mean, however, that it is the result of any one feature of their experience in Israel. Reports concerning Ethiopian refugees in the United States, Germany, Canada, and resettlement camps in Ethiopia itself all mention a disturbingly high rate of suicide. Given the vast differences that separate these countries and their refugee programs, it seems unlikely that a common denominator will be found on this level.

Analysis of a few of the suicides that have occurred since Operation Moses seems to support the link between at least some of these incidents and the kinds of absorption difficulties discussed above. On December 14, 1991, for example, a Christian Ethiopian who feared he would be returned to Ethiopia if his Beta Israel wife carried out her threat to divorce him, murdered her and then committed suicide. Later the same month, an Ethiopian Jew engaged in a violent quarrel with his wife struck her, knocking her unconscious. Fearing that he had killed her, the man himself committed suicide.[95] Other cases earlier the same year included a father of eight who killed himself following an extended period of unemployment, and another whose suicide appears to have been connected to having tested positive for HIV.

One theme that emerges in many cases is the feeling the victims had of being trapped and powerless. Unable to live in an honorable fashion in a country whose rules and customs remain unfamiliar, the Ethiopian seeks to exert at least a measure of control by dying with honor. In contrast to the usual norm by which attempted suicides outnumber deaths by nearly ten to one, among Ethiopians the proportion narrows to two or three to one. The teen suicides found in many Western countries are also comparatively rare among the Ethiopians. It is the older generation, and for reasons we have discussed above, particularly the men, who are most vulnerable to the loss of hope and honor.

Finally, it must be remembered that suicides are both a symptom of difficulties and a cause of difficulties. Viewed from the perspective of the family, suicide is like a stone thrown into a pond, leaving in its wake orphans, widows and widowers, one-parent families, and bereaved elders. It produces yet one more chink in the fragile structure of Ethiopian family life.

---

[95]On violence within Ethiopian families, see Westheimer and Kaplan, *Surviving Salvation*, pp. 109–13.

CONCLUSIONS

Major efforts have been made to facilitate the speedy integration of the Ethiopians into Israeli society. In some matters their adjustments have come easily, while in others, traditional preferences remain strong. So, for example, women are not averse to relinquishing their familiar leather baby carriers, worn on their backs, for strollers, but they generally insist on preparing *enjera*, the Ethiopian pancake bread, rather than go over to pitas, as have so many of the other ethnic groups in Israel.[96] In religious matters they have generally been ambivalent. Youngsters have been eager to learn about Jewish customs and observances—*tefillin*, *mezuzot*, Hanukkah—with which they were previously unfamiliar, but have been reluctant to incorporate them into their daily lives. Their fathers have assiduously avoided taking on many new practices.

Despite the fact that the vast majority of Ethiopian children study in the national religious school system, a notable process of secularization seems to be taking place among the younger generation of Ethiopians. Even as many resist the acceptance of new practices as taught in school, they simultaneously reject the ways of their fathers, which may seem outdated. This tendency toward secularization is often accelerated when they serve in the army, and many young men remove their *kippot* for good at this stage.

The dilemmas faced by Ethiopian Jews in the religious realm are further complicated by the challenges to their traditional social structure and patterns of family life. Almost everyone who has met or worked with Beta Israel immigrants has commented on the upheavals they have weathered in their domestic lives.[97] The changes undergone by Ethiopian families in Israel—as couples divorce and remarry, children assert an unprecedented degree of independence, and women redefine their roles—lie at the heart of the Ethiopian experience in Israel. Moreover, the Ethiopians' move to Israel has not only redefined roles within the family but has also radically altered the family's relationship with the surrounding society. In Ethiopia, the Beta Israel were united by a shared faith and a broad network of kinship ties. Families and households were the foundation of rural communal society and played a far greater role in the life of the individual than they do in most industrial societies. Families served as schools, workshops, clinics, reformatories, and credit organizations. In Israel most of these functions have

---

[96]Cf. Tsili Doleve-Gandelman, "The Role of Ethiopian Women in the Production of the Ethnic Identity of Their Immigrant Group in Israel," in *Other Perspectives in Gender and Culture: Rewriting Women and the Symbolic*, ed. J.F. MacCannell (New York and Oxford, 1990), pp. 242–57.
[97]For a more detailed discussion of these issues, see Westheimer and Kaplan, *Surviving Salvation*.

become the primary responsibility of other institutions. Families that have been forced to give up many functions must adjust themselves to a new position in the wider community.

At this point in their absorption process, a tension continues to exist between the deep-rooted sentiments that still tie the newcomers to their former way of life in Ethiopia and their frequently stated desire to be like other Israelis. At one extreme of the tension is the specter of their becoming a totally separate group, isolated and ostracized.[98] At the other end is the fear that the Ethiopians will renounce all of their traditions and become— except, of course, for color—indistinguishable as a group from the majority of other Israelis.[99] While there is little consensus in Israel as to what the precise outlines of a successful absorption would be, there can be little disagreement that either of these extremes would represent a dangerous and costly failure.

Looking back at the decade since Operation Moses, it can be seen that many of the immigrants who arrived with or prior to that airlift have made significant progress. Their success was to some extent overshadowed in the immediate aftermath of Operation Solomon, when the issues of crowded housing, inadequate educational facilities, and high unemployment once again made headlines. Amid a spate of hunger strikes, protest marches, and violent demonstrations, past achievements were quickly forgotten. Dire predictions were made that the caravan sites would become explosive slums, racial powder kegs with no precedent in the history of the State of Israel.[100]

On the whole, these pessimistic forecasts have not been borne out. Many of the problems that surfaced immediately after Operation Solomon were the almost inevitable result of so large an influx and the short-term problems it produced. While hardly conforming to a utopian vision of the ingathering of the exiles, the absorption of Ethiopian immigrants has had its successes. Ethiopian immigrants are today no longer viewed as a curiosity, but as a familiar part of Israel's ethnic mosaic. They have been accepted in cities and towns throughout the country and contribute in growing numbers to the Israel Defense Forces. Government policies designed to move immigrants from caravan sites to permanent housing have succeeded in part.

As of January 1994, most Ethiopian immigrants had been in Israel less

---

[98]On the "marginalization" of the Beta Israel, see Alex Weingrod, "The Context of Ethiopian Jews in Israel: Immigrants, Israelis, Ethiopian Jews," in *Between Africa and Zion* (forthcoming).

[99]In Ethiopia the Beta Israel were highly acculturated but had not socially assimilated. The challenge facing them in Israel is to assimilate without completely acculturating.

[100]See, for example an interview (in Hebrew) in *Yediot Aharonot*, June 3, 1992, with Uri Gordon, head of the Immigration Department of the Jewish Agency and former head of Youth Aliyah, entitled "Are We Setting Up for the Ethiopians the *Ma'abarot* [camps] of the Year 2,000?"

than three years. Thus, it is still too early to predict the outcome of their integration into their new homeland (a process that will continue for years if not decades). The questions of whether the Ethiopians will achieve their goals by dint of their long-standing, characteristic patience or their newly emergent violence, or whether they will be left adrift regardless of what kinds of actions they take, stand as a concluding reminder that much is yet to be accomplished before one can speak with satisfaction about the ingathering of the Jews of Ethiopia in the land of Israel.

Review
of
the
Year

UNITED STATES

Civic and Political

Intergroup Relations

T HE AMERICAN JEWISH COMMUNITY faced challenges on a number of fronts in 1992. The presidential and congressional elections forced a shift in priorities on the communal agenda toward an expanding range of domestic concerns. Black-Jewish relations continued along a rocky path: expressions of anti-Semitism in the African-American community accompanied by efforts at reconciliation between the two groups. Support for Israel, relations with the Vatican, church-state issues, and various civil-rights matters also occupied the Jewish community in the course of the year.

1992 Elections

As was the case in 1988, the 1992 general elections—particularly the presidential campaign—presented some problems for the Jewish community. Chief among these were the candidacies of conservative columnist Patrick J. Buchanan and former Klan leader David Duke (see "Political Anti-Semitism," below) and the injection of religion into the political process.

THE CAMPAIGN

Pat Buchanan, after garnering 37 percent of the vote in the New Hampshire Republican primary vote on February 17—compared with incumbent George Bush's 53 percent—received sizable "protest" votes in March 3 primaries in Colorado, Georgia, and Maryland, but none exceeding 36 percent. On Super Tuesday, March 9, Buchanan won sizable protest votes in five southern states and Oklahoma, Missouri, Massachusetts, and Rhode Island; his support all but eliminated the vote for Louisiana state representative David Duke, who received between 2 and 11 percent (9 percent in his home state). But Buchanan faded rapidly thereafter and was not a factor in the nomination process. He resurfaced, however, to the consternation of Jewish groups across the political spectrum, at the Republican convention (see below).

In the Democratic primaries on Super Tuesday, March 9, the Jewish vote split between Gov. Bill Clinton of Arkansas, the front-runner, and former Massachusetts senator Paul Tsongas. In a key battleground for Jewish votes, Florida, Clinton narrowly beat out Tsongas, winning half of the overall vote to Tsongas's one-third, and 46 percent of the Jewish vote to Tsongas's 44 percent, while former California governor Jerry Brown took 11 percent of the Jewish vote. (In other races, it is estimated that Tsongas did better among Jews than Clinton.)

In a Connecticut surprise on March 24, Jerry Brown, picking up Tsongas support (Tsongas had dropped out of the race the previous week), was the victor and also edged out Clinton in the Jewish vote. In New York—a state with a much more diverse Jewish community, one more readily responsive to Clinton's message on urban affairs—the Jewish vote was decisive in a Clinton victory on April 7. Exit polls placed the Jewish vote at more than 50 percent for Clinton, 29 percent for Tsongas (no longer in the race), and a meager 10 percent for Brown. (Overall, Clinton won 41 percent, Tsongas 29 percent, and Brown 26 percent.)

Analysts drew two lessons from the returns: first, through his support of Israel, articulated at length to Jewish groups prior to the campaign, Clinton established himself as a favorite candidate of the community; and second, Jesse Jackson, whom Brown picked as a running mate, remained "an albatross" around the neck of any candidate who embraced him, in the words of David Zwiebel, Agudath Israel of America's government affairs director.

The relationship of Clinton and the Democratic party to the Jewish community was both informed and reinforced by the candidate's meetings with major Jewish organizations throughout the year. The choice of Sen. Al Gore (D., Tenn.) as vice-presidential candidate—a known quantity to Jews, with a good record on issues of importance, such as the U.S.-Israel relationship—was a plus. And the Democratic national convention, held in New York City in July, drafted and passed one of the strongest pro-Israel party platforms in recent history, one that was free of the rancor over pro-Palestinian resolutions that had plagued the party in 1988. The platform included a plank affirming the "special" U.S.-Israel relationship, admonishing the Bush administration for not being an "honest broker" in the peace process, declaring Jerusalem to be the capital of Israel, condemning anti-Semitism, and calling upon the United States to assist in the absorption of Jewish immigrants into Israel. "It's a big change from 1988," observed Stuart Eizenstat, domestic-policy adviser in the Jimmy Carter White House. "The platform represents the work of the National Jewish Democratic Council and other Jewish organizations, and the fact that Jesse Jackson is not a major player."

The candidacy of Texas billionaire H. Ross Perot raised questions for the electorate as a whole and for Jews as a group. Perot, who was in, then out, and finally in, as an independent candidate, consistently affirmed his support of Israel. But allegations with respect to an anti-Semitic firing from Perot's computer company, Electronic Data Systems, surfaced in early July, and the New York State Division of Human Rights determined that there was "probable cause" to believe that EDS discriminated against an Orthodox Jewish woman who refused to work on Sukkot.

As for Perot's politics, Earl Raab, director of Brandeis University's Perlmutter Institute, offered this analysis: "Perot represents a dangerous tendency that a lot of alienated people find attractive. . . . He represents a counter-revolutionary tendency that should be dismaying to all Americans and especially to Jews. He bypasses the coalition process in favor of the 'participatory democracy' of an electronic town hall. . . . It is the political equivalent of a lynch mob, in which 'Jewish issues' would no longer be a serious part of the equation."

THE REPUBLICAN CONVENTION

Even before the Republican national convention, held in Houston in late August, Jews were troubled about President George Bush's views on religion and state. In January, one day before he delivered his 1992 State of the Union Address, he told 1,600 delegates to the National Religious Broadcasters, a largely evangelical group, "One cannot be America's president without a belief in God, without a belief in prayer." The president drew criticism from some Jewish groups for apparently forgetting that the Constitution proscribes a religious test for public office.

At the convention itself, the religious theme was taken up by Bush surrogates, mainly Patrick J. Buchanan and fundamentalist minister Pat Robertson, head of the Christian Coalition. In a speech on August 17, kicking off the convention, Buchanan characterized the campaign as a "religious war" and attacked Democrats' opposition to public funding for private and parochial schools as a deviation from "Judeo-Christian values . . . not the kind of a change we can abide in a nation we still call God's country." Robertson, speaking to the convention on August 19, reiterated Bush's religious themes in a speech that angered many in both parties, including Jewish Republicans, who backed away from Buchanan's "religious war."

On August 22, Bush re-injected religion into partisan politics. Speaking before a convention of evangelical religious leaders in Dallas, the president said that he was struck that "the other party [the Democrats] took words to put together their platform but left out three simple letters: G-O-D." Bush and the Republican party were rebuked by leaders of the National Council of Churches, who stated in an August 25 letter, "It is blasphemy to invoke the infinite and holy God to assert the moral superiority of one people over another, or one political party over another."

CONGRESSIONAL RACES

The anti-incumbency mood sweeping the nation, together with redistricting and a number of retirements, contributed to a large number of changes in the U.S. House of Representatives and Senate. Among the 55 voluntary departures and 7 involuntary ousters resulting from primary contests were four strong supporters of Israel: Dante Fascell (D., Fla.), chairman of the House Foreign Affairs Committee since 1984; Larry Smith (D., Fla.), a victim of the House bank scandal who was also at risk due to redistricting, and whose decision in late April not to run for reelection was viewed as a major setback for the pro-Israel community; Mel Levine (D., Calif.); and Vin Weber, a conservative Minnesota Republican who sought to get the GOP leadership to champion Israel's cause.

Among the primary races watched closely by Jewish groups were the Democratic race in Pennsylvania, where political unknown Lynn Yeakel won an upset victory over Lt. Gov. Mark Siegel, largely by attacking incumbent Republican Arlen Specter over the 1991 Clarence Thomas sexual-harassment hearings; and a toughly fought primary in New York's 12th congressional district, in which nine-term Brooklyn congressman Stephen J. Solarz (D.) was fighting for his political life. Solarz's seat was in a district that had been heavily Jewish but was now newly shaped as a Hispanic district to conform to the provisions of the 1965 Voting Rights Act. His five Democratic rivals were all Hispanic. On primary day, September 15, Solarz lost to Nydia M. Velasquez, the Commonwealth of Puerto Rico's former representative in New York. Also in New York, on the eve of the New York primary, Rep. Ted Weiss (D.), a liberal congressman who had represented Manhattan's 17th (newly drawn and renumbered as the 8th) district since 1974, died. Weiss, who won the primary nonetheless, was succeeded in Congress by State Assemblyman Jerrold Nadler. Finally, on primary day in Illinois, March 17, six-term black congressman Gus Savage, considered by observers of the political scene to be the most antiwhite, anti-Jewish, and anti-Israel member of Congress, was defeated by a 2–1 margin by community activist Mel Reynolds.

ELECTION RESULTS

Tuesday, November 3—election day, 1992—had Jewish voters giving massive support to Gov. Bill Clinton of Arkansas, who won an overwhelming majority of electoral votes, even as he received only 43 percent of the popular vote. Exit polls variously placed the Jewish vote for Clinton at from 78 percent (*New York Times*) to 86 percent (American Jewish Congress). President George Bush received 10–15 percent and independent candidate H. Ross Perot 4-10 percent of the Jewish vote. The lopsided Jewish support of Clinton was the highest Jewish showing for any Democrat since Lyndon Johnson received 90 percent in his 1964 landslide victory over Barry Goldwater. (Estimates of the Jewish vote for Michael Dukakis in 1988 were 65, 71, and 72 percent; similar estimates applied to Walter Mondale in 1984.)

A study conducted by the National Jewish Democratic Council, a political advocacy group, revealed that Jews—who make up 2.4 percent of the population—accounted for 4 percent of the total casting ballots and 7 percent of Clinton's nationwide vote, and possibly provided the winning margin in two key state races, Georgia and New Jersey.

Analysts suggested that many Jewish voters were retaliating against the Bush administration for its position on loan guarantees to Israel rather than positively supporting Clinton. However, according to political analyst Joshua Muravchik, Bill Clinton was able to appeal to many Jewish voters by "distinguishing himself from liberal orthodoxy," particularly "on the critical subject of race," which he did by allowing Jesse Jackson only minimal exposure during the campaign and at the Democratic convention. On welfare reform, military strength (notwithstanding his advocacy of defense cuts), his alliance with the middle class, and other issues, Clinton established his nonliberal persona "and found victory in the center," said Muravchik.

THE NEW CONGRESS

The Jewish position in the 103rd Congress was slightly enhanced. Jews retained the 33 seats they had held in the House of Representatives of the 102nd Congress, as 11 newcomers replaced some of the well-publicized retirees. The number of Jews in the Senate increased from eight to ten, making Jews a full 10 percent of the upper House.[1] In one Senate race that bucked a pattern of incumbent triumph, conservative Republican senator Bob Kasten of Wisconsin—one of Israel's most powerful and devoted allies in Washington—lost to Russell Feingold, a progressive state senator. And highly significant was the victory in California of two Jewish women, both Democrats, Rep. Barbara Boxer and former San Francisco mayor Dianne Feinstein, in the race for two Senate seats.

Two emotionally charged races took place in New York and Pennsylvania. In New York, Sen. Alphonse D'Amato (R.), winning 40 percent of the Jewish vote— the key to his victory—narrowly defeated Attorney General Robert Abrams, a Jew. D'Amato received the lion's share of pro-Israel PAC money. In Pennsylvania, Sen. Arlen Specter (R.), a Jew, defeated Democratic challenger Lynn Yeakel, who had strong support from women. Jews in Pennsylvania were divided over the race, but Specter had strong backing from the organized pro-Israel community, and Yeakel's support for Israel was in some doubt. The unexpected defeat of Rep. Bill Green (R., N.Y.) was mourned by the pro-Israel community; Green had played an important role in crafting the foreign-aid program. Also defeated was Rep. Tom Downey (D., N.Y.), a strong supporter of pro-Israel initiatives and of the emigration of Soviet Jews.

All of the Jewish newcomers in the House and Senate, as well as the incumbents, were vocal supporters of Israel, but they represented a new crop of liberal, domestically oriented political activists. The image of a "disciplined Jewish political community," in the words of political observer Morris Amitay, appeared to be eroding, because the Jewish vote had become more independent. And Abba Cohen, Agudath

---

[1]Jewish senators in the 103rd Congress: Barbara Boxer (D., Calif.), Russell Feingold (D., Wis.), Dianne Feinstein (D., Calif.), Herbert Kohl (D., Wis.), Frank Lautenberg (D., N.J.), Carl Levin (D., Mich.), Joseph Lieberman (D., Conn.), Howard Metzenbaum (D., Ohio), Arlen Specter (R., Pa.), and Paul Wellstone (D., Minn.). The retirement of Warren Rudman (R., N.H.) was more than offset by the election of the three new senators, Feingold, Boxer, and Feinstein.

Israel of America's Washington representative, said that he was "not optimistic about the new class [of members of Congress] coming in. Although they talk of pro-Israel issues, they have no proven record."

THE CHRISTIAN COALITION

The election activities of television evangelist Pat Robertson's Christian Coalition were of concern to Jewish groups and their coalition partners during the campaign. Founded in 1989, the Christian Coalition had eclipsed the now defunct Moral Majority, which had been a force on the political religious right during the 1980s. Robertson's group, which aimed at electing "pro- family Christians" and achieving "working control" of the Republican party by 1996, became a force on Republican central committees in more than half a dozen states and placed some 300 members as delegates to the Republican convention. The increased visibility of the fundamentalist political movement was manifest in the prominent role played by Robertson and the coalition at the convention, at which Robertson delivered a prime-time address in which he articulated many Christian Coalition themes.

Coalition groups, which claimed 250,000 members in 49 states, worked through the tactic of placing "stealth candidates" in hundreds of local elections around the country. According to People for the American Way, a liberal public-affairs advocacy group, the Christian Coalition elected some 40 percent of the approximately 500 candidates it fielded, mostly to local offices such as school boards. The Christian Coalition also aggressively backed anti-gay ballot initiatives in Oregon and Colorado.

Jewish groups chided Mississippi governor Kirk Fordice for his declaration on November 17, at a meeting of the Republican Governors Association, that "the United States of America is a Christian nation. . . . The less we emphasize the Christian religion, the further we fall into the abyss of poor character and chaos."

THE NEW ADMINISTRATION

At year's end, as the president-elect announced the key members of his foreign-affairs team, Jewish groups were generally confident that the U.S. commitment to Israel would remain strong. At the same time, questions were raised about Warren Christopher, named secretary of state, and Anthony Lake, named national security adviser, based on their previously expressed views. Two other Clinton appointments raised questions for the Jewish community. The nomination in December of University of Wisconsin-Madison chancellor Donna Shalala as secretary of human services drew mixed reviews from Jewish groups. Concerns were expressed about Shalala's support for campus speech codes and an ethnic-studies requirement as well as relaxed admissions requirements for blacks and hiring goals for faculty "of color." But Steven Morrison, executive director of the Madison Jewish Community Council, asserted, "Shalala is clearly an advocate for the Jewish agenda." An article in the English-language *Forward* (December 18), on Johnetta Cole, president of Spellman College in Atlanta, who had been tapped for a key role in the Clinton transition operation and was reportedly a leading candidate for secretary of education, disclosed Cole's past support of hard-line Communist front organizations, including the U.S. Peace Council, reportedly a pro-PLO group. Shalala was ultimately nominated to her post; Cole was not.

Other Political Matters

An item on the congressional agenda in 1992 was campaign finance reform, a matter of fierce dispute among Jewish groups, mainly over the question of limitations on political action committees (PACs). The Congressional Campaign Spending Limit and Election Reform Act of 1992, never a favorite among lawmakers, was passed by the Congress in April but vetoed by President Bush in May.

SOCIAL-POLICY ISSUES

Jewish groups took positions on various social-policy issues that were not specifically "Jewish" concerns but about which there were strong feelings in the Jewish community.

In the November elections, homosexual rights were on the ballot in two states. Oregon voters rejected Ballot Measure 9, which would have amended the state constitution to require that government discourage homosexuality. Despite the intense efforts of a broad-based coalition—including Jewish groups in the state—43 percent of the voters supported the measure. In Colorado, Amendment 2, denying homosexuals preferential treatment or protection against discrimination, was approved. The National Jewish Community Relations Advisory Council (NJCRAC), acting on behalf of national and community member agencies (with the Union of Orthodox Jewish Congregations of America, a congregational body of the centrist Orthodox movement, dissenting) adopted in September a policy in opposition to sexual-orientation discrimination; however, religious institutions were exempt from the policy.

In the area of reproductive rights, the U.S. Supreme Court decision in *Planned Parenthood of Southeastern Pennsylvania v. Casey* on June 29 generated a furor of activity on Capitol Hill and among pro-reproductive-choice groups—including many Jewish organizations—around the country. In one of the most controversial decisions issued in 1992, the Court, by a 5–4 margin, upheld the constitutionality of nearly all components of a Pennsylvania law requiring a woman to notify her husband before she could have an abortion, parental consent for minors, counseling by the doctor about alternatives to abortion followed by a waiting period of at least 24 hours, and reporting on abortion procedures and patients by health clinics. The bitterly divided Court upheld the challenged provisions of the Pennsylvania law, with the exception of the spousal notification requirement. In so doing, it paved the way for states to enact laws patterned after Pennsylvania's that would regulate or restrict access to abortion.

According to Alfred A. Moses, president of the American Jewish Committee, "While claiming to re-affirm *Roe*. . . the decision in fact overturns that portion of *Roe v. Wade* which treated the right to choose as a fundamental right." Numerous Jewish organizations as disparate as New Jewish Agenda, Hadassah, Women's American ORT, and the Anti-Defamation League filed *amicus* briefs challenging the Pennsylvania law. However, Agudath Israel of America's general counsel, David Zwiebel, representing a view shared by many in the Orthodox community, maintained that abortion is not a fundamental right and that to allow abortions without restrictions is "unwise public policy." "Laws that undermine the sanctity of life send a message that is profoundly dangerous to society," added Zwiebel.

The *Casey* decision served to mobilize support for passage of the Freedom of Choice Act (FOCA), which would prohibit states from restricting abortion prior to fetal viability. But threatened with presidential veto, FOCA came to the floor of neither the House nor the Senate. Other legislation related to reproductive choice fared poorly as well; legislation reversing the "gag rule," the Bush administration policy prohibiting health-care workers at clinics that receive Title X funds from providing counseling on abortion services, died when the House failed to override a presidential veto.

Jewish groups were disappointed with President Bush's veto on September 22 of the Family and Medical Leave legislation that had been vigorously supported by a coalition of Jewish and other groups since its first appearance in the 99th Congress in 1986. Advocates of the measure, which would provide for up to 12 weeks of unpaid leave to care for a new baby or a family illness, looked to the new Congress and administration for passage.

Soviet Jewry

Debate continued over Israel's request to the United States to guarantee, by acting as co-signatory, a loan for $10 billion to assist in the absorption of immigrants—primarily from the former Soviet Union.

In the fall of 1991, President Bush demanded, and Congress agreed to, a 120-day waiting period, to permit movement on the peace process, specifically, the direct Israeli-Arab peace talks in Madrid on October 30. At the beginning of 1992, Jewish groups had urged the president to move on the loan-guarantee request and the second session of the 102nd Congress to act on it. The administration, however, had conditions for approval of the request which did not please the Shamir government (still in power in Israel), namely—as stated by Secretary of State James Baker in February 24 testimony before the House foreign operations subcommittee—linkage of loan guarantees to "a halt or end to settlement activity" in the occupied territories. Subsequent administration proposals, including a plan in March agreeing to $1 billion immediately without linkage, and the rest linked to restriction of settlement activity, was rejected by the Israelis. Bush further solidified the impasse when he remarked, on March 17, that linkage was a "long-standing policy," directly related to Middle East peace.

The election of a new government in Israel in June dramatically changed the political landscape with respect to the issue. With Prime Minister Yitzhak Rabin at best ambiguous (Rabin said that he opposed "political" settlements), administration officials had, in the words of analyst Morris Amitay, "significant wiggle room." When the Israeli government announced in early August a limit on the building of settlements, the stage was set for an agreement to be reached on the loan-guarantee issue, as it was in a meeting of Bush and Rabin in Maine on August 11. The agreement included a crucial provision consistent with administration policy: the cost of any further settlement construction would be deducted from the guarantees, in order to ensure that the United States would not be in the position of financing settlements in the territories.

In a speech on September 8 to B'nai B'rith, President Bush called on Congress to approve the guarantee of $10 billion of loans. Senate approval of the foreign-aid bill including the guarantee request (FY 93 Foreign Operations Appropriations) came exactly three weeks later by a vote of 87–12. On October 1, the measure was reconciled with the slightly different House bill passed earlier, and President Bush signed the measure into law on October 6. It authorized guarantees of $2 billion over each of the next five years, with discretion to the president to suspend the loan program if he determined that "the terms and conditions have been breached." This signified a U.S. demand for a virtual freeze on the construction of Jewish housing across the Green Line.

On another front, Jewish groups advocated vigorously for refugee legislation—the so-called Lautenberg Amendment—that had implications for Jews and others from the former Soviet Union. The legislation, responding to troubling conditions for persecuted groups, would facilitate the granting of refugee status to Soviet Jews and other groups, including Soviet evangelical Christians, Ukrainian Catholics, and certain classes of Indo-Chinese. The bill, first introduced by Sen. Frank Lautenberg (D., N.J.) as an amendment to the 1990 Foreign Appropriations Act, and valid for that year only, was next included in the 1991 measure, where it again had a "sunset" provision, calling for annual reauthorization. In 1992 the amendment was included as part of both the Foreign Operations Appropriations Act and the Freedom Support Act and was cosponsored by Rep. Howard Berman (D., Calif.). The amendment was extended for two years in October.

Crisis in Bosnia

As the crisis in Bosnia-Herzegovina deepened this year, with reports of "ethnic cleansing" evoking memories of the Holocaust, Jewish groups mobilized in response. Even as they were developing stances with respect to issues such as lifting the arms embargo and creating "no-fly zones," 18 Jewish organizations participated in a "call to action" at a rally held August 5 outside the United Nations in New York. Benjamin Meed, president of the American Gathering of Jewish Holocaust Survivors, one of the rally's organizing groups, summed up the "call": "Mankind is divided into three groups: the murderers, the victims, and the bystanders. Murderers can only act if the bystanders permit them to." The rally was accompanied by an ad placed in the *New York Times* on August 5 by the American Jewish Committee, the American Jewish Congress, and the Anti-Defamation League, calling for "every necessary step, including the use of force," in "stopping the death camps" in Bosnia, and calling upon representatives of humanitarian organizations to investigate accounts of conditions in the camps.

In November, the American Jewish Congress was the first Jewish organization to call for the administration to reverse its arms-embargo policy in responding to the Bosnian crisis. Most Jewish organizations held off articulating support for this or other measures at the request of the American Jewish Joint Distribution Committee, which was concerned about the fate of Jewish communities in Bosnia, primarily in the capital, Sarajevo. However, by year's end, 19 of 24 sponsoring organizations of a rally held on December 22 at the still-incomplete U.S. Holocaust Memorial Museum in Washington endorsed a 12-point statement, "Bosnia, a Plea to the United States," asking the U.S. government to "formulate and announce an American policy adequate to the crisis in Bosnia." The statement called for military intervention, if necessary, and the prosecution of those involved in war crimes. As the year drew to a close, Jewish support grew for lifting the arms embargo. Said Kenneth Jacobson, international affairs director of the Anti-Defamation League, "enabling the Bosnian Muslims to become armed is a way of saving Muslim lives."

While the Jewish community cooperated with Catholic, Protestant, and Muslim groups in activism on the Bosnia issue—the four faith communities joined in a Sabbath for Prayer and Petition for Bosnia on the weekend of December 4–6— Christian groups stopped short of calling for military action. The National Council of Churches, in an August 6 letter to President Bush, urged the United States to give financial and diplomatic support to the United Nations.

Black-Jewish Relations

CROWN HEIGHTS AFTERMATH

The year following the August 1991 events in the Crown Heights section of Brooklyn was a period of attempted healing between blacks and Jews, even as anger and bitterness reemerged because of new developments. Most troubling was a Brooklyn jury's acquittal in October of the prime suspect in the murder of Yankel Rosenbaum, a young Orthodox Jew who had been set upon, beaten, and murdered on the first night of the Crown Heights riot. (See AJYB 1993, pp. 91–94.)

Tensions in Crown Heights simmered during the months following the riot, and flared in the aftermath of discrete events—the stabbing murder of a Hassidic woman in February; a late March attack on a Hassidic man; the arrest of a Hassid for participating in the gang-beating of a homeless black man suspected of burglary, in early December; and most notably, the acquittal of Lemrick Nelson. Nelson, a 17-year-old black, had been indicted on four counts—intentional murder, murder by depraved indifference, and first- and second-degree manslaughter—in the August 19, 1991, stabbing murder of Yankel Rosenbaum. On October 29, following a trial in New York State Supreme Court (the trial level in New York State), in which the credibility of the police was repeatedly questioned because of allegedly sloppy investigative work, Nelson was acquitted of all charges.

The reaction of Jewish groups was one of deep disappointment. The verdict, said Judah Gribetz, president of the New York Jewish Community Relations Council, "is a blot on the record of the system of justice." Officials of the Anti-Defamation League, the Union of American Hebrew Congregations, the National Jewish Community Relations Advisory Council, the American Jewish Committee, and other organizations expressed shock and dismay at the verdict and called upon the U.S. Department of Justice to investigate whether Rosenbaum's civil rights had been violated.

Indeed, the day after the Nelson acquittal, Attorney General William P. Barr announced that the Justice Department would conduct an inquiry into the Rosenbaum death in order to determine whether there were civil-rights violations in the case; and on November 17, New York State governor Mario Cuomo ordered a state inquiry into both the Nelson trial and allegations that the New York City police had been hampered by higher-ups in their response to the Crown Heights events, thereby exacerbating the riots. Cuomo ordered his director of criminal justice, Richard Girgenti, to probe the entire incident. On November 20, a class-action suit was filed in federal court by the Crown Heights Jewish Community Council, charging that Mayor David Dinkins and then police commissioner Lee Brown had conspired not to protect Jews from the mob and that civil rights of Crown Heights residents had been violated.

A December 16 meeting in Crown Heights between Jewish leadership and the mayor failed to resolve anything. However, national Jewish groups, in an effort to prevent the further widening of already gaping rifts, defended Dinkins from charges of anti-Semitism leveled by some in the community. In a full-page advertisement in the *New York Times* (December 10) entitled "Enough!" the American Jewish Congress asserted that the charges were "offensive" and called upon blacks and Jews to "resolve our conflicts and heal our wounds . . . black leaders must reject false charges of racism and condemn anti-Semitism in the black community, just as Jewish leaders must reject racism and false charges of anti-Semitism in the Jewish community."

The implications of the Crown-Heights aftermath for black-Jewish relations were mixed. The Reverend Jesse Jackson, often regarded as an irritant in the relationship, was involved in an "active and constructive" manner in an effort to keep the controversy from tainting black-Jewish relations nationally, according to Diana Aviv, an official of the National Jewish Community Relations Advisory Council. Although most analysts agreed that Crown Heights was unique, the current tense state of black-Jewish relations around the country could not be ignored. Most observers agreed with American Jewish Committee official Murray Friedman, who said, "We're going to have to realize that the [black-Jewish] alliance cannot be reasserted in the way it once existed. . . . We may need a degree of separation, a cooling-off period."

JESSE JACKSON

Jesse Jackson's activities during the year included an aggressive—"near manic," in the words of one observer—courtship of the Jewish community. In addition to his activities with respect to Crown Heights, Jackson met with numerous Jewish groups throughout the year in efforts aimed at repairing a relationship that was seriously compromised in 1979, when Jackson was photographed hugging Yasir Arafat, and 1984, when, as a presidential candidate, he called New York City "Hymietown" and refused to distance himself from Louis Farrakhan.

In a July 7 speech clearly aimed at reconciliation with the Jewish community, Rev. Jackson told a conference on anti-Semitism and prejudice, convened in Brussels by the World Jewish Congress, that "racism and anti-Semitism are scientifically and morally wrong," and praised Zionism as a "liberation movement." (This was in marked contrast to his 1980 characterization of Zionism as "a kind of poisonous weed choking Judaism.") Calling for "joint action" with the Jewish community, Jackson said, "The shrill voices of the extreme must not take our eyes off the real institutional threats." The reaction of Jewish leaders to Jackson's remarks was a mixture of praise and caution; they suggested that his credibility would be enhanced if he were to deliver his message of opposition to anti-Semitism in black neighborhoods and to black audiences.

Within a week of his July 7 speech in Brussels, Jackson again—this time at the Democratic National Convention—reached out to Jews, speaking movingly about the Holocaust and proffering optimistic observations about Israel's new government. Finally, in December, Jackson and the American Jewish Congress, in a clear attempt to define black-Jewish relations in terms of political action rather than violent reaction, unveiled a joint legislative agenda. Most Jewish leaders praised Jackson's effort to reach out to Jews. "For five years, he has bent himself into a pretzel trying to re-forge the [black-Jewish] alliance," said UAHC president Rabbi Alexander Schindler, and "the reason that it's been more intense recently is that he's finding a response." Other Jewish leaders, while welcoming Jackson's activities, were more cynical in their analyses, suggesting that Jackson was wooing the Jewish community as part of a strategy aimed at securing a position with the incoming Clinton administration.

ANTI-SEMITISM IN THE BLACK COMMUNITY

Prof. Leonard Jeffries, Jr., chairman of the City College of New York's Black Studies Department, who was severely criticized in 1991 for teaching anti-Semitic ideas, was again a focus of controversy. Although Jeffries' term as department chairman had been extended in October 1991 by a probationary one-year period, on January 27 City College president Bernard W. Harleston informed the Board of Trustees of the parent City University of New York (CUNY) of his intention to remove Jeffries from that position. On March 23, the CUNY board voted to replace Jeffries with Edmund W. Gordon, a retired Yale professor, with Jeffries remaining a tenured full professor at the City College. In early June, Jeffries sued the college, claiming that his demotion was punishment for controversial views he had aired and was therefore a violation of his First Amendment right to freedom of expression. Jeffries sought $25 million in damages and reinstatement as chairman. *Jeffries v. Harleston* was viewed as a potentially seminal case in defining the parameters of professors' rights and responsibilities at a time when campus tensions over "political correctness" and multiculturalism were growing.

Concern was expressed by Jewish organizations over reports from New York, Philadelphia, Pittsburgh, Washington, D.C., and Los Angeles that an arm of Louis Farrakhan's Nation of Islam, an antiwhite, anti-Semitic black-Muslim organization, had bid for, and in some cases had been awarded, contracts to provide security at housing projects funded by the federal government through the Department of Housing and Urban Development (HUD). A number of Jewish groups, including the American Jewish Committee and the Anti-Defamation League, called upon HUD Secretary Jack Kemp to scrutinize, and invalidate if necessary, proposed federal contracts if, in the words of the American Jewish Committee (September 22), "the discrimination and religious enterprises of the parent company infect this enterprise." At year's end the matter had not been resolved.

Mayor Sharon Pratt Kelly of Washington, D.C., ignited a firestorm of protest when, on July 11, she issued a proclamation honoring Dr. Abdul Alim Muhammad, "minister of health and human services" and a national spokesman for the Nation of Islam. The proclamation was issued within days of rejection of a similar proclamation by the City Council. Following meetings with Washington Jewish leaders, Kelly issued an "open letter to the African-American and Jewish communities," in which she said that she had sought to acknowledge Muhammad's antidrug and anti-AIDS work and had condemned his anti-Semitic comments. "While we welcome [Kelly's] response," commented the Jewish Community Council of Greater Washington, "it was a serious mistake to honor an individual with a well-documented history of bigotry and anti-Semitism." Similar concern was expressed in October, when Atlanta mayor Maynard Jackson wrote a letter to Minister Louis Farrakhan welcoming him to Atlanta for the Nation of Islam's annual convention. While Jewish groups did not question the right of the Nation of Islam to hold a meeting, they did chastise Mayor Jackson for welcoming and embracing Farrakhan.

Two prominent African-American academics—Henry Louis Gates, Jr., of Harvard and Cornel West of Princeton—published articles analyzing and repudiating anti-Semitism in their community. In a July 20 *New York Times* op-ed article that received significant attention, Gates, a professor of English and chairman of Harvard's Afro-American Studies Department, shot well-aimed arrows at those blacks who spread anti-Semitic canards—charging them with demagoguery and "opportunism"—and argued forcefully that the ultimate damage done by black anti-Semitism is to the political culture of blacks themselves. West, a professor of religion and director of Princeton's Afro-American Studies Department, in an article in *Tikkun*, "Black Anti-Semitism and the Politics of Resentment" (January-February, 1992), argued that black anti-Semitism, by weakening the buffer between racism and social justice, "plays into the hands of the racists, who appeal to . . . the silent depression that plagues the majority of Americans." While Gates and West were praised in Jewish and other white quarters for bringing the issue into the open, they were reviled by a number of African-American spokespersons. Typical was the comment—directed at Gates—of former Harvard Law School professor Derrick Bell, who said, "Blacks should be very careful about criticizing each other because whites love it so much when they do." Gates received a number of death threats as well.

OTHER MATTERS

Amid tensions reflecting fundamental—some analysts suggested even inherent—difficulties in the black-Jewish relationship, positive developments were taking place on the local level. In Los Angeles, in the course of the riots that followed the April 29 verdict acquitting four police officers in the beating of Rodney King, a black man, Jewish communal leaders developed action plans to get quantities of food and other necessary goods to riot-stricken areas. In New York, on May 28, the UJA-Federation, a local fund-raising and community-planning Jewish communal umbrella body, joined with five groups representing African-American, Hispanic, Asian, Catholic, and Protestant charities in the Joint Federation of Public Policy Partnership, in an effort to improve the services provided to the city's multiracial and multireligious population. The partnership launched a diversity-training program, viewed by observers of intergroup relations as a model for such programming.

In August, Jewish and black health-care professionals traveled to South Africa to help train blacks in health-care fields. The program, Medical Education for South African Blacks, was funded by a foundation grant. Commenting on black-Jewish activities around the country, Rabbi Lynn Landsberg, associate director of Reform Judaism's Religious Action Center, said, "The [black-Jewish] alliance may be seriously troubled nationally—that's obvious. But you wouldn't know it from the hundreds of programs conducted on the local level in virtually every community."

Two arts events during the year were regarded as efforts to heal the breach between blacks and Jews. A documentary film, "The Liberators: Fighting on Two

Fronts in World War II," released in November and aired on PBS television on November 11, Veterans' Day, tells the story of the all-black army divisions—which themselves had been subject to official discrimination—that liberated the Buchenwald and Dachau concentration camps in the closing months of World War II. The film was viewed by observers of black-Jewish relations as a vehicle for reconciliation. At year's end, however, questions were being raised about the accuracy of some of the historical information.

"Bridges and Boundaries: African-Americans and American Jews," an exhibition at the Jewish Museum in New York, under the joint auspices of the museum and the National Association for the Advancement of Colored People, traced the complex relationships between blacks and Jews in America. While there was some criticism of the show by Jewish groups—the Jewish Labor Committee contended that there were inaccurate portrayals of aspects of the labor movement, including allegations of discrimination—Jewish representatives said that "the positive side of bridge-building outweighs the negative side."

Anti-Semitism and Extremism

ASSESSING ANTI-SEMITISM

By most major criteria, anti-Semitism continued to diminish. An Anti-Defamation League study, "Survey on Anti-Semitism and Prejudice in America," conducted by the Boston polling firm Marttila and Kiley and released in November, corroborated the long-term downward trend of attitudinal anti-Semitism that has characterized American society for the past 45 years.[2]

The index of anti-Semitic beliefs used in the Marttila/ADL study grouped respondents into one of three categories—"not anti-Semitic," "middle," and "most anti-Semitic"—based on the number of critical responses they gave to 11 specific questions about Jews. Twenty percent of those surveyed accepted six or more stereotypes, qualifying those individuals as "most anti-Semitic"; 41 percent—the "middle group"—held between two and five stereotypes and "are considered to be neither prejudiced nor unprejudiced—not an audience to be worried about"; and 39 percent held none or one of the critical responses, and were judged to be "virtually free of prejudicial attitudes toward the Jewish community." The study reaffirmed findings from previous polls. For example, as levels of education rise, anti-Semitism declines; and Americans over 65 are twice as likely as those under 65 to be anti-Semitic. With respect to the African-American community, Marttila found that blacks are twice as likely as whites to hold anti-Semitic views, but blacks and whites

---

[2]See AJYB 1993 for details on the American Jewish Committee/National Opinion Research Center 1991 study, *What Do Americans Think About Jews?* (New York: American Jewish Committee, 1991).

alike tend to be less anti-Semitic as levels of education rise.

Some analysts questioned the validity of any study based on an "index of anti-Semitic beliefs," since respondents placed in the "most anti-Semitic" category by virtue of answering yes to at least six out of the eleven questions may have given up to five pro-Jewish responses as well. Similarly, among those classified as "not anti-Semitic," some anti-Jewish attitudes may have been expressed. Analysts suggested that attitudinal surveys could not claim more than a marginal few as either "anti-Semitic" or "not anti-Semitic," and that a more sophisticated conceptual scheme was called for.

The *1992 New York Intergroup Relations Survey*, conducted by the Roper Organization for the American Jewish Committee, released in October, had some disturbing findings about attitudes toward Jews in the major center of Jewish population. Forty-seven percent of New York City residents viewed Jews as having "too much influence in New York City life and politics," with 63 percent of blacks affirming this view. The 47-percent figure was more than twice that for other racial or ethnic groups. The data from the New York study were mixed, however; Roper found that Jews are the most admired group on several characteristics surveyed, including "intelligence" and not being "prone to violence." The Roper/AJC poll stands in sharp contrast to a 21-percent "too much influence" response in a 1990 national survey conducted by the National Opinion Research Center, and 31 percent in the 1992 ADL poll.

With respect to Jewish perceptions of anti-Semitism, 54 percent of New York Jews said that anti-Semitism is "somewhat of a problem," and 37 percent asserted that it is a "very serious problem." These numbers are slightly higher than, but generally consistent with, national data in this area.

One traditional index of anti-Semitism, the number of discrete incidents of anti-Semitism, declined for the first time in six years, according to the annual audit of anti-Semitic incidents compiled by the Anti-Defamation League (ADL). The total of 1,730 incidents was 8 percent lower than the record number of 1,879, recorded in 1991. Cases of vandalism against Jewish institutions and property and instances of "harassment" also declined during 1992.

EXTREMIST GROUPS

The Anti-Defamation League estimated that the total membership of all hate groups around the country was fewer than 20,000, roughly unchanged since 1990. Nonetheless, the ADL cautioned that there had been an increase over the past two years in the numbers of young people aligning themselves with violence- and hate-promoting "skinhead" groups (some 3,000–3,500 individuals), groups that were often drawn to associate with more established "hate" organizations, such as Tom Metzger's White Aryan Resistance (WAR).

Another indicator of the number of "sympathizers" with such groups is the circulation size of *Spotlight*, the organ of the anti-Semitic and racist Liberty Lobby.

The reported 1992 figure of 80,000, a slight decrease from 1991 (and significantly lower than the 200,000 circulation reported during the 1970s), suggested that there was yet a sizable number of Americans in the penumbra of extremism in the United States.

While passage of hate-crimes legislation was advocated by Jewish groups (see "Legislative and Judicial Activity," below), analysts of extremism suggested that the effect of such laws would be minimal. "Extremism is tautologically extremist," offered Earl Raab, director of Brandeis University's Perlmutter Institute for Jewish Advocacy, "and these groups will act notwithstanding the passage of some law."

Finally, in July, Tom Metzger, John Metzger, and the White Aryan Resistance (WAR) appealed the $12-million judgment secured against them and two Oregon skinheads in October 1990 in an Oregon state trial court. The ADL together with the Southern Poverty Law Center filed an *amicus* brief in the case, *Berhanu v. Metzger*.

POLITICAL ANTI-SEMITISM

With the beginning of both the year and the presidential-campaign season, a debate developed within the Jewish community over whether to meet with Republican presidential candidate Patrick J. Buchanan. Buchanan had over the years angered American Jews with his anti-Israel stance, his defense of accused Nazi war criminals, attacks on the U.S. Justice Department Office of Special Investigations charged with prosecuting Nazi war criminals, and his 1990 accusation that only Israel and its " 'amen' corner" in America were pressing for war with Iraq. The debate was triggered by a December 24, 1991, letter from Menachem Rosensaft, past president of the Labor Zionist Alliance and founding chairman of the International Network of Children of Jewish Holocaust Survivors, to Shoshana Cardin, chairwoman of the Conference of Presidents of Major American Jewish Organizations, in which Rosensaft praised the 1991 decision of the Presidents' Conference not to meet with white supremacist David Duke, also a Republican presidential candidate. (The Presidents' Conference provides presidential candidates with a public forum to address issues of concern to the Jewish community.) Rosensaft asserted in his letter, "Buchanan is no better than Duke . . . indeed, I believe he is far more dangerous."

Joshua Muravchik, an analyst of political anti-Semitism, sought to distinguish Buchanan from Duke: "If Buchanan would recant [his anti-Semitism], we might be skeptical, but it would be hard for the Jewish community not to accept his apology. With Duke, it would take more than an apology."

Jewish groups were hesitant to identify Buchanan as an anti-Semite until an incident in early March. On March 2, at a campaign rally in Marietta, Georgia, Buchanan told a group of Jewish protesters that his rally was "of Americans, by Americans, and for the good old U.S.A." On March 3, the American Jewish Congress branded Buchanan "as genuine and authentic an anti-Semite as they come

. . . [he] is not only an anti-Semite but also racist and contemptuous of women."
The American Jewish Committee, on March 4, said that Buchanan's suggestion that
American Jews who disagreed with him were not patriotic Americans "is plainly
anti-Semitic and has no place in the political process." Buchanan's presidential
campaign failed, although at the peak of his campaign he gained 37 percent of the
vote in the New Hampshire primary.

David Duke was successful in 10 of 14 attempts to get his name onto state ballots
for 1992 Republican presidential primaries. However, having failed to win a single
delegate, Duke announced on April 22 that he was dropping out of the race.
Although he still had a core constituency, for the moment at least, Duke remained
outside the electoral arena.

A brief flap erupted in March over a report that Secretary of State James Baker,
in a closed meeting with Republican officials, employed an obscenity to dismiss
American Jewish claims on the Bush administration. According to former New
York mayor Edward I. Koch, writing in the *New York Post* on March 6, Baker said,
"F— them [the Jews]: They didn't vote for us." Baker immediately denied the
report, and, in a March 8 letter to the ADL, said that he had been "deeply offended
by the false and malicious press story." Baker's denial, which was accepted at face
value by most Jewish leaders, did little, however, to reassure American Jewry about
the secretary's motives with respect to Israel.

Finally, Chicago congressman Gus Savage (D., Ill.) continued to make anti-
Semitic remarks, referring, for example, to the "Jewish money" raised by his primary opponent, Mel Reynolds. A chief federal circuit court judge in Florida, John
Santora, Jr., got into hot water over remarks he made about Jewish judges. Santora
apologized for his remarks but did not step down.

HOLOCAUST DENIAL

Denial of the Holocaust—styled as "revisionism" by its proponents—was manifest in 1992 in the efforts of Californian Bradley R. Smith to place his 4,000-word
essay asserting that the Holocaust did not take place as an advertisement in a
number of college newspapers. (Smith claimed that gas chambers were "life-saving"
fumigation shelters.) Smith's ads were turned down by college newspapers at Harvard, Brown, Yale, and the University of California and were accepted at Cornell,
Duke, Northwestern, and Michigan. Jewish groups suggested that the best approach
to the Smith ad was that of the *Daily Targum* at Rutgers University in New Jersey,
which rejected the Smith tract as an advertisement but ran the text in its news
columns, along with editorial denunciation and comment by invited authors.

A "summit meeting" of Holocaust revisionists, together with black and white
racists, held on February 1 in Los Angeles, failed to live up to its advance billing.
Three of the featured 13 speakers—including Willis Carto, founder of the white
racist and anti-Semitic Liberty Lobby, and Prof. Leonard Jeffries of the City University of New York—failed to appear, and the 15 listeners who materialized at the

conference were considerably outnumbered by media people.

There were new developments this year in a federal case involving free speech, contractual rights, and Holocaust "revisionism": *Simon Wiesenthal Center for Holocaust Studies, American Jewish Committee, et al. v. McCalden and McCalden v. California Library Association*. In 1984, David McCalden, cofounder in 1978 of the Institute for Historical Review—a pseudo-scholarly organization that claims the Holocaust is a myth and a hoax—contracted for exhibit space at a meeting of the California Library Association (CLA). He also announced plans to give a presentation on the premises entitled "Free Speech and the Holocaust," which he described as "an overview of the severe censorship and intellectual terrorism which inhibits any objective, open discussion of this controversial subject." McCalden alleged that the American Jewish Committee and the Los Angeles-based Simon Wiesenthal Center engaged in contract interference and violated his civil rights by informing the CLA that if the contract were not canceled the conference would be "disrupted." The space granted McCalden for the 1984 meeting was withdrawn. A federal district court dismissed McCalden's original complaint, but in January, the U.S. Ninth Circuit Court of Appeals let stand an earlier appeals-court ruling that overturned the district court's decision.

Jewish groups—the Anti-Defamation League, the National Jewish Community Relations Advisory Council, the American Jewish Congress, and the Jewish Community Relations Committee of the Jewish Federation Council of Greater Los Angeles, in addition to the defendants American Jewish Committee and Wiesenthal Center—petitioned the U.S. Supreme Court for *certiorari* (review) in the case, asserting that Jewish organizations ought not be punished for exercising their First Amendment free-speech rights—in this case to oppose anti-Semitic propaganda—and that planned demonstrations were lawful so long as there was no incitement to imminent violence. In late May the Supreme Court denied *certiorari* in the case. Richard Foltin, governmental affairs director of the American Jewish Committee, said, "At stake [in the Court's decision were] substantial and weighty issues of free speech. The message is that the right to protest is reserved for the Holocaust deniers, and not for those who would oppose them."

LEGISLATIVE AND JUDICIAL ACTIVITY

By 1992, the federal government, 47 states, and a number of municipalities had passed some form of "hate-crimes," ethnic intimidation, or bias-motivated violence laws. The constitutionality of some of the state and municipal statutes was called into question by a decision handed down by the U.S. Supreme Court on June 22 in *R.A.V. v. City of St. Paul*. In its first consideration of a hate-crimes statute, the High Court struck down the St. Paul, Minnesota, Bias-Motivated Crime Ordinance, a statute that prohibited the display of offensive graffiti or symbols likely to arouse "anger, alarm, or resentment in others on the basis of race, color, creed, religion, or gender," and specifically cited the swastika and the burning cross. In *R.A.V.*, a white teenager who burned a cross on a black family's lawn was prosecuted under the St. Paul ordinance.

While the decision to invalidate the ordinance was unanimous, the ruling revealed deep splits within the court on the issue of hate crimes. Justice Antonin Scalia, speaking for a five-justice majority, said that the St. Paul ordinance violated free-speech rights by singling out certain kinds of offensive expressions for punishment. Justice Scalia asserted that, even within the category of "fighting words,"[3] government may not selectively "silence speech on the basis of its content," even if that speech or other expression is abhorrent, and permit other forms of speech. Scalia averred that states and cities seeking to legislate against bias-motivated crime would not be able to rely on the "fighting-words" exception if it was applied in a selective manner. Four justices in *R.A.V.* focused on flaws in the St. Paul ordinance itself, which they characterized as "fatally overbroad," and thus capable of deterring expression deserving of constitutional protection. They suggested that it was possible to draft hate-crimes laws that would avoid the constitutional defect of the St. Paul ordinance.

Jewish defense organizations had mixed reactions to the ruling. The American Jewish Committee acknowledged that the St. Paul ordinance was flawed, and that "speech, however repugnant, should not be susceptible to criminal penalty." Nevertheless, said AJCommittee legal director Samuel Rabinove, "there's a line to be drawn, and St. Paul failed to draw that line properly." The Anti-Defamation League had filed an *amicus* brief in the case supporting a "fighting-words" interpretation of the law. The American Jewish Congress welcomed the decision, albeit with some reservations. AJCongress had filed an *amicus* brief opposing the ordinance.

Jewish groups supported the "penalty-enhancement" approach as more likely to pass constitutional muster under the guidelines articulated in *R.A.V. v. St. Paul*. Hate-crimes legislation introduced in April in the 103rd Congress by Representatives Charles Schumer (D., N.Y.) and James Sensenbrenner (R., Wis.) and by Sen. Paul Simon (D., Ill.) would oblige federal judges to increase the penalty for those found guilty of any crime where the defendant acted because of the victim's race, religion, national origin, sexual orientation, gender, or ethnicity. Approximately two dozen states had hate-crimes laws with penalty-enhancement provisions.

The day after the ruling in *R.A.V. v. St. Paul*, the Wisconsin supreme court became the first state court to invalidate its state's hate-crimes law, which called for enhancing the penalty in bias-motivated crimes. Jewish groups welcomed the December 14 decision of the U.S. Supreme Court to review *Wisconsin v. Todd Mitchell*, which would have implications for the 27 states that had penalty-enhancement statutes on their books. The American Jewish Committee, the American Jewish Congress, and the National Jewish Community Relations Advisory Council had

---

[3]That is, conduct that itself inflicts injury or tends to incite violence. The U.S. Supreme Court has held that "fighting words" do not merit protection under the free-speech clause of the First Amendment. Other exceptions to the clause are libel and obscenity.

joined an ADL brief asking the Court to grant *certiorari* in the case. The Supreme Court withheld a decision on review of *Ohio v. Wyant* (see 1993 AJYB, p. 96), pending its decision in *Mitchell*. The Ohio statute, likewise struck down by the state's supreme court, was also based on the penalty-enhancement approach.

In *Oregon v. Plowman* and *Oregon v. Hendrix*, handed down this year, the Oregon supreme court upheld that state's penalty-enhancement law. A penalty-enhancement-law case in Florida, *State of Florida v. Stalder*, was pending in the Florida state supreme court.

The Federal Bureau of Investigation released in early January the first full year's data on hate crimes, as required by the Hate Crimes Statistics Act passed by Congress in 1990, a measure that had broad support among Jewish groups. The FBI reported 4,588 hate crimes for 1991 (the first year for which statistics were kept)—mostly crimes of "intimidation"—with racial bias accounting for the motivation of 60 percent of the crimes, religious bias for 20 percent, and ethnic and sexual-orientation bias, 10 percent each. Of interest to observers of anti-Semitism was the fact that antiblack offenses accounted for 39 percent of the total; "antiwhite" and "anti-Jewish" offenses, 19 and 17 percent, respectively.

ANTI-SEMITISM ON THE CAMPUS

The number of anti-Semitic incidents reported on college campuses in 1992 numbered 114 at 60 campuses, according to the Anti-Defamation League, a 12-percent increase over the 1991 total of 101, also at 60 campuses. Much anti-Semitic activity continued to occur around well-defined "flash points," such as invited speakers who carried an anti-Semitic message, and was increasingly linked to the debate over "multiculturalism." One such speaker was City College of New York professor Leonard Jeffries, who was on the campus speaking circuit, appearing at Harvard, the University of Michigan, and at campuses in Florida, California, New York, and New Jersey.

One institution of higher learning, the University of Wisconsin, in September repealed its rule against "hate speech," adopted in 1989 and one of the first such codes in the country. The Wisconsin rule, specifically barring speech intended to create a hostile learning environment by demeaning a person's race, sex, religion, color, creed, disability, sexual orientation, or ancestry, was dropped in the aftermath of the U.S. Supreme Court's decision in *R.A.V. v. St Paul* (see above).

OTHER DEVELOPMENTS

A public discussion of anti-Semitism in opinion magazines, op-ed pages, and the media generally, using Pat Buchanan, among others, as a foil, had been given significant impetus in a December 1991 article by William F. Buckley, Jr., in the *National Review*: "In Search of Anti-Semitism" (see AJYB 1993, p. 94). Debate continued in 1992 when Buckley published "Chapter II: In Pursuit of Anti-Semitism" in the magazine's March 16 issue, a compilation of responses to the original article. (The two essays, with some additional material, were published in book form in 1992.)

In "What Is Anti-Semitism? An Open Letter to William F. Buckley, Jr." (*Commentary*, February 1992, and excerpted in Buckley's book), Norman Podhoretz argued for the pivotal role played by Israel in contemporary anti-Semitism. Podhoretz asserted, "Criticisms of Israel based on [a] double standard, rooted . . . in ancient anti-Semitic propaganda, deserve to be stigmatized as anti-Semitic." Other observers of anti-Semitism in the United States regarded criticism of the policies of the State of Israel—even harsh criticism—as entirely legitimate. The threshold beyond which anti-Israel rhetoric became anti-Semitism, in this view, was anti-Zionism, namely, a basic challenge to the legitimacy of the State of Israel—and therefore the peoplehood of the Jews.

On February 27, in response to the David Duke and Pat Buchanan phenomena, the American Jewish Congress and the Wilstein Institute of Los Angeles convened a scholarly consultation on "The Danger of Increasing Appeals to Anti-Semitism and Racism in Public Life." In Brussels, July 6–8, the World Jewish Congress convened "My Brother's Keeper: Anti-Semitism and Prejudice in a Changing World: The Common Challenge." And the Anti-Defamation League, in cooperation with the Nathan Perlmutter Institute for Jewish Advocacy and Brandeis University's Cohen Center for Modern Jewish Studies, held the Salzburg Conference on Anti-Semitism in Boston on November 6. Internationally, UNESCO, an agency itself long considered a hotbed of anti-Israel polemics, convened a conference in June, "Educating for Tolerance: The Case of Resurgent Anti-Semitism." The UNESCO conference was sponsored jointly with the Simon Wiesenthal Center.

Jewish groups responded angrily to anti-Semitic and racist remarks made in November by Marge Schott, owner of the Cincinnati Reds major-league baseball team. Schott reportedly used the terms "money-grubbing Jews" and "nigger," according to a dismissed employee who had filed suit against the Reds for discriminatory front-office practices. After a meeting between Schott and Jewish and black leaders in Cincinnati on November 20, Dr. Michael Rapp, executive director of the Cincinnati Jewish Community Relations Council, said: "Notwithstanding the odiousness of her comments, the hatefulness of her sentiments, Schott was willing to recognize that there were problems in her past expressions, and to work with us in seeking remedies."

And last, two prominent figures from different worlds—rock star Sinead O'Connor and chess genius Bobby Fischer—made the news with public expressions of bigotry. O'Connor, wearing a Star of David, tore up a photograph of Pope John Paul II during an October 3 national television appearance; Fischer spewed anti-Semitic verbiage at a September press conference in Yugoslavia.

Protestant-Jewish Relations

The relationship of American Protestants and American Jews continued to reflect the bi-axial pattern of the past decade and more: harsh criticism of Israel sometimes emerging from national Protestant bodies; at the same time, evidence of close cooperation in communities around the country.

MAINLINE DENOMINATIONS

A program for Protestant-Jewish relations was outlined in an address delivered by the Reverend Joan Brown Campbell, general secretary of the National Council of Churches (NCC), the umbrella body for Protestant and Orthodox groups in the United States, to the Executive Committee of the National Jewish Community Relations Advisory Council (NJCRAC) on September 21. Campbell called for strengthening relations nationally between Protestant and Jewish groups, citing specific areas—particularly social and economic justice—in which communal interests coincide; and, in a candid call, a joint effort aimed at addressing "the deep concern we have for the growing Christian 'right' and the potential that we see for intolerance."

Campbell's call notwithstanding, Jewish groups were troubled throughout the year by the NCC's role in developing statements on loan guarantees, the peace process, and other issues related to the Middle East. An "Open Statement of Religious Leaders to President George Bush," brokered and passed by the NCC on January 28, called upon the president to "oppose housing loan guarantees to Israel until it halts construction and expansion of settlements in the West Bank, Gaza, and East Jerusalem." Jewish groups had long opposed the linking of humanitarian issues, such as loan guarantees for housing and jobs for immigrants, with the political issue of Israeli settlements. In addition, said (Reform) Union of American Hebrew Congregations officials Rabbis Alexander M. Schindler and Gary Bretton-Granatoor, "no less saddening is the manner in which this 'open letter' came to the fore, without any consultation with the Jewish community," disregarding an established consultative process between the NCC and Jewish organizations. The NCC statement was signed by the Presbyterian Church (U.S.A.), the Lutheran Council, the Episcopal Church, the Mennonites, the American Baptist Church, the United Church of Christ, the Reformed Church of America, and the Unitarian-Universalist Association.

National denominational bodies debated and passed resolutions this year that seemed to betray growing impatience with Israel over lack of movement in the peace process. At the quadrennial meeting of the United Methodist Church, held in Louisville, May 5–15, a draft resolution calling upon the U.S. government "to cease all loan guarantees or aid of any kind that can assist the State of Israel in its illegal building of settlements and its continuing occupation of Palestinian, Syrian, and Lebanese territories" failed to pass the full convention, purely for parliamentary reasons, but did receive strong support.

The General Assembly of the Presbyterian Church (U.S.A.), the main denominational body for Presbyterians in America, in June adopted a statement commending the president and the Congress "for refusing loan guarantees for Israel until the building of settlements on the occupied territories has come to a halt," and calling on the U.S. government to press for an end to the Israeli occupation of southern Lebanon and the West Bank and Gaza. The 1992 Presbyterian statement contrasted with the less harsh and more balanced statement regarding the Arab-Israeli conflict adopted by the body in 1991.

The World Council of Churches, meeting in Geneva in late August, adopted a statement, "Christian-Jewish Dialogue Beyond Canberra 91," which received mixed reviews by Jewish groups. Observers noted positive language in the statement: strong condemnation of "anti-Semitism in all its forms," encouragement of churches to oppose the "emerging anti-Semitism" of Eastern Europe, and a rejection of supersessionism in its affirmation that the Jewish covenant with God "continues" as the "vocation of the Jewish people." At the same time, questions were raised by Jewish groups about statements viewed as critical of Israel.

COALITION ACTIVITIES

A number of interfaith program initiatives in public-policy areas emerged during 1992. The Common Ground for the Common Good, developed from a Ford Foundation study, was announced on October 24. In this program, the National Council of Churches (NCC), the National Conference of Catholic Bishops (NCCB), the Synagogue Council of America (an umbrella of the rabbinic and congregational bodies of Orthodox, Conservative, and Reform movements in the United States), together with the National Jewish Community Relations Advisory Council, undertook to develop public-policy approaches on poverty and social welfare in the United States. The National Religious Partnership for the Environment was organized as a vehicle for education and action on environmental concerns. The partnership, organized in October, consists of the NCC, the U.S. Catholic Conference, the Evangelical Environmental Network, and the Coalition on the Environment and Jewish Life, a consortium of the Religious Action Center of Reform Judaism, NJCRAC, and the (Conservative) Jewish Theological Seminary. In the Interreligious Health Care Access Program, launched in January, the NCC and the Religious Action Center (the public-affairs arm of Reform Judaism) pledged cooperative efforts of Jews and Christians in pressing for equal access to health care. The coalition did not formally endorse any health-care proposal.

Catholic-Jewish Relations

The election in November of Archbishop William H. Keeler of Baltimore, the titular Primate of the United States, to a three-year term as president of the National Conference of Catholic Bishops and of that body's public-affairs arm, the U.S.

Catholic Conference, symbolized the growing cordiality between American Catholics and Jews. Keeler, who had headed Catholic-Jewish relations for the conference's committee on ecumenical and interreligious affairs, was widely regarded as a friend of the Jewish community, and his election to the prestigious presidential post was viewed as validation of the American Jewish community's importance to the Catholic Church. There was also movement this year on the establishment of full diplomatic relations between the Vatican and the State of Israel, on resolving the Auschwitz convent issue, and in other areas.

VATICAN RECOGNITION OF ISRAEL

Some progress was made toward normalizing relations between the Holy See (the formal state and diplomatic entity of the Roman Catholic Church) and the State of Israel, long an issue between American Catholics and Jews. Of significance was the visit of New York's John Cardinal O'Connor to Lebanon, Egypt, Jordan, and Israel from December 27, 1991, to January 7 (in Israel January 5–7), 1992. At a briefing in New York to Jewish groups on his return, O'Connor asserted, "There is a definite change in the Vatican's orientation toward Israel." Specifically and significantly, with respect to normalization of Vatican-Israel relations, O'Connor was encouraging. "The issue [for the Vatican] is no longer the status of Jerusalem," he reported, "but guarantees of free access to Jerusalem's holy sites to Christians, Muslims, and Jews; and the protection of Christian communities in the Middle East." The Vatican had earlier, in 1987, asserted that there was no "theological bar" to full normalization of diplomatic relations, and had throughout insisted that it gave de facto "recognition" to the State of Israel.

A key step in the normalization process was the establishment, in July, of a "permanent bilateral working commission" that would look into "issues dealing with the situation of the Church and its institutions," including the status of Church property; the status of Jerusalem; access to holy places; and other matters. No timetable for normalization of relations was offered, but Dr. Eugene Fisher, secretary for Catholic-Jewish relations of the National Conference of Catholic Bishops, speculated that it would happen "much sooner rather than much later." Jewish groups welcomed the establishment of the permanent working commission.

OTHER MATTERS

The ongoing question of the Carmelite convent at the Auschwitz/Birkenau death-camp site in Poland remained without closure in 1992. Construction of a Carmelite convent on the site of a new "Center for Information, Meetings, Dialogue, Education, and Prayer" in the town of Oswiecim, near the death-camp site, progressed but at year's end was not completed, and the nuns remained in their old convent.

A July mission, constituting the highest-level joint delegation of American Catholics and Jews to visit Poland, addressed a number of issues in Polish-Jewish relations, including the convent matter, anti-Semitism in Poland, the maintenance of Jewish cemeteries, and educational programs on Jews and Judaism in Polish seminaries. Participants included Archbishop William Keeler and other NCCB representatives; Archbishop Henryk Muszynski, emerging as a leader in Poland's church hierarchy; representatives of the Polish Jewish community; and representatives of American Jewish national organizations, including the Anti-Defamation League, the American Jewish Committee, and the National Jewish Community Relations Advisory Council.

Official Catholic documents were reviewed by Jewish groups in 1992 in terms of their ramifications for Jews. Chief among these was the new Catholic *Catechism for the Universal Church*, seven years in preparation, signed by Pope John Paul II in October and released (in French) in November. (See AJYB 1992, pp. 192–93, for details on the draft catechism considered in 1990.) Interreligious analysts noted, on the positive side, the repeated emphasis on Christianity's roots in Judaism and, incorporating the language of Vatican II, rejection of the charge of deicide, but felt that the catechism language did not go far enough. According to Rabbi Leon Klenicki of the Anti-Defamation League, "It would have been appropriate to include a condemnation of anti-Semitism at that point [i.e., the repudiation of deicide]. It would help educators understand that the anti-Judaism of the New Testament opens the door to anti-Semitism, as it has through the centuries."

Jewish analysts were divided in their views on the catechism's continued use of supersessionism. While some noted that there was no reference in the catechism to Judaism after the coming of Jesus, others, including Rabbi A. James Rudin, the American Jewish Committee's director of interreligious affairs, reminded observers, "This is a Christian document, so of course it states that the ultimate religious truth is Jesus and Christianity." Summing up the views of most analysts, Rudin concluded that the catechism "consolidates, rather than retreats from, Vatican II—it gives final authority to what we've worked on for thirty years—but doesn't break any new ground in Christian-Jewish relations."

Jewish groups welcomed Pope John Paul II's denunciation of anti-Semitism on several occasions. On October 28, the 27th anniversary of the Vatican II document "Nostra Aetate," the pope characterized current expressions of anti-Semitism in Western Europe as "profanations which offend the memory of victims of the Holocaust." The pope reiterated his condemnation in a meeting with World Jewish Congress officials on November 12; and in meetings with German bishops the same month, called upon them to combat anti-Semitism in their country.

The National Conference of Catholic Bishops, possibly responding to the emergence of the Labor government in Israel and expectations of movement in the peace process, did not debate issues related to Israel and the Middle East at its annual meeting in November and did not adopt a stance critical of Israel, as many observers had expected.

Finally, Rabbi Marc H. Tanenbaum, an internationally recognized pioneer in Christian-Jewish relations, died on July 3. Tanenbaum had served as national interreligious director for the American Jewish Committee and took a leadership role in Vatican-Jewish affairs. (See "Obituaries," elsewhere in this volume.)

Church-State Separation Issues

"ESTABLISHMENT-CLAUSE" MATTERS

The constitutionality of prayer at public-school graduations was tested in 1992 by the U.S. Supreme Court in a Rhode Island case, *Lee v. Weisman*. In a 5–4 decision handed down on June 24, the court affirmed federal district and appeals court rulings that delivery of an invocation and benediction by clergy at a junior high-school graduation violated the "establishment clause" of the First Amendment and was therefore illegal. The case originated when a Jewish couple in Providence, the Weismans, protested against prayers offered at the public school graduation ceremonies, several years apart, of their two daughters.

In bringing the case, the Justice Department had seen it as an opportunity for the justices to scrap or at least revise the so-called *Lemon* test of constitutionality. But Justice Anthony M. Kennedy, writing for the majority in *Lee v. Weisman*, said that there was no need to revisit the test articulated in the *Lemon v. Kurtzman* precedent.[4] "The controlling precedents as they relate to prayer and religious exercise in public schools compel the holding here that the policy . . . is an unconstitutional one," asserted Kennedy. He rejected the proposition that inclusion of government-sponsored prayer in a graduation ceremony is a legitimate accommodation of religion, stating that an agency of the government may not compel anyone to participate in a religion or in a religious exercise, and that even nonsectarian invocations and benedictions violate the First Amendment.

For the most part, Jewish public-affairs organizations hailed the court's decision in *Lee v. Weisman*. "Secular" Jewish groups—the American Jewish Committee, the American Jewish Congress, the Anti-Defamation League, the National Jewish Community Relations Advisory Council—together with numerous Christian, educational, and civil-liberties groups, had filed *amicus* briefs in support of the Weismans and hailed the ruling. The congregational arm of the Reform movement, the Union of American Hebrew Congregations, supported the Weismans' position as well. Orthodox organizations, however, which have to a greater or lesser degree opposed bans on religious activity in the public schools, expressed disappointment with the ruling. They argued that the *Lemon* test had been used by those intolerant

---

[4]As articulated in *Lemon v. Kurtzman* (1971), in order for a law or other governmental activity to be constitutional, it must have a secular purpose, its effect must not advance religion, and it must not foster or result in excessive government entanglement. Violation of any one of the three *Lemon* prongs causes the law or activity to be unconstitutional. While Jewish groups would not like to see *Lemon* replaced, an earlier, simpler test has been preferred: government may not favor one religion over another, or religion over nonreligion.

of religion per se and had welcomed Supreme Court review of the case as an opportunity to reevaluate the test itself.

A number of graduation-prayer cases continued to work their way through the federal courts. Jewish groups were exercised over the November decision by the U.S. Fifth Circuit Court of Appeals to affirm a federal district court ruling in *Jones v. Clear Creek Independent School District*, that a school-district "resolution" permitting a nondenominational prayer offered by a student at the student body's initiative was constitutional. The circuit court's reasoning in *Clear Creek*—a strikingly different conclusion from that in *Lee v. Weisman*—apparently rested on the fact that the school itself was neither supporting prayer nor dictating its content (as in *Lee v. Weisman*) but was merely accommodating the wishes—and free speech—of its students. A petition for U.S. Supreme Court review was pending in *Clear Creek*.

The graduation-prayer issue was viewed with concern by Jewish organizations, which took note of the increasingly widespread practice of such events. "This has become the June version of the 'December Dilemma,' " said ADL legal director Steven Freeman, referring to the problems associated with Christmas-holiday observances in the schools.

Three cases accepted in 1992 for review by the U.S. Supreme Court deal with other aspects of the relationship between religion and government. In *Zobrest v. Catalina Foothills School District*, the question is whether mandated government assistance to a deaf student, under the Individuals with Disabilities Education Act, may be provided constitutionally on the premises of a religiously sponsored school, or only in a public or secular private school. Lower courts had declared the use of the funds in religious settings unconstitutional. Jewish groups were divided on *Zobrest*. The American Jewish Committee and the Anti-Defamation League joined as *amici* on the side of the school district; the American Jewish Congress entered on the side of the deaf student, Zobrest.

Lamb's Chapel v. Center Moriches Union Free School District addresses questions of conflict between free-speech, establishment-clause, and free-exercise clause protections. In *Lamb's Chapel*, an evangelical Christian church challenged a New York State school district's refusal to make a high-school auditorium available for a movie with a Christian theme. Lower courts had denied access to the religious group, holding that public schools are limited public forums not open to religious use. The stance of most Jewish groups permitted the fair-market rental of public-school facilities to any community group during evening and weekend hours. Nonetheless, there was no consensus among Jewish organizations on *Lamb's Chapel*. Only two organizations, the Anti-Defamation League and the Union of American Hebrew Congregations, elected to enter the case as "friends of the court" on the side of the school district. (For the third case, *Church of the Lukumi Babalu Aye v. Hialeah*, see below, " 'Free-Exercise' Matters.")

Although most of the cases denied for review by the Supreme Court in 1992 involved decisions that Jewish groups generally favored, two exceptions were noteworthy. The Supreme Court declined to review, to the disappointment of Jewish groups, *Cammack v. Waihee*, in which a federal appeals court in 1991 upheld the constitutionality of declaring Good Friday a Hawaii state holiday. And in *Murray v. Austin*, the Fifth Circuit Court of Appeals held that the inclusion of religious imagery in a city seal did not violate the establishment clause because, under the *Lemon* test, it did not have the primary effect of advancing religion.

The 1992 holiday season saw more reports than usual of Christmas- and Hanukkah-related activity—and questionable holiday observances in the schools. In many cases these crossed the limits articulated by the Eighth Circuit Court of Appeals in *Florey v. Sioux Falls School District* (1980), which permit religious material, such as music, for educational purposes, only for the "advancement of the students' knowledge of society's cultural and religious heritage." Complicating the matter was a letter sent on November 17 to all 14,712 school superintendents in the country by the American Center for Law and Justice, written by Jay Alan Sekulow, lawyer for the Christian fundamentalist organization. In his letter, Sekulow asserted that "certain national groups have been pressuring local school districts to censor any religious observances of Christmas," misrepresenting the position of Jewish and other civil-liberties groups and the *Florey* rules as well. Jewish groups engaged school boards around the country on this issue.

The issue of educational "choice"—the term of art for public aid in the form of vouchers to parochial schools—made no headway this year, either in Congress or in state legislatures. Most Jewish groups continued to oppose federal support for private or parochial school attendance.

In the area of kosher food regulation by government, the New Jersey supreme court overturned a lower court ruling that had found New Jersey's Consumer Fraud Act and related regulations governing the sale of kosher food to be constitutional. In its July 22 ruling on *Ran-Dav's Country Kosher, Inc. v. State of New Jersey*, the supreme court, by a 4–3 margin, decreed that, because the New Jersey statute and regulations defined *kashrut* in accordance with a specific religious subgroup (in this case, Orthodox Judaism), and set forth a religious procedure to determine the standards of *kashrut*, the regulation violated the establishment clause. The State of New Jersey appealed *Ran-Dav* to the U.S. Supreme Court. Although Jewish groups have supported "kosher laws" as legitimate protection of consumers against fraud, they were divided on support of the New Jersey statute, because of the "Orthodox" stipulation. With respect to federal legislation on consumer fraud, one bill, spearheaded by Agudath Israel of America, that would require the public disclosure of certification information, made no headway in Congress this year.

There was some action on the Chabad/Lubavitch-menorah front in 1992, as the Lubavitch organization continued to erect Hanukkah menorahs in a number of communities around the country, generally (although not always) in proximity to Christmas trees or other holiday artifacts, in order to satisfy the technical requirements laid down in *Lynch v. Donnelly* (1983) and *ACLU v. County of Allegheny and City of Pittsburgh* (1989). New developments occurred in a case that dated back to the 1990 holiday season, *American Jewish Congress v. City of Beverly Hills* (California). In that year, the city approved a permit for Chabad to erect a 28-foot menorah on public property directly across from city government buildings. The American Jewish Congress filed a lawsuit challenging the constitutionality of the display and of the city's policy.

A federal district court subsequently held that a menorah standing alone would not pass constitutional muster, but that it would be acceptable if a Christmas tree were standing next to it, and if no religious ceremony were held. When Chabad in 1991 did not fully comply with these stipulations, the case was scheduled for trial. A settlement was reached in which the menorah would be displayed if Chabad met a number of conditions, including a disclaimer and a provision that the menorah be moved from the park where city hall was a background, but this settlement fell through at the eleventh hour in December 1991. In December 1992, without any hearing, a U.S. District Court granted summary judgment in favor of the city, permitting Chabad to display its menorah, provided that it was placed in proximity to a Christmas tree and that a disclaimer sign was erected.

In Cincinnati, after a federal judge ruled in December that the city could not prevent Chabad from erecting its menorah on downtown Fountain Square, several Klan groups indicated their intention to erect a cross in the plaza. One group applied for and won a permit, using the same religious-freedom argument employed by Chabad. The ten-foot-high wooden cross stood for less than five hours on December 21 before an angry onlooker damaged it, prompting the police to remove it as a safety hazard. Jewish groups joined in demonstrations of religious leaders protesting the Klan cross.

Most Jewish groups viewed placement of religious symbols—including placement together with other religious symbols or secular artifacts—as a violation of the establishment clause. The Union of Orthodox Jewish Congregations of America (UOJCA), a centrist Orthodox synagogue group, said that, while it agreed with the consensus position on religious symbols, it would not go to court against Chabad.

On the general question of religious symbols in public parks, considered to be "open forums" and therefore arguably different from government buildings such as city halls, a number of other cases were working their way through federal courts in 1992. In May, the full U.S. Seventh Circuit Court of Appeals, rehearing the case of *Doe v. Small*, reversed its earlier decision that prohibited a display in a public park in Ottawa, Illinois, of 16 large paintings depicting the life of Jesus. The Seventh Circuit now ruled that its previous injunction against the display was overbroad because it amounted to a total ban on religious speech in a "quintessential public forum . . . far removed from the seat of government." A number of Jewish groups had entered the case as *amici* and were disappointed in the appeals court's ruling.

In July the New York State Court of Appeals upheld a lower court's invalidation of a 1989 state statute that had created a special school district in the Hassidic village of Kiryas Joel. The district was intended to provide remedial education only—no religious study—for handicapped children of the Satmar Hassidic group who live in the cohesive community. The decision in *Grumet v. Board of Education of the*

Kiryas Joel Village School District, expected to be appealed to the U.S. Supreme Court, was supported by Jewish defense agencies and opposed by Orthodox religious groups.

Finally, in July New York State passed its second *"get"* law within a decade, going beyond the 1984 law barring the granting of a civil divorce if there was any "barrier to remarriage," which was understood to include refusal of a spouse to give a Jewish divorce. The new legislation amending the state's Domestic Relations Law requires judges to take into account a party's refusal to give or accept a *get* when dividing up the assets of a marriage. Orthodox Jewish groups were divided on the legality and efficacy of *"Get* II." Agudath Israel of America opposed the measure, maintaining, among other things, that under Halakhah—Jewish law—the validity of a *get* given under duress is called into question. Other Orthodox Jewish groups supported the law.

"FREE-EXERCISE" MATTERS

Jewish groups viewed passage of the Religious Freedom Restoration Act (RFRA) as one of the highest legislative priorities of the 102nd Congress. It had been drafted by a broad coalition of groups in 1990 for the purpose of legislatively reversing the U.S. Supreme Court decision in *Employment Division of Oregon v. Smith*, the "peyote" case. That ruling effectively eviscerated the free-exercise clause of the First Amendment by declaring that the state was not required to prove "compelling state interest" in order to deprive a person of a religious right. (See AJYB 1992, pp. 201–02, and AJYB 1993, pp. 113–14.) Under the sponsorship of Rep. Stephen J. Solarz (D., N.Y.) and Senators Edward Kennedy (D., Mass.) and Orrin Hatch (R., Utah), progress was made during the second session of the 102nd Congress on moving RFRA through the legislative process, despite continued opposition and indeed intransigence on the part of the U.S. Catholic Conference, the public-affairs arm of the National Conference of Catholic Bishops. That body maintained that RFRA would be used to establish a religiously based right to abortion were *Roe v. Wade* overturned.

RFRA did not come up for a vote by the time the 102nd Congress adjourned, largely because of the reluctance of Sen. Joseph Biden (D., Del.)—who had been slated as an original sponsor, but dropped out—to move the measure through his Senate Judiciary Committee. It was also suggested that the White House, never enthusiastic about RFRA, urged Sen. Alan Simpson (R., Wyo.) to put a hold on the bill in the Judiciary Committee. The wall-to-wall pro-RFRA coalition, "The Coalition for the Free Exercise of Religion," was able to recruit 195 cosponsors in the House and 27 in the Senate, but these were insufficient to move the legislation. RFRA received a boost for the forthcoming 103rd Congress when, during his campaign, Democratic candidate Bill Clinton articulated support for the measure.

In a related development, the Maryland General Assembly defeated, by a 66–63 vote, "Religious Freedom Restoration" legislation in March. Although the Maryland legislation enjoyed broad support, with the Baltimore Jewish Council active in coalition efforts on behalf of the bill, the issue of reproductive choice was instrumental in its defeat. RFRA-type bills were also in play during 1992 in Rhode Island and New Mexico.

According to a publication of the authoritative Congressional Research Service, *The Religious Freedom Restoration Act: A Legal Analysis*, released in April, no fewer than 38 cases in federal and state courts had either been decided using the new *Smith* standard or had in some way been influenced by *Smith*.

In March the Supreme Court accepted for review *Church of the Lukumi Babalu Aye v. Hialeah*, addressing questions of laws specifically targeting a religious group. In 1991 the Eleventh Circuit Court of Appeals affirmed a federal district court decision upholding a series of Hialeah, Florida, ordinances banning animal sacrifice. The ordinance directly targeted religious practices of the Santeria Church (a Caribbean offshoot of Roman Catholicism), including ritual animal sacrifices. Jewish groups joined in a coalition *amicus* brief in the Santeria case, arguing that, unlike the Oregon "peyote" law upheld by *Employment Division of Oregon v. Smith*, the ban was not "religiously neutral" but targeted a specific religion or religious practice.

Two cases involving the Boy Scouts were watched closely by Jewish groups, because of their implications for the ability of Jewish organizations to limit membership or services to Jews and not be charged with discrimination. In *Welsh v. Boy Scouts of America*, a Cub Scout den refused to admit Elliott Welsh because he would not take the scout oath; Elliott's parents were agnostics and he refused to use the word "God." A U.S. district court in Illinois ruled in March that the Boy Scouts are not a public "place of public accommodation or entertainment," and are therefore outside the Title II provision of the Civil Rights Act of 1964, which prohibits discrimination based on race, religion, or national origin in public settings. Elliott Welsh was therefore not protected by Title II.

The second case involved the Randall twins, who were dismissed from the Cub Scouts in Orange County, California, because they refused, as atheists, to recite the scout oath. In *Randall v. Boy Scouts of America*, a California state court in May held that the Boy Scouts of America is a business under the state law, and therefore could not exclude individuals because of their religious beliefs. Marc D. Stern, co-legal director of the American Jewish Congress, articulated the dilemma for Jewish groups: "These are situations in which our deeply held principles on religious liberty and opposition to discrimination need to be tested against the needs of our communal agencies." Appeals were expected in both cases.

OTHER MATTERS

Garrison (originally *Teagarden*) *v. Commissioner of Internal Revenue* reached the U.S. Tax Court in 1992. *Garrison*, a case that, according to analysts of tax issues, could affect tax deductibility of payments to synagogues for High Holiday seats and to churches for pew rentals, was one of a number of cases being litigated by the Church of Scientology. The Scientologists' claims in *Garrison* were an outcome of the U.S. Supreme Court decision in *Hernandez v. C.I.R.* (1989), in which the court ruled that payments for "auditing," a central Scientology practice, were not a charitable contribution for a religious sacrament but a quid-pro-quo exchange for a service and therefore not deductible under the tax code. The Scientologists contended that numerous religious organizations, including Jewish groups, require quid-pro-quo payments in exchange for religious services. Jewish groups presented testimony arguing that payments to synagogues are made without specific exchange or tangible benefit.

On September 13–14, leading experts on church-state law and public advocacy gathered at the American Jewish Committee for a national consultation, "Religious Liberty in the 1990s," to consider the current status of church-state law.

Civil Rights

Several cases challenging the creation of a new village, Airmont, by the town of Ramapo, New York, were all still pending this year. The new village's zoning regulations, which forbade holding worship services in private residential dwellings, were clearly intended to discourage Orthodox Jews from living in the community. *United States v. Village of Airmont*, filed December 17, 1991, alleged violation of the Orthodox residents' rights under the Federal Fair Housing Act (FFHA), claiming that Airmont was formed for the express purpose of excluding Orthodox Jews from its boundaries. It marked the first time the Justice Department had brought action under the FFHA alleging religious discrimination and the first time the Justice Department had moved specifically to protect the rights of Orthodox Jews.

Two cases in an ongoing legal battle involving Jews for Jesus, the proselytizing messianic "Hebrew-Christian" group, and the Jewish Community Relations Council of New York (JCRC) made their way through the courts. In one case, *Jews for Jesus v. Jewish Community Relations Council of New York*, the New York State Court of Appeals, the state's highest court, ruled that the JCRC did not violate state antidiscrimination laws when it asked rabbis to urge their Christian colleagues not to rent out church space to Jews for Jesus for an interfaith Passover seder. The case had its origins in a 1985 JCRC memo, which also asked Long Island rabbis to alert local caterers to the fact that Jews for Jesus and the Chosen People Ministries (a proselytizing organization formerly known as the American Board of Missions to the Jews) might try to rent space. The Court of Appeals decision ruled that JCRC did not deny Jews for Jesus access to a place of public accommodation.

The New York JCRC did not fare as well in the other case, argued in federal courts, *Jews for Jesus v. Jewish Community Relations Council of New York*, in which the U.S. Second Circuit Court of Appeals awarded Jews for Jesus the right to go to trial in an antidiscrimination and civil-rights suit against the New York JCRC. The case stemmed from an incident in 1987, when Jews for Jesus was scheduled to hold its annual "East Coast Ingathering" at the now defunct *glatt* kosher Stevens-ville Hotel in the Catskill Mountains. JCRC director Michael Miller reportedly advised the hotel that Jewish groups would not patronize the establishment if it hosted Jews for Jesus; the hotel canceled the Jews for Jesus contract. Jews for Jesus sued the JCRC in 1988, alleging violation of its civil rights. The suit was dismissed by a district court in 1991 on the grounds that the JCRC was exercising its First Amendment rights. On July 9, Jews for Jesus won the appellate court ruling.

VOTING RIGHTS ACT AND REDISTRICTING

At least one Jewish community, that of Greater Miami, was implicated in a federal court case involving reapportionment under the Voting Rights Act of 1965, and redistricting was a matter of concern to Jewish communities around the country during the 1992 election season. Interpretations by the U.S. Supreme Court of the 1982 amendments to the Voting Rights Act of 1965—which eliminated the require-ment that discrimination be proved before remedies are applied—enable legislatures and courts to redistrict, or create entire new legislative districts, so that minority-group members are more likely to be elected. In some such situations, other groups, not "protected" under the federal statute, have assertedly been deprived of represen-tation as a consequence.

One of the first cases headed toward U.S. Supreme Court review in this highly sensitive area directly involves the Jewish community of Dade County (Miami), Florida. *Wetherell v. de Grandy* tests the validity of a redistricting plan for the state legislative seats from Dade County developed by a federal district court in Florida, which created Hispanic districts at the expense of other, including Jewish, commu-nities. The district court's order was stayed by the U.S. Supreme Court, which seemed likely to accept the case for review in 1993.

Jewish groups had mostly supported the Voting Rights Act and many of them the 1982 amendments as well. An exception was the American Jewish Congress, which opposed the amendments and, joined by the Greater Miami Jewish Federa-tion, filed an *amicus* brief in support of Supreme Court review of *de Grandy*. Most other Jewish organizations had not adopted positions on reapportionment under the Voting Rights Act and did not enter the case in its early stages.

One Jewish member of Congress, nine-term Democratic representative Stephen J. Solarz, was a victim of interpretation of the Voting Rights Act by the New York State Legislature when it redrew the 12th congressional district based on the 1990 census. The district, originally heavily Jewish but now newly shaped as a Hispanic district—snaking through Manhattan, Brooklyn, and Queens, lurching from neigh-borhood to neighborhood to take in a Hispanic block or two—was sought by five Democratic rivals, all Hispanic. (The district is in fact approximately 55 percent Hispanic.) On primary day, September 15, Solarz lost to Nydia M. Velasquez, the Commonwealth of Puerto Rico's former representative in New York.

To some observers, the Solarz defeat suggested that the impact of such redistricting plans would be the continued polarization of politics along racial lines. Duke University law professor William Van Alstyne said, "Inadvertently, we are driving back toward segregation." Jewish groups that had long opposed quota systems of any kind were watching Voting Rights Act developments closely but were generally muted in their responses. They clearly did not want redistricting to turn into a black-Jewish or other minority-group issue, with potential for further damage to relations between Jews and those groups.

OTHER MATTERS

The proposed revival, announced in August, of a New York State mandatory "set-aside" plan for state contracts for selected minority groups was cause for expressions of dismay on the part of the American Jewish Committee and the Anti-Defamation League. The state had suspended the plan in 1989, following a U.S. Supreme Court decision that contractual rights of white contractors were violated under such programs. The Court had said, however, that local governments could revive such programs if they gathered sufficient evidence of past discrimination; governments across the land—including New York State—spent the past three years doing just that. American Jewish Committee governmental affairs director Richard Foltin explained the Jewish groups' opposition: "There is an unquestionable history of discrimination in the city, state, and country, so it is necessary at times to enable these groups to have a fair chance. But the programs can only go so far before they become quotas where merit is not an issue." Jewish organizations were monitoring similar situations around the country.

Jewish organizations were divided over the validity of "race-based" college and university scholarships. The current debate focused on a set of guidelines issued in December 1991 by Education Secretary Lamar Alexander, in an effort to resolve confusion over how to increase campus diversity while adhering to the provisions of Title VI of the Voting Rights Act of 1964, which prohibits any discrimination on the basis of race. Alexander essentially split the difference between extreme positions: the Education Department would prohibit schools from using race as an exclusive factor for awards from their general pool of scholarship funds, but would permit private donors to earmark specified race-exclusive awards.

During the period of public commentary on the proposed rules, which ended in early March, Jewish groups took varying positions. The Union of American Hebrew Congregations, which generally viewed the use of scholarship funds to promote the racial diversity of a campus as appropriate, found the limitation to privately funded awards too narrow a restriction. The American Jewish Congress, which generally held that the allocation of funds on the basis of race constitutes discrimination, backed the guidelines as sufficiently limiting. The Anti-Defamation League argued that even privately funded aid should not be permitted if it is distributed on the basis of race. The American Jewish Committee's national affairs director, Gary Rubin, argued against this view: "Minority-based scholarships aren't that much different than scholarships set aside for athletes or to increase geographical diversity."

Finally, the Jewish community mourned the passing on September 3 of Joseph L. Rauh, Jr., 81, a leading figure in civil-rights causes and an individual with whom Jewish groups had worked closely, through the Leadership Conference on Civil Rights (a national coalition of some 200 civil-rights organizations), in laying the basis for much of the landmark civil-rights legislation passed during the 1960s. Hyman Bookbinder, former Washington representative of the American Jewish Committee, recalled that Rauh's leadership, through his 40-year service as general counsel of the Leadership Conference, "provided unbroken continuity of co-operation between the major elements of the Jewish and the black communities. Black leadership knew, from Joe Rauh's role, that the Jewish community was always present in every important civil-rights battle." (See "Obituaries" section, elsewhere in this volume.)

Nazi War Criminals

The Office of Special Investigations (OSI) of the U.S. Department of Justice continued its probes of individuals suspected of being Nazi war criminals and who were alleged to have lied about their past when they entered the United States or applied for citizenship. Through 1992, 43 Nazi war criminals had been stripped of their citizenship and 32 deported from the United States, with an additional 86 cases in which OSI had sought removal. Three individuals were extradited to other countries for trial. OSI investigations were in process on 419 suspected Nazi war criminals; 19 cases were active at the end of 1992.

In January the OSI decided to drop the case of Leonid Petkiewytsch, 68, because it felt it could not persuasively prove that Petkiewytsch had engaged in acts of persecution at the Kiel-Hassee labor camp during World War II. A federal appeals court in 1991 had blocked Petkiewytsch's deportation. A federal district court judge in Florida in August entered a deportation order against Antenas Mineikis, who had been denaturalized in January. The government had charged Mineikis with involvement in acts of persecution while serving as a member of a Lithuanian police battalion during the war. A federal district judge in New York on October 8 revoked the citizenship of Sergis Hutyrczyk, 68, who admitted that he had been an SS guard at the Koldyczewo concentration camp in Byelorussia during the war.

The OSI moved in a number of denaturalization cases during the year. In June it commenced proceedings in a U.S. district court in Philadelphia against Jonas Stelmokas, 75, charging that in 1941–42 Stelmokas had been a platoon commander in a Lithuanian *Schutzmannschaft* (protective detachment) battalion, responsible for the murder of Jews in Kovno. Within days of the Stelmokas proceedings, the OSI began denaturalization proceedings in a U.S. district court in Manhattan against Jakob Riemer, 73, for concealing his Nazi activities in order to gain entry to the United States in 1952 and obtain citizenship in 1959. Riemer reportedly served in the Trawniki SS unit and participated in the murder of Jews in ghettos in Warsaw and Czestochowa in Poland.

Denaturalization proceedings were begun as well against the following: George Lindert, 69, in a U.S. district court in Cleveland, for concealing his service as an SS guard when he entered the United States in 1955 and successfully applied for citizenship in 1962; Nikolaus Schiffer, 72, in in Philadelphia, for concealing his service in a Nazi "Death's Head" battalion when he applied for U.S. citizenship in 1956; Jozsef Szendi, 77, in Nashville, Tenn.; and Anton Bless, 67, in the District of Columbia. Szendi, the first Hungarian to be charged with being a Nazi war criminal, had reportedly been a member of the Royal Hungarian Gendarmerie and had personally transported deported Jewish civilians from Budapest to the German SS in Poland. Bless, who fled the country for Germany before his hearing, was charged with serving in an SS "Death's Head" battalion in Auschwitz. He concealed this service when he successfully applied for U.S. citizenship in 1964. In December the Justice Department revoked Bless's citizenship. A deportation trial in U.S. district court in Binghamton, New York, against Mikelis Kirstiens opened in December after having been twice postponed because of Kirstiens' ill health. Kirstiens was accused of falsifying his service in a Latvian militia unit that collaborated with the SS. Kacys Palciauskas, who was stripped of his U.S. citizenship for lying about his collaboration—as wartime mayor of Kovno, Lithuania—in the deaths of 10,000 Jews in the Kovno ghetto, died on January 7.

Notwithstanding these proceedings, Jewish groups were concerned that the investigations into the Justice Department handling of the Demjanjuk case (see below) could undermine the Nazi-hunting efforts of the OSI. The American Jewish Committee, the American Jewish Congress, and the Anti-Defamation League, in a joint statement issued on July 1, called for OSI investigations and prosecutions to continue and for the government "not to lose sight of OSI's vital mission." OSI director Neal M. Sher, who worked closely with Jewish groups on a number of investigations, expressed concern that the passage of time, as well as the Demjanjuk investigation, could cloud OSI's activities, even in "a year in which we filed more cases than in any other year."

Finally, the CIA announced in September that it would unlock its long-secret Nazi files.

DEMJANJUK CASE

New questions emerged during the year about the identity—and possible misidentification—of John Demjanjuk, the retired Cleveland auto worker who was tried and convicted in 1988 in Israel for the crimes of "Ivan the Terrible," the notorious Treblinka death-camp guard. (Demjanjuk was sentenced to death on April 18, 1988, but the sentence was delayed by Israel's High Court of Justice in 1989, pending investigation of new evidence that Demjanjuk was a victim of mistaken identity. In 1991, the Israeli court rejected a Demjanjuk application but said that it would hear "new evidence" in 1992. See AJYB 1993, pp. 117–18, for details.)

In March, Demjanjuk's Israeli lawyer, Yoram Sheftel, making use of newly released evidence from the former USSR, asked Israel's High Court of Justice to release Demjanjuk, based on written documents identifying a man named "Ivan Marchenko," whose photograph bore no similarity to that of Demjanjuk, as the operator of the Treblinka gas chambers. The new evidence included the testimony of *"Wachmanner,"* Soviet prisoners of war who worked as concentration-camp guards. (Israeli prosecutors had maintained that "Marchenko" or "Marczenko" was the maiden name of the defendant's mother, which Demjanjuk sometimes used as his own.) In an effort to verify the claim of mistaken identity, in late April the prosecution sent two representatives to Ukraine to examine KGB archives and files; the files, however, could not be found. On June 1, the High Court of Justice began its final hearing on Demjanjuk's appeal, concluding on June 9. At year's end the court had not rendered its decision, although Justice Aharon Barak, in surveying the new evidence, said that even if it were questionable, it could raise the reasonable doubt sought by the defense to invalidate the conviction. Barak's statement was interpreted by observers to indicate that the court did indeed entertain doubts about the identity of "Ivan."

This viewpoint gained credibility because of events in the United States. On June 5, the U.S. Sixth Circuit Court of Appeals in Cincinnati, on its own initiative, reopened Demjanjuk's extradition case. Justice Department officials asked the appeals court to let stand the extradition order for Demjanjuk, arguing that an Israeli court was the proper venue for deciding the case. Demjanjuk's lawyers countered, at a fact-finding hearing held August 11, by charging the Justice Department with withholding crucial evidence that would have prevented their client from being extradited to Israel in 1986.

On August 17, the appeals court took the unusual step of appointing a special master, U.S. District Court Judge Thomas A Wiseman, Jr., to investigate allegations of Justice Department misconduct, specifically, whether the Justice Department had "misled" the court during the 1986 extradition hearings by withholding evidence that Demjanjuk was not "Ivan the Terrible." In its order, the Sixth Circuit rejected the Justice Department's contention that the court did not have the jurisdiction to review the extradition case. On August 20, Demjanjuk's lawyers asked the appeals court to permit him to return to the United States if his conviction were overturned by Israel's High Court of Justice. On August 31, the appeals court ruled that such an order would be "premature" in the absence of any indication by Israel of any intention to release Demjanjuk. Hearings on the allegations of Justice Department misconduct began on October 15.

Other Holocaust-Related Matters

The Finance Ministry of the German government, in an agreement signed in November with the Conference on Jewish Material Claims Against Germany, pledged to pay millions of dollars to European Jews who had survived Nazi persecution but were never compensated or who received minimal compensation. Thousands of victims of Nazism who lived after the war in the former Soviet Union and Eastern Europe never received indemnification because they were unable to file applications by the 1965 deadline stipulated in the 1952 reparations agreement. Rabbi Israel Miller, chairman of the Claims Conference, said, "Now that their governments are free, [the survivors] are able to request what others have received in terms of compensation. . . . This historic agreement will make it possible for some of the most severely persecuted victims of Nazism—almost all of them elderly and needy—to live out their days in dignity." The accord was reached under article 2 of the implementation agreement to the German Unification Treaty reuniting East and West Germany, in which the German government agreed to negotiate with the Claims Conference for these payments.

Finally, cartoonist Art Spiegelman, himself a child of Holocaust survivors, was awarded a special Pulitzer Prize for his work. Two books, *Maus: My Father Bleeds History* and *Maus II: A Survivors Tale. And Here My Troubles Began*, chronicle the life of Vladek Spiegelman, an Auschwitz survivor, from his experiences in Poland to his immigration and new life in America. Much of Spiegelman's work was serialized in the Jewish English-language weekly, the *Forward*.

The Pollard and Manning Cases

There were several developments this year in the case of Jonathan J. Pollard. (See AJYB 1992 and 1993 for details on the case.) On March 20, Pollard lost his most recent appeal. By a 2–1 decision, the U.S. Court of Appeals for the D.C. Circuit refused to reverse a 1990 district court decision denying his motion to have his 1986 plea of guilty to espionage set aside. On October 13, the Supreme Court declined to review *U.S. v. Pollard*. In December Pollard filed a petition with the U.S. Department of Justice, asking President George Bush to commute his sentence to time served. Bush rejected the petition.

Throughout the year, activists on Pollard's behalf, including a number of Jewish groups—mostly rabbinic organizations on the local level—were increasingly active in his behalf. Most national Jewish groups, however, chose not to become involved. "For us the threshold issue is institutional anti-Semitism," said Jeffrey P. Sinensky, national civil-rights director of the Anti-Defamation League, articulating the view of many groups. "We have called for full and open exploration of all the factors in this case, but absent a concrete finding of anti-Semitism we cannot intervene in the case." Groups calling upon the organized Jewish community to intervene actively included the (Reform) Central Conference of American Rabbis and (Orthodox) Agudath Israel of America.

In a case that had some resemblance to that of Pollard, supporters of Robert and Rochelle Manning, indicted in January in Los Angeles on murder charges, protested their extradition from Israel to the United States. U.S. authorities sought to try the

Mannings for a 1980 bomb murder related to a business dispute; federal prosecutors believed that Robert Manning could be linked as well to the 1985 bomb murder of American-Arab Anti-Discrimination Committee official Alex Odeh. The Mannings' supporters argued that Jewish law forbade turning over Jews to non-Jewish courts.

JEROME A. CHANES

The United States, Israel, and the Middle East

THE YEAR 1992 WAS THE FIRST in the decades-old Arab-Israeli conflict in which the parties were actively involved in negotiations for peace. It was also a year in which American-Israeli relations took an upward turn following the victory of Israel's Labor party and its leader, Yitzhak Rabin, in June. This change was highlighted by the meeting of Prime Minister Rabin with President George Bush in Kennebunkport, Maine, culminating in a U.S. agreement to approve loan guarantees to Israel. The positive mood was affirmed with the election in November of Bill Clinton to succeed Bush as president of the United States, with Clinton advocating a strengthened relationship. The peace talks that began with high hopes on October 30, 1991, had thus far yielded no tangible results; however, the Israelis continued to assert optimistically that a breakthrough was likely in the months ahead on either the Palestinian or Syrian front.

The Peace Process

As the year began, Arab and Israeli negotiators were expected to begin a third round of talks in Washington, D.C., on January 7. While the earlier sessions in Madrid and Washington had yielded no results and had generally been characterized by rhetorical flourishes and procedural wrangles, the very fact that negotiations were accepted as an ongoing reality was itself astounding.

In the bilateral talks that broke off on December 18, 1991, Israel and Syria, and Israel and Lebanon had been engaged in discussions on substantive issues, though without having begun to bridge their differences. Israel and the joint Jordanian-Palestinian delegation, however, had not resolved their procedural dispute about how to organize their talks and had been meeting in a corridor in the State Department, rather than entering a formal negotiating room. Israel maintained that the Palestinian question had to be settled in conjunction with Jordan, while the Palestinians, in their pursuit of an independent state, argued for meeting with the Israelis alone. Israel offered a compromise proposal, which provided for an opening meeting of the heads of the delegations, then a full session of all three delegations, followed by separate meetings between Jordanians and Israelis and Palestinians and Israelis. At the latter meetings, two Palestinians would attend the Jordanian talks and two Jordanians would attend the Palestinian talks. As the new year began, the Palestinians were said to be considering the proposal.

As usual in the Middle East, nothing came easily. On January 2, five days before the talks were to resume, a Jewish settler was shot to death in the Gaza Strip. This was the fourth settler fatally attacked over a ten-week period. The following day,

Israel's defense minister, Moshe Arens, ordered the expulsion of 12 Palestinians whom Israel accused of terrorist involvement. Immediately, the Palestinian delegates to the talks announced that in protest they had suspended plans to go to Washington on January 7 and indicated that the PLO, which they called "the legitimate political leadership of the Palestinian people," would make the final decision as to whether the delay would be temporary or a full-blown boycott. Washington strongly condemned the Israeli action and "urged Israel, at the highest levels, to reconsider and rescind its decision."

Other participants in the negotiations—Syria, Jordan, Lebanon—announced on January 4 that they were postponing their departure to Washington. None, however, indicated any intention of scuttling the talks. Hanan Ashrawi, chief Palestinian spokeswoman, said it was her "surmise" that the Palestinians and others would end up going to Washington after the U.S. condemnation of Israel's decision. For its part, Israel rejected Washington's call to withdraw the deportation order, Arens saying that there was "no room for debate about this," that Israel was "committed to taking all steps that are likely to spare lives."

On January 6, in what was characterized as the harshest criticism of Israeli policies ever made at the United Nations Security Council by the United States, the Bush administration joined the other 14 members of the council in backing a resolution that "strongly condemn[ed]" the deportation order. Diplomats noted that previous resolutions used the word "deplore," a far milder rebuke than "strongly condemn." The U.S. vote was seen as an effort to bring Arab negotiators back to the table. American ambassador to the UN Thomas Pickering said that the United States voted for the UN resolution, which called on Israel to refrain from deporting any Palestinian citizen from the territories, after having "respectfully urged the government of Israel immediately and permanently to cease deportations." Observers also noted that Washington did not wait to be prodded by the Arabs to give its support to a resolution highly critical of Israel. This rapid American response, together with the strongest Security Council criticism of Israel approved by Washington, seemed to impress Arab representatives, who indicated the next day that they would resume peace talks shortly. In Damascus, a Syrian government spokesman was quoted as saying that, after consultation among the Arab parties, "it has been agreed that Arab delegates will go to Washington within the next two days." Not surprisingly, Israeli reaction to the U.S. vote was very different. Yossi Ben-Aharon, head of the Israeli team negotiating with Syria, said in an interview that "we can only express our bitterness, our anger and our regret that the United States continues to pay a price to bring the Arabs to the negotiating table at the expense of Israel and our terror victims."

As the resumption of talks was awaited, Israel protested to the United States not only because of its support for the resolution but also over the language in the preamble referring to the West Bank, Gaza, and Jerusalem as "occupied Palestinian territories." State Department spokeswoman Margaret D. Tutwiler explained that the phrase was "merely demographically and geographically descriptive, and not indicative of sovereignty." Observers noted, however, that the effort to explain the language raised questions, since the demographic and geographic character of the territories were as much a matter of dispute as their sovereignty, with both sides pointing to demographic and geographic evidence to bolster their competing claims for sovereignty.

THIRD-ROUND TALKS CONVENE

On January 13, talks resumed in Washington. Israel and the Palestinians found themselves in their first ever direct substantive negotiations. This happened after an agreement on a negotiating formula was reached to accommodate both Israel's demand that the Palestinians be considered part of a joint delegation with Jordan and the Palestinian preference for a separate status and agenda. First, all three delegations met for about half an hour. Then Israelis met separately with Palestinians, with two Jordanians also present; and the following day, Israelis met with a Jordanian delegation, with two Palestinians present. Zalman Shoval, Israel's ambassador to Washington, summed up the mood: "We have finally left the corridor of the State Department and entered the corridor to peace." Hanan Ashrawi, claiming victory for her side, said that the Israelis "have recognized the fact that only Palestinians can speak for themselves and negotiate on their behalf."

On January 14, all four tracks to the talks resumed: Israel-Syria, Israel-Jordan, Israel-Lebanon, Israel-Palestinians. A pattern that was to remain fairly consistent throughout the year was developing. The parties would spend the day talking. Then each would hold a press briefing in which it would give its impression of what took place, whether any progress had been made, and what the other side was doing wrong or right. By the end of the first day, the only reported bright spot was in the Israeli-Jordanian discussions. Jordanian spokesman Marwan Mouasher told the press that his delegation had offered Israel a "vision of peace when the issues between us are resolved," which he said "would certainly include full cooperation including diplomatic relations." This delineation of the meaning of peace was important to Israel. Indeed, Israel continued to look for such a statement from Syria before considering proposals about the Golan Heights but, as earlier, none was forthcoming. Syrian negotiator Mowaffak Allaf told reporters that this Israeli request concerned the fruits of the peace process, not the beginning.

Meanwhile, on the Palestinian front, Hanan Ashrawi called on Israel to immediately cease all settlement activities: "If they continue to steal the land literally from beneath our very feet, there is no reason to discuss any arrangements because the land will be gone." When asked whether the Palestinians would be prepared to suspend the *intifada*, as the United States had suggested, in return for a suspension of Israeli settlements, she replied: "I think that you should ask the Israelis what they should give. The *intifada* is a natural and normal reaction, a response to a very abnormal situation which is the situation of occupation." Israel continued to maintain that settlements were a matter for the final-status negotiations.

At the same time, it was reported that the Palestinians had presented, for the first time, their plan for self-rule in the territories in which, according to Ashrawi, all the powers that were being exercised by the Israeli military or civil administration would "be transferred to the Palestinian authority." Shoval said that this proposal was unacceptable because it was hard to distinguish it from a plan for Palestinian sovereignty and independence; in effect, it asked Israel to cede full control of the territories to the Palestinians.

On January 15, Secretary of State James Baker, ending his detachment from the talks, met separately with the heads of the delegations, urging conciliation. Israeli negotiators, upset with the original delay of the round because the Arabs absented themselves, eager to move the meetings to a Middle East venue, and seeing no progress, agreed to stay for only one day beyond the scheduled end of the talks on the 15th.

The next day saw the end of the four-day round of talks. Not only were there no agreements, there was a general increase in the nastiness between the parties, as reflected in the respective press conferences following the meetings, and uncertainty about when or where they would meet again. The Arabs continued to insist on Washington as the venue, with Israel looking for a spot closer to the Middle East.

Further complicating matters were developments on the Israeli political scene. On January 16, the right-wing Tehiya party, with three Knesset seats, withdrew its support for the government, to prevent it from offering a plan for Palestinian self-rule. A second right-wing party, Moledet, with two seats, followed suit the next day, depriving Prime Minister Yitzhak Shamir of his majority.

On January 27, the Shamir government survived a no-confidence vote, the first since the defection of the two right-wing parties. At the same time, negotiations continued between the Likud and Labor parties over a date for elections, initially set for November. Two days later, a tentative agreement was reached to move elections up to June 23, a compromise between Labor's desire for an even earlier election and Likud's desire to delay.

Meanwhile, the secretary of state sought to revive the bilateral talks. On February 12, the State Department indicated that it had proposed that the fourth round of talks be held in Washington beginning February 24. Within days, Israel, Syria, Lebanon, and Jordan announced their intention to attend. The Palestinians hesitated, claiming on February 18 that they might stay home in protest of Israel's arrest of two West Bank academics—Mohammed Khomani and Jamal al-Shoulaki—recently added to the Palestinian negotiating team. Hanan Ashrawi said the process was on the "brink of collapse." Israeli officials, however, accused the Palestinians of creating tension in the hope that Washington would pressure Israel to release the men, held by Israel as accused organizers of terrorist actions.

FOURTH ROUND OF TALKS

On February 24, the Palestinians appeared at the table, showing once again that none of the parties wanted to appear recalcitrant to their American hosts. The principal development of this round took place on the first day, when Israel presented the Palestinians with a paper outlining Israeli ideas for Palestinian self-rule. This proposal differed markedly from an earlier proposal submitted to the Israelis by the Palestinians. The latter was seen as seeking to create a foundation for a Palestinian state through a virtually total withdrawal of Israeli forces to be replaced by an elected Palestinian government, while the Israeli plan was described as giving Palestinians greater control over regulatory agencies and civil services while depriving them of any ability to lay the foundations for an independent state.

Two days later, the Palestinian negotiators called on Assistant Secretary of State for Near Eastern Affairs Edward Djerejian to say that the Israeli proposal did not treat them as "human beings" with national rights. The Israeli representatives, for their part, asserted publicly that the Palestinians were just interested in scoring propaganda points and trying to draw the Americans into the negotiations, instead of talking about the substance of the Israeli proposal. Despite the contentiousness, it was reported that Baker had no plans to intervene in the talks; rather he would encourage the bilateral talks in the hope that the parties would move away somewhat from opening positions and provide an opportunity for the United States to come forward with what Baker called "bridging proposals."

On March 3, the Palestinian delegation presented Israel with a more detailed version of its self-government proposal of January. Included were specifics for setting up an election process, complete with international observers; an interim self-government with legislative functions and power over "land, natural resources, water, subsoil, territorial sea, exclusive economic zone and air space"; an independent judiciary and police force; the cessation of all Israeli settlement activity in the territories; the return of seized property; and the release of political prisoners and detainees.

Following discussions about the proposal, Israeli negotiator Eli Rubinstein expressed his government's negative reaction because, he said, the proposal amounted to a framework for an independent Palestinian state. He added: "The notion of an independent Palestinian state, with all it connotes in terms of our security and national interests, is unacceptable to us." The gap was evident in the comments by the head of the Palestinian negotiating team, Haidar Abdel-Shafi: "The transition process must lead to a Palestinian state."

When the fourth round of talks ended on March 4, the parties not only remained as divided on substance as they had been when they began four months earlier, they were also unable to agree on where and when to meet again. Reacting to the lack of progress, Baker summoned each of the parties to his office to urge them to agree to at least one more round of negotiations before the Israeli national election on June 23. It was understood that once the elections took place, it would take time to put together a new Israeli government, which would soon be followed by a series of Jewish holidays and then the eve of the U.S. election, so that serious negotiations would not be possible until November or December.

As to the talks themselves, the gap between the parties was described as wide, both between Israel and the Arab states and between Israel and the Palestinians. Jordanian spokesman Mouasher summed it up: "I guess it's safe to say that expectation for some progress to take place in this round has been met with disappointment. Although we did explore a lot of ideas in this round on an informal basis, still I find myself repeating what I said at the conclusion of the last round— profound disagreements occur and exist over the principles that underlie the whole peace process." Israel and Syria continued exchanging interpretations of UN Resolution 242 and its disputed applicability to the Golan Heights.

The day after the talks ended, newspaper headlines indicated that Baker, in his meetings with the Palestinians, criticized them for "posturing" and urged them to focus more on negotiating specific proposals with Israel than on their broader goal of establishing an independent state. Officials at the State Department also chastised the Palestinians for presenting a plan on self-rule that it called unrealistic, a thinly disguised vehicle for independence aimed not at the Israelis but at their own Palestinian public. Abdel-Shafi, speaking to the Arab-American Institute, rejected the criticism, saying that it was "not true at all, and the record is straight." In this atmosphere, Djerejian told reporters that, despite the disappointment in the talks, there was hope in that "real substance" was on the table, "even if the parties have not found ways to explore the details to start narrowing the gaps between their positions."

On March 12, King Hussein of Jordan made his first trip to Washington since the Gulf War, meeting with Bush and Baker. Reports indicated that he told Secretary Baker that he and Yasir Arafat were considering declaring a confederation between Jordan and the West Bank as a way to give impetus to the talks and as a way to build pressure on Israel to return land. Some Palestinian leaders in the territories reacted negatively to the reports on the grounds that such an initiative could undercut their efforts to establish the Palestinians as an independent, sovereign party separate from Jordan. Saib Erakat, a member of the Palestinian delegation, called the proposal "premature" at a press conference in Jerusalem on March 16. Meanwhile, an unnamed senior PLO official in Tunis predicted that the PLO Central Council would not endorse the confederation proposal "because it will complicate the peace process." The proposal was seen as an effort to revive, during the Israeli election campaign, Labor's position on a "Jordanian option" for resolving the Palestinian dispute.

FIFTH ROUND OF TALKS

Pursuing its goal of having one more round of talks before the Israeli election, the State Department announced on March 30 that the United States had proposed convening a fifth round in Washington on April 27 but would insist on moving subsequent talks closer to the Middle East. This was a compromise between the Israeli desire to shift the talks to the Middle East and the Arabs' preferring to stay in Washington.

Three days later, State Department spokeswoman Tutwiler announced that the Arabs and Israelis had agreed to hold a fifth round in Washington beginning on the 27th and had agreed, in principle, to move future negotiations closer to the Middle East. She reported that all the parties had submitted informal lists of proposed alternative sites for the sixth round and that the lists showed some "commonality."

On April 7, amid the hubbub surrounding the peace process, Yasir Arafat regained center stage when a plane on which he was traveling disappeared from radar screens as it was crossing from the Sudan into southern Libya. The following day, nearly 12 hours after the private plane crash-landed in a sandstorm, the PLO leader was found alive by a Libyan patrol in the Libyan Desert. He was described as bruised but not seriously injured. The State Department insisted that it had played no role in the rescue. It was reported that a Palestinian official had sought American help through former president Jimmy Carter, who called the White House, but that the White House had not reached a decision by the time the plane was found. Unnamed Bush administration officials indicated that there was a feeling of ambivalence about Arafat's fate, leading to indecision as to whether to use American satellites to find Arafat's downed plane.

Hani al-Hassan, a PLO Executive Committee member, who only two weeks earlier had distributed a scathing critique demanding that the organization allow wider participation in its decision making, reflected the widespread Palestinian reaction to the survival of Arafat: "We all have something to say about the peace process and in favor of more consultations, but I and everyone else [are] relieved that he is fine." Another unnamed PLO official noted how feelings of desperation had quickly set in with the news of Arafat's disappearance, indicating that this accident "proved he was still the most important leader of the organization." On the Israeli side, Defense Minister Moshe Arens told reporters, before word arrived that Arafat was alive, that if it turned out Arafat was dead, "I don't think that anyone in Israel is going to mourn. He headed a murderous organization for years that bears the responsibility for the deaths of hundreds, if not thousands, of people."

The immediate effect of the accident was the PLO decision on April 9 to postpone a crucial meeting of its 94-member Central Committee, which had been expected to challenge the policies of Arafat. The decision apparently reflected the resurgence of support for the PLO chief after the crash and the reluctance of his most vociferous opponents to confront him at that time. For Bassam Abu Sharif, a senior political adviser to Arafat, the crash showed that only Arafat had the power to pick a new generation of leaders, "because his choices will be accepted by the Palestinians inside the Israeli-occupied territories and in the diaspora." In the days following the incident, however, demands for a wider PLO leadership surfaced within the organization. Nayef Hawatmeh, head of the hard-line Democratic Front for the Liberation of Palestine, a PLO component, said that the rise of a collective leadership had become "imperative," and that without it, the Palestinian situation "could not be sustained." Chief of the Palestinian delegation to the talks Dr. Haidar Abdel-Shafi said that what was needed was a closing of Palestinian ranks around a mechanism for a democratic process which, he pointed out, "would not be undermined by surprise events."

Meanwhile, in Washington, awaiting the resumption of talks, the State Department announced on April 21 that the parties had agreed to shift the talks to Rome after the fifth round. Tutwiler said that no date had been scheduled for the discussions in Rome, but that the United States believed it was important to "maintain the momentum of the peace process." It was expected, however, that the sixth round would be delayed for some time after the Israeli election.

Two days before the fifth round of talks resumed, Syrian president Hafez al-Assad and Palestinian spokeswoman Ashrawi continued the public war of words with Israel. Assad said in a speech in Damascus that only full Israeli withdrawal from occupied Arab land would bring peace to the Middle East. He added that "if the Madrid and Washington peace talks have proved sterile, this is due to Israeli rulers' intransigence and insistence on placing obstacles on the road of peace." And Ashrawi accused Israel of not really being interested in peace. With the propaganda war apparently winning out over real negotiations, the Bush administration was getting impatient. Djerejian commented that the parties had had "ample time to assess their positions," and now "they have got to get on with it."

As the talks commenced, Israel offered to work with the Palestinians on a mutually agreeable schedule for municipal elections in the territories. Underlying the proposal, it was reported, was the Israeli belief that it would take a long time to reach agreement on a plan for broad self-government powers for the Palestinians and, therefore, giving Palestinians a measure of local self-rule could fill the void, helping to relieve Palestinian frustrations and helping the Israeli public get used to the idea of Palestinians governing themselves. Ashrawi, however, the next day called the Israeli proposal "a public relations exercise" aimed at sidetracking the negotiations from the goal of Palestinian self-rule. She said that her delegation saw the Israeli idea as an attempt to delay indefinitely elections for a Palestinian self-governing authority, while allowing Shamir's government to appear forthcoming. Not wanting to appear intransigent, however, the Palestinians did not reject the proposal outright.

Benjamin Netanyahu, the Israeli delegation's spokesman, explained his country's approach: "In no way does our proposal nullify negotiations over elections, borders and other issues in the territories. We haven't posed [the municipal election idea] as a condition. I think such elections would facilitate the process, but we're not linking the two."

On April 30, the fifth round ended. No progress was reported, but Netanyahu emphasized the positive, while Ashrawi and Syria's chief negotiator, Mowaffak Allaf, were extremely critical of Israel and negative about the accomplishments of the talks. Observers tended to see these different public stances as partly connected to the coming Israeli elections, with Netanyahu trying to convince the Israeli electorate that it was accomplishing something, while the Palestinians and Syrians were seeking to undercut Shamir's appeal.

Interestingly, unnamed senior administration officials told the *Washington Post* that the just-concluded round was very positive in tone and content and showed "serious engagement" by all sides. This assessment paralleled that of Israeli officials but was sharply at odds with the views of the Arab participants. One American official stressed how important it was that "this time, the Palestinians put ideas on the table, as well as the Israelis." He emphasized that, among the Palestinian delegates, there was a new tendency to play down polemics and show greater flexibility, in contrast to the previous round when the United States criticized the Palestinians for "posturing" and "playing to the media."

NEW ISRAELI GOVERNMENT

As expected, the peace talks were put on hold by the upcoming Israeli elections. On June 23, the Labor party won a clear victory over Likud, creating the possibility of a center-left coalition committed to a different approach to the peace talks. Early returns gave Labor 45 seats to Likud's 32 (the final count gave Labor 44), with 12 seats going to the left-wing Meretz party, and 5 to Arab parties, adding up to 62 seats, a parliamentary majority and more than enough to block Likud from regrouping the religious-right alliance that it had led for the past two years. The next morning, Rabin pledged that the coalition he would try to create would "include all the positive forces in the nation that identify with our way: further peacemaking while safeguarding our security." Echoing his basic campaign theme, he said, "We will change the order of national priorities," referring to his commitment to shift government money from settlement-building to social and economic needs in Israel proper.

Meanwhile, in Washington, unnamed administration officials expressed satisfaction with the outcome, citing as reasons for believing that the Labor victory sharply increased the prospects for progress in the talks the better personal relations between Rabin and Bush, Rabin's commitment to freezing settlements, and his general willingness to compromise. They indicated that the United States would press for an early resumption of the talks and expected a Rabin visit to Washington soon.

Arab leaders gave a mixed welcome to the Labor victory. Osama el-Baz, senior adviser to Hosni Mubarak, said the change would "give a strong push to peace efforts and the reaping of a golden opportunity to achieve historic reconciliation between Israel and the Arabs." Arafat described the result as a vote "against war and the terrorism of Shamir." Foreign Minister of Jordan Kamal Abu Jahn said the development was "good," but added that "the test now is how serious the coming Government will be about its commitment to Middle East peace." And Syrian foreign minister Farouk al-Sharaa applauded Shamir's defeat but said, "We cannot judge in advance the policy to be adopted by Rabin on the peace process."

While Rabin worked to form a coalition government and announced that he would slash the special subsidies that the Shamir government had given to Jewish settlers, the Shamir policy became the subject of headlines once again when the Likud leader was quoted in *Ma'ariv* as saying to a reporter that had he won, he would have pushed to greatly increase the number of settlers while delaying negotiations: "I would have conducted the autonomy negotiations for ten years, and in the meantime we would have reached half a million souls in Judea and Samaria." In contrast, Likud leader and defense minister Moshe Arens announced his retirement, acknowledging that the election showed that a significant part of the public did "not see the slogan 'Greater Land of Israel' as an adequate or sufficient response in grappling with the complexity of problems associated with Palestinians in the territories."

On July 2, in his first public speech since the Labor victory, Rabin called for continuous peace talks that would yield an autonomy agreement with the Palestinians within a year. When and where the talks would resume was uncertain. On July 10, Rabin completed his negotiations with the left-wing Meretz party and the Sephardic religious party Shas, thereby ensuring a Labor-led coalition government. Reports indicated that the agreements left Rabin wide latitude in the peace talks.

On July 12, one day before he was to take over as prime minister, Rabin unveiled his cabinet to a jubilant Labor party conference. The cabinet, which was described as decidedly dovish on peace issues, included Shimon Peres—Rabin's longtime rival—as foreign minister. The government, which controlled 62 seats, consisted of Labor, Meretz, and Shas. It was widely reported, however, that Rabin would continue to seek a broader government to include the hawkish Tzomet party and the Orthodox United Torah Judaism, to offset the heavy leftist character of the coalition.

On July 13, Rabin took over as prime minister. In his inaugural speech, he pledged to waste no time in the search for peace and appealed to Palestinians to take Israeli offers of limited self-rule seriously and not "lose this opportunity that may never return." His was a call for a change in direction, a clarion call to the country to stop thinking that "the whole world is against us." He asserted: "We must overcome the sense of isolation that has held us in its thrall for almost half a century. We must join the international movement toward world peace, reconciliation and cooperation that is spreading over the entire globe these days, lest we be the last to remain, all alone, in the station."

Rabin underlined his appeal for peace by inviting Palestinian leaders and heads of neighboring states to Jerusalem "for the purpose of talking peace," and on his part offered to go immediately to Amman, Damascus, and Beirut. He urged the Palestinians to take up what he called Israel's fair and viable proposal of autonomy. The same day, President Bush called Rabin to congratulate him, indicating that he would send Baker to the Middle East the following week to get the process rolling again and would invite Rabin to visit him in his Maine summer home in early August.

The new momentum generated by the Rabin election and the upcoming Baker visit was bolstered by the announcement on July 16 that Mubarak had invited Rabin to meet with him in Cairo in order to press ahead with talks before Baker's arrival in Cairo. The meeting would be only Mubarak's second with an Israeli prime minister, the first having been in 1986, with Shimon Peres, in Alexandria. An Egyptian spokesman said of the meeting: "We never extended the offer to former prime minister Shamir because we never believed he was seriously interested in discussing peace." The two leaders met in Cairo on July 21 for a 90-minute session. The meeting was described as "informal" by both men, focusing on an exchange of views rather than details. Mubarak praised Rabin's freeze on new settlements as a "good step." Mubarak also indicated that Rabin had invited him to visit Israel and said: "Whenever I find it convenient, I will go to Israel. My response is positive to Mr. Rabin." No date, however, was set for a trip, and Egyptian officials reportedly said that until a date was set, the issue would probably not prompt wide debate.

On July 19, Baker began his five-nation tour in Jerusalem. In a talk with reporters en route to Israel, Baker made clear his feelings: "It's a pleasure to be going to Israel under circumstances in which I anticipate that we will not be met with the opening of a new settlement or settlements, but rather a suspension of contracts for the construction of new houses or settlement activity—something that I think can only inspire trust and confidence." Hours before Baker's arrival, Rabin announced that he was suspending all new building of Jewish settlements in the territories, pending a review by the government of exactly what was being built and where. Following two hours of talks with Rabin, Baker cited the changes in Israeli policy and hoped "that we could begin to hear some new and different signals coming from those on the Arab side."

On the morning of July 21, Baker left Jerusalem for Amman. In a news conference later that day with King Hussein, Baker declared his opposition to any new Israeli settlements, even those considered important to its security. He called settlements "an obstacle to peace." He talked as well about the fresh chance for peace offered by the new Israeli government and commented, after his four-hour meeting with the Jordanian ruler, that the parties should and would take advantage of the opportunity.

In Syria on July 23, Baker met with Foreign Minister al-Sharaa. At a news conference afterward, Baker asserted that he had received positive signs in his visits in the region. Sharaa, not surprisingly, focused on the need for Israeli flexibility and, when asked what gesture Syria might make, said the Arab countries had done enough by agreeing to negotiate with Israel. Later in the day, under heavy guard, Baker motored into Lebanon, the first visit to that country by a U.S. secretary of state since 1983. The purpose was to show U.S. support for President Elias Hrawis's effort to reestablish Lebanese independence by inducing Syria to move its troops out of Beirut. On his last stop, in Saudi Arabia, Baker summed up his message to the parties: "It is time to come together again quickly and actually see some nitty-gritty negotiating." A senior official accompanying Baker indicated that they knew Israel was ready to be flexible, that this had been confirmed by Rabin, but it remained uncertain that the Arab side was ready to match Rabin's gestures. As to the issue of where the talks would continue, it was reported that Rabin probably would be willing to return to Washington if the Arab side felt strongly about it.

On July 25, the foreign ministers of Syria, Jordan, Lebanon, and Egypt and Palestinian representatives met in Damascus to assess the Baker visit. In a joint communiqué, the ministers welcomed the Baker tour, saying it had revitalized the peace process. Concerning the new Israeli government, they noted its declared intentions but added that they "await practical proof. . . ."

On July 28, the White House announced that Rabin would visit President Bush in Kennebunkport on August 10–11. In the days leading up to Rabin's first meeting as prime minister with the president, Israel took several steps that highlighted its new approach. On August 3, it named Itamar Rabinovich, a Tel Aviv University legal scholar, to replace Yossi Ben-Aharon as head of the talks with Syria. This move was seen as reflecting a willingness to be more flexible and to give more importance to the Syrian talks than Rabin himself had earlier indicated. It was also seen as a response to Syrian warnings against leaving the negotiations with Damascus for a later phase. Several days later, Rabin negotiated a compromise with Palestinian leaders to end a strike, without the use of force, by a thousand Palestinian students at Al Najah University in Nablus. And on August 9, the government said it would propose changing a law that prohibited individual citizens from meeting with PLO officials. Deputy Foreign Minister Yossi Beilin said, "We have a deep obligation to change this stupid law."

On August 10, Rabin arrived in the United States and met with President Bush in Maine. The 24-hour stay at the president's summer home was intended to signal an end to the tensions in U.S.-Israeli relations, as well as to project the image of a warm, personal relationship contrasting with the obvious tense one that existed between Bush and Shamir. The president said afterward that it was "a true pleasure for Barbara and me to spend this time with the Prime Minister and Mrs. Rabin . . . our time together can best be described as a consultation between close friends and strategic partners." Bush denied that the meeting would help him in his reelection campaign, though all observers took it for granted that this was an important motivation. Most significantly, the two leaders announced their agreement on the much delayed package of $10 billion in loan guarantees (see below).

Two days later, speaking in Washington at a National Press Club luncheon, Rabin promised to be "more forthcoming" in the pending negotiations with the Palestinians on autonomy, including the commitment to offer the Palestinians general elections the following year for an administrative council that would "run their daily life" in the territories during the interim period. Later in the day, Rabin met with Democratic presidential candidate Bill Clinton for an hour, during which Clinton expressed strong support for the peace process.

SIXTH ROUND OF TALKS

In the intervening period, agreement in principle had been reached among the parties to resume the peace talks on August 24 in Washington. Despite some reservations on the part of Arab foreign ministers over the U.S. decision to move forward on the loan guarantees, Syria's al-Sharaa said that there was no move afoot to boycott the sixth round of talks.

With James Baker leaving his position as secretary of state in order to run the Bush reelection campaign, Acting Secretary Lawrence Eagleburger took over supervision of the talks. Prior to the new talks, he said that they were resuming "in the context of an Israeli Government that is prepared to be far more forthcoming." He predicted that the issue of Palestinian self-rule would be a focus.

As Israel prepared for the next round, its leaders said they were serious about wanting to reach quick agreements, especially on a form of self-government for Palestinians. Yossi Beilin said that the Arabs "won't find a more moderate Government than the current one . . . for them, this is a moment of truth, and I hope they do not want to postpone it." "To improve the atmosphere" in the territories and the mood in the talks, Rabin on August 23 loosened restrictions on Palestinians entering Israel, revoked expulsion orders issued in January against 11 Palestinians, and freed about 800 prisoners.

On August 24, the talks opened in Washington. On August 25, Israel gave Palestinian negotiators a detailed set of proposals for Palestinian self-rule in the territories. These provided for elections by April or May, 1993, to an administrative council that would allow Palestinians to run many aspects of daily life. The proposal fell far short of the Palestinian desire for a 180-member parliament with full legislative powers, but was consistent with the model of the Camp David accords for the interim period. While Israeli and Palestinian delegates exchanged comments in public, reflecting different approaches but conciliatory in tone, Arafat blasted the United States in a speech in Geneva. "We consider there to be a flagrant bias in favor of the Israeli position and a cause or a reason to abort the peace process," he said, referring to the loan guarantees.

By the end of the first week of talks, the optimistic tone on the Palestinian negotiations had vanished. Ashrawi referred to a "deadlock," criticizing the Israeli proposal for not recognizing the land rights of the Palestinians and not including Jerusalem. Eli Rubinstein, Israel's negotiator, expressed frustration with the Palestinian negotiators, indicating that while the Israeli plan did not offer the Palestinians everything they wanted, "it is a sea change from the existing situation."

In Jerusalem, on September 2, Rabin issued an unusually strong criticism of the Palestinian negotiators for raising issues that could not lead to an agreement and for not considering more seriously the best deal for self-rule they had ever received. Prime Minister Rabin noted that the problem seemed to lie in the tensions between the Palestinian delegation and the PLO in Tunis: "The Palestinians in the territories are more pragmatic than those in Tunisia. Some elements in Tunisia are still an obstacle to some of the Palestinians in the territories to reach an agreement." The same day, Peres added that when the Palestinians veered from the autonomy question to raise issues like Jerusalem's future status, they were "really endangering the very foundation of the negotiations."

Meanwhile, in the area of Israeli-Syrian negotiations it was reported that, for the first time, Israel acknowledged that UN land-for-peace resolutions applied to the Golan Heights. However, Israeli officials in Jerusalem made clear that their willingness to discuss some territorial concessions did not mean that they were prepared to hand back the strategic heights or to end Israel's presence there.

On the Syrian side, a document submitted to Israel by the Syrian delegation was described by Israeli negotiator Rabinovich as the first tangible sign that the Syrians were really "engaged" in negotiations with Israel. Israeli officials pointed in particular to a line in the Syrian paper stating that the Syrians understood that Israel, like Syria, had "security concerns" and that Damascus was ready to talk about them, provided that they did not compromise Syrian interests and territory. A government newspaper in Damascus in fact asserted that Syria would accept nothing less than a full Israeli withdrawal, because "peace cannot be converted from a sacred cause into a matter for bargaining." Responding to optimistic assessments on the Syrian talks offered by some U.S. and Israeli officials, Rabin on September 7 said that, while the general mood had improved, Syria, in its document, offered to accept a peace agreement but "not open boundaries, not embassies, not commercial and cultural relationships."

Beginning on September 9 and continuing for several days, Rabin made a number of comments in Israel that seemed intended to give new life to the talks. Possibly out of frustration over the lack of progress in the Palestinian negotiations, and sensing a need to focus more on Syria, Rabin indicated that his government would be willing to give back parts of the Golan Heights. On the 9th, in the Knesset, responding to opposition charges that the government was preparing a sellout by announcing its willingness to make concessions to the Arabs, Rabin strongly suggested that Israel was willing to return at least part of the Golan Heights to Syria for peace: "Our purpose is indeed to make the most of the chance. We are not starting from the assumption that in return for peace, we can give only peace when it comes to Syria. The idea of 'peace for peace' (Likud's approach to Syria) does not work where Syria is concerned. I never heard of anyone interpreting the Syrian reading of 242 and 338 as meaning 'peace for peace.' "

Reiterating his position the following day in an interview with IDF Radio, Rabin said that, in exchange for a peace treaty with open borders, diplomatic relations, and normalization, Israel was ready "for a certain territorial compromise." He added, "We've never defined lines and we won't define lines, nor enter [discussions] regarding the territorial issue before we know that Syria is now ready for a peace treaty such as I have described." Meanwhile, Assad told a visiting group of Druse residents of the Golan Heights that Syria sought "the peace of the brave" with Israel. Learning of the Syrian leader's comments, Rabin said that his willingness to talk openly about peace was a "positive development." And Peres on Army Radio described the recent period as "the best ten days in the relationship between Syria and Israel."

On September 14, after a ten-day recess, Israel presented to Syria a new eight-page outline of its views on peace, including a vision of peace, the terms of peace including a territorial dimension, and a proposed agenda for negotiations. Speaking in Jerusalem, Rabin made clear Israel's key points: First, Israel would not consider withdrawal from the Golan until the real terms of a peace accord with Syria became clear; and second, any peace treaty would have to stand on its own and could not be linked to progress in talks with other Arabs. "As long as these two issues will not become clear to us," he said, "we will not enter into any territorial discussions." Syria's chief negotiator, Mowaffak Allaf, called the Israeli paper insufficient, claiming that there was no mention whatsoever of the word "withdrawal." The talks appeared stuck on each side's requirement that its demands should be discussed first—Syria wanting Israel's commitment to withdrawal from the Golan before discussions on details of peace; and Israel saying Syria must first spell out terms of peace.

In Paris, on September 15, Foreign Minister Roland Dumas of France disclosed that he had paid a surprise visit to Damascus on the 14th in a bid to mediate differences between Israel and Syria. Deputy Foreign Minister Beilin of Israel said in Washington that an informal back channel for discussions with Syria was "vital," naming Egypt, France, or the United States as possible links. He described the prospect of a peace agreement with Syria as so important that "we would be wasting a lot if we were not using all connections," and adding that negotiations "will be very difficult with just formal" arrangements. Rabin, however, reacted against this proposal by the Foreign Ministry for a back channel and sent a public message to the Syrians: "I want to clarify, especially to the Syrians, that the talks are via one, and only one, channel between the Syrian delegation and the Israeli delegation. All sorts of middlemen are not relevant to the negotiations."

Meanwhile, soon after Rabin announced that Resolution 242 would apply to the Golan Heights, Arafat, suspecting a Syrian-Israeli deal, had the Palestinian delegates insist that 242 also be applied to the West Bank and Gaza. Washington was reported to be outraged by this development, and Djerejian told the Palestinians that the issue of Israeli withdrawal was not part of the autonomy talks. By September 21, after consultations with Tunis, the Palestinian delegation abandoned its demand that Israel affirm its willingness to give up land in the West Bank and Gaza for peace.

As the sixth round of talks ended on September 24, there was no Syrian-Israeli breakthrough, despite the excitement aroused two weeks earlier. Rabinovich noted, "Progress has not matched our expectations. But if you look at the round as a whole, I'm pleased."

SEVENTH ROUND OF TALKS

The seventh round of talks, the last before the U.S. presidential election on November 3, began on October 21. Days earlier, concern was expressed by all sides that time was running out. Regarding the Syrian talks, Itamar Rabinovich suggested that something had to give before too long, because there was domestic opposition to any territorial compromise on the Golan, and time was "not unlimited for the Israeli government." On the Palestinian discussions, Hanan Ashrawi argued that there would have to be some sort of breakthrough by December in the Israeli-Palestinian talks; otherwise, she cautioned, the negotiations risked running out of steam because the U.S. presidential winner, no matter who, would concentrate on America's domestic problems. Complicating matters was the rising tension between Palestinians and Israelis, reflected in a hunger strike by prisoners and the stabbing of an Israeli in northern Israel.

At the same time, paradoxically, it was understood that, with the U.S. election so near, there would be no major breakthroughs in the seventh round. Although Rabin indicated before the talks that the "negotiations with Damascus appear more promising," on October 31, the first anniversary of the talks, Rabin on Israel Radio criticized the basic approach set at the opening conference in Madrid, saying it had not produced results. Indicating that Israel would prefer to have talks with one country at a time, he reflected a deepening frustration with the peace process. As the American election neared, the only good news came from an agreement in writing between Israel and Jordan that their goal was a formal peace treaty within the framework of a comprehensive Israeli-Arab settlement.

On November 3, Bill Clinton was elected president of the United States. In a congratulatory message the next day, Israeli leaders voiced the hope that U.S. ties would be, in Rabin's words, as "close as always." In a telephone conversation with Rabin on November 9, the president-elect said that he wanted the Arab-Israeli peace talks to move forward with "no delay." Meanwhile, George Stephanopoulos, Clinton's spokesman, said Clinton would support "anything that makes sure there is no delay in the peace process." This was seen as a message to the Arabs and Israelis not to drag their feet by waiting for a Clinton administration to emerge before deciding what concessions to make.

On November 9, the talks, which had been in recess for the U.S. elections, resumed. The first day was marked by warnings from Israel to Lebanon and Syria that Israel was prepared to make life intolerable in Lebanon if Shiite guerrillas continued to launch rockets against northern Israel as they had the day before. On the same day, Arafat, in Paris, strongly criticized Hamas, the Palestinian Islamic fundamentalist movement, warning the group of unspecified retaliation if its acts of violence, including the killing of Palestinians in the territories, were to continue.

On November 13, in an interview with the *Washington Post*, Rabin took a pessimistic view of the outlook for talks with Syria and the Palestinians, blaming Assad and Arafat for the lack of progress. Regarding Assad, he compared his actions to those of Sadat between 1972 and 1978: "President Assad of Syria until this moment hasn't done one percent of what President Sadat did, talking to the people of Israel, talking to his own people and convincing both peoples of both countries that here is a leader that wants peace. The opposite has happened." He noted that Assad had encouraged Palestinian terrorist groups based in Damascus in their opposition to the talks and had permitted Hezballah guerrilla attacks in southern Lebanon. As for Arafat, Rabin accused him of not allowing the delegation to move forward on the issue of self-government. The battle of words continued in Washington. On November 17, Syrian negotiator Allaf said the negotiations had been "stymied" by Israel's refusal to surrender territory. And Rabinovich suggested that the Arabs were marking time until the Clinton administration took office in January.

The president-elect's views on the process were aired in an interview published on November 13. The election of Rabin, he said, had breathed new life into the negotiations and he offered the opinion that "it's time for the Arabs to make more moves toward Israel." One such move, he said, would be for one of the Arab countries to "break the ice and end the boycott against Israel. That would be the best thing they could do." He reiterated the U.S. role as an honest broker and on occasion as a catalyst. And he described peace as more than a hostile truce: it required the end of the boycott and normal economic and trade relations between Israel and the Arabs.

As expected, the seventh round of talks ended on November 19 with little progress and increased recriminations, attributable to the intense fighting in southern Lebanon initiated by pro-Iranian Hezballah guerrillas; and by uncertainty on both sides about the policies of the incoming Clinton administration. A day later, Arab negotiators, speaking at a news conference to mark completion of the seventh round, said they might break off negotiations in the spring if gains were not made promptly once the Clinton administration took office. Allaf said that "Arab patience cannot last forever." Abdel-Shafi of the Palestinian team called for the United States to put pressure on Israel.

EIGHTH ROUND OF TALKS

Several weeks later, on December 7, the eighth round of talks began. To protest the lack of progress, the Palestinians sent a rump delegation of only four representatives rather than the usual fourteen. They also called for U.S. intervention. Aside from this, the general expectation was that the parties were merely going through the motions of negotiating until Clinton took office. Also casting a shadow over the talks was the December 7 ambush-killing of three Israeli soldiers by Islamic gunmen in Gaza. In Rome, Rabin blamed terrorist groups intent on bringing about the talks' collapse, but he said Israel would not pull out of the negotiations because to do so would hand "a prize to those who like to kill peace in the region." The Likud opposition quickly attacked him, blaming the terrorist raids on his many concessions to the Palestinians since he came to power in July.

On December 8, Israel closed off the Gaza Strip and confined hundreds of thousands of Palestinians to their homes as the army searched for the killers of the three soldiers. Four days later, the army lifted the curfew, and clashes ensued between stone-throwing Palestinians and Israeli soldiers. The next day, Muslim fundamentalists of Hamas kidnapped an Israeli border policeman, Nissim Toledano, and threatened to kill him unless Israel released Sheik Ahmed Yassin, the founder of their movement, who was serving a life sentence. Toledano's body was found on December 15, alongside a highway near Jerusalem. Waves of anti-Arab anger rolled across Israel.

On December 16, in reprisal for the killing, Israel announced that it would deport 415 Palestinians linked to militant Islamic groups. The Arab delegates to the talks met separately with President Bush on December 17 to appeal to Bush to halt Israel's action. The Arabs then boycotted the final session of the eighth round, Abdel-Shafi warning that the deportations could "deal a death blow to the peace process." In a press conference in Little Rock, President-elect Clinton criticized the expulsions. While expressing his understanding of Israeli frustration and anger at Hamas terrorism, he said he was "concerned that this deportation may go too far and imperil the peace talks." Speaking on behalf of the president, Marlin Fitzwater called on Israel to end the expulsions, saying they "risk complicating the search for peace."

Reaction elsewhere was extremely critical. The UN Security Council voted to "strongly" condemn the expulsions, demanded that those expelled be readmitted to the territories, and asked Secretary-General Boutros Boutros-Ghali for the first time to consider sending a representative to Israel to discuss "this serious situation" with the government and report back to the council. Lawrence Eagleburger of the State Department said that, with the expulsions, Israel had "played into the hands of the very people who are trying to wreck the process." Israeli officials responded by criticizing the Security Council resolution, expressing disappointment that it ignored the nature and deeds of Hamas.

Palestinian leaders continued to protest the deportations. Abdel-Shafi, head of the Palestinian delegation to the peace talks, said the deportations had made it "impossible" for the negotiations to continue. Faisal al-Husseini warned at a news conference on December 23 that the Middle East talks were dying and that Palestinians had choices other than negotiation, including "the armed struggle option." Meanwhile, Boutros-Ghali announced on December 22 that he was sending Under Secretary-General James Jonah to Israel to help resolve the deportation issue. It was reported that the Israeli government had agreed to his visit.

On December 27, Jonah met in Jerusalem with Rabin and Peres to discuss the fate of the deportees. The two leaders rejected the UN resolution because it was one-sided and did not take into account the violence of the deportees. Peres emphasized that Hamas "wants not only to murder the peace process, but also everyone who supports the peace process, whether Jews or Arabs."

In Israel, some observers saw the decision to oust the fundamentalists as the beginning of movement toward establishing relations with the PLO. In particular, Rabin's left-wing coalition partner, Meretz, told him on December 21 that Israel had little alternative but to begin direct talks with the PLO. Rabin, however, repeated his opposition to such contacts.

By year's end, not only were the bilateral talks on hold because of the deportation issue, but there was a general feeling of disappointment that many rounds of discussions, even with a new Israeli government, had yielded no tangible results.

Multilateral Talks

Parallel to the bilateral negotiations, at the start of 1992, the multilateral talks involving 30 nations began in Moscow at the end of January. These talks were conceived as a way to buttress the bilateral talks and as an opportunity to involve in the process other Arab states as well as leading nations around the world. The underlying premise of these discussions was that, if the Middle East were truly to enter a new era in a changing world of regional cooperation, the problems beyond those of war and peace had to be addressed by many nations.

Before the first multilateral meeting took place, however, an obstacle arose regarding the makeup of the Palestinian delegation. On January 26, it was reported that the PLO executive committee was meeting in Tunis to assess whether it should approve a restricted delegation—as in the bilateral talks in Madrid and Washington—or whether it should insist on broader representation, including Palestinians from East Jerusalem and outside the territories. It was pointed out that such issues as refugees, economic development, the environment, and arms control affected the whole region and required broader Palestinian representation. The United States and Russia, cosponsors of the meeting, made clear that the terms for participation could not be changed. While an expanded Palestinian delegation did show up in Moscow, the Palestinians announced that they would not attend the conference because they were being barred from it. Baker said that the Palestinians had refused to attend according to the terms set out in the invitation and added that he was "disappointed" that they had missed yet another opportunity to advance their cause.

Twenty-four nations were represented in Moscow on January 28. Sitting together for the first time were representatives of Saudi Arabia and Kuwait, as well as other Arab states, and representatives of Israel. Syria and Lebanon, however, refused to participate, the Syrians arguing that participation awaited progress on the bilateral front. The meeting lasted two days, during which it was decided to establish working groups to meet and deal in the coming months with five regional problems: arms control and regional security; economic development; water resources; environmental issues; and refugees.

Although Palestinians did not participate, it was reported that Secretary Baker had pledged to Ashrawi and Faisal Husseini that, in those talks involving refugees and economic development, the United States and Russia would support the inclusion of Palestinians from outside the territories. Israeli officials, however, immediately expressed their opposition to any change in the "Madrid formula" governing the talks.

In April, as the bilateral talks stalled, trouble appeared regarding the multilaterals as well. On April 27, the United States and Russia formally issued invitations for the five different regional talks. Dates and places were set: economic development in Brussels on May 11; arms control in Washington on May 11; sharing water resources in Vienna on May 12; refugee problems in Ottawa on May 13; and environmental issues in Tokyo on May 18. And what had been reported following the Moscow regional conference was confirmed. Baker indicated that the Palestinians could bring outside Palestinians to the working groups on refugee matters and economic development, provided they were not members of the PLO. The next day, Israel's foreign minister, David Levy, told Baker that Israel would not take part in those talks if this were to occur. Ambassador Zalman Shoval of Israel explained the reason for excluding outside Palestinians: "It is very clear to us, and I think it should be very clear to anybody who knows anything about it, that the insistence of the Palestinians to include outside Palestinians or diaspora Palestinians in this process is in order to get the right-of-return question back into the whole process through the back door. . . . And Israel will not agree to that."

Baker reportedly told Levy that the U.S. administration would not force Israel to talk with anyone it did not want to, but that he did not intend to alter his position on Palestinian participation in the working groups. On May 6, Israel gave formal notice that it would boycott those two phases of the regional talks in which Palestinians from outside the territories would be taking part.

Five days later, May 11, two sessions of the multilateral talks opened. In Washington, the session on arms and regional security met, with the Syrian and Lebanese delegations boycotting the talks on the grounds that not enough progress had been made in the bilateral talks, and the Palestinians not present, even as part of a Jordanian delegation, because only states with military establishments were invited. A Palestinian delegation arrived in Washington unannounced to protest their exclusion. Yezid Sayigh, coordinator of the group, argued that Israel claimed that it "cannot accommodate our natural rights because this would endanger Israeli security. We are willing to take up that theme and discuss it. We have to deal with issues of security and confidence-building as Palestinians."

The talks were attended by 13 Middle Eastern nations, as well as China, India, Japan, Turkey, and the European Community. The talks were described as lacking rancor or vitriol. The purpose of the talks, as described by American officials, was to present ideas for discussion on topics including methods of arms control, the framing of agreements for dealing with unexpected military incidents, and the installation of hotlines like those used by American and Soviet leaders during the Cold War. However, it was noted that many delegates expressed skepticism that the region's arms could be substantially limited without a comprehensive peace accord.

The Washington talks lasted four days. Unnamed American officials indicated that the sessions exceeded expectations in the participants' willingness to acknowl-edge that negotiations had to seek eventual reduction of the region's arsenal of mass-destruction weapons. It was also agreed that stability required exchanging confidence-building proposals as the first step toward achieving serious arms control in the strife-torn region.

On the same day, the talks on the regional economy opened in Brussels with Israel not participating because of the presence of outside Palestinians, and Syria and Lebanon not participating as part of their total boycott of the multilaterals.

On May 13, the talks on refugees in Ottawa were also boycotted by Israel because of the outside Palestinians. The procedural matter in this case was directly tied to the Arab desire to raise the controversial matter of the right of Palestinians to return to the homes they had left during the 1948 war. The Israeli fear, that the refugee talks would focus on the right of return, intensified when State Department spokes-woman Tutwiler said, in response to a question as to whether Washington still supported a 1948 UN Resolution that upheld the principle of return, "The United States has supported General Assembly Resolution 194 since it was adopted on December 11, 1948. We continue to support it." Immediately, Israeli officials pro-tested and asked their embassy in Washington to request a prompt explanation of the statement.

The following day, Tutwiler clarified her comment. She reiterated U.S. support for two UN resolutions endorsing the so-called "right of return," but stressed that "the issues raised in many other UN resolutions related to the Arab-Israeli conflict, and can only be resolved through a process of direct negotiations among the parties themselves." Observers noted that the U.S. position did not mean it favored the return of the 1948 refugees to Israel, but instead wanted a formula for compensation —which the international community would pay—to be found.

Prime Minister Shamir summed up the Israeli view: "The term 'right of return' is an empty phrase that is utterly meaningless. It will never happen, in any way, shape or form. There is only a Jewish 'right of return' to the land of Israel." Reports indicated that Labor party candidate Yitzhak Rabin was furious that the adminis-tration, by raising the issue of return one month before the Israeli election, had handed Shamir a substantial gift. Shlomo Avineri, a pro-Labor professor and former director-general of the Foreign Ministry, reflected this attitude: "It shows either complete insensitivity to Israeli domestic politics or utter stupidity."

Concerned about the impact of this controversy, the State Department reportedly pressed Palestinian delegates to the Ottawa talks to lower their profile on the issue. Salim Tamari, one of the delegates, indicated later on that at the talks that day the Palestinians had focused on the right to return to the "State of Palestine," not to their original homes in Israel proper, and that the number of returnees would be a subject for negotiations in the context of the peace process. Meanwhile, Yossi Ben-Aharon, director-general of the Prime Minister's Office, indicated that Israel sought a public disavowal by the United States: "We want this whole affair over UN Resolution 194 to end, but this can only be done if the U.S. rectifies the impression it left this week. Otherwise, the peace process will be hurt as will the credibility of the U.S. as an honest broker."

On May 18, the State Department moved to defuse the dispute. Tutwiler, in a prepared statement, said that UN Resolution 194 was not part of the current peace talks: "What's important here is the process of direct negotiations between the parties themselves. That process has clear terms of reference . . . [which] specifically name only two resolutions, 242 and 338. It is these resolutions, not the many, many other resolutions passed by the United Nations over the years, that constitute the agreed terms of reference for the peace process." It was noted that Resolutions 242 and 338 do not require Israel to accept the return of refugees. Tutwiler added that, until the Israeli election on June 23, she would try to refrain from responding to every question on the peace process, to avoid inadvertently instigating any controversy by her answers. Apparently, the brouhaha over Resolution 194 occurred when a reporter's question was referred to the State Department's International Organization Division, which checked out what the U.S. stand on the resolution had been and concluded that Washington still supported it.

No further regional talks were held in the summer while Israel went through its election process and the Rabin government began to organize itself. With panels on refugees and economic development scheduled for November, the question of Israeli participation, in light of the presence of outside Palestinians, was an issue for the new government to address. Egyptian foreign minister Amre Moussa made a hastily arranged visit to Israel on October 8 to discuss the issue; at the end of the day, in a move to preserve the momentum of the talks, Israel withdrew its previous objections to the participation by outside Palestinians in the regional talks. Peres, in making the arrangement, cautioned that Israel, as before, would not sit down with residents of East Jerusalem or with members of the Palestine National Council, the legislative arm of the PLO.

On October 30, 40 nations attended the opening of multilateral talks on development in Paris. The head of the Israeli delegation, Bank of Israel governor Yaakov (Jacob) Frankel, stressed that the Middle East could not avoid regional cooperation such as was under way in Europe, North America, and Asia. He called economic boycotts "counterproductive and utterly nonconsistent with the peace process." The Jordanian delegate, Dr. Fayez Tarawneh, said Jordan would not cooperate with the Israelis right now because this "would indicate normalization before peace," which was what Israel wanted while it continued to occupy lands. Meanwhile, the World Bank suggested establishing a Middle East reconstruction bank, modeled on the European Bank for Reconstruction and Development created in 1991 to promote market economies in the former Communist states of Eastern Europe.

Finally, on November 12, Israel participated in the talks on refugee issues in Toronto, the first time since 1948 that Israel had participated in such a session. A day earlier, Israel had walked out, on the grounds that the Palestinians had violated the agreement by having Mohammed Hallaj, a member of the Palestine National Council, in the delegation. Israel returned the next day after it received assurances that Hallaj was no longer a participant in the talks. Israel indicated that it saw the talks as a forum to find practical ways to alleviate living conditions for Palestinian and other refugees in the region, not to discuss the right of return.

Israeli Arms Sales to China

In March, reports began to circulate that the Bush administration had ordered an investigation of possible Israeli transfer of American-made Patriot missile technology to China, in violation of U.S.-Israeli agreements banning diversion of such technology to a third country. After Saddam Hussein's first Scud missile attacks on Israel during the Gulf War, the United States gave Israel two batteries of Patriot missiles to help protect it from further attacks. Under the terms of the arrangement, Israel promised in writing not to transfer the weapons or related technology to another country. Reportedly, the White House ordered an investigation after an intelligence report indicated that the transfer might have occurred. On March 13, a spokesman for Israeli defense minister Arens dismissed the report as false: "Israel did not transfer a Patriot missile or the technology of the missile to China. These reports are lies and totally baseless."

Senior administration officials were divided about the charge, some giving it credence, others impressed by Israel's "very authoritative and direct denial." It was probably significant that the issue surfaced at a time when tensions between Washington and Jerusalem were high as a result of the loan-guarantees issues (see below).

Israeli officials stepped up their criticism of the administration on this matter on March 15. One unnamed member of the cabinet said after a meeting that the technology dispute was "a deliberate campaign of slander against Israel." Health Minister Ehud Olmert said that it showed that "something much deeper here is wrong in the basic attitude" of the Bush administration toward Israel. And Benjamin Netanyahu said that what he called the "deliberate campaign of slander against Israel" was intended "to undermine Israel's position in the American public and in the American Congress."

On March 16, Arens met with Defense Secretary Richard Cheney in Washington and afterward repeated denials that Israel had sold Patriot missiles or technology to China. He said that he told Cheney there were "no grounds at all" for the suggestion. He indicated that Israel "would be ready" to have a U.S. team visit Israel to check the allegations. Meanwhile, in Israel, Shamir called the allegations "lies and false accusations."

On March 22, a team of U.S. Army inspectors began an investigation into the allegations in Israel. The 15-member team engaged in four days of inspection. Israeli officials were said to be confident in the result, calling on Washington to make the findings public and some even insisting on a U.S. apology. American ambassador to Israel William Harrop spoke on Israeli television: "If it turns out that intelligence, which we had obtained and which was a cause of worry to us, proves to be completely groundless, I would think an apology would not be out of line." Tutwiler, however, said, on March 26, that an apology was out of the question, noting that the person who owed an apology to Israel was the "irresponsible leaker" who made the allegations public. She added that she was not aware of any Israeli request for such an apology and said that the United States had not and did not intend to offer one.

On April 2, the State Department announced that its investigators had found "no evidence that Israel had transferred a Patriot or Patriot missile technology" to China and added that the matter was closed. Tutwiler offered conciliatory remarks, saying that the Israeli government had "a clean bill of health on the Patriot issue." And she thanked Israel's Defense Ministry for its "superb cooperation" during the investigation. It was reported that administration officials were eager to make such statements in an effort to deflate the tensions between the two governments.

Israeli officials welcomed the State Department announcement on the same day. Defense Ministry spokesman Danny Naveh said that the "clear announcement of the State Department speaks for itself." He added that when Moshe Arens became defense minister two years earlier, he stressed the need to adhere to the policy on transfer of U.S. technology "very strictly." To some, however, the sour taste of the affair remained. Netanyahu told Israel Radio, "I don't appreciate the attempt to cover Israel with a cloud of innuendo."

Loan Guarantees

The major issue of conflict between the Bush administration and the Shamir government in 1991 had been Israel's request for $10 billion in loan guarantees to help in the resettlement of Jews from the former Soviet Union. In particular, the conflict centered on the administration's insistence that any consideration of the loan guarantees depended on Israel ceasing to build new settlements in the territories. As 1991 came to a close, the stalemate continued, the administration refusing to move forward, the Shamir government insisting on the need and the right of Israel to increase settlements. On January 2, 1992, Shamir won parliamentary approval for a 1992 government budget that provided for 5,000 of 7,500 publicly financed housing units to be constructed in the territories. This decision was seen as exacerbating the conflict over loan guarantees between Bush and Shamir.

For their part, the leaders of the American Jewish community, through the Conference of Presidents of Major American Jewish Organizations, on January 6 urged the White House to act quickly on the loan-guarantee request now that the 120-day waiting period agreed to by Congress the previous October—to allow the peace process to get off the ground—had passed. In a meeting between a conference group and White House chief of staff Samuel Skinner, the Jewish leaders emphasized that they looked to the administration to work out an agreement with Israel. This was a significant change from September, when the community sought to have Congress force the issue. The new strategy reflected awareness that Congress was now focusing on domestic priorities and was unlikely to take the lead in securing the guarantees.

On a visit to Israel in early January, Sen. Phil Gramm (R., Tex.) reinforced the notion that the two leaders had to work out a compromise: "With the President, the loan guarantees may pass Congress. Without him, it is impossible." Gramm added that, in light of Israel's recent budget actions, Bush was certain to insist on assurances that the U.S.-backed loans would not be used to finance settlements in the territories. A spokesman for Shamir, responding to Gramm's comments, indicated that Israel's position remained the same: "Our firm position is that no linkage should be made between a humanitarian matter such as immigrant absorption, and political questions."

However, reports began to surface that Israel, bowing to political reality, was in fact seeking to negotiate a compromise with the administration. The compromise would resemble the plan of Sen. Patrick Leahy (D., Vt.), which would deduct from the loan guarantees an amount equal to what Israel spent on settlements. In addition, it was reported that a deal might involve only one year for $2 billion. Observers noted that, even if there were agreement in principle on such an approach, negotiations would be difficult over such details as determining settlement-construction costs, whether an agreement should cover all new settlement activity, and whether building in East Jerusalem should be included.

On January 20, Shamir told cheering Jewish settlers that nothing could stop Israel's home building in the territories. This was widely read as a signal to the Bush administration that Shamir would reject any effort to link the loan guarantees to a settlement freeze. Finance Minister Yitzhak Modai added that if Washington insisted on a settlement freeze as the price for the loan guarantees, he would rather forego the assistance, no matter the economic consequences. Meanwhile, the Israeli daily *Ha'aretz* published Finance Ministry figures for housing starts in the territories that showed there had been 5,435 in the first 9 months of 1991, easily outpacing the 3,230 starts there in the previous two years combined; overall, there were 12,985 units in an advanced stage of construction from January to September 1991. These reports and comments were significant because they appeared only days before a crucial meeting on the subject between Baker and Israeli ambassador Zalman Shoval.

On January 24, Baker met with Shoval and reportedly told him that if Washington was going to support Israel's request, it needed assurances that the money would not be spent to further a policy—Israeli settlement building—that ran counter to American principles. The comments by Baker did not, according to reports, include any final terms and conditions, because he wanted to let the Israelis suggest how they might meet American concerns. Shoval afterward described the meeting as "constructive," emphasizing the administration's commitment in principle to help Israel in the task of absorbing the immigrants.

Two days later, Shamir expressed optimism that he could negotiate a compromise with the administration. He made clear again that Israel was "not speaking about any freeze of settlements. Please forget about it." But he said that the two governments had to "engage in a common effort to find a formula that will not contradict U.S. policy or this principle of ours." Reports focused on the idea that the administration would allow Israel to complete construction already under way but would penalize it for the amount spent on such construction and bar new construction.

On February 6, the day before Shoval was to meet Baker again, Senator Leahy endorsed the administration's plans to insist on a halt to new settlements as a condition for the loan guarantees. He said that if the Israelis thought they could get an easier deal from Congress, they should "forget it." On the same day, Baker told the House Foreign Affairs Committee that while Israel always repaid its loans—a positive factor in the making of a U.S. decision—that was "because we appropriate the money up here with which to repay ourselves."

The next day, Shoval provided Israel's counterproposals. Reportedly he told Baker that Israel might consider a slowdown, but not a total halt, in new housing starts; that Israel should be allowed to complete those houses already under way, using the number of 13,500; and that Israel would accept the Leahy deductions, but that they should kick in after the completion of the 13,500 dwellings. The administration, meanwhile, estimated that there were only 6,000 unfinished houses and apparently would deduct the cost of their completion.

Israel's health minister, Ehud Olmert, offered a pessimistic assessment in a meeting with American Jews on February 10 in Jerusalem. He accused President Bush of deliberately provoking a confrontation and said he no longer expected Israel to receive the guarantees.

On February 21, Baker and Shoval met for the third time, but the talks failed to break the impasse. Shoval reportedly offered to slow down new building, but Baker demanded a total halt. The meeting came one day after Leahy told Baker that "time is running out" for Congress to act on the request for the current year. Leahy indicated that if Israel and the administration could not reach agreement in the next few days, he probably would propose legislation imposing severe limits on Israel's ability to use any U.S. guarantees if it continued to build settlements.

On February 24, in testimony before the House foreign operations subcommittee, Baker laid out the administration's conditions. He said the administration would "support loan guarantees of up to $2 billion [a year] for five years if there is a halt or an end to settlement activity." Baker added that, if the Israeli government felt it could not accept a total freeze on settlement construction, Washington was prepared to offer an option: a far smaller amount in American loan guarantees, for only a year of time—on the condition that only those settlement units under way would be completed and that all new construction would have to be frozen. It was noted that this marked the first time in U.S.-Israeli relations that a U.S. administration had chosen to use economic aid as a tool to try to change Israeli political actions in the territories.

The hearing saw a nasty exchange between Secretary Baker and Cong. Larry Smith (D., Fla.), reflecting how upset some strong supporters of Israel were. Smith suggested that Baker's position jeopardized his ability to be an honest broker in the peace process. Baker replied: "Nobody else is asking us for $10 billion in addition to the $3 billion to $4 billion that we give every year with no strings attached." Smith said he found the answer "extremely offensive." A few more hostile remarks were exchanged.

By early March, comments coming from Israeli leaders suggested that they were ready to abandon their request in the face of U.S. demands. Shamir told Army Radio on March 8 that he thought "almost all political factions in Israel would not accept a situation in which the American administration would dictate our policy, whether about settlements today, or about other territorial issues tomorrow." Ariel Sharon said two days earlier that he would "give up on the matter," and added, "I would announce, 'Thank you very much' and make a very big effort to raise these funds from other sources." And Shoval said in Washington that if there were "tough conditions" in a compromise bill being worked on in Congress, it was possible that Israel would "have to reassess its request." On March 10, however, after a meeting with the Knesset's Foreign Affairs and Defense Committee, Shamir said, "There's no reason for us to give up on these loan guarantees."

On March 16, the administration redrafted a compromise plan by Congress, which would grant Israel $1 billion in the guarantees immediately, without linking them to a freeze, and give the president the authority to provide the rest of the guarantees on the condition that Israel restrict its settlement activity. Israeli defense minister Arens, in Washington, reacted strongly, saying that Israel would "not beg, or crawl for help" and would rather abandon its quest for the loan guarantees than "renounce the right of Jews to live in Judea and Samaria." The following day, after meeting with Baker, Arens said in radio interviews broadcast in Israel that Washington's insistence on no new settlements amounted to "impossible terms" that "no Government in Israel could accept."

In a news conference on March 17, Bush said he still wanted to go forward on the loan guarantees, but only on terms consistent with U.S. opposition to new construction: "I don't think they're dead. We've always wanted to go forward with loan guarantees." But he added: "We have a long-standing policy that feels that settlements are counterproductive to peace. This is not a new policy. This is a long-standing policy, and I am determined to see that that policy not be altered. However, if there's room within that policy to do what we'd like to do, which is to support the people coming home, we'd like to do that. So we'll just have to wait and see."

The president's comments seemed to seal the doom of the loan-guarantee request, at least while Bush was president and Shamir prime minister. On March 23, speaking in Jerusalem to hundreds of Evangelical Christian pilgrims, Shamir called the Bush demand for a freeze on settlements "an attempt to determine Israel's borders and the ultimate status of the areas in question in advance of negotiations. We shall never agree to such a step." On April 17, in an interview in the *Jerusalem Post*, Shamir accused the United States of refusing Israel's request because the administration had already promised Arab countries it would withhold the guarantees unless Israel stopped building settlements. He reiterated that "there was some kind of promise. The Arabs say so."

New opportunities for the loan guarantees opened up with the election of Yitzhak Rabin on June 23. In his election campaign, Rabin had repeatedly said that government money being spent on settlements should be used instead to absorb immigrants. While his exact position on settlements was yet to be determined, the Labor party clearly opposed Likud settlement policy. Early on after his victory Rabin expressed his opposition to "political" settlements, without defining them, but adding that he only supported settlements that enhanced Israel's security.

On July 16, three days before Baker's visit to Israel to meet with the new prime minister, Rabin declared a temporary halt to contracts for government-subsidized housing, marking the first step toward reducing expansion of settlements. Clearly, it was intended as a signal to the U.S. secretary of state about the shift in direction that would lead to a resumption of negotiations on the loan guarantees. Three days later, and only hours before his meeting with Baker, Rabin and his cabinet ordered a review of all previous decisions to build settlements.

After two days of talks between the prime minister and secretary of state, an unnamed senior U.S. official reported that a deal was in the making that would give Israel the guarantees in exchange for broad limits on settlement activity, but not a total freeze. It was also reported that the conclusion and announcement of a deal would be left for a meeting between Rabin and Bush in August in Kennebunkport.

On July 23, the new government announced its settlement policy. It said it would stop all planned construction, numbering nearly 6,700, but would complete 8,700 new housing units in progress. Baker, in Jiddah, Saudi Arabia, hailed the decision but said more details would be required before the administration decided whether the action met its conditions for granting the loan guarantees.

Two weeks later, as Rabin left for the United States for meetings with President Bush, the government announced a new limit on the building of settlements, suspending allocation of state land for privately financed construction. This was intended to prevent the raising of money for private ventures to offset previously announced curbs on government-financed construction.

In Kennebunkport, Maine, after a day of talks, the long-discussed loan-guarantee plan was agreed to in principle. On August 11, in a joint press conference, Rabin and Bush announced that a full accord had been reached. Bush said they concurred on "basic principles" and asked for swift action on the guarantees in Congress. Under the new proposal, Israel agreed that the cost of continuing settlement construction would be deducted from the amount of the guarantees, so that the United States would not finance settlements. The actual deduction was to be established by a "joint mechanism" of the two governments, rather than by Washington alone. Moreover, Israel's contribution to the costs that would be assessed to the U.S. budget for guaranteeing the loans would be limited to 3.5 percent of the face amount of the loan guarantees.

Observers noted that the terms of the agreement were softer than those presented to Shamir and were the result of Rabin convincing Bush and Baker that, except for a possible few token cases, his government intended to stop settlements. Also, Rabin had apparently satisfied the administration that the units to be completed were in such an advanced state of construction that abandoning them would entail substantial financial losses and legal complications.

On September 8, in a speech to B'nai B'rith, almost one year after he caused a a stir by publicly criticizing the pro-Israel lobby for pressuring him on this very issue, Bush said that he would formally ask Congress for $10 billion in loan guarantees for Israel.

F-15 Sale to Saudis

An old issue—the sale of F-15 fighter jets to Saudi Arabia—reemerged early in the year. In November of 1991, McDonnell Douglas had announced that the Saudis were seeking U.S. government approval to buy 72 F-15s. The announcement triggered an immediate outcry from Israeli supporters on Capitol Hill, including a letter originated by Sen. Howard Metzenbaum (D., Ohio) and signed by 67 senators, opposing the sale. The opposition caused a division within the administration, with Pentagon officials pressing for a quick go-ahead and Secretary Baker advocating a slower approach that would avert attempts in Congress to pass legislation blocking the sale. Debate on the issue was intense in February and March 1992, those in favor of the sale arguing that congressional opposition would be weakened by concern about recession and unemployment. Pentagon officials, pushing for the sale, argued that the production lines at McDonnell Douglas would begin closing, possibly as soon as summer. McDonnell Douglas officials said that as many as 7,000 workers, most at a plant in St. Louis, could lose their jobs by 1994 if the sale did not go through. State Department officials continued to oppose an imminent sale, fearing it would damage the peace talks.

In April, although there was still no notification to Congress, even informally, of plans to sell the Saudis the F-15s, 237 members of the House sent a letter to Bush expressing concern about such a prospect. In the letter of April 9, the members said, "The sale of additional F-15 aircraft to Saudi Arabia is incompatible with any meaningful arms control policy"; it would represent "a significant escalation of the regional arms race."

Consistent with reports that the administration was interested in a piece-by-piece military sale, the Pentagon announced on June 2 that the administration intended to sell Saudi Arabia $1.8 billion worth of helicopters, missiles, rockets, and small military vehicles, as well as support services for F-15 and F-5 fighter aircraft. Congress was informed of the proposed sales and had 30 days to block them, but no such action was anticipated. Early in the summer, however, it appeared that the administration would wait until after the U.S. elections to approve the sale, which McDonnell Douglas insisted would come too late to avert layoffs. But the election of Rabin, followed by the Bush approval of the loan guarantees to Israel, provided a political opening to push the sale through, the argument being that the loan guarantees would insulate the administration from criticism from pro-Israel lawmakers. And the election-year focus on the economy, it was said, would raise the political cost of not approving the sale. Cong. Mel Levine (D., Calif.), a leading opponent of arms sales to the Arab countries, conceded that the president had enough votes in Congress to allow the sale to go through: "In a tough economy, the sale would be tougher to block."

On September 2, with expectations that Bush would shortly notify Congress formally of plans to sell the 72 aircraft for an estimated $5 billion, Rabin, speaking in Jerusalem, left the clear impression that Israel had decided not to lobby actively in Congress against the sale. "I don't like lost battles," he said, pointing to a "real change" in the political climate in Washington as a result of the Saudi role in supporting the coalition against Iraq. He also referred to a conversation with House majority leader Richard Gephardt (D., Mo.), who "made it clear to me" that the arms sale had become a major election-year economic issue because of the large number of jobs at stake. He added that he had "met congressmen, senators, Jews and non-Jews, and they said to me, 'this time we are not coming out' " against the sale. And he noted that both presidential candidates were "on record" in favor of it. Rabin also made clear that Israel remained opposed in principle to the deal because it was a "continuation of the vicious circle of the arms race" and because the weapons were being sold to an Arab country still in a state of war with Israel.

On September 11, Bush canceled an appearance at a trucking company in Joplin, Missouri, at the last minute and flew to the McDonnell Douglas aircraft plant in St. Louis for about half an hour to tell a cheering crowd that he was approving the sale of 72 F-15 planes to Saudi Arabia. The White House insisted that his action had nothing to do with the campaign, calling it a way to provide a "credible Saudi defensive deterrent" that helped protect vital U.S. interests. Spokesman Fitzwater indicated that the jobs involved were a "major factor" in the decision. It was noted that Bush announced the sale at a time when it posed the least political risk. With Labor in power and the peace process in flux, and with Congress unlikely to oppose a job-saving plan in an election year, strong opposition was unlikely. The day of the announcement was the same day that the administration sent the loan-guarantee legislation to Congress.

Meanwhile, in Washington, Secretary of Defense Cheney met with Ambassador Shoval, reportedly to discuss compensation to allow the Israeli military to keep its qualitative edge. The next day, Israel criticized the U.S. decision, but its statement was seen as intended more to remind Bush of his promise to preserve Israel's military superiority over its Arab neighbors than to prevent the transfer of the planes to the Saudis. On September 14, it was reported that the United States and Israel were negotiating a major military cooperation package, and on September 26, the White House announced that it had agreed to send army helicopters to Israel and to store other military equipment there. The White House called the agreement a "significant effort in reaffirming the U.S. commitment to a strategic partnership with Israel." The announcement pointed to other elements of the agreement: "advanced defense equipment" would be stockpiled or prepositioned in Israel for use, with

American approval, if needed in a crisis; a commitment to establish closer ties between the armed forces of the two countries; cooperation on improved technology; and new talks on ways Israel could take part in, or benefit from, the Strategic Defense Initiative.

The way in which this sale of F-15s to Saudi Arabia eventuated, as compared with the monumental struggles of past years over arms sales to Arab states, reflected the new realities in the diplomatic sphere and in the countries involved: the Gulf War and its consequences; the peace talks in process; American domestic economic pressures; a Labor government in power in Israel.

KENNETH JACOBSON

Communal

Jewish Communal Affairs

CONTINUING THE TREND OF RECENT YEARS, the American Jewish community in 1992 focused increasing attention on problems of Jewish identity and continuity. While the strength and security of Israel remained high priorities—especially given the growing hostility between the U.S. and Israeli governments—and the fate of convicted spy Jonathan Pollard aroused considerable grassroots interest, organized American Jewry worried most about its own ultimate survival in an open, democratic society.

Loan Guarantees

Having lost the battle to secure $10 billion in loan guarantees for Israeli absorption of Soviet immigrants in September 1991, the organized Jewish community was leery of challenging President George Bush on this issue again. After a January 6 meeting with White House chief of staff Samuel Skinner, the Conference of Presidents of Major American Jewish Organizations announced that it would not press for a quick vote in Congress on the loan guarantees, despite the fact that the president had promised to reconsider the matter in January. A week later, the conference sent a mildly worded letter to Bush urging the administration to "proceed expeditiously in its deliberations and its discussions with Israel and to support the necessary legislation to be enacted by Congress." The letter stressed that the loan guarantees were a "humanitarian concern." Shoshana Cardin, chairwoman of the Conference of Presidents, arrived in Israel on January 20 to convey the U.S. administration's views on the subject to Prime Minister Yitzhak Shamir.

When Shamir stated publicly that none of the funds from the loan guarantees would be used in the territories, but that he would not place a freeze on settlements, as requested by Bush, the chances for American approval dimmed, and American Jewry split over how to react. Americans for Peace Now accepted a settlement freeze as a legitimate condition for loan guarantees. Americans for a Safe Israel, a pro-Likud organization, released a poll indicating that a solid majority of American Jews felt that "Israel should not give up any of the disputed territories." Some observers expressed serious doubts about the poll's validity. Meanwhile, the New Israel Fund sponsored a public debate between former *Moment* magazine editor Leonard Fein and Tom Dine, executive director of the American Israel Public Affairs Committee (AIPAC), on whether it was legitimate for American Jews to criticize Israel publicly. Dine argued that such public criticism generates "splits among ourselves," while Fein countered that a Jewish community that stifled dissent risked its credibility. Shoshana Cardin insisted that there was a consensus on loan guarantees: the American Jewish leadership, she said, "remains unanimous in supporting Israel's request."

Her assessment was overly optimistic. In mid-February, the annual plenum of the National Jewish Community Relations Advisory Council (NJCRAC)—the umbrella organization that seeks to build consensus among the 117 local community relations councils and 13 national agencies for whom it speaks—addressed the issue. Preparations for the plenum uncovered a high degree of disagreement. The American Jewish Congress—which had recently participated in meetings in Riyadh in an effort to involve Saudi Arabia in the peace process—the Union of American Hebrew Congregations, and community relations councils in Milwaukee and Detroit sought an explicit resolution urging a freeze on settlements in the territories, a step that the Union of Orthodox Jewish Congregations of America, for one, considered "an effort to undermine Israel." Israeli diplomats expressed concern that a vote against settlements might encourage the administration to harden its position on loan guarantees. A conference call among members of NJCRAC's Joint Program Plan Committee resulted in a decision not to vote on the question of settlements, but rather to send a transcript of the debate on the subject to the Israeli government—unless two-thirds of the delegates insisted on a vote, which was highly unlikely.

The NJCRAC debate took place on February 19. Over the course of an hour and a half, approximately 50 speakers addressed the plenum. Those advocating silence about the settlements outnumbered those seeking a freeze by more than two to one, with each side accusing the other of endangering the loan guarantees for Israel. NJCRAC then unanimously passed a resolution urging the United States and Israel to work out an agreement on the guarantees.

The next week, the annual study mission of the Conference of Presidents of Major American Jewish Organizations arrived in Israel, ostensibly "to see firsthand the facts on the ground." In their public statements, the Americans backed the official Israeli line and strongly denounced the linkage between the humanitarian need for loan guarantees and a freeze on settlement activity. Privately, however, the mission participants urged Israeli leaders to show restraint on settlements. In his speech to the group, Prime Minister Shamir repeated his pledge not to use the loans beyond the Green Line, but made no commitment on halting the settlements.

The mission was still in Israel when Secretary of State James Baker made linkage explicit, announcing that Israel would have to make a choice: loan guarantees or more settlements. A halt to all building in the territories would trigger the full $10-billion guarantee; the completion of housing already begun would reduce the amount. Mainstream American Jewish organizations voiced displeasure at what they considered an artificial intrusion into the peace process; settlement activity, they believed, was an issue to be negotiated by the parties concerned. From Israel, the Presidents' Conference charged that the administration was "presenting demands that Israel cannot meet."

The National Council of Jewish Women and the Zionist Organization of America sent delegations to Washington to lobby for loan guarantees, even as the Jewish Peace Lobby, which advocated a two-state solution to the Israeli-Palestinian controversy, circulated a letter signed by over 250 rabbis urging the next U.S. president, whoever he might be, to oppose new Israeli settlements in the territories. The internal debate within the Jewish community even prompted a page-one story in the *New York Times* (March 2) headlined "Uneasy Debate for Jews in U.S. on Loans Issue." It quoted David A. Harris, executive vice-president of the American Jewish Committee, describing American Jewry as "caught between a rock and a hard place. People are not fully happy with some of the ways Israel is behaving, but they don't have confidence in the script being written by the Administration either."

On March 5, the Conference of Presidents held a private meeting with Dennis Ross, director of the State Department's policy-planning staff. The next day, Shoshana Cardin and Malcolm Hoenlein, executive director of the conference, conducted what Hoenlein described as "a very intense exchange" with Secretary Baker, who proved unwilling to bend on the settlements issue. That same day, former New York City mayor Ed Koch reported in his *New York Post* column that Baker had said to White House advisers, apropos the Jews: "F— 'em. They didn't vote for us." Despite Baker's denial, the charge was widely believed and drew harsh criticism, even from Jewish organizations that agreed with the administration's stand on settlements. "Baker reflects a vision of his role that simply is irreconcilable with his office," commented Rabbi David Saperstein of the Union of American Hebrew Congregations. To make matters worse, when Israel's Labor party leader, Yitzhak Rabin, was in Washington to address the United Jewish Appeal's Young Leadership Conference, the administration leaked the charge—later shown to be baseless—that Israel had illegally transferred American military technology to other countries.

As the leading Democratic presidential aspirants vied for Jewish votes with criticisms of the administration's treatment of Israel, Jewish organizations recognized that the loan guarantees would not be passed before March 31, the expiration date for Congress's continuing resolution for funding foreign aid. "The request will be made again," said Shoshana Cardin in the name of the Conference of Presidents, "maybe in June or September." Jewish leaders made no secret of their anger at the administration's refusal to accept congressional proposals for a compromise on loan guarantees, and accused President Bush of going back on a pledge not to link the guarantees to the issue of settlements.

Both the Israeli government and American Jewry gave serious thought to alternate ways of funding the resettlement of Jewish immigrants in Israel without the guarantees. While Joel Tauber, incoming national chairman of the United Jewish Appeal, said there was "no way to replace the $10 billion," Michael Siegal, national campaign chairman of Israel Bonds, declared: "We have the capacity. There will be no problem in appealing to the marketplace to raise the money." The Council of Jewish Federations entered the picture as well, with the announcement that almost all of its member federations had agreed collectively to guarantee up to $900 million in bank loans to help immigrants to Israel pay their resettlement bills—though this money would not be used to build the infrastructure that the U.S. government's loan guarantees were designed to provide.

Fury at the administration's failure to act on the loan guarantees erupted at the national convention in late March of the dovish American Jewish Congress, which was on record in opposition to further settlements in the territories. Although both Robert Lifton, the group's president, and Henry Siegman, the executive director, favored a resolution backing a settlement freeze, a majority of the 300 delegates defied the leadership and voted to make no public statement on the issue until after the Israeli elections in June. Disappointed, Lifton commented, "I'm not satisfied, but it was a decision within the membership, and we'll abide by it. . . . I'm not allowed to say anything about it, but if you look at our previous statements, we haven't retracted them."

AIPAC, which held its annual policy conference in Washington, D.C., in April, came under close scrutiny in the Jewish media for the failure of the loan guarantees. As the preeminent pro-Israel lobby in the capital, what was its responsibility for the series of miscalculations that had put the administration and American Jewry at loggerheads? While AIPAC's director, Tom Dine, attributed the scuttling of the loan guarantees to a turn in American public opinion against foreign aid generally, others felt that AIPAC's over-aggressiveness had unnecessarily alienated the president. There was considerable speculation that AIPAC and the broader pro-Israel community, disillusioned with the Bush administration, would seek closer ties with the Democrats in this presidential election year.

Election Politics

Indeed, presidential politics came to play an increasingly prominent role in American Jewish deliberations over Israel. Seeking to counteract the growing barrage of Jewish criticism, President Bush wrote a letter—obviously intended to be publicized—to a prominent Jewish Republican who had expressed discomfort at Bush's stance on Israel. In the letter, which was made public on March 30, Bush insisted that "our fundamental commitment to Israel is just that—fundamental." Since Israel had the most to gain from a peace settlement, he went on, it should not take provocative steps in the territories that might sabotage the chances for peace. "I will do all that I can," wrote Bush, "to see that the current strains do not grow worse but, on the contrary, are put behind us. . . ." American Jewish leaders expressed appreciation for the sentiments, but felt, in the words of the American Jewish Committee's David Harris, that "deeds are still more significant. We will have to wait and see." In succeeding weeks, a number of high-ranking administration officials, in private meetings with Jewish leaders, at public forums, and in media interviews, continued to press the case that the Bush policies were, on balance, in Israel's best interests.

Meanwhile, the president's leading Democratic challenger, Arkansas governor Bill Clinton, articulated his own vision for the Middle East in an address in New York City on March 31. Accusing the administration of Israel-bashing and even of exploiting anti-Semitism, Clinton asserted his support for loan guarantees and argued that the humanitarian task of resettling Soviet Jews should not be held hostage to the peace process. While the Jewish community applauded Clinton's critique of the Bush policies, some were disappointed that he nevertheless considered the Israeli settlements obstacles to peace and refused to call for the U.S. embassy to be moved to Jerusalem.

In May Jewish organizations offered testimony before the Democratic platform committee in an effort to have their points of view reflected in the national platform. AIPAC, NJCRAC, and other mainstream bodies urged the Democrats to confirm the special U.S.-Israeli relationship, support loan guarantees, and insist on direct Israeli-Arab negotiations without imposition of solutions from outside. Americans for Peace Now wanted the Democrats to espouse Israeli security along with "the legitimate rights of the Palestinian people in the West Bank and Gaza Strip," while the Jewish Peace Lobby urged the party to endorse the Bush policy conditioning loan guarantees for Israel on a settlement freeze.

The stunning electoral triumph of Yitzhak Rabin and his Labor party in the June elections in Israel had a dual impact on the American Jewish community. First, the replacement of a government committed to continued settlement of the territories by one likely to be far more amenable to a "land for peace" deal was taken both as a harbinger of better U.S.-Israeli relations and as vindication by the dovish Jewish organizations that had called for a settlement freeze. Second, the election results immediately touched off speculation about a shakeup of leadership in the establishment organizations of American Jewry, which, having become identified with Likud positions over the years, would now have to work in tandem with a Labor-led coalition.

Henry Siegman, executive director of the American Jewish Congress, articulated the euphoria of the American Jewish left. When Rabin's victory was announced, Siegman predicted that "the traditionally warm relations between the U.S. and Israel will be quickly resumed and the Administration will act promptly on the loan guarantees." Savoring the shift of government in Israel and the chagrin of American Jewish hard-liners, he noted sarcastically: "Suddenly even those American Jews who supported the Likud are saying that they were Labor supporters after all."

Immediately after the election, Israeli newspapers carried stories about pressures from Israel for the removal and replacement of the top executives at AIPAC and the Presidents' Conference, Tom Dine and Malcolm Hoenlein, on the grounds that their sympathies for Likud had gone beyond the bounds of what was strictly necessary. In addition, the papers predicted similar changes in the lay leadership of

AIPAC and the election of a Labor sympathizer as the next chairperson of the Conference of Presidents.

While these reports proved to be unfounded, Yitzhak Rabin did make clear that his election signaled a lessened role for American Jewry in Israeli-American relations. Rabin paid a visit to President Bush in August, and the new Israeli leader's flexible position on the issue of settlements provided the occasion for the president to announce, at long last, his support for the loan guarantees for Israel. But the prime minister also used his American stay to criticize Jewish leadership. Both in a private session with AIPAC leaders and at a public meeting with the Conference of Presidents, Rabin sharply condemned the American Jewish strategy that he felt had mishandled the loan guarantees in 1991 and evoked administration animosity in the bargain. Those who heard him at the public meeting were taken aback both by his angry tone and his insistence that Israel would make its own policy and convey it directly to the U.S. government. Israel no longer wanted to use the American Jewish community as an intermediary. "Rabin and Pro-Israel Group Off to Testy Start," was the headline in the *New York Times*. On September 7, speaking by satellite to B'nai B'rith International's biennial convention, Rabin tried to mitigate the damage by explaining that he was upset with only "one organization"—obviously AIPAC—and that he actually admired "the devotion" of the American Jewish community to Israel.

Even more harmful to AIPAC than Rabin's criticism was a blow inflicted by its own president, David Steiner. Eager to impress a potential donor with the magnitude of the organization's clout, Steiner said, in a taped phone conversation, that AIPAC was negotiating with the Clinton campaign over who would serve as secretary of state in a Clinton administration, and that he, Steiner, had personally convinced Secretary of State Baker to approve a $1-billion strategic cooperation agreement with Israel. The tape recording was made public on November 4—the day after Clinton was elected president—and Steiner immediately resigned, admitting he had made up the stories to impress the donor. On November 22, Steven Grossman was named as his successor. Since Grossman, a Massachusetts businessman, was an active Democrat as well as a prominent supporter of territorial compromise by Israel, the appointment was widely interpreted as a strategic move by the pro-Israel lobby to establish better relations with the new governments in Washington and Jerusalem.

American Jews and the Zionist Movement

The World Zionist Congress—the first of whose meetings in 1897 marked the start of the movement that led, 50 years later, to the creation of a Jewish state—met in Israel in the summer of 1992, just as it had every fifth year, even after the establishment of the State of Israel. Shorn of its mission as the political expression of world Jewry by the coming of the state, its major role now was selecting the leadership of the World Zionist Organization (WZO), which in turn selects half of the officials of the Jewish Agency, the other half of whom are designated by Diaspora fund-raisers, who are chiefly affiliated with local federations. Influence over the Jewish Agency means control over dollars: the agency had a $730-million budget, allocated to it by the United Jewish Appeal (UJA), to be used for the absorption of immigrants in Israel. In the 1987 elections for American delegates to the World Zionist Congress, two new parties, those affiliated with the Reform and Conservative streams in American Judaism, made major gains at the expense of such mainstream Zionist groups as the Zionist Organization of America and Hadassah, the women's Zionist organization. The 1987 result was widely interpreted as a protest against the Orthodox establishment in Israel and as a mandate for religious pluralism there.

In preparation for the 1992 congress, the mainstream American groups proposed choosing the American delegates through an electoral college that would reflect the proportionate strength of the various factions in the previous congress, rather than through direct election by all members of Zionist organizations. While the ostensible reason for shelving a popular vote was to save the more than $1 million that had been spent to run the 1987 election, ARZA, the Zionist group affiliated with Reform, viewed the electoral college plan as a stratagem to block further gains it thought it would make in a democratic election.

Angry charges were exchanged by both sides. When the plan for an electoral college was upheld by the Zionist Supreme Court, ARZA expressed its continuing dissatisfaction with the status quo by pushing for the election of Reform rabbi Richard Hirsch to replace Simcha Dinitz as chairman of the WZO and the Jewish Agency. At the congress, in July, Hirsch offered to drop his candidacy if Dinitz would agree to direct elections for the next congress, so that the WZO might reflect "the real strength of the various religious streams in the Diaspora." Dinitz refused, the vote was taken, and Dinitz won 382–101.

The fireworks over ARZA's challenge obscured a more fundamental change in American Zionism that found expression at this congress, namely, the American delegates' preoccupation with the battle against assimilation in the United States. Rather than seeking to liquidate the Diaspora in classical Zionist fashion, or even seeking primarily to build American support for Israel in the traditional American Zionist way, the Americans now wanted the Jewish state to provide a Jewish anchor for their youth through cultural programs and trips to Israel. The presence at the congress of Seymour Reich, a former chairman of the Conference of Presidents, was especially noteworthy. Reich, who had made his mark in the Jewish community-relations field and had never before sought a leadership role in any strictly Zionist organization, was representing B'nai B'rith, which had never before sent delegates to a Zionist Congress. Reich spoke of the new challenge that he and American Zionism had to take on, saying, "It's easier to fight anti-Semitism than to fight the problems of the Jewish family."

In October the Jewish Agency Assembly meeting in Jerusalem pitted the Zionists of Israel and the Diaspora against the primarily American fund-raisers. Convinced that the agency's operation was hampered by bureaucratic duplication and partisan political patronage, the fund-raisers sought to save some $700,000 a year by eliminating several department chairmanships and having these departments run by the professionals already on staff. This aroused the ire of the Zionists, who charged that the wealthy fund-raisers were seeking to wrest control of Zionism from the broad mass of volunteers who constituted the rank and file of the Zionist movement in the Diaspora. A full-scale confrontation over the issue was avoided when both sides agreed to maintain the status quo pending further study.

The Pollard Case Continued

With a federal appeals court due to rule on Jonathan Pollard's appeal of his life sentence for passing classified information to Israel, the campaign to secure his release picked up steam. Pollard's supporters claimed that government prosecutors, in demanding the harshest possible sentence, had violated an agreement not to do so in return for a guilty plea. And the harsh prison term for Pollard, contrasted to shorter sentences meted out to others who spied for friendly countries, aroused suspicion that anti-Semitism might have played a role.

Emanating originally from the grassroots Jewish community rather than from Jewish organizations, the pro-Pollard movement had by early 1992 gained the support of several rabbinic bodies and other Jewish institutions. In February the Union of Orthodox Jewish Congregations of America became the first member organization of the Conference of Presidents to call for Pollard's release. The major Jewish community-relations organizations, professing sympathy for Pollard's personal plight but unconvinced that he was the victim of anti-Semitism, declined to get involved. Seventy-eight prominent American Jews and organizations did sign on to a friend-of-the-court brief for Pollard. Leading the campaign was Seymour Reich, immediate past president of the Conference of Presidents, who charged that "Pollard got a raw deal" and announced that "enough is enough."

On March 22, a three-judge panel of the U.S. Court of Appeals for the District of Columbia turned down Pollard's appeal 2 to 1. Pollard's supporters expressed bitterness. Harvard law professor Alan Dershowitz, who assisted in the preparation of Pollard's case, claimed that, had the organized Jewish community mobilized behind Pollard, the decision might have gone the other way. And Reich went so far as to charge that the mainstream Jewish groups had discouraged Christian leaders from speaking up for Pollard. NJCRAC, the umbrella organization reflecting the views of the community-relations organizations, still held back from endorsing Pollard's release. After the appeals-court ruling it issued a press release backing "full, open, and fair hearings, before appropriate tribunals, on the legitimate questions that have arisen in this case. We are aware that the judicial process has not run its course in this matter. We are encouraged that the process may still go forward, and we hope that following a review of the record, the U.S. Supreme Court will grant *certiorari* and accept this case for adjudication."

Pollard's family and supporters organized events across the country to mobilize public opinion in favor of his release. They garnered an important ally in Nobel laureate Elie Wiesel, who began speaking out for Pollard's release "only on humanitarian grounds" after an April 7 visit to his prison cell. A key aspect of the strategy to help Pollard was the involvement of prominent non-Jews, thereby making it less a purely Jewish issue and more a question of miscarriage of justice. Thus, a mass rally on the Upper East Side of Manhattan on June 22 that attracted 2,000 people featured addresses by Wiesel and the prominent Christian broadcaster Pat Robertson. At the event, Seymour Reich publicly castigated the major Jewish community-relations organizations for their failure to participate.

Despite the public campaign to free Pollard, on October 13 the Supreme Court declined to hear the appeal. The only hope now was a presidential pardon. And since President Bush was in the final weeks of a desperate effort to win reelection, there was speculation that the Bush campaign might favor such a pardon as a means to demonstrate the president's compassion and his sympathy with the Jewish community. On October 23, the *New York Times* published a full-page ad calling for Pollard's release, signed by 575 rabbis and 65 rabbinic organizations. Yet no pardon was forthcoming before the election.

After election day, when Bush was defeated by Bill Clinton, Pollard's champions asked both the outgoing and the incoming presidents for a pardon. Bush's December pardon of former secretary of defense Caspar Weinberger for withholding information from Congress added further impetus to their efforts. After all, it was none other than Weinberger who had asked the trial judge to treat Pollard severely on the grounds that the spy had caused incalculable harm to the nation. But 1992 ended with Pollard still in jail, with no prospect of freedom any time soon.

Jewish Continuity

The findings of the 1990 National Jewish Population Survey continued to vex American Jews. The news that over 50 percent of young Jews were marrying out of the faith, and that relatively few of the offspring of such marriages were raised as Jews, generated wide-ranging and sometimes acrimonious debate— and considerable coverage in the general and Jewish media—about strategies to strengthen American Jewish identity and thereby secure the Jewish future.

Writing in *Moment* magazine (August), Barry Kosmin, the demographer who led the team that conducted the survey, put the findings into historical perspective: "In a society where religion is an individual attribute, and more Jews regard themselves as members of a cultural group (72 percent) than as members of a religious group (47 percent), the boundaries of the Jewish population have become permeable." He compared the situation to the pre-Christian Roman Empire, with its "free marketplace of religious ideas" and the relative freedom of Jews to live their lives as they saw fit. Kosmin pointed to one optimistic finding of his survey, that over 70 percent of American Jews said that being Jewish was important in their lives. But he offered no suggestion as to how that vague sentiment might be actualized, how the Jewish community could reach "some of America's most sophisticated citizens and one of its most attractive consumer markets."

A front-page story in the *New York Times* (October 18) by religion editor Peter Steinfels focused on the threat that intermarriage posed to Jewish survival and the efforts of the Jewish community to reach out to intermarried couples. Reform congregations, noted Steinfels, had long been committed to such inclusionary activities, and most of the almost 600 programs around the country geared to intermarrieds were under Reform auspices. The only question remaining, for Reform, was one of degree: to what extent should non-Jewish spouses of Jews participate in Jewish religious life? "Can non-Jewish parents recite blessings or honor the Torah during a child's bar or bat mitzvah? Can non-Jews hold synagogue offices or vote on important issues?" were among the specific issues they raised.

Steinfels also cited the opinions of the skeptics. Rabbi Jerome Epstein, executive vice-president of the United Synagogue of Conservative Judaism, challenged the proponents of programs for the intermarried, asking, "Where are the great successes of outreach after more than a decade?" Dr. Steven Bayme, director of the American Jewish Committee's Jewish communal affairs department, decried the tendency to accept the fact of intermarriage as an inevitable aspect of living in an open society. He suggested that if the opposition to intermarriage collapsed totally, the rate of such marriages would soar beyond 90 percent. Though endorsing carefully targeted programs to intermarried families that showed some interest in Jewishness, both Bayme and Epstein rejected the participation of non-Jews in the synagogue.

During the year, a number of new studies of the American Jewish community provided more reasons for concern besides the narrow issue of intermarriage. Two of these were surveys published by the American Jewish Committee. *Organizational Affiliation of American Jews: A Research Report*, which surveyed the affiliation patterns of a national sample of 1,114 Jews, found that although 70 percent were affiliated in some way with the Jewish community, the Jewish connection had little effect on their everyday lives: the majority did no volunteer work, attended no meetings, and contributed little money. Jewish affiliation, then, could be regarded as wide but rather shallow. *The High Cost of Jewish Living*, which analyzed the expenses incurred in living a Jewish life in the Philadelphia area, suggested that dues for synagogues and Jewish community centers and the fees for Jewish schools and summer camps were so high as to discourage affiliation. The report concluded by asking, "Is living Jewishly beyond the reach of a significant segment of American Jewry? Has exclusion because of cost led to alienation from the Jewish community and Jewish causes?" The response of leaders in other communities to the study indicated that the problem was not unique to Philadelphia.

A demographic study of the nation's most important Jewish community provided some cause for concern: New York City Jewry was slowly shrinking. Considered the most solidly Jewish metropolis in the nation, with the highest levels of Jewish identification and the lowest intermarriage rate, New York Jewry was nevertheless declining numerically. A population study conducted by the New York UJA-Federation showed a loss of 222,300 Jews since 1981, 13.5 percent of the Jewish population. Although this outflow was part of a larger population movement from the city—in which the rate of Jewish exodus was actually lower than that of other non-Hispanic whites—communal leaders took it seriously. The UJA-Federation convened a high-level strategic planning group to study the implications of the data for programming and fund-raising.

Concern about fund-raising was widespread throughout the Jewish community because of the new complexities posed by demographic changes. For some years it had been clear that wealthy Jews, not as intensely committed to Jewish causes as their counterparts in earlier generations, were giving more to nonsectarian causes than to Jewish philanthropies. This long-term trend, combined with the lingering economic recession, cut into the fund-raising of federations and other Jewish charities in 1992. Perhaps the hardest-hit community was Los Angeles, where severe cuts had to be made in allocations, and staff members of communal agencies—professional and well as clerical—were let go. Other communities, while not as desperate, also sought ways to cut costs. In this climate of fiscal stringency, the *Forward* (November 13) caused a stir of indignation by publishing the six-figure salaries—obtained from publicly available IRS filings—of the executive heads of ten major Jewish organizations.

Prof. Gary Tobin of Brandeis University, in a study commissioned by UJA, found that the national UJA-Federation system, though raising more money than ever before—indeed, as it turned out, more than any other American charity—was getting a steadily declining percentage of the Jewish philanthropic dollar. "There's now more money being raised from Jews by non-Jewish causes," he said, "and we must stop it." Tobin urged federations to hire more fund-raising staff, give donors a heavier dose of "stroking," and insist on higher levels of giving from those who could afford it.

Prof. Gerald Bubis—director of the School of Jewish Communal Service of the Hebrew Union College in Los Angeles—asserted in *Moment* magazine (December) that the fund-raising problem went far deeper. "Jewish philanthropy is in trouble," he wrote, "and the worst is yet to come." While the American Jewish community still placed Israel at the center of its fund-raising, he maintained, more and more American Jews had little or no emotional attachment to the Jewish state. Accompanying Bubis's article were dramatic charts providing graphic evidence for his assertions. True enough, giving over the 1971–1991 period had climbed steadily upward. But when adjusted for inflation, there was actually a decline, if special campaigns like Operation Exodus were not included. And what of the future? Bubis noted that the few super-rich philanthropists devoted to the Jewish community were dying off, and that their successors were professionals, who, by the nature of their income, tend to give considerably less than the self-employed businessmen who were the mainstays of Jewish philanthropy in the past. Bubis warned that without creative new ideas for raising money, "there may well be a massive retrenchment of services when they are needed as never before."

Making Jews More Jewish

Both those seeking chiefly to minimize the incidence of intermarriage and those seeking to improve the chances that intermarrying Jews would still identify as Jews and give to Jewish causes were agreed on one premise: that ways must be found to strengthen the Jewish identification of young people before marriage. Their search for strategies to maximize the prospects for Jewish continuity focused first on Jewish education.

From the teachers' standpoint, Jewish education was unlikely to improve unless the community put more resources into it. The annual conference of the Coalition for the Advancement of Jewish Education, held in August, heard bitter complaints of low salaries, few if any health plans or pensions, the consequent need to juggle two or even more jobs to make ends meet, and the lack of respect from students who knew that their teachers were not valued in the community.

Whether more money alone, in the absence of new approaches to using it, was likely to solve the problem, was questionable. Morton Mandel, a philanthropist eager to help raise the quality of Jewish education, had funded a 1990 study of American Jewish education, out of which came the Council for Initiatives in Jewish Education. The council had announced that in 1992 it would choose three "lead" communities to serve as models for others to follow. These communities would receive professional assistance from the Council of Jewish Federations, the Jewish Community Centers Association of North America, and the Jewish Educational Service of North America in formulating programs and seeking grants from foundations for innovative projects that might be replicated in other cities. On August 25, Atlanta, Baltimore, and Milwaukee were declared the winners.

Jewish educators were showing increased interest in the concept of "family education," that is, educating parents and children together as a unit, using Shabbat dinners, holiday activities, social events, and other functions to draw entire families into participation in Jewish religious and communal life. While most such initiatives targeted unaffiliated families, Torah Umesorah, a major national association of Orthodox Jewish day schools, adopted a similar parent-education program to deal with the new phenomenon of large numbers of unobservant and Jewishly uneducated parents sending their children to day schools.

Jewish life on the college campus also came in for scrutiny from those worried about Jewish continuity, as Jewish communal leaders saw from the examples of their own children and grandchildren the frequent erosion of Jewishness during the college years. While much had been written about anti-Semitic and anti-Zionist incidents on the campus, relatively little had been said about the loss of Jewish identity there. In early May, Hillel, the national Jewish student organization, discussed the problem at its National Leadership Conference in Washington. A task force set up to improve Hillel's effectiveness suggested broadening its function beyond the provision of religious services to encompass cultural and ethnic functions, which might draw Jewish students with no interest in synagogue services. Some worried, however, that turning Hillel into the equivalent of a black or Hispanic student organization could be perceived as giving a Jewish imprimatur to the multiculturalist agenda. Meanwhile, Hillel had to adjust to the drastic curtailment of funding from its parent organization, the financially strapped B'nai B'rith. It hoped to compensate by raising funds from federations to maintain and even enhance programming at colleges located in their areas, while shutting down chapters that were no longer viable.

Another result of the search for ways to inspire young Jews was the emergence in 1992 of a new genre of Jewish literature, the autobiographical essay setting forth what being Jewish means to the writer. Such statements demonstrate, first, the variety of ways in which people of different ages, backgrounds, and outlooks identify with their Jewishness, and second, the fact that one can live a fulfilling, successful life as part of American society without sacrificing Jewish identity. It is assumed that the reader—a college student, young adult, or simply an unaffiliated Jew—will identify with one or another of the essay writers as a Jewish role model and be inspired to live a more Jewish life.

Thus, the cover story of the December 1992 issue of *Moment* magazine was "Why Be Jewish?" It included accounts of the personal Jewish odysseys of nine famous and not-so-famous Jews, running the gamut from sociologist Samuel Heilman's description of his Judaism as a "recurrent personal victory over oblivion," to theologian Irving Greenberg's assertion that Judaism " 'discovered' and taught the world about the God behind nature, the author of the redemption plan," to writer Hillel Halkin's confessed inability to articulate a reason to be Jewish and his warning that "when you need reasons, you're in trouble."

The American Jewish Committee used the autobiographical approach for a series of advertisements on the op-ed page of the *New York Times* under the heading "What Being Jewish Means to Me." The first, appearing on September 27, the eve of Rosh Hashanah, featured a photo of Nobel Laureate Elie Wiesel along with a statement by him articulating the synthesis of Jewish particularism and general humanitarian concern that characterizes Judaism. "The mission of the Jewish people has never been to make the world more Jewish," noted Wiesel, "but to make it more human." The second AJCommittee ad appeared on December 6. In it, U.S. senator Joseph I. Lieberman of Connecticut, an observant Jew, explained how prayer, religious ritual, and an ethnic culture helped sustain him as he worked on Capitol Hill. Both ads, which urged readers to contact the committee for further information about Jewish life, elicited numerous letters and phone calls.

In this atmosphere of heightened anxiety over Jewish continuity, it came as no surprise that the 1992 General Assembly (GA) of the Council of Jewish Federations (CJF)—held in New York City, November 10–15—devoted a full day to the problem. Since the GA, which annually attracts around 3,000 Jewish communal volunteers and professionals, is the closest thing to a North American Jewish "parliament," its agenda is generally an accurate barometer of the mood of the community.

"A full day on a single theme is very rare for a General Assembly," noted CJF president Charles Goodman. "But Jewish identity and continuity is an issue of such magnitude for the future of the North American Jewish community that it was clearly necessary . . . to provide an opportunity for a variety of approaches and for wide-ranging discussions." This was the first time that the General Assembly had ever been held in New York, and the planners took the availability of local talent into consideration when planning the program. After a November 12 morning plenary on "Building Renewed Jewish Communities and New Jewish Meaning: An Historic Challenge for the Federation Movement," the rest of the day was devoted to five forums, and then small-group dialogues and study sessions, on aspects of Jewish identity, led by rabbis and Judaic scholars from the New York area.

The major address at the plenary was delivered by Shoshana Cardin, the outgoing chairwoman of both the Conference of Presidents of Major American Jewish Organizations and the National Conference on Soviet Jewry. Coming as she did from the world of Jewish political activism, her expressed misgivings about overemphasis on such matters had a powerful impact. Cardin suggested that the organized Jewish community shift its emphasis to helping Jews identify as Jews. She challenged the delegates: "You in this room, your leaders, your peers, your co-workers, your colleagues, have agreed that this is in fact the priority." She urged federations to join forces with synagogues to implement Jewish outreach programs so that every Jew will "understand what it is to be Jewish" and no one "who defines himself or herself as a Jew" will feel excluded.

Perhaps Cardin's most controversial point was her proposal that Jewish knowledge be one of the criteria for the selection of Jewish leaders, in addition to organizational and financial know-how. Adding credibility to her argument was the knowledge that Cardin herself had recently accepted the chairmanship of CLAL, the National Jewish Center for Learning and Leadership, an organization dedicated to educating Jewish communal leaders Jewishly through the study of classic Jewish texts and analysis of their relevance to current concerns in the community.

This General Assembly's emphasis on Jewish continuity struck a positive chord among the participants, many of whom enjoyed the small-group Jewish study sessions so much that additional ones were improvised on the spot throughout the week. And President Chaim Herzog of Israel, addressing a plenary session at Radio City Music Hall, reinforced the message when he declared that Jewish education was the top priority for both Israeli and Diaspora Jews. "Your future and our future depends on it," he said. Yet despite the high level of enthusiasm, there were few concrete proposals for enhancing Jewish identification, a fact suggesting to some observers that the challenge of transmitting Jewish values and spirituality might not be amenable to the kinds of organizational and fund-raising strategies used so effectively by the Jewish community for political and philanthropic ends.

The one specific programmatic suggestion that drew considerable interest was the encouragement of trips to Israel by young Jews. Charles Bronfman described to the GA the work of his CRB Foundation in this area. After five years of research that cost $1.5 million, Bronfman could assert that "the Israel experience holds great promise for heightening awareness, strengthening identity, and making a significant contribution to contemporary Jewish life, education, and Jewish continuity." Hoping to increase the number of North American Jewish teenagers who visit Israel from the current 8,000 a year to at least 50,000 by the end of the decade, the foundation, the United Jewish Appeal, and the Council of Jewish Federations had agreed to a pilot program providing grants to 12 local communities to help pay for the trips, as well as for advertising and new staff positions to run the programs, on condition that each local community put up three dollars for every one dollar it received in grants. Peter Geffen, the CRB Foundation official in charge of Israel programs, defined the aim clearly: to make a trip to Israel "a basic tenet of being a young Jewish person in this country."

A change in the CJF bylaws ensured that whatever steps it might eventually take to enhance Jewish continuity or deal with any other matter would reflect a broad consensus of the American Jewish leadership. Whereas CJF was previously run by a board of directors not clearly accountable to any specific constituency, the new system provided for a board of delegates representing each of the federations, with membership weighted according to the size of the community and its campaign. Observers suggested that the CJF was now the closest thing to a democratic national Jewish congress that American Jewry had ever had.

Homosexuals in Jewish Life

The issue of gay rights, so emotional and divisive in the general society, continued to stir debate in the Jewish community as well.

On January 19, the board of directors of the Federation of Reconstructionist Congregations and Havurot adopted a statement, "Homosexuality and Judaism: The Reconstructionist Position," that argued for an end to all distinctions between heterosexuals and homosexuals in Jewish life. This went beyond the Reform movement's position, which accepted homosexuals for the rabbinate while affirming the heterosexual ideal. Explaining the biblical abhorrence of homosexuality as a product of faulty premodern science, the Reconstructionist report asserted, instead, the contemporary idea that "homosexuality is a fundamental constituent of somebody's psychological makeup, not something that can be changed, not a segmented part of their life." Therefore, the Reconstructionists asserted, holiness can inhere in a same-sex relationship, just as it can between a man and a woman, and gays and lesbians, not just straights, can contribute to the strength of the Jewish family. The Reconstructionists also produced a workbook for synagogue programming that would "encourage gay and lesbian Jews to celebrate their unique life-cycle events" and introduce "the stories of gay and lesbian Jews into our people's history."

The Conservative movement was still plagued by this issue in 1992, caught in the tension between halakhic proscription and openness to change and unable to take any step beyond espousing "civil equality" for gays. As one rabbi put it, this was "the most emotion-laden issue" ever to come up, "even more so than the ordination of women." On the one hand, traditionalist forces, led by Rabbi Joel Roth, professor of Talmud at the Jewish Theological Seminary (JTS) and incoming dean of its rabbinical school, maintained that the biblical condemnation of homosexuality remained in place no matter what modern science might say, and that the only way for gays to avoid sin was celibacy. On the other hand, members of a gay club at the seminary, as well as some gay rabbis and sympathizers, proclaimed their opposition by wearing lapel pins on which one triangle of a Jewish star was pink, the color of the badges homosexuals were forced to wear by the Nazis. The homosexual students—who would not have been accepted as students had they revealed their sexual orientation when applying for admission—complained that pressure to conform was so intense at JTS that some of them dated members of the opposite sex so as to avoid detection, and that two gays had been made so uncomfortable they left the school.

In March, a majority (13 out of 23) of the Rabbinical Assembly's Committee on Law and Standards, which sets Conservative religious policy, voted to back Rabbi Roth's reassertion of the traditional position. While homosexuals would be welcomed to participate in synagogues, schools, camps, and youth groups affiliated with the movement, no openly gay applicant would be admitted to the rabbinical or cantorial schools, and Conservative rabbis were prohibited from conducting "commitment ceremonies" for gay and lesbian couples. It was left up to individual rabbis to decide whether to hire homosexuals as teachers and youth leaders, and whether to grant them lay leadership positions and synagogue honors.

While a proposal to equalize the status of homosexuals in the movement received only the one vote of its sponsor on the committee, a third viewpoint, articulated by Rabbi Elliot Dorff, provost of the seminary's University of Judaism in Los Angeles, garnered eight votes, and thereby, according to the rules of the Committee on Law and Standards, was also considered "adopted." Dorff cited recent scientific evidence that homosexuality is an inborn trait and suggested that this takes it outside the biblical category of "abomination." His plan called for maintaining the status quo pending further study of the broad issue of human sexuality by a new committee that reflected a wider spectrum of the movement's constituency: JTS, the lay people active in the United Synagogue of Conservative Judaism, and the pulpit rabbis who constitute the Rabbinical Assembly.

Immediately, the United Synagogue executive vice-president, reflecting the predominant lay view that there were far more important issues facing the Conservative movement, and the chancellor of JTS, deploring the blurring of lines between Conservative and Reform Judaism caused by the failure to articulate a single, unequivocal traditionalist stance, announced that their institutions would not participate. The supporters of the Dorff position insisted nevertheless that they would proceed with their new committee. Rabbi Gordon Tucker, leaving his post as dean of the JTS Rabbinical School, compared those unwilling to join in the search for new knowledge about sexuality to Galileo's contemporaries who refused to look through his telescope. Eleven faculty members at JTS issued a public letter supporting the Dorff plan and denying that the accession of Joel Roth as dean of the rabbinical school signaled that only the traditionalist position was welcome at the institution. Dorff, meanwhile, was delighted that his view had attained official recognition. "There is now a *teshuvah* (rabbinical response) on the books," he said, "that says engaging in homosexual acts is not *toeva* (abomination)."

The May convention of the Rabbinical Assembly (RA) made clear that, on the whole, Conservative rabbis were more open to gay rights than the movement's academicians or laity. The rabbis voted unanimously to implement the special committee suggested in the Dorff proposal. The RA also voted 64–50 to place rabbis in any congregation that requests one, "without consideration of the sexual orientation of its members," a matter that had never before been addressed officially by the movement. However, unwilling to assert authority on halakhic issues not within its purview, the RA appended a clause to the resolution declaring the decision void should the Committee on Law and Standards decide that it breached Jewish law.

The decision to allow placement of Conservative rabbis in predominantly gay synagogues came a bit too late for Congregation Beth Simchat Torah in New York City, whose 1,100 members made it the largest gay synagogue in the country. In March the synagogue chose Sharon Kleinbaum from among over 50 applicants as its first rabbi. An open lesbian, Kleinbaum was a graduate of the Reconstructionist Rabbinical College and a member of the Reform movement's Central Conference of American Rabbis. She responded to the considerable media attention that her appointment attracted—including an article and photo in the *New York Times* (March 29)—by declaring: "I am not a rabbi for any particular sexual orientation. I am a rabbi." She was officially installed in September.

The Orthodox response was blunt. Rabbi Binyamin Walfish, executive vice-president of the Rabbinical Council of America, condemned "the so-called rabbi of this so-called synagogue." Noting that Orthodoxy had room for homosexuals so long as "they stay in the closet," Walfish compared a gay synagogue to one established by "pork-eaters." And when the National Jewish Community Relations Advisory Council adopted a statement condemning discrimination on the basis of sexual orientation, the Union of Orthodox Jewish Congregations of America (UOJCA) abstained. Explaining that it opposed discrimination, the Orthodox group pointed out that Jewish law prohibited homosexual activity, "and we cannot join in a statement that could be misinterpreted to imply otherwise." Had the NJCRAC declaration not included support for an exemption for religious institutions, the Orthodox union would have exercised its veto and scuttled the decision.

Denominational Developments

ORTHODOX JUDAISM

As the Jewish movement least touched—though hardly unaffected—by the demographic ravages plaguing the rest of American Jewry, Orthodoxy spent much of its energy on the internal battle between its modern and its more traditionalist wings.

Dr. Norman Lamm, president of Yeshiva University (YU), the flagship institute of modern Orthodoxy, declared at the national convention of the Rabbinical Council of America that the "entrenchment and fortress psychology" of the sectarian Orthodox "is a sign of weakness." Declaring that only moderate Orthodoxy could serve as a bridge between the world of tradition and the other branches of Judaism, Lamm urged his audience not to allow themselves to be intimidated by the right. Ironically, it was Dr. Lamm who found himself accused by those in his own ideological camp of aiding and abetting the right.

At the beginning of 1992, the fate of Yeshiva University's Bernard Revel Graduate School was still unclear. The only Orthodox-sponsored coed graduate school of Jewish studies in the United States, Revel was ordered in 1991 to end its degree-granting programs, which would be replaced by courses in "Jewish thought" that would lead to a certificate rather than a diploma. Though President Lamm, who made the decision, cited financial factors for the change, students, alumni, and many others in the modern Orthodox community argued that the loss of this recognized school, which utilized modern critical modes of scholarship, would signal a victory for sectarian Orthodoxy, which had always insisted on traditional, uncritical educational methodology and separate education for men and women. But peaceful student sit-ins and wide publicity brought results. According to Lamm, the outcry in opposition to the change brought forward donors willing to support the school, and now, for the first time, Revel would have its own board of directors to look after its fiscal health.

The next intra-Orthodox confrontation took place within the Rabbinical Council of America (RCA), and this time the sectarians won. In 1991 an Orthodox "Roundtable" under the aegis of the RCA had suggested halakhically acceptable ways to reach out to intermarried Jews. In May 1992, a letter protesting the work of the roundtable was circulated, signed by 14 prominent talmudists at Yeshiva University. "We declare," the letter concluded, "that intermarriage is anathema to the Jewish community and those who marry outside the faith have separated themselves from *Hashem* (God) and his people." By September the pressure from the right was so great that the RCA issued a press release calling it "regretful" that the roundtable document, intended only for "internal discussion," had created the impression that there had been any change in the organization's opposition to "any generalized notion of alternative reactions in dealing with intermarriages. Any public impression of either substance or mood given by the paper that intermarriage is somehow mitigated in our time and place is unequivocally repudiated."

Significant new research by Prof. Samuel Heilman, sponsored by the American Jewish Committee, suggested that those forces within Orthodoxy least willing to seek accommodation with the non-Orthodox were likely to grow with time. Comparing the attitudes of rabbis with those of rabbinical students, Heilman found that the students—the rabbis of the future—were far more hard-line in their attitudes toward the other denominations than those already in the pulpit. And in a newspaper article (*Baltimore Jewish Times,* October 2, 1992), Heilman theorized about the sociological dynamic involved. As increasing numbers of the moderate Orthodox have entered the professions, he suggested, Jewish education has been taken over largely—by default—by the most insular elements of Orthodoxy, those who shun the outside world. Many of the children of the modernists, exposed to such educational influences, either turn to the right themselves, or else, feeling alienated, leave Orthodoxy completely, claimed Heilman.

LUBAVITCH MESSIANISM

On March 3, Chabad-Lubavitch Hassidim, who fervently believe in the imminent coming of the Messiah—who could very well be, they feel, the Lubavitcher Rebbe himself, Menachem Mendel Schneerson—were stunned by the news that their 89-year-old leader had suffered a stroke that paralyzed the right side of his body. His public appearances ceased as doctors treated him in his Crown Heights, Brooklyn, headquarters. Since the childless rabbi had apparently made no plans for the succession, there was much speculation about what would happen to the movement with his passing. His own followers, who prayed fervently for his recovery, refused to speculate, and, when pressed, suggested that the question was meaningless, since the Messiah was almost here. On May 19, the Rebbe was taken out-of-doors in a wheelchair for the first time since the stroke. His assistants said that he was able to read his mail but could not yet dictate replies.

Meanwhile, some Lubavitch leaders—sensing perhaps that, with an incapacitated leader and no successor, the movement had to demonstrate its continuing vitality—escalated the public messianic campaign. Glossy literature, full-page newspaper ads, billboards, subway posters, and loudspeakers on caravans of buses urged people to help the Rebbe get well and to bring the Messiah by studying Torah, giving charity, and performing good deeds. The great man's illness, they argued, was but a test of faith. Cooler heads among the Lubavitch leaders, fearful that this campaign could discredit the movement and hurt fund-raising, tried to calm things down. By April, two factions had coalesced: the radicals, led by Rabbi Shmuel Butman, openly stated that the Rebbe was the Messiah; the moderates, led by Rabbi Yehuda Krinsky, would go no further than the position that the world must be made ready for the Messiah's arrival.

With the coming of fall, speculation centered on whether Rabbi Schneerson would be well enough to attend High Holy Day services. The faithful were overjoyed to see him appear—for an hour the first day of Rosh Hashanah and 90 minutes the second day—on a specially constructed balcony above the main Lubavitch synagogue. On Yom Kippur and each day of Sukkot, he made 90-minute appearances, and on the last two days of Sukkot his followers greeted him by singing "King Messiah." From then on, the song became a regular feature of Lubavitch gatherings whenever Rabbi Schneerson was seen. Rumors spread that the Rebbe had been seen making hand motions when he heard the song, which was interpreted by many as a sign that he was accepting the messianic mantle. Rabbi Krinsky and other moderates denied that it meant anything.

CONSERVATIVE JUDAISM

The role of gays and lesbians was not the only matter of concern for the Conservative movement in 1992. In June, severe financial constraints induced the Jewish Theological Seminary to stop funding over a third of the budget of the Masorti movement, the Israeli branch of Conservative Judaism. Masorti would now have to raise these funds directly in the United States. And in October, the Masorti-Conservative relationship underwent a different kind of strain when the Masorti Halakhah Committee declared that Conservative Jews in Israel may not ride to synagogue on the Sabbath—unlike American Conservative Jews, who had been allowed to ride to the synagogue by a ruling in 1950. The Masorti rabbis explained that, unlike the case in suburban America, very few Israelis do not live within walking distance of a synagogue. And as for Masorti Jews who do not live near Masorti congregations and do not want to patronize Orthodox synagogues, the committee went on, "people for whom Shabbat observance is important will move to another home in order to live close to the synagogue of their choice." "Our job is not to justify lack of observance by our constituents," declared Rabbi David Golinkin, chairman of the Halakhah Committee in Israel. This was the first halakhic dispute ever between American and Israeli Conservative authorities, and it was not even clear whether the Israelis had the right to go against the American precedent.

The impulse "not to justify lack of observance" was felt in American Conservative Judaism as well. In a hard-hitting address to the board of directors of the United Synagogue, Rabbi Jerome Epstein, the executive director, put the Conservative synagogues on notice that they could be expelled for not adhering to the standards of the movement. He specified those derelictions that could lead to ouster: not having a religious school that requires attendance six hours a week for five years prior to bar/bat mitzvah, accepting non-Jews as members, recognizing children of non-Jewish mothers as Jews, and public congregational desecration of the Sabbath. "We stand for something," Epstein insisted, "and we have to become more committed to emphasizing that we do."

One reason for the frustration of people like Epstein was the fact that many of the most observant Conservative Jews, angered at the decision to ordain women, had formed their own organization in 1983, which officially broke with the Conservative movement in 1990, and, calling itself the Union for Traditional Judaism (UTJ), set up the Institute of Traditional Judaism to train rabbis. In 1992 the UTJ—made up of 8,000 families and 350 rabbis—broadened its scope by incorporating the Fellowship of Traditional Orthodox Rabbis, an organization of between 50 and 100 modern Orthodox rabbis unhappy with the growing ascendancy of the Orthodox right wing. Rabbi Ronald Price, the UTJ executive vice-president, declared: "Through this agreement we have taken a major step toward unifying the traditional halakhic community and marshaling the resources available therein, to teach open-minded observant Judaism to the entire Jewish community."

REFORM JUDAISM

The Reform movement in 1992 was primarily concerned with how to cope with the high intermarriage rate. Reform temples in many communities had considerable numbers of intermarried families as members, and the movement had a multi-pronged strategy to deal with the phenomenon. In February the Commission on Reform Jewish Outreach issued three publications on aspects of intermarriage. One, on outreach, stressed the importance of inculcating a sense of Jewish peoplehood among converts and children of intermarriage, who often conceive of Judaism only as a matter of faith. The second publication, on the role of the non-Jew in the synagogue, argued for the inclusion of non-Jewish spouses of Jews, so as to "draw them closer to us and involve them in Jewish life." The third, on how to talk to adolescents about interdating and intermarriage, explained how to get teenagers to examine their own Jewish identity and thus "increase the likelihood that they will be advocates for Judaism in their lives."

Intermarriage was also the main theme of the annual convention of the Central Conference of American Rabbis (CCAR) in April. Keynote speaker Steven Bayme, director of Jewish communal affairs for the American Jewish Committee, challenged the Reform rabbis to dispel the image of Reform as "weak, watered-down" Judaism by speaking out against intermarriage and insisting on conversion of the non-Jewish spouse. Echoing Bayme, Rabbi Walter Jacob, the CCAR president, called for clear boundaries separating Jews from non-Jews. "Should a non-Jew be a member of a congregation?" he asked, and provided his own answer: "No."

RECONSTRUCTIONIST JUDAISM

The major contribution to Jewish theology in 1992 came from the Reconstructionist movement. Rabbi Arthur Green's *Seek My Face, Speak My Name* was the first serious attempt to arrive at a contemporary understanding of Judaism based not on rationalism, ethics, or Halakhah, but on the Jewish mystical tradition. Rabbi Green, who was serving as president of the Reconstructionist Rabbinical College when he wrote the book, asserted that all the "events" recorded in the Bible were "metaphors for a truth whose depth reaches far beyond them." He argued for a "nondualistic" worldview that would eliminate the traditional distinction between the material and the divine: " 'God' and 'world,' " wrote Green, "are different modes of the only Being there is." He denied that God had any plan for the world or that God acted in history. Rather, God is experienced in "human intimacy," care for the environment, and a respect for life that mandates vegetarianism. Revelation does not come from on high, but, like an artist's inspiration, emerges from within the human soul. Green wrote: "I do not know a God who 'commands' specific religious behavior or forms of worship." In his view, the messiah will be "the human self most fully open to the One, perhaps the human self that stands at the very far edge of transcending what we understand as 'human' altogether. . . ."

Although Green's views were his own, not those of the movement, they reflected a growing interest in mysticism in recent years, which coexisted, not always comfortably, with the naturalism and rationalism of Mordecai Kaplan, the movement's founder.

LAWRENCE GROSSMAN

Jewish Population in the United States, 1993

BASED ON LOCAL COMMUNITY counts—the method for identifying and enumerating Jewish population that serves as the basis of this report—the estimated size of the American Jewish community in 1993 was 5.8 million. This is about 5 percent more than the 5.5 million "core" Jewish population estimated in the Council of Jewish Federations' 1990 National Jewish Population Survey (NJPS).[1]

The difference, small though it is, between the national and aggregated local figures is partly explained by the lag in data gathering and reporting on the local level. As more local communities conduct studies over the next few years, declines and increases that have already occurred will be documented, and the updated statistics will most likely show national and regional patterns more in line with NJPS findings. However, since there are definitional issues as well as a lack of uniformity in local research, the aggregate counts may never exactly match the NJPS national totals.

The demographic results of the NJPS suggested that the population was growing slightly due to an excess of Jewish births over Jewish deaths during the late 1980s. However, extrapolation from the age structure suggests that for the mid-1990s, zero population growth in numbers has been realized, with a balance between the annual numbers of births and deaths. At the same time, some growth in numbers is occurring through Jewish immigration into the United States. The most obvious example is that of refugees from the former Soviet Union, for whom the annual quota is currently set at 40,000 Jews each year.

The NJPS used a scientifically selected sample to project a total number for the United States, but could not provide accurate information on the state and local levels. Therefore, as in past years, in this article we have based local, state, and regional population figures on the usual estimating procedures.

While the Jewish federations are the chief reporting bodies, their service areas vary in size and may represent several towns, one county, or an aggregate of several counties. In some cases we have subdivided federation areas to reflect the more natural geographic boundaries. Some estimates, from areas without federations, have been provided by local rabbis and other informed Jewish community leaders. In still other cases, the figures that have been updated are from past estimates provided by United Jewish Appeal field representatives. Finally, for smaller communities where no recent estimates are available, figures are based on extrapolation from older data. The estimates are for the resident Jewish population, including those in private households and in institutional settings. Non-Jewish family members have been excluded from the total.

---

[1]See Barry A. Kosmin et al., *Highlights of the CJF 1990 National Jewish Population Survey* (New York, Council of Jewish Federations, 1991).

The state and regional totals shown in Appendix tables 1 and 2 are derived by summing the individual estimates shown in table 3 and then making three adjustments. First, communities of less than 100 are added. Second, duplicated counts within states are eliminated. Third, communities whose population resides in two or more states (e.g., Kansas City and Greater Washington, D.C.) are distributed accordingly.

Because population estimating is not an exact science, the reader should be aware that in cases where a figure differs from last year's, the increase or decrease did not come about suddenly but occurred over a period of time and has just now been substantiated. Similarly, the results of a completed local demographic study often change the previously reported Jewish population figure. This should be understood as either an updated calculation of gradual demographic change or a correction of a faulty older estimate.

In determining Jewish population, communities count both affiliated and nonaffiliated residents who are "core" Jews as defined in NJPS.[2] In most cases, counts are made by households, with that number multiplied by the average number of self-defined Jewish persons per household. Similarly to NJPS, most communities also include those born and raised as Jews but who at present consider themselves as having no religion. As stated above, non-Jews living in Jewish households, primarily the non-Jewish spouses and non-Jewish children, are not included in the 1993 estimates presented in the appendix below.

Local Population Changes

Six communities reported increases of more than 1,000 this year. The community reporting the largest numeric increase was that of the Boca Raton-Delray Beach area at the southern end of Florida's Palm Beach County, which raised its population count from 60,000 to 70,500. The remaining portion of Palm Beach County and the Gulf Coast community of Tampa also show significant growth. The new estimate for each of these Florida communities reflects actual Jewish population growth, documented by a substantial increase in the number of Jewish households on the respective federation lists.

The new larger figures for Raleigh, North Carolina, and Somerset County, New Jersey, were also substantiated through expanded communal lists. The large increase for Sacramento, California, was documented in that community's recently completed Jewish population study. The communities with the largest percentage increases are all on the West Coast. Along with Sacramento, these include Corvallis, Oregon, and Napa County and the Vallejo areas of California.

The other communities showing significant but less dramatic Jewish population increases are primarily in the South and West. These include Naples-Collier County, Brevard County, and Orlando, Florida; Atlanta, Georgia; New Orleans, Louisiana;

---

[2]Born Jews who report adherence to Judaism, Jews by choice, and born Jews without a current religion ("secular Jews").

Las Vegas, Nevada; Albuquerque, New Mexico; Charlotte, North Carolina; and Columbia, South Carolina. Several communities outside these regions also had increases: Kalamazoo, Michigan; Manchester, New Hampshire; and Lancaster, Pennsylvania.

No community reported a significant loss in Jewish population. The biggest decline was in the Los Angeles metropolitan region, where, based on several independent measures, the Jewish population count was reduced by about 2 percent, a drop of 11,000. This decline may be the result of migration out of Los Angeles and other parts of southern California to the northern part of the state as well as to the Pacific Northwest.

The drop of over 5,000 in Middlesex County, New Jersey, represents a correction of the previous estimate, which was found to be based on questionable methodology.

Continuing the trend of recent years, most of the communities reporting declines were in the Northeast and Midwest. These include Bridgeport, Connecticut; Kankakee, Illinois; Evansville and Lafayette, Indiana; Leominster, the Lynn-North Shore area, and North Berkshire County, Massachusetts; Bayonne, New Jersey; Poughkeepsie-Dutchess County, Niagara Falls, and Rome, New York; Akron and Canton, Ohio; and Butler, Pennsylvania. Declines outside of these regions occurred in Santa Barbara, California, and Beaumont, Texas.

BARRY A. KOSMIN
JEFFREY SCHECKNER

APPENDIX

TABLE 1. JEWISH POPULATION IN THE UNITED STATES, 1993

State	Estimated Jewish Population	Total Population*	Estimated Jewish Percent of Total
Alabama.................	9,000	4,138,000	0.2
Alaska	2,400	587,000	0.4
Arizona	72,000	3,882,000	1.8
Arkansas	1,800	2,399,000	0.1
California................	919,000	30,677,000	3.0
Colorado	51,000	3,470,000	1.5
Connecticut..............	97,500	3,281,000	3.0
Delaware.................	9,500	689,000	1.4
District of Columbia........	25,500	589,000	4.3
Florida..................	622,000	13,488,000	4.6
Georgia	75,000	6,751,000	1.1
Hawaii..................	7,000	1,160,000	0.6
Idaho...................	500	1,067,000	(z)
Illinois..................	268,000	11,631,000	2.3
Indiana.................	17,500	5,662,000	0.3
Iowa....................	6,000	2,812,000	0.2
Kansas..................	14,000	2,523,000	0.6
Kentucky................	11,500	3,766,000	0.3
Louisiana................	16,500	4,287,000	0.4
Maine...................	8,000	1,235,000	0.6
Maryland................	212,000	4,909,000	4.3
Massachusetts	270,000	5,998,000	4.5
Michigan	107,000	9,437,000	1.1
Minnesota	32,500	4,480,000	0.7
Mississippi...............	1,400	2,614,000	0.1
Missouri.................	61,500	5,193,000	1.2
Montana.................	500	824,000	0.1
Nebraska	7,000	1,606,000	0.4
Nevada..................	21,000	1,327,000	1.6
New Hampshire	8,000	1,111,000	0.7
New Jersey	437,000	7,789,000	5.6
New Mexico	7,000	1,581,000	0.4
New York	1,640,000	18,119,000	9.1

State	Estimated Jewish Population	Total Population*	Estimated Jewish Percent of Total
North Carolina	20,000	6,843,000	0.3
North Dakota	600	636,000	0.1
Ohio	129,000	10,941,000	1.2
Oklahoma.	5,500	3,212,000	0.2
Oregon	17,500	2,977,000	0.6
Pennsylvania	330,000	12,009,000	2.8
Rhode Island	16,000	1,005,000	1.6
South Carolina.	9,000	3,603,000	0.3
South Dakota.	350	711,000	(z)
Tennessee	17,500	5,024,000	0.4
Texas	109,000	17,658,000	0.6
Utah	3,500	1,813,000	0.2
Vermont	5,500	570,000	0.9
Virginia.	68,500	6,377,000	1.1
Washington	33,000	5,136,000	0.6
West Virginia.	2,500	1,812,000	0.1
Wisconsin.	35,000	5,007,000	0.7
Wyoming	500	466,000	(z)
U.S. TOTAL	**5,840,000	255,082,000	2.3

N.B. Details may not add to totals because of rounding.

*Resident population, April 1, 1992. (*Source:* U.S. Bureau of the Census, *Current Population Reports,* series P-25, no. 1044.)

**Exclusive of Puerto Rico and the Virgin Islands, which previously reported Jewish populations of 1,500 and 350, respectively.

(z) Figure is less than 0.1 and rounds to 0.

TABLE 2.   DISTRIBUTION OF U.S. JEWISH POPULATION BY REGIONS, 1993

Region	Total Population	Percent Distribution	Jewish Population	Percent Distribution
Northeast	51,118,000	20.0	2,813,000	48.2
New England	13,200,000	5.2	405,000	6.9
Middle Atlantic	37,918,000	14.9	2,408,000	41.2
Midwest	60,713,000	23.8	678,000	11.6
East North Central ..	42,753,000	16.8	556,000	9.5
West North Central..	17,960,000	7.0	122,000	2.1
South	88,143,000	34.6	1,215,000	20.8
South Atlantic	45,061,000	17.7	1,043,000	17.9
East South Central...	15,529,000	6.1	39,000	0.7
West South Central ..	27,554,000	10.8	133,000	2.3
West	55,108,000	21.6	1,134,000	19.4
Mountain..........	14,381,000	5.6	155,000	2.7
Pacific	40,726,000	16.0	979,000	16.8
TOTALS............	255,082,000	100.0	5,840,000	100.0

N.B. Details may not add to totals because of rounding.

TABLE 3. COMMUNITIES WITH JEWISH POPULATIONS OF 100 OR MORE, 1993
(ESTIMATED)

State and City	Jewish Population	State and City	Jewish Population	State and City	Jewish Population
ALABAMA		CALIFORNIA		Oakland (incl. in	
*Birmingham	5,200	Antelope Valley	700	Alameda County,	
Decatur (incl. in		Bakersfield-Kern		under S.F. Bay Area)	
Florence total)		County	1,400	Ontario (incl. in	
Dothan	150	Berkeley (incl. in		Pomona Valley)	
Florence	150	Contra Costa County,		Orange County	75,000
Huntsville	750	under S.F. Bay		Palmdale (incl. in	
**Mobile	1,100	Area)		Antelope Valley)	
**Montgomery	1,000	Carmel (incl. in Mon-		Palm Springs[N]	9,850
Sheffield (incl. in		terey Peninsula)		Palo Alto (incl. in	
Florence total)		*Chico	500	South Peninsula,	
Tuscaloosa	300	Corona (incl. in		under S.F. Bay Area)	
Tuscumbia (incl. in		Riverside total)		Pasadena (incl. in	
Florence total)		***El Centro	125	L.A. Metro Area	
		*Eureka	500	total)	
ALASKA		Fairfield	800	Petaluma (incl. in	
**Anchorage	2,000	Fontana (incl. in		Sonoma County,	
*Fairbanks	180	San Bernardino		under S.F. Bay Area)	
Juneau	100	total)		Pomona Valley[N]	6,750
Ketchikan (incl. in		*Fresno	2,500	*Redding area	150
Juneau total)		Lancaster (incl. in		Redwood Valley	200
		Antelope Valley)		Riverside	2,000
ARIZONA		Long Beach (also		Sacramento[N]	21,300
Cochise County	260	incl. in Los Angeles		Salinas	750
*Flagstaff	250	total)[N]	13,500	San Bernardino area	
Lake Havasu City	100	Los Angeles Metro			3,000
*Phoenix	50,000	Area	490,000	*San Diego	70,000
Prescott	250	*Merced County	190	San Francisco Bay	
Sierra Vista (incl. in		*Modesto	500	Area[N]	210,000
Cochise County)		Monterey Peninsula		Alameda County	
*Tucson	20,000		2,300		32,500
***Yuma	100	Moreno Valley (incl. in		Contra Costa County	
		Riverside total)			22,000
ARKANSAS		Murietta Hot Springs		Marin County	18,500
Fayetteville	150		400	N. Peninsula	
Hot Springs	130	*Napa County	950		24,500
**Little Rock	1,350				

[N]See Notes below. *Includes entire county. **Includes all of 2 counties. ***Figure not updated.

State and City	Jewish Population
San Francisco.	49,500
San Jose	33,000
Sonoma County	9,000
S. Peninsula	21,000
*San Jose (listed under S.F. Bay Area)	
*San Luis Obispo.	1,450
*Santa Barbara	4,500
***Santa Cruz.	1,200
***Santa Maria.	300
Santa Monica (also incl. in Los Angeles total)	8,000
Santa Rosa (incl. in Sonoma County, under S.F. Bay Area)	
Sonoma County (listed under S.F. Bay Area)	
South Lake Tahoe.	150
*Stockton.	1,200
Sun City	200
Tulare & Kings counties	300
Ukiah (incl. in Redwood Valley total)	
Vallejo area	900
*Ventura County .	9,000

COLORADO

State and City	Jewish Population
Aspen	250
Boulder (incl. in Denver total)	
Colorado Springs	1,500
Denver[N]	46,000
Evergreen.	100
*Ft. Collins	1,000
*Grand Junction.	250
Greeley (incl. in Ft. Collins total)	
Loveland (incl. in Ft. Collins total)	
Pueblo	250

State and City	Jewish Population
Telluride	100
Vail	100

CONNECTICUT

State and City	Jewish Population
Bridgeport[N]	10,250
Bristol (incl. in Hartford total)	
Cheshire (incl. in Meriden total)	
Colchester	300
Danbury[N]	3,500
Danielson.	100
Darien (incl. in Stamford total)	
Greenwich	3,900
Hartford[N]	26,000
Hebron (incl. in Colchester total)	
Lebanon (incl. in Colchester total)	
Lower Middlesex County[N]	1,650
Manchester (incl. in Hartford total)	
Meriden[N]	3,000
Middletown	1,300
New Britain (incl. in Hartford total)	
New Haven[N]	24,000
New London[N]	4,000
New Milford area	600
Newtown (incl. in Danbury total)	
Norwalk[N]	9,500
Norwich (also incl. in New London total)	1,750
Rockville (incl. in Hartford total)	
Shelton (incl. in Valley area)	
Southington (incl. in Meriden total)	

State and City	Jewish Population
Stamford/New Canaan	9,600
Storrs (incl. in Willimantic total)	
Torrington area.	580
Valley area[N]	550
Wallingford (also incl. in Meriden total) .	500
Waterbury[N]	3,000
Westport (incl. in Norwalk total)	
Willimantic area	700

DELAWARE

State and City	Jewish Population
Dover[N]	650
Wilmington (incl. rest of state)	9,500

DISTRICT OF COLUMBIA

State and City	Jewish Population
Greater Washington	165,000

FLORIDA

State and City	Jewish Population
Boca Raton-Delray Beach (listed under Southeast Fla.)	
Brevard County .	4,140
*Crystal River.	100
**Daytona Beach .	2,500
Ft. Lauderdale (listed under Southeast Fla.)	
Ft. Myers-Lee County.	5,000
Ft. Pierce.	500
Gainesville.	1,600
Hollywood (listed under Southeast Fla.)	
**Jacksonville	7,300
Key West.	500
*Lakeland	800
*Miami-Dade County (listed under Southeast Fla.)	

State and City	Jewish Population	State and City	Jewish Population	State and City	Jewish Population
Naples-Collier County 3,500		Brunswick 100		Rock Island (incl. in Quad Cities)	
Ocala-Marion County 200		**Columbus 1,000		Rockford[N] 1,000	
Orlando[N] 18,850		**Dalton 180		Southern Illinois[N] . . 750	
Palm Beach County		Fitzgerald-Cordele . 125		*Springfield 1,000	
(listed under		Macon 900		Waukegan 400	
Southeast Fla.)		*Savannah 3,000			
**Pasco County . . 1,000		**Valdosta........ 100		INDIANA	
**Pensacola........ 775				Bloomington 1,000	
*Port Charlotte-Punta		HAWAII		Elkart (incl. in	
Gorda 400		Hilo 280		South Bend total)	
*St. Petersburg-		Honolulu (includes		Evansville 450	
Clearwater..... 9,500		all of Oahu) ... 6,400		**Ft. Wayne 900	
**Sarasota 12,000		Kauai............ 100		**Gary-Northwest	
Southeast Florida		Maui 210		Indiana 2,200	
.... 533,000				**Indianapolis... 10,000	
Boca Raton-Delray		IDAHO		**Lafayette 400	
Beach...... 70,500		**Boise 220		*Michigan City..... 280	
Ft. Lauderdale[N]		Lewiston (incl. in		Muncie........... 160	
.... 140,000		Moscow total)		South Bend[N] 2,000	
Hollywood[N] . . 66,000		Moscow 100		*Terre Haute....... 250	
Miami-Dade County					
.... 189,000		ILLINOIS		IOWA	
Palm Beach County		Aurora area....... 500		Ames (also incl. in	
(excl. Boca Raton-		Bloomington-Normal		Des Moines total). 200	
Delray Beach)		 230		Cedar Rapids 420	
.... 67,800		Carbondale (incl. in		Council Bluffs (also	
Stuart-Port St. Lucie		S. Ill. total)		incl. in Omaha, Nebr.	
.... 3,000		*Champaign-Urbana		total) 150	
Tallahassee 1,640		 1,300		Davenport (incl. in	
*Tampa 15,000		Chicago Metro Area[N]		Quad Cities, Ill.)	
Venice (incl. in		 261,000		*Des Moines..... 2,800	
Sarasota total)		**Danville......... 100		*Iowa City 1,200	
*Vero Beach 300		*Decatur 200		**Sioux City 570	
Winter Haven (incl.		***DeKalb 200		*Waterloo 170	
in Lakeland total)		East St. Louis (incl.			
		in S. Ill.)		KANSAS	
GEORGIA		Elgin[N] 600		Kansas City (incl. in	
Albany........... 190		Freeport (incl. in		Kansas City, Mo.)	
Athens........... 300		Rockford total)		Lawrence......... 175	
Atlanta Metro Area		*Joliet 500		Manhattan........ 100	
.... 67,500		Kankakee........ 100		*Topeka........... 500	
Augusta[N] 1,400		*Peoria............ 900		Wichita[N] 1,300	
		Quad Cities[N] 1,250			
		**Quincy 105			

State and City	Jewish Population	State and City	Jewish Population	State and City	Jewish Population

KENTUCKY
Covington/Newport
(incl. in Cincinnati,
Ohio total)
Lexington[N] 2,000
*Louisville....... 8,700
Paducah (incl. in S. Ill.)

LOUISIANA
Alexandria........ 150
Baton Rouge[N]... 1,200
Lafayette (incl. in
S. Central La.)
Lake Charles area.. 200
Monroe 525
**New Orleans.. 13,000
*Shreveport........ 905
South Central La.[N]..250

MAINE
Augusta.......... 200
Bangor......... 1,000
Biddeford-Saco (incl.
in S. Maine)
Brunswick-Bath (incl.
in S. Maine)
Lewiston-Auburn .. 500
Portland........ 3,900
Rockland......... 110
Southern Maine (incl.
Portland)[N] 5,500
***Waterville 300

MARYLAND
*Annapolis 2,000
**Baltimore..... 94,500
Cumberland....... 265
*Frederick......... 900
*Hagerstown....... 325
*Harford County . 1,200
Howard County . 7,200
Montgomery and Prince
Georges counties
.... 104,500

Ocean City 100
**Salisbury 400
Silver Spring (incl. in
Montgomery County)
Upper Eastern Shore[N]
.... 130

MASSACHUSETTS
Amherst.......... 750
Andover[N] 3,000
Athol area (also incl.
in Worcester County
total) 300
Attleboro area..... 200
Beverly (incl. in
Lynn total)
Boston Metro Region[N]
.... 228,000
Brockton[N] 8,000
Brookline (also incl. in
Boston total).. 26,000
Cape Cod-Barnstable
County........ 3,000
Clinton (incl. in
Worcester County)
Fall River area .. 1,780
Falmouth (incl. in
Cape Cod)
Fitchburg (also incl.
in Worcester County
total) 300
Framingham (incl. in
Boston total)
Gardner (incl. in
Athol total)
Gloucester (also incl.
in Lynn total).... 450
Great Barrington (incl.
in Pittsfield total)
*Greenfield 1,100
Haverhill 1,500
Holyoke.......... 600
*Hyannis (incl. in
Cape Cod)

Lawrence (incl. in
Andover total)
Leominster (also
incl. in Worcester
County total) 300
Lowell area 2,000
Lynn-North Shore
area[N] 20,000
*Martha's Vineyard . 260
New Bedford[N] .. 3,300
Newburyport...... 280
Newton (also incl. in
Boston total).. 34,000
North Adams (incl. in
N. Berkshire County)
North Berkshire
County.......... 400
Northampton 700
Peabody (incl. in
Lynn total)
Pittsfield-Berkshire
County....... 3,300
Plymouth area..... 500
Provincetown (incl. in
Cape Cod)
Salem (incl. in
Lynn total)
Southbridge (also
incl. in Worcester
County total) 105
Springfield[N].... 11,000
Taunton area.... 1,300
Webster (also
incl. in Worcester
County total) 125
Worcester area[N] 10,100
*Worcester County
.... 13,700

MICHIGAN
*Ann Arbor 5,000
Bay City 200
Benton Harbor area
.... 450

State and City	Jewish Population	State and City	Jewish Population	State and City	Jewish Population

**Detroit Metro Area
.... 94,000
*Flint........... 1,710
*Grand Rapids... 1,500
**Jackson 200
*Kalamazoo 1,100
Lansing area 2,100
*Marquette County . 150
Midland.......... 100
Mt. Clemens (incl. in
Detroit total)
Mt. Pleasant[N] 100
*Muskegon 220
*Saginaw 150

MINNESOTA
**Duluth.......... 500
*Minneapolis.... 22,000
Rochester........ 550
**St. Paul 9,200
Winona (incl. in
LaCrosse, Wis. total)

MISSISSIPPI
Biloxi-Gulfport 150
**Greenville 160
**Hattiesburg 130
**Jackson 550

MISSOURI
Columbia........ 400
Hannibal (incl. in
Quincy, Ill. total)
Kansas City Metro
Area........ 19,100
*St. Joseph 265
**St. Louis 53,500
Springfield 300

MONTANA
*Billings........... 240
Butte 110
Helena (incl. in
Butte total)

NEBRASKA
Grand Island-Hastings
(incl. in Lincoln total)
Lincoln 800
Omaha[N]........ 6,500

NEVADA
Carson City (incl. in
Reno total)
*Las Vegas 20,000
**Reno 1,400
Sparks (incl. in
Reno total)

NEW HAMPSHIRE
Bethlehem 100
Claremont 150
Concord.......... 450
Dover area........ 600
Exeter (incl. in
Portsmouth total)
Franconia (incl. in
Bethlehem total)
Hanover-Lebanon .. 360
*Keene............ 150
**Laconia 270
Littleton (incl. in
Bethlehem total)
Manchester area . 3,500
Nashua area 1,000
Portsmouth area ... 950
Rochester (incl. in
Dover total)
Salem (also incl.
in Andover, Mass.
total) 150

NEW JERSEY
Asbury Park (incl. in
Monmouth County)
*Atlantic City (incl.
Atlantic County)
.... 15,800

Bayonne (listed under
Hudson County)
Bergen County (also
incl. in Northeastern
N.J. total).... 83,700
Bridgeton......... 200
Bridgewater (incl. in
Somerset County)
Camden (incl. in
Cherry Hill total)
Cherry Hill-Southern
N.J.[N]........ 49,000
Edison (incl. in
Middlesex County)
Elizabeth (incl. in
Union County)
Englewood (incl. in
Bergen County)
Essex County[N] (also
incl. in Northeastern
N.J. total).... 76,200
East Essex.... 10,800
Livingston.... 12,600
North Essex .. 15,600
South Essex... 20,300
West Orange-Orange
.... 16,900
Flemington 900
Freehold (incl. in
Monmouth County)
Gloucester (incl. in
Cherry Hill-Southern
N.J. total)
Hoboken (listed under
Hudson County)
Hudson County (also
incl. in Northeastern
N.J. total).... 12,040
Bayonne 1,740
Hoboken 1,100
Jersey City 5,700
North Hudson
County[N] 3,500

State and City	Jewish Population	State and City	Jewish Population	State and City	Jewish Population
Jersey City (listed under Hudson County)		Plainfield (incl. in Union County)		Broome County)	 2,600
Lakewood (incl. in Ocean County)		Princeton area...	3,000	Brewster (incl. in Putnam County)	
Livingston (incl. in Essex County)		Somerset County (also incl. in Northeastern N.J. total)....	10,500	*Buffalo........	17,000
Middlesex County[N] (also incl. in Northeastern N.J. total)........	51,000	Somerville (incl. in Somerset County)		Canandaigua (incl. in Geneva total)	
		Sussex County (also incl. in Northeastern N.J. total).....	4,100	Catskill	200
Monmouth County (also incl. in Northeastern N.J. total)........	33,600	Toms River (incl. in Ocean County)		Corning (incl. in Elmira total)	
		Trenton[N]	6,000	*Cortland	200
Morris County (also incl. in Northeastern N.J. total)....	33,500	Union County (also incl. in Northeastern N.J. total)....	30,000	Dunkirk..........	100
				Ellenville	1,600
Morristown (incl. in Morris County)		Vineland[N]	2,150	Elmira[N]	1,100
Mt. Holly (incl. in Cherry Hill-Southern N.J. total)		Warren County....	400	Fleischmanns......	120
		Wayne (incl. in Passaic County)		Fredonia (incl. in Dunkirk total)	
Newark (incl. in Essex County)		Wildwood	425	Geneva area	310
New Brunswick (incl. in Middlesex County)		Willingboro (incl. in Cherry Hill-Southern N.J. total)		Glens Falls[N]	800
Northeastern N.J.[N]	359,000			*Gloversville	380
		NEW MEXICO		*Herkimer.........	180
Ocean County (also incl. in Northeastern N.J. total).....	9,500	*Albuquerque	5,000	Highland Falls (incl. in Orange County)	
		Las Cruces.......	525	*Hudson	500
Passaic County (also incl. in Northeastern N.J. total)....	17,000	Los Alamos.......	250	*Ithaca area	1,700
		Santa Fe	900	Jamestown........	100
Passaic-Clifton (also incl. in Passaic County total) ..	8,000			Kingston[N]	4,400
		NEW YORK		Lake George (incl. in Glens Falls total)	
Paterson (incl. in Passaic County)		*Albany........	12,000	Liberty (also incl. in Sullivan County total)	2,100
Perth Amboy (incl. in Middlesex County)		Amenia (incl. in Poughkeepsie-Dutchess County)		Middletown (incl. in Orange County)	
Phillipsburg (incl. in Easton, Pa. total)		Amsterdam	170	Monroe (incl. in Orange County)	
		*Auburn	115	Monticello (also incl. in Sullivan County total)	2,400
		Beacon (incl. in Poughkeepsie-Dutchess County)		Newark (incl. in Geneva total)	
		*Binghamton (incl. all		Newburgh (incl. in Orange County)	

State and City	Jewish Population
New Paltz (incl. in Kingston total) New York Metro Area[N]	1,450,000
Bronx	83,700
Brooklyn	379,000
Manhattan	314,500
Queens	238,000
Staten Island	33,700
Nassau County	207,000
Suffolk County	100,000
Westchester County	94,000
Niagara Falls	200
Olean	120
**Oneonta	250
Orange County	10,000
Pawling	105
Plattsburg	260
Port Jervis (also incl. in Orange County total)	560
Potsdam	200
*Poughkeepsie-Dutchess County	4,000
Putnam County	1,000
**Rochester	22,500
Rockland County	83,100
Rome	150
Saratoga Springs	600
Seneca Falls (incl. in Geneva total)	
**Schenectady	5,200
South Fallsburg (also incl. in Sullivan County total)	1,100
Sullivan County	7,425
Syracuse[N]	9,000
Troy area	800
Utica[N]	1,900

State and City	Jewish Population
Walden (incl. in Orange County)	
Watertown	120
Woodstock (incl. in Kingston total)	
NORTH CAROLINA	
Asheville[N]	1,300
**Chapel Hill-Durham	3,000
Charlotte[N]	5,000
Elizabethtown (incl. in Wilmington total)	
*Fayetteville	320
Gastonia	190
Goldsboro	120
*Greensboro	2,500
Greenville	240
*Hendersonville	200
**Hickory	100
High Point (incl. in Greensboro total)	
Jacksonville (incl. in Wilmington total)	
Raleigh-Wake County	5,750
Whiteville (incl. in Wilmington total)	
Wilmington area	500
Winston-Salem	440
NORTH DAKOTA	
Fargo	500
Grand Forks	130
OHIO	
**Akron	5,500
Athens	100
Bowling Green (also incl. in Toledo total)	120
Butler County	900
**Canton	1,650
Cincinnati[N]	23,000

State and City	Jewish Population
**Cleveland[N]	65,000
*Columbus	15,600
**Dayton	6,000
Elyria	200
Fremont (incl. in Sandusky total)	
Hamilton (incl. in Butler County)	
*Lima	210
Lorain	600
Mansfield	180
Marietta (incl. in Parkersburg, W.Va. total)	
Marion	125
Middletown (incl. in Butler County)	
New Philadelphia (incl. in Canton total)	
Norwalk (incl. in Sandusky total)	
Oberlin (incl. in Elyria total)	
Oxford (incl. in Butler County)	
**Sandusky	130
Springfield	200
*Steubenville	150
Toledo[N]	5,500
Warren (also incl. in Youngstown total)	400
Wooster	135
Youngstown[N]	4,000
*Zanesville	100
OKLAHOMA	
Norman (also incl. in Oklahoma City total)	350
**Oklahoma City	2,500
*Tulsa	2,750

State and City	Jewish Population	State and City	Jewish Population	State and City	Jewish Population
OREGON		Jeanette (incl. in		incl. in Pittsburgh	
Ashland (incl. in		Greensburg total)		total)	175
Medford total)		**Johnstown	415	Wayne County	500
Corvallis	700	Lancaster area. . .	3,000	Waynesburg (incl. in	
Eugene.	3,000	*Lebanon.	350	Washington total)	
Grants Pass (incl. in		Lehigh Valley . . .	8,500	West Chester (also	
Medford total)		Lewisburg (incl. in		incl. in Chester	
**Medford.	1,000	Sunbury total)		County).	300
Portland.	12,000	Lock Haven (incl. in		Wilkes-Barre[N] . . .	3,200
**Salem	530	Williamsport total)		**Williamsport	350
		McKeesport (incl. in		York.	1,500
PENNSYLVANIA		Pittsburgh total)			
Allentown (incl. in		New Castle	200	RHODE ISLAND	
Lehigh Valley total)		Norristown (incl. in		Cranston (incl. in	
*Altoona	400	Phila. total)		Providence total)	
Ambridge[N]	350	**Oil City	100	Kingston (incl. in	
Beaver Falls (incl. in		Oxford-Kennett Square		Washington County)	
Upper Beaver County)		(incl. in		Newport-Middletown	
Bethlehem (incl. in		Chester County)		. . . .	700
Lehigh Valley total)		Philadelphia Area[N]		Providence area	
Bucks County (lower		. . . .	250,000	. . . .	14,200
portion)[N]	14,500	Phoenixville (incl. in		Washington County	
*Butler.	180	Chester County)		. . . .	1,200
**Chambersburg. . . .	125	Pike County	300	Westerly (incl. in	
Chester (incl. in		Pittsburgh[N]	45,000	Washington County)	
Phila. total)		Pottstown	650		
Chester County (also		Pottsville	225	SOUTH CAROLINA	
incl. in Phila. total)		*Reading	2,800	*Charleston	3,500
. . . .	4,000	*Scranton	3,200	**Columbia	2,500
Coatesville (incl. in		Shamokin (incl. in		Florence area	220
Chester County)		Sunbury total)		Georgetown (incl. in	
Easton (incl. in Lehigh		Sharon (also incl.		Myrtle Beach total)	
Valley total)		in Youngstown, Ohio		Greenville	1,200
*Erie	850	total)	260	Kingstree (incl. in	
Farrell (incl. in		State College	550	Sumter total)	
Sharon total)		*Stroudsburg.	400	**Myrtle Beach	425
Greensburg (also incl.		Sunbury[N].	200	Rock Hill (incl. in	
in Pittsburgh		Tamaqua (incl. in		Charlotte, N.C. total)	
total)	425	Hazleton total)		*Spartanburg.	330
**Harrisburg.	6,500	Uniontown area . . .	250	Sumter[N].	160
Hazleton area	300	Upper Beaver County			
Honesdale (incl. in		. . . .	200	SOUTH DAKOTA	
Wayne County)		**Washington (also		Sioux Falls.	150

State and City	Jewish Population

TENNESSEE
Bristol (incl. in
  Johnson City total)
Chattanooga 1,350
***Johnson City.... 210
Kingsport (incl. in
  Johnson city total)
Knoxville....... 1,630
Memphis 8,500
Nashville 5,600
Oak Ridge........ 200

TEXAS
Amarillo^N 150
*Austin 5,000
Bay City (incl. in
  Wharton total)
***Baytown........ 300
Beaumont 500
*Brownsville 325
College Station-Bryan
  400
*Corpus Christi .. 1,400
**Dallas........ 35,000
El Paso 4,900
*Ft. Worth 5,000
Galveston......... 800
Harlingen (incl. in
  Brownsville total)
**Houston^N..... 42,000
Kilgore (incl. in
  Longview total)
Laredo........... 160
Longview......... 150
*Lubbock......... 480
Lufkin (incl. in
  Longview total)
Marshall (incl. in
  Longview total)
*McAllen.......... 475
Midland-Odessa ... 150
Port Arthur....... 100
*San Antonio ... 10,000
Tyler 400

Waco^N 300
**Wharton 100
Wichita Falls...... 260

UTAH
Ogden 150
*Salt Lake City... 3,300

VERMONT
Bennington 300
*Brattleboro 350
**Burlington 3,000
Manchester area ... 250
Montpelier-Barre .. 550
Newport (incl. in
  St. Johnsbury total)
Rutland 550
**St. Johnsbury 100

VIRGINIA
Alexandria (incl.
  Falls Church,
  Arlington, and Fairfax
  counties) 35,100
Arlington (incl. in
  Alexandria total)
Blacksburg........ 300
Charlottesville... 1,000
Chesapeake (incl. in
  Portsmouth total)
Colonial Heights (incl.
  in Petersburg total)
Fredericksburg^N ... 500
Hampton (incl. in
  Newport News total)
Harrisonburg (incl. in
  Staunton total)
Lexington (incl. in
  Staunton total)
Lynchburg area.... 275
**Martinsville...... 100
Newport News-
  Hampton^N 2,000

Norfolk-Virginia Beach
  19,000
Petersburg area.... 550
Portsmouth-Suffolk
  (also incl. in Norfolk
  total) 1,900
Radford (incl. in
  Blacksburg total)
Richmond^N..... 8,000
Roanoke........ 1,050
Staunton^N 370
Williamsburg (incl. in
  Newport News total)
Winchester^N 200

WASHINGTON
Bellingham 400
Ellensburg (incl. in
  Yakima total)
Longview-Kelso (incl.
  in Portland, Oreg.
  total)
*Olympia.......... 450
Port Angeles...... 100
Pullman (incl. in
  Moscow, Idaho total)
*Seattle^N 29,300
***Spokane........ 750
*Tacoma 1,100
Tri Cities^N........ 300
Vancouver (incl. in
  Portland, Oreg. total)
**Yakima 100

WEST VIRGINIA
Bluefield-Princeton . 200
*Charleston........ 950
Clarksburg........ 110
Fairmont (incl. in
  Clarksburg total)
Huntington^N 300
Morgantown 175
Parkersburg....... 130
**Wheeling 275

State and City	Jewish Population	State and City	Jewish Population	State and City	Jewish Population
WISCONSIN		La Crosse	120	Waukesha (incl. in	
Appleton area	400	*Madison	4,500	Milwaukee total)	
Beloit	150	Milwaukee[N]		Wausau[N]	240
Fond du Lac (incl. in			28,000		
Oshkosh total)		Oshkosh area		WYOMING	
Green Bay	320		170	Casper	100
Janesville (incl. in		*Racine	375	Cheyenne	230
Beloit total)		Sheboygan		Laramie (incl. in	
*Kenosha	180		140	Cheyenne total)	

Notes

CALIFORNIA

Long Beach—includes in L.A. County: Long Beach, Signal Hill, Cerritos, Lakewood, Rosmoor, and Hawaiian Gardens. Also includes in Orange County: Los Alamitos, Cypress, Seal Beach, and Huntington Harbor.

Palm Springs—includes Palm Springs, Desert Hot Springs, Cathedral City, Palm Desert, and Rancho Mirage.

Pomona Valley—includes Alta Loma, Chino, Claremont, Cucamonga, La Verne, Montclair, Ontario, Pomona, San Dimas, and Upland. Portion also included in Los Angeles total.

Sacramento—includes Yolo, Placer, El Dorado, and Sacramento counties.

San Francisco Bay Area—North Peninsula includes northern San Mateo County. South Peninsula includes southern San Mateo County and towns of Palo Alto and Los Altos in Santa Clara County. San Jose includes remainder of Santa Clara County.

COLORADO

Denver—includes Adams, Arapahoe, Boulder, Denver, and Jefferson counties.

CONNECTICUT

Bridgeport—includes Monroe, Easton, Trumbull, Fairfield, Bridgeport, Shelton, Stratford, and part of Milford.

Danbury—includes Danbury, Bethel, New Fairfield, Brookfield, Sherman, Newtown, Redding, Ridgefield, and part of Wilton; also includes some towns in neighboring Putnam County, N.Y.

Hartford—includes most of Hartford County and Vernon, Rockville, Ellington, and Tolland in Tolland County, and Meriden area of New Haven County.

Lower Middlesex County—includes Branford, Guilford, Madison, Clinton, Westbrook, Old Saybrook, Old Lyme, Durham, and Killingworth. Portion of this area also included in New London and New Haven totals.

Meriden—includes Meriden, Southington, Cheshire, and Wallingford. Most included in Hartford total and a portion also included in New Haven and Waterbury totals.

New Haven—includes New Haven, East Haven, Guilford, Branford, Madison, North Haven, Hamden, West Haven, Milford, Orange, Woodbridge, Bethany, Derby, Ansonia, and Cheshire.

New London—includes central and southern New London County. Also includes part of Lower Middlesex County and part of Windham County.

Norwalk—includes Norwalk, Weston, Westport, East Norwalk, Darien, Wilton, part of Georgetown, and part of New Canaan.

Valley Area—includes Ansonia, Derby, Shelton, Oxford, Seymour, and Beacon Falls. Portion also included in Bridgeport and New Haven totals.

Waterbury—includes Bethlehem, Cheshire, Litchfield, Morris, Middlebury, Southbury, Naugatuck, Prospect, Plymouth, Roxbury, Southbury, Southington, Thomaston, Torrington, Washington, Watertown, Waterbury, Oakville, Woodbury, and Wolcott.

DELAWARE

Dover—includes most of central and southern Delaware.

DISTRICT OF COLUMBIA

Greater Washington—includes Montgomery and Prince Georges counties in Maryland, Arlington County, Fairfax County, Falls Church, and Alexandria in Virginia.

FLORIDA

Ft. Lauderdale—includes Ft. Lauderdale, Pompano Beach, Deerfield Beach, Tamarac, Margate, and other towns in northern Broward County.

Hollywood—includes Hollywood, Hallandale, Cooper City, Dania, Davie, Pembroke, and other towns in southern Broward County.

Orlando—includes all of Orange and Seminole counties and part of Lake County.

GEORGIA

Augusta—includes Burke, Columbia, and Richmond counties and part of Aiken County, South Carolina.

ILLINOIS

Chicago—includes all of Cook and DuPage counties and a portion of Lake County.

Elgin—includes northern Kane County, southern McHenry County, and western edge of Cook County.

Quad Cities—includes Rock Island and Moline (Ill.), Davenport and Bettendorf (Iowa).

Rockford—includes Winnebago, Boone, and Stephenson counties.

Southern Illinois—includes lower portion of Illinois below Carlinville, adjacent western portion of Kentucky, and adjacent portion of southeastern Missouri.

INDIANA

South Bend—includes St. Joseph and Elkhart counties and part of Berrien County, Mich.

KANSAS

Wichita—includes Sedgwick County and towns of Salina, Dodge City, Great Bend, Liberal, Russell, and Hays.

KENTUCKY

Lexington—includes Fayette, Bourbon, Scott, Clark, Woodford, Madison, Pulaski, and Jessamine counties.

LOUISIANA

Baton Rouge—includes E. Baton Rouge, Ascension, Livingston, St. Landry, Iberville, Pt. Coupee, and W. Baton Rouge parishes.

South Central—includes Abbeville, Lafayette, New Iberia, Crowley, Opelousas, Houma, Morgan City, Thibodaux, and Franklin.

MAINE

Southern Maine—includes York, Cumberland, and Sagadahoc counties.

MARYLAND

Upper Eastern Shore—includes towns in Caroline, Dorchester, Kent, Queen Annes, and Talbot counties.

MASSACHUSETTS

Andover—includes Andover, N. Andover, Boxford, Lawrence, Methuen, Tewksbury, Dracut, and town of Salem, New Hampshire.

Boston Metropolitan Region—includes all towns south and west of Boston within approximately 30 miles, and all towns north of Boston within approximately 20 miles. All towns formerly part of Framingham area are now included in Boston total.

Brockton—includes Avon, Brockton, Easton, Bridgewater, Whitman, and West Bridgewater. Also included in Boston total.

Lynn—includes Lynn, Saugus, Nahant, Swampscott, Lynnfield, Peabody, Salem, Marblehead, Beverly, Danvers, Middleton, Wenham, Topsfield, Hamilton, Manchester, Ipswich, Essex, Gloucester, and Rockport. Also included in Boston total.

New Bedford—includes New Bedford, Dartmouth, Fairhaven, and Mattapoisett.

Springfield—includes Springfield, Longmeadow, E. Longmeadow, Hampden, Wilbraham, Agawam, and W. Springfield.

Worcester—includes Worcester, Northborough, Westborough, Shrewsbury, Boylston, W. Boylston, Holden, Paxton, Leicester, Auburn, Millbury, and Grafton. Also included in the Worcester County total.

224 / AMERICAN JEWISH YEAR BOOK, 1994

MICHIGAN

Mt. Pleasant—includes towns in Isabella, Mecosta, Gladwin, and Gratiot counties.

NEBRASKA

Omaha—includes Douglas and Sarpy counties. Also includes Pottawatamie County, Iowa.

NEW HAMPSHIRE

Laconia—includes Laconia, Plymouth, Meredith, Conway, and Franklin.

NEW JERSEY

Cherry Hill—includes Camden, Burlington, and Gloucester counties.

Essex County—East Essex includes Belleville, Bloomfield, East Orange, Irvington, Newark, and Nutley in Essex County, and Kearney in Hudson County. North Essex includes Caldwell, Cedar Grove, Essex Fells, Fairfield, Glen Ridge, Montclair, North Caldwell, Roseland, Verona, and West Caldwell. South Essex includes Maplewood, Millburn, Short Hills, and South Orange in Essex County, and Springfield in Union County.

Middlesex County—includes in Somerset County: Kendall Park, Somerset, and Franklin; in Mercer County: Hightstown; and all of Middlesex County.

Northeastern N.J.—includes Bergen, Essex, Hudson, Middlesex, Morris, Passaic, Somerset, Union, Hunterdon, Sussex, Monmouth, and Ocean counties.

North Hudson County—includes Guttenberg, Hudson Heights, North Bergen, North Hudson, Secaucus, Union City, Weehawken, West New York, and Woodcliff.

Somerset County—includes most of Somerset County and a portion of Hunterdon County.

Trenton—includes most of Mercer County.

Union County—includes all of Union County except Springfield. Also includes a few towns in adjacent areas of Somerset and Middlesex counties.

Vineland—includes most of Cumberland County and towns in neighboring counties adjacent to Vineland.

NEW YORK

Elmira—includes Chemung, Tioga, and Schuyler counties. Also includes Tioga and Bradford counties in Pennsylvania.

Glens Falls—includes Warren and Washington counties, lower Essex County, and upper Saratoga County.

Kingston—includes eastern half of Ulster County.

New York Metropolitan Area—includes the five boroughs of New York City, Westchester, Nassau, and Suffolk counties. For a total Jewish population of the New York metropolitan region, please include Fairfield County, Connecticut; Rockland, Putnam, and Orange counties, New York; and Northeastern New Jersey.

Syracuse—includes Onondaga County, western Madison County, and most of Oswego County.

Utica—southeastern third of Oneida County.

NORTH CAROLINA

Asheville—includes Buncombe, Haywood, and Madison counties.

Charlotte—includes Mecklenburg County. Also includes Lancaster and York counties in South Carolina.

OHIO

Cincinnati—includes Hamilton and Butler counties. Also includes Boone, Campbell, and Kenton counties in Kentucky.

Cleveland—for a total Jewish population of the Cleveland metropolitan region, please include Elyria, Lorain, and Akron totals.

Toledo—includes Fulton, Lucas, and Wood counties. Also includes Monroe and Lenawee counties, Michigan.

Youngstown—includes Mahoning and Trumbull counties. Also includes Mercer County, Pennsylvania.

PENNSYLVANIA

Ambridge—includes lower Beaver County and adjacent areas of Allegheny County. Also included in Pittsburgh total.

Bucks County (lower portion)—includes Bensalem Township, Bristol, Langhorne, Levittown, New Hope, Newtown, Penndel, Trevose, Warrington, Yardley, Richboro, Feasterville, Middletown, Southampton, and Holland. Also included in Philadelphia total.

Philadelphia—includes Philadelphia City; Montgomery, Delaware, Chester, and Bucks counties. For a total Jewish population of the Philadelphia metropolitan region, please include the Cherry Hill, Salem, and Trenton areas of New Jersey, and the Wilmington area of Delaware.

Pittsburgh—includes all of Allegheny County and adjacent portions of Washington, Westmoreland, and Beaver counties.

Sunbury—includes Shamokin, Lewisburg, Milton, Selinsgrove, and Sunbury.

Wilkes-Barre—includes all of Luzerne County except southern portion, which is included in Hazleton totals.

SOUTH CAROLINA

Sumter—includes towns in Sumter, Lee, Clarendon, and Williamsburg counties.

TEXAS

Amarillo—includes Canyon, Childress, Borger, Dumas, Memphis, Pampa, Vega, and Hereford in Texas, and Portales, New Mexico.

Houston—includes Harris, Montgomery, and Ft. Bend counties, and parts of Brazoria and Galveston counties.

Waco—includes McLennan, Coryell, Bell, Falls, Hamilton, and Hill counties.

VIRGINIA

Fredericksburg—includes towns in Spotsylvania, Stafford, King George, and Orange counties.

Newport News—includes Newport News, Hampton, Williamsburg, James City, York County, and Poquoson City.

Richmond—includes Richmond City, Henrico County, and Chesterfield County.

Staunton—includes towns in Augusta, Page, Shenandoah, Rockingham, Bath, and Highland counties.

Winchester—includes towns in Winchester, Frederick, Clarke, and Warren counties, Virginia; and Hardy and Jefferson counties, West Virginia.

WASHINGTON

Seattle—includes King County and adjacent portions of Snohomish and Kitsap counties.

Tri Cities—includes Pasco, Richland, and Kennewick.

WEST VIRGINIA

Huntington—includes nearby towns in Ohio and Kentucky.

WISCONSIN

Milwaukee—includes Milwaukee County, Eastern Waukesha County, and Southern Ozaukee County.

Wausau—includes Stevens Point, Marshfield, Antigo, and Rhinelander.

Review
of
the
Year

OTHER COUNTRIES

Canada

National Affairs

CANADA'S CONSTITUTIONAL CRISIS completed a new phase in 1992. Still hoping to get Quebec to endorse the 1982 constitution, which had been enacted without that key province's concurrence, the government held a national referendum in October on a package of constitutional amendments known as the Charlottetown accord. The major elements of the package included recognition of Quebec as a "distinct society"; an enhanced role for the provinces through reform of the Senate to make it an elected body with equal representation from each province; a change in the method of appointing Supreme Court justices and a transfer of some powers from the federal to the provincial governments; and granting of self-government to aboriginal peoples.

Proponents of the package contended that, after the failure of the Meech Lake accord in 1990 and Quebec's ensuing movement toward sovereignty, it was Canada's last best chance to satisfy Quebec's interests and thereby avert the threat of separation. As a result, the vote took on almost apocalyptic implications. Despite the calls to vote Yes in order to save Canada, most Canadians (about 54 percent) voted No, many in the belief that the accord weakened the power of the federal government. Six of the provinces, including Quebec and Alberta, voted No. The strongest support for the deal was found in parts of Atlantic Canada, which feared being cut off should Quebec separate. After the referendum's failure, there was widespread support for the idea of shelving the constitutional question, which had exhausted politicians and citizens alike for a decade. But Quebec's opposition Parti Québécois remained committed to the French-speaking province's independence and planned to hold a referendum on that question within a year of its next election victory, which it hoped would occur in 1994.

From the perspective of the Jewish community, Canadian unity was highly valued. With nearly 30 percent of the country's Jews living in Quebec, the prospect of Quebec independence, with its anticipated deleterious effect on the well-being of the community, remained anathema to the bulk of the Jews. Hence it was not surprising that the Canadian Jewish Congress (CJC), which speaks for the community on political and governmental issues, came out strongly for the Yes position. President Irving Abella described Charlottetown as "probably the most important

229

constitutional question in Canadian history since 1867. We owe it to ourselves as Canadians, not just as Jews, to vote to keep Canada together." Although some Jews were ambivalent about the accord—because of fears that the "distinct society" concessions to Quebec and other provisions would weaken the protection of individual rights in the country—ultimately it appeared that most Jews did vote Yes, accepting the view that support for the federalist side demanded such an action.

On other matters, a new political group, the Reform party, encountered some criticism from Michael Lublin, a disgruntled member, who claimed that racism and anti-Semitism were widespread at many levels. Tom Flanagan, the party's director of research, responded that in fact the party had been vigorous in expelling members of the racist Heritage Front who had joined, as well as a member who had defaced a Toronto synagogue. He claimed that Lublin's accusations were motivated by personal bitterness. Earlier, party leader Preston Manning had made it clear that he personally rejected anti-Semitism and racism and that his party did not adhere to such views.

Israel and the Middle East

Prime Minister Brian Mulroney named Norman Spector as ambassador to Israel in January, the first Jew to hold the post. Spector, who speaks Hebrew, had been Mulroney's chief of staff. Reactions to the appointment from official Arab spokespersons were quite pointed. James Kafieh, president of the Canadian Arab Federation, charged that Spector, who had no diplomatic experience, was chosen simply because of "his record as a loyal supporter of Israel." He also wondered whether Spector would "be serving Canadian or Israeli interests" and concluded that "his primary interest will be in serving the interests of the international Zionist movement. . . ." Jewish organizations welcomed the appointment. In February the prime minister responded to the critics, stating that the assignment would "eliminate the doubt in anyone's mind as to where we should stand on certain issues. Norman Spector is remarkably well-qualified to serve as Canada's ambassador to Israel." He used the opportunity of a diplomatic reception to reiterate his commitment to a strong relationship with Israel.

Spector, in an interview with the *Canadian Jewish News*, stated that he had no doubt that the Department of External Affairs had systematically excluded Jews from top diplomatic assignments in Israel. He said that Mulroney had been delighted to break the existing practice. Spector's assertion about diplomatic personnel practices was supported by a letter to the *Toronto Star* from foreign-service officer Aharon Mayne, who claimed that superiors had discouraged him from any involvement with Middle East affairs. B'nai Brith's director of governmental relations, Ian Kagedan, who had talked with several foreign-service officers with similar complaints, argued that what is "most troubling is that within the culture of External Affairs is the thought that Jews can't be fully Canadian."

Canada was actively involved in the Arab-Israeli peace negotiations throughout the year. Michael Bell, the outgoing ambassador to Israel, became an adviser to the Canadian delegation to the peace talks. He was optimistic early in the year, expressing the view that both sides were making a real effort to succeed. As part of the multilateral negotiations, Canada was asked to chair the working group on refugees. Bell, in a February interview, indicated that Canada was trusted by the Israelis and the Arabs "as a country that is fair-minded and solution-oriented."

The refugee talks held in Ottawa in May ran into trouble early. Israel declined to participate because Canada invited an "expanded Palestinian delegation," including representatives from outside the territories. Israel maintained that the multilaterals should operate according to the Madrid rules, which barred so-called diaspora Palestinians from the talks. However, both the United States and Canada contended that the multilaterals did not operate under the same rules. An underlying question was whether Palestinians have a right of return to Israel if they claim that they lived in that territory before 1948. As the Israeli embassy in Ottawa put it: "Inclusion of Palestinians from outside the Territories as partners to the peace process bestows legitimacy to their inevitable claim . . . for the 'right of return.' " The talks continued without Israel's presence, with Canada issuing a final communiqué expressing a broad consensus that negotiations on the refugees should not wait for progress in the bilateral negotiations. Both Syria and Lebanon were also absent as a protest against what they regarded as insufficient Israeli flexibility in the bilateral talks.

A number of specific refugee or asylum claims came up during the year. Wahid Kahlil Baroud, reportedly a former bodyguard for PLO head Yasir Arafat, applied for refugee status with his family, was allowed into Canada on bond, failed to appear at two immigration hearings, and was then arrested. He had reportedly been involved in terrorist actions in the past. Another Palestinian, Mahmood Abo Shandi, had been detained upon his arrival in 1991 with false papers, when he asked for political asylum, claiming to be in danger from the Mossad in Norway because of his previous PLO activities. The government opposed his claim on the grounds that he was "likely to engage in acts of espionage or subversion. . . ." Following a hearing on his claim in January, Shandi, who had been a Fatah colonel, was ordered deported by a federal court judge, who found, based on evidence presented by the government, that he had been more active in the PLO than he acknowledged. He was deported in February.

Another Palestinian terrorist, Mohammad Issa Mohammad, was more successful, clearing one of the two hurdles on the way toward refugee status. Even though he had taken part in a 1968 attack on a Greek plane in Athens in which an Israeli man died, a two-member immigration panel held in November that there was a credible basis for his claim. Jewish organizations urged the Immigration and Refugee Board to reject his application at the next stage.

Israel and Canada explored the possibilities of concluding a free-trade agreement, similar to the Israeli-U.S. pact of 1985, when Industry and Trade Minister Moshe Nissim visited Ottawa in March. International Trade Minister Michael Wilson stated that Canada had too many other priorities at the time, though he did hold out hope for improved trade relations. In that light, the Canada/Israel Technology Co-operation Forum, held in March, provided an opportunity for Israeli companies to meet with Canadian counterparts in order to stimulate business. Cooperation in the legal area was also moving apace through the Canada-Israel Legal Co-operation Program. Law professor Irwin Cotler, who organized it, hoped that the exchange of ideas between lawyers and jurists in the two countries would culminate in Israel's eventual adoption of a bill of rights modeled on the Canadian version. The first undertaking of the group was a conference in Israel in December, involving top legal minds, on the treatment of human rights in the two countries.

Canada's agreement in September to sell three armed frigates to Saudi Arabia prompted an outcry from the Canada-Israel Committee (CIC). Executive Director Rob Ritter accused the government of a double standard because it authorized sales to Arab countries but not to Israel. Israeli ambassador Itzhak Shelef also opposed the sale, on the ground that the Saudis were still in a state of war with Israel.

The head of the Security Intelligence Review Committee told a parliamentary committee in May that the Mossad had operated illegally in Canada in 1990, specifically, that agents conducted activities without Canadian permission. The admission substantiated a charge by controversial author Victor Ostrovsky, who published an exposé of the Mossad, that two agents had come to his home to persuade him not to publish the book. Israeli officials were reportedly rebuked for the actions.

Anti-Semitism

There was a major new development in the case of Ernst Zundel, who was appealing his 1988 conviction for "spreading false news" through his Holocaust-denial publications. The Supreme Court of Canada declared in a 4–3 decision that the law under which he had been convicted was unconstitutional, that it violated protections of freedom of expression in the Charter of Rights and Freedoms. Jewish community spokespersons expressed outrage at the judgment. They had been backing the various legal actions against Zundel for nine years and had seen him convicted twice, only to see both convictions ultimately overturned on appeal. David Satok of the Canadian Jewish Congress Ontario Region declared that "Congress will no longer allow the likes of Ernst Zundel or anyone like him to spread hatred against our community," after laying a new complaint against Zundel under another section of the criminal code.

James Keegstra was convicted for a second time under the antihate provisions of the code in July, for promoting hatred against Jews as a high-school social-studies teacher. He was fined $3,000, but an appeal was planned. His case, too, had been in the courts for nearly a decade. Meanwhile, a New Brunswick court upheld an administrative decision to dismiss Malcolm Ross from his teaching job because of his anti-Semitic writings. He appealed to the provincial court of appeal, which heard the arguments in September and then reserved judgment.

British revisionist historical writer David Irving attempted another cross-country speaking tour in November. The ensuing uproar focused a great deal of attention on his Holocaust-denial efforts. The Simon Wiesenthal Center in Toronto tried to have him barred from the country on the grounds that a German law under which he had been convicted was equivalent to Canada's antihate law. The government agreed and notified Irving, who was by then in the United States, that he would not be admitted, thus jeopardizing planned speeches in at least seven locations. Irving managed to sneak into Canada and to speak in Victoria and Toronto before being taken into custody and deported to Britain. In a separate matter, Irving sued federal multiculturalism minister Gerry Weiner for defamation in connection with an earlier visit.

Anti-Semitic incidents continued to occur, although B'nai Brith Canada's annual accounting showed a decline in the total number of instances of harassment or vandalism, after annual increases since 1987. On a countrywide basis there were 150 incidents of harassment and 46 of vandalism, for a total of 196, compared with 251 in 1991. But this was still the third highest number in the 11 years that the survey had been conducted. The bulk of the incidents (97) occurred in Toronto, while Montreal and Ottawa had 25 each. A decline in the western provinces was attributed to tougher law enforcement.

Desecrations of cemeteries and synagogues distressed Jews in Montreal, where eight tombstones were defaced in February, and in Winnipeg, where a major synagogue was vandalized by neighborhood teenagers in April. Three Toronto area synagogues were defaced in June, and a Jewish community building in Ottawa was vandalized in July. A neo-Nazi rally planned for the end of July, in the town of Ste. Anne de Sorel, Quebec, attracted only about 70 participants. Vigorous action by the local authorities helped to discourage attendance.

A vacant house owned by a Kitchener, Ontario, Jewish woman who publicly opposed the speaking activities of David Irving burned down in November as the result of arson. In Ottawa, in December, many Jews and Jewish organizations received anti-Semitic material in the mail. Anti-Semitic stickers were also affixed to Jewish-owned businesses in the city.

A Jewish employee of the New York subsidiary of ScotiaMcLeod Inc., a large Canadian brokerage firm, alleged that anti-Semitic attitudes and practices were tolerated in the company. He contended that he and other employees had been targets of ethnic slurs on more than one occasion. After Simon Israel, the employee, was dismissed from his job, Jewish organizations in Canada intervened with the parent company. Eventually, two employees who had been accused of making anti-Semitic remarks were demoted. Several Jewish community officials claimed that such action came only after adverse media publicity, and that the company was only interested in damage control, rather than in rooting out discriminatory attitudes.

A doctoral dissertation at Université Laval in Quebec created controversy when its acceptance was inordinately delayed and some members of the committee advocated its rejection. The author, Esther Delisle, wrote on "Anti-Semitism and Extreme Right-Wing Nationalism in Quebec from 1929–39," arguing that anti-Semitism was central in the intellectual life of Quebec during that period, especially due to the influence of the late Lionel Groulx, a priest and historian who had a great influence on the development of Quebec nationalism. She also documented the frequency of anti-Semitic expressions in the Montreal newspaper *Le Devoir* during the 1930s, stating that "it was like *Der Sturmer*." The thesis was eventually accepted and then published as a book. Many Quebec intellectuals were outraged by her charges against Groulx, making her the object of considerable opprobrium.

Nazi War Criminals

Jacob Luitjens, a former professor in British Columbia who had collaborated with the Nazis in his native Holland during World War II, was stripped of his Canadian citizenship and deported to the Netherlands to stand trial, culminating a four-year legal struggle. After the Federal Court rejected his appeal in April, he was finally deported in November, in response to an extradition request from the Netherlands. Subsequently, he was jailed in Amsterdam while he appealed a 1948 conviction in absentia and a life sentence. The appeal was denied by a Dutch court at the end of the year. Nazi rocket scientist Arthur Rudolph, who tried to visit Canada, was also deported.

Imre Finta, who was acquitted in 1991 of charges under Canada's war-crimes legislation, faced an attempt by the Crown to appeal the verdict. Although the Ontario Court of Appeal refused to grant a new trial, on the grounds that any judicial error did not affect the outcome, the Supreme Court of Canada agreed in December to hear the appeal. Charges against Michael Pawlawski, accused of participating in the killing of 500 Jews and Poles in Belorussia in 1942, were dropped by the Crown following adverse rulings by the judge that made it impossible to present a case. Subsequently, Pawlawski was awarded costs by the court. In a new case, Radislav Grujicic, originally from Yugoslavia, was charged with ten counts of murder and other crimes for his activities as a police officer between 1941 and 1944.

In an analysis of the government's handling of war criminals during the five years since the passage of the law, B'nai Brith's David Matas was highly critical of the lack of action by the prosecutors and unsatisfactory progress in dealing with actual and potential cases. "There is no area of the law where action is more lethargic," he charged.

JEWISH COMMUNITY

Demography

First results from the 1991 census contained some surprises, most notably a reasonable growth in the Jewish population, a smaller than anticipated decline in Montreal, and large numbers of people who indicated some Jewish ethnic background but did not classify themselves as Jews by religion.

The census asks two questions that enable one to identify Jews: a religion question, which is usually straightforward, and an ethnicity question, which has changed from one census to the next and is a source of some ambiguity. In 1991, respondents were permitted to list a single response to the ethnicity question about the group to which their ancestors belonged or to give multiple responses. The number of people giving Jewish as a single response was 245,840, while those listing Jewish as one of two or more responses numbered 123,725. The total of 369,565 represents the high end of the estimate of the Jewish population because it undoubtedly includes among those giving multiple responses some people whose Jewish identity is extremely marginal. The religion question showed 318,070 Jews, which is certainly the lower end of the range. An accurate number is somewhere in between, including some of those who did not list their religion as Jewish but did give a Jewish ethnic identification.

In a recent analysis of the 1991 census data, Prof. Jim Torczyner and associates at McGill University cross-tabulated the ethnicity and religion measures to produce a combined Jewish variable that encompasses those who identify themselves as Jewish on both questions, those who are ethnically Jewish but give no other religion, and those who give their religion as Jewish. Thus, secular Jews with no religious affiliation are included, but Jews who have adopted another religion are excluded. On that basis, the total number of Jews in 1991 was 356,315, an increase of 44,215, or 14.2 percent, since 1981, using consistent methodology. (Jews represent about 1.3 percent of the Canadian population.) It should be noted that 49,460 people who list a Jewish ethnic origin identify with a religion other than Judaism. Of the 356,315 Jews, 281,680 give both religious and ethnic identities, 36,390 list Jewish religion but another ethnicity, and 38,245 list Jewish ethnicity but no religion.

The greatest percentage growth in the Jewish population between 1981 and 1991 occurred in Toronto (26.4), Ottawa (26.6), and Vancouver (31.0). People moving from Montreal and various smaller communities, plus immigrants, produced the large increase among the Jews of Ontario, with Hamilton and London experiencing double-digit percentage increases. Montreal, on the other hand, declined by 2.1 percent, but that was a lower drop than had been anticipated. The Montreal Jewish population fell from 103,425 in 1981 to 101,210 in 1991. As a result, Toronto is now home to nearly 46 percent of Canada's Jews, and Montreal's share is down to about 28 percent (in contrast to the 1970s, when the proportions of Jews in the two cities were about equal).

Eleven cities (defined as Census Metropolitan Areas, CMAs) have Jewish populations of 1,500 or more. The following table is based on the analysis of Torczyner and his colleagues.

The Jews of Canada continue to be an aging population: 17.3 percent are over 65 and 17.5 percent between 35 and 44, compared to 10.8 percent and 16.2 percent in the general population. At the same time, 21.0 percent of Jews are younger than 15, the same proportion as in the general population, and the proportions of 45–64-year-olds are similar, 19.1 percent among Jews and 19.9 percent in the population at large.

The Jews continue to have higher education levels than the rest of the population: 52.1 percent of Jews aged 25–44 hold university degrees, compared to 16.5 percent of the total population. In general, of people over 15 years of age, Jews are two and a half times as likely to have a bachelor's degree or some college and four times as likely to have an advanced degree as the general population. In terms of occupation, they are three times as likely to be professionals and twice as likely to be managers and administrators.

Some 18,270 people listed Israel as their birthplace, including 16,770 who are permanent residents and 1,500 who are in Canada on some kind of temporary permit. This statistic of course understates the Israeli population in Canada, because it omits those who were born outside of Israel, made *aliyah*, lived in Israel, and subsequently emigrated to Canada.

Some 6,595 people listed Yiddish as their home language while another 1,425 listed Yiddish and another language. Interestingly, 6,955 listed Hebrew as their home language and 1,790 listed Hebrew and another language. This is probably the first time that the number of Hebrew speakers outnumbered the Yiddish speakers

Census Metropolitan Areas	Jewish Population	Percent Change from 1981
Toronto	162,605	+26.4
Montreal	101,210	− 2.1
Vancouver	19,375	+31.0
Winnipeg	15,050	− 6.2
Ottawa	11,555	+26.6
Calgary	7,155	+18.0
Edmonton	5,430	+16.4
Hamilton	5,145	+10.6
London	2,670	+14.6
Windsor	1,785	−16.0
Halifax	1,755	+20.6

in Canada by any measure. However, 25,375 people listed Yiddish as their mother tongue (down from 32,760 in 1981), while 11,895 listed Hebrew. All told, there were 53,420 people in Canada who said they could speak Yiddish and 52,455 who could speak Hebrew. The most Yiddish speakers (23,485) were in Montreal, while Toronto had the most Hebrew speakers (26,345). In Winnipeg, which once boasted a vibrant Yiddish-speaking community, only 3,330 reported that they could speak Yiddish.

Communal Affairs

One of the dominant themes during the year was the financial crisis faced by the community. As the economy generally sputtered in recession, the fallout in the community was serious. The problem was exacerbated by the restructuring necessitated by the free-trade pact with the United States. The crowning blow was the collapse of the Reichmann financial and real-estate empire in Toronto, though the Reichmann disaster was only the most visible sign of a process that affected the community deeply. Given the dependence of local federation fund-raising campaigns on the big givers, the economic downturn caused serious pressures on community agencies, in terms of both demand for services and resources available. Agencies noted an upsurge in requests for financial assistance, vocational counseling to find alternative employment, and help in dealing with the psychological and family problems related to job loss and deteriorating personal financial situations. Such difficulties even reached into the middle and upper-middle classes.

The recession's effects were felt in organizational budgets, which often had to be cut back just as demands for services and financial assistance were reaching record high levels. Schools, for example, found that families were less able to pay their tuition fees, while community funds to offset these shortfalls were less likely to be available. Organizations serving senior citizens were equally hard hit, and health-care agencies found it necessary to reduce spending at a time when their services were in demand. In Montreal, the budget of Federation CJA for local needs was reduced by about $400,000 to just over $12 million between 1991 and 1992. Some agencies saw their allocations drop by as much as 12 percent.

In Toronto, when the federation was compelled by its auditors to write off $6.8 million in unpaid pledges to the United Jewish Appeal from earlier years, it became necessary to reduce the annual allocation to Israel as the alternative to crippling local agencies. Israel, through the United Israel Appeal, had expected to receive about $16 million; instead its allocation was slashed to $9 million. That compared with $11.5 million in 1991 and $17 million in 1990. Part of the problem was the diversion of funds to Operation Exodus, which had an impact on the regular campaign, but part was also due to the recession.

The financial bind of institutions that had depended on Reichmann largesse prior to the bankruptcy of Olympia and York Developments Ltd., the family real-estate company with worldwide holdings, complicated the situation immensely. Previously the Reichmanns reportedly donated millions of dollars annually to an array of community institutions, primarily but not exclusively Orthodox. Schools such as the Yeshiva and Mesivta Yesodei HaTorah, the Bais Yaacov School, and the Kolel Avreichim found themselves several million dollars in debt due to the abrupt cessation of subsidies from the Reichmann family interests. As the Reichmann funding dried up, institutions turned to the federation for support, precisely when the federation itself was experiencing serious difficulties. At the same time, the families utilizing the institutions were ill-equipped to undertake substantially higher financial burdens. A further problem in Toronto was the reduction by the United Way of allocations to its affiliated agencies, including Jewish ones.

Canadian Jewish Congress held its triennial plenary assembly in Toronto in May. In an interview before the plenary, outgoing president Les Scheininger raised questions about some of the trends in the community, in particular the focus on organizations for their own sake; he called on fellow activists to ensure that the purpose of service to the community was foremost in the mission of the various bodies. He also expressed fear that the financial crisis would lead to less emphasis on education, which he viewed as the primary tool to combat assimilation and intermarriage. At the plenary itself, the new president, Irving Abella, stressed the challenge of Jewish continuity and promised to focus programming on youth, especially on the nation's university campuses.

The plenary passed a number of resolutions on the Middle East, anti-Semitism, human rights, and community relations. The most controversial and divisive resolution was one that was defeated 72–28. Backed by Canadian Friends of Peace Now, it called for Israel to cease "further settlement in the territories during peace negotiations." Debate on the resolution from both sides was intense.

Sociologist Steven M. Cohen and pollster Martin Goldfarb presented findings from recent surveys concerning Jewish life in Canada. Goldfarb pointed to the importance of visiting Israel as a factor in maintaining an individual's Jewish identity and commitment at home. In general he found that Jewish ritual practice in Canada was quite high throughout the different age cohorts. Cohen, reinforcing the point, asserted that Canadian Jews were more deeply committed to Jewish values and institutions than American Jews.

The Montreal community continued to be concerned about its future. The revived threat of Quebec independence during the constitutional turmoil of the early 1990s highlighted the heavy toll that political uncertainty can take on the vitality of community life. The knowledge that young people had moved out of the community in significant numbers during the past 20 years was a source of consternation, not only because decline in any part of the community is troubling, but also because of the likely effect on the community's future of a shortage of young people and a gap in that age cohort.

Between 1990 and 1992, various groups under federation auspices began investigating the problem and developing strategies to combat it. What emerged was a project known as ProMontreal. One of the key objectives of the new group was to identify job opportunities for young people, especially with Jewish employers, who were most likely to be responsive to initiatives from the community. Other objectives included the promotion of positive aspects of living in Montreal, especially from a Jewish perspective, and the stimulation of an appreciation for the French language and Quebec culture. Overall, backers of the ProMontreal initiative hoped that they could stem the tide of outmigration among the young and perhaps even attract some of the Jewish students from elsewhere who attend university in Montreal to settle in the city. Even after the defeat of the October constitutional referendum, which generally had been supported by the city's Jews, there was a more positive feeling in the community than there had been for a few years. Certainly the deliberate community efforts were one factor in the change of mood.

The attempt to revive spirits in the Montreal community was accompanied by a greater appreciation of the role of the Sephardim in community life. The predominantly French-speaking group, a rapidly growing segment of the community, had become more assertive in general and seemed more aware of its strategic situation as a link between the Jews and the majority French Québécois society. Senior community leader Charles Bronfman addressed the annual meeting of the Communauté Sépharade du Québec (CSQ) in February, calling on French-speaking Jews to seek an enhanced role in the federation and communitywide fund-raising. "You have a major responsibility in helping to ensure the continuity of a vibrant and vital Jewish community in Montreal," he told them. Joseph Gabay, the new president of the CSQ, lamented the underrepresentation of Sephardim in key community bodies and committed himself to trying to remedy the situation.

Both of the major federations changed their names during the year. Toronto Jewish Congress became the Jewish Federation of Greater Toronto (JFGT) in order both to make clear that it has no connection with the Canadian Jewish Congress and to stress the expansion of Jewish life beyond the city's traditional boundaries. In Montreal, Allied Jewish Community Services changed to Federation CJA, a name that could be used in either English or French and that emphasized the connection between the fund-raising of the Combined Jewish Appeal and the spending of the federation. In Toronto, the JFGT and CJC's Ontario Region agreed on a new division of responsibilities, shifting control over cultural activities, including Yiddish programming, archives, and Holocaust-related events, from CJC to the federation. The Council of Jewish Federations, based in New York, made its Canadian office in Toronto more autonomous by setting up a separate Canadian division known as CJF Canada. Backers of change believed that the new structure would be helpful in dealing with issues that are unique to Canada or are different from similar issues in the United States.

In an abrupt move, CJC Ontario Region dismissed Edmond Lipsitz as its executive director in June, for reasons that were not fully explained publicly. Some officers complained that they had been left out of the process that led to the decision. The matter was taken up by the council in July, but the termination remained in effect.

The Canadian Zionist Federation (CZF) canceled its planned election of delegates to the World Zionist Congress. In a February decision, the CZF simply allocated the seats by agreement among the constituent groups, thus saving the $250,000 cost of holding the election. The action was permitted under World Zionist Organization rules because a consensus existed. The allocation of delegates was as follows: United Torah Coalition—5, Kadima—4, Mercaz-Canada—3, Labor-Zionist Movement—3, Herut-Likud—2, Zionist Organization of Canada—2, Friends of Pioneering Israel—1, Confederation of United Zionists—1. The total of 21 delegates represented an increase of two over Canada's allocation to the 1988 Congress.

In other communal affairs, new Jewish community centers were dedicated in Hamilton, Ontario, and in Kelowna, British Columbia, the latter serving the growing community in the Okanagan region. The Canadian Association for Ethiopian Jews disbanded after 12 years, satisfied that its efforts had succeeded in helping to resettle the community in Israel.

Education

Ontario's Jewish community continued to press for provincial government aid to the day schools, but without success. A key underlying consideration was the fact that Roman Catholic schools in Ontario did receive state support. Early in the year, a group of parents, aided by CJC, initiated a lawsuit to try to compel government funding, on the grounds that existing policy violated the Charter of Rights and Freedoms, specifically, equality and freedom-of-religion guarantees. In the case, heard in the Ontario Court of Justice in May, lawyer John Laskin argued that compulsory school attendance, coupled with a commitment to freedom of religion, obligated the government to fund the schools. The decision of the court, handed down in August, went against the Jewish parents, who decided to appeal. Justice William Anderson accepted the assertion that rights had been denied, but found the limitations on rights to be "acceptable" within the meaning of the constitution. Meanwhile, in Montreal, the Association of Jewish Day Schools (AJDS) was exploring the possibility of associate status with either the Protestant or Catholic school board, in order to gain access to increased funding. Financial pressures prompted the move for the schools, which received partial funding under the Private Education Act. Quebec government approval would be required for any new arrangement.

Several new educational facilities opened during the year. In Montreal, the Hebrew Academy erected its own building on land purchased from Federation CJA after renting for many years, while United Talmud Torahs expanded and remodeled its Herzliah High School's Snowdon campus. The first Jewish day school in Richmond, British Columbia, opened in the fall.

Five ultra-Orthodox schools in Toronto faced severe financial problems due to the ending of Reichmann funding. Yeshiva Bnei Zion of Bobov threatened to close because of an inability to meet its obligations. These schools had not been funded by the Board of Jewish Education because they failed to meet the necessary criteria. Some 2,000 children attended the five schools in question.

Community Relations

In the aftermath of the failure of the Meech Lake accord in 1990, some Jewish leaders began to work together with other ethnic groups in order to promote national unity and enhance understanding of the complexity of the Quebec problem among Canadians in the rest of the country. The lead for this initiative came from CJC people in Montreal, who forged a coalition that also included the Hellenic Canadian Congress and the National Congress of Italian Canadians. After traveling across the country for over a year, the coalition was ready to swing into action to enlist ethnic support for an agreement to renew the Canadian federation. The message was straightforward: keep Canada united but recognize Quebec's uniqueness. In February, the coalition submitted a comprehensive brief to a federal committee exploring the parameters of a renewed Canada. It also was instrumental in building ethnic support for the October referendum. Despite the failure of the Charlottetown accord, the exercise proved useful in that it produced an unprecedented degree of cooperation between the three ethnic communities on matters of common interest.

A Mordecai Richler publication again precipitated a community-relations crisis for Montreal's Jews. This time it was the appearance of his book *Oh Canada! Oh Quebec!* in which he enlarged on the themes that he had identified the previous year in his controversial *New Yorker* article. Even though the main thrust of the book was criticism of Quebec's language laws, Richler's assertions about anti-Semitic influences in the province remained the major focus of debate. His writings provoked intense discussion as to whether Quebec had really changed from the 1930s and 1940s, when anti-Semitism was prevalent. Critics contended that Quebec society had indeed changed, while Richler still observed incidents that made him uncomfortable.

There were other discussions about the place of Jews in Quebec as well. In May, Université du Québec political scientist Julien Bauer and CJC community-relations professional Jack Jedwab had a sharp exchange at a public meeting in Montreal. Bauer contended that Jews remained marginalized in Quebec politics, that anti-Semitism was common among the elite, and that Jews suffered disabilities in some respects. Jedwab countered that French Québécois genuinely wanted to achieve rapprochement with Jews more than ever before. In a panel discussion held in Toronto, also in May, McGill professor Harold Waller argued that Quebec nationalism did not threaten Jews as Jews, even though most, including French-speaking Jews, were strongly opposed to the idea of Quebec independence. Jedwab went even further, suggesting that Montreal was the best place on the continent to "maintain a Jewish identity." Both speakers agreed that, although the declining Jewish population should be lamented, it did not necessarily mean that the community had no future. At a meeting in January, a Parti Québécois vice-president tried to convince Jewish community leaders that independence was inevitable and that Jews should support it and become part of the movement. The 150 leaders present gave him a cool reception, reflecting continuing hostility toward the idea.

A number of issues involving the media arose during the year. The Montreal newspaper *La Presse* apologized for a front-page cartoon linking Richler and Hitler that appeared in October. In November, Montreal broadcaster Claude Jasmin described Hassidic Jews as racist during a broadcast. Earlier in the year, he had referred to Jews as "racists . . . especially practicing Jews." Both CJC and B'nai Brith were sharply critical of the incidents.

In other developments, Ontario finally decided to allow Sunday shopping, thereby concluding a lengthy battle that involved Sabbath observers, among others. Manitoba decided to abolish prayer in the schools. In Toronto, in April, an observant lawyer's request to adjourn a court proceeding late on Friday afternoon was denied. Bert Raphael, president of the Jewish Civil Rights Educational Foundation of Canada, declared that "this shows that anti-Semitism is alive and well in Toronto in 1992." The Quebec government's failure to provide kosher food to Jewish prison inmates provoked some internal conflict between Lubavitch representatives and federation officials over how to deal with the problem.

The Quebec government and Federation CJA in Montreal cooperated in efforts to bring about 400 Jews from the former Soviet Union to settle in Quebec. Russian Jew Dmitri Berman was finally able to leave the Canadian embassy in Moscow after many months of trying to avoid what he regarded as an unfair prosecution. He then was able to go to Israel.

Religion

The Conservative movement faced serious disaffection within the Toronto rabbinate. Canadian Jewry in general is somewhat more traditional in patterns of religious observance and synagogue practices than American Jewry, and the Toronto members of the Conservative Rabbinical Assembly (RA) had strong reservations about the direction of the movement, especially in terms of egalitarianism. At a meeting of the Ontario Region of the United Synagogue of Conservative Judaism in Richmond Hill in June, rabbis Erwin Schild and Benjamin Friedberg criticized recent developments within their movement. Rabbi Schild expressed the view that "we seem to have lost our sense of direction and are steering by the winds of change rather than tradition." Rabbi Friedberg added that "instead of teaching Halakhah, we're trying to change it. We're watering things down." A threat by several rabbis to withdraw from the RA, at a meeting of the 18 RA members in Ontario held later in June, would have replicated an earlier split by the Conservative cantors of the Toronto area. According to Rabbi Wayne Allen, the regional chairman, among the issues that motivated the rabbis were ideology, decision-making processes, and the general direction of the movement. Rabbi Lawrence Troster said that the immediate stimulus for withdrawal was the adoption earlier in the year by the movement's Committee on Jewish Law and Standards of resolutions dealing with gender equality, homosexuality, and human sexuality.

An August visit to the discontented rabbis by Rabbi Joel Meyers, executive vice-president of the RA, quieted things briefly, although Rabbi Allen reported continued unhappiness among many of his members. There were reports that several rabbis would join the rabbinic fellowship of the Union for Traditional Judaism (UTJ). Then Rabbi Allen resigned as regional chairman at the end of August, stating that "the gap is irreparable. There's no going back." In an effort to keep the dissident Toronto rabbis within the fold, Chancellor Ismar Schorsch of the Jewish Theological Seminary of America visited Toronto in December. He warned his colleagues not to join the UTJ, which he described as "marginal." He added, "We need the Yiddishkeit of Toronto."

Despite frantic efforts to raise necessary funds, the Conservative Shaareh Haim Synagogue, in the Toronto suburb of Richmond Hill, was forced to close in June. A Reform congregation, Rodeph Shalom, that had served the Montreal suburb of Dollard des Ormeaux for 26 years, decided to close after its membership had dwindled to only 38. It sold its building to a new Sephardic congregation and donated its ritual articles to the Reform movement, after holding its last service in July. Meanwhile, approximately 300 gays formed a new synagogue in Toronto, Congregation Keshet Shalom. In total there were approximately 65 Orthodox, 10 Conservative, and 10 Reform synagogues in Toronto. The new Vancouver Traditional Congregation decided to affiliate with the UTJ and to restrict the role of women in the service. The leadership of the new synagogue tried to establish a middle ground between contemporary Orthodox and Conservative practice, exemplified by distinct sections for separate and mixed seating.

Five medical doctors in the Toronto-Hamilton area became the first Reform Jews to be certified as *mohelim* (ritual circumcisers) by the Berit Milah Board of Reform Judaism. Quebec's newly revised Civil Code removed from religious congregations the responsibility to register births and deaths for official state purposes.

Culture

The 500th anniversary of the expulsion of the Jews from Spain was commemorated in Montreal by the yearlong series of events known as Sepharad '92, which was jointly sponsored by Federation CJA and the Communauté Sépharade du Québec (CSQ) in an effort to enhance the appreciation of Sephardic Jewish culture. The events included an exhibition of the works of the painter Raphael Abecassis entitled "*De l'Exil à aujourd'hui*" (From the Exile to Today), a special Mimouna celebration at the end of Passover, lectures, a film series, puppet workshops, and a photographic exhibit about the Jews of Morocco. An exhibit produced by the Spanish Foreign Ministry was shown in Montreal, Toronto, Ottawa, and several U.S. cities.

The Stars of the Ester Kaminska Theater from Warsaw made their first Canadian appearance, presenting *The Joys of Yiddish* in Toronto in June. The same month, Yiddish theater director Dora Wasserman and French-Canadian playwright Michel

Tremblay collaborated on a production of a Yiddish translation of Tremblay's *Les Belles Soeurs* (The Beautiful Sisters) in Montreal. A new film by Simcha Jacobovici, *The Sephardim—A Passion for Life*, traces the Sephardic odyssey since the expulsion of 1492. The National Film Board's documentary *Des lumières dans la grande noirceur* (A Vision in the Darkness) tells the story of Lea Roback, a political activist, trade unionist, and feminist looking back on her accomplishments at the age of 89.

Srul Irving Glick's symphonic poem "The Reawakening" had its premiere by the Toronto Symphony Orchestra, under guest conductor Victor Feldbrill, in January. Another new Glick composition, "Artist's Life: A Portrait in Six Poems," is based on the work of the late Yiddish poet Rochel Korn. Its premiere was in Montreal in November. The Hazzan Mendelson Music Foundation of Montreal sponsored an International Jewish Song Competition in November. Some 170 songs were entered, with the top 15 being performed at the competition. Five songs, written by artists from England, Canada, the United States, Australia, and Israel, won prizes.

Queen's University in Kingston, Ontario, established a chair in Jewish studies. The first professor to hold the chair is Reena Zeidman, a specialist in rabbinics. Prof. Emil Fackenheim returned to Toronto from his home in Jerusalem to speak at a symposium on the occasion of his 75th birthday in March. He stressed the importance of the Holocaust and the Six Day War as formative events in his intellectual development.

Montreal's Saidye Bronfman Center, dedicated to the arts, celebrated its 25th anniversary in February with a gala evening of ballet and musical presentations. "Tur Malka" (Royal Mountain, in Aramaic), an exhibition commemorating 200 years of Jewish life in Montreal, opened in May at the Jewish Public Library. In a lecture on the Jewish experience in Canada, in April, in Montreal, Prof. Irving Abella of York University described what he considered to be the golden age of Canadian Jewry, the 1840s, when Jews were in the vanguard of the fight for human rights. Turning to the present, he observed that "Canadian Jews are the envy of every Jewish community in the world. . . ."

Publications

Gerald Tulchinsky's *Taking Root: The Origins of the Canadian Jewish Community* traces the development of the community from 1760 to 1920, trying to distinguish the Canadian experience from the American. The fact that Canada was more likely than the United States to foster separate ethnic identities helped maintain a more intense Jewish life and a strong commitment to Zionism.

Ruth Wisse confronts controversial contemporary issues in *If I Am Not for Myself: The Liberal Betrayal of the Jews*, in which she argues that Israel's well-being is endangered by the guilt of Jewish liberals in both Israel and the Diaspora, at a time when Arab hostility still constitutes a danger and anti-Semitism has taken on new forms.

The Stones That Speak, by David Rome and Jacques Langlais, chronicles two centuries of the "common history" of Jews and French Québécois and asserts that, despite historical and contemporary tensions, Quebec has been a hospitable place for Jews to live. In contrast, Mordecai Richler's *Oh Canada! Oh Quebec! Requiem for a Divided Country* accentuates the negative aspects of Quebec nationalism, especially the language laws of the last 15 years.

The theme of anti-Semitism in Quebec is documented in much greater detail in *Le traître et le Juif: Lionel Groulx, Le Devoir et le délire du nationalisme d'extrême-droite dans la province de Québec, 1929–1939* (The Traitor and the Jew: Lionel Groulx, *Le Devoir*, and the Development of Extreme Right-Wing Nationalism in the Province of Quebec, 1929–1939) by Esther Delisle. She focuses on the influential daily newspaper *Le Devoir*, citing over 1,000 anti-Semitic articles, many on the front page and many written by Groulx, the father of modern Quebec nationalism. Alan Davies edited *Antisemitism in Canada: History and Interpretation*.

Other nonfiction works published during the year included *The Jews in a Polish Private Town: The Case of Opatow in the Eighteenth Century* by Gershon Hundert, which won the J.I. Segal Award from the Jewish Public Library in Montreal; *Que sais-je? Les partis religieux en Israel* by Julien Bauer; *Itineraires sépharades 1492–1992* by Yossi Levy and Yolande Cohen; *Unholy Alliances* by Warren Kinsella, which demonstrates how Libya funds right-wing and anti-Semitic groups in Canada; *The Un-Canadians* by Len Scher, the story of the harassment of leftists by government agencies during the McCarthy period; *Religion and Culture in Jewish Family Law* by John Syrtash; *Canadian Families in Transition* by Ben and Rachel Schlesinger; *Fackenheim: German Philosophy and Jewish Thought*, a festschrift in honor of the philosopher's 75th birthday, edited by Louis Greenspan and Graeme Nicholson; and *Phoenix from the Ashes* by Saul Levine.

Among new works of fiction were *Ship of the Hunted* by Yehuda Elberg; *The Number Game* by Abraham Boyarsky; and a work based on the life of a Jewish pioneer, *Aaron Hart: Sieur de Becancour/La Vie Mouvementée du Premier Juif Etabli au Québec au XVIIIe Siècle* by Michel Solomon. New works of poetry included Ray Shankman's *For Love of the Wind*, Shel Krakofsky's *The Reversible Coat*, and Henry Pollack's *The He and the She of It*. Solly Levy published a book of songs, plays, and poetry entitled *Those Were the Days*. The book was written in Haquetia, a language spoken by Spanish Jews before the expulsion.

New reference books included David Mendel Harduf's *English-Yiddish, Yiddish-English Dictionary*, volume 4. The feminist quarterly *Fireweed* devoted its volume 35 to the topic of Jewish women. It was the first collection of feminist Jewish writings published in Canada.

Marianne Langner Zeitlin won the City of Toronto Book Award for her novel *Next of Kin*. Rabbi Gedalia Felder won the Penina Rubinoff Memorial Prize in Biblical and Rabbinic Scholarship posthumously for *Yesodai Yeshurun: A Collection of Comments and Notes on Maseches Avos*.

Personalia

Judge Rosalie Silberman Abella was appointed to the Ontario Court of Appeal, that province's highest court. Other judicial appointments included Joel Guberman to the Quebec court and Sheila Ray to the Ontario criminal court. Ray is the first Sephardi Jew to serve as a judge in Ontario. Jacqueline Holzman was elected mayor of Ottawa, the first Jewish woman to hold that position. Ruth Wisse left McGill University to inaugurate a new chair in Yiddish studies at Harvard University, and Cheryl Jaffee became curator of the Jacob M. Lowy Collection of Hebraica and Judaica at the National Library. Bernard Dolansky was elected president of the Canadian Dental Association. Dror Zeigerman was appointed consul general of Israel in Toronto, succeeding Benjamin Abileah.

Irwin Cotler was appointed to the Order of Canada; the Order of Ontario was conferred on Rose Wolfe and Harry Rasky and the Order of British Columbia on Joseph Segal. Dorothy Reitman received the Governor General's Award in Commemoration of the Persons Case for her work to achieve equality for women. Bert Raphael was awarded the Law Society Medal by the Ontario bar association. King Hassan II of Morocco conferred the Al Istihqaq Al-Watan Medal, one of his country's highest honors, on Simon Keslassy. Dr. Ken Rosenthal won the Canadian Foundation for AIDS Research Industry Research Award.

Within the community, Irving Abella and Charles Zaionz were elected president and chairman of the national executive of the Canadian Jewish Congress. Other new CJC leaders include Gerda Frieberg as chairwoman of the Ontario Region and Manuel Shacter as her counterpart in Quebec. Rabbi Allan Nadler was appointed research director of the YIVO Institute for Jewish Research in New York, and Rabbi Howard Joseph became president of the Canadian Christian-Jewish Consultation. Gabe Nachman was elected president of B'nai Brith Canada, and Gerald Halbert became president of UIA Canada. Manuel Prutschi added the job of executive director of the Ontario Region of CJC to his community-relations job there. George Wasserstein became chairman of the National Budgeting Conference.

Among leading Jews who died in 1992 were the following: Florence Hutner, former executive director of the United Jewish Welfare Fund and the first woman to head a major Jewish organization in Canada, in January, aged 84; Dr. Martin Fischer, psychiatrist, in January, aged 78; Samuel Lewin, a longtime official of CJC, in February, aged 80; Barbara Frum, one of Canada's leading broadcast journalists, in March, aged 54; Jack Cowan, a founder of *Canadian Jewish Outlook* and former president of the United Jewish People's Order, in March, aged 91; Harry Orlinsky, eminent Bible scholar, in April, aged 84; Henry Blatt, founding president of B'nai Brith Canada, in April, aged 81; Dave Stitz, community leader, in April, aged 66; Cecil Linder, acclaimed actor, in April, aged 71; Hy Fogelman, community professional, in May, aged 66; Joseph Diamond, noted educator and founder of the Jewish Teachers Seminary, in May, aged 87; Sam Malmed, a one-man *bikur holim* society, in May, aged 95; Max Frieberg, a leader of Herut-Likud Canada, in June, aged 70;

Louis Soupcoff, community activist, in June, aged 78; David Weiss, social worker, in July, aged 77; Rabbi Mordechai Weinberg, dean of Yeshiva Gedolah Mercaz Hatorah, in July, aged 63; Sam Berger, owner of a professional sports team and former president of the Canadian Football League, in August, aged 92; Jaan Saber, engineering professor, in August, aged 46; Faye Tanenbaum, philanthropist, in September, aged 89; Jack Burke, pioneer educator, in October, aged 77; Joseph Tanenbaum, businessman and noted philanthropist, in November, aged 87; Jacob Rabinovitch, Yiddish journalist, in November, aged 83; Morris Lax, president of the Shiloh Institutions for Israel, in December, aged 71; and Rabbi Eli Bohnen, former president of the Rabbinical Assembly, in December, aged 83.

HAROLD M. WALLER

Western Europe

Great Britain

National Affairs

TWO PIVOTAL DATES IN 1992 were April 9, the date of the general election, which resulted in a close Conservative victory; and September 16 ("Black Wednesday"), when the pound sterling was forced out of the fixed-rate European Monetary System. In April the Tories, led by Prime Minister John Major, returned to power, defying the predictions of the pollsters but with a much reduced overall majority of 21. Neil Kinnock resigned as Labor leader, to be replaced by John Smith. The campaign was marked by successful and sustained Conservative attacks on Labor's alleged tax-and-spend policy. Much was also made of signs of the onset of economic recovery, but this did not materialize, and the continuing high level of interest rates (barely reduced from 10.5 percent to 10 percent in May) squeezed the life out of the faint revival in consumer spending. In fact, unemployment increased by 35,000 in the first 11 months of 1992, and manufacturing output at year-end was almost no higher than in 1979, when the Tories first came to power.

The summer was spent trying to reconcile the need of the domestic economy for a looser monetary policy with the constraint imposed by membership in the European system. This precarious balance was upset by several events: the Danish rejection of the Maastricht treaty in a referendum on June 2, a further increase in German interest rates in July, and the unilateral devaluation of the Italian lira by 7 percent early in September. The pound sterling meanwhile sank to the bottom of its permitted level against the deutsche mark. On the morning of September 16, speculation against the pound forced a rise in interest rates to 12 percent and in the afternoon to 15 percent. In the evening the chancellor announced the suspension of the pound sterling from the Exchange Rate Mechanism.

The immediate consequence was the devaluation of sterling by some 17 percent. But this did make it possible to reduce interest rates by 3 percentage points to 7 percent (lowest in about 15 years) by the end of the year, without adding to inflation. At 3 percent, inflation was at its lowest in six years. On the other hand, unemployment in December had risen to 2.291 million, with 10 percent of the labor force out of work. Premier John Major's popularity suffered, as did that of the Tories generally.

Israel and the Middle East

Although in March Foreign Secretary Douglas Hurd told the *Jewish Chronicle* that the atmosphere between London and Jerusalem had "considerably improved" over the past few years, Israel's actions in the occupied territories remained a major stumbling block. A Foreign Office spokesperson described Israel's January decision to expel 12 Palestinians from the occupied territories, for the killing of several settlers, as "particularly provocative." British diplomats at the United Nations, where Britain currently held the Security Council presidency, were instrumental in formulating a resolution condemning the expulsion order. Britain suggested to the UN secretary-general that a smaller consultative committee be convened to "ensure Israeli respect" for the Geneva Convention in the occupied territories. And Prime Minister John Major wrote a controversial letter to the Zionist Federation encouraging the main Jewish organizations to tell the Israeli government that the expulsions would damage both Israel's image and hopes for peace.

In March the Foreign Office announced that Britain was withdrawing its troops from the international peacekeeping force, the Multinational Force of Observers, in the Sinai Desert, as the government was satisfied that conditions were stable. A spokesperson stressed that this did not mean a lessening of British commitment to peace and security in the Middle East. Prime Minister Major, who sent a message to Israeli premier Yitzhak Shamir describing the late Menahem Begin as "a man of great vision whose historic contribution to the cause of peace will never be forgotten," said that his government was dedicated to Israel's success and its right to live peacefully within recognized boundaries. "We believe that a successful outcome to the present peace process is in Israel's greatest and long-term interest. We do not believe that the establishment of new settlements in these territories will help advance the peace process." In June he called on the Arabs to abandon their trade boycott against Israel in exchange for curbs on Israeli settlements in the West Bank and Gaza Strip, which were, he said, "a major impediment to the peace process."

The June election of the new Israeli government seemed to signal a new era in Anglo-Israeli relations. "I believe we now have the chance to further strengthen links with Israel," Major said, indicating that the European Community (EC), under British leadership, would play an active role in the Middle East peace process, which would be given "very high priority." Israeli foreign minister Shimon Peres, visiting Britain in August at the personal invitation of Foreign Secretary Hurd, told the *Jewish Chronicle* that Israel would like to see the Europeans playing a considerable role in the building of the new Middle East, while senior Israeli diplomats pressed British cabinet ministers to help Israel achieve closer links with the EC. The warm welcome accorded the new Israeli prime minister, Yitzhak Rabin, in Britain, in December, when Major accepted an invitation to visit Israel in the spring, was seen as reflecting Britain's approval of the Israeli government's more flexible approach to the overall peace process, even as they differed on the status of Jerusalem and recognition of the PLO. Foreign Office minister Douglas Hogg told the House of Commons in November that the government did not recognize Israel's rule over any part of Jerusalem or its status as Israel's capital. "Jerusalem as a whole is a special case," he said, "and its status has yet to be determined. We believe the city should not be divided. Its status must be addressed in the peace process." In December Britain voted in favor of a Security Council resolution declaring Israel's jurisdiction over Jerusalem illegal.

British policy on the PLO would remain unchanged, Foreign Secretary Hurd said in March, since the PLO had made a "huge mistake" in supporting Saddam Hussein in the Gulf War. The ban on ministers meeting with PLO representatives remained, though other British officials maintained contacts through which they urged the PLO not to obstruct the peace process. Despite a June attempt by Dr. Nabil Shaath, chairman of the Palestine National Council's political committee, to persuade high-ranking Foreign Office diplomats to lift the ban, in October the Foreign Office declined to allow the PLO's London representative, Afif Safieh, to accompany visiting Bethlehem mayor Elias Freij to a meeting with Hogg.

Britain would continue supplying weapons to her traditional friends in the Gulf, Hurd said in March. The ban on arms sales to Israel remained, but was not a "live issue," and Britain was willing to sell oil to Israel. Pro-Israel MPs called for reconsideration of the ban in November, when the government announced a judicial inquiry into allegations that ministers had allowed arms-making equipment to be exported to Iraq, contravening the weapons embargo against Saddam Hussein's regime. Although in November Defense Minister Jonathan Aitken told the House of Commons that the government would maintain the ban until Israeli troops were withdrawn from southern Lebanon, a change in policy was signaled in December. Major told Rabin that there was no longer any block on Britain purchasing Israeli arms, and Raphael, Israel's armament development authority, was one of 20 companies invited to bid on a £2-billion contract to supply the British army with armored vehicles.

Britain was party to the unanimous Security Council vote in December condemning Israel's expulsion of over 400 alleged Hamas and Islamic Jihad supporters but abstained on a Security Council resolution calling for the PLO to be included in a UN-sponsored peace conference.

In October the British Broadcasting Corporation announced its choice of American professor and pro-Palestinian activist Edward Said to give the prestigious Reith Lectures in 1993. Chief Rabbi Jonathan Sacks had been Reith lecturer two years earlier.

The British Labor party's attitude to the Middle East changed markedly after Rabin's victory in the Israeli general elections in June, which new foreign-affairs spokesman Jack Cunningham called a "watershed." No motions critical of Israel or praising the PLO were presented at the party's annual conference in October, and the traditionally pro-Palestinian Fire Brigade Union passed a motion welcoming the peace talks and hoping for a comprehensive and lasting peace. The Israel Labor party's "fraternal representative," Ephraim Sneh, was given a warm reception at the Blackpool Labor party conference. By contrast, a delegation from the National Association of Local and Government Officers (NALGO) did not plan to meet with Histadrut officials when it visited Palestinian labor activists in the occupied territories in April, and three Labor MPs and several trade-unionists formed part of a fact-finding mission that visited PLO leader Yasir Arafat in Tunis in October.

Liberal-Democrat foreign-affairs spokesman Sir David Steel introduced Palestinian spokeswoman Hanan Ashrawi at a public meeting held in London in June, as part of a campaign by Palestinian diplomats and supporters to win EC sympathy and political backing.

The Council for Jewish-Palestinian Dialogue was launched in May, with a 12-member executive board, headed jointly by Palestinian activist Saida Nusseibeh and Jewish academic Tony Klug, and including June Jacobs, an executive member of the Board of Deputies of British Jews.

Nazi War Criminals

Scotland Yard's war-crimes unit recorded considerable activity this year. In July Earl Ferrers, minister of state at the Home Office, told the House of Lords that more than 90 alleged Nazis living in Britain were currently under examination and that detectives had examined 343 cases since the War Crimes Act was passed in 1991.

In March, unit leader Detective Superintendent Eddie Bathgate was consulting with officials in Jerusalem. By July, when it was reported that the unit had sufficient evidence to prosecute 12 suspected war criminals living in Britain, Bathgate was in the former Soviet Union, meeting with local prosecutors and studying KGB files on suspected Nazis. The same month, Bathgate's deputy, Detective Superintendent David Sibley, was in Israel, meeting with the Israel Police's Nazi-hunting unit and talking to witnesses of wartime atrocities in Europe.

In July Lord Milligan ruled that Glasgow-based Scottish Television (STV) had not libeled Anton Gecas by describing him as a war criminal. Lithuanian-born Gecas, a 75-year-old former mining engineer living in Edinburgh since 1947, brought the £600,000 action after an STV documentary, "Crimes of War," alleged that he was responsible for the deaths of 50,000 Jews and partisans in the former Soviet Union. The case made Scottish legal history when the evidence-gathering commission of the Court of Sessions moved to Vilnius, Lithuania, because witnesses were too old and frail to travel. Following the verdict, Jewish Board of Deputies chief executive Neville Nagler said that the case showed it was possible for a British court to assess evidence fairly on events that had occurred in Eastern Europe decades before. Ephraim Zuroff, director of Jerusalem's Simon Wiesenthal Center, who in March claimed that a new list of several dozen suspected Nazi war criminals existed in British government archives, urged the Scottish war-crimes team to put

Gecas on trial quickly, in case he fled the country. But in September the Scottish Office said that investigators were still some way from presenting any case for prosecution to Scotland's leading law officer, the Lord Advocate.

Anti-Semitism and Racism

Reports by both the London-based Institute of Jewish Affairs (published in June) and the New York-based Anti-Defamation League of B'nai B'rith (published in December) found less anti-Semitism in Britain than elsewhere. Nonetheless, 250 anti-Semitic incidents were reported nationwide in 1992, most of them in London, said Commander David Stevens, head of the police community involvement branch, in March. According to Board of Deputies defense director Michael Whine, the number of anti-Semitic incidents reported to the board's community security organization had reached an all-time high in 1991, though most were minor and nonviolent. In general, said Whine, the number and range of anti-Semitic activities in Britain could not be compared to those on the Continent.

The 1992 incidents included anti-Semitic daubings on synagogues (Elstree Progressive in March, Hertsmere Progressive in June, Croydon Federation in August); tombstone desecrations (West Ham cemetery in May, Cardiff's Ely cemetery in November); abuse shouted at congregants (Boreham Wood and Elstree Synagogue in April); and arson (the Kosher Luncheon Club in Whitechapel in June). In November half a pig's head and daubings were placed on the Holocaust Memorial in Gladstone Park, Dollis Hill, north-west London; and pigs' feet and daubings were found at Yakar Study Center, Hendon. In December the Serious Crime Squad investigated malicious Hanukkah cards sent to some 200 prominent British Jews.

The activities of extreme right-wing groups believed responsible for most of these actions were watched with concern. In February Bexleyheath police raided a British National party (BNP) bookshop in Welling, south-east London, seizing racially inflammatory material. But the National Front (NF) fielded only 15 candidates in the April general election, compared with 301 in 1979, and polled a total of 4,684 votes. BNP presented a further 13, including, in Dewsbury, Yorkshire, the Dowager Lady Birdwood, convicted in 1991 of distributing anti-Semitic literature. With BNP recording a total of 7,005 votes, Whine said the far right was no longer "an issue at general elections." However, although Labor won a council by-election in London's Docklands in October, BNP polled 657 votes, its best election result for a decade, beating the Conservative candidate into third place. In October the Jewish Board of Deputies sought a meeting with senior Scotland Yard officials to discuss why the police were "facilitating" neo-Nazi meetings in halls hired under false pretenses. Their concern followed a BNP rally, attended by 400 people, in the General Assembly Rooms, Church House, Westminster, London, home of the Church of England General Synod, booked in the name of the "Anglo-Baltic Exchange." Two hundred policemen surrounded the building to protect BNP members from antifascist demonstrators.

The Board of Deputies campaign to persuade the government to toughen up racial-hatred laws received a setback in October. Following a meeting between a board delegation and Home Office officials, board chief executive Neville Nagler reported that the Home Office was "not convinced that the existing laws were insufficient," though it promised to continue the dialogue and monitor the situation. The Commission for Racial Equality, in its September review of the 1976 Race Relations Act, recommended that the government make racially motivated violence a specific criminal offense, strengthen the act to stamp out racial discrimination in the workplace, and set up an independent review of the working of the law on incitement to racial hatred. In November a parliamentary branch of the Anti-Racist Alliance was launched in the Commons and immediately demanded a new law against racial harassment. The same month, the group demonstrated outside London's German embassy against neo-Nazi violence in Germany.

The rebirth of the Anti-Nazi League (ANL) in January provoked controversy. It was accused of being a front for the extreme left Socialist Workers' party, which was active in the campus anti-Zionist campaign. The Board of Deputies regarded the group's reemergence as likely to split existing broad-based opposition to neo-Nazi activity. In February the Union of Jewish Students (UJS) told its members to shun ANL and urged support for Anti-Fascist Action and the antifascist magazine *Searchlight*.

At times antifascist activities ended in violence. In February ANL members distributing leaflets in the East London borough of Tower Hamlets were attacked by BNP members; in March three men were charged with assault. In April violence broke out at a BNP Bethnal Green election meeting where campaign literature claimed that the "Tory and Labor parties were controlled by communists, Zionists, and international companies who . . . are actively hostile to the British people." In May four UJS members were beaten up following an antiracist demonstration and a BNP counterdemonstration in central London. In August 13 people were arrested in London's East End as more than 500 antifascists massed outside Bethnal Green's council hall to protest BNP's by-election meeting. In September four men were arrested after an attack on an ANL stall in the East End, and 44 arrests were made when Anti-Fascist Action occupied Waterloo Station concourse in an attempt to halt skinheads en route to hear the neo-Nazi band Skrewdriver. National Front plans to march past the Cenotaph on Remembrance Sunday and lay a wreath in memory of the war dead were condemned in Parliament; some 100 marchers persisted and were outnumbered by protesters in ensuing clashes. In July, Southwark Crown court cleared *Searchlight* editor Gerry Gable of charges of attacking a policeman in May 1991, due to insufficient evidence.

Holocaust revisionism was a live issue. Defense Minister Alan Clark faced an outcry from both sides of the House of Commons for attending a January party to launch the revised edition of *Hitler's War* by Holocaust revisionist historian David Irving. He "utterly rejected" Irving's views, he averred. In response to a June announcement that a Holocaust revisionist seminar would be held in London in

July, with Irving as the main speaker, a motion was introduced in Parliament calling on the government to prevent this "obscene event." The Board of Deputies organized a demonstration, attended by several hundred people, outside Irving's Mayfair home. Some 300 people joined another demonstration, organized by the board, UJS, and the Association of Jewish Ex-servicemen and Women (AJEX), outside International Student House, central London, where 200 participants attended the seminar; seven arrests were made.

In July historians, Jewish groups, politicians, and others protested the announcement that the *Sunday Times* of London had hired Irving to transcribe and translate diaries of Hitler's minister of propaganda, Joseph Goebbels, which were uncovered in a Moscow archive. Jewish leaders urged Home Secretary Kenneth Clarke to act against Holocaust deniers, and a Board of Deputies delegation warned that Holocaust revisionists planned to make the United Kingdom their headquarters. A House of Commons motion attacked as "tasteless and offensive" a *Sunday Times* advertising poster showing Goebbels against a swastika; ANL members defaced billboards featuring the poster throughout London. Poale Zion and the Jewish Socialist Group, in liaison with Anti-Racist Alliance, organized a protest outside the *Sunday Times* Wapping headquarters. The paper responded to the outcry by publishing a two-page feature on the worldwide threat of Holocaust revisionism, in addition to the two-part serialization of the diaries. The *Sunday Times* and editor Andrew Neil, said Sir Ivan Lawrence, chairman of the House of Commons Home Affairs Committee, had been "shamed" by the intense criticism of the decision to hire Irving. Meanwhile, Irving contemplated legal action over a contractually agreed-upon credit that never appeared in the newspaper. A line at the end of each article indicated that Irving had transcribed and translated the diary excerpts; he felt he should have been credited as their editor and had his historical views on the diaries published as well. In November, during a speaking tour of North America and Australia, Irving was arrested in Canada and deported back to Britain because of his alleged criminal background and the likelihood of his breaking Canadian law by inciting racial hatred. The same month, ANL published *Holocaust Denial: The New Nazi Lie*, an inexpensive and accessible introduction to the threat of Holocaust revisionism.

JEWISH COMMUNITY

Demography

The estimated number of Jews in Great Britain was 300,000. The downward trend in synagogue marriages of the past two decades continued, according to figures issued by the Community Research Unit of the Board of Deputies of British Jews. In 1992, 1,031 marriages took place under Jewish religious auspices, compared with 1,082 in 1991. Orthodox marriages accounted for 79 percent and Progressive marriages for 21 percent of the total. Figures for religious divorce obtained from both Orthodox and Reform *batei din* (rabbinical courts) show 271 *gittim* issued in 1991 against 261 in 1990.

Burials and cremations under Jewish auspices decreased to 4,219 in 1992 from 4,431 in 1991. Births, estimated on the basis of figures for circumcision, rose to 3,427 in 1991 from 3,096 in 1990.

Regional studies showed declining populations. Figures issued by the Community Research Unit in February put the number of Jews in Leeds at 10,000, a drop of 30 percent from 1985. A census by Birmingham's local representative council indicated a community of under 3,000, nearly a third aged between 60 and 79 and only 6 percent in the 15–19 age group.

Communal Affairs

The economic recession continued to dominate the community scene both in London and the provinces. In February the Jewish crisis hotline, Miyad, reported that calls had doubled to an average 200 monthly over the past year, with concern at the time of the Gulf War and recession-related problems the major contributory factors. Prime worries now were layoffs and job insecurity, leading to anxiety and family breakup, said Jeffery Blumenfeld, director of Miyad's parent agency, the Jewish Marriage Council.

The financial situation of Nightingale House, the Home for Aged Jews, was the worst in his 30 years with the organization, said executive director Asher Corren in February. In June Norwood Child Care executive director Sam Brier reported that members of 1,135 families sought help from Norwood in 1991, a 17-percent increase over 1990. "People who used to support us with contributions, fund-raising, and volunteer work are coming to us for help," said Jewish Care executive director Melvyn Carlowe. To alleviate the situation, Care opened an unemployment support group in August, administered by the Hendon-based Shalvata counseling service. Individual synagogues also organized help initiatives for job-seekers.

Jews in the Former Soviet Union

The changed situation in the former Soviet Union, as well as financial difficulties in Britain, caused organizations engaged in assisting Soviet Jews to rethink their programs. In July the National Council for Soviet Jewry, which was at the forefront of the movement in the 1970s and early 1980s, changed its name to the National Council for Jews in Former Soviet Lands. Its new constitution reduced the executive to "a smaller group of those actually involved in the area," said chairman John Fenner, and the group was now much better equipped to provide "effective positive action to help both those who want to leave and those who want to stay in the former Soviet Union."

In August the British Student and Academic Campaign for Jews of the Former

Soviet Union scaled down its national organization, eliminating the position of national organizer and closing its offices. At the same time, it opened a Jewish youth center in Kiev to teach young Ukrainian Jews about Judaism. Efforts on behalf of Soviet Jews were divided between assisting those who remained in the former Soviet Union and those who emigrated to Israel, through fund-raising and other activities.

In April the Manchester City Council called on its St. Petersburg counterpart to investigate reports of anti-Semitic demonstrations and also made a plea for more Jews to be allowed to emigrate. In December, at a meeting with Russian ambassador Boris Pankin, arranged by the Women's Campaign for Soviet Jewry, the 35s, a delegation of four MPs discussed Moscow's continuing refusal to allow some Jews to emigrate. In December, too, Foreign Secretary Hurd promised members of the Manchester 35s to "explore every available channel" to help Russian Jews being denied exit visas.

Community Relations

In January the Board of Deputies announced its willingness to hold talks with the newly formed Muslim Parliament, which claimed to represent Britain's two million or so Muslims and was to some degree modeled on the Jewish body. In February the board's president, Judge Israel Finestein, hosted a lunch for deputies and black lawyers, for the purpose of getting acquainted and exchanging views. Similar discussions had already taken place with Hindu leaders. February also saw the launching, at the initiative of Greville Janner, MP, of the Maimonides Foundation, whose purpose was to cultivate links between British Jews and Muslims. In August, a letter in the London *Times* calling on the British government to spearhead action against war crimes in Bosnia was signed by Progressive rabbi Hugo Gryn and leading British Muslims. In September the Board of Deputies organized a symposium on "Israel, Islam and the Jewish community."

In October Home Secretary Kenneth Clarke reintroduced the government Asylum Bill in Parliament in an amended form. The bill, which aimed to cut the number of political refugees allowed sanctuary in Britain, was originally introduced in 1991. Although the bill now included new concessions aimed at meeting objections raised by the Board of Deputies and other lobbies, in November, when the bill received its second reading in the Commons, communal leaders still vowed to continue the fight against its "iniquities." The board had campaigned against the bill since its inception, with Judge Finestein writing to the Home Secretary in January that it contravened the spirit of the 1951 UN Convention on Refugees, which "was adopted to ensure no group would suffer the same fate as those many Jewish people who had no refuge and lost their lives." In August the Zionist Federation appealed to Prime Minister Major to admit refugees from war-ravaged Bosnia and to avoid repeating the policies that prevented Holocaust victims from finding safe havens.

Religion

Financial problems beset the centrist Orthodox United Synagogue (US), Britain's largest synagogue association, throughout the year. In February the US council approved the sale of part of the Great Synagogue's silver collection to the Jewish Museum. The same month, in a drive to control spending, the council demanded that its officers release details of salaries and expenses paid to the organization's 1,500 employees, including the chief rabbi and the US London Bet Din's chief executive. This was agreed to in March, against the wishes of US president Sidney Frosh, on condition that the figures remain confidential. In March the US's deficit was revised upward to £1.6 million (from £1.3 million reported in December 1991), partly because of the failure of several synagogues to pay their expected contributions toward central services. In June the audit committee chairman, Norman Roberts, warned that, despite spending cuts, the US was likely to exceed its budgeted deficit of £254,000 in 1992 because of continuing losses on its kosher slaughtering operation, the slowness of some synagogues to repay cash advances, and membership arrears of over £1 million. United Synagogue membership fell by more than 500 to 34,018 in 1991.

Such was the situation when the Kalms Report, a major study of the US, was published in September. Prepared by Stanley Kalms, the head of Dixons, a major retail outlet, and a former US officer, the 300-page report described the organization as "moving relentlessly towards insolvency and loss of members far more rapidly" than other synagogue organizations. The US's "market share" of the Jewish community was in sharp decline amid wide dissatisfaction with a remote head office, cold, unwelcoming communities, and a "drift to the right" away from its traditional tolerant ethos, the report said. To reduce its £9-million debt, the report advised introducing a five-year program of cutting expenditures and increasing membership. It also called on US members to support a completely revamped organization, one that placed more emphasis on individuals and communities, that reduced central control over local communities, and that placed greater responsibility for decision-making in local hands. Local synagogues should become "independent trust communities," managing their own administration and finances, the report said.

The US central structure should be radically reduced, the report further suggested, with the US retaining responsibility solely for burials and possibly *kashrut* and ceding its other responsibilities, such as education, to independent bodies. The report envisaged an enhanced Chief Rabbinate, one more independent of the US, though the US would remain its principal supporter, and with increased responsibilities, including support for adult education and rabbinical placements. The role of women should be reviewed and promptly recast, said the report's authors, enabling them to participate fully in the US council and local management committees.

The report received a mixed reception. The United Synagogue's lay leaders, headed by Frosh, resigned en bloc, while Chief Rabbi Jonathan Sacks greeted it as a "pivotal document of the decade of renewal." In October, however, he described it as "a lay document, couched in terms of finance, management and marketing." It lacks, he said, "a spiritual dimension." US rabbinical council chairman Rabbi Alan Plancy said, "We as religious leaders must take [the spiritual and religious future of Anglo-Jewry] in hand, not the laymen." The Union of Jewish Students (UJS) voted unanimously to fight Kalms's proposal that the US pull out of student chaplaincy funding.

US council elections in October reflected the divided reaction. Seymour Seideman, one of the report's authors, defeated outgoing joint vice-president Alan Grant, who was more critical, to become the youngest president in US history. However, the 53-year-old Seideman, a financial consultant, stressed that he would "initiate the widest possible debate before embarking on any of the changes" the report suggested. In December the US council unanimously approved an austerity budget involving the loss of 12 jobs at US headquarters, the Chief Rabbi's office, and the London Bet Din, and spending cuts of £800,000.

In February Chief Rabbi Sacks launched a comprehensive review of the role of Jewish women, the first practical initiative of his "decade of renewal." Rosalind Preston, the first female vice-president of the Board of Deputies, was appointed to head a commission including women from all backgrounds. The London Bet Din head, Dayan Chanoch Ehrentreu, agreed to serve as adviser on matters of Jewish law, the chief rabbi announced. "Renewal starts with Jewish women," Sacks said. "They are the builders of our values, our homes, our families." Preston, who was assembling task forces of women to look at their roles in education, the family, marriage and divorce procedures, the synagogue and religious life, and other areas, hoped to present Rabbi Sacks with a report in 18 months.

The optimism engendered among Jewish women by this initiative was dampened in November when the first-ever women-only Sabbath service, scheduled to be held on US premises in Stanmore Synagogue, Middlesex, was canceled following intervention by the chief rabbi, other senior rabbis, and the London Bet Din, who wanted to "discuss the matter further." It was reported that the chief rabbi planned to rule on the issue early in 1993.

The April announcement of Sacks's second major initiative, a charity walk for unity, also provoked controversy when it emerged that the Jewish Lesbian and Gay Helpline was banned from participating. Helpline was not an "appropriate charity for the Chief Rabbi to give recognition to," explained Rabbi Pinchas Rosenstein, one of the walk organizers. Despite protests over this decision by Habonim/Dror, the Union of Jewish Students, and a delegation of Progressive rabbis, an estimated 4,000 participants joined Sacks on a three-and-a-half-mile walk around London's Hyde Park in July, which raised £100,000 for 120 Jewish charities.

Sacks's third initiative, announced in May, was a national program of Chief Rabbinate awards for excellence. This would honor groups and individuals who had achieved the highest standards in youth work, synagogue life, welfare, education, and work for Israel. "Anglo-Jewry has not understood the importance of motivating people," Sacks said. "We don't have a forum for the community to say congratulations." The program, which would be held every two years, would be open to groups under the chief rabbi's patronage and organizations included at the "discretion of the Chief Rabbi."

Meanwhile, in April Sacks announced a series of projects to be implemented in the subsequent six months: a scholarship program to enable young people to study in Israel, initiatives in business ethics and adult education, and a reshaped rabbinic training program. In September he established a department for rabbinic development in his office, its aim to develop the talents of local rabbis so as to make "our synagogues more open, welcoming, accessible, varied and full of life."

In June the Barnet Council public-works committee approved plans for a northwest London *eruv* (a symbolic boundary converting a public into a private area, in which it is permitted to carry certain items and push prams and wheelchairs on the Sabbath). The proposed *eruv*, which would cover an area of $6\frac{1}{2}$ square miles, incorporating Golders Green, Hendon, parts of Hampstead Garden Suburb, and Cricklewood, where some 10,000 Jews lived, still required approval by the council's planning authority and the Department of Transport. The project would be funded by the US.

Britain's Sephardi community was divided over the nature of Sepharad '92, the year-long program of events marking the 500th anniversary of the expulsion of Spanish Jews. Dayan Pinchas Toledano, head of the Sephardi Bet Din, boycotted a special Sabbath service at the Spanish and Portuguese Synagogue in London, attended by the Spanish ambassador. "I do not feel we should be celebrating," he said, and it was "absolutely inappropriate" for the ambassador to attend. But Rabbi Dr. Abraham Levy, spiritual head and communal rabbi of London's Spanish and Portuguese Jews' Congregation, denied that Sepharad '92 was a celebratory event. "It is a commemoration not only of the horrors of persecution but also of the glorious achievements of our ancestors in Spain." In April, Britain's oldest synagogue, the Spanish and Portuguese Bevis Marks, erected in 1701, was badly damaged when an IRA bomb blast devastated an area of the City of London.

In November the US, the Federation of Synagogues, and the Spanish and Portuguese synagogues agreed that rabbinic responsibility for *shehitah* operations would be shared on an equal basis between the chief rabbi and his Federation and Sephardi counterparts. The conflict over kosher slaughter began in 1989 when the US launched a breakaway operation following disagreement over rabbinic control. The US was expected to shut down its loss-making operation within a few months, leaving the London Board for Shechitah as the sole provider of meat for central Orthodoxy. In three years, the US lost over £500,000 on its meat operations.

In February the British Masorti (Conservative) movement moved its headquarters to larger premises. The movement had over 3,500 congregants in its London synagogues, said Michael Rose, chairman of the Assembly of Masorti Synagogues.

The Reform Synagogues of Great Britain (RSGB), with nearly 26,000 members, celebrated its 50th anniversary this year by opening a £500,000 youth and education building at the Sternberg Center in Finchley, north-west London, in July. The building contains the headquarters of the Center for Jewish Education, the teachers' training center, a resource library, and the Reform movement's youth department offices, as well as a mikveh (ritual bath).

In March the Liberal Jewish Synagogue in St. John's Wood, north-west London, elected its first woman head, Rita Adler. In December Rabbi Jacqueline Tabick was the first woman elected to head the Council of Reform and Liberal Rabbis.

Education

There were 24,000 children enrolled in full- or part-time Jewish education, 10,000 fewer than 30 years ago when the Anglo-Jewish population was larger, said a report by the Jewish Educational Development Trust's (JEDT) think tank, published in August. Of the total 42,800 British Jewish children in the 5–17 age group (compared with 58,500 in 1962), 80 percent received formal Jewish education at some stage. The report's statistics, based on research by Dr. Stephen Miller, head of social sciences at London's City University, showed a growth in the Jewish day-school population, mainly due to the right-wing Orthodox. Some 43 percent of children in Jewish schools came from right-wing Orthodox homes, while only 1 percent attended the only Progressive school, Akiva. More children were now enrolled in day schools than in the part-time system, which served half the number of children it did 30 years earlier. In 1962, 36 percent of the 5–17 age group attended part-time classes and 15 percent were in day schools. Currently, part-time classes accounted for 26 percent of that age group and day schools 30 percent. All in all, some 16,000 Jewish pupils were enrolled in day schools, in 29 nursery schools, 36 primary schools, and 25 secondary schools. Jewish nursery schools, with 38 percent of the preschool Jewish population, were the most popular form of Jewish education; however, based on Miller's research, only 24 of every 100 children who entered Jewish nursery school would be attending a Jewish school at sixth-form level (ages 16–17). Likewise, less than half those in full- or part-time Jewish education at age 7 would still receive Jewish education at age 14, the report stated.

The 80-page report based on these findings and compiled by think-tank chairman Fred Worms found that Jewish education was gripped by "an unprecedented funding crisis" that threatened its future and affected almost every communal educational organization. The report described an "extraordinarily fragmented" educational system in which money was wasted because organizations failed to cooperate. It proposed the formation of a national council for Jewish education, involving Orthodox and Progressive organizations, lay leaders, and education professionals, whose central purpose would be fund-raising and avoiding unnecessary competition. There was no suggestion that constituent groups would interfere in the content of education. The report's second main proposal was a change in emphasis away from opening new schools and toward recruiting and training teachers, and it offered a number of measures to implement this.

Jews' College, which had 150 students in July, announced in October that practical rabbinics would in future form half of its three-year course leading to ordination. There were currently ten British-based trainee rabbis at the college, which prepares rabbis for the US and other centrist Orthodox communities.

The Joe Loss Fellowship in Jewish Music was established at the City University as part of the music department's ethnomusicology course. A full-time lectureship in medieval Jewish studies was set up in the Department of Hebrew and Jewish Studies at University College, London. In August a £1-million chair in business ethics and social responsibility was created at the London Business School by Stanley Kalms, who was also among the sponsors of an eight-week lecture series on Jewish business ethics, arranged by Integrity in Action under the auspices of the Chief Rabbi's Office.

In June Manchester University don Philip Alexander was appointed to succeed David Patterson, who retired as president of the Oxford Centre for Post-graduate Hebrew Studies in December.

Publications

The H.H. Wingate/Jewish Quarterly Prize for nonfiction was awarded to Robert Wistrich for *Antisemitism: The Longest Hatred*, after Tudor Parfitt's *Journey to the Vanished City*, announced as co-winner, was disqualified because it was not published in the period stipulated by the terms of the award. The £40,000 David Cohen British Literary Prize, funded by a Hampstead physician and former Board of Deputies member, was launched in cooperation with the Arts Council. It will go to a living British writer to honor his or her whole body of work.

Biographical works published during the year included *Arendt*, David Watson's study of Hannah Arendt; *Lender to the Lords, Giver to the Poor*, a biography of Samuel Lewis by Gerry Black; *Warrior Statesman: The Life of Moshe Dayan* by Robert Slater; *Dreyfus: A Family Affair, 1789–1945* by Michael Burns; *Herbert Samuel: A Political Life* by Bernard Wasserstein; *Epstein: Artist Against the Establishment* by Stephen Gardiner; *Wellesley Aron: Rebel with a Cause* by Helen Silman-Cheong; and *Lord George Gordon*, by Yirmeyahu Bindman. Ramin Jahanbegloo's *Conversations with Isaiah Berlin* and S.J. Goldsmith's *Essays in Disapproval* have biographical relevance.

New autobiographies were *Tango Down the Corridor* by Joan Gordon; *Memories of the Gorbals* by Jack Caplan; *Crossing*, the third volume of Jakov Lind's autobiography; *An Economist's Testimony* by S. Herbert Frankel; *Bow Jest* by Paul Zetter; *Shared Lives* by Lyndall Gordon; and *There Was a Young Man from Cardiff*, autobiographical fiction by Dannie Abse.

Fiction published during the year included *The Journey* by Ida Fink; *The Red Pagoda* by Robert Mendelsohn; *The Very Model of a Man* by Howard Jacobson; *The Jewess: Stories from Berlin and New York* by Irene Dische; *Loving Brecht* by Elaine Feinstein; *My Golden Trades* by Ivan Klima, a collection of stories set in Czechoslovakia; *The Volcano Lover* by Susan Sontag; *Inheritance* by David Pryce-

Jones; *Augustus Rex* by Clive Sinclair; *Roth* by Glyn Hughes; *A Little Space for Issie Brown* by Anthony Simmons; *Mendelssohn Is on the Roof* by Jiri Weil; *Mother Russia* by Bernice Rubens; and *The Last Honeymoon* by Shelley Weiner.

New works on religious themes were *Judaism and Ecology*, edited by Aubrey Rose; *Crisis and Covenant: Jewish Thought After the Holocaust* by Chief Rabbi Jonathan Sacks; *Religion and the Individual* by Louis Jacobs; and *How to Get Up When Life Gets You Down* by Progressive rabbis Lionel Blue and Jonathan Magonet.

Historical studies included *War, Jews, and the New Europe: The Diplomacy of Lucien Wolf, 1914–1919* by Mark Levene; *1492: The Year and the Era* by Barnet Litvinoff; and *The Sephardim* by Lucien Gubbay and Abraham Levy. Geoffrey Alderman's *Modern British Jewry* and the *Survey of Jewish Affairs, 1991*, edited by William Frankel, analyze the contemporary scene. Local history included two books on Oxford: *The Jews of Oxford* by David M. Lewis and *Then and Now* by Freda Silver Jackson.

Historical studies of the Hitler period were Eric Silver's *The Book of the Just*, on the "silent heroes" who saved Jews from Hitler; *Benevolence and Betrayal* by Alexander Stille, an account of five Jewish families in wartime Italy; *The Germans and the Final Solution* by David Bankier; and *The Roots of Appeasement* by Benny Morris. Personal accounts of the period included *Three Lives in Transit* by Laura Selo; *Witnesses: Life in Occupied Krakow* by Miriam Peleg-Marianska and Mordecai Peleg; *A Time to Speak* by Helen Lewis; *By the Moon and the Stars* by Eva Hayman; *On Thin Ice* by Henry Stanhope; and *The Poison Seed: A Personal History of Nazi Germany* by Marianne Walter. *The Trial of God* by Elie Wiesel and *At an Uncertain Hour, Wine from Two Glasses*, and *I'm Not Even Grown Up*, all by Anthony Rudolf, are related approaches to living with the memory of the Holocaust. *Justice Delayed* by David Cesarani examines moves to bring war criminals to trial.

Works on refugees from Nazi Germany included *The Face of Survival* by Michael Riff, and *Refugee Scholars: Conversations with Tess Simpson*, edited by R.M. Cooper. Simpson was assistant secretary to the Society for the Protection of Science and Learning set up in 1933 by Sir William Henry Beveridge (later Lord Beveridge) to help refugee academics.

New studies of anti-Semitism were *Political Discourse in Exile: Karl Marx and the Jewish Question* by Denis Fischman, and *The Jew's Body*, in which Sander Gilman examines anti-Semitic myths spawned by the notion that Jews are physically and mentally "different."

Poetry published during the year included *Trial by Verse* by Geoffrey Hoffman; *The Proper Blessing* and *A Bit of Dialect* by A.C. Jacobs; *The English Earthquake* by Eva Salzman; *Roots in the Air* by Michael Hamburger; *The Lens Breakers* by Jon Silkin; *Fathers* by Daniel Weissbort, who also edited *The Poetry of Survival: Post War Poets of Central and Eastern Europe*; *Offshore* by Anne Atik; *Crossing Point* by Myra Schneider; and *Jaguar of Sweet Laughter* by Diane Ackerman. In *Watermark*, poet Joseph Brodsky paints a portrait of Venice in poetic prose.

Works relating to Israel included *Israel: A Concise Political History* by Yossi Beilin; *The Road Not Taken* by Itamar Rabinovich, a study of the failure of Israel's early negotiations with the Arab states; *From Palmerston to Balfour: Collected Essays of Mayir Verete*, edited by Norman Rose; *Labor and the Political Economy in Israel* by Michael Shalev; *Arabs and Jews in Israel*, vol. 2: *Change and Continuity in Mutual Intolerance* by Sammy Smooha; *Stalemate: The War of Attrition and Great Power Diplomacy in the Middle East, 1967–70* by David A. Korn; *Israel and Africa: The Problematic Friendship* by Joel Peters; *The Kibbutz Movement: A History*, vol.1: *Origins and Growth, 1909–1939* by Henry Near.

Books on London's East End and Yiddish culture included *An East London Album*, compiled by Peter Marcan; *Three for the Price of One*, Anna Tzelniker's personal history of the Yiddish theater; *Jewish Books in Whitechapel: A Bibliography of Narodiczky's Press*, compiled by Moshe Sanders and edited by Marion Aptroot; *On Foot in the East End* by Robert Philpotts; *Jewish Eastenders*, edited by Aumie and Michael Shapiro; and *Skeet—A House in the Country*, an anthology of former Brady Club members' reminiscences. In the field of Yiddish, Oxford Yiddishist Dovid Katz published *Eldra Don*, a collection of Yiddish short stories, under the pseudonym Heershdovid Menkes; and David G. Roskies edited *S. Ansky: The Dybbuk and Other Writings*.

Literary translations included *Flow Tide: Poems and Prose of Claude Vigée*, translated and edited by Anthony Rudolf; *Primo Levi: Collected Poems*, translated by Ruth Feldman and Brian Swann; and *Out of the Depths* by Joseph Chaim Brenner, translated by David Patterson, the first of a series of English translations of Hebrew writings published in the 50 years before World War II, edited by Patterson.

Books on East European Jewry were *The Enigma of Soviet Jewry*, a collection of articles by Schneier Levenberg; *Bolsheviks and British Jews: The Anglo-Jewish Community, Britain and the Russian Revolution* by Sharman Kadish; *Journey to Poland* by Alfred Doblin; and *The Struggle for Soviet-Jewish Emigration, 1948–1967* by Yaacov Ro'i.

The Homeless Imagination in the Fiction of Israel Joshua Singer by Anita Norich is a work of literary criticism. Matthew Stevens edited the *Jewish Film Directory*.

Personalia

Former Conservative chancellor of the exchequer Sir Nigel Lawson and Sir Geoffrey Finsberg, for 22 years Conservative MP for Hampstead and Highgate, were made life peers. Labor peeress and former health minister Baroness Serota was appointed Dame of the British Empire. Knighthoods went to Nottingham industrialist and philanthropist Harry Djanogly for his work in philanthropy; Louis Blom-Cooper, former barrister, journalist, and chairman of several government committees; and Ivan Lawrence, Tory MP for Burton. Sir Peter Taylor was named Lord Chief Justice.

Among British Jews who died in 1992 were Nat Franks, leading 1930s middleweight boxer, in January, aged 79; David Deutsch, film producer, in January, aged 65; Mark Hertzberg, for 40 years reader at St. John's Wood Synagogue, in January, aged 81; Georg Schwarzenberger, emeritus professor of international law at London University, in January, aged 83; Philip Goldberg, Federation of Synagogues elder, in February, aged 87; Bernard Krikler, historian and Wiener Library supporter, in February, aged 65; Rev. Max Modell, Bristol Synagogue minister for 24 years, in February, aged 83; Fritzi Gordon, top international bridge player, in March, aged 86; Samuel Magnus, judge and writer on legal topics, in March, aged 81; Sam Kramer, one-time president and chairman of the National Union of Hebrew Teachers, in March, aged 79; Jim Joel, grand old man of racing, in March, aged 97; Miles Elton, founder of the Ranulf Association, in March, aged 73; Jack Graham, leading Maccabi supporter and worker, in April, aged 72; Morrice Adelman, Glasgow Zionist, in April, aged 52; Rixi Marcus, first woman World Bridge Federation grand master, in April, aged 81; Max Catto, author, in April, aged 84; Shmuel Lowensohn, dedicated Zionist and co-editor of *I Came Alone*, in May, aged 69; Abraham Gluck, Lubavitch personality, in May, aged 68; Alan Howard, founder-chairman of Conscience, the interdenominational committee for Soviet Jewry, in June, aged 54; Elie Kedourie, emeritus professor of politics, London School of Economics, and Middle East expert, in July, in Washington, aged 66; David Sala, leading Sephardi communal figure, in July, aged 78; Hans Feld, Zionist worker and founder-member, Association of Jewish Refugees and Leo Baeck Institute, in August, aged 90; Rose Adler, for 35 years prominent in Federation of Hungarian Jews in Great Britain, in August, in her 80s; Lilian Hill, architect of Jewish Welfare Board's work for the old, in August, aged 90; Samuel Prais, Birmingham communal figure, in August, aged 93; David Degalla, for 36 years Jews' Temporary Shelter secretary, in September, aged 80; David Goldstone, Manchester Jewish personality, in September, aged 84; Felix Mitchell, communal worker and Reform Synagogues of Great Britain personality, in October, aged 69; Barry Shenker, communal worker, chairman, British Mapam movement, 1985–90, in October, aged 48; Clifford Barclay, businessman and founder of Oxford's Templeton College for Management Studies, in October, aged 84; Frank Levine, Anglo-Jewish communal worker, in October, aged 74; Fay Stern, street-trading adviser and charitable worker, in November, aged 86; David Bohm, leading physicist, in November, aged 85; Alec Rozansky, founder-member, Stanmore and Canons Park Synagogue, in December, aged 81; Mark Lesnick, 1920s flyweight boxer, in December, aged 85; Prof. Albert Latner, medical practitioner in clinical biochemistry, in December, aged 80; Prof. Arthur Bloom, leading British hemophilia authority, in December, aged 62; Lord Lloyd of Hampstead, academic lawyer, in December, aged 77; and Asher Loftus, communal philanthropist, in December, aged 78.

MIRIAM & LIONEL KOCHAN

France

National Affairs

FOUR SUBJECTS DOMINATED the news in France in 1992. One was the difficult economic situation, marked by the continuing long-term growth of unemployment. The second was the ongoing debate over the admission of foreigners to France. The third was growing disillusionment with President François Mitterrand's Socialist government over its handling of various "affairs," such as the Habash affair (see below); the revelation that blood known to be potentially contaminated with AIDS had been distributed in 1985 through a state-controlled agency; and the uncomfortable results of inquiries into the illegal financing of political parties.

The fourth subject of public concern was the debate over ratification of the Maastricht treaty creating a European Union. The September referendum showed a deepening distrust of the European idea among the French public. Whereas in previous years opinion polls had shown a strong majority in favor of the European project, in the referendum only 51 percent of the voters finally said yes, while the main political parties were divided. Two sets of local elections took place in March. Both produced disturbing results for the Socialist government, and both showed the voters seeking alternatives to the parties of both right and left that had ruled France since 1945. Most analysts linked the distrust of the "classical" parties to the public's growing impatience with the continuing rise in unemployment and the failure to end the economic crisis.

Both right and left took a beating in the regional elections, a one-round proportional ballot. The Socialists won 18.3 percent of the vote, down 11.5 from 1986, while the RPR/UDF alliance (Union pour la France, a coalition of the two main parties of the right) won 33 percent, down 8 percent from 1986. The surprises were the Greens' 14.7 percent and the 13.9 percent for the National Front (FN), which enabled both to take seats in regional councils, where they were in a good position to influence decision making.

The cantonal (*département*) elections produced similar results in the first round but smaller votes in the second round for the Greens and the FN, and thus fewer seats in the district councils. Even though FN leader Jean-Marie Le Pen did not win his anticipated 20 percent in the cantonal balloting, the results of both elections were considered a success for the FN, illustrating its growing roots in the country and its achievement of a permanent place in French political life.

Faced with his government's poor showing in the elections, in May President Mitterrand responded by replacing unpopular Prime Minister Edith Cresson with

Finance Minister Pierre Bérégovoy, who was perceived as being more experienced in economic matters, smoother in personality, and more in touch with the public.

Israel and the Middle East

In comparison with 1991 (the Gulf War and French involvement in the conflict), this year saw a decline in French preoccupation with the Middle East. Part of the public still showed interest in the *intifada*, but the main theater of activity was the peace negotiations in Madrid, where France had, at best, a very limited role to play. The only notable developments were in economics and technology, with the two countries agreeing to undertake new exchange programs in these areas.

THE HABASH AFFAIR

On January 29, the press disclosed that George Habash, leader of the Popular Front for the Liberation of Palestine (PFLP), was a patient in a Red Cross hospital in Paris. Faced with strong public hostility to France's giving shelter and medical help to a well-known terrorist, both the prime minister and the president denied knowing anything about Habash's presence or even having been consulted. On January 30, four high-ranking officials were dismissed from their positions over the matter. Former minister Georgina Dufoix, who was then serving both as an aide to President Mitterrand and as president of the French Red Cross, had to resign from both positions. The others were François Scheer, secretary-general of the Ministry of Foreign Affairs; Bernard Kessedjian, an aide to Minister of Foreign Affairs Roland Dumas; and Christian Vigouroux, chief of staff in the Ministry of Interior.

Although Habash himself was questioned by a judge on the same day, about alleged terrorist activities in France, he was allowed to leave France and to go back to Tunis on February 1.

Widely discussed in the media, the Habash incident was termed by former Socialist prime minister Michel Rocard "a most serious affair." It threw a spotlight not only on the apparent lack of coordination between different government authorities but also on the ambiguous attitude of officials toward terrorist organizations and states. François Mitterrand's statement, on February 4, that "there is no more Habash affair" showed, to say the least, a certain degree of irritation with the persistent attention. A senatorial commission of inquiry heard Minister of Interior Philippe Marchand acknowledge "a general failure of judgment," and former prime minister Edith Cresson described the affair as "the sum total of individual errors." When the commission submitted its final report on June 24, it expressed regret that the "principle of ministerial responsibility" had not been respected; in other words, that only civil servants had had to resign as a consequence of it.

MITTERRAND IN ISRAEL

President François Mitterrand's second official trip to Israel did not arouse as much interest as the first one in 1983. To a certain extent it was viewed as routine and was even described by the press as a "trip of normalization." Although the results of the trip were judged to be generally positive, Mitterrand had to face fierce attacks from the Israeli press, which denounced his support of the PLO and the creation of a Palestinian state. He himself expressed disappointment that Europe in general and France in particular were being kept out of the peace process.

Anti-Semitism and Racism

The statistics of the Ministry of Interior showed a decrease in the overall number of violent anti-Semitic incidents (23, as against 40 in 1991), with the incidents unevenly distributed over the year. Five violent actions were recorded between January and September, but there were eight in September and ten between October and the end of December. There did not seem to be any particular explanation for that pattern, except possibly some linkage to the debate over the role of France in the deportation of the Jews during World War II (see below), or the influence of antiforeigner incidents in Germany, or the debate over the referendum on Europe. None of this could be proven, however. There was also an increase in the number of desecrations of Jewish cemeteries: two in March and April, but six between August 30 and the end of December, including Herrlisheim in Alsace (where 193 graves were damaged) and two cemeteries in Cronenbourg, near Strasbourg. Daubings in one of the cemeteries in Cronenbourg at the end of December indicated a connection with Israel's recent expulsion to Lebanon of 415 Palestinian members of the Hamas movement.

Public anti-Semitic utterances from the National Front were far more elusive than in previous years. Still, Jean-Marie Le Pen, addressing his supporters in La Trinité-sur-Mer on August 23, charged that "those who claim secure and guaranteed borders for Israel [are] also those who want to destroy the borders of France." After the desecration in Herrlisheim, Jean Kahn, the president of the Representative Council of French Jews (Conseil Représentatif des Institutions Juives de France, CRIF), told an interviewer in the daily Le Monde (September 2): "One cannot avoid establishing a connection between this desecration in Alsace and the racist events in Rostock in Germany. The statements made by Mr. Le Pen on August 23 in La Trinité are also an incitement to racial hatred." Le Pen sued Kahn for libel—unsuccessfully—for this statement.

The annual public-opinion poll on intolerance and racism conducted by the Consultative Commission on Human Rights of the Prime Minister's Office, which includes questions on the Jews, showed continuity with previous trends: 19 percent of those questioned expressed antipathy to the Jews (16 percent in 1991, 18 percent in February and October 1990); and 22 percent somewhat or completely agreed that there were too many Jews in France (21 percent in 1991, 24 percent in February and October 1990).

Anti-Semitism was the focus of an international conference organized by UNESCO in Paris, in June, in cooperation with the Simon Wiesenthal Center, on the theme: "Education for Tolerance: The Case of the Rebirth of Anti-Semitism." Léon Poliakov, Alexandre Adler, Jeane Kirkpatrick, and Simon Wiesenthal were among the speakers.

Holocaust-Related Matters

This year was the 50th anniversary of the first convoy that left the French camps of Drancy and Compiègne on March 27, 1942, carrying to Auschwitz 1,112 Jewish men (of whom 22 came back). The anniversary was marked by several commemorative events; it also set off an intense public debate on both the role and the culpability of the Vichy French regime in the persecution of the Jews in France.

Beginning in March, a number of commemorations took place, national and local, in academic and nonacademic frameworks, initiated by the Jewish community or by national and/or municipal authorities.

On March 27, the Contemporary Jewish Documentation Center (Centre de Documentation Juive Contemporaine, CDJC) inaugurated new, expanded quarters, combining its former building with an adjoining one. The new structure houses the CDJC—library, an archive on the destruction of European Jewry, a new photography lab, and increased space for meetings and audiovisual presentations—and the Memorial to the Unknown Jewish Martyr, a monument and area for commemorative gatherings. The CDJC was created clandestinely in Grenoble in 1943, at the initiative of Rabbi Isaac Schneersohn, in order to gather and preserve all documents and archives pertaining to the persecutions and genocide.

Together with the inauguration of its new building, the CDJC opened an exhibition called "*Le Temps des Rafles*" (The Time of the Raids), which was prepared by Serge Klarsfeld under the aegis of CDJC, with the help of the City of Paris. The exhibition was devoted to the fate of the Jews in France from 1940 to 1944 and was the most comprehensive ever organized on the subject. In the same period, *Le Premier Convoi*, a film produced by Pierre-Oscar Lévy, based on interviews with 12 of the 22 survivors of the first convoy, was shown on television.

Several conferences this year were devoted to the subject of the deportation. Among them a colloquium jointly organized by the National Institute for Oriental Languages (INALCO) and the School for Higher Studies in Social Science (EHESS), with the support of the Foundation of French Judaism (Fondation du Judaïsme Français), focused on "The Year 1942." Several experts from different countries took part in the symposium, among them Léon Poliakov (France), Renée Poznanski (Israel), Robert Paxton (U.S.A.), Maxime Steinberg (Belgium), and Michael Marrus (Canada).

An exhibition on the transit camps of Pithiviers and Beaune-la-Rolande in central

France opened in June in the neighboring city of Orléans. (Beaune-la-Rolande was known as one of the camps where Jewish children who had been separated from their parents were detained in particularly awful conditions until being deported to Auschwitz.) Also in Orléans, a permanent documentation center on the camps in the area of the Loiret was opened, at the initiative of individuals with the support of the municipality.

A center for the history of the resistance and the deportation opened in the city of Lyons in November. It was located in the building that served as Gestapo headquarters during the occupation. The center included a library, a film archive, and rooms for meetings and exhibitions. In the same period, the city of Aix-en-Provence in southern France was the scene of 46 cultural events relating to the *camp des Milles* (the "tile factory" camp), where, among many others, artists and intellectuals such as Max Ernst, Hans Bellmer, Otto Meyerhof, and Lion Feuchtwanger were detained.

The annual Buchman Prize for a work on the history of the Holocaust was awarded to historian François Bédarida. This year saw the creation of the Corrin Prize, in memory of businessman and Holocaust survivor Charles Corrin, designed specifically to promote the teaching of the Holocaust in the framework of the French educational system and oriented toward the younger generation. The first Corrin Prize was shared by a group of 16 schoolchildren from Marseilles who made a video about the deportation of 5,000 Jews from that city, and Alain Gintzburger and Juliette Battle, who created a work for the theater based on the letters sent from Drancy by 18-year-old Louise Jacobson before she was deported.

VICHY, THE REPUBLIC, AND THE JEWS

In June, some 200 Jewish and non-Jewish intellectuals, mainly historians, issued an appeal to the president of the republic, calling on him to acknowledge publicly the specific responsibility of the Vichy regime in the persecution of the Jews, and also to proclaim that "the French state is responsible for persecutions and crimes against the Jews in France." The wording of the appeal, putting the responsibility for the crimes on "the French state" in general and not specifically on the Vichy regime, posed a basic problem that was widely debated for several months. What was the place occupied by the Vichy regime in the history of French institutions? Was Vichy, as the authors of the appeal seemed to indicate, to be considered part of France's institutional continuity, a chapter in the ongoing history of the French state? Or was it an illegitimate "parenthesis," a regime that usurped authority and built itself up against the republic and against France, as many immediately claimed? The reaction of the president, who refused to respond to the appeal as requested, was a clear indication that he had chosen the second option.

A new episode in the debate started in connection with the 50th anniversary of the *grande rafle*, the mass roundup and arrest in Paris on July 16 and 17, 1942, of 13,000 Jews, who were herded into Paris's winter cycle-racing arena (Vélodrome d'Hiver, or Vel' d'Hiv'). On July 14, Mitterrand stated that the republic should not be held accountable for the crimes of the Vichy regime, since "Vichy was not the Republic." In response, the Vel' d'Hiv' 1942 Committee, created by the initiators of the appeal to Mitterrand, called again for "an official acknowledgment by the state of the crimes of Vichy." The ceremony at the Vélodrome d'Hiver on July 16, in the presence of Mitterrand and an audience of over 7,000 persons, was marred by loud booing of the president by a number of Jewish activists. Former minister of justice Robert Badinter (president of the Constitutional Council, a judiciary body, and also an active member of the Jewish community), who was one of the speakers, sharply denounced the insult to the president. But he went on to express his personal opinion, stating: "The Republic owes the victims of Vichy the teaching of the truth and the strength of justice."

The polemics started again in the fall when Mitterrand sent a floral tribute to be laid on Marshal Pétain's tomb on the island of Yeu on November 11 (anniversary of the World War I armistice). On November 12, the CRIF expressed "its intense emotion and deep pain" over the incident, adding that "this incomprehensible gesture was a wound to the survivors and the families of the victims." According to CRIF, it was "essential to ask the national representatives sitting in the National Assembly and the Senate to perpetuate, through a solemn declaration, the memory of the infamy that had been committed on the soil of France by the French state." The CRIF text made an implicit allusion to two points: the fact that François Mitterrand had been the first president of the republic to decorate Pétain's tomb regularly (previous presidents had done it only on special occasions), and the fact that a Socialist member of the National Assembly, Jean Le Garrec, had proposed a law making July 16 a national day of commemoration for the deportation, but his text was not put on the agenda of the Assembly. On November 13, Mitterrand conceded to his critics somewhat, announcing that he would look for ways of "managing differently" the contradiction between "the glory of Verdun" and "the shame of 1942."

THE TOUVIER CASE

In January, Albert Cardinal Decourtray, bishop of Lyons, received the report he had commissioned on the involvement of the Church in hiding Paul Touvier, the former head of intelligence of the *Milice*, the pro-Nazi militia in the Lyons area during World War II. The report, which was prepared by a commission of seven historians under the direction of Prof. René Rémond, concluded that certain members of the Catholic hierarchy had indeed conspired to protect Touvier and enabled him to escape detection during all the years from 1945 to 1989. (See AJYB 1993, pp. 252–53, and AJYB 1991, pp. 264–65.)

On January 26, the *chambre d'accusation* (a three-judge grand jury) of Paris reopened its investigation into the charges against Touvier for having committed crimes against humanity, with the historians' report now part of the file of evidence.

On April 13, the court dismissed the charges and Touvier was released. The tortured reasoning of the judges was considered as worrisome as the decision itself. The judges contended that the Vichy regime could not be considered among those regimes defined as guilty of crimes against humanity. Vichy had not, for example, been "seeking ideological hegemony," one of the characteristics of regimes in that category, and Jews had not been declared enemies of the state. President Mitterrand declared, on April 14, that he was "surprised, to say the least," by the decision. Cardinal Decourtray himself expressed his wish to see Touvier brought to trial, and a group of historians launched a petition drive. As a consequence of the lower-court decision, Pierre Truche, the attorney general for the Paris area (who had been the public prosecutor in Lyons during the Klaus Barbie trial), immediately turned to the *cour de Cassation*, France's supreme court, asking it to overturn the verdict. On April 24, the president of the supreme court, Pierre Drai, called for calm and announced that the court would make its decision within six to eight months, "when passions and emotions are appeased."

On November 27, the court partially reversed the lower court's ruling. It said that Touvier could stand trial for his role in the execution of seven Jewish hostages in Rillieux-la-Pape in 1944, but it let stand the lower court's version of the nature of the Vichy regime. Experts in legal matters claimed that it would now be virtually impossible to bring to justice other Vichy officials, specifically, René Bousquet and Maurice Papon, for crimes against humanity. Since April both Bousquet and Papon had been under new investigation for crimes against humanity for carrying out the deportation of 1,645 Jews from the Bordeaux area between July 18, 1942, and May 13, 1944.

THE "JEWISH FILE"

According to a report by historian René Rémond, the list of 140,000 Jews that had been found in 1991 in the archives of the Ministry of Veterans Affairs was not, as had been publicly claimed by Serge Klarsfeld, the census of Jews ordered by the Germans and carried out by Vichy officials in 1940. Klarsfeld did not accept the report's conclusion.

JEWISH COMMUNITY

Demography

There was no major change in the estimated Jewish population of France, which remained, according to most sources, 550,000–600,000. No surveys were conducted that would have provided an updated and more precise idea of the sociological and demographic evolution of the Jewish population.

Communal Affairs

The vitality of the French Jewish community could be seen in a number of developments this year. One was the opening of a new Conservative congregation in Paris (the Adath Shalom Massorati Congregation), initiated by Rabbi Rivon Krygier to meet the needs of Jews seeking new ways of being Jewish other than through ultra-Orthodoxy, the French Consistory's mainstream Orthodoxy, or the Reform movement. Additional signs of this vitality were the public lighting of a Hanukkah menorah in one of Paris's main city parks, beneath the Eiffel Tower, and the inauguration of a new synagogue and community center in Strasbourg, featuring stained-glass windows by the artist Théo Tobiasse.

There was also the successful Judéoscope, held November 7–11, in Paris, organized by Henri Hajdenberg. During the five-day festival, some 20,000 people took part in discussions, shows, debates, plays, movies, and other activities. The subjects of the forums and debates reveal the current preoccupations of French Jews, among them: "Identities," "What future for secular Judaism?" "The children of intermarriage," "The rise of the far right," and "Teaching the history of the Jewish Diaspora."

The France-Israel Building opened in November in a fancy area of the Champs-Elysées. According to its president, former government minister Lionel Stoleru, the building would be a showcase for Israel in France, as well as a place for Israeli business executives visiting Paris to learn about France. In its 3,000-square-meter space it offered a reading room with Israeli newspapers, a travel agency, a display and sale area for Israeli products, a room for public meetings, several restaurants, a business center to foster French-Israeli business ties, and other facilities.

Even as Jewish cultural and religious activities were flourishing, the community was feeling the effects of the economic recession. Community leaders in charge of Jewish social welfare claimed that the community had entered a new era. The postwar period had been one of reconstruction; that was followed by a period of integration of transplanted communities (e.g., the North Africans); now the Jewish community was faced with the classic social problems linked to poverty. The priorities of social action in 1992 were thus helping the elderly and problematic youngsters, providing job training for the unemployed, and finding housing for those who needed it. The Fonds Social Juif Unifié (FSJU), the United Jewish Philanthropic Fund, and its affiliated organizations proposed a 1992 budget of 250 million francs ($50 million), of which Fr 25 million were to be supplied by the Jewish community and the rest by the state, through subventions to specialized Jewish agencies.

SPANISH EXPULSION ANNIVERSARY

The 500th anniversary of the expulsion of Spanish Jews attracted broad attention in the Jewish press and was marked by the publication of several books. However, it did not inspire many public events or commemorations in France. The primary reason for this was lack of consensus about the significance of the date and what character the anniversary should take. There was some fear that the commemoration would become a festival and cause people to forget the essentially traumatic nature of the historic event.

Events abroad, such as the visit of King Juan Carlos of Spain to the synagogue of Madrid, and the historical commemoration organized by "By My Spirit" in Toledo (which was attended by Chief Rabbi of France Joseph Sitruk), were followed closely by French Jews. The only comparable event in France was an academic symposium at the Sorbonne, organized by the Fonds Social Juif Unifié, on "The Expulsion of the Jews of Spain and Its Consequences."

A Crisis in the Jewish Community?

The internal debate that had begun to emerge in recent years took on sharper outlines in 1992. Essentially, it was between those favoring greater insularity and religious Orthodoxy, and those—among them Jean Kahn—who argued for an open and pluralistic Jewish community in France.

In the May issue of the Jewish monthly L'Arche, the philosopher Shmuel Trigano gave his own analysis of the situation: "For a number of years now, French Jewry has been a center of missionary activity for ideologies coming from abroad (more often from the United States than from Israel) and inspired by the Hassidic or the haredi [ultra-Orthodox] movements. These aim to take over the Jews without any regard for communal consensus and the institutions of the Jewish community, ignoring its history and values as well as the nature and specific logic of the French framework in which they carry out their activities."

Trigano added that he saw the birth of "a sectarian phenomenon" in French Judaism, as a result of which "the concept of community itself was suffering a setback." He noted the unique character of French Jewry, "heir to the old Israelite consistory, revised and corrected by Vichy and the Shoah," a community that "has integrated the East European traditions" but one that has also "become the depository of the entire North African tradition," and a community that has, since 1970, "been home to a movement of Jewish renewal and rediscovery." Trigano concluded that there was a crisis in the Jewish community and blamed "a lack of democracy" as one of the main causes.

Events this year in both the Central and Paris Consistories—the official religious arms of French Jewry—indirectly illustrated the cause of Trigano's unease. In elections for the presidency of the Central Consistory, on June 21, Jean-Pierre Bansard defeated incumbent Jean-Paul Elkann, 111 to 69. (Elections to the Central Consistory are conducted through a college of 200 electors, among them the chief rabbi of France, the chief rabbis of the regions, representatives of the Consistory itself, and delegates of the affiliated congregations.) The new president was born in Oran (Algeria) in 1940; he had been vice-president of the Pasteur-Weizmann Honorary Committee; the founder in 1986 of the King David Club, a group open only to major donors to the United Jewish Appeal; and in 1991 was elected president of the Consistory of the Champagne-Ardennes region.

Bansard used as his campaign slogan: "The Central Consistory has lost its two strongest suits: it is no longer either efficient or representative." Although Bansard sounded an apparently neutral theme, his election, coming after that of Benny Cohen in 1990 as president of the Paris Consistory, was interpreted as a victory for the more Orthodox elements in the Consistory and those who want a more activist Consistory that will branch out from the purely religious sphere and engage in political representation of the community, alongside, or even instead of, CRIF.

The Paris Consistory faced a crisis at the end of the year related to the issue of representation. An extraordinary general assembly of that body was convened in order to ratify a modification to the bylaws that had been adopted by a tiny majority of the administrative council (14 votes to 12). According to the proposed new rule, only those who were sponsored by three community presidents could be candidates in the consistory elections that were to take place in 1993. Given that the 70 presidents of communities are appointed by the president of the Paris Consistory and the Paris chief rabbi, opponents of the proposal objected that the new rule would make it impossible for anybody who disagreed with the present presidents not only to be elected but even to be a candidate. "If they don't want somebody to be a candidate, it is very easy for them to put pressure on the presidents so that they refuse to give their support," commented Moïse Cohen, an opponent of Benny Cohen, in an interview in the weekly *Tribune Juive* (December 17). The general assembly was marked by serious disturbances. The modification to the bylaws was finally adopted, but in a vote that took place in dubious circumstances. Opponents decided to lodge an appeal in civil court to have the results of the vote invalidated.

Community Relations

Racism remained a matter of concern. In November the president of CRIF, Jean Kahn, expressed his sympathy and total solidarity with the Muslim community in France, following the desecration of graves of North African soldiers killed while serving in the French military. In his Rosh Hashanah message, Kahn had expressed deep concern over the rise of racism and intolerance in France and on the European continent in general, particularly in Germany.

Xenophobia in Germany and the decision of the German authorities to send Romanian Gypsies who had found refuge in Germany back to Romania led a number of young French Jews to demonstrate in October in the German city of Rostock, which had been the scene of violent anti-immigrant demonstrations a few weeks before. The French demonstration led to incidents with the German police, and three French demonstrators were arrested. During the General Assembly of CRIF, which took place on November 29, Jean Kahn stated that he had intervened with authorities for the youngsters' release; at the same time, he said, he would have preferred it if the demonstration in Rostock had been conducted in dignity—which had not been the case on the part of the Jewish demonstrators, he felt. He also firmly denounced the violent anti-German incidents that had been initiated in Paris against the buildings of the Goethe-Institut and the French-German Chamber of Commerce.

The situation in former Yugoslavia was also a matter of deep concern, although not touching the French Jewish community directly. In numerous speeches and articles, writer and philosopher Alain Finkielkraut denounced Serbian propaganda's exploitation of what he called "the alleged anti-Semitism of the Croatians," which depicted all modern Croatians as Oustachis (the pro-Nazi Croatian militia) and created a situation in which most Europeans, among them Jews, were reluctant to intervene against the Serbs.

Although Finkielkraut failed to convince most Jews—who were still sensitive to the memories of World War II and the pro-Nazi involvement of a vast number of Croatians—CRIF president Kahn showed no hesitation, particularly after the Serbs started their "ethnic cleansing," in acting on both the humanitarian and the political levels. He flew several times to former Yugoslavia, taking part in actions to save local Jews as well as in general humanitarian initiatives, together with foreign and local representatives of various religious groups. In August, when the press released information about the Serb-built concentration camps for civilian Muslims and Croatians, Kahn said, "The basic principles of human rights are being denied" and called for intervention. He repeated his dismay over the situation in his Rosh Hashanah message.

A declaration on Europe that was released early in September, which Kahn signed together with Bishop Joseph Duval (president of the French Episcopal Conference) and Pastor Jacques Stewart (president of the French Protestant Federation), included the following statement: "The war that is bathing former Yugoslavia in blood, the atrocities that are taking place there, the 'ethnic cleansing' that is being carried out, the camps that have sometimes been called concentration camps, which are being built, all that is unbearable to us." After the CRIF General Assembly on November 29, Kahn issued a new statement on Yugoslavia, in the name of the French Jewish community, reiterating the facts and calling on France "to go beyond purely humanitarian action" and "to take the initiative of forming an international coalition that would intervene in the name of the right of intervention which France has acknowledged and adopted."

Jean Kahn expressed himself both personally and in his official capacity in favor of the ratification of the Maastricht treaty. Three weeks before the referendum, CRIF issued a statement that, while emphasizing the total freedom of choice of Jewish voters, also pointed out that "moving from the Economic European Community to an economic, monetary and political union of a European whole" would make it possible for Europe "to curb any kind of hegemony in Europe, to prevent conflicts, and to assert itself in the world of the 21st century."

Culture

Three Jewish communities—in Créteil (a suburb of Paris), Toulouse, and Marseilles—organized "Jewish culture weeks" at different times of the year, featuring lectures, presentations of new books, movies, musical shows, and theatrical works on various aspects of Jewish culture. The events took place either in community centers or in non-Jewish halls.

Centre Rachi, the Jewish cultural center for academics and students in Paris, had an exhibition on "Art and Judaica from Israel." Artist Théo Tobiasse had an important retrospective in the small resort city of Cagnes sur Mer, in southern France, with 155 works exhibited. The Amédée Maratier Prize of the Kikoïne Foundation was awarded to painter Abraham Haddad.

The 32nd colloquium of French-speaking Jewish intellectuals, in December 1991, had as its subject "Morals and Politics in Danger?" The group's 33rd colloquium, in 1992, was on the question of "Disoriented Time," which was discussed by, among others, Henri Atlan, André Kaspi, and André Fontaine (former editor of the daily *Le Monde*). A symposium sponsored by the FSJU, the United Jewish Philanthropic Fund, took place in the Senate building in Paris. It dealt with the problem of "The Jews in Europe Today and Tomorrow," with the participation of Rita Thalmann, Alexandre Adler, Pierre Lellouche, and Béatrice Philippe.

The 1992 WIZO Book Award for French writers was given to Elisabeth Gille, author of *Le Mirador*, a biography of her mother, the writer Irène Nemirovski, a Russian refugee in France and a member of the émigré intelligentsia, who discovered her Jewishness through persecution and lost her life in the Holocaust. B'nai B'rith's Emil Domberger Book Award was given to Pierre Birnbaum for *Les Fous de la République*, a history of upper-level Jewish civil servants at the end of the 19th and beginning of the 20th centuries.

At the beginning of December, the Medem Library, with over 20,000 volumes the most important collection of Yiddish literature in Europe, organized two open-house events that attracted many visitors. The library had been created in 1929 with 300 volumes brought to Paris by Jewish immigrants from Poland. By 1940, it had gathered some 5,000 books, which were hidden and saved throughout the war with the help of a non-Jewish sympathizer. In 1982 it became a cultural center and was named for Vladimir Medem, a prominent leader of the Bund who died in the United States in 1923. The Medem Library, which also serves as a center for the teaching of Yiddish language, is supported by the French Arbeter Ring.

The Jewish press in France continued to experience difficulties. *Combat pour la Diaspora*, a journal created in 1981 by a group of young Jewish intellectuals interested in Jewish communities in the Diaspora, was forced to discontinue when the subvention it was getting from the Ministry of Culture was not renewed. The weekly *Tribune Juive* went through a number of changes. After 27 years, its director, Rabbi Jacquot Grunewald, decided to retire (although he continued as a columnist), and the weekly, which had serious financial problems, was taken over by a new team of professionals whose declared purpose was "to open a forum for dialogue that would bring together the most extreme opinions."

Publications

In connection with the anniversary of the expulsion of Spanish Jews, several new books were published relating to the Sephardi world. *Les Juifs d'Espagne 1492–1992: Histoire d'une Diaspora* (The Jews of Spain, 1492–1992: History of a Diaspora) is a collective work of some 700 pages, prepared by a team of experts under the editorship of Henry Mechoulan, on the various communities that were born as a consequence of the expulsion; *Séfarades d'hier et d'aujourd'hui* (Sephardim of Yesterday and Today) by Haim Vidal Sephiha and Richard Hayoun contains the biographies of 70 well-known Sephardi Jews; *Marranes* (Marranos) is an album of photographs taken by Frédéric Brenner of the last crypto Jews remaining in the 1980s in the Belmonte region of northeast Portugal, with a text by Yosef Haim Yerushalmi; *Une vie judéo-espagnole à l'Est: Gabriel Arié*, by Esther Benbassa with the collaboration of Aron Rodrigue, examines, through the diary and correspondence of Gabriel Arié (1863–1939), a Turkish businessman, communal leader, teacher, and historian, the influence of liberalism on the emancipation of an eastern community; and the novel *La Sultane* by Catherine Clément offers a romantic portrait of the exiled Dona Gracia Mendès.

New works on the history of the Jews in France included *Les fous de la République: Histoire politique des juifs d'Etat, de Gambetta à Pétain*, Pierre Birnbaum's study of Jewish families whose members served enthusiastically as high-level civil servants in the late 19th century and the first half of the 20th century; and Perrine Simon-Nahum's *La Cité investie. La Science du Judaïsme française et la République* ("Integrating into Society," a study of the French *Wissenschaft des Judentums* movement). Institutional history is represented by *Histoire du Rabbinat français (XVIè–XXè siècle)* (A History of the French Rabbinate, 16th–20th Centuries) by Roger Berg, with a preface by former chief rabbi Jacob Kaplan (the author had been secretary-general of the Central Consistory for 14 years). A biography of Bernard Lazare, one of the first to get involved in the defense of Alfred Dreyfus in 1894, was published by Jean-Denis Bredin. The relationship between the French people and the Zionist idea is the subject of Catherine Nicault's *La France et le sionisme 1897–1948: Une rencontre manquée?* (France and Zionism: A Missed Encounter?). Another approach to the subject of Zionism in France, seen from a purely contemporary Jewish point of view, is provided by Roger Ascot, journalist and novelist, in his caustic essay *Le sionisme trahi, ou les Israéliens du dimanche* (Betrayed Zionism, or the Sunday Israelis), published in 1991.

New books about different Jewish communities or specific periods in history included Paul Sebag's history of the Jews in Tunisia, *Histoire des Juifs de Tunisie, des origines à nos jours*; Daniel Tollet's *Histoire des Juifs en Pologne du XVIè siècle à nos jours* (History of the Jews in Poland from the 16th Century to Our Times);

Enzo Traverso's *Les Juifs et l'Allemagne: de la "symbiose judéo-allemande" à la mémoire d'Auschwitz* (The Jews and Germany: From "Judeo-German Symbiosis" to the Memory of Auschwitz); Jacques Derogy and Hesi Carmel's *Bonaparte en Terre Sainte* (Bonaparte in the Holy Land); and André Chouraqui's summary of the relations between the Vatican and the State of Israel, *La Reconnaissance* (The Recognition).

Among many new works on the period of World War II were Claude Singer's *L'Université et les Juifs: Les silences de la mémoire* (The University and the Jews: The Silence of Memory), on institutional and individual attitudes toward the Jews during the occupation; Annette Wieviorka's *Déportation et Génocide: Entre la mémoire et l'oubli* (Deportation and Genocide: Between Remembrance and Forgetfulness), an analysis of the different psychological outcomes for deported partisans and Jewish survivors of concentration camps; Adam Rayski's *Le Choix des Juifs sous Vichy* (Jewish Choice Under Vichy), an attempt to answer the question: how were three-quarters of the Jews in France able to escape deportation? Sabine Zlatin, who was in charge of the house in Izieu from which the Jewish children in her care were deported by order of Klaus Barbie, published her story in *Mémoires de la dame d'Izieu*, with a preface by François Mitterrand. The decision of the Paris court clearing Paul Touvier of the charge of committing crimes against humanity is analyzed and sharply challenged by Théo Klein, a lawyer and former president of CRIF, in *Oublier Vichy? A propos de l'arrêt Touvier* (Forget Vichy? On the Touvier Decision). The Vichy period is the subject of a collection of essays edited by Jean-Pierre Azéma and François Bédarida, *Vichy et les Français*. The review *Pardès* devoted its issue number 16 to the Jews in France during World War II, under the editorship of André Kaspi, Annie Kriegel, and Annette Wieviorka.

New publications about anti-Semitism included *Faux et usage d'un faux: Introduction et études sur les Protocoles des Sages de Sion* (Forgery and the Use of Forgery: Introduction and Studies of the Protocols of the Elders of Zion), edited by Pierre-André Taguieff; and *L'Antisémitisme en France pendant les années trente* (Anti-Semitism in France in the Thirties) by Ralph Schorr. *La Beauté de Cham* (The Beauty of Ham) by Maurice Dorès explores the relations between Jews and blacks throughout history, with one chapter devoted to the relationship of blacks to the State of Israel.

A general historical and sociological overview of the Jewish people is provided in the first two volumes of *La Société juive à travers l'histoire* (Jewish Society Throughout History), edited by Shmuel Trigano. The same author published *Philosophie de la Loi: l'origine de la politique dans la Tora* (Philosophy of the Law: The Origin of Politics in the Torah). In *L'Histoire promise*, Catherine Chalier refutes the notion of the passivity of the Jewish people through the ages. The linguistic, legal, and historical aspects of the "lex talionis" are explored by Raphaël Drai ir *Le Mythe de la loi du talion*.

Marc-Alain Ouaknin pursues his historical-philosophical reflections in *Tsim tsum*, an introduction to Hebrew meditation in the tradition of Rabbi Nahman o

Bratslav, and in *Méditations érotiques*, an essay on Emmanuel Levinas and his approach to the Talmud.

The series of short paperbacks on different subjects initiated by the publisher Albin Michel issued these new titles: *Les Caraïtes* by Emanuela Trevisan-Semi; *Les Juifs de Paris à la Belle Epoque* by Béatrice Philippe; *Martin Buber* by Pamela Vermes; *Rachi* by Simon Schwarzfuchs; and *L'Hébreu, 3,000 ans d'histoire* by Mireille Hadas-Lebel.

In addition to a collection edited by Jacques Eladan, *Poètes juifs de langue française* (French-speaking Jewish Poets), poetry was represented by two books of Claude Vigée: *Dans le silence de l'Aleph* (In the Silence of Aleph), poems influenced by Rabbi Nahman of Bratslav, and *La Terre et le Souffle* (The Land and the Breath). A third book by Vigée, *Héritage de feu* (Heritage of Fire), contains collected essays, poems, interviews, and talks with the Yiddish author Abraham Sutzkever.

New works of fiction included *Rendez-vous au métro Saint-Paul* (Rendez-vous in the St. Paul Station) by Cyrille Fleischmann, a collection of short stories about the small world of Parisian Jews; *L'Insomniaque du Danube* (Insomniac of the Danube) by Edgar Reichmann, an exploration of the author's triple identity as a Romanian, a Jew, and a Frenchman; *Deborah et les anges dissipés* (Deborah and the Dissolute Angels) by Paula Jacques, a novel that takes place in the old Jewish area in Cairo in 1948, recipient of the Prix Fémina; *Dans la plus stricte intimité* (In the Closest Intimacy) by Myriam Anissimov, an autobiographical work by an author born in 1943 in a refugee camp; and *Le Testament de Liou-Liao-Lian* by Léon Leneman, a translation into French of a Yiddish memoir of the 1941–1947 period in the Soviet Union.

Personalia

The following French Jews were made knights in the Order of the Legion of Honor: Aaron Lublin, a former resistance fighter; Joseph Sitruk, chief rabbi of France; Claude Riveline, teacher in the Ecole Polytechnique and a member of the planning committee of the annual colloquiums of French-speaking Jewish intellectuals; Rita Thalmann, historian; Nathan Khaiat, director-general of Oeuvre de Secours à l'Enfance, a leading Jewish child-welfare institution; Jacques Marburger, board member of the Association of Veterans of the Jewish Resistance; and Ernest Gluck, president of the Nantes Jewish community. The following were made officers in the Order of the Legion of Honor: Pierre Kauffmann, former secretary-general of CRIF; Isabelle Vichniac, journalist, *Le Monde* correspondent at the international organizations in Geneva; Albert Memmi, sociologist and author; and Roger Berg, former secretary-general of the Central Consistory.

The following were elected to office in the Jewish community: Pierre Drai, first president of the Paris court of appeal, as president of the French Friends of the Hebrew University of Jerusalem; Manek Weintraub, as president of the French section of the World Jewish Congress; Jean Kahn (by a huge majority and with no opposition) to a second term as president of CRIF; Pierre Aidenbaum, a son of one of the founders of LICRA (the International League Against Racism and Anti-Semitism), as president of LICRA; and Simon Pinto as president of UEJF (the Union of French Jewish Students). Chief Rabbi Michel Guggenheim (son of the late Chief Rabbi René Guggenheim), a member of the Paris Beth Din and a teacher of Hebraic law and Talmud, was appointed director of the rabbinical seminary in Paris.

Among prominent Jews who died in 1992 were Charles Corrin, Holocaust survivor and creator of the Corrin Prize for a pedagogical work on the Holocaust; Rachel Gordin, founder of one of the best-known Jewish kindergartens in Paris, combining religious teaching with Montessori methods; Aby Wieviorka, an expert in Yiddish studies, author of numerous translations from Yiddish into French, who helped to revive the Yiddish Medem Library; Raymond Lindon, attorney and a high magistrate, member of the central committee of Alliance Israélite Universelle and a former leader of the Jewish National Fund, aged 81; Edouard Roditi, born in Paris to American parents of Turkish origin, art critic, essayist, and poet, aged 81; Emmanuel Eydoux (Roger Eisinger), a teacher at ORT and a poet who won the Grand Prize for literature of Provence in 1977; Abraham Moles, emeritus professor of communications at the University of Strasbourg and a former member of the planning committee of the colloquiums of French-speaking Jewish intellectuals, aged 72; and Rabbi Saul Naouri, chief rabbi of Nice between 1958 and 1965. Rabbi Abraham Deutsch, born in Mulhouse, died at the age of 90 in Jerusalem, where he had settled in 1970. He served as chief rabbi of Strasbourg from 1945 to 1970, where he founded the Akiba Day School and the *Bulletin de nos Communautés*, which later became the weekly *Tribune Juive*.

NELLY HANSSON

The Netherlands

National Affairs

THE YEAR 1992 BROUGHT no major upheavals, either political or economic, to the coalition government of Christian Democrats (CDA) and Labor (PvdA) headed by Premier Rudolf Lubbers. In the country as a whole, domestic problems and several disasters occupied public attention.

Facing a serious budget deficit, in part brought on by a reduction in exports, in part by overspending for social welfare, in September the government announced major cuts in spending. The government's economizing policies resulted in a number of strikes for higher wages, among them one by public transport workers, and cost the Labor party some 10,000 members.

The European Community's summit conference, held in December 1991 in Maastricht, at the southeasternmost tip of Dutch territory, aroused little interest in Holland itself, and the agreement evoked little discussion among the Dutch. The treaty of European union was approved almost without debate by the vast majority of the members of the Second Chamber of Parliament 11 months later, in November of this year.

The most serious domestic problem, one that almost caused a government crisis, was that of the large number of persons—some 900,000 out of a population of 15 million—receiving disability payments of 70 percent of their last earned wages up to the age of 65, when they become eligible for old-age pensions. Proposals put forward by the CDA and supported by the Liberals (VVD), that all those under 50 years of age receiving disability payments should be medically reexamined after some years, were vigorously opposed by Labor and the Federation of Trade Unions. In the end it was decided that all existing payments would be maintained, but that new cases would receive lower payments. A parliamentary commission of inquiry was appointed to examine why the number of disability cases was so high.

Another controversial subject of long standing, euthanasia, was resolved, at least in principle, this year. It was decided by a majority of the Second Chamber of Parliament that euthanasia would remain a punishable offense according to the Penal Law, but doctors who performed it at the explicit will of a person who was incurably ill would not be prosecuted if they practiced the greatest possible caution, consulted colleagues, and after carrying it out immediately reported it to the Regional Health Inspector.

Other issues that evoked public debate were health care, the environment, and crime, and the proposed introduction of individual identification documents, among other reasons to help identify illegal immigrants. This latter met with such vehement objection by the civil-liberties-conscious Dutch that it had to be dropped.

The number of persons applying for political asylum upon arrival in Holland in 1992 was about 20,000, against some 23,000 in 1991. Among them were a large number from Somalia. To the 20,000 could be added 14,000 inhabitants of former Yugoslavia who came at the invitation of the Dutch government or of relatives or friends and who were supposed to return to their country of origin when peace was achieved. All or most of the political refugees had to be accommodated in special absorption centers until a definite decision on their application was made, which might take as much as two years, as those rejected had the right to appeal.

Over 600 Jews from the former Soviet Union had come to Holland directly from Russia in the past few years and applied for political asylum. At the end of this year the Dutch Ministry of Justice decided that all those who had arrived in the country before June 1 would be granted political asylum, the first time since 1945 that such a large group was granted political asylum collectively. While awaiting a decision on their petition for asylum, the Russian Jews usually stayed in absorption centers around the country and were often visited by the Jewish Social Welfare Foundation and the IPOR, the Inter-Provincial Chief Rabbinate of the Ashkenazi community. Quite different treatment was accorded those Russians—not all of them Jewish or halakhically Jewish—who came to Holland from Israel, beginning in autumn 1991, claiming they had been discriminated against there. They were refused asylum, and a first group of 43 was forcibly returned to Israel in February 1992. Others, however, managed to go into hiding in Holland.

DISASTERS

The Netherlands was hit this year by three major disasters that claimed human lives. The first and largest, which attracted worldwide attention, was the crash of an El Al Boeing 747 cargo aircraft over the Bijlmer district of Amsterdam on Sunday evening, October 4. When the plane hit the juncture of two ten-story apartment buildings, some 80 apartments were demolished and 160 were made uninhabitable. The number of dead was smaller than first reported: 43 in all, including eighteen children, three El Al crew members and one female passenger, the bride of an El Al employee; the number of seriously wounded, mainly burn victims, was four. Practically all the victims were *allochthones*, Third World immigrants, who were a majority of the 90,000 largely transient residents of this part of the Bijlmer district, a modern neighborhood constructed during the past 25 years at the southeastern tip of Amsterdam. Even before this disaster, the Amsterdam municipality had decided to demolish two large apartment buildings in the area that were no longer habitable because of vandalism and neglect.

The fire brigade, ambulances, and police came immediately to the scene of the crash, as did social workers, to assist those seeking missing relatives and to provide temporary shelter and food. Next morning the site of the disaster was visited by Queen Beatrix and her eldest son, as well as Premier Lubbers and Mayor Ed van

Thijn. The Israeli ambassador, Michael Bawly, had come to the site within two hours of the disaster.

On the following Sunday an impressive memorial ceremony was held. At their request, representatives of all the ethnic communities that had been affected by the disaster took part in their own manner, with speakers, music, and dances reflecting Holland's multiracial, multiethnic society. Among those present were Prime Minister Lubbers, Princess (former Queen) Juliana, nearly all the Dutch cabinet ministers, the Israel minister of transport, Yisrael Kesar, and other dignitaries. A Muslim imam recited selections from the Koran; Rabbi L.B. van de Kamp recited the *Yizkor* prayer, and Cantor Hans Bloemendal chanted Psalm 23 in Hebrew. About 13,000 persons attended. Earlier that day the site where the plane crashed was turned into a sea of flowers.

Generous help for the victims, in kind and in money, was made available almost immediately, the Amsterdam municipality, for one, providing alternative housing and living expenses. Private firms and individuals donated large amounts of clothing and furniture. El Al donated a total of Fl. 750,000 (over $400,000) to 525 persons claiming to be victims, separate and apart from its possible legal responsibility, and later also distributed toys and sweets to the children in the apartments involved. El Al and Boeing jointly offered, through an established Dutch law firm, to pay damages to all victims or their surviving relatives, in accordance with Dutch law. Other Amsterdam law firms, with the help of three American firms specializing in aircraft-disaster claims, warned their clients not to accept this offer, because under American law they would receive much higher compensation. The offer of El Al and Boeing for a settlement was therefore rejected by most victims.

The root cause of the disaster, for which a commission of inquiry was set up, had not yet been determined by the end of the year. The voice cockpit recorder was never found, though the police offered a reward for its return.

Another aircraft disaster claiming many victims occurred on December 21, when a Dutch Martin Air charter plane with 327 passengers planning to spend Christmas vacation in Portugal crashed at the southern Portuguese airfield of Faro, probably owing to sudden squalls. Of the 327 passengers, practically all of them Dutch nationals, 55 were killed and 90 seriously wounded; two stewardesses among the 13 crew members were killed.

The third disaster was a serious railway accident south of Schiphol, in the early morning of November 30; five persons were killed and 33 wounded.

Israel and the Middle East

Foreign Minister Hans van den Broek visited the Middle East, including Israel, in January, at the request of the European Community (EC), to explore what that body could contribute to the peace process in the Middle East. In Israel he met with Prime Minister Yitzhak Shamir and Foreign Minister David Levy, whom he urged to stop building settlements in the occupied areas, and in eastern Jerusalem with a

Palestinian delegation headed by Faisal Husseini, whom he urged to make efforts to end the *intifada*. Van den Broek visited Israel again early in September to make the acquaintance of the new prime minister, Yitzhak Rabin, and the new foreign minister, Shimon Peres.

Israel and the Netherlands signed an agricultural research agreement in November, for exchanges of experts in the fields of greenhouse horticulture, irrigation, water resources, and vegetable diseases.

Despite the policy barring meetings with official PLO representatives, Palestinians Hanan Ashrawi and Nabil Shaath, the latter a high-ranking PLO official, were received by Van den Broek in The Hague on May 25. They urged Holland and the EC to pressure Israel to withdraw from the occupied areas and to expedite the peace process.

The Second International Water Tribunal, held in Amsterdam February 17–21, accused 11 countries, including Israel, of improper use of water. Israel was condemned because it had refused to connect some Arab settlements in the Galilee—which it claimed were built illegally—to the national water system and because of its water-use policies in the occupied areas.

A number of anti-Israel demonstrations took place during the year. On March 27, some 300 Muslim men, women, and children associated with the Vathek mosque in The Hague, following a call by Ayatollah Khomeini to attack Israelis everywhere, held a demonstration in front of the Israeli embassy in The Hague, shouting "Death to Israel" and similar slogans. The police kept them at a distance but did not interfere or make any arrests. Afterward the UMMON (Union of Moroccan Muslims in the Netherlands) and the WIM (Union of Muslims from Suriname) condemned the demonstration.

On December 23, following the expulsion of 415 Hamas members from Israel, a number of Palestinians and members of the Green Left party and Pax Christi demonstrated in front of the Israeli embassy. On December 30, ten Palestinians started a three-day hunger strike at the PLO office in The Hague, protesting the expulsion and demanding that the Netherlands break off trade relations with Israel and recall its ambassador from Tel Aviv.

Women in Black, a small, largely Jewish group, continued to hold monthly one-hour demonstrations against Israel's occupation of the West Bank and Gaza. These took place every second Friday of the month, in the center of Amsterdam. On June 5, the group demonstrated in front of the Israeli embassy in The Hague.

A Palestinian Trade Center opened July 1 in Rotterdam, financed for the first two years entirely, and then for another four years partly, by the Netherlands Ministry for Development Aid to Third World Countries. The center would promote exports from the occupied areas to Holland and through it to other European countries, mainly of citrus, vegetables and fruit, textiles, and sport shoes. Two Palestinians, one from the West Bank and one from Gaza, who headed this office, were trained for this task for six months in Holland. In April a counterpart office, the Palestinian Trade Promotion Organization, was established in the occupied areas. The Ministry for Development Aid also gave subsidies to a variety of organizations in the occupied areas, mainly in the Gaza Strip, among them the Palestinian Red Crescent and a group providing free legal assistance to parents of children arrested by the Israelis. The same ministry supported a variety of pro-Palestinian activities in the Netherlands. One was a symposium on the Palestinian problem at the University of Amsterdam, which for over ten years had had a relationship with the University of Bir Zeit. One of the main speakers was Prof. Edward Said of Columbia University in New York. The ministry also subsidized publication by the Netherlands Palestine Committee of a collection of stories by Palestinian women about their experiences during the Israeli occupation. The Netherlands Palestine Committee continued to publish its quarterly *Soemoed* (Steadfastness), which highlighted the alleged violations of human rights by Israel in the occupied areas.

Controversy arose over a joint project of the Dutch pro-Israel Christians for Israel Foundation and the Jerusalem Foundation in Israel—to establish a "Holland Village" in southern Jerusalem, opposite Bet Safafa, to provide temporary housing for Ethiopian Jewish immigrants—when it was learned in Holland that part of the site was in territory occupied by Israel in 1967. A widespread campaign in the Dutch news media against the project led the Netherlands government and the Netherlands Council of Churches to distance themselves from it, and the goal of raising ten million guilders was not achieved.

The Knesset election in Israel in June was featured prominently in the Dutch news media, largely because of the perception that a change of government would increase the chances for peace. The expulsion of some 415 Hamas members to Lebanon in December also aroused enormous interest. The media continued to give considerable attention to the *intifada*, in particular the IKON, a small progressive broadcasting company maintained jointly by progressive Protestant and Roman Catholic churches, which devoted much of its limited broadcasting time to the Palestinians. On the other side, the pro-Israel Protestant Evangelische Omroep (Evangelical Broadcasting Company) or EO, presented several pro-Israel TV programs. It also ran a TV fund-raising campaign for a new gerontological wing at the psychiatric hospital in Kfar Shaul near Jerusalem.

The chairman of the Netherlands-Israel Friendship Society, Dr. G.J. de Loo, the mayor of Lueuwarden, who had held this position for several years, was succeeded by Dr. D. Dolman, who until 1989 had been chairman of the Second Chamber of Parliament. The society, which had branches in several cities, reported a decrease in membership and the "graying" of its remaining members.

Nazi War Criminals

The collaborator Jacob Luitjens, now 72, who was sentenced in absentia to life imprisonment in 1948 after he had managed to escape abroad, was extradited by Canada to Holland in November. In 1944–45 Luitjens had been a *Landwacht*—a member of the Dutch Nazi supernumerary police—in the province of Drenthe, and as such had hunted out persons in hiding, both Jews and others; he was also convicted of killing at least one German deserter. He was arrested after liberation but managed to escape to Paraguay; around 1960 he settled in Canada, where he became a teacher of biology at the University of Vancouver. Although his presence there was discovered some years ago, and Holland asked for his extradition, he had in the interim received Canadian citizenship, and Canada does not extradite its own nationals. However, when it was found that he had failed to mention his Dutch conviction on the application for Canadian citizenship, his citizenship was revoked and the way cleared for his extradition. On his arrival in Holland he was imprisoned in Grainguen.

Racism and Anti-Semitism

Racism, which is generally regarded as taboo in Holland, posed relatively few problems this year. The extreme right-wing Centrum party and the Centrum Democrats were hopelessly divided among themselves and of negligible influence. The one seat won by the Centrum Democrats in the 150-member Second Chamber of Parliament was held by Hans Janmaat, a rather ridiculous figure who lacked the charisma of Jean Le Pen in France, Franz Schönhuber in Germany, or Filip Dewinter in Belgium. The latter tried unsuccessfully to establish a counterpart of his Flemish Bloc in Holland, also with a view to a larger representation of the extreme right in the European Parliament. The main issue of all these extreme-right parties was not anti-Semitism but opposition to the large influx of immigrants from Third World countries. They had some success in the poorer neighborhoods of the large cities, where certain sections were now largely inhabited by *allochthones*. It was estimated that if parliamentary elections had been held this year, the extreme right might have won five or six seats.

Antiracist demonstrations attracted large crowds concerned about the growing sentiment against foreigners. A demonstration in The Hague on March 21 drew some 50,000 participants, including Premier Lubbers and several cabinet ministers. The theme of the gathering was "United Against Racism. For a Multicolored Society." When Premier Lubbers mounted the rostrum to deliver his address, he was pelted with tomatoes and rotten eggs by demonstrators who charged that Holland was not tolerant enough. Frits Bolkestein, too, the chairman of the Liberal party in Parliament, was greeted with yells. He was frequently called a racist because he had criticized Muslim parents for keeping their daughters aged 12 and up at home and for practicing female circumcision.

On November 18, the Senate unanimously adopted a resolution condemning all racism and xenophobia. The word "anti-Semitism," which appeared in the original text of the motion, was left out in the final version in order to make the resolution as general as possible.

The introduction to the 1992 annual report of the Netherlands Ashkenazi Israelietisch Kerkgenootschap (NIK), the largest organized Jewish community in Holland, states that anti-Semitism in the Netherlands was "no cause for concern." According to the report's authors, religiously motivated anti-Semitism hardly existed any longer; the extreme right had become much more cautious in its statements; and the anti-Semitism of the left, which was mainly directed against Israel, was not much in evidence at present. No cases of personal violence or threats had been reported lately, and denial of the Holocaust by Dutch nationals (to be distinguished from those in other countries) dated from several years back.

The only exceptions, the report continued, were the problems on the soccer fields, but the efforts of the R. Netherlands Football League to counter these expressions of anti-Semitism offered hope for gradual improvement. Of course prejudice of various types still existed, but anti-Semitism in the Netherlands was confined to isolated incidents and was not structural. The report went on to urge that anti-Semitic incidents be reported but not exaggerated, even within the Jewish community itself.

People with Jewish-sounding names in five Dutch cities received anti-Semitic pamphlets in the mail from the Flemish Foundation for Free Historical Research in Antwerp, a revisionist organization headed by Siegfried Verbeke. Entitled *The Six Million Holocaust* and *American Expert Ends the Legend of the Gas Chambers*, the leaflets asserted that the Holocaust was a "pack of lies" designed to serve as "an endless source of income for the Antwerp survivors and their descendants." The CIDI (Center for Information and Documentation on Israel), whose director, Ronny Naftaniel, also engaged in combating anti-Semitism and racism in Holland, joined with the Anne Frank Foundation and the Landelijk Bureau Bestrijding Racisme (Countrywide Bureau for Combating Racism) in filing a civil suit against the Belgian foundation, based on the Dutch laws outlawing racism and discrimination. In November the president of the Hague district court forbade further distribution of the leaflets in the Netherlands. Verbeke appealed to the Hague higher district court.

In March, three graves in the Jewish cemetery in Beek, near Maastricht and the Belgian border, were desecrated, and eight tombstones were daubed with swastikas. At the same time, a monument to Jewish deportees in Meerssen, near Beek, was defaced with swastikas.

JEWISH COMMUNITY

Demography

The total number of Jews in the Netherlands was estimated to be about 25,000, the large majority of whom were unaffiliated with the organized Jewish community.

The official Ashkenazi community, the NIK, reported its membership as 5,734 (5,788 in 1991): 3,051 in Amsterdam and the adjoining suburb of Amstelveen, and nearly 400 each in the Hague and Rotterdam areas. The remainder were divided among 30 congregations, 9 of them medium-sized, with between 100 and 215 members each, and 21 still smaller.

The Sephardi community had some 600 members, including a number of recent immigrants from Muslim countries, and only one congregation, that in Amsterdam. The Liberal Jewish community had between 2,000 and 2,500 souls, in six congregations, of which only two, those in Amsterdam and The Hague, had full-time resident rabbis and held regular Sabbath or Friday-evening services.

Communal Affairs

On September 24, the *Netherlands Official Gazette* published the government decision to allow ritual slaughter—both by Jews and by Muslims—for export as well as for domestic use. Slaughtering for export, which was practiced mainly by Jewish slaughterers, for Jewish communities in Switzerland and also for Israel, had been a controversial issue for several years. The Netherlands Ashkenazi community (NIK) was a member of the European Board of Shehita, domiciled in Brussels.

The Ashkenazi Synagogue and Communal Center in Rotterdam at the ABN Davids Square, which was constructed with the help of a government subsidy in 1953 to replace two synagogues that had been destroyed in the German bombardment of the center of Rotterdam in May 1940, had become much too large for the congregation. As a result largely of emigration and of movement to the Amsterdam area, in particular of younger members, membership had dropped from 800 to barely 400. What with maintenance seriously in arrears, it was decided to reduce the space by dividing the synagogue in two, using half of it as a sanctuary and half as a social hall. The work was carried out with assistance from the Rotterdam municipality and the NIK. The renovated building was officially opened on December 21.

On September 20, the dedication took place of the restored synagogue in Breda, in the southwest part of the country, to be used both as a synagogue and a cultural center. The prewar synagogue, which had stood empty since 1942, was renovated at the initiative of the Rebuilding Breda Synagogue Foundation, which was established in 1986, and whose board consisted of representatives of various groups in the area. Financial assistance was also given by the NIK.

The Sephardi community of Amsterdam continued to raise funds to repair the roof and walls of its Esnoga, dating from 1675. The government and the Amsterdam municipality together contributed Fl. 3.5 million and private donors Fl. 4 million (approximately $4 million altogether). A fund-raising campaign, undertaken with the help of a public-relations firm, adopted the slogan "Provide a roof for the Esnoga," inviting people to buy one or more roof tiles. As a symbol of government support for the project, the first tile was purchased by Minister of Welfare and Culture Hedy D'Ancona.

The Liberal synagogues in both Amsterdam and The Hague also needed major renovation and were relying on societies of friends to raise the required funds. The campaign in The Hague was launched in the presence of the American Jewish author Chaim Potok, whose new novel, *The Trope Teacher*, was first published in

Dutch. The proceeds of the Dutch edition were to go toward the synagogue restoration.

The Cheider, the Orthodox day school under Lubavitch auspices, which was established in Amsterdam in 1983 with only five pupils, now had nearly three hundred pupils and had outgrown its premises. The foundation stone for a new building was laid on November 4 in a well-attended ceremony, by U.A. Cohen, who had been the guiding spirit of the school since its inception, and by Mrs. N. Ginjaar (née Maas), a former undersecretary of education, who had shown an active interest in the project for several years.

The Netherlands Zionist Organization (NZB) officially became the Federation of Netherlands Zionists (FNZ) on March 8, as had been decided by a majority of the delegates to its annual conference in 1991. The new body was to have a general board composed of representatives of the various affiliated groups, in accordance with their membership count. To represent unaffiliated Zionists, who formed the vast majority of the NZB members, the BONZ (Organization of Independent Zionists) was established.

On March 1, a new Moadon (clubhouse), specially built for the Zionist youth group Habonim, was opened in the southern Amsterdam suburb of Buitenveldert, where large numbers of Jews now live. It replaced a clubhouse in a residence elsewhere in Amsterdam which was no longer suitable. The 45th anniversary of the establishment of Habonim in Holland was celebrated both in Israel, by former Habonim members who had settled there, and in Amsterdam, by those who had stayed in Holland or had returned. Attendance at both celebrations was high.

Holocaust-Related Matters

On June 12, the Westerbork transit camp, from which some 100,000 Dutch Jews had been deported to extermination camps in the east, was reopened in a new and expanded form and renamed the Westerbork Commemoration Center. Attending the ceremony were Princess Margriet (a younger sister of Queen Beatrix), the governor of the province of Drenthe, and the Israeli ambassador. The construction cost of over Fl. 2 million, which included the reconstruction of the camp watchtowers and some of the barracks, was paid for by the government and by non-Jewish and Jewish institutions and individuals. A monument on the site consists of a map of the Netherlands formed by 102,000 bricks, all but a few hundred of them bearing a Magen David, in memory of the over 100,000 deported Jews. The idea was conceived by Louis de Wijze, who as a boy had been an inmate of the camp. A commemorative stamp for the Westerbork camp, one of a series of stamps commemorating the German occupation, was issued on August 28.

Memorial monuments for deported Jews were unveiled inter alia in Brielle, Delfzijl, and at the former Jewish psychiatric hospital Het Apeldoornsche Bosch, from where all the patients and some 50 staff members, none of whom survived, were deported in January 1943.

The Netherlands government contributed about $1 million toward the restoration of the Auschwitz concentration camp in Poland.

The Conference of Hidden Children was held in Amsterdam, August 23–25, a sequel to a similar conference held in New York in June 1991. This time only persons who, as children, had been kept in hiding in the Netherlands were present—over 500 of them—many now living abroad, in particular in Israel and the United States. The conference was opened by Ed van Thijn, the mayor of Amsterdam, who as a Jewish hidden child himself had found shelter at 18 different addresses during the war. The conference was subsidized by the Jewish Welfare Foundation (JMW) and the ICODO, the (non-Jewish) Information and Coordination Organization for Service to War Victims. It received considerable attention in the news media, though apart from the opening session it was closed to the press.

The Ministry of Social Welfare and Culture (WVC) renewed its grant to the JMW for its "Second Generation" project, which brought together children of survivors for a weekend conference once a year and ran monthly meetings in cafés in various cities for groups with names like "Mazzel" and "Naches." These gatherings offered a forum for discussing common traumas and problems and also served as a meeting-place for people of Jewish origin between the ages of 20 and 40 who otherwise had few links with the Jewish community. The cafés proved a great success and attracted nearly a thousand participants.

As in previous years, the Israeli ambassador awarded Yad Vashem medals, many of them posthumously, to "Righteous Gentiles" who saved Jewish lives during the German occupation. Since most of the living honorees were now quite aged, instead of one central ceremony in Amsterdam, there were now several regional ceremonies, making it easier for them to attend.

To mark the 50th anniversary of Anne Frank's family going into hiding in what has become known as the Anne Frank House, the Anne Frank Foundation (not a Jewish group) published a booklet in six languagues, including Japanese, on the history of the Frank family and the history of the house, which now draws 600,000 visitors a year. The Amsterdam Municipal Council voted a sum equivalent to $200,000 to help save the chestnut tree at the back of the Anne Frank House that is mentioned by Anne in her diary, which was threatened by oil leaking from a fuel tank behind a nearby house.

Jewish-Christian Relations

On November 24, the OJEC, the Consultative Council of Jews and Christians, took leave of its chairman, the Reverend Simon Schoon, a Protestant clergyman who had headed it since its establishment 11 years earlier, when he returned from serving as minister at the Christian settlement of Nes Ammim in western Galilee in Israel. On this occasion, he received the Sigmund Sternberg Prize of the International Council of Christians and Jews from the hands of the Dutch minister of justice, Ernst Hirsch Ballin. Schoon was succeeded by the Reverend Hendrik Vreekamp, who had been secretary of the Dutch Reformed Council for the Church and Israel since 1984. In his farewell address, Rev. Schoon suggested that the OJEC had made very little progress in its 11-year existence—not in Protestant and Roman Catholic circles and not in Jewish circles. Christian groups still practiced some covert forms of missionary activity, he maintained, whereas Jewish circles were still suspicious of OJEC's intentions. Marion Kunstenaar, who had been the OJEC's secretary for most of its existence, was succeeded by Mrs. H. Gelderblom (née Lankhout), a member of the Dutch Senate for the D'66 party. Both women belonged to the Liberal Jewish community.

Culture

Three important exhibitions opened this year at the Jewish Historical Museum in Amsterdam, all accompanied by illustrated catalogues. The first was "The Old Testament in Paintings by 17th-Century Dutch Masters"; the second, "Russian Jewish Avant-garde Artists Between 1990 and 1928"; the third, "In the Footsteps of An-Ski." The last also served to celebrate the sixtieth anniversary of the establishment of the museum and the fifth anniversary of its transfer to its present premises. It showed Jewish folkloristic material collected by a Jewish ethnographic expedition led by S.J. Rapaport (S. An-ski) in the Ukraine between 1911 and 1914 on behalf of the Jewish Ethnographic Society presided over by Baron H. de Guenzburg. Part of the material had been stored for years in the State Ethnographic Museum in Leningrad, where it was discovered under the new liberalization policy, and had its first public showing in Amsterdam. The exhibition was scheduled to be shown in Cologne, Frankfurt, New York, and Israel.

The Dutch-Jewish filmmaker Willy Lindwer made two documentaries of Jewish interest this year, one on the history of the Spanish and Portuguese Jews in the Netherlands, and one titled *My Shtetl Delatyn*. In the latter, Lindwer takes his 84-year-old father and his 13-year-old daughter to visit his father's birthplace, the village of Delatyn in eastern Galicia, and also to Stryj, Lwow, Przemysl, and Krakow, places where his father stayed for some time before finally settling in Amsterdam in 1930. Hardly anything of Jewish life remains in any of these places.

On the occasion of its fifth anniversary, the Netherlands Society for Jewish Genealogy published a special issue of its quarterly, *Misjpoge*, on *Jewish Contributions to Dutch Civilization* (in the fields of painting, literature, music, architecture, and the cabaret).

The Dutch-Jewish weekly *Nieuw Israelietisch Weekblad*, the only Jewish weekly in the Netherlands, suffered a serious loss with the unexpected death of its chief editor, Maurits Kopuit, at the age of 62. He had operated the paper since 1973, working with an all-female editorial staff. He was succeeded by 41-year-old Tamarah Benima, who had been on the staff from 1980 to 1985 and afterward was a regular contributor to the paper. The editorial staff now consisted entirely of women, several of them young, and not all of them Jewish.

Publications

The most important new publication this year was the *Encyclopedia of the Jews of the Netherlands*, in a Dutch edition of some 600 pages. The *Pinkas Hakehilloth be-Holland* was first published in Hebrew in 1985 as one of the volumes in the *Pinkasei Hakehilloth (Encyclopedia of Jewish Communities)* series published by Yad Vashem, and was compiled by Dr. Joseph Michman, his son Dan Michman, and the late Hartog Beem. Like the Hebrew-language book, the Dutch volume consists of two parts: a detailed survey of the history of the Jews in the Netherlands, arranged according to periods, and an alphabetical lexicon of all local Jewish communities that existed before 1940, with an ample bibliography.

The Dutch volume is not merely a translation of the Hebrew edition. Chapters containing information familiar to Dutch readers were shortened, and a lengthy chapter was added, written by Johan Sanders, the secretary of the Netherlands Ashkenazi community, on developments from 1955 to 1991. The number of Jewish communities dealt with was expanded from 139 to 194; the bibliography was expanded and brought up to date. The publication was made possible by contributions from the Prince Bernhard Fund and other organizations, both non-Jewish and Jewish, and the NIK guaranteed the sale of 1,800 of the 3,000 copies that were printed.

A Bibliography of Dutch-language Books Published Between 1983 and 1991 on Jewish Subjects and Israel, by Hanna Blok and Deborah Hersch, contains well over 1,100 titles. Henriette Boas published *Veertien Bewust-Joodse Vrouwen*, profiles of 14 Jewish women who were active in Jewish affairs in Holland before 1940 and some of them after 1945 as well, with supplements on Dutch-Jewish women's organizations and periodicals.

Other new works of interest were *The Jewish Burial Ground of The Hague at the Scheveningseweg* by Francina Menko (née Puttmann), and *Beelden uit de Nacht* (Images from the Night), concentration camp memories by Eli A. Cohen, who had published several earlier books on this subject.

The subjects of new monographs about Jewish communities that no longer exist, written by local historians, included Assen (F.J. Hulst and N.M. Lumil), Avereest (P.M. Kaska), De Kanaalstreek, in the province of Groningen (E.F. Boon and G.A. van den Berg), and De Pekela's, in the province of Groningen (E. Schut).

A novel by the Dutch-Jewish author Leon de Winter, *De ruimte van Sokolow* (Sokolow's Space), became a best-seller. As in previous years, a large number of novels by American-Jewish and Israeli authors were translated into Dutch.

Personalia

Simon Wiesenthal received the Erasmus Prize, worth Fl. 200,000, from the hands of Prince Bernhard, the governor of the Praemium Erasmianum Foundation, on September 17. He was honored "for his relentless struggle, in the spirit of Erasmus, to promote human dignity, tolerance, and freedom of expression, and his fight against discrimination and the persecution of minorities."

Rabbi Meir Just was made a knight in the Order of the Netherlands Lion on the occasion of the 30th anniversary of his arrival in the Netherlands. He had served as communal rabbi of the Amsterdam Ashkenazi community and later as its chief rabbi, and was currently chairman of the Chief Rabbinate of the Netherlands.

Television producer Ralph Inbar received the Golden Rose of Montreux for a program about the Amsterdam Jewish surgeon Sally van Coevorden.

Among prominent Jews who died this year were Nico Boeken, past director of the Jewish Social Welfare Foundation (JMW) and a leading member of the Liberal Jewish community of Amsterdam, aged 72; Hans Evers, since 1968 a member of the Amsterdam Ashkenazi Congregation Council and its chairman 1980–1985, as well as chairman of the Amsterdam branch of the Netherlands Zionist Organization and a board member of the OJEC, aged 67; Paolo Gorin, an opera singer for many years and since 1969 chief cantor of the Liberal Jewish community of Amsterdam, aged 75; Maurits Kopuit, chief editor of the Dutch-Jewish weekly *Nieuw Israelietisch Weekblad* since 1973, aged 62; and Prof. Herman Musaph, professor of sexual psychiatry at the University of Utrecht and a leading member of the Liberal Jewish community, aged 77.

HENRIETTE BOAS

Italy

National Affairs

THE ITALIAN POLITICAL SCENE in 1992 was one of considerable turmoil, fed by growing public disenchantment with a government that operated a vast patronage system, that fostered ties with business and organized crime, and that was viewed as largely ineffective.

In the April 5 general election, with an astonishingly high voter turnout of 87.2 percent, the Christian Democratic party (DC), which had dominated Italian politics since World War II, suffered its worst setback, winning less than a third of the vote. With its coalition partners—Socialists (PSI), Social Democrats (PSDI), and Liberals (PLI)—it managed to cling to office, but only by a bare majority. Most political commentators felt that the new government was stillborn from the start, since it did not represent a genuine majority, and predicted that new elections would soon be needed.

The beneficiaries of DC and PSI losses were small parties representing regional interests. The Lombard League-Northern League made the largest gains, increasing its share of the vote and pushing the Christian Democrats into second place in Lombardy, Italy's wealthiest region. The right-wing Italian Social Movement (MSI) also received a considerable increase in votes. Both the MSI and the Lombard League could be considered ideological descendants of the old Fascist party, and both accepted the concept of a homogeneous "Italian" population, with no place for outsiders.

President Francesco Cossiga, a Christian Democrat who had been openly critical of the government's corruption and a strong advocate of major reform of the system, resigned on April 28, a day after Prime Minister Giulio Andreotti stepped down. Following a monthlong deadlock between proreform deputies and senators and supporters of the status quo, on May 25 they elected a compromise candidate, Oscar Luigi Scalfaro, a 73-year-old Christian Democrat and a devout Catholic. The choice of the new president was surprisingly well received by the general populace. In June Socialist Giuliano Amato was appointed prime minister, and Emilio Colombo (DC) became the new foreign minister.

A series of political and economic scandals shook the country during the year, in which many politicians and public officials were accused of taking bribes and kickbacks from some of the country's leading businesses. The "Tangenti" scandal (from the Italian word for bribery) started in Milan and spread throughout the whole of the country. In Rome five members of Parliament, including the secretary of the Socialist party, Bettino Craxi, were accused of involvement in the affair.

The Mafia continued its campaign of assassination of leading public and political personages, including, on May 23, the country's leading anti-Mafia judge, Giovanni Falcone, together with his wife and three bodyguards. The killings triggered a wave of protests, and President Scalfaro appealed to the country for a "new resistance" against the *Piovra* (octopus). The government approved new, stronger measures that would give greater powers to police and prosecutors to confront organized crime. By the end of the year, the Anti-Mafia Commission was taking testimony from informers willing to name names, accusing politicians, magistrates, and public officials from all parties.

The Italian economy remained in recession in 1992. In spite of this, a report from ISTAT (the Italian Statistical Institute), which appeared in September, ranked the Italian economy sixth among the industrialized nations.

Israel and the Middle East

The new president of Italy, Oscar Luigi Scalfaro, was a man with sympathetic views toward Israel. In January, as a founder and leader of the Friendship for Israel Parliamentary Association, he had led members of this group on a visit to Israel, where they were warmly received by then prime minister Yitzhak Shamir and other members of the government. In an interview with the Italian-Jewish monthly *Shalom* upon his return, Scalfaro explained that his feelings for Israel stemmed from his belief as a Catholic that "Jews and Christians have inseparable family ties, like those between parents and children." When, on the completion of his term at the association, he was invited by the Jewish National Fund to plant an olive tree from Jerusalem in Italy, he took the unprecedented step of opening the gates of the Quirinale, the presidential residence, to have it planted in the garden there.

Foreign Minister Emilio Colombo arrived in Israel on August 31, where he met with Prime Minister Yitzhak Rabin and Foreign Minister Shimon Peres, opening what was to be a series of discussions between the new Israeli government and the European Community (EC). This first meeting focused on Israel's participation in the economic sphere of the EC and on the important role that Europe could play in the negotiations with the Arab countries. Rabin encouraged European initiatives in developing the quality of life in the territories and helping to reduce their economic dependence on Israel. Colombo supported the idea of Israel's participation in the European economy, but added that only real advances in the peace negotiations (then taking place in Washington) would allow progress in that area.

Foreign Minister Peres visited Rome at the end of October, where he was received by Pope John Paul II (see "Jewish-Catholic Relations," below) and was warmly welcomed by President Scalfaro and leaders of the Italian government, as well as by representatives of the Italian Jewish community.

A significant step in Israeli-Italian relations was the signing of a protocol on economic cooperation. This occurred at the end of the meeting of the Italy-Israel Bilateral Commission for Economic Cooperation, held in Jerusalem, November 3–6.

The Italian delegation, led by Deputy Foreign Minister Giuseppe Giacovazzo and the Italian ambassador to Israel, Pier Luigi Rachele, met with Deputy Foreign Minister Yossi Beilin and the Israeli members of the commission and discussed, among other things, the problem of the Arab boycott and Italian financing of a canal to connect the Red Sea with the Dead Sea. This project, which would cost some $2 billion, could be implemented only after the normalization of relations between Jerusalem and Amman.

In December Rome was one of the first European capitals to be visited by Yitzhak Rabin after his becoming prime minister. In his three-day visit, he met with President Scalfaro, Prime Minister Amato, and Foreign Minister Colombo. He invited the Italian leaders, together with the rest of Europe, to play a more active role in the peace process, especially in the financial and economic spheres, and reiterated his statements made in Israel in August concerning the need for EC investment in the region. In his meeting with Amato, Rabin asked for his support in helping to change the 1975 agreement limiting Israel's exports, and received backing for his request for improving economic and research and development relations between the two countries.

During this visit Rabin expressed a wish to visit the memorial at the Fosse Ardeatine, the caves in Rome where 335 Italian partisans, both Jewish and Christian, were buried after being killed by the Nazis in a reprisal action during World War II. He was accompanied to the mausoleum by the mayor of Rome and a group of several hundred Jewish and non-Jewish youths who came to express solidarity with Israel.

While in Rome, Rabin, on behalf of the Israeli government, recognized and presented awards to several people who, between 1945 and 1948, had helped make possible the success of "Aliyah Bet," the illegal immigration of Jews to then Palestine under the British Mandate. One outstanding individual in the group was the much decorated general Alberto Li Gobbi. While still a captain in the Italian army, where he was a transport officer, he managed to gather groups of Jewish refugees as they crossed the border from northern Europe and move them to various locations along the coast, where they were able to board boats leaving clandestinely for Palestine.

One Italian was honored in 1992 by the Israeli authorities as a "Righteous Gentile," 95-year-old Guelfo Zamboni. In 1943, he was the Italian consul in Salonika, Greece, which was under German occupation. The Jewish population at the time, which numbered around 50,000, had been subjected to increasingly restrictive and punitive measures, culminating in forced roundups and deportation. At the risk of his own life, he repeatedly entered the district of the city where Jews were interned before being shipped to German and Polish death camps and provided them with false certificates, managing to save 280 of them. The courage of Consul Zamboni (his humanitarian initiative continued for months) was the basis of the film *The Righteous Enemy*, which was shown on television in many Western countries.

Fiamma Nirenstein, a distinguished journalist and writer with a special interest in Italian and Israeli art and culture, arrived in Tel Aviv in June to take up her appointment as the new director of the Italian Cultural Institute.

Anti-Semitism and Racism

There was a definite increase in anti-Semitic incidents in 1992. On February 29, several hundred skinheads (Naziskins)—dressed in neofascist uniforms and shouting anti-Semitic slogans—marched through the center of Rome to the Piazza Venezia, to stand beneath the balcony of the Palazzo Venezia, Mussolini's favorite site for addressing crowds. There were also cases of desecration of Jewish cemeteries in various parts of the country, with headstones being daubed with painted anti-Semitic slogans. The major incident occurred in November, after the results of an opinion poll on anti-Semitism commissioned by the Italian newsweekly *L'Espresso* were inaccurately reported in other Italian papers throughout the country. The survey, as reported in *L'Espresso*'s November 8 edition, gave the misleading impression that "10.5 percent of all Italians, or six million people, think Jews are foreigners and should leave the country." It later transpired that it was not 10.5 percent of all respondents, but 10.5 percent of the 44.2 percent who had replied affirmatively to a previous question, i.e., around 4.5 percent (or two million) of the Italian adults between the ages of 14 and 79. Since other polls conducted during the past two decades had shown under 10 percent of Italians with anti-Semitic attitudes, the new figures were not considered cause for alarm. As Chief Rabbi Elio Toaff of Rome put it, the proportion of anti-Semites in Italy was comparable to the proportion "endemic to any democratic society." Still, the *Espresso* survey also showed that, in the eyes of many Italians (44.2 percent), Jews are seen as having "common cultural, social and political characteristics that distinguish them from the rest of the population."

In this period, the media played up Italian anti-Semitism as a growing phenomenon. As if to prove them correct, certain anti-Semitic fringe groups stuck large yellow stars on a number of Jewish shops throughout Rome, together with the message "Zionists leave Italy." This prompted a counterreaction by a group of young Jews who marched into the headquarters of the Movimento Politico Occidentale (Western Political Movement, MPO), the only overtly anti-Semitic group in Italy, composed largely of young Nazi-skinhead-revisionists. These young Jews wreaked havoc inside the building, and even destroyed some of the cars parked outside.

A large demonstration against anti-Semitism and racism, which was held simultaneously in several large Italian cities on November 9, the anniversary of *Kristallnacht*, ended the week of high media exposure of anti-Semitism in Italy. Rabbi Toaff, accompanied by the mayor of Rome and leaders of both houses of Parliament, told a large group of young people gathered in front of Rome's Great Synagogue, "This turnout is proof of what the people of Rome think of that small, criminal riff-raff of anti-Semites and racists." All the speakers present stressed Italy's determination that the horrors of the past would "never again" be repeated. In this, they echoed the motto printed on the signs held up by members of the crowd, many of whom were also waving red "CGIL" (Italy's largest labor union) banners or signs identifying various Christian ecumenical and interreligious groups.

Italy's top officials were quick to offer reassurance to the Jewish community on the government's position. President Scalfaro made a private visit to the headquarters of the Jewish community organization of Rome on September 7. He met there with Chief Rabbi Toaff, president of the Rome Jewish community Sergio Frassineti, and other members of the community council. The purpose of this meeting was to enable Scalfaro to express his unconditional solidarity with Italy's Jewish citizens in a period of escalating anti-Semitism. At the same time, he noted that, compared with anti-Semitic occurrences in other parts of Europe, the Italian situation was not particularly alarming.

In a meeting on November 3 with Tullia Zevi, president of the Union of Italian Jewish Communities (Unione delle Comunità Ebraiche Italiane, UCEI), Prime Minister Amato reaffirmed his government's solidarity with the Jewish community, "regarded as an integral part of the national community." In an official statement, he underlined the need for maximum effort by all official state bodies to counteract racist activity, illegal under Italian law. He also stressed the need to increase popular awareness of the problem through extended educational efforts. The UCEI (together with several political parties) demanded, in a press communiqué, that the MPO be outlawed, because its ideology was based on "an apologia for racism and fascism."

JEWISH COMMUNITY

Demography

Some 31,000 Jews were affiliated with their local Jewish communities. The total number of Jews in Italy, taking into account those not affiliated, was believed to be around 35,000.

Communal Affairs

President Scalfaro received a courtesy visit from the executive of the Union of Italian Jewish Communities (UCEI), headed by president Tullia Zevi, at the Quirinale on September 16. The atmosphere of the meeting was friendly and cordial, and the Italian president again confirmed his closeness to the Jewish community. He added that he considered Jews to be a significant component of the Italian social fabric, one whose history and culture were not sufficiently recognized in the country.

The meeting of the executive bodies of the European Jewish Congress (EJC) and World Jewish Congress (WJC), held in Jerusalem in February, confirmed Tullia Zevi, the Italian representative to the EJC, and Gerhart Riegner of Switzerland,

WJC official, as co-presidents of the EJC Commission for Interreligious Relations. The main topics of the meeting were the problem of anti-Semitism in Europe and preparations for an international conference on anti-Semitism to be held in Brussels in July. Zevi and some of the other European delegates objected to holding the conference at this time, because of the current high levels of nationalism and racism on the continent. They suggested, as an alternative, that a public-opinion survey be conducted on all aspects of anti-Semitism and racism in Eastern and Western European countries, the results of which should be incorporated in a "white paper" to be presented to the secretary-general of the United Nations and to heads of state.

A delegation of the EJC to the European Parliament in Strasbourg, in April, discussed the growth of the right in Europe, and stressed the need to harmonize the laws against racism and anti-Semitism throughout Europe. The delegation proposed creating a central body to monitor and act against racism, anti-Semitism, and all types of prejudice, to be supported and financed by the appropriate institutions within the European Community. The parliament agreed to set up such a body, and said that the first aim of the organization would be the preparation of the proposed white paper. There was also some discussion of the Arab boycott and of Europe-Israel relations. The delegation ended its visit by inviting all members of the Parliament to attend the forthcoming Brussels conference on anti-Semitism.

July saw three major meetings in Brussels: the executive of the World Jewish Congress, the executive of the European Jewish Congress, and the international conference titled "My Brother's Keeper—Anti-Semitism and Prejudice in a Changing World." This last was attended by a large Italian contingent that included the president of the Center for Contemporary Jewish Documentation (CDEC), a Milan-based research institute, Luisella Mortara Ottolenghi, and researcher Adriana Goldstaub; Tullia Zevi and Amedeo Mortara of the UCEI; and the Italian and Euro parliamentarian Marco Pannella. The president of the Italian Senate, Giovanni Spadolini, sent a message condemning anti-Semitism and promising his support for all efforts made to suppress it. At the end of the conference, Zevi stated that she felt the whole event had consisted of nothing more than a lot of talk and the expending of considerable sums of money for practically no tangible results and no clear plans for future action.

The new Israeli ambassador to Italy, Aviezer (Avi) Pazner, was welcomed to Rome on January 28 in a ceremony hosted by Tullia Zevi together with Chief Rabbi Elio Toaff, Roberto Lovari, and the Hon. Oscar Luigi Scalfaro, president of the Friendship for Israel Parliamentary Association.

"Italian Jewry—What Is Its Future?" was the title of a national conference organized in Rome at the end of the year by the UCEI. The official purpose of this three-day conference was to discuss Jewish life and the prospects for survival in the Diaspora, but the meetings also examined the purpose and future of the UCEI. The conference was attended by a much higher percentage of youth than had been anticipated, and was colored by their liveliness, openness, and active participation in the sessions, which dealt with the many cultural, political, and religious problems facing Italian Jewry. The final document of the conference stressed the need to strengthen the ties between the individual communities and the UCEI in order to ensure maximum circulation of ideas and information and maximum interaction between members of the various Jewish communities and the central body.

The 25th anniversary of the expulsion of Libyan Jews to Italy was observed in Rome on October 31. The event, which was primarily social, was under the auspices of the Rome municipality and was attended by leading Italian political and cultural figures. The evening included a photographic exhibition and a film about the customs and culture of the Libyan Jewish community and ended with a buffet and dancing.

Community Relations

The UCEI and leaders of Italy's three main labor unions (CGIL, CISL, and UIL) agreed to carry out educational programs aimed at developing "healthy relations between ethnic and religious minorities." The UCEI also continued negotiations with the Italian Ministry of Education for the creation of an audiovisual program for schools on the history and culture of Jews in Italy and Europe, for which final approval was given in November. This project was also supported by the St. Egidio Community, an important Catholic organization that had been making efforts to persuade the Italian Bishops' Conference to include accurate material on Judaism in the nationwide courses on the Catholic religion taught in the public-school system.

Jewish-Catholic Relations

"Anti-Semitism is un-Christian" became a new slogan for the Catholic Church, following the pope's statement, "Anti-Semitism is a sin against God and man," which was made during his speech commemorating the 27th anniversary of "Nostra Aetate" on October 28. The pope's strong condemnation of anti-Semitism was echoed in statements made by major church dignitaries and in articles in *Osservatore Romano*, the official Vatican newspaper.

Another unprecedented turning point in Jewish-Catholic relations occurred in February, when a joint interfaith mission went to Central Europe (Poland, Czechoslovakia, and Hungary). The delegates included Monsignor Pier Francesco Fumagalli, secretary of the Vatican Commission for Religious Relations with the Jews, and representatives of Jewish organizations, together with Tullia Zevi and Dr. Gerhart Riegner, co-presidents of the European Jewish Commission on Interreligious Relations.

The initiative for the tour came from the International Catholic-Jewish Liaison Committee (ILC), and was a direct consequence of the upsurge in European anti-Semitism that followed the breakup of the Communist regimes in Eastern and Central Europe, a breakup in which the Catholic Church played a significant role.

(The ILC had come into being in 1971 as a result of meetings between the Vatican Commission for Religious Relations with the Jews and the International Jewish Committee for Interreligious Consultation—IJCIC, currently chaired by Edgar Bronfman—and actively promoted communication and cooperation between Catholics and Jews.) The interfaith delegation met with church primates as well as government representatives and leaders of the Jewish communities in the three countries. Of special interest was the meeting with the primate of Poland, Josef Cardinal Glemp, who had in the past been accused of making anti-Semitic remarks, who now talked about "our big brothers the Jews, whose faith and culture represent a constructive element in the development of European civilization." He also condemned all forms of anti-Semitism and expressed "sincere regrets for all the anti-Semitic events that had taken place on Polish soil."

During these meetings, the government representatives of the three countries assured the delegation that, despite the increase in emergent anti-Semitic attitudes and activity resulting from the new freedom, all such activity would be considered illegal. A joint declaration issued at the conclusion of the mission stated that the Catholic Church in these countries would make efforts to publish and disseminate literature in the local languages, stating the Church's attitude to the Jewish people in accordance with the principles set out by the Vatican Ecumenical Council. It went on to say: "Xenophobia, anti-Semitism and racism and extreme forms of nationalism require a joint response from all the religious communities, in order to support laws guaranteeing religious, civil and human rights for all members of the population."

The 14th general meeting of the ILC was held May 4–7 in the United States, in Baltimore, home of America's oldest Catholic seminary and a large, active, liberal Catholic minority. In his opening statement, the Vatican's Edward Cardinal Cassidy referred to the 500th anniversary of the expulsion of the Jews from Spain and said that the Church was considering a response to this tragic act of intolerance. The accent of the meeting was on the continuation of Jewish-Catholic dialogue, on the Holocaust and the Church's reactions during and after, and on Vatican-Israel relations. The final document stated that a forthcoming declaration by the Vatican regarding the Holocaust and anti-Semitism would be official doctrine for all Catholics.

The ILC met again on November 12 in the Vatican, where the topics discussed included cooperation in promoting human rights and in the fight against racism and anti-Semitism. Among the initiatives suggested was the adoption of an "annual day dedicated to Jewish-Catholic dialogue and cooperation," following the example set by the Episcopal Conference of Italy in 1989.

The use of a medieval anti-Semitic expression in a speech by Salvatore Cardinal Pappalardo caused feelings of anger and discomfort among Italian Jews and led many members of the Catholic community to protest strongly his use of the offensive metaphor. Speaking at the funeral of Judge Falcone in Palermo, in May, Cardinal Pappalardo referred to the Mafia as the "Synagogue of Satan." In response to a letter of protest from UCEI president Zevi, the cardinal stated in an open letter of apology, which he released to the press, that he had never intended any disrespect to the Jews, who are the ancestors of Christianity, but was using the word synagogue in its wider sense, that of a public meeting place. He continued, "In order to eliminate all ambiguity, in the official transcript of the speech to be published in the Diocese newsletter, the phrase will be replaced by an equivalent one, such as the 'Church of Satan.' "

The Vatican, to a great extent as a result of the bilateral Arab-Israeli negotiations taking place, had begun to review its approach to the Middle East situation and had become a more active participant in the peace process. One move in this direction was the Vatican-authorized visit to Israel by the archbishop of New York, John Cardinal O'Connor, before coming to Rome to meet with Pope John Paul II in January. While in Israel, O'Connor held successful meetings with Prime Minister Yitzhak Shamir and President Chaim Herzog.

In April the pope met with the Israeli ambassador to Italy, Avi Pazner, who called on him at the Vatican. In the same month, one of the pope's top advisers, Joseph Cardinal Ratzinger, arrived in Israel for an unofficial visit.

In July the Permanent Israel-Vatican Bilateral Committee was formed, with the express purpose of studying and jointly defining issues of reciprocal interest. Israeli foreign minister Shimon Peres visited the Vatican in October in order to discuss with the pope ways to expedite the normalization of diplomatic relations between the Vatican and Israel. Peres personally extended an open invitation to the pontiff to visit Jerusalem. The official communiqué at the end of the session stated that the meeting was characterized by a positive atmosphere and extreme cordiality between the two participants, and concluded with the announcement that there would be an exchange of representatives, to be followed later by a "full" diplomatic delegation.

A meeting of the bilateral committee held in November at the Foreign Ministry in Jerusalem was memorable for its being the first formal visit to Israel by Vatican dignitaries. The Vatican delegation, headed by Director of Foreign Affairs Monsignor Claudio Celli, was received by Deputy Foreign Minister Yossi Beilin, with whom they discussed, in a relaxed and optimistic atmosphere, the situation of the Church in Israel and the administered territories.

Culture

Cultural activities this year focused on the commemoration of the 500th anniversary of the expulsion of the Jews from Spain. Various exhibitions and conferences organized by individual Jewish communities, together with national and international cultural institutions and with the cooperation of local authorities, attracted a large number of visitors and participants from all parts of Europe and the world.

One of the first events of the year was an international conference held in Genoa, in May, on the subject "*Le vie difficili della convivenza*" (The Difficult Path of Coexistence). It dealt with the evolution of coexistence between the three monotheistic religions in Spain before 1492—Islam, Judaism, and Christianity—with special reference to the prospects for similar cultural and religious coexistence in the present. The conference attracted high-level participants from all three religions.

Another international conference, the fifth "Italia Judaica," also took as its theme a subject related to the expulsion. It was held in June in Palermo, Sicily, under the auspices of the Italian Cultural Heritage Ministry, Tel Aviv University, and the Hebrew University of Jerusalem, within the framework of Italy-Israel cultural accords. The subject of the conference, "The Jews in Sicily Before Their Expulsion in 1492," was relevant to the Spanish expulsion, since 15th-century Sicily, like most of southern Italy, was under the rule of Ferdinand and Isabella of Spain.

The 19th international congress of the Italian Association for the Study of Judaism took place in Potenza, in southern Italy, September 20–24. The subject was "The History of the Jewish Communities in the Southern Italian Peninsula from Their Establishment up to 1541." Academics and researchers from Europe and Israel gathered at the Basilicata University to explore the history of these communities, which, after absorbing many of the Jews from Spain in 1492, were themselves wiped out by the expulsion order of October 31, 1541.

Two important cultural events were offered by the Jewish community of Livorno during the year. The first was the opening of a new Jewish museum, and the second was the hosting of an international conference, in November, on "The Inquisition and the Jews in Italy," with sessions held partly in Livorno and partly in Pisa.

The work of the National Jewish Bibliographic Center (Centro Bibliografico dell'Ebraismo Italiano) of Rome, cataloging the archives and libraries of Jewish communities throughout Italy, was extended this year to include the Tuscany region. Since more and more of the smaller Jewish communities were going out of existence, there was a pressing need to expedite the work in order to save as much as possible. The center received aid and some financing from the Italian Cultural Heritage Ministry.

Continuing collaboration between the Centro Bibliografico and the Hebrew University of Jerusalem was seen in the initiation of a three-year project for the collection and recording of Italian Jewish liturgical and popular music. This material would be the start of the music section of the bibliographic center in Rome.

An exhibition on the history of the Jews in Merano was opened in New York on January 7, at the Elaine Kaufmann Cultural Center, by Federico Steinhaus, president of the Merano Jewish community.

Il Libro della Memoria, a volume containing the names of all the Jews deported from Italy between the years 1943–1945, published in 1991, was presented to the president of the Yad Vashem Holocaust Memorial Center in Jerusalem by its author, Liliana Fargion, and Luisella Mortara Ottolenghi, the president of the Center for Contemporary Jewish Documentation (CDEC), on behalf of the organization. The event, which was organized together with the Center for Italian Jewish Studies in Jerusalem, was attended by the Italian ambassador, Pier Luigi Rachele.

The last major activity of the year was Jewish Culture Week, November 4–11. Organized by the Cultural Center of the Rome Jewish community, together with the Gramsci Institute Foundation, and held under the auspices of the Italian Ministry of Culture, it offered a panoramic view of the Jewish contribution to Italian arts, science, and culture during the preceding 35 years. The "week" comprised four main events: a book exhibition of over 1,000 volumes, entitled "Jewish Culture Through Italian Publishing, 1955 to 1990"; a study day devoted to various aspects of Jewish literature and what it is that makes a book "Jewish"; a two-day symposium, "Jewish Culture and Scientific Culture in Italy," on the impact of the 1938 racial laws on the academic life of the country; and an exhibition arranged by the Rome Jewish Youth Center showing the secret journeys of Spanish Jews after their expulsion.

The *Platea Estate*, Rome's summer theater festival, which each year highlights works from another country in its foreign section, this year featured works by major Israeli playwrights. Plays by Daniel Horovitz, from the Haifa Municipal Theater, and Hanoch Levin, one of the country's leading writers, were performed at the Teatro Colosseo in Italian translation.

Publications

The proceedings of the seventh international congress of the Italian Institute for the Study of Judaism were published at the beginning of the year. The subject was "Jewish Manuscripts, Fragments and Books from 15th and 16th Century Italy."

Several books were published to mark the 500th anniversary of the expulsion of the Jews from Spain and also on Christopher Columbus, claimed by some researchers to be of Jewish origin. Rabbi Nello Pavoncello of Rome published a booklet, *Gli ebrei spagnoli a Roma e le loro scole* (The Spanish Jews of Rome and Their "Shool"). *Sepharad addio* (Farewell Spain) by Guido Nathan Zazzu tells of the arrival of the Spanish Jews in Genoa. *Miti e utopie della scoperta* (Myths and Utopia of the Discovery) by Juan Gil considers aspects of Columbus the Navigator and his time. Using previously unpublished documents, the author arrives at the conclusion that Columbus was a Jew.

The well-known Leo S. Olschki publishing house of Florence published the ninth volume of the "Proceedings of the St. Uffizio [the legal tribunal of the Catholic Church] Against the Jews of Venice," covering the years 1608–1632. In this monumental work, Pier Cesare Ioly Zorattini, the researcher who found the original documents, expands and comments on them.

Abraham Berliner's classic *History of the Jews of Rome*, first published over one hundred years ago in German, appeared this year in its first Italian edition: *Storia degli ebrei di Roma*. This account of Roman Jews and the Church's attitude toward them over the centuries was warmly welcomed by the Rome Jewish community.

The literary quarterly *Rassegna Mensile d'Israel*, published by the UCEI, dedicated its September issue to Israeli Hebrew literature. It included essays and articles by well-known Israeli and Italian Jewish writers.

Silvio Ferrari's *Vaticano e Israele* (The Vatican and Israel) is a carefully researched, detailed examination of the difficult relations between the two states in the period between the end of World War II and the 1991 Gulf War.

Judaica Minora (Jewish Trivia) contains three essays by Vittore Colorni. The first two are about the Jews of Sabbioneta and Bozzolo, small towns in the north of Italy, while the third is a study of the changes occurring in Jewish surnames of geographic or toponymic origin.

Personalia

Italy's candidate for the 1992 "Prix Femme d'Europe" was Tullia Zevi, president of the UCEI and a member of the executive of the European Jewish Congress. The prize is usually given to a woman from one of the 12 EC member countries, for activities contributing to human rights and the promotion of solidarity among nations. This year, in a departure from the usual practice, it was presented to two women from Eastern Europe.

Among prominent Jews who died this year were Fritz Becker, a leading member and official of the World Jewish Congress from 1946 to 1986, who was active in Catholic-Jewish relations, in January, in Rome, aged 71; Rabbi Emanuel Menachem Artom, an active Zionist, an emissary for the Jewish Agency, chief rabbi of the Venice and Turin communities, and author of an Italian-Hebrew/Hebrew-Italian dictionary as well as several liturgical and educational texts, in July, in Jerusalem, aged 76; Baruch Joseph Sermoneta, professor of medieval philosophy at the Hebrew University and authority on the Jews of Italy, who immigrated to Palestine in 1939, in October, in Jerusalem, aged 68.

Two non-Jews who died this year had a special relationship with the Jewish community. Beniamino Carucci, who died in Rome, in July, aged 70, was the first Italian publisher to pay serious attention to Jewish works, producing the first Italian series on Jewish themes and subjects. A charming and cultivated man, he was married to a Jewish woman, and their children were brought up as Jews. Giorgio Perlasca, who was designated a "Righteous Gentile" in 1991, died in August in Padua. Known as the "Silent Hero" and "the Italian Raoul Wallenberg," he saved some 5,000 Hungarian Jews from deportation during World War II (see AJYB 1991, pp. 291–92).

RACHELE MEGHNAGI SMULIAN
DAVID SMULIAN

Federal Republic of Germany

National Affairs

IN 1992, GERMANY'S SECOND YEAR of unification, important developments took place in spheres ranging from foreign policy to the treatment of foreigners to abortion laws. Many of these were related to the dynamics of nation and state building, as Germany assumed its new role as the wealthiest and most powerful state in post-1989 Europe.

In foreign affairs, the most dramatic new development was the participation of the German military in international peacekeeping operations, first in the former Yugoslavia and later in Somalia. In January Germany became the first European state to recognize Slovenia and Croatia. In July Germany began to take part in the humanitarian airlift to Sarajevo. Additionally, Bonn sent a destroyer and three reconnaissance planes to monitor the UN embargo on Serbia and Montenegro. And in December Chancellor Helmut Kohl announced the initiation of humanitarian aid to be delivered by German military personnel to Somalia. These moves provoked heated discussion within Germany. The Bonn government justified its actions with the argument that since the use of arms was excluded, these measures did not constitute military actions and thus did not require parliamentary consent.

In September Foreign Minister Klaus Kinkel addressed the UN in New York, emphasizing Germany's wish to assume all the rights and obligations of a UN member, which could include a seat on the Security Council. In November Kinkel visited China and Japan, and in December the German Parliament ratified, by a large majority, the Maastricht treaty on a European economic, political, and currency union.

State elections were held in Baden-Württemberg and Schleswig-Holstein in April. In both states, the governing Christian Democratic and Social Democratic parties (CDU and SPD) suffered large losses, and the far-right parties made dramatic gains, winning seats in the state parliaments. One-third of the electorate did not vote. These results were repeated in the Berlin local elections in May, the first joint elections in Berlin since 1946. The major parties lost heavily; the right and the PDS (the successor to the Communist party of the former German Democratic Republic) made significant gains, and there were more nonvoters than in any previous postwar election.

In 1992, six million foreigners resided in Germany. One-half of them had lived in West Germany for at least 15 years. Throughout the year, the immigration of asylum seekers remained high (440,000), as did the displacement of eastern Germans to the western states and the resettlement of ethnic Germans from states of the former Eastern Bloc (149,182 in the first nine months). The growth of the non-native population evoked varying responses as Germans sought to find a public consensus regarding who had the right to live in the unified Germany.

Late August witnessed a pogrom against asylum seekers in Rostock. In late November another attack occurred, this time against resident Turkish citizens in Mölln, a town in western Germany. Significant sectors of the German population distanced themselves from these actions by organizing anti-xenophobia and antiracist demonstrations (see "Anti-Semitism and Extremism," below).

Over the same months, negotiations were held among the major political parties aimed at drafting legislation to limit the number of asylum seekers and other foreigners to be admitted to Germany. An agreement was reached in December. "Refugees of wars" would have a separate status and would be admitted for a limited period of time; "asylum seekers" (the largest category) would retain the right to political asylum only if they arrived directly from countries deemed "insecure"; naturalization of long-term "foreign residents" would be made easier; the flow of "ethnic Germans" would be controlled (partly indirectly, through treaties which would make it more attractive to them to remain where they were); and the number of "contract laborers" in Germany would be limited to 100,000.

Israel and the Middle East

Despite frequent declarations of good faith and reaffirmations on both sides of Germany's "special relationship" with Israel, German-Israeli relations in 1992 started out cool, and by June had reached a 25-year low.

Several issues and incidents contributed to the increasing tensions. In February three German business executives were arrested and charged with having illegally shipped parts suitable for the construction of rockets to Iraq in 1991. In April Israeli foreign minister David Levy criticized Chancellor Helmut Kohl's reception of Austrian president Kurt Waldheim in Germany. In February, in the course of what started out as a commercial dispute between Lufthansa Airline and the Association of Israeli Travel Agencies, Lufthansa was accused of using anti-Semitic stereotypes in its advertising (two days before Holocaust Memorial Day). Ultimately the conflict over the distribution of Lufthansa's "group price" tickets was resolved with a compromise, and it was revealed that Lufthansa's offending advertisement had been commissioned from an Israeli artist.

A constant irritant in German-Israeli relations in 1992 was the Arab boycott of Israeli products. In July Bonn issued a directive prohibiting boycott provisions in trade agreements with other countries. The Federation of German Wholesale and Foreign Trade rejected this policy, claiming that boycott provisions did not damage Israel and that the new directive would put German exporters at a disadvantage when competing with other European countries. In November, during a visit to Riyadh, Economic Minister Jürgen Möllemann announced that, in the future, only the place of origin would appear on goods exported from Germany, instead of the previous declaration "not from Israel." Möllemann had been chairman of the German-Arabian Society for many years before becoming economic minister in 1991.

Another serious issue was Bonn's continuing refusal to make restitution payments for residents of the former GDR, though talks proceeded regarding other forms of aid.

On a three-day visit to Germany in September, Prime Minister Yitzhak Rabin met with President Richard von Weizsäcker, Chancellor Kohl, Foreign Minister Kinkel, and Defense Minister Volker Rühe. In Berlin, Rabin spoke with the president of the German Parliament, Rita Süssmuth, and with leaders of the Social Democratic party. He also addressed the Socialist International, which was meeting at the Reichstag (the building that housed the prewar German parliament), met with the board of directors of the Central Council of Jews in Germany, and visited the former concentration camp at Sachsenhausen. The Israeli prime minister did not ask for German credits but did call for more German investment in Israel, especially in industry and tourism. He also asked for German humanitarian support for the creation of new jobs and for the integration of Jewish immigrants from the former Soviet Union, and he voiced dismay over recent right-wing and anti-Semitic incidents in Germany.

Throughout the year, Israeli officials expressed concern about the increasing manifestations of right-wing radicalism and anti-Semitism in Germany. The opposition Likud called for limiting official relations with Germany, and Israeli minister of education Shulamit Aloni urged the government to call for a travel boycott of Germany, should Bonn fail to take more serious action against right-wing radicalism and anti-Semitism. The Knesset issued a statement expressing Israel's "recognition of those forces in German public life which are active in combating racism and anti-Semitism," but by this time, relations had become so tense that a Knesset delegation postponed its planned trip to Germany.

By the time of Foreign Minister Klaus Kinkel's visit to Israel in November, German-Israeli relations had taken a turn for the better. The Israelis did not bring up the matter of restitution payments for former East German residents, and Kinkel's talk with Israeli foreign minister Shimon Peres centered on "cooperation." Kinkel pledged that Germany would help Israel with the absorption of immigrants from the former Soviet Union; that funds for German-Israeli research and development would be doubled; and that the Bonn government would encourage German investment in Israel. Kinkel also agreed to push for lifting the Arab boycott of Israeli products. Kinkel's visit was followed by the arrival in Israel of Klaus Naumann, inspector general of the German Army. This was the first visit to Israel of such a high-ranking German military officer. Naumann was greeted by Chief of Staff Ehud Barak and other high Israeli officers.

Despite tensions in their political relations, Germany and Israel remained important trading partners. German investment in Israel (largely in housing, banking, and industry) totaled $312.5 million, and in recent years 130,000–160,000 German tourists visited Israel annually. Cultural and citizen exchanges continued their high level of activity in Germany's western states and increased in the new federal states. By June the Deutsch-Israelische Gesellschaft (Germany-Israel Society) had opened chapters in all the new states. Partnerships linked 87 German cities, communities, and districts with 62 Israeli localities. German-Israeli youth exchanges, which involved 7,000 German and 3,000 Israeli young people per year, continued high, with strong participation, especially of eastern Germans.

An active program of German-Israeli cultural exchanges continued. Among the more important events were the following: In February the Hotel Kempinski in Berlin hosted an Israel Week, featuring Israeli chefs and musicians. In March the folklore group Anachnu Kahn performed, writer Amos Elon gave a reading, and painter Uri Shaked opened an exhibit in Munich. The Akko Theater Center staged its controversial play *Arbeit macht frei vom Toitland Europa* (Work Makes One Free of Death-Land Europe) in Berlin. In May the Israeli play *Die Vermummten* (The Masked Figures) opened in Hamburg; and the Leipzig Opera Ensemble performed *The Marriage of Figaro* and *The White Rose* at the Israel Festival in Jerusalem. Seven Israeli artists presented at the *Dokumenta*, Germany's major international art exhibit, in Kassel. In June an exhibit titled "Positions Israel," involving 13 contemporary Israeli artists, opened in Berlin. In July a photo exhibit about Jerusalem, featuring the works of photographer Hans Günther Kaufmann and text by writer Shalom ben Chorin, was shown at the Jewish Museum in Frankfurt.

Germany and Israel continued to honor each other's citizens. Friedrich Schiller University in Jena awarded a posthumous doctorate to Israeli trade-unionist Benjamin Herzl Berger. Berger, a former student in Jena, had been forced to flee Germany before receiving his Ph.D. He settled in Palestine, where he became an editor of *Davar*, the trade-union newspaper. Gebhard Ziller, secretary of state in the Ministry of Science in Bonn, received an honorary doctorate from Bar-Ilan University. Israel's Righteous Gentile Award was bestowed on Margit David of the former East Germany. During the Nazi years, her family hid Jews in their cellar and provided them with false identification papers. To date, 2,000 individuals had received this award, including 260 Germans. The David family was recognized only recently due to the lack of official relations between Israel and East Germany. A German high-school student, Jan Bernd Bessling of Münster, won an Israeli essay competition for a composition about his class trip to the former concentration camp Stutthof (near Danzig).

Anti-Semitism and Extremism

Attacks on asylum seekers, foreign residents, and (secondarily) Jews took place on a daily basis throughout 1992 and dominated newspaper headlines after mid-August. Over 20,000 acts of violence with proven or suspected right-wing motivation were registered. Over one-third of these offenses involved arson or bombing; most of the perpetrators were between 12 and 20 years old. By December the total number of militant right-wing Germans was estimated at 6,000, and some 41,000

German citizens were registered with the Federal Republic's 77 right-wing parties and organizations. Public discussion centered on the attacks and their perpetrators and also on the official reluctance, in particular of the federal government, to protect the victims (and potential victims) or to combat the radical right with a rigor similar to that deployed against the radical left in the 1970s and 1980s.

A shocking episode occurred in late August in Lichtenhagen, a high-rise suburb of Rostock. For several days, 500 right-wing youths firebombed—and ultimately burned down—a building housing 300 foreigners. All evidence suggested that this attack had been well organized. Nevertheless, the police arrived at the scene several hours late; local citizens even gathered to watch. One spectator told a reporter: "It's like a public holiday here!" Mecklenburg-Vorpommern's minister of the interior, Lothar Kupfer (CDU), emphasized the need to curb "the uncontrolled flow of foreigners" to his state. In the aftermath, Rostock's police chief was fired, and 32 youths were arrested. Two were charged with attempted murder and the rest with severely disturbing the peace. Further attacks on asylum seekers took place in several communities in eastern Germany.

In mid-November it was confirmed that members of Germany's armed forces had participated in 22 right-wing incidents—mostly in the attacks on the residences for asylum seekers, but also in desecrations at Jewish cemeteries. They committed these acts, however, in off-hours and wearing civilian attire. Alisa Fuss, president of the International League for Human Rights and a founder of the Berlin Jewish Group, called for a nationwide strike to express public outrage at the attacks and at the inadequate response of public officials.

Another incident that attracted national and international attention took place in late November in Mölln, a small town in Schleswig-Holstein. Three Turkish residents, a woman and two children, died when two houses were set afire. Nine other Turkish citizens were injured when they jumped out of windows to escape the flames. Unlike previous attacks, in which the target was asylum seekers housed in barracks in the eastern states, this incident took place in western Germany and was aimed at the resident foreign population. The victims had been living and working in Germany for up to 20 years. Two men (25 and 19 years old, respectively) were arrested. In the days and weeks following this event, demonstrations against xenophobia and racism were organized in several German cities, and two right-wing parties (National Front and Democratic Alternative) were outlawed. Further attacks on foreigners took place in Gelsenkirchen, Vreden, Eberswalde, and Neuruppin. In Neuruppin the victims were ethnic German immigrants from the former Soviet Union.

After the incident at Mölln, Ralph Giordano, a writer of Jewish descent, sent an open letter to Chancellor Kohl, advising him that many Jews in Germany were planning to resort to armed self-defense. Ignatz Bubis, president of the Central Council of Jews in Germany, called on Germans to demand that the state adopt a tougher policy against right-wing radicalism. The Israeli government also appealed to Bonn and to German society to combat violence from the right. The final week of 1992 saw a series of large candlelight demonstrations and cultural events in Germany's major cities condemning racism and xenophobia. In December the Bonn government announced the establishment of two bodies: a new subcommittee to deal with combating right-wing radicalism and a coordinating group under the leadership of the Office for the Protection of the Constitution, with the participation of the Office for Combating Crime (Bundeskriminalamt) and the Federal Prosecutor's Office.

According to a January 1992 survey of 2,000 western Germans and 1,000 eastern Germans, conducted by the Emnid Institute in Bielefeld, most Germans were ashamed that "Germans had committed so many crimes against Jews" but did not feel guilty and wanted to "close the file" on that part of German history. Of those surveyed, 73 percent rejected the idea that the unified Germany should make restitution payments for the GDR; 91 percent felt that Jews from the former Soviet Union should not be privileged over other foreigners; 32 percent responded that worldwide, Jews have too much influence; another 32 percent said that if Jews are hated and persecuted, it is partly their fault; 42 percent felt that the Nazi regime had its good and bad sides. Fewer eastern Germans than western Germans, however, wanted to "close the file" on Germany's past, and more eastern Germans felt a special responsibility toward the Jews.

Against the background of these attitudes and the general climate of violence, the number of anti-Semitic crimes in Germany soared in 1992. In Munich, just before Passover, inhabitants of the Jewish old-age home received letters containing Hitler texts; in the days before Rosh Hashanah, fliers circulated in the city charging that kosher slaughter involves animal torture. Also in September, anti-Semitic pamphlets were found in the Hohenschönhausen district of eastern Berlin. Throughout the year Jewish monuments were damaged, and 80 desecrations of Jewish cemeteries were reported. There were also two incidents in which German radio stations broadcast anti-Semitic material. In September, on a program called "Schalom," DLF (Deutschlandfunk) editor Joseph Biolek characterized Jews as left-wingers who tend to distort the German past. And in December a program on the popular RTL station featured a sympathizer of the right-wing Republican party who, broadcasting under the pseudonym Aaron Moschel, told the radio audience: "The Germans are Jew-haters. We have to defend ourselves."

Two troubling incidents occurred in the city of Rostock. In October, a group of young French Jews—members of the groups Tagar, Betar, and Sons and Daughters of Deported Jews from France—came to that city to protest Germany's September 24 agreement with Romania, which facilitated the repatriation of Romanian Gypsies from Germany. The protesters, led by the French Nazi hunters Serge and Beate Klarsfeld, became involved in skirmishes with the police after they tried to occupy Rostock's city hall and to hang a sign condemning the agreement and recalling Nazi crimes against the Gypsies. Several demonstrators were taken into custody; all but three were released within 48 hours. In Paris, demonstrators demanding the release of the last three French Jews broke a window of the Goethe Institute, and 200

French Jews protested in front of the German embassy. The incident ended with the release of the three French Jews ten days after the incident began. The Berlin rabbi who visited the three in jail wondered at the sudden efficiency of the Rostock police, given their helplessness in August (see above). He reported that the young men had been held in cells with seasoned criminals and had been advised to remove their *kippot*, so as not to "provoke" the other prisoners.

In the first week of November, the new president of the Central Council of Jews in Germany (Zentralrat der Juden in Deutschland), Ignatz Bubis, visited Rostock as a guest of the city. He criticized Rostock's racist riots in August and the arrest of the French Jewish protesters. During a press conference at city hall, Rostock city councillor Karl-Heinz Schmidt (CDU) asked: "Mr. Bubis, you are a German citizen of the Jewish faith. Your home is Israel. Is that right? What do you think of the daily violence between Palestinians and Israelis?" Bubis responded angrily: "In other words, you want to know what business I have here?" Bubis tried to clarify the difference between religious belief and citizenship, and said, "My home is in Frankfurt and Judaism is no nationality." He went on to say that remarks like Schmidt's encouraged right-wing extremist behavior. The next day Schmidt resigned his office under pressure, and Mayor Klaus Kilimann asked Jewish citizens for forgiveness. Shortly after this incident, the Middle German Broadcasting Company (MDR) canceled Bubis's appearance—scheduled for January 1993—but reinvited him after the cancellation was publicized.

The antiforeigner and anti-Semitic attacks of autumn 1992 included fires set at the sites of two former concentration camps. The so-called Jewish barrack in Sachsenhausen was torched in late September. The next day, hundreds of Jewish and non-Jewish demonstrators held a rally at Sachsenhausen to express their outrage. No German politicians appeared. A planned demonstration two weeks later, sponsored by the state parliaments of Berlin and Brandenburg, the Central Council of Jews in Germany, unions, and about 20 church-related groups, drew a disappointing 5,000 participants. Three weeks after the attack at Sachsenhausen, a fire was set at Ravensbrück. The news was withheld from the public for two and a half days.

Throughout the hot autumn, the president of the Central Council of Jews in Germany was everywhere. Bubis attended rallies against xenophobia and anti-Semitism, gave press interviews, and appeared on radio and television. He condemned the racist attacks; he urged all citizens to force the federal and local governments to protect victims and potential victims of violence in Germany; he spoke out strongly against changing Germany's asylum law; and he publicly urged that German citizenship be granted to all children born in Germany, regardless of their parents' origins.

Holocaust-Related Matters

This year saw the termination of two Nazi war-crimes trials in Germany. In January the regional superior court in Hannover announced that, after ten years, it would end the trial of 69-year-old former SS Corporal Heinrich Niemeyer. This had been one of the longest-running trials in the history of the Federal Republic. Niemeyer was accused of having shot Jewish prisoners during an evacuation march from Auschwitz in January 1945. The court claimed he was suffering from health problems that rendered him unable to stand trial.

In May the trial of SS Sergeant Josef Schwammberger, at the regional court in Stuttgart, ended after almost a year. The 80-year-old Schwammberger, an Austrian by birth, was convicted of 25 murders and of complicity in several hundred others and sentenced to life imprisonment. He was originally charged with 45 murders and complicity in 3,000 other deaths. Schwammberger admitted only that from 1941 to 1944 he was commander of the forced-labor camps Rozwadow and Przemysl in occupied Poland. Following the sentencing, protesters gathered outside the courthouse and called for Schwammberger's release.

The Central Office for the Prosecution of Nazi Crimes (in Ludwigsburg) announced in April that in the future there would "probably be no more big Nazi trials." Central Office officials explained that those who held high offices under the Nazis were now in their nineties and not fit to stand trial, and that the failing memory of older witnesses hampered prosecution efforts. Since May 8, 1945, 163 life sentences had been passed by West German courts on Nazi criminals. Twelve people were condemned to death but were saved when the death penalty was abolished in West Germany in 1949. By contrast, the German Democratic Republic had sentenced 12,900 Nazi criminals. Up to 75 percent of the sentences, however, were for less than ten years in prison, and many of those sentenced had fled to West Germany and were tried in absentia.

In March, 70-year-old State Parliamentary Deputy Gustav Just, a prominent Social Democrat in Brandenburg, admitted that during World War II he had voluntarily participated in the execution of Jews in Ukraine; he referred to the incident as "old hat." Just stepped down from state government after days of criticism and calls for his resignation by the CDU, FDP, and PDS and by Heinz Galinski, president of the Berlin Jewish Community and of the Central Council of Jews in Germany. This development marked a new phase in the politics of Germany's eastern states, where, previously, officials were forced out of office for Stasi (GDR state security) rather than Nazi involvement. The Central Council of Jews in Germany protested the fact that criminal investigation of Just's past was initiated but soon dropped.

Also in March, Chancellor Helmut Kohl welcomed Austrian president Kurt Waldheim to Munich for an "unofficial working visit." This trip, which broke the international isolation of Waldheim, was the Austrian president's first visit to Germany since he assumed office in 1986, though the two leaders had met in Austria. Waldheim came to Munich to accept an award from the conservative Peutinger Foundation and was a guest of Kohl and of Bavarian prime minister Max Streibl at a luncheon. The visit provoked bitter criticism from Jewish organizations, from the Israeli government, and from the press.

Chancellor Kohl's response to the reproaches was sharp: "I as chancellor decide on whom I meet here in Munich." He further charged that an emissary of the World Jewish Congress had "traveled to East Berlin in late 1989 and politicked against unification in a scandalous manner." This accusation was documented by papers from East Germany, but was denied by Maram Stern, the emissary involved. The Central Council of Jews in Germany said it knew nothing of Stern's GDR visit. Heinz Galinski said that Chancellor Kohl could meet with whom he wished, but the Jewish community could criticize him for it.

This year also saw new German legislation regarding compensation to categories of victims of Nazism that had not previously received reparations payments. In March, payments of DM 1,400 per month (DM 800 for widows and widowers of victims) were extended to victims of Nazism from the former East Germany. In November the German Ministry of Finance and the Conference on Jewish Material Claims Against Germany reached an agreement on compensation payments to Jews who were persecuted by the Nazi regime but who, as citizens of states in the former Eastern Bloc, had received little or no restitution. On the basis of a clause in the German unification treaty, the Bonn government earmarked DM 100 million ($63 million) for these payments, which were to be made between 1993 and 1999 to persons who had been incarcerated in concentration camps for at least 6 months or imprisoned or in hiding for at least 18 months.

In September three Jewish women, now in their seventies, filed a suit with the Bremen Regional Court seeking compensation for forced labor during World War II. The claimants demanded a nominal DM 15,000 ($10,000) each. If successful, the case could set a precedent for payments of millions of marks, since several thousand foreign forced laborers in Nazi Germany are still alive.

Incidents involving revisionist history of Nazi Germany centered this year around two right-wing personalities. In January the German Federal Archive in Koblenz announced that the purported memoirs of Adolf Eichmann, which British revisionist historian David Irving had recently presented to the public and to the archive as a new find, were "nothing new," but were from a 1980 book, *I, Adolf Eichmann*. In May Irving was fined DM 10,000 in Munich for having proclaimed in spring 1990 that there never were gas chambers. Irving had traveled to Germany that year to participate in a right-wing demonstration in Berlin, which was subsequently canceled by the authorities.

Over the summer, the right-wing publisher Alfred Detscher of Munich was convicted of incitement, of provoking racial hatred, of damaging the memory of the deceased, and of slander. The charges were based on articles and notices published by Detscher in 1991 denying the Holocaust. Detscher was fined DM 10,000 and sentenced to 12 months' probation.

Concern about the public rehabilitation of Nazis was raised by the announcement in July that a pilgrimage site and museum had been erected in honor of Arno Breker, a prominent Nazi sculptor who died in 1991 and whose works had been banned from German museums since 1945. The edifice was built in Nörvenick (North Rhine-Westphalia).

JEWISH COMMUNITY

Demography

The total number of Jews in Germany, including those not affiliated with the organized Jewish communities, was estimated to be well over 40,000.

On December 31, 1992, the total membership of Germany's organized Jewish communities was 37,498. This represented an increase of 3,806 over the figure for 1991, and it included 4,551 immigrants from abroad, most of whom had come from the former USSR during the previous few years. The distribution of this membership, including the number of immigrants, was as follows: Baden 1,675 (up 306 since 1991), including 335 immigrants; Bavaria 5,545 (down 68), 202 immigrants; Berlin 9,834 (up 440), 702 immigrants; Bremen 218 (up 54), 53 immigrants; Frankfurt 5,633 (up 311), 377 immigrants; Hamburg 1,691 (up 298), 297 immigrants; Hesse 2,167 (up 257), 222 immigrants; Cologne 1,626 (up 189), 230 immigrants; Lower Saxony 1,069 (up 297), 219 immigrants and 54 members of the new Jewish community in Oldenburg; North Rhine 4,107 (up 602), 643 immigrants; Saar 291 (up 68), 71 immigrants; Saxony-Thuringia (Dresden, Erfurt, Chemnitz, Leipzig) 287 (up 55), 70 immigrants; Saxony-Anhalt, Brandenburg, Mecklenburg-Vorpommern (Halle, Magdeburg, Potsdam) 152 (down 13), 50 immigrants; Westphalia 1,767 (up 610), 623 immigrants; and Württemberg 1,015 (up 336), 368 immigrants.

Soviet Jews

The Federal Administrative Office reported that, as of December 31, 1992, immigration documents had been issued to 47,015 Jews seeking to leave the former Soviet Union. The administrative office had no information on how many of these people actually entered Germany or what happened to them after their arrival. The Central Welfare Board of Jews in Germany confirmed that, as of October, 12,000–15,000 Jews from the former USSR had immigrated to Germany, but not all of them were registered as members of a Jewish community. For example, 73 immigrants were sent to the city of Reutlingen, which had no Jewish community. The Welfare Board made an effort to settle as many of the immigrants as possible in the eastern states, to strengthen and rejuvenate the small Jewish population of what had been East Germany. The immigrants, however, tended to leave the eastern states and head west. The economic situation in the eastern states was generally precarious, and the seven small Jewish communities in the east had few resources for integrating the newcomers. In eastern Berlin, for example, over the year, 190 Soviet immigrants arrived, while 166 left, resulting in a net gain of 24.

The Jewish communities struggled with the problems posed by the dimensions of the immigration, such as finding the new arrivals apartments and jobs. Also, although the Soviets were supposed to apply for immigration papers before leaving for Germany, many were still arriving with three-month tourist visas. Regularizing these people's status entailed prolonged struggles with German bureaucracies. In several places, the arrival of Soviet Jews literally doubled the size of the Jewish population, creating an urgent need for larger religious and communal facilities.

In April the federal government announced that Jews arriving from the former Soviet Union would have a status similar to that of *Kontingentflüchtlinge* (quota refugees), but would have to retain their previous passports instead of being issued new international passports. This decision was based on objections from the CIS that, since the Soviet Union had signed the Geneva Convention, its citizens could not be considered refugees. By December, after much political and bureaucratic wrangling, all the Soviet Jewish immigrants in Germany had obtained full *Kontingentflüchtling* status.

Communal Affairs

The death on July 19 of Heinz Galinski, president of both the Berlin Jewish community and the Central Council of Jews in Germany, marked a major turning point in the history of postwar German Jewry. Galinski was born in 1912 in West Prussia and came to Berlin in 1938. An Auschwitz survivor, Galinski had led the Berlin Jewish community since 1949. (From 1953 to 1991 he headed the West Berlin community; East Berlin maintained a separate Jewish community.) He became president of the Central Council of Jews in Germany in 1988.

When Galinski took on the Berlin post, that Jewish community was considered— and considered itself—a *Liquidationsgemeinde* (a community in liquidation). Under Galinski, however, it became a solid and expanding institution; by 1992 it numbered almost 9,000 members—by far the largest Jewish community in Germany. Galinski built a community of Jews of heterogeneous backgrounds and political orientations—most of them nonreligious Jews—on the basis of an extensive infrastructure of social services. Within the community, Galinski was criticized as an autocrat, and it was no secret that, during his time in office, at least 11 rabbis came and left, following confrontations with him. Most Jewish intellectuals in Berlin kept their distance from the Jewish community. To non-Jewish Germans, Galinski served as a living and voluble reminder of the German Holocaust and of the Federal Republic's obligations to its Jewish communities. German politicians hated Galinski but were forced to take him seriously and to bestow considerable privileges and public funds on the Federal Republic's small Jewish population.

Galinski's funeral was attended by 1,000 mourners, including Chancellor Helmut Kohl, President Richard von Weizsäcker, President of the German Parliament Rita Süssmuth, Mayor of Berlin Eberhard Diepgen, President of the state of Brandenburg Manfred Stolpe, President of the state of Thuringia Bernard Vogel, former mayors of West Berlin Klaus Schütz and Hans-Jochen Vogel, President of the Berlin House of Representatives Hanna-Renate Laurien, and Israeli ambassador Benjamin Navon. At a memorial service for Galinski in late November, Rita Süssmuth appealed to Jews not to leave Germany, despite the increase in anti-Semitic violence. Two days earlier, a plaque was unveiled at the house where Galinski had lived until his deportation in February 1943.

Galinski's successor as president of the Central Council of Jews in Germany, Ignatz Bubis, had been president of the Frankfurt Jewish community for several years. Born in 1927 in what is today Poland, Bubis survived the Nazi years in a forced labor camp. After the liberation, he came to Germany, where he became a wealthy entrepreneur, specializing in real estate. He became active in Jewish organizations in Germany in the 1960s. Unlike his predecessor, who kept a discreet distance from party politics, Bubis was an active member of the Free Democratic party in Hesse. Where Galinski identified himself as a "Jew in Germany," Bubis called himself a "German citizen of the Jewish faith." Although among Jews Bubis was often accused of being too friendly to German politicians, he was very popular with the non-Jewish public. A charismatic speaker, he was constantly invited to participate in public events and television talk shows.

Jerzy Kanal, the new president of the Berlin Jewish community, born in 1921, is a Polish Holocaust survivor. He came to Berlin in 1953 and had been a member of the community's council of representatives for three decades.

In October the Berlin Jewish community opened a Jewish elementary school in the eastern part of the city, in a building which in the prewar period had housed a Jewish boys' school. In December the cornerstone was laid for a new building for the Jewish elementary school that had opened in 1986 in West Berlin. The school was renamed the Heinz Galinski School. The Berlin Jewish community also announced plans to open a Jewish high school as soon as possible.

The Central Welfare Board of Jews in Germany (Zentralwohlfahrstelle der Juden in Deutschland) celebrated its 75th anniversary in 1992. Closed down by the Nazis, the board reopened in 1951 to provide for the needs of Holocaust survivors in Germany. As the Jews of the Federal Republic became stabilized and prosperous, the board eventually outlived its usefulness. In 1990, though, it was reactivated to integrate the thousands of Jews who began to arrive in Germany from the former USSR. By 1992 it had 50 permanent employees.

Members of the Dresden Jewish community—which doubled in size this year due to Soviet immigration—expressed resentment over the fact that all formerly Jewish properties in Dresden were being handed over to the Jewish Claims Conference. The community faced considerable financial difficulties, which rental income from some of these properties could alleviate.

The Halle Jewish community—with 25 members, the smallest Jewish community in Germany—marked its 300th anniversary in 1992. The celebrations, opened by Prime Minister of Saxony-Anhalt Werner Münch, included lectures, discussions, concerts, special theater performances, prayer services, and a parade through the city. A volume documenting the history of the Jews in Halle was issued for the occasion.

Two new Jewish communities were established in 1992. In May the city of Baden-Baden rededicated its newly renovated synagogue. The restoration work had been subsidized by the city administration, the German-Israeli Society, and the Council of Jews in Baden. The renovated building was to be used for prayer services and cultural events. Once the renovations were completed, a founding meeting was held to establish a permanent Jewish community. In Oldenburg, a new Jewish community was organized with 40 founding members. There had been a postwar Jewish community in Oldenburg, but most of its members died and the community was dissolved in the 1960s. In recent years, the opening of a new university in Oldenburg and the immigration of Jews from the former Soviet Union brought a new population of Jews to the area. Oldenburg's city council promised the new Jewish community a synagogue, to be restored and ready for use in 1995.

In February a delegation of 60 leaders of the American Jewish Committee visited Germany for four days. In Bonn, the Americans met with Chancellor Helmut Kohl and expressed concern over increasing right-wing radicalism in Germany. In Berlin, in a meeting with Heinz Galinski, the delegation promised to help find rabbis and Hebrew teachers for the Jewish communities in the new states.

In February Chancellor Kohl spoke with Galinski regarding the situation of Jews in the former Soviet Union and promised food packages for the CIS Jewish communities. In March a delegation of the U.S. Conference of Presidents of Major Jewish Organizations visited Berlin as guests of the Konrad Adenauer Foundation. The presidents met with representatives of Germany's Foreign Ministry, with bankers, with Berlin mayor Eberhard Diepgen, with Berlin's immigration commissioner Barbara John, and with Galinski.

In April Galinski visited Poland as a guest of Polish president Lech Walesa, meeting with representatives of the government and with leaders of the Jewish community. He laid a wreath at the Warsaw Ghetto monument and visited Auschwitz, where he had been an inmate.

Community Relations

The tensions and contradictions—old and new—in the situation of Jews living in the postunification Federal Republic were highlighted by several incidents this year.

One involved a controversy over the building of a shopping center on the site of a former Jewish cemetery in the neighborhood of Ottensen in Hamburg. The cemetery, which dates from 1663, was in use until it was confiscated by the Nazis in 1934 and destroyed. After the war, the land, then unrecognizable as a cemetery, was returned to Hamburg's Jewish community. In 1950, the trustee agency Jewish Trust Corporation sold the land to a builder who resold the property in 1988. The current owner's plans to construct a large shopping center on the site angered some residents of Ottensen—a poor area with a large immigrant population. The shopping mall was publicly opposed by some members of the Greens on the grounds that it would drive up rents and benefit mostly real-estate speculators.

When it was discovered in the spring that the site had once been a Jewish cemetery, the Greens alerted Athra Kadisha, a Jerusalem-based Orthodox group that works to preserve holy places. Athra Kadisha, in turn, mobilized Orthodox Jews from several countries to protest at the site. By early May, hundreds of Orthodox Jews from England, Israel, Belgium, and Canada were protesting outside Chancellor Kohl's office in Bonn, as well. On May 21, Hamburg's police headquarters advised local police stations to immediately report any information regarding the arrival or sojourn of Orthodox Jews in Hamburg. After weeks of demonstrations, confrontations, suggestions, and counter suggestions, at the end of May Chief Rabbi of Jerusalem Itzhak Kolitz came to Hamburg to inspect the site. He agreed to the construction, but "with a heavy heart." He stipulated, however, that the bones in the earth not be removed to another cemetery: hence, no digging could proceed on a large part of the building site.

In Berlin, conflict continued regarding the legal status of the maverick, self-designated Orthodox Jewish community Adass Jisroel. This congregation, located in the eastern part of Berlin and represented by the Offenberg family, was recognized by the GDR government in 1989 as the successor to the Jewish community of the same name that was dissolved by the Nazis in 1939. This recognition brought Adass corporate status and five valuable pieces of real estate. However, Adass Jisroel was never recognized by the Central Council of Jews in Germany or by the Jewish Claims Conference, which also laid claim to the five properties. In October the Berlin Senate announced that it would not recognize Adass Jisroel as successor to the prewar Orthodox community and would revoke its corporate status, but would not try to recover the real estate. The Offenberg family contested this decision in administrative court. Fearful of a scandal, the court put off making any legal judgment. For the time being, the Senate promised Adass Jisroel DM 110,000 to modernize its heating system and provide a paid employee for its cemetery.

Another confrontation in Berlin involved the renaming of streets in the district of Wilmersdorf. The local SPD suggested restoring the pre-Nazi names of three streets named for resident Jewish families—Morgenroth, Friedenthal, and Duncker. Many local residents, however, opposed the renaming and engaged a lawyer to represent them. When historian Götz Aly defended the renaming at a neighborhood meeting, referring to the murder of European Jewry, a local resident shouted: "We should be able to discuss street signs without having Auschwitz rubbed under our noses!"

A sharp contrast in spirit was shown by an anonymous female politician on Berlin's Alternative List (the Berlin equivalent of the Greens party) who turned over her inheritance—which was based on "Aryanized" Jewish property confiscated in the 1930s—to a new foundation helping Jewish women to study in Berlin.

In Frankfurt, at the Börneplatz, the Museum Judengasse (Jew Alley Museum) opened in November, as a branch of the Frankfurt Jewish Museum. Museum Judengasse comprises 500 square meters in the basement of the postmodern high-rise erected over the remains of what had been Frankfurt's Jewish quarter in the Middle Ages. The new structure had been built despite vehement protest from Frankfurt's Jews. (See AJYB 1989, pp. 344–45.) Worked into the concrete of the structure are reconstructions of the foundations of five of the Judengasse's 19 houses. The museum's first exhibit, "Stages of Forgetting," included video clips of Jewish demonstrators being carried from the construction site by German police in 1987.

Another area of tension was the fate of former synagogues. In Ingolstadt, a former synagogue was destroyed without the permission of the local authorities when the building was converted first to a pinball casino and then to a café. After protests from the local Jewish community, the authorities fined those responsible DM 100,000 and promised the community that the original structure would be restored. In March the Central Council of Jews in Germany complained that in Hesse the CDU was opposing the restoration of former synagogues, even in cases where agreement to renovate already existed. Further, it accused the CDU of giving the impression that the restoration of synagogues competed with other public projects.

In December the Central Council of Jews in Germany protested the demolition of a former synagogue in Malchow (Mecklenburg-Vorpommern). The owner of the building had been given permission to demolish the structure, which he described as a "storage shed," though it covered an area of 300 square meters. When the local authorities claimed they had no idea that the building was a former synagogue, the Central Council countered that it had filed papers to reclaim the structure in 1991.

Jewish-Christian Relations

The Lutheran Church's network of Societies for Christian-Jewish Cooperation continued its work, but at a low level of activity. The proliferation of new Jewish cultural organizations—many of them quite dynamic—had led to a situation where some communities now had several groups organizing conferences, exhibits, lectures, and the like, with Jewish content, though not necessarily in a religious framework.

In January the Rhine state synod of the Lutheran Church released a declaration acknowledging that, during the Nazi years, Lutherans had not assisted Jews and had not stood by Christians of Jewish descent. Also in January, the Lutheran Academy at Arnoldshain held a conference on "Awareness of the Holocaust in Postwar Germany." In February the Siegen Society for Christian-Jewish Cooperation organized a seminar on "The Arab-Israeli Conflict After the Gulf War," with Kalmon Yaron and Mahmoud Abu-Bahr (an editor with Israeli national television), both of the Martin Buber Institute of Israel, as guest speakers.

Authorities in the Bavarian town of Deggendorf announced in May that the annual pilgrimage to Gnad, a church built in 1360, would be abolished. The history of the pilgrimage goes back to a supposed desecration of the host and other alleged sacrilegious acts by Deggendorf Jews in the 14th century. The vice-general of Regensburg, Wilhelm Gegenfurter, said this was "the only consequence possible" after recent research revealed that the Jews of Deggendorf were not guilty of any of the crimes of which they were accused, including ritual murders of children. The pilgrimage would be replaced by a "Week of Faith," and a memorial stone would be erected for the murdered Jews.

The Düsseldorf Society for Christian-Jewish Cooperation helped with settling in Soviet Jewish immigrants. It organized a weekly meeting and a German-language course for 30 adults (of whom only one had a job). In September the Rhine-Neckar

Society for Christian-Jewish Cooperation organized a pilgrimage to Gurs, to commemorate the deportation of Jews from Baden-Palatinate to France. In December, against the background of increasing anti-Semitism and violence against foreigners in Germany, the Cologne Society for Christian-Jewish Cooperation held a conference—"Abraham Unites, Abraham Divides"—about relations between Christians, Muslims, and Jews. And the synod of the Lutheran Church of Brandenburg-Berlin condemned the "re-emerging hatred of Jews" and called on Christians to stand by their Jewish fellow citizens and help them build their community. For the first time, an effort was made to insert a reference to the "ongoing chosenness of Jews" as God's people into the synod's new (postunification) constitution.

Culture

As in previous years, a staggering number of cultural events with Jewish themes took place in Germany in 1992; many of these events were organized by and/or for non-Jewish Germans. Germany's three largest Jewish communities—Berlin, Frankfurt, and Munich—all held major Jewish cultural festivals. In addition, cities, towns, and communities throughout the Federal Republic organized exhibits, concerts, conferences, and lectures on Jewish themes. A festival of Yiddish song and *klezmer* music took place in Fürth in March. In August, a *klezmer* group, the Klezmorim, was founded in Quedlinburg, a small community in the Harz Mountains with no Jewish inhabitants.

In November, after years of struggle to secure financing from the Berlin senate, the cornerstone was laid for a new Jewish museum in Berlin. The estimated cost was DM 120 million. Construction was to begin in 1993 and be completed in 1996; the museum is scheduled to open in 1998.

In January the Moses Mendelssohn Center for European Jewish Studies opened at the University of Potsdam, with Julius Schoeps as director. The center seeks to promote interdisciplinary work among scholars of religion, literature, the social sciences, and history. In May a Research Office for German Jewish Contemporary History was established, to be located at the German Army University in Neubiberg. Headed by Michael Wolffsohn, it will focus on German Jewish history after 1945.

Dresden acquired two new institutions of Jewish interest. The Hannah Arendt Institute for the Study of Totalitarianism opened in November, its purpose to study the social and political structure of Nazi Germany and the GDR and their influence on the Federal Republic. And Hatikva, a place of learning and meeting, offered Dresdeners their first opportunity to participate in cultural and educational events on Jewish themes outside the framework of religious institutions. In August a European Center for Jewish Music was founded in Hannover. It will be financed by the state of Lower Saxony and linked to Hannover's College of Music and Theater.

A major controversy erupted in January when the commission that selects the

German film to be an Oscar nominee decided not to nominate *Europa, Europa* (German title: *Hitlerjunge Salomon*). *Europa, Europa* was voted the best foreign film of 1991 by the U.S. National Board of Review, and it won the Hollywood Foreign Press Association's Golden Globe Award. The film tells the story of a Jewish youth adrift in Europe during World War II, who is enrolled at an elite school for Hitler Youth and falls in love with a blond German girl. Several prominent German filmmakers and actors—including Volker Schlöndorff, Michael Verhoeven, Margarethe von Trotta, Werner Herzog, Hanna Schygulla, and Armin Mueller-Stahl—signed an open letter supporting the film, but clearly many Germans were made uncomfortable by it.

Of the hundreds of exhibits with Jewish content shown in Germany this year, the following were among the most noteworthy. "Patterns of Jewish Life," which opened in Berlin in January, was several years in preparation and cost DM 10 million ($6.3 million). Encompassing 2,000 objects, it documented the everyday life, work, and beliefs of Jews from antiquity to the present. Among many events offered in connection with the exhibit were a conference on German Jewish women in the 19th and 20th centuries; several film series, including Yiddish films, Israeli films about Holocaust survivors and their children, documentary films about the Holocaust, and pre-World War II films from the Soviet Union; and readings by contemporary German Jewish writers Jurek Becker and Irene Dische. Altogether, 350,000 people saw the exhibit, and 115,000 attended the related programs.

Another particularly interesting exhibit, at the Berlin Academy of Art, documented the history of the Jüdische Kulturbund, the cultural organization that Jewish artists in Berlin were forced to form by the Nazis. The exhibit was prepared by Henryk Broder and Eike Geisel. "Degenerate Art: The Fate of the Avant-garde in Nazi Germany," an exhibit mounted by the Los Angeles County Museum of Art, was shown in Berlin in March. And "Jewish Life in Eastern Europe," an exhibit of photos by Edward Serotta, opened at America House in December.

A major conference on anti-Semitism in Europe was organized in Berlin in September by the Center for the Study of Anti-Semitism (an institute of Berlin's Technical University), in cooperation with the Jerusalem Center for the Study of Anti-Semitism and the London Institute of Jewish Affairs. Three hundred people participated.

Holocaust Commemoration

Many individuals and institutions throughout Germany took part in remembering the Jewish victims of Nazism, and considerable public resources were committed to these commemorations. In November the Bonn government announced that it would contribute DM 10 million ($6 million) in the years 1992–96 toward restoration work at Auschwitz (the total cost of the project is DM 70 million). The first 2.5 million marks would be paid in 1993. The Norddeutsche Rundfunk (NDR, North German Broadcasting Company) collected DM 400,000 for the Auschwitz project through a radio campaign. Employees at NDR were shocked, however, by the angry reactions of many listeners. Three out of four telephone calls responding to the campaign were negative, and the announcers received several threatening calls and letters.

In January a Holocaust "learning and memorial center" was opened at the Wannsee Villa, the house in the suburbs of Berlin where the decision to carry out the Final Solution was made in January 1942. The center is supported by the Ministry of the Interior, the city of Berlin, and the Central Council of Jews in Germany. The opening ceremony was attended by Chancellor Kohl, President of the German Parliament Süssmuth, and Simon Wiesenthal.

Controversy surrounded the erection of new Holocaust monuments and the reorganization of existing memorials in former East Germany, because they raised questions about the identities and relative importance of the perpetrators and victims of recent German history. For example, the concentration camps Buchenwald and Sachsenhausen were the sites of mass liquidations by the Nazis in the years 1937–45. But from 1945 to 1950 they were used by the Soviet occupation forces as internment camps for opponents of Stalinism, including many former Nazis. (56,000 people perished in Buchenwald from 1937 to 1945, and another 10,000 from 1945 to 1950; in Sachsenhausen, 100,000 were murdered during the Nazi years and another 13,000–30,000 died during internment by the Soviets.) The question as to whether the two groups of "victims" should be remembered together or separately aroused considerable public debate.

In the case of Buchenwald, a committee of experts decided in favor of two separate memorials. The committee also announced that a plaque would be placed at the exhibit on the camp's Nazi history to commemorate Buchenwald's Jewish victims. (Until 1992 there was only a plaque to remember those Jews brought to Buchenwald in November 1938, in the aftermath of *Kristallnacht*.) In May, on the 47th anniversary of the liberation of the Ravensbrück concentration camp, a room was dedicated to the Jewish women who perished there. In the GDR years, rooms had been dedicated to the Czech and Polish victims, but, since the Jews were not recognized as a nationality, no room had been dedicated to them.

Another variant of the public debate about memorials was the conflict over the planned Berlin monument to the Jewish victims of Nazism. In 1988 a Berlin citizens' initiative, sparked by television personality Lea Rosh, proposed this monument, to be erected in the center of the city, near Hitler's bunker. The Central Council of Sinti and Roma (Gypsies) then demanded that, as victims of Nazi racism, they also should be included in the monument. This demand was opposed by the citizens' initiative and by the Berlin Jewish community. After much wrangling at the local level, the issue was resolved in Bonn. In July the federal government announced that the Berlin monument would commemorate only the Jewish victims, and that a separate memorial would be put up for the Gypsies.

November 9 (*Kristallnacht*) was widely observed throughout Germany, but this year the commemoration took a new turn. Evidently because of the great success of November 9 rallies in previous years—especially 1991 in Berlin, Cologne, and other large cities—some top politicians decided to put themselves at the helm of a similar demonstration in 1992. This rally, dubbed the *Grossdemonstration*, was under the patronage of President von Weizsäcker; announcements of the event appealed to citizens to individually oppose hatred and violence on the anniversary of "the night in which what began with burning synagogues ended with extermination camps and a world war."

Unlike previous years, in which commemorative events often included a march to a Holocaust site, this year's demonstration in Berlin began in West Berlin at the Wittenbergplatz and Gedächtniskirche (Memorial Church) and in East Berlin at the Gethsemanekirche (Gethsemane Church, the principal center of the East German dissident movement in the late 1980s). The marchers from these German and Christian sites met at the Lustgarten Square in the historic center of Berlin.

The CDU, SPD, and FDP politicians involved clearly hoped that the mere act of appearing prominently in a mass rally of this sort, with over 300,000 participants, would serve to advertise to the international community—and also to the German right—official German concern about Rostock. A substantial number of participants, however, regarded this as insincere political propaganda and resented the usurpation of the event by mainstream politicians. Speakers were loudly denounced as "hypocrites," and about 100 young radicals engaged in violence and egg throwing. Ignatz Bubis, president of the Central Council of Jews in Germany, was present at the demonstration but was not an official speaker. He addressed the rally, however, after it had been disrupted and was officially declared to have ended, saying: "I am ashamed for what happened here; we are not in the year 1938, but in 1992."

Beside the citywide commemorations, several Berlin districts put up plaques and monuments to former Jewish inhabitants. The Berlin Museum for Transportation and Technology organized an exhibit on the role of the railroad in the Final Solution, and an exhibit was mounted in honor of Raoul Wallenberg.

As in former years, several German school groups visited Poland—including the concentration camps and former Jewish ghettos. In some cases, German and Israeli school groups visited Poland together. Many German cities and communities invited their former Jewish inhabitants currently living abroad to return for a visit, free of charge. And throughout Germany, communities continued to erect Holocaust monuments, put up plaques, and organize vigils and silent marches to remember their former Jewish "fellow citizens."

Publications

As in previous years, over 150 books on Jewish subjects were published in Germany in 1992. At least half were written by non-Jews. The major genres included biographies of noteworthy German Jews; histories and documentations of destroyed Jewish communities in Germany—photo essays about Jewish cemeteries were a favorite; books about anti-Semitism and the Holocaust, including autobiographies and interviews with Holocaust survivors; religious teachings; novels about Jews (often translated from other languages); histories of Jews in Germany; and studies of Jewish identity.

Among the most important new publications of Jewish interest were *Neues Lexicon des Judentums* (New Encyclopedia of Judaism), edited by Julius H. Schoeps; *Juden in Westdeutschland. Selbstbild und Fremdbild einer Minorität* (Jews in West Germany: The Self-Image and Alien Image of a Minority) by Alphons Silbermann and Herbert Sallen; *Zwischentöne: Jüdische Frauenstimmen aus Israel* (Nuances: Voices of Jewish Women from Israel) by Silke Mertins; and three important testimonials of Jewish Holocaust survivors: *Ich war Hitlerjunge Salomon* (I Was Hitler Youth Solomon) by Sally Perel; *Im Haus des Henkers* (In the Hangman's House), interviews with Holocaust survivors in East and West Germany, by Susan Heenen-Wolff; and *Unbequem . . . Mein Leben nach dem Überleben* (Uncomfortable . . . My Life After Survival) by Inge Deutschkron. Three significant contributions to the literature on émigré Jewish intellectuals were: *Über Juden in Deutschland* (About Jews in Germany) by Gert Mattenklott; *Einige werden bleiben. Und mit ihnen das Vermächtnis* (Some Will Remain, and with Them, the Heritage), edited by Ortwin Breisbart and Ulf Abraham; and *Der Teufel in Frankreich. Erlebnisse. Tagebuch 1940. Briefe* (The Devil in France: Experiences; Diary 1940; Letters) by Lion Feuchtwanger. Also, a photo essay, *Jüdisches Leben im Osten Europas nach dem Holocaust* (Jewish Life in Eastern Europe After the Holocaust) by Edward Serotta (U.S. title: *Out of the Shadows: A Photographic Portrait of Jewish Life in Central Europe Since the Holocaust*).

Among new works of fiction were *Engel sind schwarz und weiss* (Angels Are Black and White) by Ulla Berkewicz; *Gebürtig* (Born) by Robert Schindel; *Der Tod des Akrobaten. Erzählungen* (The Death of the Acrobat. Short Stories) by Hans Sahl; *Glatte Bauchlandung* (Smooth Bellyflop) by Zwika Lipowitz; *Nicht von jetzt, nicht von hier. Roman* (Not from Now, Not from Here) by Yehuda Amichai (translated from the Hebrew by Ruth Achlama); *Der Dritte Zustand. Roman* (The Third State of Being) by Amos Oz (translated by Ruth Achlama); and *Die Frau im Kaftan. Lebensbericht einer Schauspielerin* (The Woman in the Caftan: A Report on the Life of an Actress), an autobiographical novel by Ruth Klinger (edited and with an introduction by Ludger Heid). An interesting volume of Israeli poetry, translated from the Hebrew, was *Arbeiten auf Papier: Gedichte* (Works on Paper: Poetry) by Ascher Reich. Also of note was *Literatur aus dem jüdischen Osteuropa heute* (Literature from Jewish Eastern Europe Today), a special issue of the German literary journal *Sirene, Zeitschrift für Literatur*, edited by Peter Ambros.

Significant works on the history of Jews in Germany included *Bild und Selbstbild der Berliner Juden zwischen Aufklärung und Romantik* (The Image and Self-Image of Berlin Jews Between the Enlightenment and Romanticism), edited by Marianne Awerbuch and Steffi Jersch-Wenzel; *300 Jahre Juden in Halle. Leben. Leistung. Leiden. Lohn* (300 Years of Jews in Halle: Life, Accomplishments, Suffering, Reward) by the Jewish Community of Halle; *Unternehmen Bernard* (Enterprise Bernard) by Adolf Burger; *Aufbau nach dem Untergang* (Reconstruction After the Downfall), a festschrift for Heinz Galinski, edited by Andreas Nachama and Julius H. Schoeps; *Erinnerungen deutsch-jüdischer Frauen 1900–1990* (Memories of German Jewish Women 1900–1990), edited by Andreas Lixl-Purcell; *Ravensbrücker Ballade oder Faschismus Bewältigung in der DDR* (Ravensbrück Ballads, or Working Through Fascism in the GDR), edited by Klaus Jarmatz; *Haus Deutschland oder die Geschichte eines ungesühnten Mordes* (House Germany, or the History of an Unatoned-for Murder) by Peter Finkelgruen; and *Nachtgedanken über Deutschland* (Night Thoughts About Germany) by Chaim Noll.

Personalia

The Bundesverdienstkreuz (the Federal Cross of Merit) was awarded to four German Jews in 1992: Ignatz Bubis, president of the Frankfurt Jewish Community and of the Central Council of Jews in Germany; Alisa Fuss, president of the International League of Human Rights, Berlin; Maria Brauner, of the Council of Representatives of the Berlin Jewish community; and Anna Pultuskier, president of the Women's Zionist Organization of Munich. The Warburg Prize of the Atlantic Bridge for German-American Understanding went to former U.S. secretary of state Henry Kissinger; Simon Wiesenthal won the Otto Hahn Peace Medal of the state of Berlin United Nations Association; and Rabbi Henry G. Brandt, state rabbi of Lower Saxony, received the Hedwig Burgheim Medal of the city of Giessen for his work in promoting understanding between Christians and Jews.

Various Jewish writers and artists won German prizes in 1992. Tel Aviv filmmaker Gil Alkabetz was awarded the German short film prize for his production *Swamp-Sumpf,* which he made while studying at the Art Academy of Stuttgart. Poet Hilde Domin won the Friedrich Hölderlin Literature Prize of the city of Bad Homburg. Two eastern German novelists won prizes: Stefan Heym received the Chemnitzer Ernst Art and Culture Prize of the city of Chemnitz, for his artistic work and his courageous bearing; and Barbara Honigmann (now living in France) was awarded the Stefan-Andres Prize of the city of Schweich on the Mosel. On November 8 (the eve of *Kristallnacht*), the French filmmaker Marcel Ophuls won the Peter Weiss Prize of the city of Bochum, for his ability "to bring to life the torments of yesterday and the imponderables of today." Ophuls also won the Culture Prize of the state of Hesse. The Peace Prize of the German Book Trade Association went to Israeli writer Amos Oz. George Tabori received the Büchner Prize, and Günther Anders won the Sigmund Freud Prize of the German Academy of Language and Literature in Darmstadt. Joshua (Yehoshua) Sobol was awarded the Bremen Nobel Prize for his Bremen production of *Ghetto.*

The Jewish community of Düsseldorf awarded its Josef-Neuberger Medal to Herbert Schnoor, minister of the interior of North Rhine-Westphalia, for his efforts on behalf of Jewish immigrants from the former Soviet Union. The Leo Baeck Prize of the Central Council of Jews in Germany went to the Norddeutsche Rundfunk

(North German Radio) for its broadcast *Auschwitz verfällt* (Auschwitz Is Decaying) and its connected fund-raising campaign, which collected DM 400,000 for repairs. In Munich, the Geschwister Scholl Prize was awarded for the volume *Dachauer Hefte, Studien und Dokumente zur Geschichte der nationalsozialistischen Konzentrationslager* (Dachau Volumes: Studies and Documents Concerning the History of the National Socialist Concentration Camps), which was commissioned by the International Dachau Committee and published by Barbara Distel and Wolfgang Benz. The DM 20,000 award was donated to Holocaust survivors. Charlotte Schiffler won the Moses Mendelssohn Prize of the city of Berlin for her role in the establishment of Neve Shalom, the cooperative village of Jews and Palestinians in Israel.

The death of Heinz Galinski, president of the Berlin Jewish community and of the Central Council of Jews in Germany, at age 79, represented a major loss for German Jewry (see above). Three other important figures in Jewish life in Germany died in 1992. Kurt May, the restitution expert, died at age 95. Director of the legal aid department of the Jewish Restitution Successor Organization (JRSO), in 1955 he took over the direction of the United Restitution Organization with its headquarters in Frankfurt. Jürgen Landeck, publicist, translator, and for many years director of the library of the Berlin Jewish community, died in Berlin at age 69. And Helmut Eschwege, the expert on Jewish history in the territory of the former East Germany, died in Dresden at age 79. Eschwege wrote and, after years of struggle, succeeded in publishing *Kennzeichen J* (Identification J) in 1966, one of the first documentations of Nazi crimes against the Jews to appear in the GDR. His other major works include *Die Synagoge in der deutschen Geschichte* (The Synagogue in German History) and *Selbstbehauptung und Widerstand. Deutsche Juden im Kampf um Existenz und Menschenwürde* (Self-Assertion and Resistance: German Jews in Their Struggle for Survival and Human Dignity), with Konrad Kwiet, published in Hamburg (West Germany) in 1984.

ROBIN OSTOW

Austria

National Affairs

THE PRESIDENTIAL ELECTION dominated Austrian politics in 1992. Much to the relief of most Austrians, President Kurt Waldheim announced that he would not seek a second term. Waldheim's candidacy in 1986 became embroiled in controversy following revelations about his Nazi past, as a result of which he could not fully discharge the largely ceremonial functions of his office. One such function, that of carrying out state visits, was largely denied him by European governments which refused to invite him. The United States placed him on a "watch list," thereby barring him from the country.

In the first-round election for president, the candidate of the Socialist party, Rudolf Streicher, won 40.7 percent of the vote; his conservative People's party opponent, Thomas Klestil, received 37.2 percent; and the candidate of the far-right Freedom party, Mrs. Heide Schmidt, garnered 17 percent. In the runoff, Klestil emerged victorious, with 56.8 percent of the vote to 42.2 percent for Streicher. What proved decisive for Klestil was the decision of the leader of the Freedom party, Jorg Haider, to signal support for him. During the election campaign, Klestil made Waldheim's international isolation into an issue. And while distancing himself from right-wing extremists, the People's party candidate was careful not to criticize them.

The election of Klestil, a career diplomat, removed the cloud that hung over the presidency. The new Austrian president was now welcomed in European capitals, and the strained relations that had developed between Vienna and Jerusalem following Waldheim's election were normalized.

The Freedom party gained in a number of local and provincial elections. The party, a nesting ground for many old-time Nazis and their sympathizers, sought to stir up latent xenophobic tendencies by railing against foreigners and calling for severe restrictions against them. Apologists for Nazis were also in evidence in the People's party. Two of its leaders accepted invitations to speak to a group of veterans of Hitler's SS, known as "Kameradschaft IV," which was under government investigation for violating laws against Nazi revivalism.

While not a few Austrians attributed the rise of intolerance to Jorg Haider's politics and actions, they noted that these also had the effect of provoking more public discussion about the country's Nazi past. Significant in this regard was the statement made by Chancellor Franz Vranitzky before Parliament in July 1991, which acknowledged for the first time that while many Austrians were victims of Nazi crimes during World War II, just as many were perpetrators of evil deeds. "We must not forget," he stated, "that there were not a few Austrians who in the name of this regime brought suffering to others, who took part in the persecutions and crimes. We own up to all facts of our history and to the deeds of all parts of our people. As we take credit for the good, we must apologize for the evil." The chancellor pledged restitution for suffering to those whose claims had not been met. However, no meaningful action was taken by the government to redeem this pledge.

In the economic sphere, Austria, a member of the six-nation European Free Trade Association (EFTA), continued negotiations with the European Community to win entry into that group. It was generally acknowledged that Austria would be among the first of the several applicants to gain admission.

For most of the year, Austria's economy was the envy of other European countries, defying the entrenched or deepening recessionary trends elsewhere. Starting in September, the economy began to experience serious difficulties, largely due to the slumping German economy, which accounted for nearly 40 percent of Austrian exports. As the economy contracted, unemployment reached 7 percent, a level not seen since the 1950s.

The disintegration of neighboring Yugoslavia had direct and immediate consequences for Austria. Following Germany's lead, Austria initially gave strong support to Slovenian independence, which the European Community reluctantly acquiesced in. Austria's move led to a strain in relations with the United States, which feared that this would encourage separatism and the breakup of Yugoslavia. The Slovenian issue also turned into a thinly veiled confrontation between the two government coalition partners, the Socialist party and its junior partner, the conservative People's party. Members of the latter, led by Foreign Minister Alois Mock, competed with one another in expressions of enthusiasm for the secessionist province that was once part of the Habsburg Empire. Socialist chancellor Franz Vranitzky was more circumspect about recognizing Slovenia, fearful that the disintegration of Yugoslavia could bring about unforeseen dangers. As the conflict in Bosnia intensified, and the unspeakable acts of "ethnic cleansing" carried out by the Bosnian Serb militias against the Muslims spread, a refugee problem of enormous proportions was created.

Immigration

Following the collapse of the Soviet Union and the outbreak of war in the former Yugoslavia, Austria absorbed large numbers of immigrants and refugees. From the fall of 1991 until the end of 1992 it received approximately 100,000 immigrants, some 60,000 from Bosnia alone. There was, in addition, an influx of about 70,000 Croats fleeing the war with the breakaway nationalist Serbs in the region of Krajina. The influx of large numbers of immigrants from Eastern Europe and of refugees fleeing the war in Bosnia did not, as was feared, lead to an upsurge of xenophobia such as happened in Germany. Still, there was concern that the growing number of refugees from the Balkans, coupled with the worsening economic situation, could intensify growing xenophobic trends.

The extreme right-wing Freedom party attempted to capitalize on latent antiforeigner sentiment for political purposes, following the example of right-wing parties in Germany, France, Belgium, and other European countries, which had made impressive electoral gains by using this tactic. Party leader Jorg Haider launched an inflammatory petition campaign aimed at curbing immigration and immigrants' rights, but it was met in the fall with a massive countercampaign by the other political parties, the church, Jewish organizations, and most of the media. This demonstrated the determination of many Austrians to block Haider's use of the potentially explosive immigrant issue for political purposes.

Despite the lack of popular backing for the petition, Haider's message did not go altogether unheeded. Strong support had developed for imposing restrictions on immigration from Eastern Europe. Most Austrians believed that the country had taken in as many refugees as it could absorb and that the government should clamp down on further immigration. In May the interior minister proposed an immigration law that would for the first time set quotas on the number of people allowed to settle in the country. The law would still allow some 25,000 to 30,000 foreigners to settle permanently in Austria annually, the same number that had been arriving in recent years. In June an amended asylum law went into effect, the most restrictive in Europe. The same month, Austrian soldiers began to be deployed along the country's 204-mile-long border with Hungary, to prevent illegal immigrants from entering the country.

Anti-Semitism, Neo-Nazism

Anti-Semitic attitudes, according to a poll by the Gallup Institute of Austria, remained widespread. The poll, which was conducted in 1991 on behalf of the American Jewish Committee, found "substantial portions of the Austrian population expressing strong negative attitudes toward Jews."[1] Sympathy for Israel and Zionism, moreover, was weak among most Austrians. A majority of Austrians subscribed to the idea that it was "time to put the memory of the Holocaust behind us." More positive attitudes toward Jews, Israel, and remembrance of the Holocaust were found among younger people, the better educated, and those living in Vienna.

While these sentiments appeared deep-rooted among a large segment of the population, they did not come to the surface in a threatening way. Where anti-Semitic incidents occurred, the government resolutely condemned them. The most serious anti-Semitic incident was the desecration in October at the new Jewish cemetery in Eisenstadt. In this apparently well-organized incident, more than a hundred tombstones were defaced with Nazi slogans and swastikas. Chancellor Vranitzky and other leading political and religious leaders journeyed to Eisenstadt to demonstrate solidarity with the Jewish community and expressed profound regret for what had happened.

---

[1]Fritz Karmasin, *Austrian Attitudes Toward Jews, Israel, and the Holocaust* (American Jewish Committee, New York, 1992), p. 12.

Equally disturbing to the Jewish community were expressions of Holocaust denial, especially articles in the press claiming that the mass murder of Jews in World War II never occurred. The columnist Richard Nimmerrichter, writing in the right-wing, mass-circulation daily *Neue Kronen Zeitung* under the pseudonym "Staberl," claimed that few Jews died in concentration camps from gassing but rather were the victims of hunger, disease, exhaustion, and maltreatment. The Israelitische Kultusgemeinde, the representative body of Austrian Jewry, initiated action to have the writer prosecuted for distorting the true nature of the Holocaust. After considering the matter for seven months, the state prosecutor decided not to bring charges.

By contrast, in a trial conducted in April against the editor of the extreme right-wing newspaper *Halt*, a court in Vienna found its publisher, Gerd Honsik, guilty of publishing stories denying that Jews were killed in Auschwitz. The judge sentenced the publisher to a year and a half in prison and ordered him to pay 2.3 million schillings ($230,000) for damages and court costs. Honsik was found guilty on the strength of evidence presented by the Austrian historian Gerhard Jakschitz, of the Vienna Institute of Contemporary History. Jakschitz testified that, based on historical evidence, National Socialist ideology was anti-Semitic to the core, and that Nazi Germany had engaged in the mass murder of Jews.

A provincial court convicted Walter Ochensberger for neo-Nazi activities and sentenced him to three years' imprisonment. Publisher of a newsletter called *Sieg* (Victory), he ran articles claiming that the Holocaust was a fabrication and that gas chambers never existed. Ochensberger, who was twice before acquitted on similar charges, was found guilty this time because the prosecutor was willing to accept a reduced penalty.

The trial renewed debate in the country over existing laws dealing with neo-Nazi activities. The conservative People's party wanted to reduce the penalties for such crimes, arguing that stiff jail terms only deterred juries from bringing in a conviction. A contrary view was held by the Socialist party, which feared that such a change would convey the message that neo-Nazi activities were regarded as little more than misdemeanors. The Jewish community favored the former approach, believing that less severe punishment would result in more convictions of those charged with neo-Nazi activities.

Israel and the Middle East

Relations between Austria and Israel, which had been strained as a result of the Waldheim affair, showed signs of warming in 1992, after President Kurt Waldheim announced that he would not be a candidate for reelection. (Following Waldheim's election as federal president in 1986, Israel refused to name a new ambassador to Vienna and was represented by a "chargé d'affaires ad interim." Although trade relations and most bilateral contacts continued on an even keel, high-level diplomatic exchanges came to a virtual halt. In protest over Israel's action, the Austrian government downgraded the level of its diplomatic representation in Tel Aviv.)

The improvement in relations accelerated with the election in May of Thomas Klestil, the candidate of the Austrian People's party, as Austria's new president. Actually, the groundwork for this was laid during an official visit to Israel at the end of 1991 by Klestil, the then director-general of the Austrian Foreign Ministry. Barely a week after President Waldheim stepped down from office, Israel's envoy to Vienna, Peter Aran, presented his credentials to President Klestil. In a parallel move, the Austrian envoy to Israel, Kurt Hengl, presented his credentials as ambassador to President Chaim Herzog. This signaled the full normalization of relations between Vienna and Jerusalem.

A spate of official visits by high government officials soon followed. Prof. Dr. Helmut Zilk, mayor of Vienna, made an official visit to Jerusalem, which was reciprocated by his host, Mayor Teddy Kollek. Federal Minister of Education Dr. Rudolf Scholten also visited Israel and pledged funds to rehabilitate a high school in Jerusalem's Rehavia neighborhood. These goodwill visits were topped off by the visit in December of Israeli foreign minister Shimon Peres to Vienna, where he was officially received by Foreign Minister Alois Mock. In a gesture to the Palestine Liberation Organization, with which Austria had maintained semi-official ties, Mock met the following day with Farouk Kaddoumi, the organization's leading foreign-affairs official.

Relations between the two countries remained amicable in areas of special concern to Israel and the Jewish community. Vienna continued its liberal policy of allowing Jewish organizations to provide transit facilities to Iranian Jewish immigrants. Overall, most of the articles or reports about Israel that appeared in the Austrian media were balanced and not unfriendly.

In the more conventional areas of trade, tourism, and scientific and cultural exchanges, good to excellent ties were maintained. The combined trade in both directions amounted to about $100 million annually. This figure was expected to rise now that Israel had become an associate member of the European Free Trade Association (EFTA). Austria did much to smooth Israel's request for associate-member status in that body.

There was also a much improved tone in relations on political issues between the two countries. The Austrian government strongly supported the Arab-Israeli peace process that got under way in Madrid in the fall of 1991. And while it continued to back Palestinian self-determination, Vienna adopted a lower profile on the issue.

During the Gulf War, Austria, as a nonpermanent member of the United Nations Security Council, strongly supported the resolutions aimed at curbing Iraqi aggression against Kuwait. The press, especially the state-run radio and television, and the public in general, were sympathetic to Israel following the Scud missile attacks against Israeli cities. During the fighting, a parliamentary delegation made up of members of the three main political parties went to Israel to demonstrate support. The government contributed $2.5 million for the repair of housing and schools damaged by Iraqi missile attacks.

Tourism between the two countries remained strong, with an estimated 30,000

Austrians visiting Israel and almost twice that number of Israelis traveling to Austria. The national carriers, Austrian Airlines (AUA) and El Al, maintained regular service to meet the growing tourist travel between the two countries. The Jewish Welcome Service, a branch of the Austrian Tourist Office, assisted tourists from abroad to become acquainted with Jewish life in Vienna and arranged individual and group travel from Austria to Israel. Its director, Dr. Leon Zelman, a prominent personality in the Jewish community and a survivor of the Mauthausen concentration camp, frequently addressed students on the Holocaust and Austria's treatment of Jews during the Nazi period.

The long-standing cooperation between Austria and Israel in the scientific and educational fields continued to develop. Under the direction of Vice-Chancellor Erhard Busek, who also served as the federal minister of science and research, a great deal of attention was given in 1992 to revamping and strengthening these ties. Related to this was the network of friendship societies that maintained fund-raising activities on behalf of Tel Aviv University, the Weizmann Institute, the Haifa Technion, and the Hebrew University.

Plans were under way for Austria to have a central place in the 1993 Israel Festival. As part of this undertaking, certain of Austria's foremost cultural institutions were to perform in Israel—the Vienna Philharmonic Orchestra, the Staatsoper, and the Burg Theater. Plans also called for an official visit to Israel by Chancellor Vranitzky, the first ever by an Austrian chancellor, during the festival.

JEWISH COMMUNITY

Demography

The Jewish population of Austria was undergoing significant change in terms of its size, age, and composition. It was getting larger, younger, and becoming more varied. There were 8,000 Jews registered with the Israelitische Kultusgemeinde, the official Jewish communal body, but knowledgeable observers claimed that the actual number was twice that figure. The overwhelming majority of Jews were concentrated in Vienna, with approximately 300 to 400 making their homes in the large provincial cities of Salzburg, Innsbruck, Baden, and Linz.

Whereas in the past, the main source of population growth had been immigration from the former Soviet republics, this had slowed to a trickle, and growth was now the result of increased fertility, mainly among Sephardi and Orthodox Jews. The turning point in the demographic trend was 1991, when for the first time since the prewar era, the number of births exceeded the number of deaths. It was widely accepted that the Sephardi community, which accounted for roughly a quarter of the registered community membership, would outstrip the Ashkenazi community in size in the not too distant future. This was bound to have profound ramifications in terms of the leadership of the community and its religious and social agenda. The gradual transformation in the community's ethnic composition was not unlike what happened in the years following World War II, when Jews from Central and Eastern Europe immigrated to Austria and became more numerous than the pre-1938 Jewish population. It was these migratory streams that gave renewed vitality and life to the Austrian—particularly the Viennese—Jewish community.

Communal Affairs

The Austrian Jewish community was led by an elected Board of Deputies, made up of 24 members, which selected its president. The post was held by Hofrat (Counsellor) Paul Grosz, the acknowledged spokesman for the entire Jewish community. Two groups, the Alternative List and Young Generation, which merged in 1992, held half the seats on the board, with the remainder held by the Bund (3), Mizrachi (2), Bukharim (2), Religious Group (2), Tikkun (2), and Kol Israel (1). Community elections for a new board were to be held in 1993, following which the board would proceed to elect a president. Grosz, who was awarded with the honorary title of Hofrat by the president of the Austrian Republic in 1992, was a candidate to succeed himself.

The Kultusgemeinde joined with the Jewish communities in Zurich, Munich, Prague, Bratislava, Ljubljana, Venice, and Milan to promote cooperation in matters of common concern. They formed an organization, known as the Eight Communities Seven Countries, which issued a periodic newsletter called *Faxlink* that provided information on cultural, political, and social matters.

As a sign of its growing presence in the Jewish community, on October 18 the Sephardi community inaugurated its own quarters for prayer and social activities. Dedication of the Sephardi Center, the first new synagogue built in Vienna on a new site since 1928, took place amid great ceremony. Located in the second district, the center is home to two synagogues, one for Vienna's Bukharan Jews and the other for Georgian Jews. The inauguration of the center was attended by the Austrian federal president, Dr. Thomas Klestil; the mayor of Vienna, Prof. Dr. Helmut Zilk; the federal minister of education, Dr. Rudolf Scholten; Rabbi Paul Chaim Eisenberg, chief rabbi of the Jewish community of Vienna; Paul Grosz, president of the Jewish community of Vienna; and other prominent personages. The cost of the building, 14 million schillings ($1.2 million), was paid by the federal government and the city of Vienna, the Jewish community, and private sources.

In supporting the construction of the center, the Kultusgemeinde made a tangible commitment to promoting a pluralistic Jewish community. Such a center, it was believed, would do much to help Sephardi Jews maintain and observe their traditions. Before 1938, the observance of Sephardi traditions and customs had been a pronounced feature of Austrian Jewish life.

A new congregation affiliated with the World Union of Progressive Judaism was established in Vienna. Under the leadership of Rabbi Michael Konig, the Or Hadash Synagogue opened for services in 1990. The house of worship, located in Vienna's second district, had a small but growing membership numbering 50 families. Services were conducted Friday evenings and Saturday mornings, as well as on holidays. The services and religious practices were comparable to those of left-wing American Conservative Judaism.

Culture and Education

To the accompaniment of an eight-hour musical marathon, the Jewish Culture Week opened on May 17 on Vienna's famed Seitenstettengasse, on which are located the Stadttempel and the offices of the Jewish community. The festival featured Jewish music, exhibitions of works by Austrian Jewish artists, public concerts, cantorial singing, and a book fair. This major cultural event, which formed a part of the Vienna *Festwoche*, was intended to signal the rebirth of Austrian-Jewish culture.

As part of Jewish Culture Week, and in commemoration of the 500th anniversary of the expulsion of the Jews from Spain, the Jewish Museum of the City of Vienna opened an exhibition, "The Sephardic Diaspora," organized by Dr. Felicitas Heimann-Jelinek. At the same time, there opened at the Austrian Jewish Museum in Eisenstadt an exhibition on "The Jews of Spain Before 1492."

The City of Vienna and the Kultusgemeinde agreed to relocate the Jewish Museum of the City of Vienna from its temporary quarters in the community building to a permanent site, an old palace located on Dorotheumgasse in the first district. The community's decision to accept the city's offer of the building prompted the museum's curator, Dr. Daniela Luxembourg, to resign, warning that the new facility was not adequate for the future needs of the museum. Named to succeed her was Dr. Hans Julius Schoeps, whose work in staging the exhibition "*Judische Lebens Welte*" (Patterns of Jewish Life) in Berlin in the spring of 1992 won international acclaim. The museum, whose collection of artifacts and documents had been enriched largely through the generosity of private individuals, was scheduled to open its doors to the public in the fall of 1993.

A Jewish museum opened in 1991 in Hohenem, a city located in the province of Voralberg, dedicated to promoting a greater understanding of the history and life of the Jews of the city. The event was noteworthy on two counts: little is known, even in Jewish circles, of the city's Jewish past, and few Jews inhabit the city at present.

In spite of the community's small numbers, it supported a growing network of day schools, part-time *talmud torahs*, and a yeshivah. The leading day school was the Zvi Peretz Chayes School, with an enrollment of 350 boys and girls, offering classes from kindergarten to 12th grade. The Chabad-Lubavitch school, which had a kindergarten and grades five through eight, had approximately 125 pupils. A third day school, known as the Orthodox school, also served the community. It had an enrollment of 150 pupils in kindergarten to eighth grade. The recently organized Or Hadash Synagogue ran its own afternoon Hebrew school, in which some 20 children were enrolled.

Personalia

Simon Wiesenthal, whose efforts in tracking down Nazi war criminals have brought him international renown, was the recipient of the Erasmus Prize, named in honor of the great humanist of Rotterdam. Crown Prince Bernhard of the Netherlands awarded the prize to Wiesenthal at a ceremony in the Netherlands, citing his contribution to the promotion of a more humane and open society in Europe.

Robert Schindel's novel *Geburtig* (which can be translated either as "Born of" or "Native to") became a best-seller in Austria. The Austrian-Jewish writer's novel, published by Suhrkamp in Germany, deals with the relationships among two generations of Viennese Jews, survivors of the Holocaust, their children, and their Gentile Austrian friends.

MURRAY GORDON

Eastern Europe

Former Soviet Union

National Affairs

BY 1992 IT LOOKED AS IF THE ROAD to reform in the former USSR would be longer and more difficult than anticipated. The breakup of the Soviet Union in late 1991 and its partial replacement by the much looser Commonwealth of Independent States (CIS) had created expectations both there and among many in the West that the successor states would move quickly to market economies and democratic political systems. However, in almost all of the successor states a combination of factors sent the economy into a tailspin: the introduction of some free prices and the resulting inflation, the dismissal of many employees from state-owned, unproductive enterprises, and the need to renegotiate economic relations among the independent parts of what had been a single state. The struggle between radical economic reformers, moderate reformers, and antireformers was a major political issue outside Central Asia, where other issues were more salient. In Russia, and to a lesser extent in other republics, the constant struggle between the executive and the legislature meant unstable governments and an inability to formulate, let alone implement, policy. It also seriously impeded the movement to political and economic restructuring.

In the Russian Federation, the lifting of price controls on most items sent prices skyrocketing. More goods than ever began to appear in shops, but their prices put them beyond the reach of most citizens. In the political arena, the Democratic Russia movement, the main reformist grouping, fell apart. Boris Yeltsin failed to build a democratic party or a movement that would be his political base and was forced to replace the 36-year-old economic reformer Yegor Gaidar as prime minister. The new prime minister, Viktor Chernomyrdin, a former official of the Soviet oil and gas ministry, was widely regarded as less committed to economic reform than Gaidar.

Ukraine, the second largest of the European states, was tranquil. Former Communist party ideological secretary Leonid Kravchuk held the reigns of power firmly, but resisted the introduction of economic reforms. There were tensions with Russia over the presence on its territory of formerly Soviet missiles, and over control of the former Soviet Black Sea fleet, based in the Crimean city of Sevastopol. Belarus appeared to be the most conservative of the European republics in the CIS. The former Communist *nomenklatura* remained in power, and there were few signs of economic reform.

The Baltic states of Estonia, Latvia, and Lithuania had led the way out of the Soviet Union by being the first to declare independence. Though there was a change in government in Estonia, its economy showed signs of stability coupled with serious attempts at reform. A major issue was the new citizenship law, which Russians claimed discriminated against them. Latvia's economy, which had begun to deteriorate in 1990, got worse. Proposed guidelines on citizenship would apparently disenfranchise those who came to Latvia after 1940, mostly Slavs from other republics. In Lithuania, where over 80 percent of the population is Lithuanian, more liberal citizenship requirements were adopted. Economic reform was more modest in Lithuania than in the other Baltic republics. In all three republics, Russian troops remained and were the subject of intensive talks between Russia and the Baltic states.

In Central Asia, in every republic except Kyrgyzstan, authoritarian governments ruled, headed by former high officials of the Communist party. In all parts of Central Asia, Europeans and Russian speakers felt uneasy, perceiving that official policies favored the indigenous peoples, especially in culture, education, and employment.

In the Caucasus, the conflict between Armenia and Azerbaijan over Nagorno-Karabakh continued; however, Armenia was more stable politically than her neighbors. Azerbaijan had three presidents within as many months. In Georgia, an armed rebellion against President Zviad Gamsakhurdia eventuated in the return to power of former Soviet foreign minister (and previously first secretary of the Georgian Communist party) Eduard Shevardnadze. The economic situation deteriorated, as it did in neighboring Azerbaijan and Armenia.

In Moldova, part of Romania before 1940, Russians and Ukrainians had split off and created the Dniester Moldovan Soviet Socialist Republic in 1991, which called for the restoration of the Soviet Union and its military power. In Moldova, the cultural activities of national minorities such as Russians, Ukrainians, Jews, and Gagauz were supported by the government. In the Dnester Republic, though Moldovans were the largest single nationality, Moldovan culture was suppressed.

Thus, the first year of post-Communism was marked by economic downturns nearly everywhere; ethnic violence in the southern areas of what had been the USSR; in some places, political instability; and, in others, the maintenance of or return to power of Communist officials.

Relations with Israel

Uzbekistan was the first Central Asian state to establish diplomatic relations with Israel. Kazakhstan, Kyrgyzstan, and Tajikistan followed suit, leaving Turkmenistan as the only predominantly Muslim republic that did not have relations with the Jewish state. Armenia established diplomatic relations in April. By year's end, Israel had diplomatic relations with 13 of the 15 states that had emerged from the former Soviet Union (Moldova was the other state with which Israel had no formal relations).

The Jewish Agency for Israel had 60 permanent representatives in widely scattered parts of the former Soviet Union. They were joined by agency officials who came in for brief periods, and by employees of the Liaison Office (*Lishkat Hakesher*) of Israel's Foreign Ministry. The division of labor between these two organizations was not clear, and each seemed to develop its own local clientele.

Anti-Semitism

The American Jewish Committee commissioned a survey of attitudes toward Jews, which was conducted in March and April by the Russian Center for Public Opinion and Market Research. In general, the survey found wide variation in attitudes from state to state in the former USSR and from issue to issue. The researchers found that Jews are held in high regard as workers, but many felt that Jews avoid physical work and place too high a value on money. Majorities of between 56 and 95 percent supported giving Jews equal access to employment and higher education, but only 19 to 56 percent would allow Jewish parties or social-political organizations to function. In comparison with survey results from 1990, there was a discernible increase in anti-Jewish sentiment, especially in Belarus, Latvia, Uzbekistan, and Azerbaijan. Ukraine and Moldova showed somewhat improved attitudes, while the smallest change was recorded in Russia. The researchers noted that other groups—ethnic, social, and political—are often viewed more negatively than Jews. For example, when asked to assess the level of influence that each of 15 groups has in society, 1 percent (Moldova) to 15 percent (Belarus) said Jews have too much influence, but government bureaucrats, politicians, mass media, and political parties were cited much more frequently.

Anti-Semitic graffiti and newspaper articles were reported in Samara (formerly Kuibyshev), Tomsk, several cities in Ukraine, especially in West Ukraine, and in Tallinn. Many graves in the old Jewish cemetery in Tartu, Estonia, were destroyed by vandals in July, and a bomb exploded in Tallinn's Jewish day school. The Jewish cultural club in Penza, Russia, was vandalized.

In Russia, where the media were now more free than at any time since the revolution, one result was that anti-Semitic publications appeared without hindrance. Some extreme examples were the newspapers *Russkoe Voskresenie* (Russian Resurrection) and *Russkie Vedomosti* (Russian News). The former identified itself as the organ of the "Russian National-Liberation Movement" and claimed a circulation of 40,000. It quoted from *Mein Kampf* and featured a portrait of Adolf Hitler. It called anti-Semitism "the national liberation struggle against the yoke of the kikes [*zhidy*]." "Kikes" were defined "not as a nation but as a criminal profession" who "are united by the most rabid hatred of the rest of mankind (in Russia, that means Russians)." The paper went on: "Every Russian must be an anti-Semite. If a person is not an anti-Semite, he is either a fool or a scoundrel." The party proudly identified itself as both Stalinist and Nazi, the former because "in 1937 he shot the Leninist kike swine who murdered millions of Russians by shooting them for 'anti-Semitism' or in the famine of the 1920s and 1930s," and the latter because "We are for such [national] socialism (and, in general, any system) wherein there are no kikes in power" (no. 7/15, April 1992).

Russkie Vedomosti, the organ of the "Russian party," claimed a circulation of 10,000. The party's program "recognizes the guilt of Zionism in seizing power in October 1917," and also its guilt for Soviet terror, civil war, and genocide of the Russian people. "Zionism should be tried publicly and Zionists should be deported from Russia" (no. 5, 1992).

JEWISH COMMUNITY

Demography

The last Soviet census was taken in January 1989 and enumerated 1,445,000 Jews. Emigration had reduced that number by the end of 1992 to about 970,000. The population was further eroded by internal processes, including low fertility, high mortality, and intermarriage. Demographer Mark Tolts calculated that in 1991 in the Russian republic the number of births to Jewish mothers was only 3.9 per 1,000, and the number of Jewish deaths exceeded these births by 24.2 per 1,000. In that year, only 587 children were born in Russia to families where both parents were Jews, a decline of 55 percent from 1989. The median age of Jews in the European republics was over 50, whereas in Central Asia it was a bit above 30. The age structure of former Soviet Jewry and ongoing emigration seemed to portend drastic and prolonged population decline. A possible mitigating factor is the reclaiming of Jewish identity by people who had been registered as non-Jews but now chose to identify as Jews, most often in order to qualify for emigration. No figures or reasonable estimates are available on the number who might fall into this category. However, it is unlikely that this would halt or even significantly slow the rapid decline of the Jewish population in the former Soviet Union.

EMIGRATION

In 1992, 109,360 Jews emigrated from the former Soviet Union to Israel (64,057) and the United States (45,303). It is estimated that several thousand more immigrated to Germany. According to a *New York Times* report (March 23, 1992), some 26,000 Soviet Jews had gone to Germany since the fall of the Berlin wall in 1989, though many appeared to be non-Jewish members of families in which some member was Jewish. Direct flights to Israel replaced the transit stations in Bucharest, Budapest, and Warsaw.

Several thousand Jews left war-torn Tajikistan for Israel. In Moldova and the breakaway Dniester Republic, about 2,400 Jews fled, mainly to Odessa, and about 850 continued to Israel. About 1,500 Jews in Abkhazia were caught in the fighting between Georgians and Abkhazians. The Jewish Agency evacuated some 200 to Israel.

Communal Affairs

The breakup of the Soviet Union led to the splintering of the emergent national Jewish organization, Va'ad, which had been founded in 1989. Jewish communal life began to take on a more local and regional character, paralleling the autonomist tendencies in the former Soviet Union as a whole.

In April, Va'ad of Russia (the Federation of Jewish Organizations and Communities of Russia) was established at a convention in Nizhny Novgorod (formerly Gorky). Thirty-two cities were represented by 113 delegates. They represented local Jewish religious and cultural organizations that were estimated to encompass about 6 or 7 percent of the Jewish population. Nearly half of those organizations were founded in 1989 and thereafter. A survey of the delegates by sociologists Vladimir Shapiro and Valery Chervyakov revealed that over three-quarters of the local organizations had fewer than 100 members, but that larger numbers participated in their activities, which were mostly cultural and educational. Few of the delegates reported personal encounters with anti-Semitism in the previous few months, and most regarded favorably the prospects for the development of Jewish life in their cities. Still, only a third thought that emigration would decline, and only 42 percent of the delegates averred that they themselves would never emigrate. Most saw cultural and educational activities and assistance to the needy and disabled as the primary tasks of the Jewish national movement. Interestingly, over half said their spouses were not registered on their Soviet passports as being of Jewish nationality.

The third congress of the formerly all-Soviet Va'ad convened in Odessa in May. Three hundred and twenty delegates came from as many locales in 12 republics of the former Soviet Union. (Armenia and Turkmenistan, where there are few Jews, and Lithuania, the most independent-minded of the republics, sent no delegates.) Shapiro and Chervyakov surveyed these delegates as well and found that, overall, the levels of membership in the non-Russian organizations were lower than in Russia. Most were registered with local authorities, and very few reported hostility to them or to Jewish activities on the part of those authorities. As in Russia, the main activities of the organizations were in welfare, culture, and education. Sixty percent of the delegates estimated that 30 percent or less of the Jewish population in their respective locales were involved in Jewish public, cultural, and religious life. Few reported anti-Semitic encounters, and most thought the prospects good for the development of Jewish communal life. Only about a quarter thought emigration would decrease, and the same proportion said they themselves did not intend to emigrate at any time. Perhaps surprisingly, 39 percent said they believed in God, or were inclined to such belief. Thirty-five percent had spouses not registered as Jews but, they said, only 19 percent of the spouses did not consider themselves Jewish.

The congress elected 13 directors of the Va'ad, each representing a republic. Retired colonel Yuri Sokol, who had established an independent Moscow Jewish Cultural and Educational Society, and Zinovy Kogan, leader of the Hineni group associated with the Reform movement, were elected representatives from Moscow. This was interpreted as a defeat for Va'ad cochairman Mikhail Chlenov, who, along with some others, was charged with misuse of Va'ad funds.

In Ukraine, two national organizations emerged, one headed by Yosef Zissels, associated with the Va'ad, and the other by Ilya Levitas. The Zissels group charged the Levitas group with being too closely associated with the Ukrainian government. In October the Levitas group convened a congress of Jewish organizations in Ukraine, with 72 delegates representing 22 local organizations. Levitas was elected chairman of the Jewish Societal Council, whose function was said to be to represent Jewish interests to the Ukrainian government.

In Estonia and Latvia, Jews felt threatened by policies directed against Russian speakers, since most Jews considered Russian their mother tongue, and most had come to the republics after World War II. In Lithuania, a Jewish museum was established, headed by Emanuelis Zingeris, a young Jewish member of Parliament. His cochairman of the Jewish community, the distinguished writer Grigory Kanovich, complained at a World Jewish Congress meeting in July that while all other faiths were getting back confiscated houses of worship from the government, the many synagogue buildings in Lithuania had not been returned to the Jewish community. Lithuanian law allowed former owners to reclaim nationalized private property only if they were citizens of Lithuania and resided there, thus excluding most surviving Lithuanian Jews, who lived abroad.

Religion

An association of rabbis of the Commonwealth of Independent States was formed, which included about 30 rabbis in the several republics. Adolf (Avraham) Shayevich, the last Soviet-appointed rabbi of Moscow's Choral Synagogue, was elected president of the association. Head of the *bet din* (rabbinical court) was Rabbi Pinchas Goldschmidt, who had come to Moscow from Israel.

In the cities of Brest-Litovsk and Gomel in Belarus, Jews appealed to local governments to regain control of former synagogue buildings. In the Russian cities of Khabarovsk (Siberia) and Perm similar attempts were made, and the Perm synagogue was handed over to the community.

Lubavitcher (Chabad) Hassidim continued their struggle to regain possession of 12,000 volumes in the Lenin Library in Moscow, which had been confiscated by the state from the library of Rabbi Yosef Yitzhak Schneerson, leader of the movement until his arrest and expulsion from Russia in 1929. The Hassidim organized demonstrations in front of the library in downtown Moscow. During one of these demonstrations, in February, Russian-born Israeli Ze'ev Wagner was arrested. He was released within a few days. Russian officials issued contradictory statements on what they intended to do with the books. The mayor of Moscow, Gavril Popov, and several prominent Jews criticized the Hassidim for their tactics in attempting to regain the books.

Education

There were said to be 27 Jewish day schools and over 130 Sunday and afternoon schools in the CIS. Of these, 6 day schools and 60 Sunday schools were operating on the basis of agreements between the Israeli Ministry of Education and local governments. Some of the day schools were sponsored by local communities, as in Riga and Vilnius, whereas others were supported by the Orthodox, Conservative, and Reform movements, the Jewish Agency, and the Israeli government. These movements and agencies also supported Jewish summer camps in many parts of the CIS. Jewish universities, organized and funded by local initiatives, were operating in Moscow and St. Petersburg (formerly Leningrad). Touro College of New York established a branch in Moscow. New York's Jewish Theological Seminary and the YIVO Institute sponsored and staffed a Judaica department in the Russian State University for the Humanities in Moscow.

Moscow had two day schools, several Sunday schools, and nineteen Jewish kindergartens. St. Petersburg had three day schools. The community day school in Tallinn, Estonia's capital, had been established in 1990 and enrolled 330 children. Riga's community school, a pioneer of this type of education, had 400 students. The first Jewish secondary school opened in the Ukrainian capital, Kiev, and reported an enrollment of over 500. Before 1989, not a single Jewish school of any kind had existed in the Soviet Union.

Culture

A Jewish press had emerged in the late 1980s, consisting mostly of local newspapers. The economic downturn caused some of them to cease operations, but several dozen continued to publish in 1992. St. Petersburg's *Ami* (*Narod Moi*) (My People) claimed a circulation of 20,000, and the Moscow *Evreiskaya Gazeta* (Jewish Gazette), which saw itself as a national newspaper, said it was read by 25,000–40,000 people. These newspapers reported local, national, and international Jewish news and contained regular columns on Jewish history and religion and Israeli news.

Israel's National Library concluded an agreement with the Lenin Library in Moscow to microfilm more than 2,500 rare Jewish manuscripts in the Baron Ginzburg collection. Other local and foreign scholars, as well as Judaica students from the Russian State University for the Humanities, were exploring Judaica holdings of central and provincial libraries, most of which had lain unused and even un-catalogued for decades.

The Jewish Agency for Israel and the Liaison Office of Israel's Foreign Ministry promoted cultural activities aimed at encouraging immigration to Israel. The American Jewish Joint Distribution Committee (JDC) had 12 offices that worked to assist local communities in social services, education, religion, and culture. A network of Judaica libraries in many localities was supported by the JDC.

The first international festival of Jewish music was held in Vilnius in April-May. Local musicians were joined by others from Israel, Europe, and the United States as well as other parts of the CIS. A Marc Chagall Museum and a Jewish cultural center were scheduled to open in the artist's birthplace, Vitebsk, Belarus.

After 32 years of publication, the Yiddish monthly *Sovetish Haimland* ceased publication. Declining readership, due mainly to emigration and death, rising costs, and drastic reduction in government subsidies—the defunct Soviet Writers' Union had funded the journal on behalf of the state—were given as the causes of the closure. Attempts were under way to publish a successor journal, *Di Yiddishe Gass*.

In Central Asia's largest republic, Kazakhstan, Jewish cultural associations were active in five communities. The cultural center in Almaty (formerly Alma Ata), the capital, claimed 700 members. The 4,000–5,000 Jews of Kyrgyzstan were divided about equally between Ashkenazic and "Bukharan" (Central Asian) Jews. In the capital of Bishkek (formerly Frunze), the synagogue served mostly Bukharan Jews, while the cultural center served mainly Ashkenazim. A choir, two dance groups, and a library of over a thousand volumes were sponsored by the cultural center. In Tajikistan, the civil war was driving Jews out. All cultural activities and even most religious functions came to a halt because of the chaos in Dushanbe and other cities. However, two cultural centers in Dushanbe, one Bukharan and the other Ashkenazic, were coordinating emigration and evacuation with the Jewish Agency. In the capital of Uzbekistan, Tashkent, the separate Bukharan and Ashkenazic communities maintained a vigorous level of activity. Synagogues, cultural centers, a newspaper, a library, adult education classes, and even a dating service were supported by the communities. At least seven other cities in Uzbekistan had organized communities, but they were being eroded by emigration.

ZVI GITELMAN

Eastern European Countries

IN 1992, THE THIRD YEAR after the collapse of Communism in Eastern Europe, the countries in the region were grappling with a number of issues common to them all, to greater or lesser degrees. Among these were the continuing difficult economic transformation (including questions of privatization and restitution of property that had been confiscated or nationalized by the Communist state), a political shift to the right, and rising nationalism and racism, including manifestations of anti-Semitism. Despite these difficulties, efforts to renew Jewish life in the countries were consolidated, commemorations of the Holocaust were given prominence, new initiatives were launched to preserve and protect Jewish monuments, and new endeavors came into being aimed at furthering interreligious dialogue and combating anti-Semitism.

Bulgaria

Zhelen Zhelev, a candidate of the ruling Union of Democratic Forces (SDS) party, won Bulgaria's first direct presidential election in January. Internal conflicts within the party led to a change in the government at the end of December, with Lyuben Borisov Berov unseating Filip Dimitrov as prime minister. Berov had the support of the Turkish nationalist party. The National Assembly completed arrangements for land privatization, but other promised reforms stalled, and there was growing labor unrest. The economic convulsions resulting from Bulgaria's change to a free-market economy caused shortages of many goods and services and sent annual inflation soaring to 100 percent.

JEWISH COMMUNITY

The Bulgarian Jewish community numbered about 6,000, about one-third of them over 60 years of age, many of them elderly, ailing pensioners particularly hard hit by high inflation. About 1,700 Jews received small monthly cash grants provided by the Joint Distribution Committee (JDC). Some 80 to 90 percent of Bulgaria's Jews lived in Sofia.

The community was divided between elderly Holocaust survivors, some of whom had managed to keep a few religious traditions alive during the Communist years, and younger, secularized people who had little knowledge of Judaism. (Virtually all of pre-World War II Bulgaria's 50,000 Jews survived the Holocaust; all but about 5,000 of them emigrated to Israel in the years immediately after the war.)

Under the Communists, Jews in Bulgaria were not persecuted outright, but

345

religious observance was discouraged and Jewish cultural and educational activities were limited. Only two synagogues, one in the capital, Sofia, and one in Plovdiv, remained consecrated, and only a few elderly people attended services. Jews tended to be regarded as an ethnic rather than a religious group. There was a Jewish association with branches in various towns and cities, but it was a totally secular social and political organization under the control of the state.

After the ouster of the Communists, Bulgaria's Jews, particularly the younger, postwar generations, many of whom were the children of mixed marriages, began a process of deepening self-awareness of their cultural and spiritual heritage. They had to start their learning experience virtually from scratch.

Contacts were established with international Jewish organizations, and in March 1990 a new group, Shalom, took over the premises and activities of the former state-run Jewish association. Classes, study groups, camps, and other groups were founded with the help of the JDC, which was allowed to begin operating in Bulgaria in 1990, the Memorial Foundation for Jewish Culture, and other organizations.

Shalom, supported in part by the JDC and in part by small enterprises owned by the Jewish community, had 17 branches throughout the country and remained the country's main Jewish social and cultural organization. One of its projects was the initiation of a publishing venture aimed at reprinting major Jewish works of various types. In 1991 the JDC had helped fund and organize community seders at Passover, the first time the state had allowed any public celebration of Passover and the first time most participants had ever taken part in the Passover rite. This year some 2,700 Jews attended seders in 10 different locations in Sofia and the provinces.

The revival of Jewish awareness was particularly intense among young people. Many youth groups and classes on Jewish subjects were either established or expanded. Some 450 youngsters attended three Jewish youth camps during the year, and more than 100 young people attended twice-weekly *talmud torah* classes. A Jewish elementary school was established in Sofia, with an enrollment of 125, as well as a Jewish kindergarten attended by 25 children. Membership in the Union of Jewish Students doubled. Two American JDC Service Corps volunteers began working in Bulgaria in the summer of 1992, training both adult Jewish teachers and Jewish youth leaders as well as teaching courses in Sofia and advising Jewish groups in provincial towns.

The cultural awareness of the community was enhanced by an ambitious program coordinated with the worldwide "Sepharad '92" celebration, marking the 500th anniversary of the expulsion of Jews from Spain. (Bulgarian Jews are Sephardic and many older people still speak Ladino.) The program included exhibitions of Jewish artwork and sacred objects, concerts, lectures, and seminars.

Czech and Slovak Federative Republic

Political developments leading to the dissolution of the Czechoslovak federation dominated the events of 1992. Elections in June dealt heavy losses to liberal and centrist politicians, bringing to power conservative, free-market-oriented Vaclav Klaus in the Czech Republic and populist nationalist Vladimir Meciar in Slovakia. The vote clearly demonstrated the Czech-Slovak polarization and resulted in the negotiated decision to split Czechoslovakia into the two independent states, the Czech Republic and Slovakia, as of January 1, 1993.

Jews had reason to be concerned as the movement toward autonomy for the Czech and Slovak communities gained momentum. In Slovakia, particularly, the changing political scene was marked by overt nationalism with anti-Semitic overtones. Within a year of the ouster of the Communists, Slovakia had seen a movement to rehabilitate Father Josef Tiso, the pro-Nazi World War II Slovak president who was responsible for the deportation of thousands of Jews to Nazi death camps. In March, neo-fascists rallied in Bratislava to mark the 53rd anniversary of the creation of the Slovak independent puppet state, headed by Tiso. A key speaker was Stanislav Panis, a Holocaust denier and member of Czechoslovakia's federal Parliament.

Signs of anti-Semitism, however, were countered by efforts in both the Czech Republic and Slovakia to combat it as well as to honor Holocaust victims. Various political leaders, including Slovakia's Vladimir Meciar, condemned anti-Semitism. In May President Vaclav Havel, who made it a frequent practice to condemn all aspects of racism, xenophobia, and anti-Semitism, warned of anti-Semitism in the electoral campaigns. The same month, a major international conference on anti-Semitism in Eastern Europe took place in Prague. Toward the end of the year, the Prague weekly *Politika*, the only Czech publication actively encouraging anti-Semitism, came under criminal investigation and in December was forced to cease publication. Among its articles was a spurious list of "Jews and Jewish half-breeds in contemporary Czech culture." In Slovakia, the owner of a publishing house that printed the *Protocols of the Elders of Zion* and other anti-Semitic material was also taken to court.

Several articles in the Slovak press acknowledged that Slovak collaborators were as guilty as the Nazis of crimes against Jews; nationwide TV featured a documentary on Slovak deportations; and an international symposium on the Holocaust was held in the Slovak town of Banska Bystrica.

In late March the 50th anniversary of the first wartime deportation of Jews from Slovakia (March 25, 1942) was marked with commemorative ceremonies, meetings, media coverage, and the unveiling of Holocaust memorial plaques in a number of Slovak towns. (Some 57,628 Slovak Jews were deported to Nazi death camps between March 25 and October 20, 1942.) In June, ceremonies attended by hundreds of local residents and guests from abroad marked the 50th anniversary of the deportation of Jews from the town of Kolin, east of Prague. In August workers began reinscribing the names of the 77,297 Bohemian and Moravian Jews killed by the Nazis on the walls of the historic Pinkas Synagogue in Prague. The names had originally been inscribed there in the 1950s, when the synagogue was dedicated as a Holocaust memorial, but they were removed by the Communists—probably for political reasons—during more than 20 years of restoration work on the building, when it had been closed to the public. On October 21, Slovak leader Vladimir Meciar joined Israeli ambassador to Czechoslovakia Yoel Sher in unveiling a memorial to the 6,000 Jews who were deported to Nazi camps from the city of Nitra.

JEWISH COMMUNITY

About 6,000 people in Czechoslovakia, evenly split between the Czech Republic and Slovakia, identified themselves as Jews. An unknown number of others of Jewish birth or background did not acknowledge their Jewish heritage. Half of Czechoslovakia's Jews were grouped in three main communities. The largest was in Prague, with about 1,100 formally affiliated members, followed by the slightly smaller communities in the Slovak cities of Kosice and Bratislava. Most of the rest of the country's Jews were scattered in four other communities in the Czech Republic and eleven others in Slovakia, where regular services were held, usually in small prayer rooms. The communities were grouped in the Federation of Czech Jewish Communities, based in Prague, and the Federation of Slovak Jewish Communities, in Bratislava.

Most Jews, particularly in the smaller communities, were older people, many of them survivors of the Holocaust. There was also a younger generation made up of people born after World War II and their children, many of whom began discovering or rediscovering their Jewish roots only after the ouster of the Communist regime. In the Czech Republic particularly, where Jews traditionally were highly assimilated and intermarriage was common, many of the younger people who considered themselves Jews were not Jews according to Jewish law. In late 1992, about two dozen of these individuals—and a handful of non-Jews—were studying in Prague in preparation for formal conversion. The question of who could legitimately be considered Jewish created some friction within the Prague community, as some Orthodox members refused to accept people without Jewish mothers as full-fledged community members. A Reform *havurah* was begun in Prague, aimed at instilling a Jewish identity in children of mixed-married couples who felt uncomfortable in the mainstream community.

Jewish spiritual life in both the Czech Republic and Slovakia received a boost in the latter part of 1992, when new rabbis were installed in both republics. On the eve of Rosh Hashanah, Karol Sidon took his place as rabbi of Prague, and on November 9, he was inaugurated as chief (and at the time only) rabbi of the Czech Republic. Sidon, a former dissident playwright, was the son of a Jewish father who died in the Terezin (Theresienstadt) ghetto concentration camp and a non-Jewish mother. He made a formal conversion to Judaism in 1978 and received his rabbinic ordination in Israel. In the late summer, Lazar Kleinman, a Romanian-born Orthodox Jew from Australia, was installed as rabbi of Kosice, in eastern Slovakia—at the time, the only rabbi in Slovakia. Kleinman, whose declared plan was to concentrate on transmitting Jewish culture and religion to young people, opened a Jewish kindergarten soon after his arrival. He admitted, however, that he had antagonized some of the older members of the community within two months of his arrival, particularly by his attempts to modernize the slaughtering and butchering of kosher meat.

Numerous Jewish educational and cultural groups expanded their operations throughout 1992, particularly in the larger cities. Ranging from the Czech-Israel Friendship Society to the Maccabee sports club, most of these groups were founded after removal of the repressive Communist-era restrictions on Jewish religious, cultural, and educational activities. Kosher kitchens supported by the JDC functioned in Kosice and Bratislava, while in Prague the community ran a kosher restaurant in the 400-year-old Jewish Town Hall, whose profits helped provide subsidized meals for community members. The Prague Jewish community, in fact, had become largely self-financing as of January 1, 1991, thanks to income generated by property that had been confiscated by the Communists and was restored by the new regime.

Jewish cultural events and exhibitions took place throughout the year, both in Prague and in the provinces. These included exhibitions such as "Where Cultures Meet" (an exhibit on Czechoslovak Jewish history originally mounted at Israel's Beth Hatefutsoth), the staging of new plays about Franz Kafka, and a festival of Jewish music held in Prague in November. The rock group Shalom, whose songs and logo make overt use of Jewish symbolism, sold more records, CDs, and cassettes than any other Czechoslovak band in 1992. Shalom's leader, Peter Muk, a Gentile who studied Hebrew, always wore a *yarmulke* offstage, and regularly attended Friday-night services at Prague's Reform Bet Simcha *havurah*, became a target for right-wing skinheads, who heckled the group's concerts.

A number of initiatives were undertaken to repair or conserve Jewish monuments, including a fund-raising project for the synagogue in Pilsen, on the 100th anniversary of its construction. In a ceremony in Washington, in March, the United States and Czechoslovakia signed an agreement to protect and preserve monuments, historic buildings, and other sites, primarily damaged synagogues and abandoned Jewish cemeteries. Work on a detailed survey of all Jewish monuments in Czechoslovakia was carried out under the sponsorship of the U.S. Commission for the Preservation of America's Heritage Abroad.

Hungary

The economic changes in Hungary contributed to rising unemployment, a 30-percent annual inflation rate, and a widening gap between rich and poor. Particularly hard hit were pensioners on fixed incomes, including thousands of members of the Jewish community.

Another problem that intensified in 1992 was the rise of political anti-Semitism, as exemplified by the faction of the ruling Democratic Forum party led by writer Istvan Csurka, who published anti-Semitic articles in the Democratic Forum's newspaper, made inflammatory anti-Jewish statements on radio, and wrote a manifesto-like report blaming Hungary's woes on liberals, Jews, Western financiers, and the press.

Skinhead groups also caused some concern. Police in January seized neo-Nazi propaganda leaflets, but at least two anti-Semitic newspapers were sold openly, and revisionist articles on the Holocaust appeared in the mainstream press. On October 23, black-shirted skinheads shouting anti-Semitic slogans disrupted an official ceremony marking the anniversary of the 1956 Hungarian uprising. They expressed support for Csurka and called for the resignation of President Arpad Goncz. President Goncz—labeled an agent of Tel Aviv by Csurka—had paid an official state visit to Israel a month earlier. In November Hungarian foreign minister Geza Jeszensky minimized Csurka's importance, telling an American Jewish Committee delegation that "the more anti-Semitism is mentioned, the more difficult it is to smooth the problem." Only a few days earlier, a bomb scare had forced evacuation of Budapest's Jewish community center during an address by Israeli ambassador David Kraus to a meeting sponsored by the Hungarian-Israeli Friendship Society, and leaflets attacking Jews signed by a group calling itself "Hungarian Realists" had been found on a train. They charged that Jews occupied too many top positions in Hungary's scientific, cultural, and media communities and said Hungarians would not be "slaves and servants" of the Jews.

JEWISH COMMUNITY

Hungary was the only country in East-Central Europe whose Jewish community was large enough to be a real presence. With an estimated 100,000 to 130,000 Jews, Hungary had the third largest Jewish population in Europe (outside the former USSR) after France and England. Most Budapest Jews were highly assimilated into mainstream society—as most Budapest Jews had been for decades before the Holocaust—and many had little to do with the organized Jewish community. Jews were active in the arts and professions, and there were several Jews in Parliament, including Rabbi Tamas Raj.

About 90 percent of Hungarian Jews lived in Budapest, which had all the infrastructure for a fairly normal, if still limited, Jewish life. Budapest Jews mainly adhered to the Reform—called in Hungary Neolog—rite. The Orthodox and Neolog communities had separate organizational and administrative structures. In 1992, regular services were conducted in about a score of synagogues, ranging from the Dohany Street Synagogue, the largest in Europe (now undergoing restoration), to small prayer rooms. Only three of them were Orthodox, and one Sephardic. There were two kosher restaurants in Budapest, as well as several kosher butchers, bakers, and grocers, a kosher wine merchant, and a kosher sausage factory. The Joint Distribution Committee (JDC) supported a network of kosher canteens, which in 1992 provided daily kosher meals for more than 1,000 elderly people and also functioned as social centers for the elderly. There was a Jewish newspaper, *Uj Elet*, a rabbinical seminary—during the Communist era, it was the only one in the

Eastern Bloc—with a research library, and there were several Jewish nursery, elementary, and high schools, with a total enrollment of nearly 1,200. Demand was such that enrollment could have been doubled if there were enough room and financing.

Jewish organizations, including the JDC and the World Jewish Congress, maintained offices in Budapest in the building of the Federation of Hungarian Jewish Communities.

Many Jewish community activities centered on instilling Jewish culture and religion in young people and on caring for the elderly. The Jewish summer camp at Szarvas, sponsored by the Ronald S. Lauder Foundation and the JDC, carried out a year-round schedule. Some 1,500 young people attended various programs at the camp, including 370 young Jews from other Eastern and Central European countries. Some 900 visiting parents also took part in special programs, and a special "family week" drew more than 250 children from war-torn former Yugoslavia and 70 from Czechoslovakia.

Outside Budapest, a few thousand Jews lived in scattered towns and cities, including about 20 locations where there were small organized Jewish communities of up to several hundred members, most of them elderly Holocaust survivors. Synagogues still belonging to the Jewish communities existed in many of these towns, but most were rarely used, either because the tiny size of the Jewish community made worship in a large building impractical, or because of the poor condition of the building. The major provincial Jewish communities were in Miskolc, Debrecen, and Szeged, where there were kosher canteens for community members, sponsored by the JDC. There was also an old-age home in Szeged. Jews in more isolated communities were able to get kosher meat from these towns.

In February a joint delegation representing the Roman Catholic Church and the International Jewish Committee on Interreligious Consultations met in Budapest with the primate of the Hungarian Catholic church, the papal nuncio, and leaders of the local Jewish community, as part of a fact-finding trip to Hungary, Poland, and Czechoslovakia. Throughout the year a number of cultural events and ceremonies commemorating the Holocaust took place. In January President Goncz and other dignitaries attended a ceremony held outside the Dohany Street Synagogue marking the 47th anniversary of the liberation of the Jewish ghetto from the Nazis. At the end of April, Hungarian Righteous Gentiles were honored at Budapest City Hall in the first Holocaust memorial ceremony ever held on state or city property in Hungary. Ambassador Kraus of Israel, President Goncz, and Speaker of the Parliament Gyorgy Szabad attended.

A series of Jewish-related events were held in Budapest during the first ten days of May, including a "Taste of Israel" week in which a chef from the King David Hotel in Jerusalem prepared the meals for a luxury hotel in Budapest.

Poland

As Poland continued its move toward a free-market economy, a bitter power struggle between President Lech Walesa and the government and Parliament erupted. In June the five-month-old rightist government led by Jan Olszewski was ousted after Interior Minister Antoni Maciarewicz presented Parliament with a list of public figures, including Walesa, alleged to have been secret-police informers under the old Communist regime. After lengthy political battles, a more centrist coalition led by Hanna Suchocka was installed.

Jewish-Catholic relations continued to broaden through 1992, with a number of initiatives and events. On May 25, the third annual Kosinski Jewish Heritage Award was presented by the widow of Polish-Jewish writer Jerzy Kosinski to the cochairmen of the Polish Council of Christians and Jews, Jewish leader Stanislaw Krajewski and Reverend Waldemar Chrostowski. The award honored their "dedication and devotion to the cause of preservation of the Jewish presence in Poland."

Jozef Cardinal Glemp was removed from the post of archbishop of Gniezno when the boundaries of Polish dioceses were redrawn in the spring. He was replaced in the Gniezno post, which is the diocese traditionally held by the Polish primate, by Archbishop Henryk Muszynski, president of the Polish episcopate's Commission for Dialogue with the Jews and a longtime champion of Jewish-Catholic dialogue. Some observers saw this as an indication that Muszynski might eventually be appointed Glemp's successor as primate. In February, as part of a trip to Poland, Czechoslovakia, and Hungary, a joint delegation including representatives of the International Jewish Committee on Interreligious Consultations (IJCIC) and Catholic representatives met with Muszynski and other senior Polish Catholic officials including Glemp, local Jewish community leaders, and the papal nuncio. In July a Jewish-Catholic delegation from the United States, organized by the Center for Christian Jewish Understanding at Sacred Heart University in Fairfield, Connecticut, and led by Archbishop William Keeler of Baltimore and Rabbi Jack Bemporad of Lawrence, New York, prayed and held four days of talks with Polish Roman Catholic leaders on a trip that encompassed Warsaw, Krakow, Czestochowa, and Auschwitz.

At Auschwitz, both of these interreligious groups checked on the construction progress of the new convent for Carmelite nuns, whose presence in an old theater building abutting the Auschwitz camp had for years elicited Jewish protests. The Interfaith Center for Information, Meetings, Dialogue, Education, and Prayer that was to form part of the complex housing the new convent opened in the late summer, and the new convent building itself was nearly completed by the end of the year.

Work continued on implementing changes at the Auschwitz camp museum, aimed at correcting the Communist-era disinformation that virtually denied the overwhelming Jewish character of Auschwitz victims. The deputy director of the museum said the facility needed an estimated $42 million for essential restoration and maintenance work alone. In November Germany announced that it would provide Poland with $6 million for Auschwitz restoration.

Israeli president Chaim Herzog visited Poland in May. In addition to meeting with President Walesa and other senior officials, he visited Auschwitz, where a monument commemorating this first visit by a president of Israel was erected at the building of the Auschwitz museum detailing Jewish suffering under the Nazis.

Relations between Israel and Poland grew stronger on many fronts. Tourism was up, and in December, 50 Israeli companies sent representatives to Warsaw to meet with agents of 450 Polish firms seeking joint ventures. A few Israelis were reported to have settled in Poland. In September a branch of the Polish-Israeli Friendship Society was opened in Oswiecim—the Polish town where the Auschwitz camp is located.

There were numerous Holocaust-related events throughout the year. During the last week of April and first week of May, 5,000 Jewish youths, Holocaust survivors, and visiting dignitaries from 42 countries participated in the third biennial March of the Living, a trip that took them first to Holocaust sites in Poland and then to Israel. The Polish part of the trip culminated in a two-mile march from Auschwitz to Birkenau. Elsewhere in the country, several new monuments to Jewish Holocaust victims were dedicated, and commemorative ceremonies were held. On July 19, a ceremony to commemorate the 50th anniversary of the destruction of the local Jewish community was held in Radomysl Wielki, at the monument erected in 1987 to Jewish Holocaust victims. The ceremony was attended by about 100 local towns-people, as well as 14 Jews, including survivors from the town and people who traced their ancestry to Radomysl Wielki. On November 9, a Holocaust memorial was dedicated in the old Jewish cemetery of Staszow, in a ceremony attended by 350 to 400 people. The event was covered extensively in the local media, which called it "a pioneer development in improving Polish-Jewish relations."

Such positive steps continued to be offset by isolated incidents of anti-Semitism. These included—in addition to scrawled graffiti—the desecration of Jewish cemeteries in Warsaw, Wroclaw, and elsewhere; demonstrations by skinheads and support-ers of various ultranationalist political parties; and publication of anti-Semitic tracts and periodicals. A number of public-opinion polls indicated that about half of the population disliked or distrusted both Jews and foreigners; about one-fifth to one-third could be considered anti-Semitic to some extent; and about one in seven Poles was decidedly anti-Semitic. In some cases, anti-Semitic manifestations were linked with anti-German displays by Polish nationalists. In Silesia—once part of Ger-many—there was concern at mounting ethnic German nationalism, particularly the fact that a growing number of monuments were being erected that honored German soldiers killed in World War II.

JEWISH COMMUNITY

Fewer than 10,000 people who considered themselves Jews lived in Poland, which before the Holocaust was home to 3.5 million Jews—Europe's biggest Jewish community. Only a few thousand of these currently had active contact with Jewish organizations; an unknown number of others either did not know about their Jewish identity or did not admit it.

About 85 percent of Poland's Jews were over 60 years of age; many were elderly Holocaust survivors, living isolated lives supported largely by the Joint Distribution Committee (JDC), whose welfare activities included regular cash assistance to more than 3,000 people. Despite the fact that Poland's post-Communist economic "shock therapy" seemed to be bearing fruit, with shops full of locally produced and imported goods and a rise in industrial production, by the end of 1992 inflation remained around 40 percent and unemployment had grown. Against this background, the JDC carried out a detailed evaluation of the needs of elderly Jews, most of whom existed on minuscule pensions. This raised fear among some elderly Jews that funds would be cut off.

Poland's Jewish religious organization, the Union of Jewish Religious Congregations in Poland (JRCP), an Orthodox body, maintained synagogues in four cities and prayer rooms in ten other locations around the country. Rabbi Menachem Joskowicz, a Gerer Hassid originally from Lodz, came from Israel to be rabbi of Warsaw in 1988. Friction developed between Joskowicz and Lodz-born rabbi Z.W. Moreino, who divided his time between Lodz and New York, over rival claims to the title of chief rabbi of Poland.

The JRCP got a tiny amount of income from the granting of *kashrut* certificates, mainly for kosher vodka, but otherwise all of its funding came from the JDC, which among other things payed for its infrastructure and the maintenance of functioning synagogues and cemeteries. JDC also provided the community with religious supplies and funded kosher canteens in six cities. In 1992 these provided about 70,000 free meals for needy elderly Jews and their sometimes non-Jewish spouses, few of whom kept kosher homes.

In addition to the religious organization, most of whose active members were elderly, the second main Jewish organization in Poland was the secular cultural organization, the TSKZ—the Social and Cultural Association of Polish Jews, which also received its funding from the JDC. The TSKZ, which under the previous regime was run by the Communists and was staunchly antireligious, ran clubs in about 16 cities, mostly frequented by older people. With the institution of democracy in Poland, the TSKZ lost much of its pro-Communist stigma and was freer to sponsor lectures, performances, and other cultural and educational programs.

A small but steadily growing phenomenon, which began in the late 1970s and greatly increased after the fall of Communism, was the rediscovery of Jewish roots by young people who sought to reconnect with the Jewish world. The work of the New York-based Ronald S. Lauder Foundation, which had taken the lead in initiating activities aimed at renewing Jewish life among younger people, was given impetus by the presence of American-born rabbi Michael Schudrich, who in September became the foundation's full-time representative in Warsaw. At least 400 Jews aged 15–45 took part in foundation-sponsored regular Jewish study programs in various cities, and some 220 people attended the Jewish summer camp at Srodborow, near Warsaw, which also was the scene of monthly cultural retreats. A new club, the Jewish Forum, was established in Warsaw by professionals, intellectuals, and business people attempting to attract unaffiliated Jews to some sort of association with Jewish life.

In June Krakow hosted its third biennial Jewish Culture Festival—a ten-day extravaganza of concerts, films, theater presentations, seminars, conferences, and exhibits. In July and August the Jewish Research Center of Krakow's Jagiellonian University ran its second intensive summer research program, encompassing a wide range of classes and field-study sessions on Polish Galician Jewish history. The Jagiellonian research center and the Jewish Historical Institute in Warsaw increasingly became centers of Jewish scholarship and research, though most of their staff members and students were not Jewish.

Much work was done this year on documenting and restoring Jewish monuments, including a survey of all Jewish cemeteries sponsored by the U.S. Commission for the Preservation of America's Heritage Abroad. Restitution of formerly Jewish property was a continuing issue, and in Krakow, city officials sent a letter to world Jewish organizations asking for help in locating heirs to Jewish property in the city. Also in Krakow, the Temple (Reform) Synagogue, built in 1862 and the only intact 19th-century synagogue still standing in Poland, was the scene of three concerts dedicated to the memory of the city's former Jewish community and in honor of its tiny contemporary Jewish community. They were sponsored in part by the New York-based World Monuments Fund, which began work on a full restoration of the synagogue.

Romania

Romania's economic situation continued to be one of the most difficult in the region, with annual inflation in 1992 topping 200 percent, many shortages, and a sharp drop in purchasing power. The country's rapidly aging Jewish community was hit hard by the harsh conditions, particularly as the Joint Distribution Committee (JDC) was forced to cut its budget to help meet new costs in other countries. (The JDC budget for Romania was over $4.2 million in 1990, and about $2.7 million in 1992.)

General elections in 1992 brought to power a government based on the conservative Democratic National Salvation Front, which had the support of extreme nationalist parties, although these parties were not members of the coalition. They included the anti-Semitic Greater Romania (Romania Mare) party, which won nearly 4 percent of the vote, and the nationalist Romanian National Unity party, whose primarily anti-Hungarian policy also had overtones of anti-Semitism, which won about 8 percent.

Leading government officials expressed support for the Jewish community, but anti-Semitism in various guises and manifestations remained a constant in Romania.

Anti-Semitic slogans were daubed on walls and subways, a monument in the northern city of Iasi to the 1941 pogrom there was vandalized with scrawled slogans, and tombstones in at least one historic Jewish cemetery were desecrated. Virulently anti-Semitic articles appeared in the press, particularly in the weekly newspapers *Romania Mare*, organ of the Greater Romania party, and *Europa*, as well as in numerous other extreme right-wing nationalist papers. The shrill attacks also included denials of the Holocaust. Both *Romania Mare* and *Europa* featured, among other things, repeated rabid attacks on Romania's Chief Rabbi Moses Rosen, who in March revealed that he had received death threats. (Rosen had received such threats in the past and for years traveled with a bodyguard.) Along with extreme right-wing nationalist political parties, various groups openly identifying with the fascist Iron Guard also fomented anti-Semitism.

JEWISH COMMUNITY

About 400,000 Romanian Jews survived the Holocaust, and almost all of them emigrated to Israel. Of the current population of about 14,000 to 15,000 Jews, about half lived in Bucharest. The remaining half were scattered around the country, where there were organized Jewish communities in about 60 locations, only 5 of which had more than 600 members. More than 75 synagogues were in active use, including more than two dozen where daily services were held, and virtually all of the 750 Jewish cemeteries were tended on a regular basis.

Most of Romania's Jews were over 60, many of them elderly Holocaust survivors who for some reason did not go to Israel. On the whole, the community was aging quickly and its numbers were dwindling. Members of the younger generation of Romanian Jews were, as one 24-year-old Bucharest student put it in 1991, "raised in the tradition of 'next year in Jerusalem.' It is a dream built up from childhood." They generally made *aliyah*, usually after completing their studies, though after the fall of the Communist regime, some admitted to being torn between wanting to leave— for purely economic if not religious reasons—and wanting to stay, in order to contribute to the building of a new Romania.

Under Communism, Romania's Jews lived under somewhat different circumstances than Jews in other Communist states. Romania was the only East European Communist state that did not break off diplomatic relations with Israel in the wake of the Six Day War in 1967. Dictator Nicolae Ceausescu allowed emigration to Israel (although he eventually demanded payment for each Jew permitted to leave) and permitted the JDC to engage in large-scale social work through the Federation of Jewish Communities of Romania (FEDROM). FEDROM was able to coordinate activity in local communities in a highly organized way. There were Jewish educational programs, old-age homes, clinics, kosher restaurants, meals-on-wheels programs, and even children's choirs. Ceausescu's policy toward Jews and Israel was clearly aimed at winning support in the West, and was a major factor in Romania receiving "most-favored-nation" trading status from the United States.

The success of Ceausescu's policy and the survival and relative well-being of the Jewish community were due in large part to Chief Rabbi Rosen, who, even before Ceausescu, played a delicate political game in which he traded support for the regime for better conditions for Jews and the possibility for them to emigrate. After the fall of Ceausescu, Rosen was sharply criticized by some for having been too close to the regime and for having kept silent about Ceausescu's corruption and oppressive policies. He and his supporters pointed to what was achieved as vindication of his behavior.

After the fall of the Ceausescu regime, Rosen was outspoken in warning of an anti-Semitic revival in Romania. In speeches and interviews this year Rosen continued to warn against the activities and media propaganda of the nationalist Romania Mare party and other groups. He reiterated his advice to Romania's remaining Jews to emigrate to Israel if the political climate did not improve. Rosen's 80th birthday was marked by high-profile celebrations attended by local leaders.

One question relating to a Jewish future in Romania was that of establishing new, younger community leadership to fill gaps left by death or emigration. In 1992 JDC brought a rabbi and two other functionaries to Bucharest from Israel. FEDROM operated ten kosher restaurants in various cities, which in 1992 served more than 670,000 meals. There were four Jewish old-age homes, two in Bucharest and two in the provinces, and also a network of medical clinics. About one-fifth of Romania's Jews received special winter relief grants from the JDC to enable them to heat their homes and buy food and clothing, and JDC-funded food packages for 2,900 Jews, containing sugar, cooking oil, powdered soup, and other hard-to-get staples, were increased from 8 a year to 12.

In Cluj-Napoca, in Transylvania, the Dr. Moshe Carmilly Institute for Hebrew and Jewish History at Babes-Bolyai University, the only academic institute of its type in Romania, founded in 1990, carried on with a full program of scholarly work and university courses. About three dozen students attended courses in Jewish history, art and literature, Hebrew, and biblical studies. Research work included ongoing efforts to inventory, catalogue, and register Jewish documents in the archives and libraries in Transylvania, and also to begin an inventory of Jewish architectural monuments in Transylvania. In October the institute organized an international conference on Central and Southeast European Jewish literature, art, music, and folklore. Included in the program was a concert of works by Jewish composers from Transylvania as well as an exhibition of works by Jewish painters from northern Transylvania who were killed in the Holocaust.

Yugoslavia/Ex-Yugoslavia

The civil war involving Slovenia, Croatia, and what remained of Yugoslavia (Serbia and Montenegro) spread to Bosnia-Herzegovina in the spring, touching off what would become Europe's bloodiest conflict since World War II. The 5,000 to 6,000 Jews in what had been Yugoslavia could not help but become involved in a number of ways. Jews or Jewish interests were to a certain extent exploited by Serbian and Croatian propagandists. Serbs and Croats and their supporters appeared to try to win Jewish support for their own side by accusing the other side of being more anti-Semitic.

JEWISH COMMUNITY

The most drastically affected Jewish communities were those of Sarajevo, where about 1,000 Jews lived before the war, and the scattered small outlying communities elsewhere in Bosnia-Herzegovina. Aided by Jewish leaders in Zagreb and Belgrade, the Joint Distribution Committee (JDC) organized three airlift operations of hundreds of people—Jews and non-Jews—from Sarajevo in April. Six bus convoys between August and the end of the year brought hundreds more people from Sarajevo to Split, on the Croatian coast. The last and largest convoy brought out 394 Jews and non-Jews. By the end of the year, JDC and local Jewish communities had helped about 900 Jews (and 900 non-Jews) escape from Bosnia. The JDC, meanwhile, supported by CBF-World Jewish Relief (UK), and with the cooperation of local Jewish communities in Serbia and Croatia, arranged care and housing for the refugees. A special Passover seder was held in Belgrade for Jews airlifted from Bosnia. By December, about 1,200 Jewish refugees had emigrated to Israel and elsewhere from ex-Yugoslavia.

Meanwhile, as Serbian fighters maintained sniper positions in the historic old Jewish cemetery on a hillside above Sarajevo, the local Jewish social and philanthropic organization, La Benevolencija, became a highly respected key link in distributing nonsectarian aid from a variety of sources within Sarajevo and elsewhere in Bosnia. In addition, it ran a soup kitchen and pharmacy serving more than 1,000 people a day.

Outside the war zone, Jews in Zagreb, Belgrade, and elsewhere coped with the emergency situation and tried to expand Jewish cultural and religious activities. The Jewish community-center complex in Zagreb, damaged by a terrorist bomb in August 1991, was reopened with a gala ceremony on Rosh Hashanah after a full-scale restoration.

RUTH ELLEN GRUBER

Australia

National Affairs

THE AUSTRALIAN LABOR PARTY (ALP), led by Prime Minister Paul Keating, continued in office throughout 1992. The opposing federal coalition of the Liberal and National parties was led by Dr. John Hewson. In state elections in October, the ALP retained power in Queensland but lost to the Liberals in Victoria and Western Australia. Economic issues dominated political debate at all levels, for the nation was still suffering under a severe recession, with unemployment higher than at any time since the Great Depression.

Israel and the Middle East

Addressing the biennial conference of the Zionist Federation of Australia (ZFA) in May, Prime Minister Keating maintained that Australia's policy toward the Arab-Israeli dispute was "a balanced one which takes account of political realities in the region. . . . Australia is not only committed to Israel's security, but also recognizes the right of the Palestinian people to self-determination. This allows, logically, for the possibility of their own independent state if they so choose."

Only a few days earlier, the government had announced a decision to lift the ban on official contact with the Palestine Liberation Organization (PLO) that was imposed by the Hawke administration during the Gulf War. According to Keating, this decision was "consistent with our long-established aim of encouraging the forces of moderation rather than extremism within the PLO." There had been no change in the government's basic policy, he said. "We do not accept the PLO's claim to be the sole representative of the Palestinian people, but we do accept that the organization represents the view of a significant proportion of them." He added, "Australia has long expressed its opposition to Israel's continued settlement activity in the occupied territories. As friends of Israel, we have to say that we regard such activity as an obstacle to peace."

The decision to reopen contacts with the PLO had been announced—not in Parliament but in a news release—by Minister for Foreign Affairs Gareth Evans three days before he departed on a 12-day visit to six Middle East countries, which was still in progress when Keating addressed the Zionist group. The announcement came, ZFA president Mark Leibler told Paul Keating at the conference, "as a bolt from the blue. . . .Senator Evans has given the PLO an enormous and unwarranted boost." The decision was condemned by the federal Liberal-National opposition, which accused Keating, an ALP right-winger, of "paying off his debt" to the left of his party for ensuring his election as leader. Coalition leader John Hewson assured the ZFA conference that the opposition was committed to its policy of not engaging in official dialogue with the PLO "until there is clear evidence that the PLO accepts Israel's right to exist, is genuinely committed to the peace process and is prepared to back its words on both these matters with consistent action." The opposition, he added, would press the government to reverse its decision.

The decision was the subject of an official protest to the government by Israel's ambassador, Zvi Kedar. In August Governor-General Bill Hayden, a former federal ALP leader, dismayed Jewish leaders when he met with the PLO's Australian representative, Ali Kazak, in Canberra. The meeting was the first since the lifting of the ban on contact with the PLO.

During his Middle East visit in May, Foreign Affairs Minister Evans honored an undertaking to raise the plight of Syrian Jews with the government in Damascus. His other activities, however, provoked communal anger. *Australian Jewish News* political analyst Bernard Freedman asserted that Evans "set out deliberately to promote the role of the PLO in the Middle East peace process." In Beirut, for instance, Evans said that the Israelis "mightn't like it very much, but the PLO are a reality." In Cairo he met Nabil Shaath, a senior adviser to Yasir Arafat, dubbing him a force for moderation within the PLO. In private meetings with Prime Minister Yitzhak Shamir and Foreign Minister David Levy, he repeated his oft-voiced criticism of Israeli settlement activity as an obstacle to peace and his charges of human-rights violations in the territories.

Immediately upon arrival in Israel he undertook a private tour, arranged by the Australian embassy, of UNRWA-administered Palestinian refugee camps on the West Bank. Later he met with Palestinian peace-talks negotiators Faisal Husseini and Hanan Ashrawi in Jerusalem. At a concluding press conference in Israel, Evans explained Australia's decision to renew ministerial-level dialogue with the PLO as "a recognition of its decision to back the peace process and an effort to encourage moderate Palestinian elements under the unruly organizational umbrella." He also said that despite Australia's strictures, she "is and always will be a friend of Israel," and reiterated Australia's traditional commitment to Israel's right to live in secure and recognized borders.

Evans's statements on his Middle East tour drew a barrage of criticism from mainstream Australian Jewish leaders. ZFA president Mark Leibler captured the communal mood when he termed Evans's statements "hostile, one-sided, provocative and quite antagonistic." Evans assured a joint delegation of the ZFA and the Executive Council of Australian Jewry (ECAJ) in June that there had been no change in the government's attitude. Pressed by Prime Minister Keating to redress the balance of his criticisms of Israel, Evans repeated this assurance at Jewish public meetings in Melbourne and Sydney in July and August. He also conceded that his comments lacked balance, and agreed that he should have used his media opportunities to contrast Israel's human-rights record with those of its Arab neighbors and to emphasize the precarious situation of the enemy-encircled Jewish state. Evans's assurances failed to dispel Jewish unease completely; however, when Evans addressed a Jewish audience in Sydney in August, Mark Leibler stressed that the community's differences with him had been resolved. And Leslie Caplan, president of the Executive Council of Australian Jewry paid tribute to him as a "tried, true and tested" friend of Israel.

In July Keating told a joint delegation of ZFA and ECAJ leaders that no talks would be held with the PLO unless they were for a specific purpose, and that the government would desist from such dialogue if it was deemed to imperil peace negotiations. In October Evans approved revised guidelines for Australia's voting at the UN, which were expected to result in less support for extreme anti-Israel resolutions. Under the new guidelines, for example, Australia would resist the use of "inflammatory and excessive language" as well as any description of the PLO as "the sole representative of the Palestinian people."

ARAB BOYCOTT

Documents obtained by the Zionist Federation of Australia under the Freedom of Information Act revealed that successive Australian governments, while refusing to sanction the Arab trade boycott against Israel, deliberately avoided applying antiboycott measures. Moreover, certain Foreign Affairs and Trade Department officials and other public servants had actively helped Australian companies to comply with the boycott. In February a joint delegation from the ZFA and the ECAJ raised the boycott issue with Foreign Minister Evans, who promised stronger Australian government action domestically and internationally to oppose the boycott. Evans stopped short of agreeing to introduce legislation to prohibit compliance with the boycott, but he did instruct nongovernment trade organizations, the chambers of commerce, and the Australian Manufacturers' Export Council that they must not use government-authorized certificates of origin to support the boycott. Meanwhile, the current combined trade between Australia and Israel was only $A200 million. The Australia-Israel Chamber of Commerce resolved to improve trade, and a delegation of Australian business leaders traveled to Israel in an effort to stimulate its growth.

OTHER MATTERS

Following a visit to Australia by Gideon Spiro, a representative of the Israeli Committee for Mordechai Vanunu, a group of Australian senators joined an international campaign calling for the release of the Israeli antinuclear activist and convicted traitor.

In receipt of advice from the Department of Foreign Affairs, the Department of Immigration rejected the application for refugee status of self-described Israeli intelligence agent Ari Ben-Menashe, who was living in Sydney. Ben-Menashe, who complied with an order to leave Australia, had claimed publicly that he was involved in the U.S.-Iran arms-for-hostages deal, that $A82 million worth of arms was shipped to Iran via Western Australia in 1987, and that $A8.5 million was donated to an Australian political party to facilitate the operation. He said he wanted to stay in Australia because he feared he would be "unjustly dealt with" if he returned to Israel, where he could be tried in secret for infringing that country's official secrets law.

In March Prime Minister Keating promised World Zionist Organization chairman Simcha Dinitz that he would support moves to establish regular El Al air service between Australia and Israel. Prime Minister Keating, whose support was necessary owing to the security factor, was as good as his word, and in September the federal cabinet approved the start of negotiations. In November Australian and Israeli aviation officials held talks in Canberra regarding security arrangements. Weekly direct flights between Melbourne and Tel Aviv were expected to commence in mid-1993.

Anti-Semitism and Extremism

Australia had very little anti-Semitism, by international standards. Most significant anti-Semitism stemmed from a few extremist sources. An upsurge in reported acts of intimidation against Jews and Jewish property apparently peaked during the Gulf War. However, the economic recession provided a spawning ground for racism, which was directed mainly against Asian immigrants. The right-wing, populist Australian League of Rights, which had successfully infiltrated economically distressed rural areas, remained the most significant single and continuous source of racism, as well as of anti-Semitism and anti-Zionism.

According to investigative journalist David Greason, the Citizens' Electoral Council (CEC) movement, a former subsidiary of the League, was the main backer in Australia of the extreme right-wing, anti-Semitic organization led by Lyndon LaRouche in the United States. Greason alleged that LaRouche sympathizers had seized control of CEC branches in Queensland, New South Wales, and Victoria, and that the LaRouche organization was also linked to the Western Australian Rural Action Movement. The LaRoucheites had attracted support from people connected with the Committee to Save the Children in Iraq, which in January held a rally outside the U.S. consulate in Melbourne. One speaker was Don Veith, head of a group called Friends of LaRouche in Australia. He helped to establish the Victorian Community Alliance, an independent umbrella group linked to the anti-Semitic far right, which fielded about 40 candidates in the Victorian state election in August. The Committee to Save the Children in Iraq was also associated with the pro-Libyan former far-right activist Robert Pash, who published LaRouche material in his newsletter, *New Dawn*. Also linked with the LaRouche organization were two parliamentarians: Dennis Stevenson, a member of the Australian Capital Territory Legislative Assembly, and Denis Collins, a member of the Northern Territory Legislative Assembly. Both had made anti-Semitic allegations under cover of parliamentary privilege.

The Australian Press Council, a body that arbitrates complaints about newspaper items, made the significant ruling that "if a newspaper item is found offensive by some people, that is not sufficient grounds to condemn the publication. . . ." The ruling came in response to a complaint brought by Prof. W.D. Rubinstein against the *Weekend Australian* for publishing an allegedly anti-Semitic review of his book *The Jews in Australia: A Thematic History . . . 1945 to the Present*. Rubinstein denounced the Press Council's decision, claiming that it would enable newspapers to print objectionable criticism of Jews and other minorities. "In order to obtain a sympathetic ruling," he said, "we now have to show something is out and out Nazism." In another important test case, the Press Council dismissed a complaint from Jeremy Jones, director of the Sydney office of Australia/Israel Publications, over the *Sydney Morning Herald*'s use of the term "Polish Jew" in a report on former Melbourne businessman Abe Goldberg. However, the Press Council urged "caution in the use of ethnic-religious labels" such as that under consideration, and noted that the complaint "highlights the sensitivity to such phrases and their capacity to give offense."

Invited by the Jewish quarterly journal *Generation* to comment on the way Jews and Jewish issues are depicted in the Australian media, Terry Lane, a regular Australian Broadcasting Corporation (ABC) broadcaster and newspaper columnist long noted for jibes against Israel and its supporters and against multiculturalism, inveighed against "the Zionist lobby in this country." Asserting that criticism of Israel was not tolerated, he announced that he would "never write or speak on the subject of Israel or Palestine ever again. . . . To the Zionists I say: you win. . . ."

At Melbourne University, an anti-Semitic campaign, denounced by the university authorities, was directed against three Jewish candidates for editorial positions on the student newspaper.

Michael Phillips, a Jewish Immigration Department official who publicly accused senior immigration bureaucrats of racism toward Asian asylum seekers, claimed that top bureaucrats told him that Jews should not be involved in determining refugee status because they were not impartial. Bureaucrats allegedly cited former human rights commissioner Justice Marcus Einfeld, who had called Australia's deportation of Cambodian asylum seekers a "national shame."

Allegations by federal Liberal parliamentarian Ken Aldred and Deakin University lecturer Barbara Smith that Jewish trust beneficiaries resident in Israel were involved in large-scale schemes to avoid paying Australian income tax were denied by Taxation Commissioner Trevor Boucher and his deputy. The focus of Aldred and Smith's charge was leading tax attorney Mark Leibler, whose clients, Aldred claimed, received favored treatment from the Taxation Office because Leibler was an adviser to the commissioner and a member of the National Tax Liaison Group. Leibler disputed Aldred's claim, accusing him of being extremely selective in quoting from Taxation Office documents. He added: "The context in which Mr. Aldred's observation was made was clearly designed to suggest . . . impropriety on the part of the Australian Jewish community."

Immigration

Owing to Australia's high unemployment, the federal government took steps to reduce immigration, which went into effect March 1. Among measures proposed for further cuts was a reduction in "concessional" family migration, which brought in many workers with poor English, few skills, and little immediate chance of finding jobs, among them many migrants from Russia and Eastern Europe. Nevertheless, some 1,100 Jews from the Commonwealth of Independent States (the former Soviet Union) were among the first to be allocated places in Australia's new "special-assistance" migration category. This category was intended to help people who had a special need to resettle in Australia but did not meet the United Nations definition of a refugee. The main criteria used for selecting people in the special-assistance category were: the degree of distress individuals suffered because of severe disorder or violence; whether a person was a member of a disadvantaged or oppressed minority; and the extent of the person's link with Australia. The total quota for refugee, humanitarian, and special-assistance migrants was 12,000 for the year.

Meanwhile, the Liberal opposition had committed itself to requiring an English-language test for all nonrefugee applicants. Liberals claimed that an English-language test would prevent some of the low-skilled, non-English-speakers from coming to Australia, where they either joined the unemployment ranks or were disproportionately represented in declining industries and occupations. The Liberals also advocated a two-year moratorium on welfare payments to new immigrants.

Walter Lippmann, president of the Federation of Australian Jewish Welfare Societies, criticized the "harshness" of the government's requirement for sponsorship guarantees for parents ($A3,500 per individual, $A5,000 for a couple) and urged his colleagues to continue supporting the efforts of the Federation of Ethnic Communities Councils to modify this requirement, which would seriously hamper Russian Jewish immigration. Lippmann also urged continued support by the Jewish community for a nondiscriminatory, humanitarian immigration program, including family reunion. The latter was particularly relevant to Jews from the former Soviet Union.

Nazi War Criminals

Ivan Timofeyevich Polyukovich was committed by the Adelaide Magistrates' Court to stand trial on charges of having committed atrocities against Jews in Ukraine in 1941–43; his trial was expected to take place early in 1993. The same court found that there was insufficient evidence to justify bringing to trial Mikhail

Berezowsky, who was charged with killing 102 Jews from the Ukrainian village of Gnivan in 1942. A third Adelaide resident, Heinrich Wagner, was accused of involvement in the killing of over 120 Jews, including the shooting of 19 young children of mixed parentage, in the Ukrainian village of Israylovka in 1942, and with the murder of a railroad construction worker in 1943. His committal hearing was still proceeding at year's end. All three men were charged following inquiries by the Special Investigations Unit (SIU), set up by the federal government in 1987. In accordance with a federal cabinet decision taken in 1990, the SIU closed on June 30; further investigation of possible war criminals in Australia was handed over to the federal police. The War Crimes Amendment Act, under which charges were brought, remained on the statute book.

In August the federal cabinet endorsed a decision by Attorney General Michael Duffy to abandon the investigation of an unnamed Melbourne man alleged to have committed atrocities against Jews in Latvia. The decision dismayed Jewish leaders, who made it clear to the government that they expected any future cases brought under the still existing war-crimes legislation to proceed. Attorney Bob Greenwood, former director of the SIU, declared that the man in question would have been charged with "thousands of murders," and that his would have been the biggest war-crimes trial in the world except for John Demjanjuk's in Israel. He accused the government of dropping the case because it would have been "internationally significant; they didn't want the publicity," and said he had been told by politicians that there must be some limit to expenditure in such matters and that they "cannot take any further risk of divisive influences in Australian politics." In a letter to World Jewish Congress cochairman Isi Leibler, Attorney General Duffy denied that the case had been abandoned for primarily political reasons. He claimed that "a realistic assessment" of the evidence led to the conclusion that there was little likelihood of a successful prosecution and stated that the cabinet had decided against any more special funding for war-crimes investigations, "with the exception of any inquiries necessary to support the current prosecutions."

Meanwhile, Efraim Zuroff, director of the Simon Wiesenthal Center in Los Angeles, claimed that new material available since the breakup of the Soviet Union was providing dozens of new leads that seemed to implicate former residents of Ukraine and the Baltic states now living in Australia. Zuroff castigated the closure of the SIU, and his implied charge that Australian Jewish leaders had taken a passive stance on the issue led to a heated exchange of correspondence in the *Jerusalem Post*. Zuroff's headline-grabbing tactics had long worried Australian Jewish leaders who, while zealous for war-crimes prosecutions, did not want to alienate the general public by being too visible in the cause, which they preferred to promote as humanity's in general. In the words of Isi Leibler, the Wiesenthal Center's "long, poorly researched lists of alleged criminals that sent Australian investigators on exorbitantly expensive and mostly futile wild-goose chases halfway around the world" had undermined "quiet, unpublicized" efforts to bring the perpetrators of atrocities to justice.

JEWISH COMMUNITY

Demography

The Australian federal census, taken every five years, asks an optional religious question. Results from the 1991 census, released in early 1993, showed a 7.7-percent increase in the number of persons who declared themselves to be Jewish by religion since the last census in 1986: numbers rose from 69,089 to 74,386. The number of declared Jews by religion rose in all states, with Queensland showing a remarkable 62.6-percent rise in Jewish numbers in only five years, from 2,631 to 4,278 (many of these are believed to be Jews from other states vacationing at Queensland resorts such as the Gold Coast). More Australian Jews continued to reside in Victoria (Melbourne), with 33,862 Jews (up from 32,385 in 1986, a 4.6-percent increase), followed by New South Wales (Sydney), with 29,614 (up from 28,197, or 5.0 percent); Western Australia (Perth), 4,221 (up from 3,919, a rise of 12.8 percent); South Australia (Adelaide), 1,304 (up from 1,144, a 14.0-percent rise); the Australian Capital Territory (Canberra), 530 (up from 501, a rise of 5.8 percent); and the Northern Territory (Darwin), 143 (up from 98, a 45.9-percent increase). Since 23.4 percent of Australians fail to give a religious denomination on census forms, most demographers put the number of Australian Jews far higher, at about 100,000 or more. The Jewish Welfare Society in Melbourne maintained a master list of all Jews in Victoria, believed to be about 95 percent complete; the list contained about 47,000 names, nearly 40 percent more than the 1991 census figure of 33,862.

According to a report entitled *Multicultural Australia*, issued by the Australian Bureau of Statistics and using data from the 1986 census, Jews formed the largest ethnic group (32 percent) among native-born Australians with higher education. Among Australian-born people with overseas-born parents, Jews had the lowest unemployment rate (4 percent). However, according to the Australian Jewish Welfare Society, the rate of unemployment in the Jewish community of Melbourne, Victoria (the state hardest hit by recession) was marginally higher than the national figure of 10.7 percent, reflecting the fact that the self-employed and those in senior and middle management were the worst affected.

The New South Wales edition of the *Atlas of the Australian People*, compiled by Prof. Graeme Hugo and issued this year, showed Jews as one of the most spatially concentrated ethnic groups in New South Wales. It also showed that the South African component in Australian Jewry had risen markedly since 1981. The compiler added his voice to those calling for the question on ancestry to be restored to the 1996 census; the question was included in 1986 but deleted in 1991.

Communal Affairs

Jewish communal life occurred against the backdrop of economic recession; fund-raising for welfare services and other communal requirements was difficult.

However, financial mismanagement rather than the recession was blamed when the Jewish Community Council of Victoria reported a cash-flow crisis that made it difficult to meet basic operational costs. A healthy balance in 1990 had in 1992 turned into a colossal deficit, and bank liabilities had more than doubled in two years.

Michael Marx was elected president of the New South Wales Jewish Board of Deputies, replacing Gerry Levy. Isi Leibler of Victoria was elected president of the Executive Council of Australian Jewry (ECAJ) at its year-end conference, for an unprecedented fourth term (though not consecutive, since the position alternates between Melbourne and Sydney). He replaced outgoing New South Wales president Leslie Caplan. In a break with custom, Leibler allotted portfolios and consultancies to elected and drafted councillors from New South Wales (Sydney) as well as from his home state, and the ECAJ's administrative headquarters remained in Sydney instead of moving to Melbourne, as it normally did when the presidency rotated between the two capitals. The position of Sydney-based ECAJ executive director Jeremy Jones, who had served under Caplan, was upgraded to executive vice-president. Leibler announced his intention of holding three meetings a year of the full council, instead of monthly meetings, as in the past.

The Zionist Supreme Court in Jerusalem, upholding an appeal by the Zionist Federation of Australia (ZFA), unanimously allocated an extra 11th seat to the Australian delegation at the 32nd World Zionist Congress, held in Jerusalem in July. The decision was ascribed to Australia's "excellent performance against a criteria table which includes aliya, education, membership of Zionist organizations and youth activities." At the congress, ZFA president Mark Leibler was elected to the board of governors of the Jewish Agency, joining two other Australians on that 74-member body.

Returning in January from a visit to Israel, where he had meetings with Prime Minister Yitzhak Shamir and Defense Minister Moshe Arens, World Jewish Congress cochairman Isi Leibler predicted an enhanced role for the WJC in the Asia-Pacific region in view of the enthusiasm he had found in Israel for trade and diplomatic links with Asian nations, combined with a recent softening of attitude on the part of the latter. Israeli Foreign Office bureaucrats asked Leibler to return to China and India to pursue projects he had initiated in those countries in 1991. Accordingly, in February he had talks in Beijing and New Delhi with high officials, including Chinese vice-premier Wu Xueqian and Indian prime minister Narasimha Rao.

The Jewish Crisis Center merged with the large, long-established Australian Jewish Welfare Society (AJWS) to form a single social-welfare agency for Melbourne Jews. The AJWS came under fire from Russian clients who held that legal action was wrongfully taken against them for failure to make loan repayments.

Religion

In March Chief Rabbi Jonathan Sacks of the United Hebrew Congregations of the British Commonwealth visited Australia with his wife, Elaine. He told meetings in Melbourne and Sydney, arranged by the Australian Institute of Jewish Affairs, that if Progressive Jews agreed to satisfy the requirements of Orthodoxy on the issues of divorce and conversion in the interests of Jewish unity, he would applaud their "statesmanlike, visionary and courageous" initiative. During Chief Rabbi Sacks's visit, the National Council of Jewish Women urged him to give priority to solving within Halakhah the problems associated with divorce, especially the problem of *agunot* (deserted wives).

Also during his visit, Rabbi Sacks endorsed the very narrow election victory of Rabbi Philip Heilbrunn of the St. Kilda Hebrew Congregation as president of the Association of Rabbis and Ministers of Australia and New Zealand (an Orthodox organization), following a challenge to the validity of the electoral process by supporters—mainly but not entirely Chabad-Lubavitch rabbis—of the losing candidate, Rabbi Chaim Gutnick of Elwood Talmud Torah. Reflecting the recent rightward drift of Australian Jewish Orthodoxy (which under Rabbi Heilbrunn's leadership now extended to the hitherto lax-to-moderate St. Kilda Hebrew Congregation), and especially the influence of the Lubavitcher movement, the rabbinic association's conference in March unanimously passed a resolution—moved by Rabbi Selwyn Franklin of Sydney's Central Synagogue—alerting Australian Jewry to the great potential for "messianic redemption" now at hand and encouraging the study of those parts of Torah that deal with the concepts of redemption and increased observance of *mitzvot*, with the intention of hastening the messianic redemption.

Like the adherents of Rabbi Menachem Schneerson elsewhere, the Australian Lubavitcher community viewed world events such as the Gulf War, the disintegration of the Soviet Union, and the return of Soviet Jews to Israel as indications of the imminence of the messianic redemption. In May the Melbourne *bet din* (Rabbis Sholem Gutnick, Shlomo Rudzki, and Jacob Schreiber) placed an advertisement in the *Australian Jewish News* endorsing Rabbi Schneerson as the messiah. The advertisement was greeted in the community with widespread derision. Progressive leaders such as Rabbi John Levi were openly scathing, and so were many Orthodox, among them Rabbi Selwyn Franklyn, Rabbi Ronald Lubofsky, rabbi emeritus of the St. Kilda Hebrew Congregation, and Rabbi Boruch Zaichyk of Melbourne's Mizrachi Center, who declared that the *bet din*'s statement "borders . . . on heresy," which provoked a furious rejoinder from the three *dayanim*. Before long, the story had broken in a bemused national press and was featured on national television.

Meanwhile, the Lubavitch movement had more mundane preoccupations. Denying persistent rumors of impending financial disaster, Rabbi Yitzhok Dovid Groner of Melbourne's Yeshivah Center admitted that the center had been severely affected by the recession, and that plans for additional buildings had to be postponed. Rabbi Yisroel Rosenfeld, who used his home in the outer Melbourne suburb of Waverley as a Chabad House, was forbidden by the local council to use the premises as "a place of worship," following complaints from neighbors worried about excessive noise, parking congestion, and a threat to property values.

Temple Beth Israel in Melbourne, Australia's largest Progressive congregation, also admitted to a financial crisis. Heavily in debt to the bank for loans borrowed for the expansion of its premises during the previous decade, the congregation imposed a controversial one-time levy in addition to its normal, rather steep, annual membership fee. Meanwhile, Rabbi Brian Michelson, an American, joined the temple following the departure of Rabbi Daniel Schiff. The temple's senior rabbi, Rabbi John Levi, predicted at the Australia-New Zealand Union for Progressive Judaism's Sydney conference in November that the future of Progressive Judaism in Australia would be secured by immigration from North America, which would occur because the "social structure of the United States is coming apart," and also from South America.

In June the Gold Coast Temple Shalom's new synagogue began holding regular Friday-night services. It had no minister, but Rabbi Uri Themal, head of Queensland's Bureau of Ethnic Affairs, officiated monthly. In August Bet-Yossef: The Caro Synagogue, an Orthodox congregation founded by Jews of North African and Middle Eastern origin, was opened in the Sydney suburb of Bondi in premises belonging to the Adath Yisroel Congregation. Aimed especially at former Israelis, fluent Hebrew speakers, and young couples, the congregation soon claimed a regular Sabbath attendance of 60 to 100. Services were led by members and by rabbis visiting from Israel. The congregation charged no membership fees but relied on donations to fund its activities. The estimated 40 Jews in the far north Queensland city of Cairns, who the previous year had organized High Holy Day services for the first time, continued to develop their community. They formed a district committee of the Jewish National Fund, and, under the supervision of Rabbi Moshe Cohen of Brisbane Hebrew Congregation, a representative of the Brisbane *hevra kadisha* (burial society) consecrated a Jewish burial site in the Cairns cemetery.

At the start of the year, Perth, in Western Australia, became the second Australian capital city to have an *eruv* (an area designated by rabbinic authorities within which Orthodox Jews may carry personal items and wheel baby carriages on the Sabbath). In June, Melbourne's *eruv* was extended to parts of suburban Bentleigh, East Bentleigh, and Chadstone, to meet the demands of congregants of the Chabad House in Bentleigh.

During the year, the Melbourne Hebrew Congregation celebrated the 150th anniversary of its founding. The North Eastern Jewish War Memorial Center in the Melbourne suburb of Doncaster, whose numbers had grown thanks to recent immigration from South Africa, celebrated its 30th anniversary.

The Orthodox-Progressive dialogue group in Melbourne, which was under the leadership of Isi Leibler (Orthodox) and Walter Jona (Progressive), continued to function and sponsored a major public seminar at Temple Beth Israel. But a genuine breakthrough toward conciliation on tendentious issues, such as the role and status of women in Jewish law and liturgy, remained elusive.

Jewish-Christian Relations

In April the Australian Catholic Bishops' Conference issued a set of guidelines for Catholic-Jewish relations. The guidelines strongly urged Catholic clergy, nuns, teachers, and laypeople to foster mutual understanding and respect between Catholics and Jews, to encourage interfaith dialogue, to confront anti-Semitism by instituting "a frank and honest treatment in our history books, courses and seminary curricula," to avoid proselytizing, and to "make an honest effort to understand the link between the land [of Israel] and the [Jewish] people." Conference organizers explained that the need for guidelines had become apparent for several reasons: the increased number of anti-Semitic incidents in the previous two years; growing interest in interfaith relations in Australia's increasingly pluralistic society; the large number of Holocaust survivors in Australia who "still find themselves exposed to denials of the Holocaust, attempted relativizing of the event and impatience with Jewish sensitivity"; evangelist activity; the upsurge of fundamentalism; increased awareness of Jewish concerns through contact with Jews; and "the close bonds that unite" the two faiths. Rabbi Raymond Apple, chairman of the New South Wales Council of Christians and Jews and senior rabbi at Sydney's Great Synagogue, welcomed the guidelines as a "landmark in interreligious history." The Executive Council of Australian Jewry participated in their official presentation in Sydney in November.

Formal relations with the Anglican Church also improved this year. In April a group from the New South Wales Jewish Board of Deputies and the ECAJ met with Archbishop Donald Robinson of Sydney at his request. The archbishop briefed the delegation on his visit to Israel and the Middle East earlier in the year, undertaken on behalf of the Australian Council of Churches. He had returned with a positive attitude toward Israel and a desire to improve relations with the Jewish community. In August Bishop John Reid of South Sydney successfully introduced a motion at the Anglican General Synod of Australia proposing that the church should formulate guidelines for relations with Jews.

In November the ECAJ and the Uniting Church in Australia (an amalgam of Presbyterian moderates, Methodists, and Congregationalists) agreed to improve communication. The move was encouraging because relations between the Uniting Church and the Jewish community had been badly strained owing to anti-Israel material issued by the church the previous year.

Jewish-Muslim Relations

Rabbi Brian Fox of Temple Emanuel in the Sydney suburb of Woollahra told the Community Relations Advisory Committee (CRAC) of the New South Wales Jewish Board of Deputies in August that the Jewish community should open formal dialogue with local Muslims. He expressed similar views in separate meetings with Progressive and Orthodox colleagues in Melbourne and Sydney, becoming the first mainstream Jewish leader since the Gulf War to urge such a course. Before that war there had been informal contacts between other rabbinic leaders and leading Muslims. CRAC chairman Peter Wertheim said he believed that, while there was little possibility that Jews and Muslims in Australia could agree on Middle East issues, they could present a united voice on the immigration debate and the campaign against racism.

In September Belgrade-born Sunni Muslim sociology lecturer Sheikh Abdullah Nu'man, a former member of the Islamic Council of Victoria, gave an eloquent and moving speech on "ethnic cleansing" in Bosnia-Herzegovina before a large Friday-night congregation at Melbourne's Temple Beth Israel. Invited to the temple by Rabbi John Levi, Sheikh Nu'man (who several years earlier had read a passage from the Koran in an "interfaith prayer for peace" at the temple) spoke of Muslim-Jewish cooperation in his former homeland and drew parallels between "ethnic cleansing" and the Holocaust. He also joined the congregation in worship.

Many Australian Jewish leaders, including ECAJ president Leslie Caplan, added their voices to the growing worldwide condemnation of atrocities against Muslims and others in "concentration camps" in Bosnia. Earlier in the year, some 25 Jewish and Muslim women attended an informal and unadvertised meeting sponsored by the Victorian Ethnic Affairs Commission and organized by Commissioner Molly Jedwab. Discussion covered Jewish and Muslim divorce law, dress requirements, discrimination, and the problems experienced by Muslim women during the Gulf War. Ms. Jedwab planned to establish a women's issues working group within the commission, in order to facilitate further dialogue.

Education

Monash University in Victoria opened the Center for Jewish Civilization in April and appointed Dr. Evan Zuesse as its first lecturer in modern Jewish history; he began teaching in June. Deakin University, also in Victoria, announced plans to establish a center for Jewish studies, to coordinate current and future courses. Deakin already had a Jewish studies program on its Toorak campus, but envisaged that it would require several years to develop a comprehensive sequence of courses, which it hoped would eventually be available for off-campus students via correspondence. Courses in Jewish studies were also available in New South Wales at Sydney, Macquarie, and New South Wales universities.

An estimated 90 percent of Jewish children in Australia received some form of Jewish education, through all-day schools, part-time after-school classes, or Sunday school. Figures available from the Sydney-based Australian Coordinating Committee on Jewish Day Schools indicated that the national enrollment for these schools had increased 2 percent at the start of 1992, though overall Sydney and Melbourne figures remained the same as the previous year. Queensland, with a new school—Sinai College, which opened in Brisbane in 1991—recorded an increase, while figures dropped in Adelaide and Perth. The secular Bialik College was the fastest-growing Jewish school in Melbourne, where a substantial increase at the primary level forced the addition of extra classes. While a few children had transferred to Bialik from other Jewish day schools, most of the new students came from non-Jewish private and state schools. Also in Melbourne, the Jewish Secular Humanist Society opened a Sunday school in February. Its classes, open to students between the ages of 8 and 16, had a cultural and ethical focus and included a course in modern Hebrew.

Culture

A four-day conference on Sephardic Jewry was held in Melbourne in September to mark the 500th anniversary of the expulsion of Jews from Spain. A visiting American expert on Hebrew poetry, Prof. Ezra Spicehandler, headed the panel of speakers. Barrie Kosky, acclaimed young director of the Gilgul Theater in the Melbourne suburb of St. Kilda, staged a popular production of *The Dybbuk*, which earned him two top national awards.

Early in the year, the program schedules for the Hebrew and Yiddish broadcasts of SBS (Special Broadcasting Service) radio in Melbourne and Sydney were revised, and Hebrew programs were substantially reduced. Yiddish programs were less severely cut, but there was widespread discontent among Jewish listeners over the new time slots for those programs. Consultation with SBS chiefs revealed that SBS had acted only on the basis of estimates of language groups, not on ethnic population figures. As a result, the Yiddish programs were to be restored to a Friday time slot.

Publications

Among notable Jewish books appearing this year were *The Enduring Remnant: The First 150 Years of the Melbourne Hebrew Congregation 1841–1991* by Joseph Aron and Judy Arndt; *Life Is a Corridor* by Rabbi Dr. Shalom Coleman, rabbi emeritus of the Perth Hebrew Congregation; *The Journal of an Australian Rabbi*, the posthumously published memoir of Rabbi Dr. Israel Porush, former chief minister of Sydney's Great Synagogue, issued by the Australian Jewish Historical Society; *The Future Is Past*, the self-published reminiscences of Melbourne communal personality and left-wing activist Evelyn Rothfield; *Things Could Be Worse*, a collection of interconnected stories by Lily Brett, focusing on a Jewish central character; *Between Yesterday and Tomorrow* by Matylda Engelman, a novel exploring the tensions confronting Holocaust survivors and their descendants in Australia; and *Aviva Gold*, a children's story by Jean Holkner.

Personalia

David Levine became a justice of the supreme court of New South Wales. Michael Rozenes was appointed federal director of public prosecutions. David Rosalky became head of the treasury of the Australian Capital Territory (ACT). Australia's ambassador to the United Nations, Peter Wilenski, was named head of the Department of Foreign Affairs. Prominent businessman Sir Peter Abeles retired as managing director of the international transport giant TNT and of the domestic airline Ansett Australia. In December Yehuda Avner became Israel's ambassador to Australia, succeeding Zvi Kedar.

Warrants for the arrest of former Melbourne textile magnate Abe Goldberg and a business associate, Katy Rochelle Boskovitz, were issued by the federal police, working with the Australian Securities Commission, over the multimillion-dollar collapse in 1990 of the Linter textile and investment group and alleged fraudulent borrowing and misconduct. Boskovitz was arrested, but Goldberg remained free in his native Poland (where he was reputedly the representative of a New York export company), which had no extradition treaty with Australia. (Some sources said he was surreptitiously living in California.) Robyn Greenburg, convicted of fraud following the demise of a women's investment and finance group in Western Australia, was sentenced to 17 years in prison. Some saw the harsh sentence as inspired by anti-Semitism, others by sexism.

Australian Jews who died during the year included musician and singing coach Werner Baer, a former assistant director of music at the Australian Broadcasting Corporation, choirmaster at both the Great Synagogue, Sydney, and Temple Emanuel, and founding musical director of the Sydney Jewish Choral Society, in January, aged 77; Harold Collins, Australia's oldest Jewish Gallipoli veteran and a founding member of the New South Wales Association of Jewish Ex-Servicemen and Women (NAJEX), in January, aged 99; Rose Gutnick, wife of Rabbi Chaim Gutnick of Melbourne and matriarch of a well-known rabbinic family, in January, aged 65; Lily Solvey, a communal activist known particularly for her work as organizing secretary of Victoria's United Jewish Education Board for over 30 years, in January, aged 69; Adelaide WIZO leader Esther Levy, in April, aged 73; Reb Moshe Pinchas Kantor, founder of a well-known Jewish bookstore in Melbourne and of the Caulfield Beth HaMidrash, and active for decades in Orthodox causes, in May, aged about 80; Estelle (Stella) Spray, a founder of the Gold Coast, Queensland, Progressive Jewish community and incumbent president of the Gold Coast's Temple Shalom, in July, aged 75; Sydney sculptor and arts patron Dennis (Zdanek) Wolanski, in September, aged 75. Eliezer Berkovits, the eminent American/Israeli theologian who died this year in Israel, had been rabbi at Sydney's Central Synagogue, 1946–50.

HILARY RUBINSTEIN

South Africa

National Affairs

SOME PROGRESS WAS MADE in 1992 in the move to create a new, democratic South Africa, though there were still wide gaps between the positions of the major players. In March President F.W. de Klerk held "the last exclusively white referendum," in which white voters were asked whether they supported the reform process initiated by the state president in 1990, and its culmination in a new negotiated constitution. An overwhelming 69 percent of whites voted in favor, mandating the government to enter into binding agreements with its negotiating partners. The negotiations, however, did not go smoothly: in the spring two major parties, the (Zulu) Inkatha Freedom party and the African National Congress (ANC) and its allies, withdrew from talks. At the end of September, the government and the ANC signed a "Record of Undertaking" and agreed to resume multiparty talks at a later date. In October De Klerk undertook to hold a nonracial general election within two years.

In the international arena, the demise of apartheid was rewarded by ending South Africa's isolation. More foreign governments, including the European Community, lifted economic sanctions, and South African exports increased significantly. During the first nine months of 1992, the trade surplus was 17 percent higher than in the previous year. On the political front, South African leaders were invited to address the United Nations in July; between January and August, 24 missions were established in countries previously hostile to South Africa; prominent foreign personalities as well as representatives of governments and international bodies visited the country; and South African leaders traveled widely. In sports, too, South Africans were once again participating in international competitions.

However, life in South Africa was difficult: violence and the fear of violence seriously affected the quality of life and sense of security of all sections of the population, while the continued economic recession meant not only more unemployed, but also greater difficulty in making ends meet for those who were employed. In general, the feeling of uncertainty and trepidation about the future, already evident in 1991, continued to be a primary concern for many, especially white South Africans. Despite this, emigration remained more or less at the same level as in 1991—around 4,000. Immigration, however, dropped dramatically, from over 12,000 to 7,500 in the same period.

Israel and the Middle East

A visit to South Africa at the beginning of the year by the U.S. government's assistant secretary of state for Africa, Herman Cohen, once again projected Israeli-South African military cooperation into the news. Cohen asserted publicly that South Africa had received major components of a rocket system from Israel and called for an end to this cooperation as a condition for removal of U.S. sanctions against the South African arms industry, Armscor. When the South Africans refused, President George Bush granted the waiver anyway. At about the same time, however, the U.S. government prevented Armscor from closing a multimillion-rand deal to supply Saudi Arabia.

The good relations between the South African government and Israel had been given concrete expression in the November 1991 visit to Israel by President de Klerk. In February 1992 a senior foreign ministry delegation from Israel reciprocated with a visit to Pretoria. In October the Israeli ambassador to South Africa, Zvi Gov-Ari, was awarded the Order of Good Hope, the highest decoration that can be conferred on a foreigner. It was given in recognition of the ambassador's contribution to promoting South African-Israeli relations. The ceremony followed the signing of agreements between the two countries in the fields of tourism, culture, science, education, agriculture, environmental management, trade, and industry.

Nelson Mandela, president of the African National Congress, once again stated his basic attitude to Israel and the Jews. According to a report in the Cape Town *Weekend Argus* (March 21, 1992), he emphasized that the ANC recognized the State of Israel and was mindful of the contribution made by Jews to the struggle for freedom in South Africa. He pointed out, at the same time, that Libya's Muammar Qaddafi and Cuba's Fidel Castro had been loyal friends, and said that he would not abandon them because the struggle to end apartheid was nearing its end.

Serious anti-Israel demonstrations by Muslims were reported on only two occasions: at a ceremony attended by the Israeli ambassador in Cape Town in February and at a solidarity meeting for Bosnian Muslims in October. In the first incident, 12 youths were arrested for yelling death threats, while in the second, American and Israeli flags were burned.

Toward the end of the year, Ambassador Gov-Ari was replaced by Dr. Alon Liel, who had headed the Africa desk under Shimon Peres during the "rotation" government of national unity.

Anti-Semitism

There were few reports of anti-Semitic incidents during the year. Two youths were caught in a cemetery near Johannesburg pushing over and breaking tombstones. In October anti-Semitic attacks on medical students at the University of the Witwatersrand were reported. These included defacing the posters of the South African Union of Jewish Students with "Heil Hitler" and crude anti-Semitic jokes. In addition, some students found swastikas on their lockers. In December the historic Kimberley synagogue was vandalized and defaced with Nazi-like graffiti.

A potentially serious incident occurred in neighboring Zimbabwe when President Robert Mugabe, in an attack on white farmers who were opposed to the nationalization of their land, said that commercial farmers were "hard-hearted people; you would think they are Jews." The local Jewish Board of Deputies reacted strongly and demanded an urgent meeting with the president. At this meeting, they accepted Mugabe's explanation that his remark was not meant as a slur. He had, he said, intended to compare the farmers' actions with Israeli policies in denying Palestinians a homeland. "That is the concept I used and it had nothing to do with Jews in Zimbabwe or the Jews elsewhere." He added that the world hoped for better from Israel's new government.

JEWISH COMMUNITY

Demography

The 1991 population census results, published in December 1992, showed that there were 31 million people living in South Africa and a further 6.8 million in the "independent" black homelands of Transkei, Bophuthatswana, Venda, and Ciskei. Excluding the four homelands, blacks constituted 69.9 percent of South Africa's population, whites 16.3 percent, coloreds 10.6 percent, and Asians 3.2 percent.

Unfortunately, 20 percent of whites in the 1991 census, as compared with 4 percent in 1980, did not answer the question on religion. This means that the count of 65,000 Jews is a serious underrepresentation. Two estimates of the Jewish population are, therefore, suggested. The first is based on a weighting of the census results, while the second is derived from a variety of sources, including the 1991 Sociodemographic Survey of the South African Jewish Population. According to these estimates, there were between 92,000 and 106,000 Jews in 1991. Taking 100,000 as a convenient single estimate, Jews constituted 0.3 percent of the total population and 2.0 percent of whites—significantly lower than in 1980, when the proportions were 0.5 percent and 2.6 percent, respectively.

It is difficult to estimate the number of Jews in 1992, but it is almost certain that there was some decline in numbers. In the first place, the net loss of approximately 9,000 mostly young and early middle-aged Jews through international migration since 1980 had accentuated the aging profile of the community. Secondly, if the ratio of emigration to Israel as compared to other countries was the same in 1992 as it had been between 1980 and 1991, then it may be estimated that just over 1,100 emigrated in that year. Thirdly, if patterns of Jewish immigration to South Africa resembled those of immigration generally, then only a very small and insignificant number would have arrived. Nevertheless, there was no sense of the large-scale exodus of the late 1970s or mid-1980s. Without suggesting any figure for 1992, it is highly probable that deaths exceeded births, and that there was a net loss through emigration of around 1,000 people.

Communal Affairs

Community leaders continued to emphasize in their statements and reports to the community that Jews had no reason for special anxiety. Thus, while they were watchful of anti-Israel and anti-Semitic manifestations, they insisted that there was no cause for alarm. Leaders had also broadened their contacts with the ANC and other political groups and met with senior officials on a regular basis. Communal organizations took pains to identify strongly and positively with the democratization process. Thus, for example, following the March referendum, the chairman of the South African Jewish Board of Deputies (SAJBOD), Mervyn Smith, said: "It is a vote for a positive future for all in South Africa. The President has now been given a clear mandate to continue with meaningful negotiations." He reaffirmed the board's commitment to the reform process and to the new South Africa. In a similar vein, later in the year, the South African Rabbinical Conference resolved that it was "fully committed to the ultimate achievement of a new South Africa based on freedom, democracy and equal opportunity for all its people."

Individual Jews appeared to be responding to events in South Africa in much the same ways as other South African whites of similar socioeconomic class. At the same time, while there was no sense of large-scale emigration of Jews, there did seem to be a steady exodus, particularly of young, skilled adults.

An incident reflecting the change in official Jewish attitudes was a pamphlet distributed by the South African Union of Jewish Students (SAUJS) at an end-of-year Israel United Appeal–United Communal Fund conference. The pamphlet carried the much-publicized photograph of Mandela embracing Arafat. But the accompanying message was positive: "When some people saw this picture," it read, "they were shocked and threw their hands up in horror and despair. . . ." The pamphlet went on to explain that SAUJS had accepted the responsibility of educating the emerging leadership about the Middle East and to this end had arranged for the first official ANC delegation to visit Israel in January 1993.

A much appreciated gesture of goodwill was an unsolicited Passover message from Nelson Mandela, in which he said that the ANC recognized "the particularly outstanding contribution that the South African Jewish community has made in the struggle for freedom and social justice." SAJBOD chairman Smith promptly thanked Mandela on behalf of the Jewish community. At the end of the year, ANC leaders assured an American Jewish fact-finding mission of opposition to anti-Semitism from all the major players in South Africa's transition to democracy.

In view of the changing political circumstances, the SAJBOD was engaged in proactive strategic planning to ensure that the community was adequately prepared to meet future challenges. Prof. Harold Rudolph, outgoing chairman of the Transvaal Council of the SAJBOD, suggested that the time had come to "rationalize the various activities currently in operation in the Jewish community." The Transvaal Council proposed that negotiations be undertaken between the two premier organizations—the SAJBOD and the South African Zionist Federation (SAZF)—to consider the viability of merging. In explaining the need for such a merger, Rudolph posed the following question: "If the PLO were to establish an embassy in the near future, is that an issue for the Board of Deputies or the Zionist Federation?"

Three subcommittees were established by the Board of Deputies to address welfare, religion, and educational issues. Welfare assumed increased importance because of the immigration of Russian Jews to South Africa. Between January and June 1992, 157 Russian families were registered with either the Jewish Family and Community Council or Chabad House. To meet the increasing needs, a new welfare campaign was established in the Cape Province to run parallel to that of the Israel United Appeal–United Communal Fund (IUA-UCF) campaign. In Johannesburg the *hevra kadisha* launched a massive fund-raising campaign—the first in its 104-year history. A new program, Project Tachlis, under the auspices of the SAJBOD, joined forces with Operation Snowball, a campaign organized by the Johannesburg *Star* to collect blankets for the needy.

Intensive efforts to establish dialogue both with the wider community and within the Jewish community continued under the auspices of the SAJBOD. ANC secretary-general Cyril Ramaphosa was a guest speaker at a national executive meeting of the SAJBOD and also addressed the Jerusalem Club of the IUA-UCF in Johannesburg.

A number of prominent Jewish visitors were brought to South Africa by SAJBOD. Among them, Israeli musicians Max Stern and Nathan Mishori came as part of a cultural exchange. Prof. Bernard Reisman of Brandeis University was guest speaker at a quarterly meeting of the Cape Council of the Board of Deputies. Prominent speakers addressed the IUA-UCF national conference, among them Israel Singer, secretary-general of the World Jewish Congress; Ehud Olmert, former Israeli minister of health; Baruch Gur, head of the Soviet Union and Eastern European department in the Jewish Agency; and Hirsh Goodman, editor-in-chief of the *Jerusalem Report*.

Yitzhak Navon, former president of the State of Israel, took part in the Sephardi community's commemoration of the 500th anniversary of the expulsion of the Jews from Spain. The renowned American author, Talmud scholar, practicing psychiatrist, and philosopher Rabbi Abraham J. Twerski was a guest speaker at the first scholarship dinner of the Torah Academy in Johannesburg.

Israel-Related Activity

A capacity audience of 650 people heard former Israeli prime minister Shimon Peres officially launch the 1992 IUA-UCF campaign in February. Peres called on Jews to write a second chapter of the history of Israel together. "Let's try to bring as many people as we can to Israel—not only to defend our borders but to sustain our faith."

Shoshana Cardin, chairwoman of the Conference of Presidents of Major American Jewish Organizations, launched the 1992–1993 Women's Zionist Campaign on the theme "One People, One Destiny." She addressed meetings in major centers and was a guest of honor at the Zionist Federation's Israel Independence Day celebrations in Johannesburg. Cardin had high praise for the staunch and solid commitment of the South African Jewish community to the Zionist cause—in her view, without parallel in any other Diaspora community.

Transvaal Jewish leaders signed the *Amanat Yerushalayim* (Jerusalem Covenant) at a ceremony at the Israel embassy on Yom Yerushalayim, to mark 25 years of the reunification of Jerusalem. Nachman Shai, director-general of Israel National Radio, was a guest of the SAZF at the Jerusalem Day celebrations.

John Kane-Berman, executive director of the South African Institute for Race Relations, addressed the South Africa–Israel Chamber of Commerce on "Codesa and Beyond: The Critical Issues." The group was also addressed by Harry Schwarz, South African ambassador to the United States. *Jerusalem Report* editor Hirsh Goodman and Sid Shapiro, director-general of Telfed, the Israel office of the SAZF, lectured on current events in Israel.

Education

Mervyn Smith, national chairman of the SAJBOD, told the 23rd National Conference of the South African Board of Jewish Education (SABJE) that the "new" South Africa would make different demands on Jewish education, such as possible changes in admissions policy because of government subsidies. Russel Gaddin, outgoing chairman of the board of education, said the total expenditure on Jewish education was currently 60 million rands. One of the main areas of concern was the high number of single-parent families requiring financial assistance. According to Gaddin, there had been an increased move away from government schools to Jewish schools in Johannesburg. At present, 60 percent of Jewish children of high-school age and 63 percent of primary-school age were enrolled in Jewish schools. Gaddin advocated expanding the board's subsidy program for the 3,500 Jewish children who received little or no Jewish education.

The B.M. Casper Jewish Education Development Center, named for the late chief rabbi who served the South African Jewish community for 25 years, was opened in the Hillel Berelowitz Building at King David School, Linksfield, Johannesburg. In Cape Town, the Hebrew Academy celebrated its tenth anniversary.

Chabad House, Cape Town, was totally destroyed by a fire that broke out on Tisha B'av, caused by an electrical fault. All the Torah scrolls were saved.

Religion

At a conference of the Union of Jewish Women (UJW) in Bloemfontein, national president Miriam Stern called for recognition of the changing needs of women in society and the need to improve their status. The UJW was a signatory to a petition—initiated by the International Council of Jewish Women—urging the removal of "the present, somewhat chauvinistic laws pertaining to Jewish divorce."

Stern reported that the South African Beth Din appeared to be taking more seriously some of the difficulties facing women in Jewish law.

Chief Rabbi Cyril Harris set up a special commission to deliberate on matters of common concern, including ways to impose communal pressure on husbands refusing to give a *get*, a Jewish divorce decree; standardizing religious practices; guidelines on bar mitzvah testing; and improving cooperation among rabbis.

Rabbi S. Zaidin, country community rabbi of SAJBOD, told the biennial Transvaal Council conference that during the last ten years, six synagogues in the Transvaal had been closed. Rural communities, he claimed, felt a sense of isolation.

Publications

Among new works of Jewish interest this year were a poetry anthology, *Lost and Found: A Second Generation Response to the Holocaust*, by Solly Kaplinsky, and *Lippy Lipschitz*, a biography of the eminent South African sculptor by his daughter, Tony Lipschitz Caspi. Neville Dubow edited a work on noted South African artist Irma Stern: *Paradise: The Journal and Letters (1917–1933) of Irma Stern*.

The *Zionist Record* established a relationship with the *Jerusalem Post* allowing for a number of pages from its international edition to be published in the South African paper.

Personalia

Mendel Kaplan, chairman of the board of governors of the Jewish Agency and chairman of the executive of the World Jewish Congress, received an honorary doctorate from Yeshiva University, New York. Entrepreneurs and philanthropists Eric Samson and Bertie Lubner received honorary doctorates from Ben-Gurion University of the Negev. Honorary citizenship of Ofakim, Israel, was granted to industrialist Isaac Joffe and to Mendel Kaplan.

Dr. Teddy Schneider, prominent communal leader, died in November 1991, aged 86. A widely admired physician, he received numerous international humanitarian awards for his services to society.

ALLIE A. DUBB
MILTON SHAIN

Israel

O<small>N JUNE</small> 23, 1992, <small>FIFTEEN YEARS</small> of Likud rule came to an end. The Labor party returned to power, with Yitzhak Rabin taking up where he had left off in 1977. The midyear change of government brought about a dramatic shift in Israel's international stature: relations with the United States, which had hit bottom during the first part of 1992 because of differences between the Bush administration and the Shamir government over loan guarantees, were quickly restored and improved. The international community as a whole greeted the new government and its policies with satisfaction, especially after its decision to unilaterally freeze new housing in Jewish settlements in the territories. However, expectations for a quick breakthrough in the peace process begun the previous year were dashed by the end of the year. Not only was no substantial progress achieved in the peace talks, but the very continuation of the process was overshadowed by Israel's decision to deport 400 Hamas activists to south Lebanon. Prime Minister Rabin, it seemed, was more eager than his Likud predecessors to achieve peace, but he had no intention of dropping the hard-line policies on matters of security that had earned him the confidence of the Israeli electorate in the first place.

NATIONAL SECURITY

The Intifada

The *intifada* continued unabated in 1992, despite the promise held out by the Washington peace talks and despite the midyear change of power from Likud to Labor, which brought about a significant moderation of government policies toward the territories and the Palestinians. Internecine bloodshed among the Palestinians continued to rise, as Palestinians killed almost twice as many of their own number (238) as were killed in skirmishes with the Israeli army (124).

In the politically minded West Bank, the occurrence of violent incidents was down, but the always volatile Gaza strip exploded, as armed Palestinian groups resorted more and more to deadly attacks with guns and grenades.

Twelve Israeli soldiers and twelve civilians were killed in 1992, compared to one soldier and seven civilians the previous year. The number of wounded soldiers decreased from 800 to 650, while the number of injured Palestinians rose from 1,381 to 1,605. There were 28,392 "disturbances," including 1,174 hurlings of Molotov cocktails and 94 of hand grenades, 504 incidents of shooting, 311 cases of arson, 162 detonations of explosive devices, and 1,001 "cold" attacks in which knives and axes were used.

Following the November 1991 peace conference in Madrid, Palestinian rejectionist groups, comprising the Islamic fundamentalist Hamas and Islamic Jihad movements, as well as the more radical secular groups, declared "war" on the peace process. The main instrument of this war was to be armed attacks against Israeli civilians and soldiers. The mainstream Fatah movement, which had lent its support to the Madrid process, nonetheless had not renounced the use of terror and needed to maintain the "armed struggle" against Israel in order to maintain favor with the disgruntled Palestinian public, especially in the Gaza Strip. The peace process and the new Israeli government, elected in midyear, found violent opponents on the Jewish side as well. Jewish settlers increasingly accused the government, both old and new, of "selling out" and of "abandoning" them in order to curry favor with the Arab side. The more extreme elements carried out acts of retaliation against innocent Arabs, ostensibly in order to "increase security" for Jews, but with the hidden agenda of destabilizing the government and hoping to derail the peace process.

The opposition to the peace process erupted on the first day of the new year as Doron Shorshan, a settler from the Gaza settlement of Kfar Darom, was gunned down in his car near the Dir el-Balah junction. Shorshan was the first civilian to be killed in the Gaza Strip since the beginning of the *intifada* five years earlier. In a symbolic gesture that was to become a pattern throughout the year, fellow settlers set up a "memorial" settlement in the area where the incident had occurred and were promptly evacuated from the area by the Israeli army. Responding to the murder of Shorshan, the Defense Ministry announced on January 2 that 12 Palestinians from the West Bank and Gaza would be deported because of their involvement in attacks on Jews and Arabs alike. On January 6, the UN Security Council "strongly condemned" the issuing of the deportation orders. On January 23, the government revoked a deportation order against one of the 12.

On January 14, seven Israeli settlers were wounded when shots were fired at their civilian bus near the West Bank town of Ramallah. Outraged Jewish settlers retaliated by opening fire on a private Arab car near Hebron. On January 15, Israeli Druze Mofid Kna'an was murdered near Jenin, while on a hunting expedition with friends; his assailants were not captured. A week later, four Hebron residents were wounded by gunfire from roaming bands of Jewish settlers. On January 28, an unknown Jewish group dubbed "the Hasmoneans" claimed responsibility for shots fired at the home of Bethlehem mayor Elias Freij. Two days later, an Israeli civilian, Yisrael Hirshorn, was killed at a construction site in the town of Rishon LeZion.

While public disturbances did decrease somewhat over previous years, as many Palestinians presumably decided to "give peace a chance," the opponents of peace became more armed and more dangerous. At the end of January, Israeli security forces uncovered eight heavily armed terrorist cells, complete with Israeli-made automatic weapons. The cells belonged to the opposition Democratic Front and Popular Front, as well as to the mainstream Fatah movement. Political agitation, especially at universities, was also on the rise, and on January 29, the army decided to shut down Hebron University after an army raid uncovered thousands of virulent anti-Israel pamphlets and posters.

Disagreements among the Palestinians were also wreaking havoc internally. In the third week of January, American-born professor Robert Glick, head of the archaeology department at Bir Zeit University, was killed by masked Palestinian gunmen. At the beginning of February, 17 residents of the West Bank village of Sureik were accused of stoning a fellow villager to death, after she had been accused of "collaboration." On February 8, in several separate incidents, two Arabs were killed and four seriously wounded in acts of "retribution" carried out by fellow Palestinians. A few days later the bound, gagged, and bullet-ridden body of a suspected collaborator was hurled out of a speeding car right in front of the Tul Karem police station on the West Bank.

On February 5, the army issued new open-fire guidelines, allowing soldiers to open fire on a Palestinian carrying a weapon without first giving the previously obligatory warning. By mid-February, security sources were expressing "grave concern" at the rapid rise of inter-Palestinian murders. Fifteen suspected collaborators had been killed in less than two months, they said.

On February 9, two soldiers and two civilians were wounded when an explosive device hidden in a steel pipe exploded near the Gaza kibbutz of Netzarim. On the same day, a civilian was kidnapped and stabbed on the West Bank. On February 11, an Israeli Arab, Yunes Mazrawa, was shot and killed. His body was found near the West Bank town of Tulkarm.

The violence reached a peak on February 14, in one of the most gruesome attacks ever carried out by Arab terrorists; the incident was doubly shocking because it took place inside an army base where new immigrants were undergoing basic training.

ARMY-BASE ATTACK

Despite prior intelligence warnings of an impending attack on an army base, a terrorist squad succeeded in infiltrating an army bivouac inside the Green Line, in Ramot Menashe near the town of Hadera. Two new recruits and their commander were hacked to death; the terrorists made off with their victims' weapons. The two soldiers were new immigrants from the former Soviet Union. The subsequent army inquiry revealed negligence on the part of the base commanders in their security guidelines. The incident provoked wide public discussion of the role of new immigrants in the army, and for a while elicited concern that news of the attack might cause other prospective immigrants to review their plans.

Security sources at first ascribed responsibility to the Fatah-affiliated Black Panther group operating in the territories, but investigators at the scene pointed accusing fingers at Israel's Arab community, based on evidence found near the campsite. Leading Israeli Arab figures protested the accusation, claiming allegiance to the Jewish state. Reaction was different among Palestinians in the territories, where demonstrations favoring the attack took place in the West Bank town of Bethlehem. Yasir Abed Rabbo, an official of the Palestine Liberation Organization (PLO), refused to condemn the attack, expressing "understanding" for the motives of the attackers, who lived under the "oppression of occupation."

On February 17, a Black Panther group in Jenin claimed responsibility for the attack, thus contradicting the findings of the investigators. However, their initial instincts proved to be correct. On March 4, Israeli security services and the police arrested seven suspects, all members of one Israeli Arab family, from the Israeli village of Shirpa and the town of Umm al-Faham, all members of the Islamic movement. The incident soured relations between Jews and Arabs, and for a while Arabs lived in fear of Jewish retaliation.

On February 18, the Likud government showed its unswerving commitment to the territories, despite the waves of terror. Ma'aleh Adumim, a Jerusalem suburb in the Judean hills, on the way to Jericho, was declared the first Israeli "city" in the territories. The ceremony of declaration had been scheduled for the previous October, but was postponed for fear it would upset the U.S. and Arab attendees at the Madrid conference.

New Soviet immigrants provided another victim of terror on February 21, when Genya Friedman was stabbed to death in Kfar Sava by a youth from the West Bank town of Kalkilya, who appeared to be acting on his own. Three other civilians were wounded in the attack. In this atmosphere of rising violence, on the same day as the Kfar Sava attack, three suspected Palestinian collaborators were murdered; a Palestinian was killed by army troops near Tulkarm; three Molotov cocktails were hurled at a passing Israeli vehicle; and 15 Gaza residents were wounded by army gunfire.

Two days later, violence struck again as a 23-year-old security guard, Lior Srelker, working on an oil truck south of Jenin, in the West Bank, was shot by a masked gunman. The town was placed under curfew as the army searched for the terrorist. On March 5, an Israeli soldier was killed in the southern Gaza Strip in a violent incident between an armed terrorist squad and one of the army units working undercover, "Shimshon." The disclosure of the existence of such units, in which soldiers operated disguised as Arabs, had created a public uproar the previous year, with Arab and some Israeli politicians accusing the units of serving as execution squads. The terrorists in this incident who were wounded or apprehended were suspected of killing scores of suspected Palestinian collaborators. In their possession were found automatic weapons, axes, and knives, as well as uniforms identical to those used by the Israel Defense Forces.

In March the violence continued as before, as Islamic organizations swore revenge for the February 16 Israeli killing of Hezballah leader Abbas Musawi in southern Lebanon (see "Lebanon," below). Shootings, knifings, and grenade-throwing were daily occurrences, creating political difficulties for the Likud government and increasing calls by Jewish settlers to use a "strong hand" against the Palestinians. On March 12, the army and the General Security Services carried out a wide-ranging operation in the town of Jenin. One of the most sought-after members of the Black Panther group was shot and killed. Scores of suspected terrorists were arrested. On March 15, an elite army unit shot dead three wanted terrorists in a West Bank refugee camp.

On March 17, tragedy slightly repaired the strained relations existing between Israeli Arabs and Jews since the axing attack by Israeli Arabs on the army camp. Abdel Rani Kareem, a garage owner and Arab resident of Jaffa, was murdered by a knife-wielding Gaza terrorist, outside a Jaffa night club; Kareem had come to the aid of Ilanit Ohana, a 19-year-old Jewish woman who was also killed in the attack. The perpetrator, who belonged to the Islamic Jihad organization, wounded 20 schoolchildren who were near the area before being shot dead by an Israeli border policeman on leave. The assailant had been carrying a valid permit to enter Israel from the Gaza Strip. Responding to the public outcry, on March 19, the government sealed off the strip and forbade Gazans to come to work in Israel, for a period of three days. The army heightened its surveillance of the checkposts through which the Gazans entered Israel.

The Hamas organization, known primarily for its daring terrorist actions, showed signs of gaining in political influence when it won overwhelmingly in elections for the Ramallah city council held on March 3. Violence broke out between Hamas and Fatah supporters in the wake of the elections. In elections held later in the year, however, Fatah fared better.

Throughout this period, Palestinian terrorists, apparently emboldened by the February attack on an army camp, stepped up attacks against army patrols and outposts. On April 1, four Palestinian gunmen who tried to attack a border police patrol in Rafah were killed. On the same day, a hand grenade was thrown at an army lookout post, and three soldiers were injured when their jeep caught fire under a hail of Molotov cocktails.

On April 7, PLO chairman Yasir Arafat was saved from what had been reported as a fatal air crash during a sandstorm in southern Libya; spontaneous demonstrations of joy erupted in the territories, leading to inevitable violent clashes with Israeli troops. Mass demonstrations appeared to be resuming: on April 11, 16 Palestinians were wounded by gunfire in Khan Yunis and the Nur-a-Shams refugee camp. On April 16, 6 soldiers and 11 Palestinians were wounded in mass demonstrations in the Jebalya refugee camp. Despite all this, Defense Minister Moshe Arens sought to return a semblance of normalcy to the territories. On April 20, he allowed the engineering and science departments of Bir Zeit University to reopen, overriding the objections of senior army officers who viewed the campuses as hotbeds of ferment and agitation against Israel.

On April 11, another Israeli Arab, Adnan Biaza, was stabbed to death while shopping for vegetables in Dir el Balah. On April 26, the body of 61-year-old

Avraham Greenberg was discovered in central Tel Aviv; the Islamic Jihad claimed responsibility for the killing. Mass violence reached new heights during the Passover holiday weekend at the end of April: 12 Palestinians were injured, 15 Molotov cocktails were thrown at passing Israeli vehicles, and an old woman in Gaza died after inhaling tear gas hurled at rioters.

In response to the increased attacks against soldiers, the army reissued, in late April, yet stronger open-fire guidelines authorizing soldiers to "shoot to kill," without warning, if they encountered "wanted" terrorists holding weapons in their hands. Palestinians interpreted the new rules as part of an Israeli policy of "executing" wanted Palestinians, with no regard to whether they were actually carrying out an attack.

Israeli security services again scored some successes in uncovering terrorist cells. On May 1, the GSS announced the capture of several Fatah cells in Nablus that were thought to be responsible for scores of attacks on both Jews and alleged Arab collaborators; a few days later, an 11-member Fatah squad was uncovered in Kabatiya. In five months, the security services captured 205 wanted terrorists and killed 15.

Still, the cycle of violence continued. On May 17, an Israeli animal trader was shot and killed in the Gaza Strip by members of the Hamas military wing, Iz A-din al-Kassam. A few days later, scores of Palestinians were injured by army gunfire after taking part in demonstrations commemorating the first anniversary of the May 20, 1991, murder of seven Arab laborers by the Israeli Ami Popper.

ARAB VIOLENCE, ISRAELI RIOTS

On May 23, 15-year-old Helena Rap was murdered in Bat Yam by a knife-wielding Gazan. This murder caused particular outrage among residents of Bat Yam and other Jewish cities, and riots raged throughout Israel for several days. In the immediate aftermath of the killing, 11 Arabs were injured in incidents with Israelis; an Israeli Arab from Nazareth was stabbed in Rishon LeZion. The government decided to close off the Gaza Strip, both to protect the Palestinians and to prevent further infiltration by terrorists. In Israel, the demonstrations seemed to be gaining in strength, and on May 26, thousands of Bat Yam residents scuffled with thousands of policemen; dozens were injured, scores of others arrested.

That same day, a Jewish settler in Gaza, Shimon Biran, was stabbed to death near his settlement of Kfar Darom. Biran was the settlement's rabbi. Fellow settlers went on the rampage, burning Arab fields and groves. In Bat Yam that day, 100 more demonstrators were arrested. Sensing the dangerous mood among Israelis, Palestinian leaders Faisal Husseini and Samir Abdallah publicly condemned the murder of 15-year-old Rap.

A sign that the Palestinian leadership now believed that the internecine violence was getting out of control was a "conference" of masked gunmen in Gaza, reported by the press, which saw leaders of the gangs issue a call to "minimize" killings of suspected collaborators. On May 23, PLO chairman Arafat issued a call to the leaders of the *intifada* to put a stop to the internal violence and murders of so-called collaborators. On June 7, Fatah and Hamas signed an agreement pledging an end to the killing of collaborators and promising to work together in the "efforts to end the Israeli occupation."

On the Israeli side, the open-fire guidelines of the undercover units were also raising concern. The human rights watch group B'tselem issued a special report on June 3, claiming that soldiers in these units were given a subtle message by their superiors that the killing of wanted terrorists, even if they posed no immediate danger, was permissible. The army strongly rejected the allegations, saying that soldiers were under strict orders to open fire only in cases of self-defense.

In early June the army utilized the sealing off of Gaza to seek out terrorist cells. No fewer than 71 suspects were rounded up in a single day; a few days later, on June 4, the GSS disclosed the capture of a terrorist cell that had been responsible for the murder of two Israelis. The closure of Gaza had calmed a volatile situation, but international pressure was building up on Israel to allow Palestinians to return to their jobs inside Israel. Israeli employers were discreetly conveying the same message to their government. On June 7, the government announced a partial lifting of the closure, allowing 3,000 Gazans to return to work. A few days later, more thousands were allowed in; Gazans employed in Bat Yam wisely decided to stay away for a little while longer. Prime Minister Yitzhak Shamir said, on June 9, that in any case the closure provided only a "partial solution to the crazed murderers."

The strip was not reopened, and economic pressures mounted. On June 14, thousands of Gaza residents rioted near the Erez checkpoint that connects Gaza to Israel. The same day, Israel announced that henceforth all Gazans over the age of 25 would be allowed to return to work. A few days later, the UN Relief and Works Agency, in charge of the welfare of refugees, announced emergency plans to distribute food to 120,000 families who were facing starvation because Israel was depriving them of their livelihood.

Following the June 23 election, the Palestinians greeted the defeat of the Likud and the election of Labor and its new prime minister, Yitzhak Rabin, with a mix of hope and suspicion. Rabin had been defense minister when the *intifada* broke out in December 1987, and his call to "break the bones" of demonstrators was still fresh in Palestinian memories. Nonetheless, the new prime minister had pledged during his election campaign to reach a settlement with Palestinians "within six to nine months." The Jerusalem daily *Al Fajr* predicted that Labor would form a coalition with Likud, and that things would remain the same. The *El Kuds* daily predicted superficial Israeli moderation aimed at improving relations between Israel and the United States in order to secure the $10-billion loan guarantees sought by Jerusalem.

If there was any honeymoon, it was brief indeed: 48 hours after the elections, one of the bloodiest days since the start of the *intifada* took place. A Jewish father and son, Moshe and Amikam Saltzman, were murdered in Gaza by terrorists posing as vegetable vendors. The killers were members of the Hamas Iz A-din al-Kassam group, which was forging a reputation as the most deadly of all terrorist organizations operating in the territories. That same day, a settler in Gaza was attacked with axes and moderately wounded; near the site of the attack a note was found with the inscription "This is the answer to Rabin." In Jenin, a soldier was killed in a skirmish with three terrorists who were also killed. Scores of irate Jewish settlers went on the rampage in Hebron in reaction to the renewed wave of terrorism.

On July 7, an 84-year-old citrus grower, Avraham Kinsler, was hacked to death inside the Green Line near his moshav of Batzra. That same day, the month-long truce between Hamas and the Fatah broke down, and open warfare erupted inside the refugee camps. The army decided to send in troops to stop the battles, but not before at least seven Palestinians were killed. In Amman and in the territories, the two groups once again negotiated a cease-fire.

In mid-June, the politically active a-Najah University in Nablus was the scene of one of the most dramatic showdowns since the start of the uprising. The army went onto the campus to search for wanted terrorists, claiming that at least two dozen were hiding there. To protest the action, 300 students from families of mukhtars— village chiefs—went on a hunger strike. Demonstrations erupted in which nine students were injured, and the army was effectively driven off the campus. Rabin, in his double capacity of prime minister and defense minister, defused the situation by striking a deal that allowed only six wanted terrorists to leave, provided they went on voluntary exile to Jordan. Rabin was criticized in the Israeli papers by "senior military sources" for "caving in" to the Palestinians. In moderate circles, however, optimism was expressed over the peaceful resolution of the conflict and the apparent show of Palestinian trust in the new government.

A few days later, the army killed one of the more wanted terrorists in the territories, the deputy commander of the Black Panther squads in Jenin. In a separate incident, a four-year-old Palestinian boy was killed when soldiers opened fire on a suspicious car; three soldiers were detained for investigation. All over the territories, the battle between the army and the terrorists raged on. The Palestinians were growing bolder by the day; on August 1, they infiltrated the building of the Israeli Civil Administration in Hebron, scribbling slogans on the wall before making their getaway.

While the government was battling the Palestinians, it was also facing an old/new political adversary, the Jewish settlers. The new Labor government, opposed to the expansion of what Rabin had termed "political settlements," announced plans to seriously cut back building plans both inside Israel and in the territories, for what it described as "budgetary reasons." In a move also linked with efforts to secure American loan guarantees, the government announced that 15,000 apartments previously planned would not be built; 7,000 of these had been slated for construction in the Jewish settlements. Jewish settlers vowed to fight the government's actions, which they termed "capitulation." Now the army had to allocate significant forces to control rioting settlers, both inside and outside the Green Line. The settlers launched plans to move into houses in East Jerusalem's Muslim Quarter; Rabin ordered his officials to put a stop to these "provocations."

On August 19, 55-year-old Bechor Hajaj was murdered near his village of Kfar Yavetz by two of his own Palestinian employees. A week later, the terrorists scored one of their biggest victories in the battle against Israeli undercover units: Capt. Eliahu Avram, commander of the Border Police undercover unit, was killed in a skirmish with two Black Panther men in Jenin. A few days later, terrorists kidnapped an Israeli soldier, who was found stabbed but alive in a grove in Gaza. Security sources told *Ha'aretz* that the terrorists were getting more proficient and courageous in their attacks against military patrols. The next day, another border policeman was killed in a direct confrontation with an armed terrorist. On September 12, 33-year-old new immigrant Boris Asherov was shot to death in Haifa by a Palestinian from the West Bank.

While vowing to maintain the battle against terrorists, Prime Minister Rabin was also trying to boost Palestinian confidence in the peace process. He ordered "gestures" toward the local population, including the cancellation of the deportations (August 24), partial release of prisoners with a short time left to serve, and the opening up of previously sealed-off streets and houses. On September 23, however, most of the residents in the territories joined a protest strike called by rejectionist organizations opposed to the peace process. The Palestinians were not convinced that a new era had arrived. Local leader Faisal Husseini called on PLO chairman Arafat to "apologize" to the West for his Gulf War support for Iraq, in order to increase political and economic support for the beleaguered territories.

On September 29, Palestinian security prisoners in jails throughout the country went on a hunger strike, submitting a long list of demands for improvements in their living conditions. The strike prompted widespread demonstrations of support in the territories, which quickly turned violent and exacted a steep price, with over 100 Palestinians wounded in skirmishes with the army. The strike ended after a month, after Rabin ordered the Prisons Service to accept some of the strikers' demands; once again Rabin was accused of "capitulating to terrorists."

In October, despite, or because of, the resumption of the peace talks a month earlier, the violence against Jews reached a peak. Four Israelis were murdered: On October 11, Amazia Ben Haim was killed in the Gaza settlement of Gush Katif. On October 15, Shimon Avraham, a farmer in the northern moshav Meitav, was stabbed to death in his field. Two days later, Yehudit Ostern, of Bat Yam, was burned to death when an explosive device ripped through her car near the West Bank town of Matityahu. On October 27, Motti Biton was shot to death near Jenin.

The territories were on fire. Three soldiers were killed in separate incidents. The continuing murder of Jewish farmers in their fields prompted the government to order farmers to go to work armed and alert. Pressure inside Israel for a strong hand against the Palestinians was on the rise. Rabin ordered the army to "take all measures" in order to calm the territories. However, on November 26, Rabin resorted once again to the "carrot," allowing 241 visiting spouses of residents of the territories to obtain permanent resident status. The Likud accused him of "validating" the Palestinian demand for the "right of return."

On December 7, the by-then notorious Iz A-din al-Kassam group of Hamas struck again. Three Israeli reservists were killed when their patrol car was overtaken by another car, from which deadly automatic weapons were fired. That same day, four Israeli soldiers from an elite unit were wounded in a fight with terrorists in Jenin.

The army escalated its search for Palestinians on the wanted list, and began using new and previously banned methods. On December 10, the press reported for the first time that the army was firing antitank missiles into the houses where suspected terrorists were holing up. The new tactic was to become a source of internal and international debate in the months to come.

The Deportation of the Hamas Leadership

On December 13, border policeman Nissim Toledano was kidnapped as he made his way to work in the town of Lod. Several hours after his abduction, a note was delivered to Red Crescent headquarters near Ramallah, demanding the release of Muslim leader Sheikh Ahmed Yassin, who had been in prison since October 1991. The note said that Toledano would be murdered if the demand was not met that same evening. The same day, a soldier was killed in Hebron. The Iz A-din al-Kassam group claimed responsibility for both acts.

For two days, the country watched in anxious anticipation as the army launched one of its biggest manhunts in history to find the kidnapped Toledano. Hundreds of known leaders and activists of Hamas and of the Islamic Jihad movement were rounded up and interrogated. Publicly, the government said it was "considering" the Hamas demands, although privately it was made clear, and published in the newspapers, that Israel would not give in to terrorist extortion.

On December 15, Toledano's body was found—bound, gagged, and shot—near the West Bank settlement of Kfar Edumim. Subsequent investigation revealed that Toledano had been murdered shortly after the initial deadline set by the terrorists passed. Subsequent extensions of the deadline by the terrorists were therefore not genuine, but part of the psychological battle against the Israeli government and public. Rabin reacted by saying that Israel would "retaliate gravely."

The inner cabinet met on December 15 to discuss the situation and make good on Rabin's pledge. An unprecedented decision was reached: 400 Hamas and Islamic Jihad leaders would be deported to Lebanon. Eager to contain the potentially explosive public outcry that followed the discovery of Toledano's body, the cabinet gave overwhelming approval to Rabin's proposal to deport. Sixteen ministers, including the left-wing Meretz representatives, voted in favor of the plan; Justice Minister David Libai was the sole dissenter, abstaining and protesting the intention to bypass the process of appeal to the High Court of Justice. Rabin's plan included an immediate deportation, giving only retroactive right of appeal to the deportees.

The plan was leaked to the press almost immediately, and petitions were filed with the High Court by the Association for Civil Rights in Israel and families of the deportees, seeking to stop it. The next day, the court decided, 5–2, not to block the deportations but ordered the government to explain its actions within 30 days. On the evening of December 17, scores of buses were filmed making their way to the north of the country, their passengers bound and gagged.

The deportations enjoyed almost unanimous support inside the cabinet but were greeted with dismay by the press and the rank-and-file of the leftist parties. The international community was also shocked, and the outgoing Bush administration issued a strongly worded protest. The mainstream Israeli public, however, was gratified: first polls revealed almost 90-percent support for the move. The Labor government under Rabin had dared to do what the previous Likud government had not even dreamed of doing. Palestinians in the territories were shocked; the future of the peace process appeared grim indeed.

On December 18, Israel literally "dumped" over 400 deported Hamas activists inside Lebanon, north of the Israeli-controlled security zone, near the Marj al-Zuhur checkpost. Israel had hoped that the transfer of the deportees would proceed in secret, thus preventing Lebanese attempts to repel the unwanted visitors. But as news of the deportations became public in Israel, the Lebanese government took steps to prevent the deportees from dispersing. The deportees had no choice but to set up a makeshift tent city in the no-man's-land north of the Marj al-Zuhur crossing. The camp was to attract worldwide media attention for several months to come, causing Israel severe propaganda damage and slowly transforming the image of the Hamas activists from ostensible terrorists to suffering victims.

On December 19, ten days after the fifth anniversary of the start of the *intifada*, violence erupted in the territories on a scale unknown since the late 1980s. Seven Palestinians were killed and more than 30 seriously wounded. The Fatah and the Hamas for the first time issued joint directives for action to be taken by the population.

With the Lebanese army preventing PLO and Hezballah activists from giving aid to the deportees, and the Lebanese government refusing to accept them, another attempt was made to persuade the Israeli High Court of Justice to order the Israeli government to take them back. On December 21, the South Lebanese Army (SLA) opened fire on the deportees, wounding three, and claims were made that because of the enmity between Hezballah and the SLA, the lives of the deportees were threatened. The High Court of Israel ordered the army to take steps to prevent such incidents in the future, while it considered the petitions to return the deportees. The next day, the High Court rejected the petitions, saying that since the deportees were inside the sovereign territory of Lebanon, they were not in any danger, and therefore there was no urgent need to return them. The court postponed until January its deliberations on the larger question of whether the deportations had been legal in the first place.

The Lebanese army continued its policy of quarantining the camp, ostensibly preventing food, water, medicine, and warm clothing from reaching the deportees.

Scenes of cold and hungry deportees were shown repeatedly on television screens all over the world. Surreptitiously, however, Hezballah activists were supplying the camp with food and cooking utensils.

On December 22, a special UN representative, Under Secretary James Jonah, announced his intention to visit Israel to help resolve the deportee problem. Arriving on December 27, Jonah rebuffed Israeli contentions that Lebanon was now responsible for the fate of the deportees. Rabin, for his part, rejected offers of parachuting food to the deportees via Israel, for fear that Jerusalem would thus be acknowledging its responsibility for them. Rabin assumed that the Lebanese government would ultimately have to relent and allow food convoys to reach the camp by land. On December 30, Jonah left the area, having achieved nothing; efforts to find a third country that would absorb the refugees had failed, and the Lebanese government, for its part, refused to get involved.

The deportations calmed the Israeli public, but the Israeli government, which had wished to distance the Hamas activists from its borders, found itself embroiled in a new and unanticipated controversy that refused to go away.

Other National Security Matters

LEBANON

On January 11, the London-based *Financial Times* reported that Iran and Hezballah had reached an agreement by which the Shiite terrorist organization would "renew" its operations against American and Israeli targets. Although the organization had never declared a formal cease-fire, it had reduced operations at the end of 1991 as hostage swaps were taking place. Several days after the news item appeared, two Israeli soldiers were killed in south Lebanon when an explosive device detonated near their patrol. The next day, a mukhtar of the south Lebanese village of Tir Harfa died in an explosion in his home. The Hezballah, indeed, was back in business.

On January 26, an Israeli soldier was killed in a skirmish with Hezballah terrorists. On February 8, another soldier was killed and two wounded. Hundreds of villagers just north of the Israeli-held security zone began fleeing from their homes, fearing an Israeli reprisal.

Israeli retribution, however, deviated from the norm this time around. On February 16, Israeli helicopters shot air-to-surface missiles into a convoy carrying the secretary-general of the Hezballah, Abbas Musawi. Musawi, his wife, and four-year-old son were killed, and another 18 people were wounded. It was one of Israel's most successful operations against the Hezballah, although much criticism was leveled at the government over the killing of Musawi's child. Hezballah leader Sheikh Muhammad Fadlala called for all-out Jihad against Israel. The next day, scores of Katyusha rockets landed in the security zone and on northern settlements in Israel, but there were no casualties. The army retaliated by firing over 400 artillery shells at Hezballah targets north of the security zone.

On February 18, Musawi was buried in Beirut in a funeral attended by tens of thousands of followers who demanded revenge. A previously unknown Shiite organization announced that it had executed captured Israeli navigator Ron Arad, who had been taken prisoner in October 1986. Israel responded with skepticism, announcing that the organization was unknown and that it continued to hold Iran responsible for the safety of Arad. Hassan Nasrallah replaced Musawi as secretary-general of the Hezballah.

Israel increased its forces along the northern border, and Defense Minister Moshe Arens, on a tour of the north, warned the Lebanese government that "if Israelis will be disturbed, so will the citizens of Lebanon." The warning apparently did not deter the terrorists who, on February 19, lobbed several Katyusha rockets into the northern town of Kiryat Shemonah. Three days later, Israel suffered its first civilian casualty in the north in over 11 years, as five-year-old Avia Elizada, from Moshav Granot, was killed by a rocket. A day earlier, two soldiers were killed in a skirmish with Hezballah, and Israel once again bombarded terrorist targets in the north. Seeking to defuse the escalating situation, Iranian president Hashemi Rafsanjani and Syrian president Hafez al-Assad pressured the Hezballah leadership to stop firing rockets inside Israel.

Throughout February and March, the pattern repeated itself. Hezballah fired rockets, Israel fired back, and thousands of Shiites fled their villages, fearing harsher Israeli raids, which did not come. On April 6, two Israeli soldiers were killed in a confrontation with Hezballah's sister organization, the Islamic Jihad. Israeli security sources estimated that there were about 600 active terrorists in south Lebanon. April brought reports that Syria was once again trying to curtail the activity of Hezballah and other organizations, fearing a massive Israeli reprisal that could jeopardize the peace talks.

On May 4, Amnesty International issued a report claiming that Shiite prisoners held in the El-Khiam prison in south Lebanon were being systematically tortured by their south Lebanese captors. The organization claimed that Israelis had also been present in some of these interrogations. The commander of the Israeli-backed South Lebanese Army (SLA), General Antoine Lahad, denied the charges.

Despite reports of Syrian "intervention," the Hezballah continued periodic shelling of Israeli positions both inside the security zone and on Israel's northern border. From May 19 on, Israel's response became harsher, starting with massive artillery bombardments and continuing with air raids, which in two days left at least 14 terrorists dead and dozens wounded. Some 14,000 Lebanese residents fled from the Tufah region in southern Lebanon to escape the continued Israeli raids. Prime Minister Yitzhak Shamir, in the midst of an election campaign, expressed hope that the retaliation efforts would "calm" the Hezballah. Defense Minister Arens accused Syria of transferring hundreds of Katyusha rockets, which had arrived from Teheran, into the hands of the terrorist groups.

As Israeli air attacks continued unabated, tension mounted between Israel and Syria, whose government held effective control over Lebanon. Syrian foreign minister Farouk al-Sharaa stated, on May 25, that "if Israel forces us into a war, we will not hesitate." The next day, Radio Damascus announced that Syrian units had been placed on full alert, and that reinforcements were being sent into the Beka'a Valley. Israel made clear that it did not seek a fight with Syria, but that it would continue the battle against Hezballah, wherever it might be.

On May 27, an Israeli soldier was killed in an ambush in south Lebanon. Israel retaliated with artillery, air, and helicopter attacks against terrorist targets. President Assad accused Israel of seeking a war. "If attacked, we will respond," he said. The Lebanese government called on Iran to restrain the Hezballah. The tension showed no signs of easing. Egyptian president Hosni Mubarak, in a letter sent to Prime Minister Shamir in the first days of June, warned that the continued Israeli attacks in Lebanon would escalate into a full-scale regional war. Syria and Lebanon, however, were not interested in a war, and throughout June exerted pressure on the terrorist groups to minimize their activities. The June 23 victory of the Labor party reinforced their motivation to calm the situation, although in the days following the elections, the cycle of violence continued as before. On July 21, one Israeli soldier was killed and three wounded when their patrol ran into a well-laid Hezballah ambush. The Israeli air force once again went into action.

On September 22, the Lebanese delegation to the Washington peace talks formally notified Israel that it had information that navigator Ron Arad was alive. Israeli prime minister Rabin demanded clarification, saying that Lebanon was responsible for the navigator's safety. "I hope the Lebanese are serious enough not to play with Arad's life," he said. On October 4, the leader of the Popular Front for the Liberation of Palestine, Ahmed Jibril, said in an interview that he had met with Ron Arad, and that he was feeling well. Jibril gave no further details.

The London-based *Foreign Report* magazine revealed in early August that the Hezballah was planning to step up its operations against Israel, having received new and sophisticated arms from Iran, including antitank and anti-aircraft missiles. Several weeks later, the magazine's prediction proved to be correct. On September 29, Hezballah launched one of its biggest and most sophisticated operations, with hundreds of terrorists attacking SLA positions in different areas in the security zone, for the first time using Sager-type antitank missiles. Israel retaliated with a massive bombardment of positions north of the security zone. The United States contacted the Lebanese government, urging it to stop the new conflagration in the south.

After a few weeks of quiet, the Hezballah struck again, with deadly results. On October 25, five Israeli soldiers were killed when an explosive device demolished their patrol van inside the security zone. Israel immediately sent in planes to bomb targets in Lebanon, and fears of a full-scale battle were heightened when long Israeli military convoys were spotted making their way to the north. On October 27, a Hezballah Katyusha rocket hit a house in the northern town of Kiryat Shemonah, killing Vadim Shuchman, a 14-year-old new immigrant from Ukraine. The United States, Britain, and France called on Israel not to retaliate, for fear that the peace process might be jeopardized. Israeli planes bombed targets in Syrian-held territory, but otherwise the government decided to heed the international warnings and to let Syria try and calm the situation.

On November 8, another salvo of Katyusha rockets was fired at northern settlements, but there were no injuries. The next day, another round of rockets landed inside the border. Syria promised the United States, once again, to put a stop to the Katyusha attacks. The situation throughout the next week appeared grim, but Israel once again held back. On November 15, after several days of attacks and counterattacks, calm was restored.

(On the deportation of Hamas activists to Lebanon in December, see above.)

JORDAN

The year 1991, the year of the Gulf War, had also been a turbulent year on the Israeli-Jordanian border, in which there were several bloody skirmishes with terrorists coming from Jordan. Although Israel was satisfied that the Jordanian government had not approved the attacks, there was some fear that Hussein's government was losing control over the army. One of the main reasons for King Hussein's loosened grip on his troops was the economic hardship suffered by Jordan in the wake of its support for Iraq. On March 4, Jordan announced a "revolutionary security concept," stating that it was freezing compulsory recruitment to the army. The official reason: economic hardship.

On May 3, Jordan returned to Israel a small boat that had strayed from the coast of Eilat to the southern Jordanian port of Aqaba.

On May 24, a single Katyusha rocket was fired from the Jordanian border into an uninhabited area on the Golan Heights. Israeli sources said it was an "isolated" incident and decided to play it down. Six weeks later, on July 8, a terrorist squad infiltrated from the same area and attacked an Israeli position in the southern Golan Heights, before escaping back to Jordan. On August 4, a terrorist squad crossed the border in the Jordan Salient; three terrorists were killed and two Israeli soldiers wounded. A previously unknown group called Hezballah Falastin claimed responsibility.

On September 5, a German tourist was killed north of the Dead Sea when he was spotted by an Israeli army patrol as he tried to cross the border from Jordan to Israel. Given the sporadic attacks by terrorists from Jordan, the soldiers had mistaken the tourist for another terrorist. On November 7, an Israeli patrol apprehended two Jordanian citizens who had crossed the border near the Dead Sea. They were found with a copy of the Koran and axes in their possession and were duly imprisoned. On November 30, shots were fired from across the border into the Beisan Valley region, wounding an Israeli soldier.

SYRIA

On February 12, Syria accused Israel of building nuclear weapons in order to dominate the Middle East. Throughout the year, and despite its participation in the peace process, Syria maintained its close ties with fundamentalist Iran; in March a delegation of Iranian Revolutionary Guards toured the Golan Heights, saying later that they had wanted to cut the border fences "so that we could destroy the enemy."

In April a rare occurrence of Israeli assistance to Syria took place when a small Syrian ship was saved from sinking by the Israeli navy and taken to Haifa for repairs. After the boat left Haifa, a problem emerged over payment for the cost of the repairs.

On August 12, a senior official accompanying Rabin on a visit to the United States revealed that Syria had recently carried out two experimental launches of the North Korean-made Scud-C surface-to-surface missile. The official accused Syria of funding the Islamic Hamas movement in the territories and the opposition Muslim Brotherhood in Jordan. Several days later, security sources quoted in the daily *Ha'aretz* said that the Syrian Scud-C missile would soon become operational. Western intelligence sources were quoted by the newspaper, on August 13, as claiming that, aided by North Korean scientists and technicians, Syria was building its own factory to produce Scud-C missiles. Foreign Minister Shimon Peres reacted to the reports by saying they indicated "grave designs" by Syria; he said the peace negotiations did not negate the need for preparedness by the Israeli army.

On August 16, Syria reacted by accusing Israel of engaging in a "sick campaign" concerning the Scud missiles. The daily organ of the Ba'ath party said that "Syria would not succumb to threats and will maintain its policy of safeguarding the rights of the nation." The next month, the London-based *Foreign Report* magazine reported that Syria had two fully operational factories manufacturing poison gas.

On November 23, the U.S. Congress released a report claiming heavy Syrian involvement in the international drug trade operating out of Lebanon. President Assad's brother, Rifat, was personally involved in the drug distribution, the report stated.

TERRORIST INCIDENTS ABROAD

On March 7, the security officer at the Israeli embassy in Ankara, Turkey, was killed when his booby-trapped car exploded. Various groups linked to Hezballah and the Islamic Jihad claimed responsibility, linking the bombing to the Israeli killing of Hezballah secretary-general Abbas Musawi.

On March 17, a car bomb exploded outside the Israeli embassy in Buenos Aires, Argentina, killing 28, including 4 Israeli diplomats. The Islamic Jihad organization claimed responsibility, once again citing revenge for the killing of Musawi. Foreign Minister David Levy told the Knesset on March 18 that the perpetrators were "destined for painful punishment."

OTHER SECURITY MATTERS

On January 6, it was revealed that the Pentagon was conducting an investigation into possible wrongdoing by the Israeli Defense Purchasing Mission in New York and looking into allegations of misuse of American aid money. The investigation grew out of the Rami Dotan affair, in which the Israel air force brigadier general was convicted in 1991 of bribe-taking and theft of over $10 million in American military aid monies. In June Israel rejected an American request to interrogate others involved in the Dotan scandal, citing possible risks to its national-security interests. In December an American delegation came to Israel to investigate arms-purchasing operations by the Defense Ministry.

In early February, Israel expressed concern at the American decision to sell Saudi Arabia 72 advanced F-15 fighters; in September U.S. defense officials launched talks with Israel on maintaining its air superiority. (See also "Relations with the United States," below.)

On May 2, Israel successfully tested the Israeli-made Barak seaborne antimissile missile. The missiles were to be placed on Saar 5 missile boats, then under construction in the United States. On September 23, Israel carried out its fourth experimental launch of the Arrow antimissile missile and termed the launch a success.

On June 8, the head of Israeli military intelligence, Maj. Gen. Uri Saguy, warned the Knesset's Foreign Affairs and Defense Committee that Iran could develop and produce nuclear weapons by the end of the decade. Such a development would place Israel's very existence at risk, he said.

On July 30, 2 Israelis were killed and 46 wounded in an explosion in a Military Industries factory near the coast in Herzliyah. Damage estimated at tens of millions of dollars was caused to neighboring buildings and houses.

Twelve soldiers were killed in training accidents between April and August, creating a public uproar and demands for external investigations. Prime Minister Rabin ordered the army to take all measures to put a stop to the accidents, blaming them on what he termed the notorious Israeli "trust me" attitude. In August the army decided to appoint "training safety officers" in each army unit that trains soldiers. Five Israeli soldiers from an elite infantry unit were killed on November 5 during an operational exercise at the Ze'elim training base. The soldiers were hit by a shoulder-held missile launched by another unit posing as the enemy. A military investigation later recommended disciplinary measures against three senior officers. On November 23, the *New York Times* reported that the soldiers had been training for action against the Hezballah; the next day the *Miami Herald* added that the target of the planned action was Hassan Nasrallah, the man who succeeded Abbas Musawi, the Hezballah official killed in an IDF raid in February.

On September 30, Germany announced that it would give Israel $600 million worth of military equipment and that intelligence sharing between the two countries would continue as before. Germany also announced a $140-million investment in the development of electronic warfare equipment by the Israeli Elta company.

On October 19, the U.S. Congress approved a $33-million American purchase of the Israeli-made Popeye air-to-air missile.

On November 8, Israeli helicopters rescued ten passengers from an Israeli pleasure yacht stranded off the coast of Sudan. The operation cost $2 million.

In late November the U.S. *Armed Forces Journal* reported that three Israeli military delegations had visited India. The two countries were about to conclude a $1-billion arms deal, the newspaper said.

In late December it was reported that Israeli pilots were test-flying both the F-16 and F-18 jet fighters. Israel announced that it wished to purchase 60 planes at a cost of over $2 billion.

On December 27, the army announced that compulsory military service for women would be shortened during 1993 from the current 24 months to 22 months.

DIPLOMATIC DEVELOPMENTS

The Peace Process

The first round of talks between Israel and its Arab neighbors, held in Madrid in November 1991, and the second, in Washington in December, had produced no results. Not only was there no progress on matters of substance, but in the most closely watched track, the Israeli-Palestinian negotiations, the two sides had yet to reach agreement on the modalities of the Palestinian representation, and had thus failed to convene a formal round of talks.

Israel had objected to the separate participation of the Palestinian delegation, which according to the rules of Madrid was a part of the so-called "Jordanian-Palestinian" delegation. The Palestinians, for their part, sought to break free of the constraining rules of Madrid and to be as independent as possible. In discussions leading up to the January 13 talks, which ended just a few hours before their scheduled start, a complex compromise was worked out whereby certain issues would be discussed in the forum of the joint Jordanian-Palestinian delegation, while others would be discussed directly between Israel and the Palestinian team.

BILATERAL TALKS, ROUND THREE
(Washington, January 13–16)

The third round of bilateral talks between Israel and its Arab neighbors convened in Washington on January 13. "This is the beginning," said the head of the Palestinian delegation, Haidar Abdel-Shafi, when he arrived for the start of the talks in the State Department. His Israeli counterpart, Cabinet Secretary Elyakim Rubinstein, explained to reporters that the talks would first concentrate on "matters of procedure." The start of the talks, originally scheduled for January 7, had been held up for a week as Arab delegations arrived late in protest over Israel's decision to deport 12 Palestinian activists. The Israeli delegation, arriving in Washington as originally planned, waited for a week in the American capital for their Arab interlocutors.

Palestinian and Israeli negotiators both submitted their own blueprints for Palestinian self-rule in the West Bank and Gaza. The Israeli proposal, modeled along the general lines of the 1978 Camp David accords, envisaged the establishment of an "interim self-government authority," excluded Jerusalem from any settlement, and was vague about the kind of elections that would be held to elect the "authority." The Palestinian counterproposal ensured the inclusion of Jerusalem in the interim arrangements, foresaw complete Palestinian control over land and water, and demanded the dismantling of Jewish settlements in the territories. The Israeli delegation refused to discuss the matter of settlements, claiming that this issue could be raised only in negotiations on the final status of the territories.

There was little progress on the other fronts either. Israeli and Syrian negotiators Yossi Ben-Aharon and Mowaffak al-Allaf sparred over the fate of Syrian Jews, with Allaf claiming that "there are no Syrian Jews, only Syrian citizens." Jordan asked to discuss the fate of Jewish settlements and the correct interpretation of UN Security Council Resolution 242, while Israel emphasized diplomatic recognition and economic cooperation. Lebanon demanded a complete Israeli withdrawal from the security zone in the south of the country, while Israel demanded a Lebanese guarantee against further terrorist attacks from Lebanese territory.

The sides disbanded without agreement even on the venue or date of the next round of talks. The Arab states, however, made clear that they wished to continue with the Washington talks.

MULTILATERAL TALKS, ROUND ONE
(*Moscow, January 28–29*)

The multilateral talks aimed, in broad terms, at discussing a "post-peace" Middle East in which multilateral cooperation would blossom, both within the area and with the rest of the international community. Originally an Israeli idea, the concept of the talks was embraced by the United States and Europe as a means of augmenting the direct bilateral talks and of showing the negotiating sides what the "fruits of peace" would be if they reached agreement.

From the outset, however, it was clear that the bilateral talks would cast a long shadow over the multilaterals. Two of the chief protagonists, Syria and Lebanon, announced that they would boycott the talks in protest over Israeli "intransigence" in Washington. The Palestinians, for their part, wished to exploit the multilateral forum in order to achieve what they had failed to achieve in the bilateral talks under the so-called Madrid rules: the participation of "diaspora" Palestinians—those residing in other countries—and even PLO representatives in the talks. Israel, however, claimed that the Madrid formula covered all other arenas of the peace process and refused Palestinian demands, although there was some support in

Washington for the participation of Palestinians from outside the territories. Thus, as the Moscow talks got under way, the Palestinian delegation chose not to attend. Algeria and Yemen withdrew from the talks in sympathy with the Palestinians. Even Egypt was reluctant to attend, finally deciding to go to Moscow while expressing "understanding" for the Syrian boycott.

In an effort to induce the Palestinians to attend, Secretary of State James Baker, heading the American delegation, agreed with the Palestinians to support the inclusion of diaspora Palestinians on condition that known PLO officials not attend the talks. All the other participating countries, except Israel, gladly accepted the formula; thus, the groundwork for future American-Israeli friction was laid.

Despite this, the Moscow talks constituted a diplomatic coup for Israel. For the first time, representatives of several Arab countries ended their decades-long boycott of Israel and sat together at the same table with Israeli officials. Foreign Minister David Levy, who represented Israel, found himself sitting across the table from high-ranking officials from Saudi Arabia, Kuwait, Oman, Qatar, Bahrain, the United Arab Emirates, Tunisia, Mauritania, and Morocco. Others attending included the two cosponsors of the peace process, the United States and Russia, as well as Canada, China, Japan, Turkey, and the European Community.

The conference agreed to set up five working committees that would meet in April or May: a group on arms control and regional security, which would meet in Washington; a group on refugees, which would meet in Ottawa; a group on water, which would meet in Turkey or Austria; a group on regional economic development, which would meet in Brussels; and a group on ecology, which would meet in Tokyo. Israel had objected to the establishment of a group dealing with refugees, but bowed to American pressure on this matter.

BILATERAL TALKS, ROUND FOUR
(*Washington, February 24–March 4*)

The fourth round of talks opened under inauspicious circumstances. The February 16 killing of Hezballah leader Abbas Musawi cast a pall over the talks, as did the arrest, in the territories, of two members of the Palestinian delegation. Israel, for its part, came to Washington just as Secretary of State Baker announced that Washington had decided in effect to reject Israel's request for $10 billion in loan guarantees. The atmosphere was not conducive to progress, and indeed little was achieved.

The Palestinians decided to concentrate on the issue of Jewish settlements in the territories, which Israel had refused even to discuss during the previous round of talks. Palestinian spokeswoman Hanan Ashrawi said on February 25 that the Palestinians would discuss substantive issues only after Israel agreed to address the matter of settlements as well as human-rights violations in the territories. "If Israel does not stop settlements," she said in a press conference in Washington, "there will be no discussions on any other matter." The previous day, Cabinet Secretary Rubinstein submitted a ten-page document outlining Israel's vision of the interim arrangements with the Palestinians. Contrary to the provisions of Camp David, the Israeli document made no mention of elections for the "self-governing authority," nor did it refer to the "redeployment" of Israeli troops. Israel proposed that the Palestinians should be in charge of their own civil affairs, such as taxation, justice, education, social welfare, and the like. Palestinian negotiator Haidar Abdel-Shafi said that the Israeli position was "very negative and endangered the negotiations."

On March 3, the Palestinians submitted their own counterproposal for the self-government arrangements. Their 16-page document called for free elections, control of most matters, including internal security, and the inclusion of East Jerusalem in the autonomy. Rubinstein rejected the document, calling it "a plan for a Palestinian state in all but name."

Israel and Jordan continued to bicker over the meaning of UN Resolution 242, but nonetheless began informal discussions between officials on matters of health, economy, and justice. Israel and Lebanon continued to squabble about the meaning of the 1983 Security Council Resolution 425, which called for an Israeli withdrawal from south Lebanon. The Syrian team sought to concentrate on Resolution 242, claiming that it mandated a complete Israeli withdrawal from the Golan Heights. Syrian negotiator Allaf said that Israel had come to the talks with "premeditated determination not to allow any progress."

On March 5, the heads of the delegations met with Baker, who, according to the next day's *Washington Post*, criticized the Palestinians for "posturing." The Americans also submitted a proposal for establishing a joint Israeli-Lebanese military committee to discuss security arrangments in the south. The talks once again disbanded without setting a venue or date for their next meeting.

BILATERAL TALKS, ROUND FIVE
(*Washington, April 27–30*)

In the weeks leading up to the next round of talks, Washington tried to make good on its pledge to Israel to try and move the talks to a locale in the Middle East vicinity. The administration asked Arab states to submit lists of acceptable cities in the area, hoping to cull a venue acceptable to all sides. On April 20, the administration announced that the sixth round of talks would be held in Rome. The Arabs, for their part, said that they would refuse to hold further talks with Israel until the June 23 Israeli elections took place.

In the fifth round, Israel submitted to the Palestinians a plan for holding municipal elections in the West Bank and Gaza, and offered to transfer immediately, on an experimental basis, the authority for running the health services in the territories. The Palestinians did not reject the Israeli offer of elections out of hand, saying that they would agree to municipal elections only after general political elections were held in the territories for the election of a legislative council.

On April 27, Syria announced an end to travel restrictions on Syrian Jews. The statement improved the atmosphere in the Washington talks, but there was no report of progress. Israel and Jordan discussed water rights, while Israel and Lebanon discussed the situation in southern Lebanon.

The talks ended after only four days, in the wake of a unilateral Israeli decision to return its delegates to Israel because of national holidays. Overall, the fifth round of talks, though short, took place in a better atmosphere than its predecessors and was generally considered to be the first in which substantive issues were discussed. Before the next round convened, however, Israel would have a new government with radically different policies than the one in power in April.

MULTILATERAL TALKS, ROUND TWO
(Various Sites, May)

The dispute between Israel and the United States concerning the participation of diaspora Palestinians in the multilaterals, as promised by Secretary Baker to the Palestinians in Moscow, was not settled in the four months leading up to the May convening of the five multilateral working groups. Baker had agreed that the Palestinians would be able to send their diaspora representatives to two of the five groups—refugees and economic development. On May 7, Baker sent a note to Foreign Minister Levy emphasizing that American agreement to the participation of outside Palestinians did not mean that Washington recognized the Palestinian right of return. Nonetheless, on May 9, the Israeli government decided that it would boycott the two problematic groups unless Palestinians from outside the territories were barred from participation. Israel also objected to the participation of the European Community in the forum dealing with arms control, thus straining its bilateral ties with the European countries. Syria and Lebanon, for their part, maintained their boycott of the entire multilateral process.

The economic talks, boycotted by Israel and attended by outside Palestinians, convened in Brussels on May 11 and 12; concurrently, the regional arms talks convened in Washington, with Israel but without the Palestinians, who, by an Israeli-American consensus, were kept out of these talks because they were not a "state." On the eve of the controversial refugee talks, which Israel had opposed from the outset and which it was now boycotting because of the participation of Palestinian refugees, a diplomatic crisis erupted between Jerusalem and Washington. This occurred after State Department spokeswoman Margaret Tutwiler said, at her daily briefing, that the United States supported the 1948 UN Resolution 194, which called for the return of refugees. Several days later, Tutwiler "clarified" the American position by stating that the only UN decisions relevant to the entire peace process were Security Council Resolutions 242 and 338.

In Ottawa, on May 13, Palestinian representatives refused to heed an American request and insisted that the refugee forum discuss their "right of return to Palestine." The Palestinians did not specify which areas of "Palestine" they wished to return to, because of internal differences on this matter within the Palestinian delegation. The next day, bowing to heavy American pressure, the Palestinians agreed not to demand that the "right of return" actually be placed on the agenda of the talks. The participating countries, minus Israel, agreed to explore practical ways of improving the lives of the Palestinian refugees.

Israel did participate in the water talks, held in Vienna on May 13 and 14. The participating countries agreed to discuss the establishment of an international database on water resources, regional cooperation, and ways of increasing regional water resources. In the May 18–19 talks on the environment, held in Tokyo, the delegates discussed the ecology of the Mediterranean and the Red Sea and methods of preventing pollution of the sea. On May 27, a steering committee of the multilateral process met in Lisbon, setting up the dates and venues for the next round of talks.

THE NEW ISRAELI GOVERNMENT

On June 23, 15 years of Likud rule came to an end and Labor returned to power. During the election campaign, party leader Rabin repeatedly emphasized that one of his primary targets as prime minister would be to achieve an autonomy agreement with the Palestinians "within six to nine months." Rabin appeared to be formulating a "Palestinians first" policy, by which his government would strive to achieve a breakthrough in the territories and only later deal with the other Arab partners. In his campaign, Rabin also distinguished between "security" and "political" Jewish settlements in the territories, saying that the latter were unnecessary and an obstacle to progress in the peace process. In a June 24 press conference, immediately after his election, Rabin reiterated his campaign promises.

On July 12, the police called in for questioning Palestinian spokeswoman Hanan Ashrawi and the head of the Palestinian delegation, Haidar Abdel-Shafi, in the wake of a meeting held between the Palestinian delegation to the peace talks and PLO chairman Yasir Arafat, in Amman on June 18. The two had violated an Israeli law that forbade contacts with the PLO; the new Israeli government, however, had pledged to repeal that law. The chances of the two being prosecuted were thus minimal.

The new Israeli government was greeted with ambivalence by the Palestinians as well as the rest of the Arab world. On the one hand, it was clear that Labor held more moderate positions than the Likud and genuinely sought a peace settlement; but Palestinians were wary of Rabin, who had initiated a tough response to the *intifada* during his tenure as defense minister in the late 1980s. The Palestinians were also skeptical about whether Labor's more dovish policies would be acceptable to them; they rejected Rabin's differentiation between "political" and "security" settlements.

In his July 13 inaugural speech to the Knesset, Rabin offered to visit any Arab capital in order to make peace, and invited the joint Jordanian-Palestinian delegation to come for talks in Jerusalem, an offer that was not accepted. Several days later, new foreign minister Shimon Peres reiterated the Israeli pledge to achieve a breakthrough with the Palestinians within the next year. On July 16, new housing minister Binyamin Ben-Eliezer announced a freeze on all building contracts for Jewish homes in the West Bank and Gaza. A week later, the government announced that 6,681 contracts for buildings where construction had not started would be canceled; 8,781 contracts for buildings where construction had already begun would, however, be honored. Ben-Eliezer made clear that as far as Israel was concerned, East Jerusalem was not part of the West Bank and therefore there would be no reduction in the pace of construction in the capital. The Palestinians reacted cautiously to the announcement; Ashrawi desribed it as "encouraging," while PLO chairman Arafat, who continued to demand a complete halt to Israeli construction in the territories, described the partial freeze as "a first step."

Following the formation of the new cabinet, Secretary of State James Baker toured the Middle East, July 19–23. In Amman, Baker sided with the Arabs by rejecting Rabin's differentiation between "political" and "security" settlements. He proposed, however, that in exchange for a complete Israeli freeze on settlements, the Arabs would end their economic boycott of Israel. In Damascus, on July 23, Baker reportedly solicited Syrian reaction to a proposal for phased Israeli withdrawal from the Golan Heights; according to Arab news reports, the reactions were negative. That same day, the Russian ambassador to Damascus visited Israel, stressing the Syrian wish to achieve a breakthrough in the peace talks within a few months.

Following Baker's visit, Arab foreign ministers met in Damascus and repeated the Arab demand for a complete freeze on settlements. PLO chairman Arafat, on July 30, expressed satisfaction at the change of government in Israel and said that he would be willing to meet with Rabin at anytime. On August 1, the United States and Russia issued invitations for a resumption of bilateral talks which, it was hoped, would now lead to quick and meaningful progress.

On the internal front, Rabin and his foreign minister, Shimon Peres, perennial arch-rivals for the leadership of the Labor party, agreed to maintain the division of labor that had existed in the outgoing Likud government. The Prime Minister's Office, it was decided, would be in charge of the bilateral talks, while the Foreign Ministry would be charged with running the multilaterals. As in the previous government, the allocation of responsibilities was more a result of the fierce rivalry between the prime minister and his foreign minister than a well thought-out plan of action.

On August 11, President George Bush announced that the U.S. administration had decided to give Israel $10 billion in loan guarantees. The decision raised howls of protest in the Arab world. Arab foreign ministers meeting in Damascus stated that the United States had reneged on its commitment to seek a complete settlement freeze. The ministers said that the United States could no longer be considered an unbiased mediator and proposed, without really meaning it, that the negotiations henceforth be held under the auspices of the United Nations.

BILATERAL TALKS, ROUND SIX
(*Washington, August 24–September 3; September 14–24*)

The sixth round of talks was the longest to date, lasting for a month with a ten-day break in the middle. The media reported a much-improved atmosphere at the start of the talks.

On August 17, the Israeli daily *Ha'aretz* revealed that the United States was offering to position American troops on the Golan Heights within the framework of a peace arrangement. On the eve of the talks, Prime Minister Rabin further improved the atmosphere with the Palestinians by announcing the release of 800 Palestinian prisoners. The government also announced that 280 homes in the territories that had been sealed up would be unsealed. Streets that had been closed would be reopened. On the day the talks started, Rabin announced the cancellation of deportation orders against 11 PLO activists whose deportation had been ordered in January.

One of Rabin's first steps as prime minister was to replace Yossi Ben-Aharon, the director-general of the Prime Minister's Office in the Likud government and a self-confessed hard-liner, with Itamar Rabinovich, the rector of Tel Aviv University and an expert on Syrian affairs. The appointment raised hopes that Israel would be more flexible on the issue of the Golan, which during the previous five rounds of talks had not even been discussed. Commenting on the new Israeli negotiator, the spokeswoman of the Syrian delegation, Bushra Kanafani, said on the opening day of the talks that there was a "different style" on the Israeli side. However, the major change was in substance, not style: at the start of the talks, Rabinovich told his Syrian interlocutors that Israel was now willing to acknowledge the "peace for territories" principle embodied in Resolution 242. For all practical purposes, the Golan Heights had been placed on the negotiating table for the first time. On August 25, Rabin stated that Israel would not withdraw from the entire Golan Heights, but also said that "we will not stick to every centimeter." Rabin, speaking in the Knesset, reminded his listeners that it was the Likud that had created the precedent by giving up the entire Sinai in order to reach a peace agreement with Egypt.

In Washington, Israel presented a new draft of its proposals on autonomy to the Palestinians. Israel dropped the terminology of "administrative council"—in reference to the body that would run the territories in the interim period—and was now willing to propose general political elections for the "self-governing authority." The head of the Israeli delegation to the talks with the Palestinians, Elyakim Rubinstein (who stayed on in his post in the new government), said that the council elected by the Palestinians would be able to legislate bylaws and rules but would not have the authority for "primary legislation." The Palestinians, for their part, demanded a 180-member parliament that could legislate freely. They added, however, that the matter of legislation was open to negotiation.

By the end of the first week of talks, the Palestinians reverted to their grumblings about Israeli intransigence. On August 30, the head of the Palestinian delegation,

Abdel-Shafi, said that Israel was not willing to consider "real changes." He said the new Israeli proposals fell short of what Israel had agreed to in the 1978 Camp David accords. The Palestinians once again demanded assurances that Jerusalem would be included in the final-status arrangements.

The Palestinians presented a new ten-point document on September 1; Israel did not reject the document, but news reports indicated that there were major differences between the two sides. A counterproposal submitted by Israel on September 15 offered the Palestinians, for the first time, a say in the control of water and land resources in the territories.

On the Syrian front, the head of the Syrian delegation, Mowaffak Allaf, appeared to be indicating new Syrian flexibility when he stated, on September 3, that Syria would be willing to make peace with Israel in conjunction with an Israeli withdrawal from the Golan. A day later, however, he made it clear that as far as Damascus was concerned, "peace" did not necessarily mean open borders and normalization.

In the second part of the sixth round of talks, the two sides began discussing, for the first time, theoretical future security arrangements, although no agreement was reached. The Syrian position, unacceptable to Israel, held that any security arrangements would have to be "symmetrical"—that is, of equal scope on both sides of the future border. Rabin announced, on September 7, that Israel would also be willing to negotiate with Syria on an interim settlement. On September 10, he said that peace with Syria must entail some sort of "territorial compromise." Although it had accepted the "peace for territories" formula, Israel had yet to use the word "withdrawal" in the drafting of its positions on the Golan. On September 21, U.S. ambassador to Israel William Harrop said that the Syrian demand for a prior Israeli commitment for full withdrawal on the Golan was "unreasonable."

Rabin's willingness to speak of territorial changes on the Golan created political turmoil at home, but it did not impress the Syrians. Allaf rejected a new Israeli proposal for talking points, submitted on September 14, saying that the document did not commit Israel to full withdrawal, which was a prerequisite to progress as far as Damascus was concerned. On September 17, the Syrians went so far as to break off the talks with Israel, but were subsequently persuaded by the United States to return. Following the end of the round, Allaf stated that the talks had proven, for the first time, that "peace was possible." But a few days later, Syrian foreign minister Farouk al-Sharaa said that "anyone who thinks that peace is possible without a full Israeli withdrawal from every inch of land is making a big mistake."

Away from the limelight, Israel also continued negotiations with Jordan and Lebanon. Progress was reported with Jordan on issues such as allocation of water from the Yarmuk River, but talks with Lebanon continued to be bogged down in discussions of whether Israel would commit itself to a withdrawal from southern Lebanon before Beirut proved that it could fend off terrorist attacks against Israel.

MULTILATERAL TALKS, ROUND THREE
(Various Sites, September–November)

The third round of multilateral talks got under way in largely uneventful meetings of the arms-control group, in Moscow on September 15, and the water committee, which met in Washington on the same day. The environment group met in The Hague on October 26.

Throughout the months of September and October, Egypt played a central role in ironing out the differences between Israel and the Palestinians that had led to the Israeli boycott of two multilateral committees in May. Egyptian foreign minister Amre Moussa concluded an agreement with the Israeli government by which it would agree to the participation of diaspora Palestinians in the multilateral forums, on condition that these would not be members of the PLO or of the organization's "parliament," the Palestine National Congress (PNC). Thus, on October 8, Foreign Minister Peres announced, following a meeting with Moussa, that Israel would no longer boycott the talks on refugees and on regional economic development. Israel also dropped its opposition to European—as well as Palestinian—participation in the talks on arms control and regional security. Syria and Lebanon, however, maintained their ongoing boycott of the entire multilateral process.

The regional talks got under way in Paris on October 29, with a diaspora Palestinian, Zein Myassi, in attendance. For the first time, Israeli officials sat at an official forum with a representative of the Palestinian refugees. The two sides even agreed on a World Bank survey of economic problems of the region. In Ottawa, on November 11, the Egyptian-brokered agreement appeared to break down. Mohammed Hallaj, a member of the Palestine National Council, appeared as a member of the Palestinian delegation; Israel claimed that this was a violation of the agreement and decided to boycott the first day of the talks. After many tense hours of Egyptian and American intervention, the Israelis returned to the talks, after receiving assurances from the United States that Hallaj had not been a member of the PNC since 1991.

The steering committee of the multilaterals met in London, December 3–4.

BILATERAL TALKS, ROUND SEVEN
(Washington, October 21–29; November 9–19)

On October 1, Syria rejected a call made by Rabin for a summit meeting between the leaders of the two countries. In the hiatus between the sixth and seventh rounds of talks, French foreign minister Roland Dumas launched his own diplomatic initiative to bring the Syrian and Israeli positions closer and the leaders of the two sides together, much to the displeasure of Washington. The flurry of activity on the Israeli-Syrian front worried the Palestinians, who feared a "separate" Syrian deal with Israel. PLO relations with Syria, never good, cooled even further, and Arafat canceled a planned October visit to Damascus. On October 20, Rabin told the

French daily *Le Monde* that the talks with the Syrians were "promising." According to Israeli news reports, Rabin, who had begun his prime ministership with a "Palestinians first" attitude, was now leaning toward a quick breakthrough first with the Syrians.

At the start of the seventh round, Israel submitted a new document to the Syrians which for the first time employed the specific word "withdrawal." Rabinovich made clear that Israel's willingness to withdraw did not include agreement to evacuate any Jewish settlements on the Golan. American sources, quoted in *Ha'aretz* on October 25, made clear that the simple addition of the hitherto-unspoken word would not suffice in order to reach an agreed Syrian-Israeli declaration of principles, which was now the main goal of the Israeli-Syrian talks.

The Israeli-Palestinian talks appeared for the first time to be getting down to substantive issues, as the two sides formed subcommittees to discuss details of the interim settlement as well as the overall concept of what self-rule would actually mean. Palestinian sources, quoted by *Ha'aretz* on October 27, said that Israel was showing "surprising flexibility."

But the real surprise of the seventh round was the Jordanians. On October 28, Israel and Jordan announced that they were on the verge of finalizing a detailed agenda for talks in the future. The aim of the talks, according to the document, was to reach a "peace agreement" between the two countries. Israel and Jordan also agreed to discuss the future of small slivers of land in the Arava which Jordan claimed—and Israel did not deny—had been illegally occupied by Israeli farmers in the aftermath of the 1948 war.

After taking a break for the U.S. presidential elections, the talks resumed on November 9. The defeat of George Bush and the election of Bill Clinton cast a cloud of uncertainty over the peace process, especially on the Arab side. Bush had been considered by the Arabs to be the most "pro-Arab" American president in modern times, and was widely credited, together with Secretary of State Baker, with having brought Israel, against its will, to the negotiating table. President-elect Clinton was thought to be much more "pro-Israel," especially after receiving a high proportion of Jewish votes. Concerns for the peace process were also raised in Israel, because of Clinton's self-professed intention to place greater emphasis on domestic affairs at the expense of American involvement overseas.

Although the peace talks continued on schedule, the sides conceded that little progress could be expected during the remaining months of Bush's lame-duck administration and before the new Democratic administration took power.

After the first week, Israeli officials spoke of "frustrating talks," and it was widely understood that the uncertain position of the U.S. administration was taking its toll. Syria continued to demand a full Israeli withdrawal from the Golan, while Prime Minister Rabin, in a November 14 interview with the *Washington Post*, accused Damascus of working against the talks by encouraging Hezballah actions in south Lebanon. What had started as a promising round of talks was quickly turning into an acrimonious exchange of accusations. Rabinovich said, on November 12, that the peace process had not collapsed but was definitely facing serious difficulties.

Developments with the Palestinians were not faring any better, leading the Palestinian delegation to warn, in a letter to Rabin made public on November 21, that the talks would collapse if progress were not achieved soon. PLO chairman Arafat stated, on November 25, that the talks had reached a "dead end." Rabin, in response, declared, on November 29, that the Palestinians could be repeating their "historic mistake" of 1947 when they rejected the United Nations Partition Plan.

Lebanon, for its part, rejected an Israeli proposal to set up a joint military committee, while Jordan reneged on its intention to sign the agreed agenda with Israel, concluded in the last round of talks. Jordan was also miffed at an Israeli rejection of its request to allow the repatriation of 70,000 Palestinian refugees living in Jordan. The only bright light appeared to be the start of official Israeli-Jordanian talks on water rights.

BILATERAL TALKS, ROUND EIGHT
(Washington, December 7–17)

The eighth round of peace talks convened on December 7, still plagued by the uncertainty caused by the transfer of power in the United States and now also overshadowed by violent events in the occupied territories. The Palestinians, who had unsuccessfully tried to have the talks postponed, showed up with only a four-member delegation, in protest. On December 9, two days after starting, the talks broke up for a day as the Arab delegations commemorated the fifth anniversary of the start of the *intifada*.

The Palestinians were pressing for direct American involvement, proposing that trilateral Israeli-American-Palestinian talks take place. After rejecting the proposal out of hand, Israel was surprised when State Department officials proposed that they intervene in the talks and submit a paper that would try to bridge the differences between the sides. Assuming that such an offer would not have been made without the acquiescence of the incoming administration, Rabin sent a message to President-elect Clinton asking the United States not to involve itself in the substantive matters under discussion at the negotiating table.

On December 15, the Palestinians appeared to be ready once again for substantive discussion, presenting a new proposal for an agreed declaration of principles. But the positive atmosphere lasted for less than 24 hours as news began to arrive from Israel about the government's decision to deport 400 Hamas activists. Protesting the deportations, the Arab delegations decided to end the talks on December 17. No new date was set for the next round, and the talks disbanded in an atmosphere of despair and failure. Palestinian spokeswoman Hanan Ashrawi said the talks were "on the verge of disaster."

President Bush met with the Palestinian delegation on December 19, but the meeting, which had been originally conceived as a gesture aimed at encouraging Palestinian pragmatism, was also overshadowed by the deportations. As Arab foreign ministers met in Cairo on December 24 to plan their next moves, Palestinian activist Faisal Husseini announced that the Palestinians were on the verge of a decision to "readopt the option of armed struggle."

The Arabs, however, were not willing to accept a Palestinian demand to boycott the talks until all the deportees were returned. In fact, despite the deportations, Syria was once again making positive noises about the future of the peace process: Syrian vice-president Abdul Halim Haddam said, on December 24, that Israel and Syria were in a position to reach a peace agreement, including security arrangements. On December 30, Professor Rabinovich, the head of the Israeli delegation to the talks with Syria, estimated that the two countries would achieve a peace agreement by December 1993.

Relations with the United States

Relations between the Bush administration and the Shamir government had gone from bad to worse during the latter months of 1991. Contrary to Israeli expectations, Congress bowed to the administration's request to postpone the approval of Jerusalem's request for $10 billion in loan guarantees until Washington and Jerusalem could agree to the "terms" of the guarantees, which, in effect, meant Israeli concessions on the issue of settlements in the territories. The two countries also crossed diplomatic swords on issues related to the peace process and human rights in the territories.

The loan-guarantees issue was the main source of friction between the two countries. The United States wished to attach strings to the loan guarantees that would prevent their being used, directly or indirectly, for funding construction activities in the occupied territories. Israel was willing to consider some token gestures in order to accommodate American concerns, but refused to consider an overall freeze on new construction since, after all, expanding settlement was the main political goal of the ruling Likud party.

Sen. Phil Gramm (R., Tex.), visiting Israel in early January, told Prime Minister Yitzhak Shamir that President Bush was "very upset" about the continuing rate of settlement and construction in the territories. Gramm spelled out what was already becoming quite clear to Shamir: the loan guarantees would not be given unless Israel took significant steps to "appease" the president on this matter.

Israel, for its part, stepped up its campaign in America to nudge the administration forward on the issue of guarantees, and started employing what could be described as scare tactics, emphasizing the critical importance of the guarantees to Israel's economic well-being. In January Israeli officials told American counterparts that, without the guarantees, the unemployment rate in Israel would climb from the current 10–11 percent to 16 percent or higher, that taxes would be raised, and growth would be stunted.

On January 25, Secretary of State Baker met with Israeli ambassador to Washington Zalman Shoval and offered a "compromise" formula. According to Israeli press reports, Baker suggested that if Israel undertook to stop any future building in the territories, it would be allowed to complete the projects already under way. In exchange, Baker said, the administration would approve the guarantees. Several days later, on February 2, it was unclear whether even this suggestion, which by itself was unacceptable to Israel, reflected President Bush's views. National Security Adviser Brent Scowcroft said, on February 2, that the president would not give a seal of approval to any increase in the Jewish population in the territories by means of an agreement that would allow Israel to complete housing already started.

On February 6, Shoval returned to Baker with a counterproposal, by which Israel would put a cap on the amount of money it would invest in the territories, rather than limit the precise number of housing starts. In Jerusalem, Prime Minister Shamir appeared to be facing the possibility that the guarantees might not be given at all. "If we won't receive the guarantees," he said, "we will have to look for other sources, but the immigration from Russia will not stop."

On February 8, Baker publicly asked Israel to put a stop to building in the territories, adding that monies spent by Israel on settlements would be reduced "dollar for dollar" from "American aid." It was not clear whether Baker was referring to the loan guarantees or to the annual economic aid given to Israel; the ambiguity raised concern in Israel to new heights. On February 10, *Ha'aretz* reported that Baker "had changed his mind" about the loan guarantees and was now willing to allow Israel to build an additional 6,000 housing units in the territories. On February 12, the paper reported that the administration would like to defer dealing with the loan guarantees altogether until the elections in Israel were over.

Baker and Shoval met again on February 21, but failed to achieve progress. Baker confirmed that the United States would be willing to allow Israel to finish the construction of 6,000 housing units, but subsequently there would have to be a complete freeze on new housing. According to some reports, Baker also said that monies spent on construction in the territories since the 1967 war would first be deducted from the loan guarantees. Shoval replied that any blanket freeze on settlements was unacceptable to Israel. Two days later, Shamir rephrased the Israeli position by saying that "we will not stop settling even for one day."

Baker made the American position public on February 24, and it was now clear that negotiations between the two countries on this issue had reached a dead end. The *New York Times*, on February 24, confirmed the worst suspicions of the Israeli government: the paper said that President Bush wanted Labor candidate Yitzhak Rabin to become the next prime minister of Israel. Likud officials had no doubt that Bush was actively contributing to Rabin's election campaign by refusing to budge on the matter of loan guarantees. The next day, President Bush said that he would not change his mind concerning the guarantees, even if his position harmed his chances for reelection.

Throughout March, U.S. senators Patrick Leahy (D., Vt.) and Robert Kasten (R., Wis.) attempted to reach a compromise by which Congress would give formal approval to the granting of loan guarantees, but the administration would continue negotiating with Israel the exact conditions under which they would be given. After being given the green light to proceed with their proposal, the senators were cut short on March 17 when Bush said that he had decided to reject it. Leahy said following the meeting that the loan-guarantees issue was "dead."

Several days earlier, the *New York Times* had reported that Israeli leaders were considering taking back their request for loan guarantees altogether, in light of the administration's tough stand. Defense Minister Moshe Arens, visiting Washington, replied that "we will not get down on our knees and beg for help. If the Americans attach intolerable conditions to the loan guarantees, we will raise the money by ourselves."

At the end of March, President Bush made a final offer on the guarantees, proposing that Israel be allowed to finish all housing that was already under construction at the beginning of 1992, in exchange for an immediate granting of $300 million in loan guarantees and another $9.7 billion staggered over six years. But Shamir responded that Israel would never agree to a freeze on settlements.

Relations between the two countries had reached their lowest point in years, perhaps in history. On March 8, New York mayor Ed Koch alleged in an article published in the *New York Post* that Baker had made an obscene remark about Jews in a closed meeting with Republican party workers. A senior minister in the government responded by saying that "the problem is not what Baker says against the Jews, but what he does against Israel."

In mid-March, Defense Minister Arens came to Washington against the background of another ominous development in the relations between the two countries: American allegations that Israel had violated arms export agreements by transferring restricted technology to China, including technology from the Patriot missile batteries supplied by the United States during the Gulf War. Israeli sources, quoted in *Ha'aretz* on March 16, said that the United States was conducting a "smear campaign" against Israel, based on a "web of lies."

In a meeting with Defense Secretary Dick Cheney on March 16, Arens said that the reports of illegal transfers of technology—which, he claimed, were inspired by American officials—had caused "irreparable damage." Cheney reportedly replied that the leaks had not come from the Pentagon, but from people interested "in harming relations between the two countries." Despite Cheney's disclaimer, the Pentagon announced that it was sending a team of investigators to Israel to mount an inquiry. According to Israeli reports published on March 24, the investigators found no evidence to corroborate the allegations against Israel. On March 28, the London *Sunday Telegraph* claimed that it was Saudi Arabia, not Israel, that had transferred the Patriot technology to China. On April 1, a published State Department report stated that Israel had systematically violated agreements on the illegal transfer of technologies. The next day, however, the Pentagon rejected the State Department's findings, adding that Israel's hands were clean concerning the transfer of Patriot technology to China.

Despite Shamir's stated refusal to pull back Israel's request for loan guarantees, by the beginning of April the matter was effectively dead, and Israeli officials desisted from raising the matter with their American counterparts. In April and May, election campaigns in both countries were heating up. The Likud, for its part, tried to ignore the crisis that had developed with the United States, although some of its spokespersons accused President Bush of intervening on behalf of Rabin, thus seeking to enlist votes of protest against "outside interference" in the elections. Labor utilized the campaign to accuse the Likud of "wrecking" relations between the two countries. The U.S. administration, for its part, did its best to assuage the feelings of resentment that had welled up in the American Jewish community.

Foreign Minister David Levy met with Secretary Baker twice during this period: on April 28, in Washington, and on May 24, in Lisbon. In the second meeting, Baker declared his satisfaction at the progress that had been achieved in the peace talks.

In June, tensions flared once again because of the U.S.-funded and Israeli-built Arrow missile project. A test-firing scheduled for early June was canceled due to pressure exerted by the administration, which, according to news reports, wished to "save Israel from the embarrassment" of another failed launch.

On June 17, just a week before the elections, a senior administration official was quoted as saying that, following the Israeli ballot, Bush would work to improve U.S.-Israeli relations by renewing the dialogue on the loan guarantees and by inviting the Israeli prime minister, whoever he might be, for talks in Washington.

THE NEW ISRAELI GOVERNMENT

Although they had not publicly advocated the election of Yitzhak Rabin, U.S. officials did not hide their delight at his victory in the June 23 elections. Rabin not only espoused more moderate policies on the peace process, which were much more attuned to American positions than those of the Likud, he also viewed relations with Washington as the core of Israel's foreign policy and had close personal ties with many American officials and opinion-makers. Rabin was also thought to prefer Republican administrations to Democratic ones, a result of his tenure as ambassador to Washington during the Nixon years and his negative experiences as prime minister with the Carter administration during the first few months of 1977.

In a press conference convened on the day following his victory at the polls, Rabin said one of his top priorities would be to repair relations with Washington, halt large-scale building in "political" settlements in the territories, and renew Israel's quest for the loan guarantees. On June 28, American Jewish leader Max Fisher, visiting Israel, said that Israeli-American relations would soon improve dramatically. Deputy Secretary of State Lawrence Eagleburger concurred, saying, on June 30, that, with the election of the new government in Israel, the administration would be able to restore a normal working relationship between the two countries. Eagleburger said that the two governments would be in direct contact and would no longer need the services of go-betweens, such as Congress or AIPAC.

On July 2, the new and favorable winds blowing from the administration were expressed in a meeting between Baker and Ambassador Shoval in which Baker said that the administration would try to work out a formula on settlements that Rabin would be able to accept. On July 5, senior administration officials expressed the view that relations between the Bush administration and Shamir had been based on "a pattern of deception." Rabin, the officials said, would not try to deceive the United States, and could therefore be offered a more convenient formula on the settlements. On July 13, following the formation of his new government, both Bush and Baker telephoned Rabin to congratulate him. Bush invited Rabin to come to Washington in August.

Secretary Baker made a Middle East tour in mid-July. Although Israel had wished to use the opportunity to conduct talks concerning overall relations between the two countries, Baker preferred to restrict his talks to the peace process and the loan guarantees. He told Rabin, in Jerusalem, that a "significant limitation" on building in the territories would allow Bush to announce the granting of the entire Israeli request for loan guarantees. In Amman, on July 21, Baker rejected Rabin's differentiation between "political" and "security" settlements. At the same time, Baker said that Arab states should end their economic boycott of Israel in exchange for a complete "suspension" of settlement activities in the territories.

In early August, Israeli and American officials began new negotiations on the terms for receiving the guarantees. Israel was dismayed by a new American condition that half of the monies raised through the loan guarantees—$5 billion—would have to be spent on purchases inside the United States. The governor of the Bank of Israel, Prof. Yaakov Frankel, came to Washington to discuss the issue.

Bush and Rabin met in the president's summer retreat at Kennebunkport, Maine, on August 11–12. In their talks, Rabin succeeded in putting aside the American request that half the loans raised by the guarantees be spent in America; however, the two sides were in disagreement about the "scoring" of the loan guarantees. The scoring was a percentage of the sums that could be raised through the loan guarantees, determined by the White House, that would need to be included in the U.S. budget as a sort of insurance premium against the danger of default by the borrower. Rabin presented to Bush the Israeli government's decisions on freezing settlements in the territories, which included a ban on any new housing not currently under construction.

On August 11, Bush announced that he had decided to approve Israel's request for loan guarantees. He extolled the "special relationship" between Israel and the United States, a relationship which, he said, was "between two friends who are also strategic partners." He reaffirmed America's commitment to maintaining Israel's "qualitative military superiority" over its Arab neighbors. Bush's statements did not go down very well with the Arabs, but in Israel they were welcomed as a clear sign that the bad days between the two countries were finally over.

On August 13, Rabin met with Democratic presidential candidate Bill Clinton. According to press reports, Rabin's aides acknowledged that the meeting had not gone well, despite the fact that Clinton "said all the right words." It appeared that

Rabin's preference for Republicans still influenced him, causing no small concern among Clinton's staff in the coming few months. Rabin also met with leaders of AIPAC in another meeting described by participants as "unpleasant," in which Rabin lambasted the Jewish leaders for their role in the loan-guarantees standoff between Bush and the Likud. The new Israeli government, Rabin made clear, would conduct its business directly with the administration.

On September 11, Bush announced his administration's willingness to sell 72 sophisticated F-15 fighters to Saudi Arabia, at a cost of $9 billion. Of the 72 planes, 48 were to be of the ultra-modern F-15E model, which had never before been exported abroad. The sale raised new concerns in Israel about Saudi military might, especially in the air. The United States tried to allay Israel's fears by offering sophisticated technologies and early-warning systems against missile and airplane attacks. On September 26, the two countries agreed on a $700-million supplemental arms-deal package, which included Apache helicopters and Blackhawk aircraft, within the framework of the American commitment to maintain Israel's qualitative edge. The two countries also agreed on the "prepositioning" of $300 million worth of American military stockpiles in Israel, which could be used by both countries in case of an emergency.

Israel, however, was not calmed. In early October it demanded that Cheney submit a written commitment to Congress that the Saudi F-15s would under no circumstances be used against Israel nor placed in airfields close to Israel. Eagleburger, in a letter to Rabin, reiterated the U.S. commitment to Israel and said that, henceforth, Israel would be eligible to buy sophisticated technologies on the same level as that of NATO countries. He said that in the future the United States would maintain current military aid levels to Israel.

On October 5, both houses of Congress approved the granting of $10 billion in loan guarantees to Israel, stating that the money could be used only inside the pre-1967 borders. Despite the long and costly battle waged by the administration, there was no specific mention in the bill passed by Congress of any freeze on settlement activity. The geographical provision was a long-standing American condition, attached each year to the regular aid package as well. The Likud would have agreed readily to the final wording of the American loan-guarantees bill. Together with the loan guarantees, Congress also approved the annual $3-billion military and economic aid package to Israel.

On November 3, Bill Clinton was elected president of the United States. In his first speech, he stressed his wish to see progress in the Middle East peace process. On November 9, Rabin called Clinton to congratulate him on his victory. Asked about his expectations from the Clinton administration, Rabin said that the United States should "encourage" the Middle East talks while giving the sides "latitude" to maneuver by themselves. Generally speaking, Clinton's election was greeted warmly in Israel, even by supporters of the Labor party. Despite Labor's appreciation of the possible role played by the loan-guarantees issue in their electoral victory, many shared the conviction that the Bush administration had been too "brutal" in its handling of Israel, even under the Likud. Clinton, who had won a majority of Jewish votes, was considered to be a distinctly pro-Israel president.

Rabin and his aides were concerned, however, by the president-elect's campaign promises to devote more time and effort to domestic affairs, at the expense of foreign matters. There was concern, as well, that Clinton and his advisers believed—though never said—that Rabin had let it be known that he preferred a Republican victory in the elections. Thus, even before taking power, Clinton aides were contacted by Israeli officials in Washington in an effort to arrange an early meeting between the two leaders, a short time after the president's inauguration in January.

In December the United States strongly condemned Israel's decision to deport 400 Hamas activists. Israelis were heartened, however, by Clinton's even-handed response to the deportations, the president-elect expressing sympathy for the need to combat the terrorism that had brought about the deportations.

Other Foreign Relations

The years 1991 and 1992 were watershed years for Israel's international standing, in which the trend of international isolation that began in the late 1960s and the 1970s started to be reversed. The collapse of the Soviet Union was reshaping former allegiances. In the Gulf War, in early 1991, Israel, for the first time in many years, was seen as a victim rather than an aggressor. The Madrid conference, late in the year, softened international attitudes toward the Likud government, which until then had been considered an adamant opponent of any accommodation with the Arabs. The victory of the Labor party in June 1992 brought forth a government that had well-established links to world leaders and that was portrayed as an avid peace-seeker. No wonder, then, that 1992 brought down long-standing walls and opened new frontiers for Israeli diplomacy.

Another reason for Israel's newfound popularity was the multilateral peace talks, which accompanied the more vital bilateral talks and dealt with long-range plans for a peaceful Middle East. Israel had succeeded in persuading the United States to make the existence of diplomatic relations with Jerusalem a prerequisite for participation in the talks. Many nations that might otherwise have postponed setting up links with Israel until a peace agreement was reached decided to take the plunge so as not to be left out of the prestigious multilateral forums and their promise of economic windfalls in the future.

Toward the end of the year, the deportation of 400 Hamas activists soured the new romance between Israel and the international community. The action, the scope of which had never been undertaken before, shocked the world leaders who had expected the new Israeli government to perform in a more "rational" manner than the previous Likud government.

THE EUROPEAN COMMUNITY

The European Community (EC) had effectively been locked out of the main peacemaking arena, the bilateral talks. Israel, with long-standing grievances over European policy on the Palestinian question, had done its best to minimize the European role; it found a willing partner in this in the United States, which had no wish to share peacemaking labors. The Europeans thus assumed a more commanding role in the forum left open to them, the multilateral talks. Although Israel had agreed to European participation in the multilateral forum, it further aggravated the situation when it sought to exclude the EC from the talks on arms control and regional security. On March 29, the EC foreign ministers expressed "disappointment" at this position, saying that Israel was ignoring "European stature and interests" in the Middle East.

Another source of tension between Israel and Europe was the EC wish to appoint its own ambassador to the occupied territories. This matter had been the subject of extended and often acrimonious diplomatic discussions throughout 1991. On February 10, Israel announced that the European representative would be recognized by the Israeli government but would not be allowed to set up a legation independent of the European Community embassy in Tel Aviv. On February 23, it was clear that even this arrangement was going to provide headaches to both sides, as Israel complained to the EC that its representative, Thomas Duple, had been involved in a number of "incidents" and had not coordinated his visit with the Foreign Ministry.

The June 23 election of Labor was greeted with a widespread sense of relief in Europe, European statesmen doing little to hide their satisfaction. Britain said the election results "provide an excellent opportunity for progress in the peace process." French foreign minister Dumas said, "I believe that we will now be able to implement our policies, which were the same as those which served as the basis for Labor's victory in the elections." The new government's stated intention of freezing settlements in the territories was taken as proof that European expectations would be borne out.

WESTERN EUROPE

European frustrations with the Likud were nowhere more apparent than in France, whose socialist president, François Mitterrand, was a bitter critic of Likud policies. On January 22, Mitterrand called in Israeli reporters to express French "disappointment" at having been left out of the peace talks. A few days later, already acrimonious relations between Israel and France took a turn for the worse after Paris decided to accept and then release Palestinian terrorist leader George Habash, who had come to the French capital for medical treatment after reportedly suffering a stroke. Israel lodged a formal protest with French authorities.

Later in the year, however, even before the election of the Labor party to power, relations between the two countries slowly thawed. In May France announced that it would give Israel a credit line of $500 million for investments in infrastructure and industry. By the end of the year, Israeli-French relations were in a virtual honeymoon: President Mitterrand paid an official visit on November 25; he promised a European investment fund of $1.2 billion for the development of the Middle East; and he expressed support for the attitudes of the new Israeli government. At the same time, he reiterated traditional French support for the establishment of an independent Palestinian state.

Traditionally close Israeli-German ties were strained as a result of Israel's request for 10 billion deutsche marks in loan guarantees to help in the absorption of new Soviet immigrants. On April 21, Bonn announced that it would not extend the guarantees because of Israel's policy of settling Jews in the territories. Later in the year, following Labor's electoral victory, it emerged that the true reason for German reluctance was not its criticism of Israeli policies but its lack of funds, most of which had been diverted to the enormous task of reunification with the former East Germany.

Bonn announced on August 15 that it would be hard-pressed to comply with Israel's request for loan guarantees because of urgent needs elsewhere. In September Prime Minister Rabin decided to drop the Israeli request for German loan guarantees altogether, proposing instead that funds be established for research and development in Israel. During a visit by Rabin to Bonn on September 15, Chancellor Helmut Kohl agreed to Rabin's new proposals. On November 10, *Ha'aretz* reported that Germany was resisting Israeli demands for a billion and half deutsche marks in compensation for Nazi victims who lived in the area later controlled by East Germany. Also in November, the Israeli government condemned manifestations of neo-Nazism in Germany and called on the government there to take effective measures against its spread.

Foreign Minister Shimon Peres met with Prime Minister John Major of Great Britain in London, on September 8. Major promised a British initiative against the Arab boycott of Israel as well as European support for the peace process. In December Rabin visited London and secured Major's pledge to raise the matter of racism and neo-Nazism at the upcoming meeting of the seven industrialized nations. Major agreed to lift the arms embargo on Israeli arms sales to Britain, imposed ten years earlier.

On March 30, Israeli president Chaim Herzog paid an official visit to Spain, to meet the king and queen and also to participate in ceremonies marking the 500th anniversary of the expulsion of Spanish Jewry. Herzog was criticized in Israel for what was termed "the exoneration" of Spanish responsibility for one of the greatest calamities in Jewish history.

Portuguese prime minister Anibal Kavako visited Israel on October 25, signing economic cooperation agreements with Prime Minister Rabin.

Prince Hans Adam of Lichtenstein paid an official visit to Israel at the end of November. Israelis hoped that this visit would pave the way for European kings and queens to end their unofficial boycott of state visits to Israel.

On July 29, Israel and the Vatican announced the establishment of a joint committee to examine steps leading to the establishment of full recognition and diplomatic ties between the Jewish state and the Holy See. On October 24, Foreign Minister Peres met with Pope John Paul II, who accepted an invitation to visit the Holy Land.

OTHER EUROPEAN STATES

On January 1, Turkey decided to upgrade its diplomatic relations with Israel to the ambassadorial level; until then, the Turks had maintained a legation in Tel Aviv. Turkey made the move in preparation for its participation in the multilateral talks due to convene at the end of January in Moscow. It made clear that it had its own vital interests in these talks by offering to host the first session of the committee that would deal with water-related issues in the Middle East. In mid-July, President Herzog made the first visit to Turkey by an Israeli head of state, meeting with Turkish leaders.

On January 9, Israel and Lithuania established diplomatic relations. In April Israel set up diplomatic ties with the former Soviet republic of Armenia. On April 29, Russian vice-president Aleksandr Rutskoi paid an official visit to Israel. In June, former Soviet leader Mikhail Gorbachev visited Israel, meeting with the country's top leaders.

On March 10, Israel completed its reconciliation with the former Communist bloc countries of Eastern Europe when Israel's ambassador to Italy, Avi Pazner, submitted his credentials as nonresident ambassador in Tirana, the capital of Albania. The former recluse of Eastern Europe, with a sizeable Muslim population, Albania had not maintained relations with Israel even before the 1967 war. Bulgarian prime minister Filip Dimitrov visited Israel April 17–20. On September 20, Hungarian president Arpad Goncz visited Israel, meeting with the country's top leaders and signing cooperation agreements.

In the last week of May, President Herzog made a historic and emotional visit to Poland. Speaking to the Polish Parliament, Herzog spoke of the two peoples' rich history and the tragic annihilation of Polish Jewry in World War II and warned against what he termed "the greatest danger to world peace—Islamic fundamentalism." On July 16, Israel signed a free trade agreement with the countries of the European Free Trade Association—EFTA—which called for a mutual cancellation of tariffs on all manufactured goods traded between the various countries.

On August 6, an official Israeli delegation headed by MK Yossi Sarid left for the former republic of Yugoslavia to examine ways of extending assistance to the beleaguered people of Bosnia. Ten days later, on August 18, an Israel Air Force plane laden with 18 tons of medical supplies landed in the Croatian capital of Zagreb; the supplies were handed over to the United Nations for distribution in Bosnia. On August 24, Israel decided to extend aid to Somalia as well, despite its membership in the Arab League and its traditionally hostile policies.

On May 18, Greek prime minister Constantine Mitsotakis made a first-ever visit to Israel by a Greek head of state. He signed agreements for economic, industrial, technological, cultural, and educational cooperation between the two countries.

CHINA AND INDIA

Nowhere were the changing fortunes of Israel's foreign relations more apparent than in Asia. The world's two most populous countries, China and India, eager to participate in the multilateral peace forums, were now eager to establish formal relations with Jerusalem.

Relations with China had been warming slowly since 1990, when an Israeli "academic mission" was opened in Beijing. In December 1991, following the Madrid conference, relations warmed up quickly, and the two countries announced plans to establish formal diplomatic ties, for the first time ever. On January 8, it was announced that the official signing of the necessary diplomatic protocols would take place that month, in time for China to participate in the January 28 multilateral talks in Moscow.

Foreign Minister David Levy came to Beijing on January 22, marking the first-ever public visit by a ranking Israeli in the Chinese capital. On January 24, Levy and his Chinese counterpart, Qian Qichen, signed the agreement setting up diplomatic ties at the ambassadorial level. Levy then went to the academic mission and announced that henceforth it would be the Israeli embassy; Zeev Suffoth, a veteran diplomat, was named the first Israeli ambassador. Levy took part in a highly publicized tour of famous Chinese sites in Beijing, during which he called on his experience as a former bricklayer to comment favorably on the workmanship in the Great Wall.

The Chinese ambassador to Israel submitted his credentials to President Herzog in Jerusalem on June 11. In September Qichen came on a first visit to Israel, meeting with Foreign Minister Peres to discuss the peace process. Peres told Qichen that Israel had decided not to sell Kfir jet fighters to Taiwan. On October 26, China announced that it did not object to commercial links between Israel and Taiwan. A few days later, Israel gave in to a Chinese demand that a visit by a high-ranking Taiwanese Foreign Ministry official be described as "a commercial visit."

On January 29, just in time for the multilateral talks in Moscow, Israel and India announced the establishment of formal diplomatic ties. Before this development, India had allowed an Israeli consul to operate in Bombay but throughout the years had maintained a highly critical policy toward the Jewish state. Later in the year there were numerous reports in foreign publications of wide-ranging military cooperation between the two countries, including a reported $1-billion arms sale from Israel to India. On March 23, the two countries launched their first diplomatic discussions, negotiating cooperation in education, science, and agriculture. On June 1, India formally opened its embassy in Tel Aviv.

OTHER ASIAN COUNTRIES

On April 12, Israeli ambassador to Moscow Arye Levin paid an official visit to Alma Ata, the capital of Kazakhstan, the large Muslim republic formerly part of the Soviet Union. Levin met with the top leaders of the country, and the two foreign ministries exchanged formal diplomatic notes. On September 6, the prime minister of Kazakhstan, Sergei Tereshchenko, came to Israel, where he tried to allay Israeli fears of a possible transfer of nuclear technology and weapons from his republic to Muslim states. The first Israeli ambassador to Alma Ata was appointed. Also in April, diplomatic relations were established with the republic of Azerbaijan.

Following year-long news reports of clandestine contacts with Vietnam, the two countries announced, on December 23, a first-of-its-kind barter agreement, on December 23, by which Vietnam would supply Israel with rice, coffee, and rubber while Israel would export agricultural products to Hanoi.

EGYPT

Relations between Israel and the only Arab country with which it had a signed peace agreement were, as had been the case throughout Likud rule, ambivalent. Egypt was gratified at Israel's participation in the Madrid process but was still wary of Israeli intentions and determined to be the primary voice for the Palestinians in the Arab world.

On February 5, Egypt arrested two Israeli Arabs, Faris Subhi al-Musrati and his daughter Fayiqah, on suspicion of spying for Israel. Israel vehemently denied the charges and exerted diplomatic efforts to get the charges dropped. A week later, the heads of Israel's main security services, the Mossad and the General Security Services (Shin Bet) issued a rare public statement saying that the two had never been employed by them. But two days later, on February 12, the affair became more complex when the Egyptians arrested a Jewish Israeli furniture salesman, David Ovitz, and accused him of aiding Musrati's espionage operations. Musrati's son, Majid, was also arrested.

On February 17, Egypt notified Israel officially that those arrested were suspected of "harming Egyptian security"; there was no specific mention of espionage charges. The affair clouded Israeli-Egyptian relations. Two months later Egyptian presidential adviser Osama el-Baz announced that Egypt wished to resolve the affair in order to "advance the peace process and not to damage Israeli-Egyptian ties." On May 5, three months after their arrest, the Musratis and David Ovitz were released from jail. Ten days later, on May 14, it was revealed that Israel had arrested an Egyptian citizen on charges of espionage; Cairo asked that he be released in return for the release of the Israeli suspects.

On April 14, Defense Minister Moshe Arens complained that Egypt "was not encouraging" the development of full and normal ties with Israel. Arens noted that the Egyptians had refrained from publicizing the establishment of a joint agricultural project with Israel, and that Cairo was discouraging the development of academic, cultural, and tourist ties.

The June elections were greeted with a notable sigh of relief in Cairo, which had maintained close ties with the Labor party throughout its years in the opposition. Newly elected prime minister Yitzhak Rabin chose Cairo as his first venue for a foreign visit, coming there on July 20, just after having organized his new government. It was the first visit to Cairo by an Israeli prime minister in over six years; Rabin was received warmly and held close consultations with Egyptian president Mubarak concerning the continuation of the peace process under Labor. On September 12, Deputy Foreign Minister Yossi Beilin visited Cairo; the two countries agreed to warm up their hitherto cool relations. In a speech to the Egyptian Parliament on October 7, in commemoration of the Yom Kippur War, Mubarak praised Israel's decision to "walk the path of peace." Visiting Cairo in mid-November, Foreign Minister Peres and counterpart Amre Moussa agreed to hold monthly meetings between the foreign ministers or deputy foreign ministers of the two countries.

The December deportation of Hamas activists put a special strain on relations with Egypt.

OTHER AFRICAN COUNTRIES

On January 14, Israel and Angola announced in Lisbon that they would be setting up diplomatic relations for the first time. Cape Verde made the same announcement on that day.

On April 5, Shlomo Avital presented his credentials to the president of Congo, reestablishing formal diplomatic ties that had been severed in the wake of the 1973 Yom Kippur War. On April 20, Israel and Zambia announced that they would reestablish diplomatic ties broken off in 1973. A top-level Zambian delegation visited Israel in early June.

On April 29, Foreign Minister David Levy went to Nigeria, the most populous country in black Africa, to reestablish diplomatic ties severed in 1973. The Israeli ambassador submitted his credentials on September 24.

On May 27, Israel reestablished ties with the West African country of Sierra Leone, and on September 13, Gambia entered into relations with Israel.

OTHERS

Israel and Nicaragua established formal ties in a ceremony in Washington on October 5.

UNITED NATIONS

Israel's new government was warmly received in the United Nations, the institution that had for many years been considered a hotbed of anti-Israel propaganda. In his speech to the General Assembly on October 1, Foreign Minister Shimon Peres was warmly received; for the first time, most Arab delegates did not leave their seats when he began his remarks. European countries and Russia announced that they would initiate a process of canceling all anti-Israel resolutions (the previous November, the "Zionism Is Racism" resolution had been repealed). In late November, Israel was invited for the first time to participate in UN peacekeeping forces and agreed to send Israelis to take part in these operations.

DOMESTIC AFFAIRS

Political Developments

It was inevitable that the peace process begun in late 1991 would disrupt Prime Minister Yitzhak Shamir's ruling majority. Three of the right-wing parties that made up the coalition—Tehiya, Moledet, and Tzomet—were opposed to any and all concessions in the territories or anywhere else. The strains began to show in December 1991, when the three-member Tzomet party left the coalition in protest over the peace moves and Shamir's refusal to make good on his promise to seek electoral reform. Tehiya had already decided in principle to leave the government, but had yet to make good on its threat. It was clear that the two-member Moledet party, the most right-wing of the lot, would not stay behind and prop up Shamir's Likud-led coalition.

On January 19, the two parties ended their partnership with the Likud and left the coalition, leaving it with the support of only 59 of the Knesset's 120 members. On January 21, Tehiya minister Yuval Ne'eman resigned from his post as science and energy minister, and Moledet leader Rehavam Ze'evi resigned as minister without portfolio. It was now obvious to the Likud and to the religious parties who remained in the coalition that the elections, orginally scheduled to be held in November, would have to be held earlier. After a week of haggling, the two big parties, Labor and Likud, agreed that elections would be held on June 23. On February 4, the Knesset approved the new election date. The decision to hold elections in less than five months spurred the parties into their varied decision-making processes aimed at electing leaders and lists for the Knesset elections.

LABOR PREPARES

The process was set in motion by the Labor party, which had already scheduled its historic first primaries to select the party leadership on February 24. The two main contenders for party leader were the perennial arch-rivals, Shimon Peres, the current party leader, and the former prime minister, Yitzhak Rabin. Other candidates had previously announced their intention to compete, but they gradually dropped out of the race, realizing their slim chances. The only two contenders left were Yisrael Kessar, the chairman of the all-powerful Histadrut Trade Union, and Ora Namir, former chairwoman of the Knesset's Labor and Social Affairs Committee.

The battle between Peres and Rabin had been raging for almost 20 years, since 1974, when the two vied to succeed Golda Meir, who had resigned as prime minister in the wake of the 1973 war. Rabin was the victor in that first match, but following his resignation in 1977, Peres ruled the party during 15 years of opposition. Peres was now considered the more dovish of the two, and the party appreciated his steadfast helmsmanship throughout the long years of opposition. Peres was in touch with the party activists, and close to them, unlike Rabin, who was considered aloof and distant. Rabin, for his part, enjoyed the aura of the security-minded general. But his main strength derived from the almost universal assumption, buttressed by countless polls, that he could win the election. Peres in the minds of the media and the public was a "loser," and Rabin, at least theoretically, a "winner."

If the internal elections had been held, as they had been since the party was established, in the Central Committee, there is no doubt that Peres would have won. But now, for the first time, over 100,000 party members, signed up in the 1991 recruitment drive, were going to make the decision. The contenders were thus under pressure to wage what was dubbed an American-style election campaign, complete with large newspaper ads, car stickers, and endless accusations and recriminations. On February 13, for example, Rabin's assistants were quoted by the newspapers as saying that those who supported Peres were doing so "out of compassion and pity." Peres loyalists responded by claiming that Rabin's people were "completely hysterical."

All the polls taken before the primaries predicted a victory for Rabin, but in the last few days before the actual ballot, Peres appeared to be closing the gap. This created concern among Rabin's people because, according to the rules of the primaries, the candidate who came in first had to garner over 40 percent of the vote, or face a second round against the second-place candidate. It was assumed that Peres's chances would improve in a second round because of the strong support he would receive from the Histadrut backers of Kessar.

Rabin won narrowly in the first round. With 108,000 party members voting in the primary, Rabin received 40.5 percent of the vote, Peres 34.5 percent, Kessar 19 percent, and Namir 5.5 percent. Peres pledged party loyalty and unity after the vote, but his supporters continued to claim that if Kessar or even Namir had not run, Peres would probably have emerged victorious. The supporters tried to convince the party apparatus not to force Peres to compete again in the primaries scheduled to be held on April 1, which would determine the makeup of the rest of Labor's list for the Knesset, but the committee in charge of the primaries refused the request.

In the end, the party rank-and-file, including Rabin supporters, voted overwhelmingly for Peres, giving him first place in the primaries and thus second place on the party list for the Knesset. The April 1 ballot, in which over 100,000 party members participated, produced a surprising list of young and mostly dovish candidates. Rabin was reportedly dismayed by the results, which he felt would make it harder for him to capture the "middle-of-the-road" voters away from the Likud.

The voters turned away veteran and experienced Labor politicians in favor of young leaders who were much more adept at handling modern media. Finishing right behind Peres was young firebrand Avraham Burg, a religious politician who had led many battles in favor of the separation of religion and state. Other doves, such as Namir, David Libai, and Binyamin Ben-Eliezer, came in right behind Burg. The party hawks, supporters of Rabin, had suffered a severe defeat. It was widely thought that, while Rabin had won the primaries for party leadership, it was Peres who had emerged victorious in the battle for the party list. The left-wing Meretz leader Shulamit Aloni said, on April 2, "Now we have partners in the Labor party."

THE LIKUD PREPARES

The Likud did not need the declaration of impending elections to ignite a full-scale internal war: that war had been raging continuously throughout the previous year, unrelated to national political developments. The main protagonists were three: Prime Minister Yitzhak Shamir, Deputy Foreign Minister David Levy, and Housing Minister Ariel Sharon. Shamir and Levy had crossed swords at every opportunity, the most prominent of which, in 1991, was Levy's decision to boycott the Madrid conference after learning that Shamir had decided to head the Israeli delegation himself, whereas other countries were sending their foreign ministers. Sharon, for his part, had maintained a constant barrage of criticism against Shamir, accusing him repeatedly of conducting a "soft" policy toward the Arabs and of "abandoning" Jewish lives to terrorists.

Trouble erupted immediately after the January announcement of the June 23 election date, when Defense Minister Moshe Arens announced that he would challenge Levy for the number-two spot on the Likud list. Levy, always suspicious of plots by the majority against him, reacted angrily; his supporters threatened "all out war" if the second-place spot was not promised to Levy. After a week of consultations, Levy and his supporters decided that the best way to ensure the number-two slot was to run against Shamir for the number-one position. This would prevent Sharon, who had already declared his intention to run against Shamir, from coming in "second" by virtue of his being the only contender against Shamir.

Unlike Labor, the Likud had yet to adopt reforms, and the selection of both its party leader and its list for the Knesset was still entrusted to the party's 3,000-strong Central Committee. On February 20, the committee voted for party leader; Shamir came in first with 46.4 percent of the vote; Levy was second, with 31.2 percent; and Sharon third, with 22.3 percent. Levy, who fared reasonably well, came away from the vote with the conviction that at least a third of the "realistic" spots for the Knesset should go to his supporters by virtue of his performance in the voting for party leader.

The election of the party list was carried out in two rounds: in the first round, a panel of 50 candidates, unranked, was selected. In the second round, those 50 were ranked according to a convoluted voting system known as the "septets." In the first vote, held on February 27, Levy was the 18th candidate out of 50 to be selected for the panel. Although this result did not determine his final placing on the Likud list for the Knesset, Levy reacted angrily to the result, accusing his opponents of "plotting" against him. On March 1, the committee convened again to choose the septets and to determine the final ranking of the candidates for the Knesset. Arens, operating on behalf of the Shamir camp, struck a deal with Sharon and his supporters that each would support the other's candidates. The result: Arens was chosen as number two on the Knesset list, Sharon as number three, and Levy came in only as number four.

Seeking to recover, Levy struck a deal with Moshe Nissim, one of the leaders of the Liberal party, which had merged with the Likud. And, indeed, in the second septet, the Levy-Nissim axis succeeded in surprising the Arens-Sharon coalition, placing several of its candidates in slots 8–15 on the Likud Knesset list. The next day, however, Arens retaliated by drawing Nissim away from his deal with Levy and by imposing strict discipline on his and Sharon's supporters. Arens and Sharon succeeded in routing Levy's forces altogether in the ballots for the third and fourth septets. In practice, this meant that most of Levy's supporters were pushed back to slots that were considered "unrealistic," with scant chance of making it into the next Knesset.

Levy and his supporters were overcome with shock and rage, and a movement led by Levy's brother, Maxim, openly called on the foreign minister to bolt the Likud and set up his own party. Levy allowed his supporters to speak freely to the media about the possibility of a split, but refrained from speaking for himself. On March 29, in a speech at a Herzliyah hotel, Levy shocked the Likud by announcing his intention to resign forthwith from the government. In a speech that would come to be known as the "monkeys' speech," Levy—who is of Sephardic origin—accused his rivals of ethnic prejudice and discrimination, asking rhetorically, "Are we monkeys or what?"

A major crisis was now brewing in the Likud, only two months away from the elections. Fully aware that a bolt by Levy would cripple the party's chances in the June 23 vote, Shamir and emissaries tried to persuade Levy to retract his resignation. On April 4, the two sides announced that they had reached agreement. Levy took back his resignation, and more of his supporters were allowed to take seats on important party committees.

Although Levy declared, in the wake of the compromise agreement, that "common sense had won out," he did not intend to take part in the Likud's election campaign against Labor. Despite the apparent patching up of differences, Levy's tirades against the "Ashkenazi" party leadership had left the Likud in tatters. Its traditional support among Sephardi North African voters, upset by Levy's allegations of discrimination at the top, appeared shaky, at best.

OTHER PARTIES

On February 5, the three left-wing parties—Mapam, Shinui, and the Citizens Rights Movement (CRM)—decided to form a joint list called "Meretz" for the upcoming elections. The leader of the Citizens Rights Movement, Shulamit Aloni, would lead the new party. The party conducted negotiations with the extra-parliamentary Peace Now movement, hoping for a joint front in the elections, but the talks failed.

The Tehiya party, on February 23, chose former minister Yuval Ne'eman to lead the party in the next elections. Geula Cohen came in second, and Elyakim Ha'etzni, a right-wing firebrand from the Kiryat Arba settlement near Hebron, came in third.

The National Religious party, on March 9, chose its list, with Zevulun Hammer taking first place, and Avner Shaki second. Hanan Porat, a leader of the Jewish settler movement in the territories, was relegated to fifth place, eliciting calls by settler leaders to seek another party that would represent their interests.

The two major Ashkenazi ultra-religious (*haredi*) parties, Agudat Israel and Degel Hatorah, agreed, on April 29, to form a joint list for the Knesset. The new list was given the name "Yahadut Hatorah," Torah Judaism. Rabbi Eliezer Schach, the spiritual leader of both Degel Hatorah and the Sephardi-*haredi* party Shas, sought the merger with Agudah after distancing himself from Sephardic rabbi Ovadia Yosef, who played a commanding role in Shas. On June 13, Schach was quoted as saying, "The Sephardim have yet to reach a state that they can be responsible for matters of religion or state. They still need time to learn." The statement caused an outcry among Sephardim throughout the country and created a clear ethnic split in the *haredi* community between supporters of Shas and those of Yahadut Hatorah.

Former Soviet dissident Anatoly Sharansky announced on April 17 that he would form a political party to run for the Knesset and work for the welfare of new Soviet immigrants. Sharansky's party was the third claiming to represent Soviet immigrants. On March 31, the chairman of a Soviet immigrants' society, Robert Golan, had announced that he would form a new party. And on April 14, a group called "Da" elected Yuli Kosharovsky, another former dissident, to head its list. On May 5, Sharansky announced that he had failed to put together an attractive enough list of candidates and was therefore abandoning the race.

After failing to persuade the Likud to secure him a spot on its list for the Knesset, Finance Minister Yitzhak Modai announced, on April 7, that he would run on his own list, called the "New Liberal Party."

On May 19, the Central Elections Committee announced that 30 lists would compete in the next elections, half of which had not been represented in the outgoing

Knesset. The number dropped to 28 after the High Court of Justice upheld, on June 9, the committee's decision to bar two lists—Kach and Kahane Hai—from running in the elections. The High Court held that the two groups, which claimed to be the successors of the late Rabbi Meir Kahane's anti-Arab ideology, were "racist." Three more lists dropped out of the race, leaving 25. The threshold for entering the Knesset had been raised from 1 percent of the vote to 1.5 percent.

THE ELECTION CAMPAIGN AND THE ELECTIONS

On April 9, Labor officially opened its election campaign. Presenting his party's candidates, Rabin said that Labor would emphasize Labor's "unity" and contrast it with the "divisiveness" of the Likud. Several days later it was revealed that Rabin had decided to run a tough and aggressive campaign against the Likud, specifically against Shamir, accusing him of "losing touch" and of working against peace. At the same time, Labor did its best to blur its socialist ideology, which was considered to be unpopular with the voters.

Contrary to the advice of some of its leading members, including Ronnie Milo and Benjamin Netanyahu, the Likud retaliated by launching a fierce countercampaign against Rabin, hinting at an alleged drinking problem and a suspected emotional breakdown when he was chief of staff on the eve of the Six Day War.

Both parties concentrated on getting the support of new Soviet immigrants, of whom some 250,000 were eligible to vote. Labor emphasized the high unemployment rate among new immigrants, while the Likud emphasized Labor's socialist roots, in the hope of conjuring up associations with the former Soviet Union, toward which the immigrants were presumably hostile. Likud also played up to the new immigrants' reported distrust of the Arabs, saying that Labor planned to "sell out" to the Arabs. Labor counterattacked by claiming that the massive funds funneled by the Likud to Jewish settlements in the territories were the main cause of the unemployment among immigrants. Labor also alluded to the Likud's failure to secure American loan guarantees, creating a direct link between the Likud's political ideology and the immigrants' economic plight. Labor also emphasized the internal strife in the Likud, carefully refraining from any personal attack on Levy, in the hope of attracting his disaffected supporters.

The two main parties, as well as the other parties, all employed big public relations firms to create their televised commercials, which were broadcast every evening starting in early June. Although these were aimed at arousing the interest of the electorate and getting it involved, they appear to have missed their mark. The assessment of most analysts in the media was that the public was negatively impressed by the dirty campaigning and exchange of accusations between politicians.

On June 16, Rabin and Shamir squared off in a nationally televised debate, which according to most analysts Rabin won handily. Likud activists were also quoted as expressing disappointment with Shamir's performance, saying the prime minister "hadn't said anything new."

On June 23, close to 80 percent of the country's 3,409,000 eligible voters went to the polls. At 10 P.M., television broadcaster Haim Yavin, basing himself on exit polls, told the country that there had been a "*mahapakh*"—an upset. Labor and its allies to the left had triumphed.

Labor won 34.6 percent of the vote, Likud 24.9 percent, Meretz 9.6 percent, Tzomet 6.4 percent, the National Religious party 5 percent, Shas 4.9 percent, Yahadut Hatorah 3.3 percent, Moledet and Hadash 2.4 percent each, the Arab Democratic party 1.6 percent. Tehiya, with 1.2 percent, did not pass the 1.5-percent threshold.

Rabin and Labor picked up 44 Knesset seats, compared with only 32 for the Likud. No less crucial was the fact that Labor's allies to the left won 17 seats, giving the Labor bloc an unassailable 61-seat majority and ensuring the prime ministership for Rabin. On the left, the new merged entity of three parties, Meretz, picked up 12 seats, the former Communist party Hadash, 3 seats, and the Arab Democratic party, 2 seats.

The big surprise of the election was the performance of Rafael Eitan's right-wing Tzomet party, which more than doubled its strength from three seats to eight. The Moledet party won three seats, while the Tehiya party was erased from the political map, going down from three seats to none.

The religious parties fared reasonably well, taking into account the more than a quarter of a million new immigrant voters who were largely secular. Their combined total dropped from 18 seats in the outgoing Knesset to 16 in the new one. The combined Ashkenazi-*haredi* party, Yahadut Hatorah, picked up four seats, Shas six, and the National Religious party six as well. From a political point of view, however, the religious front had lost its entire world: for the first time in Israeli political history, religious parties did not hold the balance of power. Rabin would be prime minister with or without their consent.

FORMING A NEW GOVERNMENT

On June 28, after duly consulting with all the parties, President Chaim Herzog asked Yitzhak Rabin to form a new government. Rabin made clear that he would seek to construct a large majority, indicating that he did not wish to set up a narrow government that would have to rely on the five Arab votes on the extreme left. Rabin was casting a wide net, not ruling out the right-wing parties such as Tzomet and actively courting the religious parties in the center.

Rabin's task appeared formidable. A political gulf divided Tzomet and Meretz, while a similar seemingly unbridgeable gap existed between Meretz and the religious parties. Although there was some talk among Rabin aides of the possibility that Meretz might be left out of the coalition so that Rabin could form a partnership with only the right-wing and the religious parties, such a scenario was improbable and would probably have sparked a revolt in Labor's sizeable dovish wing. On July 5, Rabin appeared to have achieved the impossible, with a draft coalition agreement that seemed to be acceptable to both the right-wing Tzomet party and the left-wing Meretz party.

Now, however, personal matters, rather than ideology, stymied Rabin. Meretz demanded that it be given the education portfolio, which was also sought by Tzomet's Eitan. Eitan made clear that without that ministry he would not join the government. Rabin decided to accede to the Meretz demand, not least because he did not wish to give Meretz the justice portfolio or foreign affairs, the only two ministries that Meretz might have accepted as substitutes for education. Rabin had bad memories of the Justice Ministry "interfering" in military affairs during his tenure as defense minister in 1988–1990. He was soon to learn, however, that handing over the education portfolio to Meretz leader Shulamit Aloni would cause him no less trouble.

Concurrently, Rabin was negotiating with all the religious parties, agreeing to defer the delicate matter—demanded by many in Labor—of recruitment of yeshivah students to the army. Rabin's negotiations with the National Religious party became bogged down in disagreement over Jewish settlements, while Rabbi Schach kept the Yahadut Hatorah faction from concluding a deal with Labor because of his opposition to Labor's secular ways. Still smarting from Schach's preelection disparagement of the Sephardim, Schach's spiritual mentor, Rabbi Yosef, decided to buck the emerging trend among the religious parties and to join Rabin's coalition.

On July 9, Rabin signed a coalition agreement with Meretz and Shas, and four days later he presented his cabinet to the Knesset. Rabin left three portfolios open as enticements for other parties to join the coalition. He kept the defense portfolio for himself, but—faced by powerful forces in his own party that supported Peres—agreed to appoint his arch-rival as foreign minister and, in practice if not in title, as the number-two man in the cabinet. Thirteen ministers were from Labor, three from Meretz, and one from Shas.

The Knesset approved the new cabinet by a vote of 67–53. Voting with the new government were the five members of the ultra-left-wing parties, who had promised to support the coalition from the outside in exchange for pledges to improve conditions among Israeli Arabs.

In the months following the establishment of the government, Rabin and Labor faced opposition from two different sources. The right wing reorganized after its defeat in order to fight concessions on the Golan Heights, which, according to news reports, Israel was about to make. The religious and *haredi* parties, for their part, launched a major political campaign against Aloni's placement as education minister. Their objections were twofold, one public and one hidden. In public, they claimed that Aloni was too antireligious to be charged with the overall education system of the country. In private, they conceded that the very fact of her being a woman played some role in their biting campaign.

In late September, Aloni made the first in a series of inflammatory remarks which would periodically shake the coalition and especially its *haredi* component, Shas. Referring to the sacred "*Yizkor*" prayer, recited to commemorate the memory of

THE NEW LABOR-LED GOVERNMENT
(installed July 13, 1992)

Prime Minister, Minister of Defense, Minister of Religious Affairs, Minister of Labor and Social Affairs*	Yitzhak Rabin (Labor)
Foreign Affairs	Shimon Peres (Labor)
Finance	Avraham Shohat (Labor)
Interior	Arye Deri (Shas)
Education	Shulamit Aloni (Meretz)
Industry and Commerce	Micha Harish (Labor)
Justice	David Libai (Labor)
Police	Moshe Shahal (Labor)
Health	Haim Ramon (Labor)
Housing	Binyamin Ben-Eliezer (Labor)
Transportation	Yisrael Kessar (Labor)
Environment*	Ora Namir (Labor)
Immigration Absorption	Yair Tzaban (Meretz)
Economic Planning	Shimon Shitrit (Labor)
Tourism	Uzi Baram (Labor)
Agriculture	Yaakov Tsur (Labor)
Energy	Amnon Rubinstein (Meretz)

*On December 26, Rabin transferred the Labor and Social Affairs portfolio to Namir, and Yossi Sarid (Meretz) was appointed Minister of the Environment.

the dead, Aloni said she did not understand why the military version of the prayer had been amended from "May the People of Israel remember their sons and daughters . . ." to "May God remember. . . ." Shas exploded in anger, and Rabbi Yosef immediately demanded that Rabin sack Aloni. Faced with a counterthreat by Meretz to leave the coalition if Aloni was removed from her post, Rabin achieved a temporary cease-fire by persuading Aloni to write a letter of apology to Rabbi Yosef.

But the animosity between Aloni and Shas continued, and Rabin was unable to reduce it. Each week brought a new crisis, created by this or that statement made by Aloni. On November 2, faced with no-confidence motions over her controversial statements, another compromise was worked out: Aloni would hand over to her deputy, a Shas man, all authority over the *haredi* education system as well as expanded influence in the secular school system's Jewish studies programs. The deputy, Rabbi Moshe Maya, created his own storm just a few days later, when he said in an interview that "secular teachers only seek adventurism in life; they have no inner content and are unable to pass on any content to others."

On October 22, the Labor party chose Nissim Zvilli as its next secretary-general, replacing Micha Harish, who had been appointed to the cabinet. Yuval Frenkel, a candidate supported by Rabin, won 43.5 percent of the vote in Labor's Central Committee, compared to Zvilli's 47.7 percent. Zvilli was supported by Peres.

On December 2, the Knesset approved by a vote of 37–36, in a first reading, the repeal of the law that forbade Israelis to have any contacts with members of the PLO. In a cabinet meeting held a week later, the government decided that, despite the amendment, it would not negotiate with the PLO.

By the end of the year, Rabin had given up hope that any of the other religious parties would join the coalition. Thus, on December 26, Meretz was given a fourth minister, and Yossi Sarid became minister of the environment. Ora Namir received the labor and social affairs portfolio, which Rabin had been holding.

In the Likud, meanwhile, Yitzhak Shamir announced his intention to resign as head of the party, and the Likud began preparing for the election of his successor, with David Levy, Benjamin Netanyahu, and Binyamin Begin considered the three top contenders. In a speech to the Likud Knesset caucus, Shamir said that he was leaving the country in very good shape, indeed "in better shape than it's ever been."

Immigration

There was a sharp drop in immigration from the former Soviet Union in 1992, down to 65,000 from 150,000 the previous year. The two main causes for the reduction were thought to be the high rate of unemployment among new immigrants, who were warning their friends and relatives still living in the republics to change or at least postpone plans to come to Israel; the tough security situation; and the continuing reforms in Russia, which gave many Jews hope of improving conditions in the future.

Altogether, 77,057 immigrants came to Israel in 1992. In addition to those from the former Soviet Union, 3,600 came from Ethiopia, 1,600 from the United States, 800 from France, 600 from Romania, 550 from the former Yugoslavia, and the balance from other countries. Of the Russian immigrants who had come since 1990, 29 percent were unemployed at the end of the year, and most of those employed were not working in the professions for which they had been trained. In the Soviet Union, 36 percent had been employed as scientific and academic workers, but only 7 percent of them were so employed in Israel. Conversely, only 3.6 percent had been employed as service workers in the Soviet Union, but 26.6 percent were so employed in Israel. Despite the large unemployment, 80 percent of new immigrants polled in January said that they "did not regret" coming to Israel. Of those who did regret their decision to come, many said they felt that "they were not needed in Israel except as a demographic factor."

In 1992, immigrants from Ethiopia, who had been perceived as docile and passive when they arrived, began demonstrating and agitating in greater numbers for improvement in their living conditions. In January the chairman of the Jewish Agency,

Simcha Dinitz, publicly complained that 11,000 Ethiopian immigrants had yet to receive permanent housing. In February and March, Ethiopians staged demonstrations and marches at various absorption centers across the country, demanding to be moved from "caravans" (mobile homes) to permanent homes. Most of the demonstrations were successful, persuading absorption officials to speed up the removal of the Ethiopians from hotels and makeshift absorption centers to permanent lodgings. It was reported that Ethiopians were proving more adept than new immigrants from the former Soviet Union in integrating in the army.

In midyear, in conjunction with the peace process, President Hafez al-Assad of Syria started allowing Jews to leave that country. By June 10, 150 of the estimated 4,000 Syrian Jews had departed, and another 1,500 had requested exit visas, according to the chief rabbi of Damascus, Ibrahim Hamara. Most of the departing Jews did not come to Israel but went to other places abroad, including the United States. By the end of August, the number of departing Jews reached 350.

Various trouble spots in the former Communist countries supplied groups of new immigrants wishing to escape war and bloodshed. Throughout the year, hundreds of Jews from the former Yugoslavia, Moldova, Uzbekistan, and Tajikistan came to Israel to escape civil war in their homelands. At the end of the year it was reported that increasing anti-Semitism in Western Europe was also spurring interest among Jews in immigration to Israel.

The Economy

The year 1992 received mixed reviews from Israeli economists. The good news was that growth rates were up and inflation was down, but unemployment continued to rise and was threatening to remain stable at an intolerable 11 percent.

On January 2, the Knesset approved the 1992 budget by a vote of 60–53. The total budget, 107 billion shekels, aimed to reduce the budget deficit to 6.2 percent of the Gross Domestic Product, compared to 6.9 percent the previous year. The budget assumed that the United States would grant Israel $2 billion in loan guarantees.

The Israeli economy grew at an annual rate of 7.9 percent, the highest growth rate among Western democratic countries. Much of this achievement, however, was due to the massive housing and construction projects undertaken to accommodate the influx of immigrants from the former Soviet Union. At year's end, housing construction appeared to be slacking off, and growth rates followed in kind. Offsetting the decline in demand for housing was the growth of Israeli exports, which had suffered the previous year from the commercial slowdown caused by the Gulf War.

The 460,000 new immigrants who arrived in Israel between 1989 and 1992 created great demand for private consumption, and an even greater demand for investment in housing. The waves of immigration should have created a similar expansion of public services, but the government kept these under strict control, so that public consumption rates were lower than that in the private sector. In 1992, however, immigration rates were down, and toward the end of the year the rise in demand for private consumption declined commensurately.

Israeli unemployment rates continued to rise, despite an increase of 4.7 percent in the number of jobs. Among the factors contributing to this trend were the expansion of social security and unemployment benefits, the growing female work force, a hiring freeze in the public sector, and a reduction in government subsidies to work-laden enterprises.

Seventy percent of the 155,000 new immigrants in the work force were employed by the end of 1992, although most were not working in their chosen professions. Inconsistencies between the demands of the Israeli market and the supply of the mostly Russian-trained work force, as well as existing levels of high unemployment, reduced the market's ability to fully absorb all of the new immigrants. Unemployment, in turn, was thought to be the prime cause of the lower immigration rates.

Inflation rates were down to 11.9 percent, compared to 19 percent the previous year. The main reasons for this dramatic change were the slow growth in nominal wages (up 1.1 percent in 1992 after declining 3 percent the previous year) and the end-of-the-year reduction in the demand for housing.

The Israeli economy showed encouraging signs of integration in the international marketplace, as exports and imports grew at similar rates (around 15 percent), and the balance of trade deficit remained stable, reaching a $6.9-billion surplus in imports at the end of 1992. Israel exported $20.8 billion worth of goods and services in 1992, and imported $27.6 billion. The foreign debt at the end of the year stood at $33 billion, with assets in foreign currency totaling $18.9 billion. The European Community continued to be Israel's major trading-bloc partner, with Israel importing $11.5 billion worth of goods and services and exporting $5.2 billion. The United States was Israel's biggest single-country trading partner, with Israel importing $3.2 billion and exporting $3.9 billion in goods and services. Of the $13 billion worth of goods exported abroad, $550 million were in agricultural products, $2.2 billion in electrical equipment, $1.5 billion in chemical and oil products, and $3.2 billion in diamonds.

On March 27, the International Monetary Fund announced that Israel could draw $243 million as compensation for the fall in earnings from exports and services during the 1990–1991 Gulf crisis and war.

In November the Knesset approved, in a first reading, the state budget for the year 1993. The package proposed a reduction in the budget deficit from 6.2 percent of GDP to only 3.2 percent. On November 11, the government announced that it would allow the value of the shekel to drop by 11 percent during the upcoming year, in order to spur growth. The government also announced a series of tax cuts and incentives, including a reduction in value-added tax from 18 to 17 percent and a 4-percent cut in corporate taxes, to be implemented during the next four years.

At the end of the year, the U.S. government approved the utilization of the first $2 billion in loan guarantees out of the total package of $10 billion in loan guarantees for five years approved by the administration.

Vital Statistics

The population of Israel at the end of 1992 reached 5,195,900, including 4,242,500 Jews, 725,400 Muslims, 140,900 Christians, and 87,100 Druze. Due to the significant drop in immigration, the rate of growth of the Jewish population dropped from 6.2 percent in 1990 and 5 percent in 1991 to only 2.4 percent in 1992. The non-Jewish growth rate remained steady at 4.3 percent. The Jewish population in Israel constituted a third of the world Jewish population.

Jerusalem led the other cities in population size; with a 2.3-percent growth rate, it reached a population of 556,000 at the end of the year, of whom 401,000 were Jews. Tel Aviv enjoyed a growth rate of only 1 percent, with a population of 356,000 at the end of the year, of whom 341,000 were Jews. Haifa had a negative growth rate of 0.5 percent, its population dropping to 249,800, of whom 225,000 were Jews.

Of the Jewish population, 2,574,000 were born in Israel, 263,000 in Asia, 335,000 in Africa, and 1,068,000 in Europe and America.

The number of males per thousand females dropped by one, from 979 to 978. Among Jewish males over age 15, 31.3 percent had never been married, compared to 23.2 percent among females. In the 25–29 age range, the never-married rate for males was 45.4 percent, compared to only 21.4 percent among females. Among those aged 45–49, however, the never-married rate among males was only 2.8 percent, compared to 4.4 percent among females. There were 30,000 divorced males, compared to 54,000 divorced females.

Israel had 1,354,000 households in 1992, with an average size of 3.58 persons, including singles. Among Jews, the average household size was 3.41; among non-Jews, 5.47. There were 75,700 single-parent households, with an average of 1.87 children under the age of 17.

The number of Israelis traveling abroad passed the one million mark in 1992, reaching 1,052,000. Tourism in Israel was up: of the 1,509,000 tourists who came, 59 percent were from Europe, 26 percent from North America, and 7 percent from Asia. Tourists stayed an average of 18.4 days in Israel, down from 21.6 days the previous year.

The number of hotels increased from 320 to 330, with 31,887 rooms and 67,113 beds. Of these, 240 were hotels recommended for tourists, with 27,258 rooms. The average tourist spent 3.7 nights in a hotel; the average Israeli, 2.4 nights. Total hotel occupancy stood at 67.6 percent of the rooms: 64.4 percent in Jerusalem, 73.2 percent in Tel Aviv, and 77.7 percent in Eilat.

Israelis had 1,176,000 cars, up a hundred thousand over the previous year. These were involved in 22,259 accidents, up from 19,147 in 1991; 507 people died on the roads, compared to 444 in 1991.

The Hebrew University in Jerusalem had 19,130 students; the Technion in Haifa, 10,470 students; Tel Aviv University, 23,440 students; Bar-Ilan University, 13,320 students; Haifa University, 9,670 students; Ben-Gurion University of the Negev, 8,220 students; and the Weizmann Institute of Science, 740 students. Another

19,000 students were enrolled in the Open University, which awarded 350 degrees.

According to a survey of leisure-time activity among Israelis over the age of 14, 92.6 percent listened to the radio, with 79.6 percent tuning in "almost every day"; 66.7 percent listened occasionally to records or cassettes, 54.1 percent watched videos, 77.8 percent read a daily newspaper, 23.8 percent were enrolled in a library, and 30.8 percent engaged in a hobby. In the area of public entertainment, 45.7 percent went to the movies at least once a year, 29.2 percent to the theater, 10.7 percent to a concert, 6 percent to a dance performance, 35.2 percent to an entertainment show, 26.8 percent to a museum, 19 percent to a spectator sport, 23.9 percent to a discotheque or night club, and 61.6 percent to a restaurant or cafe; 20.4 percent went to the movies at least once a month, and 10 percent to the theater once a month.

Other Noteworthy Events

On February 11, the Supreme Court rejected the appeal of nuclear technician Mordechai Vanunu to overturn his 18-year prison sentence. Vanunu was convicted in 1988 for selling nuclear secrets to the London *Sunday Times*.

On February 23, financier Yaakov Nimrodi bought the daily newspaper *Ma'ariv* from the estate of the deceased British publisher Robert Maxwell for $14.5 million.

On February 29, 23 Palestinians were killed following the collapse of a roof in an Arab-owned café in East Jerusalem. Arab and Jewish rescue workers cooperated in rescuing many wounded from the destroyed building.

Veteran peace activist Abie Nathan was released from prison on March 30, after serving 6 months of an 18-month sentence for meeting illegally with PLO chairman Yasir Arafat.

On May 7, Prof. Yuval Ne'eman, world-renowned physicist and leader of the right-wing Tehiya party, returned his 1969 Israel Prize in protest over the decision to grant the 1992 Israel Prize to Israeli-Arab author Emil Habibi, a supporter of Palestinian nationhood.

On July 19, the Jerusalem branch of the Hebrew Union College ordained the first woman to become a rabbi in Israel. She was 37-year-old American-born Na'amah Kelman.

On July 30, Israel won its first Olympic medal ever when judoist Yael Arad earned a silver medal in the Barcelona Olympics. Two days later, fellow judoist Oren Smadja picked up a bronze medal.

On October 4, an El Al 747 jumbo jet, laden with fuel, crashed into a housing complex in a suburb of Amsterdam. Some 70 people were killed, most of them immigrants from Suriname (the final number of fatalities was never ascertained). All three crew members, as well as a passenger on board the plane, were also killed.

Personalia

Former prime minister Menachem Begin, leader of the Likud party and the architect of peace with Egypt, died on March 9, aged 78. Begin, born in Brisk in Lithuania, was appointed commissioner of the Betar Zionist Organization in Poland in 1939; following a prolonged exile in Siberia he came to Palestine in 1943, where he took control of the Irgun Zvai Leumi underground movement and waged a relentless battle against the British. From 1948 onward, Begin led the opposition Herut party; its victory in the 1977 elections elevated him to the post of prime minister, which he held until 1983. Thousands accompanied Begin to his burial on the Mount of Olives, where he was interred in a plot alongside former colleagues in the prestate underground movement.

Other prominent Israelis who died this year included Prof. Nahman Avigad, one of Israel's leading archaeologists, in January, aged 87; poet Avot Yeshurun, winner of the Brenner, Bialik, and Israel prizes, in February, aged 82; sculptress Batya Lishinski, recipient of the Israel Prize for lifetime achievement, in April, aged 92; Prof. Shlomo Broyer, head of Tel Aviv University's applied mathematics department, in May; Prof. Avner Yaniv, deputy president of Haifa University and a world-renowned expert on security and strategy, in May, aged 49; painter Mordechai Ardon, in June, aged 96; Yaakov Hazan, veteran Zionist leader and head of the socialist Mapam party and Hashomer Hatzair kibbutz movement, in July, aged 93; Prof. Eitan Berglas, chairman of the board of Bank Hapoalim and eminent Israeli economist, in August, aged 58; former president of the Supreme Court Shimon Agranat, an architect of Israeli criminal law, in August, aged 86; Haim Tavori, former inspector-general of the Israel Police, in August, aged 73; author and journalist Yehoshua Bar Yosef, recipient of all major Israeli prizes for literature, in October, aged 80; Prof. Yoram Ben-Porath, president of the Hebrew University, in a traffic accident, in October, along with his wife and five-year-old son, aged 55; retired army major general Moshe Bar Kokhba, director-general of the Israel Railroad Authority, in November, aged 63; Yitzhak Kiester, former Supreme Court judge and an expert on Jewish law, in November, aged 88; Prof. Gad Tadeschi, recipient of an Israel Prize and preeminent expert on jurisprudence, in November, aged 85; Prof. David Meir, director-general of Jerusalem's Shaare Zedek Hospital, in December, as a result of a fatal injury in a traffic accident, aged 65; Yitzhak Ernst Nebenzahl, former state comptroller, in December, aged 85.

MENACHEM SHALEV

Jews in the Middle East and North Africa

IN THE DECADE since the *Year Book* last surveyed this subject, the Jewish population living in the Arab and Muslim countries of the Middle East and North Africa has continued its gradual decline. Essentially three factors have contributed to the diminishing numbers: attrition through death among an aging population; the lifting of government-imposed barriers to emigration; and the emigration of young adults and their families seeking better educational and economic opportunities abroad.

Throughout the region both governmental policies and popular attitudes have been affected by the momentous global and regional developments in the period under review. Most notable are the end of the Cold War and the collapse of the Soviet Union, the end of the Iraq-Iran War in 1988, the Gulf War that liberated Kuwait from Iraqi occupation early in 1991, and the opening of direct Arab-Israeli peace talks in Madrid in October of that year. These positive developments have led to improvement in the status of the Jewish communities in some Middle Eastern countries and have also aroused hope among some Israeli and Arab leaders that a comprehensive Arab-Israeli peace settlement may eventually usher in a new era of Arab-Jewish coexistence and cooperation in the region.

Others warn against premature euphoria, pointing out that most of the regimes in the region remain autocratic and face severe challenges from both radical leftists and increasingly militant Islamic political groups that oppose peace with Israel and improved relations with the democratic West. For the most extreme of these groups, the distinction between Israeli, Zionist, and Jew is often blurred. In recent years, Arab terrorists have gone so far as to target innocent Jews in Lebanon, and isolated Arab terrorist attacks occurred against Jewish worshipers in Djerba, Tunisia, and Istanbul, Turkey—two countries whose governments accord full rights to their Jewish communities.

In those Arab countries such as Algeria, Egypt, and Iraq, from which the overwhelming majority of the Jewish population emigrated in earlier years, and the tiny remnant in each country consists primarily of pensioners over 65, the numbers continue to diminish as the elderly pass on. In Libya, where only a handful survive in Tripoli, there is no organized community. In Lebanon, there is no longer a functioning community or a synagogue with regular services. Most of the few hundred Jews who remained in Beirut during the years of internecine fighting and the 1982 Israeli war with Lebanon left the country in the mid-1980s, following the Israeli withdrawal and the kidnapping and murder of leaders of the Jewish community by an Iranian-inspired radical Shiite group.

Among countries with still viable and well-functioning Jewish communities and a more healthy demographic composition are Morocco (6,500 Jews), Tunisia (1,585), and Iran (18,000). (It is difficult to obtain precise figures for the number of Jews living in Tunisia and Morocco, since some families divide their time between homes in North Africa and residences and businesses in France and other places.) The regimes in the two North African countries have been protective of their Jewish communities. In recent years they have expressed increasingly open support for the Madrid peace process and have been moving gradually to establish commercial, tourist, and quasi diplomatic ties with Israel. Nevertheless, their Jewish populations have continued to decline, primarily through the emigration of university-age students and young professionals to France, Canada, and Israel.

With the lifting of emigration restrictions in the past couple of years in Syria and Yemen, the Jews of those countries departed en masse, leaving behind small numbers of those choosing to remain.

Yemen

In Yemen, where restrictions on emigration were rigorously enforced until the late 1980s, only a few individual Jews had been permitted to leave for medical care abroad. The approximately 1,000 Jews were virtually cut off not only from their relatives who had left in the massive "Operation Magic Carpet" that brought most of Yemen's Jews to Israel in 1949–50, they were even denied normal phone and postal contact with the rest of the Jewish world. For many years, the anti-Zionist Satmar sect was the only Jewish religious group permitted to send occasional representatives to provide books and other religious articles to the few scattered Jewish communities remaining in the mountains of northern Yemen. While free to pray and study in their homes, they had no organized synagogues or schools.

Significant changes began to occur in 1989, motivated at least in part by the general decline in ideology and the move toward greater political openness and pragmatism that accompanied the breakdown of the Berlin Wall and the collapse of the Soviet Union. The decline in Soviet influence and interests in the region was the major factor for the "Yemeni version of perestroika," according to Yossi Kostiner, a Yemeni expert at the Dayan Institute of Tel Aviv University. This started in the south and extended to the north with the reunification in 1990 of the two Yemens—the Marxist-Leninist People's Democratic Republic of Yemen (South Yemen, with its capital in Aden) and the Yemen Arab Republic (North Yemen, with its capital in San'a). (In May 1994 civil war erupted and the south seceded.)

The decline of Soviet influence and aid also made Yemen eager to improve

political ties and economic relations with the United States and thus more susceptible to American pressure. After years of unsuccessful diplomatic efforts, American
citizen Yehiel Hibshoosh, an 80-year-old Yemeni Jewish historian and poet, finally
received permission in October 1989 to visit the main Jewish communities in Rayda
and Sa'ada as well as a number of smaller communities in the north. (The last Jews
in the south had left when the British pulled out of Aden in 1969.) While most of
the Jews eked out a living as artisans, silversmiths, other craftsmen, and peddlers,
they were no worse off than their Muslim neighbors. The only restriction was that
Jewish men were not permitted to carry the traditional daggers or rifles that were
the accoutrements of Yemeni men in the fiercely independent tribal areas of the
north.

Hibshoosh also found no confirmation of the rumors that had spread in the Jewish
world that Jewish orphans and young women were forcibly being converted to
Islam. The Jewish community maintained its traditional religious piety, the men and
boys easily distinguishable from their Muslim neighbors by their long *peyot* (side-
curls). He found many large families with many small children, who urgently
requested small prayer books of their own. The elders requested Torah scrolls and
the opportunity to reestablish contact with their relatives abroad. Hibshoosh met
with Foreign Minister Dr. Abdelkarim al-Iryani, who reportedly told him: "From
now on the Jews of Yemen who have relatives abroad will be able to visit their
relatives where they live, and Jews who hold a U.S. passport and have not been able
to visit Yemen will be able to visit the country."

Earlier attempts to organize group visits to Yemen from among the 5,000 Yemeni
Jews living in the United States had been encouraged by the Yemeni tourist offices,
which were eager to earn foreign currency for their economically hard-pressed
country. But these had nearly always been vetoed at the political level, ostensibly
because of tribal unrest in the northern areas, where the Jews lived, and the attend-
ant danger to visitors. This was also the official reason for the indefinite postpone-
ment of a proposed fact-finding mission by representatives of American Jewish
voluntary organizations. Unofficially, it was reported that the security forces in the
government and representatives of the Palestine Liberation Organization (PLO) in
the country had vetoed the trip because they suspected that the American Jews'
secret agenda was to prepare the ground for emigration of the Yemeni Jews, just
as similar visits had led to the exodus of the Ethiopian Jews to Israel.

In January 1990 a delegation of senior Yemeni officials, headed by Yemen Arab
Republic president Ali Abdullah Salih, came to Washington. After a meeting with
Secretary of State James Baker, Salih told a joint press conference on January 24
that they achieved "a very good understanding" with the American officials on
bilateral issues, Middle East issues, and "the peace initiative which is being discussed
these days." Baker responded that he looked forward to further improvement in
relations and pledged an increase in U.S. technical assistance to Yemen. The following day the Yemeni delegation also met with members of the House Committee on
Foreign Affairs, where Rep. Benjamin Gilman (R., N.Y.) and Rep. Mel Levine (D.,

Calif.) asked specific questions on the problems of the Jewish community and urged that Yemeni Jews be allowed to travel abroad freely. President Salih responded that while he appreciated their concern, it was not a serious issue. "I assure you they have full and equal rights according to the constitution." He declared that "we welcome any Yemenite citizen of the Jewish faith if they do not possess an Israeli passport," adding, "We'd like you to give equal attention to Palestinian rights." He asserted that "we have no different treatment between Muslims and Jews. Even Yemenite Jews who left in 1949–50, if they want to come back, they can."

Discernible but slow progress was achieved over the following months. Several small delegations of American Jews of Yemeni origin were permitted to visit northern Yemen, and three Yemeni Jewish students were permitted to come to New York for religious studies during the summer of 1991. In November a small synagogue and *mikveh* were built for the community in Rayda, and a building was rented for a school in Sa'ada. Yehieh Ibn Daud (David) Subairi, a blind man in his eighties from San'a, was finally permitted to emigrate, repeated requests by his family abroad and by Jewish organizations having fallen on deaf ears for many years. The case of "the old man" had been specifically raised by Congressman Levine with President Salih. In July 1992, upon the intervention of Roger Pinto, the Algerian-born head of the Paris-based Commission for Jewish Communities in Danger, who had been moved by the plight of a deaf and dumb boy he saw during a visit to Yemen in March 1991, the Yemeni authorities gave authorization for the boy and his uncle to go to France for special medical treatment.

International Jewish efforts to provide assistance to the Jewish communities in Yemen were hampered not only by the difficult physical conditions in northern Yemen itself, and by the ideological opposition of the Satmar Hassidim—who tried to sabotage the *aliyah* of Yemeni Jews to Israel—but also by fierce rivalry among the Yemeni Jews in the United States. It took long and frustrating efforts by American Jewish human-rights activists to get the Yemenite Jewish Federation of America, headed by Elisha Najjar, to cooperate with the International Coalition for the Rescue of the Jews of Yemen (ICROJOY), which was established in December 1988 under the leadership of Prof. Haim Tawil of Yeshiva University. (Subsequently, at the suggestion of a State Department official, the group changed its name from "Rescue" to "Revival.") In addition, Tzemah Kadi, who created the New York-based Ezrat Yehudei Teiman (Help for the Jews of Yemen), together with his wife, started a small school in Rayda as the first of a hoped-for network of schools. As Larry Cohler noted in a special report from Yemen, the factiousness of the Yemeni Jews mirrored the fragmentation and feuding among the tribal sheikhs in their native land. ("The Last Jews of Yemen," *Long Island Jewish World*, February 26-March 4, 1993.) ICROJOY was considered the most disciplined and responsible group by the State Department and by the American Jewish Joint Distribution Committee (JDC), which financially supported its efforts, as it had earlier efforts to contact Yemeni Jews.

The major breakthrough did not occur until August 1992, when Yemen began to implement its promise to permit Jewish emigration. A total of 57 Jews arrived in Israel in that year. According to Dr. Tawil, by the end of 1993 almost 500 had left Yemen and nearly all of the estimated remaining 520 were expected to leave in the near future. With the close cooperation of the Yemeni and American authorities, Gideon Taylor, the director of special projects for the JDC, organized technical and financial arrangements for the travel of the Yemeni Jews out of the country. Most subsequently went on to be reunited with their relatives in the large Yemenite community in Israel, while a few families chose to join relatives in the United States.

The relatively small movement of the Yemeni Jews was funded largely through the regular campaign of the United Jewish Appeal, in contrast to the special Operation Exodus Campaign that had been established to bring out the far greater numbers of Jewish emigrants from the former Soviet Union. Rav Tov, the relief organization of the Satmar, financed the travel of some of the families who came to the United States. As rumors of the departure of Yemeni Jews circulated in the international media, there was concern in the Jewish community that the publicity would cause the Yemeni authorities to halt the process, as had occurred a decade earlier when the Sudan stopped Ethiopian Jewish emigration because its help became publicly known. Consequently, there was surprise when Foreign Minister al-Iryani publicly confirmed that the Yemenite Jews were emigrating. "Yes, the reports are true," he told a reporter from the Associated Press at the end of March 1993. "But we do not sanction their travel to Israel."

Why did the Yemeni authorities, who in the past had been sensitive to negative reaction from the Saudis, the PLO, and the Muslim fundamentalists, make this public admission at the very time the country was preparing for its first democratic election? Economics and geopolitics were primary factors. Because the Yemeni government had sided with Saddam Hussein in Iraq's invasion of Kuwait and failed to support the allied coalition in the Gulf War, the Saudis retaliated by expelling some 800,000 Yemeni workers and cutting off aid to the San'a regime. A desperately poor Yemen now looked to the West for help in developing its oil fields; however, Yemen would not get significant American help until it improved its human-rights situation, including allowing free Jewish emigration.

In June 1992, Sen. Alfonse D'Amato (R., N.Y.) introduced a resolution in Congress calling for "full and free emigration" of Yemeni Jews as a condition of U.S. aid. Although he introduced it in the last days of the session and it was never brought to a vote, D'Amato had been able to round up 30 signatories to his amendment to the foreign operations bill. The Yemenis were certainly aware that similar demands on Syria had easily won the approval of a three-fourths majority of the Senate. Moreover, after the Arab confrontation states and the Palestinians agreed to participate in direct peace talks with Israel in Madrid in October 1991, and especially after Syria announced in April 1992 that its Jews could travel freely, maintaining Yemen's barriers to Jewish emigration became increasingly difficult to justify.

Iran

While all Iranian statistics are of questionable reliability, this is especially true for the numbers of the Jewish community. For various reasons, including a desire to demonstrate their importance and patriotism and to mask the extent of emigration, the number of those remaining in Iran has been inflated. Some Iranian Jewish scholars, such as David Yerushalmi, have placed the number of Jews before the departure of the Shah, in 1979, at between 125,000 and 130,000. He estimated that by November 1989 only 25,000 to 30,000 remained in the country. Other sources, including Lois Gottesman (AJYB 1985, p. 319), give an estimate for the prerevolutionary period of around 80,000, with about 60,000 residing in Teheran, 8,500 in Shiraz, 3,500 in Isfahan, and smaller communities scattered elsewhere. Gottesman estimated that by 1984 the total had declined to 35,000. In their article "World Jewish Population, 1992," elsewhere in this volume, the demographers U.O. Schmelz and Sergio DellaPergola note: "It is difficult to estimate the Jewish population of Iran for any given date, but it continues to dwindle. . . . The estimate for 1992 was reduced to 16,000."

Although its population is overwhelmingly Shiite Muslim, Iran is a non-Arab country. Under the Shah it pursued a pro-American orientation and avoided direct involvement in the Arab-Israeli conflict, although it did support Palestinian nationalism at the United Nations. Iran had granted de facto recognition to Israel in 1950. It maintained extensive commercial relations with Israel, for whom it was a major oil supplier, and had close but discreet political and intelligence ties with the Jewish state. Shared concern with the dangers of Soviet penetration into the region and expansionist Arab nationalism cemented Iranian-Israeli ties until the overthrow of the Shah by Ayatollah Khomeini and the establishment of the Islamic Republic in 1979. One of the first acts of the new regime was to sever all formal relations with Israel. The large unofficial Israeli embassy building was ceremoniously handed over to Yasir Arafat to serve as the embassy of the Palestine Liberation Organization. Oil shipments to Israel were canceled, as was the direct air service that El Al Israel Airlines had long maintained between Teheran and Tel Aviv. This direct link had facilitated the free movement of Iranian Jews to and from the Jewish state.

While the constitution of the Islamic Republic follows the Koran in recognizing Judaism as a revealed religion and the Jews as a protected religious minority (*ahl-al-kitab* [People of the Book] and *ahl-al-dhimma* [People of the Pact]), the Khomeini regime adopted a virulently anti-Zionist ideology, labeled Israel the "illegitimate offspring" of the "Great Satan," and called for armed struggle of the Islamic world to eradicate the State of Israel. The virulent anti-Israel propaganda campaign continued even after the death of Khomeini in 1989.

In the turbulent early years of the revolution Jews suffered from a reign of terror marked by the execution of 11 Jews, confiscation of Jewish property, and the dismissal of Jews from governmental and university positions. Many thousands of Jews emigrated in the turbulent period immediately before and after the overthrow of the Shah. The new regime barred travel to Israel and generally tightened travel restrictions following the outbreak of the Iraq-Iran war in 1980, especially banning travel by all young boys and men subject to the draft for military service. Although Jewish schools were permitted to function, they were placed under the control of the Islamic committees and were required to take in Muslim students, to remain open on the Sabbath, to include Islamic religious instruction, and to add anti-Zionist (and indeed anti-Semitic) materials to the curriculum.

Although Judaism remained an officially recognized religion and synagogues continued to function, the combination of physical danger and psychological terror prompted Jews to seek desperately for ways of leaving the country. Some managed to circumvent the barriers to Jewish emigration by acquiring Christian or Muslim identity papers and passports. Thousands of other Iranian Jews seeking freedom risked imprisonment and possible death if caught when they embarked on a hazardous journey over mountains and deserts to reach safety in neighboring countries. Successful refugees who managed to reach Turkey or Pakistan were permitted to move on to Austria and other destinations, where they were aided by the Joint Distribution Committee (JDC), the Jewish Agency, and other Jewish relief organizations to join their compatriots in the United States, Europe, and Israel. At a press conference in New York on October 2, 1987, Foreign Minister Alois Mock of Austria revealed that between July 1983 and August 1987 Austria had given temporary asylum to 5,188 Jews fleeing Iran. He stressed that his government was proceeding "without asking too many questions of Iranian refugees and without publicizing individual cases," in order not to jeopardize the flow of refugees in the future or to endanger their relatives who remained behind.

While thousands of Iranian Jews went to Israel, the majority resettled in the United States, primarily in the Los Angeles area in California and Long Island, New York. Among the early arrivals were relatives of wealthy Iranian Jews who, already in the days of the Shah, had sent their children for advanced education in the United States and had helped them establish professional and business careers. But many of those who followed in later years lacked the wealth or connections that would have facilitated their beginning a new life. Most had been robbed of their possessions, and many came with only what little they could carry with them. "The people who are leaving now had really, really tried to stay," Bruce T. Leimsidor, director of the Hebrew Immigrant Aid Society in Vienna, told *New York Times* reporter James M. Markham in an interview on November 13, 1986. He added that about two-thirds of the recent refugees had been tortured or otherwise physically mistreated in Iran.

The *Times* report of increasing Jewish emigration from Iran coincided with revelations of Israel's role as an intermediary, shipping American weapons to Iran as part of the White House effort both to secure the freedom of American hostages being held in Lebanon by pro-Iranian terrorists and to open a channel for improved communication with allegedly "moderate" elements in Teheran. Apart from its obvious strategic interest in preventing its avowed enemy, Iraq, from defeating Iran, there was speculation that the Israeli arms sale was also intended to induce Teheran to end the harassment of the Jewish community and remove the travel restrictions. A senior Israeli official denied that the increased emigration was tied to the arms deal. While some believe the Israeli contacts did help persuade some Iranian officials to turn a blind eye to the "illegal" departure of Jews, others note that there was in fact an increase in the harassment of the Jewish community in Iran at this time. Manouchehr Kalimi Nikrouz, the sole Jewish representative in the Majlis (parliament), was arrested on trumped-up charges of alleged sexual misconduct with one of his employees. Former Iranian president Abolhassan Bani-Sadr, who was then living in exile in Paris, told Reuters that the real reason for Nikrouz's arrest was to indicate the anger of the Teheran regime over the disclosure by Israeli leaders of the secret U.S. arms shipments to Iran. (*New York Times*, November 28, 1986.) (Nikrouz was eventually exonerated of all charges, released from prison, and restored to his seat in the Majlis.) Some interpreted the crackdown on the Jewish community as a calculated response by the Iranian officials implicated in the arms deal to counter the allegations of militant Islamic opponents that they were yielding to American or Zionist pressure.

After a cease-fire brought an end to hostilities with Iraq in 1988, Iran began to ease its travel restrictions. President Ali Akbar Hashemi Rafsanjani, who won reelection to a second four-year term in 1993, has sought to rebuild Iran's war-shattered economy and reestablish economic relations with the West. Consequently, some Iranian Jewish businessmen have been able to travel to the United States and Europe, though entire families are generally not permitted to travel together, and there are severe restrictions on how much money departing travelers may take with them. In recent years, not only passports but also identity cards and licenses for business have listed the applicant's religion. Jewish businessmen from Iran complain that their identification as Jews combined with a concerted government campaign discouraging Muslims from buying from or selling to Jews has significantly hurt their businesses and has also made it difficult to dispose of property. This is in addition to the economic hardship that Jews share with the rest of the population because of the country's economic problems.

The regime officially maintains its militant Islamic ideology, manifested not only in restrictions on the rights of women and persecution of the Bahai but also in its foreign policy, including support for the Hezballah (Party of God) in southern Lebanon and other militant Islamic groups that reject Israel's right to exist and actively oppose the current Arab-Israeli peace negotiations. Reports in 1993 that Iran was actively seeking to obtain a nuclear capability and that both Iran and Syria were purchasing long-range Scud missiles and other advanced weapons from North Korea and China aroused concern in Washington and Jerusalem. Unless there is a significant change in Iranian policy, the present climate of suspicion and animosity between Teheran and Jerusalem does not augur well for the long-term safety and security of the remaining Jewish communities in Iran.

Iranian Jews are concentrated in Teheran, Shiraz, and Isfahan. The Jews in the provincial cities feel even more vulnerable than those in the capital. According to Iranian Jewish émigrés, in 1986 a Mrs. Nosrat Goel was executed in Shiraz on charges of Zionism, one day after her arrest. In 1989 a Mr. Shamsa was executed there on the same charge, and in 1991 Yousef Hashimeyreti was tortured to death in Shiraz under suspicion of being a Zionist. In May 1992, Feyzollah Mechubad, the 75-year-old *shamash* of a synagogue in Teheran, was arrested and held in Evin prison. The Jewish community reportedly was told that his release could be obtained by a payment of 30 million tuman (variously valued at between $200,000 and $4 million, depending on the exchange rate applied). Before the community could complete raising this sum, he was charged with having illegal contacts with Israel, to which he confessed under extreme torture. He subsequently recanted his confession but was executed on February 25, 1994, on Purim, even though Iranian tradition prohibits execution of persons over 75 (he was 77). An autopsy reportedly revealed extensive signs of torture, including gouging of both his eyes. It is presumed that he was killed in retaliation for the massacre of Muslim worshipers at the Tomb of the Patriarchs in Hebron that had been perpetrated earlier that morning by Dr. Baruch Goldstein.

These executions, while infrequent, have had the desired effect of terrorizing the Jewish community. Adding to their fears has been the occasional publication of blatantly anti-Semitic articles in the press. On the appearance of the book *Blood for the Holy Matzoth*, by Najib Alkilani, which recounts the infamous blood libel in Damascus in 1840, the major Teheran evening daily *Keyhan* carried a lengthy article by Mohammed Reza Alvand (December 31, 1992) entitled "Israel Must Be Destroyed." The entire article is filled with vicious anti-Jewish statements and blames Israel and Zionism for all the world's evils. The Jewish community wrote a rebuttal to this article, which was only printed two weeks later—in an inconspicuous place— after intervention by the president of the Majlis and the Jewish representative in that body.

There is always an officially approved Jewish representative in the parliament, and the Association of Iranian Jews is careful to publicly endorse the government's foreign policy. For example, in the first year of his rule, Khomeini proclaimed the last Friday of the Islamic holy month of Ramadan as "Al-Quds [Jerusalem] Day," and it is marked annually with marches and demonstrations calling for Israel's destruction. The Voice of the Islamic Republic of Iran English radio service reported on May 3, 1989, that the Association of Iranian Jews (AIJ) had "today lashed out at the Zionist regime's ignorance of the sanctity of Al-Quds and voiced support for Al-Quds Day." The AIJ's statement pledged: "We, Iranian Jews, will defend the monotheistic values of Judaism against the Zionist regime's racist policies and believe that Al-Quds belongs to all monotheistic religions." The statement called on Jews throughout the world to join in the Jerusalem Day rallies and to condemn Zionism.

The government continues to enlist the local Jewish community in its international public-relations efforts. On March 2, 1993, the *Tehran Times* reported that the Association of Iranian Jews had issued a statement denouncing Western media allegations of violations of minority rights in Islamic Iran. "The propaganda tirade by colonial loudspeakers is aimed at distorting world public opinion against Iran and its ruling Islamic values," the Jewish Association statement said. The *Times* report continued: "Any fair person in his first few days of stay in Iran will find that religious minorities lead a calm and honorable life in Iran along with the rest of their compatriots." The statement noted that, according to the Islamic Republic Constitution, there are four officially recognized religious minorities in Iran—Armenian Christians, Jews, Zoroastrians, and Assyrians—"all of whom enjoy equal personal and social rights." This benevolent assessment was intended to counter continuing reports of oppression of the Bahais, who are considered heretics from Islam, and the arrest of Christians accused of attempting to convert Muslims. In its annual global survey of human rights for 1993, the U.S. State Department concluded that Iran's Islamic government continues to reinforce its hold on power through arrests, summary trials, executions, and assassinations (*New York Times*, February 2, 1994, p. A9).

Should the current Syrian-Israeli and Lebanese-Israeli negotiations result in peace agreements, they will place serious strains on the Damascus-Teheran alliance. Israel and the United States will certainly demand that Syria and Lebanon curb the activities of the Iranian Revolutionary Guard units and the Iranian-backed Hezballah and other Lebanese Islamic militants. Iranian Jews are cautiously waiting to see whether the pragmatic or the ideological elements in the Iranian ruling elite will prevail in dealing with the growing reality of Palestinian and Arab acceptance of the existence of Israel in the region.

Syria

According to a State Department estimate in September 1991, the Syrian Jewish community then numbered some 3,600, of whom 2,900 lived in Damascus, 550 in Aleppo, and 120 in the small, remote town of Qamishli, near the Turkish border. Other estimates put the total at around 4,300.

Some of the more onerous restrictions on the daily life of the Jewish community—such as the requirement that Jews needed advance written permission from the secret police to travel more than four kilometers from their homes in the Jewish quarter—were eased in recent years. Syrian Jews could travel freely within Syria, and they participated actively in the country's economy, primarily as merchants and skilled artisans in jewelry and metals. There were also Jewish doctors and pharmacists. However, Jews were barred from employment in most government offices or public bodies such as banks, and suffered from discriminatory economic and legal practices that restricted their rights to dispose of property through sale or inheritance. Jews are the only group that has their religion entered on their identity cards, although the large red letters of the past have been replaced by smaller notations in black. Jews are able to practice their religion openly.

Until recently there were two Jewish primary schools functioning in Damascus and one in Aleppo. In 1991 the Alliance school in Damascus was rebuilt and expanded by the Jewish community with financial help from the American Jewish Joint Distribution Committee. The teachers are Jewish but the principals are Muslim state officials. All synagogues and the one school still open, in Damascus, function under the watchful eyes of the authorities. For example, school attendance sheets must be delivered daily to the secret police, and agents visit the homes of those listed as ill to make sure they are really in bed and have not tried to flee the country.

One young woman from Damascus, whose husband and young daughter managed to escape a few years ago, described the feelings of the Jewish community in her testimony to the second International Conference for the Freedom of Syrian Jewry in Paris in May 1988 as follows: "Every time there is a knock on the door, mothers and fathers shake with fear for their children. Will the agents of the Mukhabarat take us to jail or some even more horrific fate? We are constantly spied upon by the authorities and our whole life is one big question mark."

In contrast to the massive emigration of Jews from the other Arab countries of the Middle East and North Africa, which reduced their numbers from nearly 900,000 in 1948 to fewer than 15,000 at the end of 1993, Syria had forbidden its Jews to emigrate since 1949. Although there had been some easing of travel restrictions in recent years, special regulations still prevented Jews from leaving freely. One problem that was given high priority by the Jewish community was the fate of young single Jewish women. This received heightened attention after four young Jewish women who were attempting to escape to Lebanon were murdered in 1974. Their burned and mutilated bodies were returned in sacks to their parents by the Syrian authorities. For years this inhibited many other women from attempting to leave illegally.

Since more young Jewish men than women successfully fled the country, and because a number of men were not marrying, hoping to start families in freedom rather than trying to escape with a wife and young children, it was feared that many Jewish women would remain single if they were not permitted to leave to seek husbands abroad. It was also feared that the shortage of Jewish men might lead some of the single Jewish women to marry Muslims or Christian Arabs. The State Department's Country Reports on Human Rights Practices for 1991, issued in February 1992, noted: "The Syrian Government closely restricts Jewish emigration, although it stated in 1989 that it would look positively at cases of family reunification and of unmarried Jewish women unable to find suitable husbands in the small Syrian Jewish community." The State Department report indicated that the number of such women allowed to emigrate "jumped dramatically in the middle of 1989, following U.S.-Syrian discussions on this issue, and 20 were given permission in 1991."

Before 1992 the Syrians rebuffed persistent requests to deal with the broader issue of Jewish emigration. Indeed, the State Department report pointed out that "there was no progress in 1991 on the issue of divided families seeking reunification," although it noted that "one case was resolved in early January 1992 when two minor children were permitted to join their parents" in the United States. The problem of divided families arose from the fact that in order to enforce the ban on Jewish emigration, the Syrian authorities required Jews permitted to travel abroad to leave behind members of their immediate family as a guarantee of their return. They also had to leave a substantial monetary deposit.

The total cost for exit permits, including official and "unofficial" payments to officials, has ranged from several hundred dollars to as high as $5,000 per person, or more than double the average per capita annual income in Syria. The State Department report acknowledged that, as a result, it is particularly those Syrian Jews "with significant holdings and financial ties in the country" who have benefited from the easing of foreign travel restrictions in recent years.

Desperate attempts to leave the country continued to occur before 1992. Those who were caught or suspected of planning to travel "illegally" were held in prison by the agents of the Mukhabarat. Amnesty International has confirmed that those arrested were subjected to brutal beatings and other forms of torture and usually denied access to legal counsel. They were routinely incarcerated for two to three years and often emerged from prison physically and mentally broken.

On November 28, 1991, apparently in response to the international advocacy efforts, and as part of a general amnesty prior to President Hafez al-Assad's virtually unanimous reelection, four Jewish men were released. Two of them, Rahmoun Darwish and Joseph Sabato, had been arrested with their wife and fiancée, respectively, on September 25, 1990, allegedly for trying to flee the country. Darwish's wife, who was seven months pregnant, gave birth in prison. The women were released a few months later, after having been kept in abusive conditions and tortured, according to the Council for the Rescue of Syrian Jewry. The other Syrian men freed in November were Subhe and Sa'id Kastika, who had been arrested at the beginning of May 1991, together with their wives, a two-year-old child, and a three-month-old baby. According to the council, "for almost three weeks they were held incommunicado, after which the women, who had been visibly beaten, and the babies were released."

Those who were held longest in prison were Selim Swed, a 51-year-old father of seven, and his younger brother, Eli, a 31-year-old bachelor. Eli had been arrested in November 1987 on his return from a trip abroad, and his brother was arrested at his pharmacy the following month. They were held incommunicado for more than two years in a damp and dark underground cell and subjected to brutal interrogation. Eli reportedly contracted tuberculosis. After numerous interventions, they were finally moved to regular cells in the Adra prison and in May 1991 were sentenced to six years and eight months, including time already served. The trial was closed to the public, but they were reportedly charged with "illegally traveling to enemy-occupied territory" and traveling without valid passports. In response to international complaints over the severity of the sentence, since they had reportedly gone to visit their relatives in Israel, Syrian officials responded that they had "gotten off lightly," since they might have been charged with espionage, which is a capital offense in Syria.

There was hope that following President Assad's unopposed reelection to a seven-year term in December 1991 the Swed brothers would be released as part of the amnesty granted to some 3,500 political detainees. However, they were explicitly excluded from the general pardon, and their harsh sentence was confirmed by the Damascus authorities in January 1992. They were finally released in mid-April 1992, on the second day of Passover. Sen. Edward M. Kennedy (D., Mass.) and 68 colleagues—more than two-thirds of the Senate—had written a joint letter to President Assad on March 26 urging him "to free the Sweds and to permit free emigration for all Syrian Jews." Progress on human rights was one of the issues the senators cited as preconditions for improvement in Syrian-U.S. relations. Alice Sardell Harary, president of the Council for the Rescue of Syrian Jewry, stated that, while the council was "grateful that Eli and Selim Swed are free at last and have been reunited with their family, we pray that this gesture is a harbinger of change in Syrian policy toward the 4,000 Jews remaining hostage in Syria."

Although the Jewish community had been scrupulously careful to stay out of domestic political activity, and no Jews were selected for any political post, they were drawn into unprecedented public action during President Assad's December 1991 reelection campaign. In view of the tight control maintained by Assad over public expression and the absence of any opposition candidate, there was much speculation as to why the financially hard-pressed regime felt the need to spend $80 million on election banners, ubiquitous giant posters of Assad, and daily mass rallies by every possible professional and trade association. One explanation is that all this display was intended to convey to the United States and the world that Assad represented stability and security, was firmly in control, and had the support of his people.

Probably the most bizarre events of the election campaign were two government-organized "spontaneous" demonstrations of support for Assad by the Jews of Damascus. The first was an evening auto rally, which the English-language *Syria Times* described as an occasion for Syria's Jews to drive their "fancy cars" through the streets of Damascus, a not-so-subtle attempt to portray the Jews as the wealthiest of the country's minorities. But when the Thursday night rally failed to attract the hoped-for Western media attention, a march on foot in broad daylight was quickly organized for the following afternoon. This was carried on Syrian television and received worldwide media attention, especially since it was the first time in history that Syrian Jews were permitted to carry banners in Hebrew, as well as in Arabic and English. The banners proclaimed the Jews' expressions of "love and honor for our great leader, Hafez al-Assad." Reuters reported that 400 Jewish schoolchildren, carrying balloons and pictures of Assad, marched with the adults, calling out, "With our souls and blood we redeem thee Hafez." The 2,000 marchers were led by Chief Rabbi Ibrahim Hamra, who shouted with the others, "Hafez Assad is the symbol of national unity." He told reporters that the Jewish community had benefited greatly from Assad's rule and would vote yes in the referendum. "Whatever we do for President Assad is not enough," he said. He pointed out that "today is Friday and it is a day to prepare for the holy day [Sabbath], but we went ahead with the rally to express our gratitude to the President, who gave us a lot." (*Daily Telegraph*, London, November 30, 1991.)

As Rabbi Hamra hinted, the timing of the rally was not chosen by the Jewish community but was set by the authorities. A few weeks later, Judy Feld Carr, who spearheaded the Canadian Jewish Congress's efforts on behalf of Syrian Jewry, received a message from a friend in Syria, "Please don't be ashamed of us; we had no choice." This activity was also clearly intended for foreign consumption—as a direct refutation of the intensified human-rights campaign on behalf of the Jews of Syria.

Prime Minister Yitzhak Shamir had pledged in speeches in Jerusalem in July and in Paris in September 1991 that Israel would work tirelessly until the Jews in Syria, like the Jews of Russia and Ethiopia, were free to emigrate. He mentioned the issue of the human rights of the Jews in Syria in his address at the Madrid peace conference in October, prompting Syrian foreign minister Sharaa to issue a categorical statement that Jews "have lived among Muslim Arabs throughout history, wherever they happen to coexist, without ever suffering any form of persecution or discrimination, either racial or religious."

A concurrent resolution of the U.S. House and Senate passed in October had called upon the Syrian government to immediately release all Jewish prisoners accused of traveling "illegally" and to grant Syrian Jews the right to travel freely. The members of Congress also urged the president to call on other countries to make similar appeals to Damascus and to seek a United Nations investigation on "the present condition of Syrian Jews and the status of respect for internationally recognized human rights in Syria." Individual members of Congress demanded that Damascus be denied U.S. economic benefits until it permitted free emigration. A State Department official wrote to concerned Jewish leaders in Chile in September, "Human rights conditions in Syria continue to be a matter of concern to the U.S. Government, and we continue to make this subject, including the restrictions placed on Syrian Jews, a prominent part of our diplomatic dialogue with the Syrian government."

The European Parliament, which had passed several resolutions on Syrian Jewry in the past, adopted a new resolution on November 21, 1991, deploring the failure of the Syrian government to permit the Jews to leave, and noting that "the perilous situation of the Jews had been made even more critical by the publication of a book by the Syrian Minister of Defense, Mustafa Tlas, which repeated the calumnies accusing the Jews of ritual murder." (The book in question, entitled *The Matzah of Zion*, recounted the infamous Damascus blood libel case of 1840, in which a Christian clergyman had falsely accused the Jews of using the blood of a Christian child to prepare their unleavened bread for Passover. At a meeting of the UN Human Rights Commission in Geneva in February 1991, the Syrian representative had recommended the book to fellow members of the commission as evidence of the malevolent nature of the Jews. As noted above, a book on the same theme was published in Iran the following year.)

Demonstrations sponsored by the European Union of Jewish Students calling for freedom for the Jews of Syria were held in front of Syrian embassies throughout Western Europe and in Moscow on December 1, the first night of Hanukkah. Similar demonstrations were held in many cities in the United States, Canada, and Latin America. On January 14, 1992, the Conference of Presidents of Major American Jewish Organizations, the National Jewish Community Relations Council, and the Council for the Rescue of Syrian Jewry joined in placing an advertisement in the *New York Times* and the *Washington Post*, headlined "There Are Still Hostages in the Middle East!" It described the 4,000 Jews of Syria as a "captive community" and demanded that "the Jews of Syria be allowed to leave now."

In the course of the bilateral Syrian-Israeli talks in Washington in January 1992, the Israeli delegation again raised the issue of Syrian Jewry and asked that the Syrian government give them permission to leave freely, "in accordance with international norms and obligations, and in accordance with a resolution passed recently by both houses of Congress." Ambassador Muwaffak al-Allaf, the head of the Syrian delegation, was sharply critical of congressional involvement in an issue he defined as a Syrian "domestic" matter. But the efforts which the Syrians made to respond to the criticism, including the well-publicized Jewish demonstration in Damascus, indicated a heightened measure of Syrian sensitivity to international public opinion. President Assad had in fact felt moved to declare to a group of Lebanese members of parliament visiting Damascus on December 12, 1991, that "everybody in Syria, including Syrian Jews, enjoys the right to leave the country." United Press International called it an "unprecedented statement," one indicating "a dramatic shift."

On the eve of the resumption of the bilateral Syrian-Israeli talks in Washington on April 27, 1992, the State Department announced that it had received confirmation from the Syrian Foreign Ministry that, in a recent meeting with the country's Jewish leaders, President Assad had declared that "all members of the Syrian Jewish community will be accorded the same rights as those enjoyed by all other Syrian citizens." The most important part of the announcement was the indication that "Syrian Jews will be allowed to travel abroad *as families*, on business and for vacation" (emphasis added). Jewish emigration was still not permitted, and departing Jews were officially issued only tourist visas, meaning that they could not take more than a limited amount of personal goods and money with them. Yet the promise to remove the requirement that immediate members of the family remain behind offered the opportunity for whole families to leave and for divided families to be reunited with their relatives in the United States and countries other than Israel. (The Jewish community of Syrian origin is estimated at over 30,000 in the metropolitan New York region alone.)

Damascus had assured Washington that, in future, Jews seeking to travel would only have to pay the normal exit visa fees. The State Department also stated that the "Syrian Government has removed difficulties encountered by its Jewish citizens with regard to the sale and purchase of property." The State Department announcement hinted at Syria's failure to live up to past promises when it concluded: "We look forward to the full implementation of these decisions affecting Syrian Jews."

The cumulative effect of interventions on behalf of Syrian Jewry may have finally convinced the Syrian president that there was more to be gained than lost by ending his anachronistic policy. Not only had other Arab states permitted their Jews to leave, but with the floodgates of the former Soviet Union open to Jewish emigration—and with some 350,000 having by then already gone to Israel—the argument that permitting Syrian Jews to leave would contribute to the military power of the Israeli enemy seemed more ridiculous than ever.

When Rabbi Hamra publicly declared his support for President Assad as the symbol of Syrian national unity, he was reflecting the true feelings of the Syrian Jewish community. There is much concern that should Assad disappear from the scene, either through natural causes or by an assassin's bullet, the country might again be racked by factional strife, and Islamic fundamentalist protest movements might come to power. The sudden death in January 1994 in an automobile crash of Assad's 33-year-old son Basil, whom the president was grooming as his successor, heightened concern over the country's political stability and intensified the Jewish desire to leave. While demanding that all remaining restrictions upon them be removed, Syrian Jews appreciate the fact that Assad has protected them from radical Palestinians and other hostile forces and fear that their position would be far worse than it is at present if the fanatical Muslim Brotherhood took over.

As noted above, in the peace talks in Madrid and Washington, Prime Minister Shamir and the Israeli delegation repeatedly demanded that Syria give its Jews the right to leave. This placed the issue squarely within the context of the Arab-Israeli dispute. This was in contrast to the strategy of the Council for the Rescue of Syrian Jewry and other advocacy groups, which had always been to emphasize that freedom for Syrian Jews was a human-rights issue that should be taken up in the context of the American-Syrian dialogue rather than in the framework of the Arab-Israeli conflict. This was necessary as long as the Syrians used the state of war between Syria and Israel as justification for their restrictions on Jewish travel, saying they had no way of assuring that Syrian Jews would not go to Israel and strengthen the military capacity of the "Zionist enemy."

Some observers believe that, in addition to seeking to improve his image in the United States, President Assad's gesture to permit Jewish families to leave was intended as a confidence-building measure in the negotiations with Israel, to induce Jerusalem to modify its stand on the Golan Heights. The June 1992 elections in Israel, which saw the defeat of the Likud party by the Labor party and the replacement of Yitzhak Shamir by Yitzhak Rabin as prime minister, held out hope of rapprochement. General Rabin, who as chief of staff in 1967 had commanded the Israel Defense Forces' capture of the Golan Heights, made it clear that his government was prepared for territorial compromise in exchange for peace, including withdrawal from the Golan Heights, subject to appropriate security arrangements. However, despite this significant ideological shift from the Likud position, the bilateral Syrian-Israeli negotiations during 1992 and 1993 failed to achieve a breakthrough. Moreover, Assad would not participate in the multilateral negotiations on such vital regional issues as shared water resources, environmental problems, economic development, arms control, and refugees, arguing that Israel should not benefit from the fruits of peace before it had met Syrian demands.

The remaining Syrian Jews once again became pawns in this larger dispute. Between April 27, 1992, and mid-October 1992, some 2,850 Syrian Jews were given permission to travel, according to the State Department's Report on Human Rights for 1992, issued in January 1993. The report noted that "the Government, however, remains opposed in principle to Jewish emigration, and Jews must have their applications for passports and exit visas approved by Syrian military intelligence." In the second half of October, the Syrian authorities suddenly reduced the number of new exit permits to a couple a week, mostly for individuals. Knowledgeable Middle East observers attributed the slowdown to the impending American presidential elections and Assad's subsequent attempt to use the release of the remaining Jews as a bargaining chip in his relations with the new administration in Washington.

Assad's reneging on his promise spurred renewed diplomatic and political efforts on behalf of Syrian Jewry. On May 23, 1993, Senators Edward Kennedy (D., Mass.) and Charles Grassley (R., Iowa), together with 71 other members of the Senate, sent a letter to Clinton urging him to address directly the issue of Syrian Jewry. On July 15, President Clinton sent a strong reply to the signatories of the Senate letter affirming his commitment to Syrian Jews, assuring them that "I have not, and will not, let this matter slip from our attention." The response from Damascus to high-level American diplomatic interventions remained the same. Both President Assad and Foreign Minister al-Sharaa assured Secretary of State Warren Christopher on his first official visit to Damascus, in February 1993, as they had President George Bush and Secretary James Baker, that no new ban had been imposed, and that the reduction in exit permits was due solely to "bureaucratic" problems. Yet by early December there was still no discernible change, and the Syrians were doling out the exit permits one at a time.

After a four-hour meeting with Assad on December 5, 1993, Secretary Christopher told reporters in Damascus that the Syrian leader had pledged to issue exit visas for all remaining Jews by the end of the month. Although there was indeed an increase in exit permits issued in the following weeks, 1993 ended with several hundred Syrian Jews still awaiting documents.

Frustration over the continuing delays and the apparent reimposition of the requirement that some family members remain behind prompted the organized Jewish community in the United States to hold a rally at the Syrian Mission to the United Nations on Sunday, December 5. The rally was cosponsored by 28 national and local Jewish groups, including such umbrella organizations as the Jewish Community Relations Council of New York and the Conference of Presidents of Major

American Jewish Organizations. Set for the weekend before Hanukkah, a time traditionally devoted to recalling Jewish triumph over religious persecution, the rally also coincided with the Assad-Christopher meeting in Damascus. American political and religious leaders joined more than 400 members of the Jewish community gathered on a cold and rainy day, carrying banners that proclaimed "President Assad Keep Your Word" and "Freedom for Syrian Jews."

Alice Sardell Harary, president of the Council for the Rescue of Syrian Jewry, described the hardships caused by the disruption of the emigration process. Those who had already left gave up their money, their businesses, their homes, and all their assets in order to "breathe the sweet air of freedom." The 1,400 who were still awaiting permission to leave to join their families abroad found their daily life disrupted. She noted that the school in Aleppo had closed and that there was only one kosher butcher to serve the remaining Jews in the three cities of Damascus (1,100), Aleppo (around 150), and Qamishli (fewer than 100). Many Jews were out of work and non-Jews would no longer extend them credit, knowing that they wanted to leave. (Prior to the mass departures, it was estimated that 50 percent of the Jewish population was middle class, 10 percent upper class, and about 40 percent at or near the poverty level.)

To illustrate the sorry state of the remaining remnant of the ancient Syrian Jewish communities, she noted: "Just six months ago we had ten baby boys who had not yet had a *bris* [circumcision] because there was no longer a *mohel* [ritual circumciser] in Syria. The oldest of the babies was eight months. It took so many months before the Syrians would agree to grant a foreign *mohel* a Syrian visa."

By the end of 1993, according to the State Department, more than 85 percent of the Jewish community had been granted exit permits, while 500–600 requests still awaited approval. Mrs. Harary confirmed to the author that, as of the beginning of February 1994, all Jews requesting exit permits had already received them. While some 1,100 Jews were still in Syria, most were expected to leave within a few months, some reportedly waiting for the end of the school year and warmer weather. It is estimated that some 300 to 400 Jews—primarily the wealthy and well established—will choose to remain in Syria.

Should a formal peace agreement be concluded between Syria and Israel, and if Damascus lifts the ban on travel to Israel, some Syrian Jewish sources in New York believe that about half of the recent immigrants will choose to resettle in Israel rather than remain in Brooklyn.

Morocco

Anxiety and concern for the future cast a constant shadow over the daily lives of the small Jewish communities even in those Arab countries where generally moderate and pro-Western rulers have tried to protect them. Although Morocco has a relatively free press, several political parties, and labor unions, King Hassan II crushed a 1972 coup attempt and has used draconian measures to quell perceived threats to his regime. The long-term stability of that regime will depend on his ability to improve the economic opportunities for a growing population by attracting increased foreign investment and tourism and to meet the popular demand for greater political participation and free expression. At the same time, he will have to restrain Islamic fundamentalists and other extremist elements that may threaten his regime.

In 1990–1991 Morocco felt the repercussions of the Gulf crisis, which exacerbated existing weaknesses, with high inflation and widespread unemployment continuing to fuel an economic malaise. The king managed to straddle the fence during the Gulf War, condemning the Iraqi invasion and sending troops to Saudi Arabia, but then announcing that Moroccan troops would never fire a shot against an Arab brother. Hassan permitted popular demonstrations in support of Saddam Hussein, in which some 300,000 Muslim fundamentalists reportedly participated, and as a result of which property was damaged and some 30 Muslims were killed. Although some of the demonstrators shouted anti-Semitic slogans, the king's police prevented the demonstration from turning into a pogrom.

After the war, he positioned himself quickly in support of the American-sponsored peace efforts, with Morocco joining 11 other Arab countries in the multilateral stage of the peace process, which convened for the first time in Moscow in January 1992. Hassan officially received Prime Minister Yitzhak Rabin and Foreign Minister Shimon Peres in Rabat in September 1993, on their return from the Washington signing of the Declaration of Principles with PLO chairman Yasir Arafat. The French-language Moroccan paper *Le Matin du Sahara et du Maghreb* reported on September 9 that the executive of the World Gathering of Moroccan Jewry had met in Paris and issued a declaration full of effusive praise for the king's "courageous," "visionary," and "pioneering" activities in support of the historic Palestinian-Israel rapprochement and pledging its support for broadening the peace process to include all the Arab states of the region.

The appointment in 1993 of Serge Berdugo, the leader of the Jewish community, as minister of tourism and the appointment of other Jews as financial advisers to the king reflected the hope that as peace took root, Moroccan Jews in France, Israel, and Canada, as well as many American and Western European Jews who were not of Sephardi origin, would increasingly be attracted to visit Morocco as tourists and even to invest in the country's development. The king has eagerly encouraged tourism and investment from American Jews and from Moroccan Jews living abroad.

Within the Jewish community, the pattern of institutional closure continued, as the population slowly decreased in size, falling to around 6,500 in 1993, according to Linda Levi of the Joint Distribution Committee. In Morocco, as in other countries with a dwindling Jewish population, there was a tendency to move from the small provincial towns to the major cities, where viable community institutions still functioned. In 1991 the JDC closed the homes for the aged in Rabat, Fez, and Marrakesh and transferred the residents to a home in Casablanca. The school in

Meknes was also closed. Tangier was the only community in the provinces to retain its homes for the aged, which JDC helped fund.

The Casablanca community continued to display a dynamism beyond its size, with more than 20 synagogues functioning on a daily basis, and 1,296 students attending Jewish day schools during the 1993–94 academic year. This represented nearly all the community's school-age children. Because of the financial pressures, the JDC actively encouraged consolidation in the four subsidized school systems: Otzar Hatorah, Lubavitch, Ittihad (formerly known as the Alliance Israélite Universelle), and ORT. A new Lubavitch youth center was opened in Marrakesh in 1992, and the JDC also helped fund their youth centers in Casablanca and Meknes, as well as summer camp programs for some 400 children sponsored by various Jewish groups. More than 500 Moroccan Jews received welfare assistance from the local community with JDC help; some 1,700 needy persons of all ages benefited from health services provided by OSE (Oeuvre Secours aux Enfants), with JDC support.

The two Spanish enclaves of Ceuta and Melilla had a combined Jewish population of around 1,500. In response to efforts to encourage communal self-sufficiency, the Melilla community in 1992 informed JDC that it now could manage to finance its own communal needs, but in Ceuta the JDC continued to provide part of the costs of Hebrew classes for 40 youngsters.

Algeria

Most of the 140,000 Jews who were living in the country when Algeria won its independence in 1962 moved to France. Although the governing National Liberation Front (FLN) was in the early years an ardent champion of the Palestinians in the Arab-Israeli conflict, the secular, socialist Algerian regime was careful to protect the local Jewish community. For instance, in May 1988, when the last functioning synagogue was desecrated by vandals who tore Torah scrolls, ripped prayer books, and broke furniture, Minister of the Interior El-Had Khedri met with Roger Said, the president of the local Jewish community, to promise that the police would seek out the vandals. The police arrested eight teenagers and charged them with robbery after stolen Jewish objects were found in local stores.

Beginning in the late 1980s, Algeria experienced growing political turbulence and the spectacular ascent of Muslim fundamentalists in the Islamic Salvation Front (FIS), which pledged to turn Algeria into a Muslim state run according to Sharia law. The success of the fundamentalist party, even among many nonobservant Algerians, is attributed to various factors, including high long-term unemployment (over 30 percent) among the rapidly growing and youthful population, disillusionment with the unfulfilled pan-Arab and socialist promises of the FLN, and widespread reports of favoritism and corruption among the FLN elite that had governed the country since independence.

An Islamic takeover in January 1992 was prevented by an army-led coup that first unseated President Chadli Benjedid, then declared a state of martial law, appointed a five-man junta, and finally arrested FIS leaders. After the military outlawed Islamic groups in 1992, they began an armed insurrection, and the country was placed in a state of emergency.

According to first-hand reports from Algiers, the small and aged Jewish community, which in 1990 numbered around 150 persons, had declined to fewer than 100 in 1993, through natural deaths or emigration. The remnant of this once flourishing community has kept a low profile and has not thus far been directly touched by the fighting. However, they suffer from the unstable political situation and the deteriorating economy. Most of the Jews are over 60, and all but two have French citizenship. (They continue to be free to move to France.)

The Joint Distribution Committee provides supplementary cash grants to seven elderly Jews lacking sufficient means. Subsidized medical care is provided to the remaining Jews when needed by the local Little Sisters of the Poor, a Catholic religious order.

In 1991, as the FLN loosened the reigns of control and the first multiparty political election campaign swung into high gear, anti-Semitic slogans became a regular tool in the arsenal of the opposition groups. There were no physical attacks on the local Jews, the aim being to focus on the "international Jewish mafia." Opposition and independent papers carried anti-Semitic articles, including reprints of the Protocols of the Elders of Zion. The Islamic Salvation Front propaganda regularly invoked "the Jews as Middle East invaders and as the rivals of Islam." Shortly before his arrest on June 30, 1991, FIS leader Sheikh Abbas Madani accused the authorities of dispersing Muslim demonstrators with smoke grenades purchased from "American Jews." In subsequent clashes, Muslim fundamentalists taunted members of the security forces as "dogs, Jews and heretics." Roger Pinto, the head of the Paris-based Commission for Jewish Communities in Danger, complained that the embattled government "doesn't denounce anti-Semitism" and gloomily predicted that "the ongoing instability can only serve to strengthen existing tensions." (Edith Beck, "The Freedom to Be Anti-Semitic," *Jerusalem Report*, December 26, 1991.) Algerian Jews recall that anti-Jewish riots after the 1967 Six Day War resulted in much damage and the conversion of all but one synagogue into mosques.

Tunisia

The total Jewish population of Tunisia had declined to around 1,585 by the end of 1993.

In a bloodless coup in November 1987, Habib Bourguiba, Tunisia's "president for life," was deposed by Zine el-Abidine Ben Ali, his prime minister. The ailing 84-year-old "father of the nation" had ruled Tunisia since leading the country to independence from France in 1956. He had actively protected the Jewish community in the face of anti-Israel demonstrations in 1967. However, growing Islamic fundamentalism in recent years and virulent anti-Semitism, fanned by inflammatory broadcasts from neighboring Libya, resulted in several incidents against Jewish institutions.

The most serious of these occurred during Simhat Torah prayers in October 1985 in the ancient El-Ghriba synagogue on the island of Djerba. A crazed Tunisian security guard, posted by the government to protect the 140 worshipers, suddenly turned his weapon on the congregation, killing 4 persons and wounding 11. The gunman also killed a Tunisian policeman who tried to resist, whose police car he grabbed to flee toward the Libyan border, where he was finally captured. He was convicted and sentenced to a mental institution. The incident came a few days after Israeli forces had bombed the PLO headquarters on the outskirts of Tunis, in retaliation for a Palestinian terrorist attack on three Israeli civilian tourists in Cyprus. One unconfirmed report said that the synagogue gunman was the brother of a Tunisian guard killed in the Israeli raid on the PLO headquarters. Whatever the reason, it demonstrated how vulnerable innocent local Jews in the Arab world are to repercussions of the Arab-Israeli conflict. The incident also caused the Tunisian authorities to have serious second thoughts about the wisdom of their offering to host the PLO after it was kicked out of Beirut in 1982. The presence of militant Palestinians and potential terrorists in the country had reportedly hurt Tunisia's image as a mecca for tourism, which was the country's main source of foreign exchange.

Within days of assuming power in 1987, Ben Ali met with the leaders of the Jewish community to assure them that he would continue to protect them. While Ben Ali has maintained the country's generally pro-Western orientation, he also restored relations with Libya, which had been broken off by Tunisia in protest against Col. Muammar Qaddafi's campaign of subversion. For a while he also eased up on local fundamentalists, whom he had helped to suppress when he served as Bourguiba's minister of the interior.

However, in the face of renewed Islamic militancy, Ben Ali intensified his vigilance and has quietly worked with the pro-Western governments of Morocco and Egypt in an attempt to stem the Islamic tide in the Maghreb. In 1991 and 1992, the government again resorted to draconian measures designed to eradicate the now outlawed An-Nahda Islamic party from the political landscape, including press restrictions and the imprisonment of 265 party leaders for plotting to assassinate the president and overthrow the government. In elections held in March 1994, Ben Ali won virtually unanimous reelection. The ruling Constitutional Democratic Rally Party won heavily in elections to the Chamber of Deputies, with four opposition parties taking 19 out of 163 seats under a new liberalized electoral system.

Although the potential for Islamic resurgence remains a concern, there is no immediate threat to the Jewish community. Both the government and the Jewish community look forward to benefits deriving from the success of the Arab-Israeli peace process. The government hopes to reap financial dividends, in which Tunisian Jews and their tens of thousands of relatives abroad may well play a helpful role. A recent sign of the priority given by the government to attracting Jewish tourism and investment was the red-carpet welcome given Chief Rabbi Joseph Sitruk of France in September 1992 on his first visit to Tunisia since he left the country as a youth in 1959. Sitruk was escorted to the presidential palace in Tunis by motorcycle outriders with sirens blaring, and the state media gave extensive coverage to his visit. Ben Ali reportedly believes that the former Tunisian Jews—particularly those who prospered in the French textile industry—could be attracted to invest in his country. As a further sign of his eagerness for rapprochement with the Jewish world, Ben Ali promised to release the assets of Tunisian Jews resident in France and made a pledge of $200,000 to restore the capital's Jewish cemetery. As for the nearly 100,000 Tunisian Jews who emigrated, Ben Ali told Sitruk, "They are at home here, and can come whenever they want." It soon became clear that this welcome also extended to Tunisian Jews who had settled in Israel.

Although Tunisia never opened formal diplomatic relations with Israel, Israeli officials were welcomed to participate when Tunisia hosted multilateral discussions on refugee issues in 1993, and four Tunisian students participated in agricultural training courses in Israel under the auspices of the Israel Foreign Ministry.

The historic el-Ghriba Synagogue in the Hara Sghira section of Djerba has long drawn Tunisian Jews from across the country, from France, and even from the United States to participate in the special three-day *hiloula* celebrations around Lag B'Omer (the 33rd day following the first day of Passover). (According to an ancient legend, the original synagogue, rebuilt on the same site in 1920, contains a stone from Solomon's Temple, which was brought by a mysterious Jewish woman who carried it with her from Jerusalem at the time of the Babylonian destruction of the Temple in 586 BCE. The stone is believed by some to possess the magical power to grant wishes.) What is unusual is that in May 1993 the Tunisian authorities actively encouraged the participation of Tunisian Jews from Israel as well. Indeed, the kitchens of seven tourist hotels in this resort area were made kosher especially for the occasion to accommodate the 2,000 Jewish visitors from abroad. The government also invited a group of American Jewish writers to cover the events, to meet with government officials, and to tour the Jewish communities in Tunis and Djerba. In this Tunisia was following the example of Morocco, which had carried out a similar program in 1980, resulting in a significant increase in American Jewish tourism to that country.

As in Morocco, the declining population forced a consolidation of institutions. In Tunis the JDC is helping to finance the remodeling and enlargement of one old-age home in order to accommodate the residents of another building, which will be sold. The JDC also provided support for the only remaining Jewish school in Tunis, a Lubavitcher institution with 75 children aged 3 to 16, most of whose families came to Tunis from Djerba. Funds were also provided to two schools in the Hara Kbira section of Djerba, a girls' school and a yeshivah for boys, with a combined enrollment of 245, and *talmud torah* classes for seven youngsters in Hara Sghira.

It should be noted that, although the total Jewish population of Tunis—estimated at 700–900—exceeds that of Djerba, with a Jewish population of only 670, the far higher percentage of Jewish children going to day schools in the latter reflects the different character of the two communities. The Jews in the capital are generally

Francophone and more assimilated, while the Arabic- and Hebrew-speaking Djerban Jews remain traditional and place a high value on Jewish observance and scholarship. There are also demographic differences, the Jews of Tunis tending to be older on average with small families, the Djerbans younger, with large families and many young children. When they emigrate, the Jews of Tunis tend to go to France, while those from Djerba prefer to settle in the Holy Land.

The JDC provided financial assistance to 185 indigent Jews, mainly single elderly persons, and also helped subsidize the salaries of two ritual slaughterers and provided Passover supplies. Other communal needs were paid for by Tunisian Jews themselves. However, as the local economy continued to deteriorate, they turned increasingly to Tunisian Jews in France to finance special needs, such as new heating equipment for the old-age home and for help in cleaning up the Tunis Jewish cemetery.

The Jewish population in outlying Tunisian towns continued to dwindle, with only some 70 remaining in Sousse, 55 in Sfax, 50 in Zarzis, and 40 in Nabeul.

Egypt

The local Jewish communities in Egypt are a pale shadow of their ancient glory. Only some 250 persons, mostly aged, remain, chiefly in Cairo and Alexandria. There is also a tiny Karaite community.

The Joint Distribution Committee gave assistance to some 50 elderly and impoverished individuals, providing health care in partnership with the local communities, and covering 90 percent of the costs of two small homes for the aged. (The Alexandria home was closed in 1992.) The JDC also helped organize festival meals and group recreation for the elderly population, consisting largely of widows living alone.

Since the conclusion of the Egyptian peace treaty with Israel in 1979, the community is no longer as isolated as it had been, and Jewish tourists and business executives from various countries, including relatives from Israel, have often helped in providing a *minyan* for Sabbath services in the main synagogue in Cairo. The ancient Ibn Ezra Synagogue, site of the famous *genizah*, has also recently been restored and reopened to visitors.

Although President Hosni Mubarak has taken an active role in seeking to mediate between Israel and the PLO and between Israel and its Arab neighbors, the fate of the members of the aging Jewish community depends more on Mubarak's success in domestic affairs—in countering the growing fundamentalist challenge to his regime and maintaining the principles of secularism and religious pluralism which he officially endorses.

Iraq

After the conclusion of the Iraq-Iran war in 1988, Saddam Hussein approved restoration of a synagogue in Baghdad, and Jews were again permitted to travel. According to a report in the Israeli newspaper *Ma'ariv* (December 12, 1991), 26 Iraqi Jewish men and women had arrived in a European country after obtaining official permission to leave Iraq. They said that only 81 Jews remained in Baghdad, most of them in their seventies.

The allied bombing of Baghdad in January 1991 as part of Operation Desert Storm did not damage the main synagogue, although its windows were shattered by the blast of nearby bomb explosions. However, the war revived concern not only for the physical safety of the tiny Jewish community but also for the fate of its valuable historical archives and its many precious Torah scrolls. Haham Solomon Gaon of Yeshiva University in New York has tried for years to get Iraqi permission to export these materials, urging major Jewish organizations to undertake a more active campaign to protect the cultural heritage of this ancient Jewish community.

Lebanon

During 1993 the Lebanese authorities authorized the removal of 50 Torah scrolls from Beirut and their export to other Jewish communities. This was mute but poignant evidence of the dissolution of this ancient and once flourishing Jewish community.

In October 1991 there were reportedly only two Jews—an elderly brother and sister—still living in the Wadi Abu Jamil section of West Beirut, where the main synagogue had closed in 1984. There are reportedly between 50 and 100 Jews living in Christian East Beirut, their average age being around 65. The dozen or so younger Jews are mainly students at the city's universities. Explaining his decision to remain, one young Jew told an Israeli reporter, "There have been Jews here for the past 2,300 years. We're one of the 17 officially recognized sects. We don't want them to become 16 one day." (*Jerusalem Report*, October 24, 1991.) In addition, some Lebanese Jewish businessmen whose families reside in Europe make periodic trips to Beirut in hopes of participating in the massive reconstruction effort that is now under way, on the assumption that peace will finally come to that troubled country.

The last American hostages held by Shiite groups in Lebanon were released in 1991, and toward the end of 1993 Syrian president Assad offered his help and that of the Lebanese authorities to ascertain the whereabouts of seven Israeli soldiers captured or missing in action; however, there has been absolutely no progress in determining the fate or even recovering the bodies of nine Lebanese Jews kidnapped in Beirut in the mid-1980s. On July 24, 1987, Joseph Mizrahi, acting president of the Lebanese Jewish community, asked the present author to convey a personal appeal to UN secretary-general Pérez de Cuéllar urging him "in the name of the most elementary human rights" to use all of his moral authority to help the Jewish community recover the remains of the murdered Jews so that they could be laid to rest "in accordance with Jewish traditions."

The Organization of the Oppressed on Earth, which in July 1989 announced that it had hanged U.S. Marine Lt. Col. William Higgins as an "American spy," kidnapped nine Lebanese Jews in 1984 and 1985. Ideologically and operationally linked to the Iranian-backed Hezballah (Party of God), a group bearing this name first surfaced in Beirut in December 1985, when it announced the execution of two of the Lebanese Jews it had kidnapped earlier. Two additional Lebanese Jewish hostages were killed by this group in February 1986, because, it said, Israel failed to meet its demands to release all Lebanese and Palestinian prisoners held in southern Lebanon. Only the first three victims were found, dumped on the streets of Beirut. The coroner reported that the body of the third victim, Abraham Benisti, bore signs of torture and that he had been shot twice and strangled.

The Organization of the Oppressed claimed that those executed had all been "spies" for Israel, but a close investigation of their personal backgrounds demonstrates that none of the victims had been involved in Lebanese politics or in the Arab-Israeli conflict. The only thing they had in common was that they were born Jewish and had remained in Muslim-controlled West Beirut after most Lebanese Jews had fled the strife-torn city. The random nature of the attacks on the helpless Jews was made clear in a statement by the group on December 28, 1985, warning that unless all its demands against Israel were met, it would kill not only those it had already kidnapped but would strike against other Jews "on whom we may lay our hands."

Among the best known and most highly respected of the Jewish victims was Dr. Elie Hallak, a pediatrician who was called "the doctor of the poor" because he often treated without fee needy Lebanese and Palestinian patients, irrespective of their religious or political affiliation. In a poignant public challenge to the kidnappers, his wife, Rachel, described his benevolent career and the unsuccessful efforts by his many friends to secure his release. Her open letter was published in the Lebanese press and in *Le Monde* (Paris), March 5, 1986.

Well-placed Lebanese sources believe that the motivation of the Organization of the Oppressed was not purely ideological or political. More mundane motives were also at work: The poor Shiites coveted the homes and communal properties of the once prosperous Jewish community and sought to pressure the kidnap victims— who included the president, vice-president, and secretary of the Jewish community—to turn over title to property and bank accounts to persons designated by the terrorists.

This radical Shiite band claimed to have executed a total of nine Jews whom it had abducted, but, as noted, only three bodies were ever recovered. The terrorists refused to release the bodies of any of the later victims, declaring that they would not do so until Israel withdrew from "all occupied territory." In a statement published in *An Nahar* on June 20, 1987, the Organization of the Oppressed reiterated its refusal to release the bodies and vowed to "continue to chase the Zionist invaders and their agents wherever they may be until this cancerous gland is uprooted."

Until a few years ago there were persistent but unconfirmed reports that Isaac Sasson, 72, president of the Jewish community, who was kidnapped in 1985, and some other Jewish hostages might still be alive. Salim Jammous, 65, the secretary-general of the Lebanese Jewish community, was abducted near the main synagogue in the Wadi Abu Jamil section of West Beirut on August 15, 1984. Since his body has not been found and no announcement has been made of his death, his sister continues to believe that he may still be alive. She has continued to write letters to the press urging that his fate be placed on the table in the current Syrian-Israeli and Lebanese-Israeli peace talks. In Paris, Roger Pinto in 1993 continued to urge European governments to press for information on the Jewish hostages.

In a statement on August 11, 1991, President George Bush underscored that "there will not be—there can't be—totally normalized relations [with Iran or Syria] as long as people are held against their will." Mr. Bush called on those with influence "to work for the release of all hostages, regardless of their nationality." The president also called for "an accounting of those who may have died while in captivity."

The relatives of the missing Lebanese Jews believe Syrian president Assad can play a crucial role in bringing this about. Syria's effective control of Lebanon was demonstrated when Syrian security forces warned that they would attack the head-quarters of radical Shiite groups unless the terrorists promptly released Jérôme Leyraud, a French doctor who had been kidnapped on August 8, 1991, in Beirut, and threatened with death by a new terrorist group opposing additional hostage releases. Dr. Leyraud was freed within 60 hours.

To keep the issue before the public, Roger Pinto organized a demonstration in Paris on June 7, 1993, which was attended by several leading French personalities and relatives of the Lebanese Jewish hostages. On July 7, Pinto and Bernard Gahnassia, secretary-general of Siona, the French Zionist group, met with Cornélio Somaruga, president of the International Committee of the Red Cross, in Geneva, and asked him to pursue the question of the fate of the Jewish kidnap victims with the Lebanese, Syrian, and Iranian governments. It remains to be seen whether the recent rapprochement between the United States and Syria and the hoped-for peace agreements between Syria and Israel and between Israel and the Syrian-dominated Lebanese government will finally bring an end to the ordeal of the Lebanese Jewish hostages and their families.

GEORGE E. GRUEN

World Jewish Population, 1992

T HIS ARTICLE PRESENTS UPDATES, for the end of 1992, of the Jewish population estimates for the various countries of the world.[1] The estimates reflect some of the results of a prolonged and ongoing effort to study scientifically the demography of contemporary world Jewry.[2] Data collection and comparative research have benefited from the collaboration of scholars and institutions in many countries, including replies to direct inquiries regarding current estimates. It should be emphasized, however, that the elaboration of a worldwide set of estimates for the Jewish populations of the various countries is beset with difficulties and uncertainties.

Since the end of the 1980s, important geopolitical changes have affected the world scene, particularly in Eastern Europe. The major event was the political breakup of the Soviet Union into 15 independent states. The Jewish population has been sensitive to these changes, large-scale emigration from the former USSR being the most visible effect. In the present article, each republic of the former USSR is included as a separate country and listed in Europe or Asia, as appropriate. Similarly, new estimates appear for the several successor states of the former Czechoslovakia and Yugoslavia.

In spite of the increased fragmentation of the global system of nations, about 94 percent of world Jewry is concentrated in ten countries. The aggregate of these major Jewish population centers virtually determines the assessment of the size of total world Jewry, estimated at 12.9 million persons at the end of 1992. The country figures for 1992 were updated from those for 1991 in accordance with the known or estimated changes in the interval—migrations, vital events (births and deaths), and identificational changes (accessions and secessions). In addition, corrections were introduced in the light of newly accrued information on Jewish populations. Corresponding corrections were also applied retrospectively to the 1991 figures, which appear below in revised summary (see table 1), so as to allow adequate comparison with the 1992 estimates.

---

[1]The previous estimates, as of 1991, were published in AJYB 1993, vol. 93, pp. 423–45.

[2]Many of these activities are carried out by, or in coordination with, the Division of Jewish Demography and Statistics at the A. Harman Institute of Contemporary Jewry, the Hebrew University of Jerusalem. The authors acknowledge with thanks the collaboration of the many institutions and individuals in the different countries who have supplied information for this update.

In recent years, new data and estimates have become available for the Jewish populations of several countries. Some of this ongoing research is part of a coordinated effort to update the profile of world Jewry that began at the outset of the 1990s.[3] Two important sources that have yielded results on major Jewish populations are the official population census of the Soviet Union held in 1989 and the National Jewish Population Survey (NJPS) in the United States completed in 1990. The respective results basically confirmed the estimates we had reported in previous AJYB volumes and, perhaps more importantly, our interpretation of the trends now prevailing in the demography of world Jewry.[4] More recently, results of national censuses were released for Canada and Australia, and Jewish sociodemographic surveys were completed in South Africa and Mexico. While allowing for improved population estimates for the year 1992 under review here, these new data highlight the increasing complexity of the sociodemographic and identificational processes underlying the definition of Jewish populations—hence the estimates of their sizes— the more so at a time of enhanced international migration.

A full review of the major conceptual problems appeared in the 1992 volume of AJYB and will only be briefly summarized here. Users of population estimates should be aware of these difficulties and of the consequent limitations of the estimates.

Presentation of Data

The detailed estimates of Jewish population distribution in each continent and country (tables 2–7 below) aim at the concept of "core" Jewish population. We define the core Jewish population as the aggregate of all those who, when asked, identify themselves as such; or, if the respondent is a different person in the same household, are identified by him/her as Jews. The core Jewish population includes all those who converted to Judaism or joined the Jewish group informally. It excludes those of Jewish descent who formally adopted another religion, as well as other Jewish individuals who did not convert out but currently disclaim being Jewish. The so-called extended or enlarged Jewish populations—including Jews, ex-Jews, non-Jews of Jewish parentage, and the respective non-Jewish household members—may result in significantly higher estimates (not reported below).

---

[3]Following the 1987 international conference on Jewish population problems, sponsored by the major Jewish organizations worldwide, an International Scientific Advisory Committee (ISAC) was established. Cochaired by Dr. Roberto Bachi of the Hebrew University and Dr. Sidney Goldstein of Brown University, ISAC coordinates and monitors Jewish population data collection internationally. See Sergio DellaPergola and Leah Cohen, eds., *World Jewish Population: Trends and Policies* (Jerusalem, 1992).

[4]See U.O. Schmelz, "Jewish Survival: The Demographic Factors," AJYB 1981, vol. 81, pp. 61–117; U.O. Schmelz, *Aging of World Jewry* (Jerusalem, 1984); Sergio DellaPergola, "Israel and World Jewish Population: A Core-Periphery Perspective," in *Population and Social Change in Israel*, ed. C. Goldscheider (Boulder, 1992), pp. 39–63.

We provide separate figures for each country with at least 100 resident core Jews. Residual estimates of Jews living in other smaller communities supplement some of the continental totals. For each of the reported countries, the four columns in the following tables provide the United Nations estimate of midyear 1993 total population,[5] the estimated end-1992 Jewish population, the proportion of Jews per 1,000 of total population, and a rating of the accuracy of the Jewish population estimate.

There is wide variation in the quality of the Jewish population estimates for different countries. For many Diaspora countries it would be best to indicate a range (minimum-maximum) rather than a definite figure for the number of Jews. It would be confusing, however, for the reader to be confronted with a long list of ranges; this would also complicate the regional and world totals. Yet, the figures actually indicated for most of the Diaspora communities should be understood as being the central value of the plausible range of the respective core Jewish populations. The relative magnitude of this range varies inversely to the accuracy of the estimate.

ACCURACY RATING

The three main elements that affect the accuracy of each estimate are the nature and quality of the base data, the recency of the base data, and the method of updating. A simple code combining these elements is used to provide a general evaluation of the reliability of the Jewish population figures reported in the detailed tables below. The code indicates different quality levels of the reported estimates: (A) base figure derived from countrywide census or relatively reliable Jewish population survey; updated on the basis of full or partial information on Jewish population movements in the respective country during the intervening period; (B) base figure derived from less accurate but recent countrywide Jewish population investigation; partial information on population movements in the intervening period; (C) base figure derived from less recent sources, and/or unsatisfactory or partial coverage of Jewish population in the particular country; updating according to demographic information illustrative of regional demographic trends; (D) base figure essentially conjectural; no reliable updating procedure. In categories (A), (B), and (C), the years in which the base figures or important partial updates were obtained are also stated. For countries whose Jewish population estimate of 1992 was not only updated but also revised in the light of improved information, the sign "X" is appended to the accuracy rating.

---

[5]See United Nations, Department for Economic and Social Information and Policy Analysis, *World Population Prospects; The 1992 Revision* (New York, 1993). Estimated total populations for the new successor states of the former USSR, Czechoslovakia, and Yugoslavia were obtained from Michel Louis Levy, "Tous les pays du monde," *Population et Sociétés*, no. 282 (Paris, 1993).

Distribution of World Jewish Population by Major Regions

Table 1 gives an overall picture of Jewish population for the end of 1992 as compared to 1991. For 1991 the originally published estimates are presented along with somewhat revised figures that take into account, retrospectively, the corrections made in 1992 in certain country estimates, in the light of improved information. These corrections resulted in a net increase in world Jewry's 1991 estimated size by 65,500. This change resulted from upward corrections for Canada (+46,000), Mexico (+2,000), Russia (+19,000), Azerbaijan (+10,000), and Ethiopia (+3,000); and downward corrections for Iran (−1,000) and South Africa (−13,500). Some explanations are given below for the countries whose estimates were revised. The geographic breakdown in table 1 is slightly different from that in previous AJYB volumes, the main change being the division of the former USSR into its European and Asian components. In addition, due to the nearly complete emigration of Jews from Ethiopia, we withdrew the previous "Central Africa" category and incorporated the tiny residual in North Africa. The 1991 data, too, are presented here in the new format.

The size of world Jewry at the end of 1992 is assessed at 12,922,000. According to the revised figures, between 1991 and 1992 there was an estimated gain of 7,000 people, or about +0.1 percent. Despite all the imperfections in the estimates, it is clear that world Jewry has reached "zero population growth," with the natural increase in Israel barely compensating for the demographic decline in the Diaspora.

The number of Jews in Israel rose from a figure of 4,144, 600 in 1991 to 4,242,500 at the end of 1992, an increase of 97,900 people, or 2.4 percent. In contrast, the estimated Jewish population in the Diaspora declined from 8,770,400 (according to the revised figures) to 8,679,500—a decrease of 90,900 people, or 1.1 percent. These changes primarily reflect the continuing Jewish emigration from the former USSR. In 1992, the Israel-Diaspora estimated net migratory balance amounted to a gain of about 49,500 Jews for Israel.[6] Internal demographic evolution produced further growth among the Jewish population in Israel and further decline in the Diaspora. Recently, instances of accession or "return" to Judaism can be observed in connection with the emigration process from Eastern Europe and the comprehensive provisions of the Israeli Law of Return (*Hok Hashvut*). The Law of Return grants immigrant rights to all current Jews and to their Jewish or non-Jewish spouses, children, and grandchildren, as well as to the spouses of such children and grandchildren. The return or first-time accession to Judaism of some of such previously unincluded or unidentified individuals appears to have contributed to a moderate slowing down in the pace of decline of the relevant Diaspora Jewish populations, and some further gains to the Jewish population in Israel.

Just about half of the world's Jews reside in the Americas, with over 46 percent

---

[6]Israel Central Bureau of Statistics, *Statistical Abstract of Israel 1993*, no. 44 (Jerusalem, 1993), p. 44.

TABLE 1. ESTIMATED JEWISH POPULATION, BY CONTINENTS AND MAJOR GEO-
GRAPHICAL REGIONS, 1991 AND 1992

Region	1991			1992		% Change 1991–1992
	Original	Revised				
	Abs. N.	Abs. N.	Percent	Abs. N.	Percent	
World	12,849,500	12,915,000	100.0	12,922,000	100.0	+0.1
Diaspora	8,704,900	8,770,400	67.9	8,679,500	67.2	−1.1
Israel	4,144,600	4,144,600	32.1	4,242,500	32.8	+2.4
America, Total	6,319,000	6,367,000	49.3	6,409,700	49.6	+0.6
North[a]	5,885,000	5,931,000	45.9	5,976,000	46.2	+0.7
Central	49,700	51,700	0.4	51,700	0.4	—
South	384,300	384,300	3.0	382,000	3.0	−0.6
Europe, Total	2,009,800	2,028,800	15.8	1,924,800	14.9	−5.1
EC	986,900	986,900	7.6	992,300	7.7	+0.5
Other West	44,000	44,000	0.3	44,000	0.4	—
Former USSR[b]	868,100	887,100	6.9	780,400	6.0	−12.1
Other East and Balkans[b]	110,800	110,800	0.9	108,100	0.8	−2.4
Asia, Total	4,298,100	4,307,100	33.3	4,378,600	33.9	+1.7
Israel	4,144,600	4,144,600	32.1	4,242,500	32.8	+2.4
Former USSR[b]	121,900	131,900	1.0	109,600	0.9	−16.9
Other[b]	31,600	30,600	0.2	26,500	0.2	−13.4
Africa, Total	129,000	118,500	0.9	114,300	0.9	−3.5
North[c]	11,900	14,900	0.1	11,200	0.1	−24.8
South[d]	117,100	103,600	0.8	103,100	0.8	−0.5
Oceania	93,600	93,600	0.7	94,600	0.7	+1.1

a U.S.A. and Canada.
b The Asian regions of Russia and Turkey are included in Europe.
c Including Ethiopia.
d South Africa, Zimbabwe, and other sub-Saharan countries.

in North America. One-third live in Asia—including the Asian republics of the
former USSR (but not the Asian parts of the Russian Republic and Turkey)—most
of them in Israel. Europe, including the Asian territories of the Russian Republic
and Turkey, accounts for about 15 percent of the total. Less than 2 percent of the

world's Jews live in Africa and Oceania. Among the major geographical regions listed in table 1, the number of Jews in Israel—and, consequently, in total Asia—increased in 1992. Moderate Jewish population gains were also estimated for North America, the European Community, and Oceania. South America, Eastern Europe, Asian countries out of Israel, and Africa sustained decreases in Jewish population size.

World Jewry constitutes about 2.3 per 1,000 of the world's total population. One in about 435 people in the world is a Jew.

Individual Countries

THE AMERICAS

In 1992 the total number of Jews in the American continents was estimated at over 6.4 million. The overwhelming majority (93 percent) resided in the United States and Canada, less than 1 percent lived in Central America (including Mexico), and about 6 percent lived in South America—with Argentina and Brazil the largest Jewish communities (see table 2).

United States. The 1989–1990 National Jewish Population Survey (NJPS), sponsored by the Council of Jewish Federations and the North American Jewish Data Bank (NAJDB), provided new benchmark information about the size and characteristics of U.S. Jewry—the largest Jewish population in the world—and the basis for subsequent updates.[7] According to the official report of the results of this important national sample study, the core Jewish population in the United States comprised 5,515,000 persons in the summer of 1990. Of these, 185,000 were not born or raised as Jews but currently identified with Judaism. An estimated 210,000 persons, not included in the previous figures, were born or raised as Jews but had converted to another religion. A further 1,115,000 people—thereof 415,000 adults and 700,000 children below age 18—were of Jewish parentage but had not themselves been raised as Jews and declared a religion other than Judaism at the time of the survey. All together, these various groups formed an extended Jewish population of 6,840,000. NJPS also covered 1,350,000 non-Jewish-born members of eligible (Jewish or mixed) households. The study's enlarged Jewish population thus consisted of about 8,200,000 persons. The 1990 Jewish population estimates are within

---

[7]The 1989–1990 National Jewish Population Survey was conducted under the auspices of the Council of Jewish Federations with the supervision of a National Technical Advisory Committee chaired by Dr. Sidney Goldstein of Brown University. Dr. Barry Kosmin of the North American Jewish Data Bank and City University of New York Graduate Center directed the study. See Barry A. Kosmin, Sidney Goldstein, Joseph Waksberg, Nava Lerer, Ariella Keysar, and Jeffrey Scheckner, *Highlights of the CJF 1990 National Jewish Population Survey* (New York, 1991); and Sidney Goldstein, "Profile of American Jewry: Insights from the 1990 National Jewish Population Survey," AJYB 1992, vol. 92, pp. 77–173.

TABLE 2. ESTIMATED JEWISH POPULATION DISTRIBUTION IN THE AMERICAS, END 1992

Country	Total Population	Jewish Population	Jews per 1,000 Population	Accuracy Rating
Canada	27,755,000	356,000	12.8	A 1991
United States	257,840,000	5,620,000	21.8	A 1990
Total North America	285,721,000ᵃ	5,976,000	20.9	
Bahamas	268,000	300	1.1	D
Costa Rica	3,270,000	2,000	0.6	C 1986
Cuba	10,907,000	700	0.1	C 1990
Dominican Republic	7,621,000	100	0.0	D
Guatemala	10,029,000	800	0.1	C 1983
Jamaica	2,495,000	300	0.1	B 1988
Mexico	89,998,000	40,000	0.4	A 1991 X
Netherlands Antilles	175,000	400	2.3	D
Panama	2,563,000	5,000	2.0	C 1990
Puerto Rico	3,626,000	1,500	0.4	C 1990
Virgin Islands	107,000	300	2.8	C 1986
Other	25,330,000	300	0.0	D
Total Central America	156,389,000	51,700	0.3	
Argentina	33,487,000	211,000	6.4	C 1990
Bolivia	7,705,000	700	0.1	B 1990
Brazil	156,578,000	100,000	0.6	C 1980
Chile	13,813,000	15,000	1.1	C 1988
Colombia	33,985,000	6,500	0.2	C 1986
Ecuador	11,310,000	900	0.1	C 1985
Paraguay	4,643,000	900	0.2	B 1990
Peru	22,913,000	3,000	0.1	B 1988
Suriname	446,000	200	0.5	B 1986
Uruguay	3,149,000	23,800	7.7	C 1990
Venezuela	20,618,000	20,000	1.0	C 1989
Total South America	309,574,000ᵃ	382,000	1.3	
Total	751,684,000	6,409,700	8.5	

a Including countries not listed separately.

the range of a sampling error of plus or minus 3.5 percent.[8] This means a range between 5.3 and 5.7 million for the core Jewish population in 1990.

Since 1990, the international migration balance of U.S. Jewry should have generated an actual increase in Jewish population size. According to HIAS (Hebrew Immigrant Aid Society), the main agency involved in assisting Jewish migration from the former USSR to the United States, the number of assisted migrants was 32,714 in 1990, 35,568 in 1991, and 46,083 in 1992.[9] These figures include a small number of individuals who settled in Canada, and, more significantly, are based on the "enlarged" Jewish population concept, incorporating non-Jewish members of mixed households. The actual number of former Soviet Jews resettling in the United States was thus somewhat smaller, though still quite substantial.

In retrospect, it can be seen that the influence of international migration between 1971 and 1990 was less than might have been expected. The first National Jewish Population Study, conducted in 1970–71, estimated the U.S. Jewish population at 5.4 million; the 1990 NJPS estimated a core Jewish population of 5.5 million, a difference of 100,000. However, since Jewish immigration contributed 200,000–300,000 in this period, it is clear that the balance of other factors of core population change over that whole 20-year period must have been negative. First detailed analyses of the new NJPS data actually provide evidence of a variety of contributing factors: low levels of Jewish fertility and the "effectively Jewish" birthrate, increasing aging of the Jewish population, increasing outmarriage rate, declining rate of conversion to Judaism (or "choosing" Judaism), rather low proportions of children of mixed marriages being identified as Jewish, and a growing tendency to adopt non-Jewish rituals.[10] A temporary increase in the Jewish birthrate occurred during the late 1980s, because the large cohorts born during the "baby boom" of the 1950s and early 1960s were in the main procreative ages; however, this echo effect is about to fade away, as the much smaller cohorts born since the late 1960s reach the stage of parenthood.

Taking this evidence into account, our estimate of U.S. Jewish population size at the end of 1992 starts from the NJPS benchmark core Jewish population of 5,515,000, and attempts to account for Jewish population changes that occurred in the latter part of 1990—after completion of NJPS—in 1991, and in 1992. Assuming a total net migration gain of about 60,000 Jews from the USSR, Israel, and other origins for the whole of 1990, we apportioned 20,000 to the final months of that year.

[8]See Kosmin et al., p. 39.

[9]See HIAS, *Annual Report 1992* (New York, 1993). See also Barry R. Chiswick, "Soviet Jews in the United States: An Analysis of Their Linguistic and Economic Adjustment," *Economic Quarterly*, July 1991, no. 148, pp. 188–211 (Hebrew), and *International Migration Review*, 1993 (English).

[10]See Goldstein, AJYB 1992; see also U.O. Schmelz and Sergio DellaPergola, *Basic Trends in U.S. Jewish Demography* (American Jewish Committee, New York, 1988); and Sergio DellaPergola, "New Data on Demography and Identification Among Jews in the U.S.: Trends, Inconsistencies and Disagreements," *Contemporary Jewry*, vol. 12, 1992, pp. 67–97.

A further 40,000 were added for 1991, and 45,000 for 1992, to account for immigration net of emigration, as well as some further attrition based on current marriage, fertility, and age-composition trends in the U.S. core Jewish population. We thus suggest an estimate of 5,620,000 Jews in the United States at the end of 1992. This estimate is still conditional on further detailed scrutiny and interpretation of the NJPS findings.

The research team of the North American Jewish Data Bank, which was responsible for the primary handling of NJPS data files, has also continued its yearly compilation of local Jewish population estimates. These are reported elsewhere in this volume.[11] NAJDB estimated the U.S. Jewish population in 1986 at 5,814,000, including "under 2 percent" non-Jewish household members. This was very close to our own pre-NJPS estimate of 5,700,000. The NAJDB estimate was updated as follows: 1987—5,943,700; 1988—5,935,000; 1989—5,944,000; 1990—5,981,000; 1991—5,798,000. These changes in the main do not reflect actual sudden growth or decline, but rather corrections and adaptations made in the figures for several local communities—some of them in the light of NJPS regional results, others based on new local community studies. It should be realized that compilations of local estimates, even if as painstaking as in the case of the NAJDB, are subject to a great many local biases and tend to fall behind the actual pace of national trends. This is especially true in a context of vigorous internal migrations, as in the United States. In our view, the new NJPS figure, in spite of sample-survey biases, provides a more reliable national Jewish population baseline.

Canada. Results of the 1991 Canadian census were released, providing a new baseline for the estimate of the local Jewish population. As customary in Canada, the census included questions on both religion and ethnic origin, besides information on year of immigration of the foreign-born and languages. An intensive special processing of the data concerning Jews was produced by a joint team of researchers from McGill University's Consortium for Ethnicity and Strategic Social Planning, Statistics Canada, and Council of Jewish Federations Canada, directed by Prof. Jim Torczyner.[12] The new census enumerated 318,070 Jews according to religion; of these, 281,680 also reported being Jewish by ethnicity (as one of up to four options to the latter question), while 36,390 reported one or more other ethnic origins. Another 38,245 persons reported no religion and a Jewish ethnic origin, again as one of up to four options. After due allowance is made for the latter group, a total core Jewish population of 356,315 was estimated for 1991—an increase of 44,255 (14.2 percent) over the corresponding estimate of 312,060 from the 1981 census. A

[11]The first in a new series of yearly compilations of local U.S. Jewish population estimates appeared in Barry A. Kosmin, Paul Ritterband, and Jeffrey Scheckner, "Jewish Population in the United States, 1986," AJYB 1987, vol. 87, pp. 164–91. The 1993 update appears elsewhere in the present volume.

[12]Jim L. Torczyner, Shari L. Brotman, Kathy Viragh, Gustave J. Goldmann, *Demographic Challenges Facing Canadian Jewry: Initial Findings from the 1991 Census* (Montreal, 1993).

further 49,640 Canadians who reported being Jewish by ethnic origin but identified with another religion (such as Catholic, Anglican, etc.) were not included in the 1991 core estimate. Including them would produce an extended Jewish population of 405,955.

In comparison with the 1981 census, the 1991 data revealed an increase of 21,645 (7.3 percent) in the number of Jews defined by religion. A more significant increase occurred among those reporting a Jewish ethnicity with no religious preference: 22,610 persons, or more than twice (+ 144.6 percent) as many as in 1981. The increase was comparatively even larger among those reporting a partially Jewish ethnic ancestry and among ethnic Jews with another religion. Besides actual demographic and identificational trends, changes in the wording of the relevant questions in the two censuses may have influenced these variations in the size of both the core and the ethnically (or, in our terminology, extended) Jewish population of Canada.[13]

Most of the 1981–1991 Jewish population increase was due to international migration: out of the total increase of 44,255 core Jews, 25,895 (59 percent) appear to have arrived in Canada since 1981. The principal country of origin is the former USSR (6,230), followed by Israel (4,975), the United States (3,630), and South Africa (2,855).[14] Practically all the rest of the Jewish population growth consists of ethnic Jews who did not report a religion, including many whose reported Jewish ethnicity is only one among several others. The latter are quite certainly children of intermarriages, whose frequency indeed increased in Canada by about 33 percent over the 1980s.[15] All this implies that the 1981–1991 demographic balance of the Jewish population living in Canada in 1981 was close to zero or slightly negative. Taking into account as well the increasingly aged Jewish population structure, it is suggested that since the 1991 census, the continuing migratory surplus may have roughly offset the probably negative balance of internal evolution. Thus, for the end of 1992, we adopted an estimated round figure of 356,000—sufficient to make Canada the world's fifth largest Jewish population.

Central America. A Jewish-sponsored population survey of the Jews in the Mexico City metropolitan area was completed in 1991.[16] The results point to a community definitely less affected than others in the Diaspora by the common trends of

---

[13]The results of preceding censuses can be found in Statistics Canada, *1981 Census of Canada; Population: Ethnic Origin; Religion* (Ottawa, 1983, 1984); and Statistics Canada, *Population by Ethnic Origin, 1986 Census: Canada, Provinces and Territories and Census Metropolitan Areas* (Ottawa, 1988).

[14]See Torczyner et al., *Demographic Challenges. . ., Appendices,* p. 22.

[15]See Torczyner et al., *Demographic Challenges. . .,* p. 20.

[16]Sergio DellaPergola and Susana Lerner, *Perfil demografico, social y cultural de la poblacion judia de Mexico, 1991; Resultados segun comunidades de muestreo, Informe sumario* (Jerusalem-Mexico, 1993). The project, conducted cooperatively by the Centro de Estudios Urbanos y de Desarrollo Urbano (CEDDU), El Colegio de Mexico, and the Division of Jewish Demography and Statistics of the A. Harman Institute of Contemporary Jewry, The Hebrew University, was sponsored by the Asociacion Mexicana de Amigos de la Universisad Hebrea de Jerusalen.

low fertility, intermarriage, and aging. Some comparatively more traditional sectors in the Jewish community still contribute a current surplus of births over deaths, and overall—thanks also to some immigration—the Jewish population has been quite stable or even moderately increasing. The new Jewish population estimate was put at 37,500 in the Mexico City metropolitan area and at 40,000 nationally. This amounts to an upward revision of 2,000 compared with our last estimate. Official Mexican censuses over the years have provided rather erratic and unreliable Jewish population figures. This was the case with the 1990 census, which came up with a national total of 57,918 Jews (aged five and over). As in the past, most of the problem derived from unacceptably high figures for peripheral states. The new census figures for the Mexico City metropolitan area (33,932 Jews—aged five and over—in the Federal District and State of Mexico) are quite close—in fact are slightly below—our survey's estimates. Panama's Jewish population—the second largest in Central America—is estimated at about 5,000.

South America.[17] The Jewish population of Argentina, the largest in that geographical region, is marked by a negative balance of internal evolution. A number of local surveys conducted at the initiative of the Asociacion Mutual Israelita Argentina—AMIA, the central Jewish community organization—consistently point to growing aging.[18] Since the 1960s, while the pace of emigration and return migration was significantly affected by the nature of economic and political trends in the country, the balance of external migrations was generally negative. Accordingly, the estimate for Argentinian Jewry was reduced from 213,000 in 1991 to 211,000 in 1992.

In Brazil, the official population census of 1980 showed a figure of 91,795 Jews. Since it is possible that some otherwise identifying Jews failed to declare themselves as such in the census, a corrected estimate of 100,000 was adopted for 1980 and has been kept unchanged through 1992, assuming that the overall balance of Jewish vital events and external migrations was close to zero. The national figure of approximately 100,000 fits the admittedly rough estimates that are available for the size of local Jewish communities in Brazil.

On the strength of fragmentary information available, the estimates for Uruguay and Peru were slightly reduced, while those for Venezuela, Chile, and Colombia were not changed.

---

[17]For a more detailed discussion of the region's Jewish population trends, see U.O. Schmelz and Sergio DellaPergola, "The Demography of Latin American Jewry," AJYB 1985, vol. 85, pp. 51–102; and Sergio DellaPergola, "Demographic Trends of Latin American Jewry," in J. Laikin Elkin and G.W. Merks, eds., *The Jewish Presence in Latin America* (Boston, 1987), pp. 85–133.

[18]Rosa N. Geldstein, *Censo de la Poblacion Judia de la ciudad de Salta, 1986; Informe final* (Buenos Aires, 1988); Yacov Rubel, *Los Judios de Villa Crespo y Almagro: Perfil Sociodemografico* (Buenos Aires, 1989); Yacov Rubel and Mario Toer, *Censo de la Poblacion Judia de Rosario, 1990* (Buenos Aires, 1992).

EUROPE

Of the approximately two million Jews estimated to be in Europe at the end of 1992, 54 percent lived in Western Europe and 46 percent in Eastern Europe and the Balkan countries—including the Asian territories of the Russian Republic and Turkey (see table 3). In 1992 Europe lost 5.1 percent of its estimated Jewish population, mainly through the continuing emigration from the former USSR. As a consequence, for the first time, literally, in many centuries, there are now more Jews in Western than in Eastern Europe.

European Community. At the end of 1992, the 12 countries that form the European Community (EC) had an estimated combined Jewish population of about one million. Overall, only very minor change was recorded as against the 1991 estimate, although different trends affected the Jewish population in each member country.[19]

The estimated size of French Jewry has been assessed for several years at 530,000. Since the breakup of the USSR, France has had the third largest Jewish population in the world, after the United States and Israel. Monitoring the plausible trends of both the internal evolution and external migrations of Jews in France suggests little net change in Jewish population size since the major survey that was taken in the 1970s.[20] A study conducted in 1988 at the initiative of the Fonds Social Juif Unifié (FSJU) confirmed the basic demographic stability of French Jewry.[21]

Periodic reestimations of the size of British Jewry are carried out by the Community Research Unit (CRU) of the Board of Deputies. Based on an analysis of Jewish deaths during 1975–1979, the population baseline for 1977 was set at 336,000 with a margin of error of plus or minus 34,000.[22] The vital statistical records regularly compiled by the CRU show an excess of deaths over births in the range of about 1,000–1,500 a year. Further attrition derives from emigration and some assimilatory losses. Indeed, a study of Jewish synagogue membership indicated a decline of over 7 percent between 1983 and 1990.[23] A new national estimate, mainly based on an evaluation of Jewish death records in the period 1984–1988, was recently completed by the CRU, suggesting an estimate of 308,000 for 1986.[24] Allowing for a further continuation of these well-established trends, we adopted a provisional revised

---

[19]See Sergio DellaPergola, "Jews in the European Community: Sociodemographic Trends and Challenges," AJYB 1993, vol. 93, pp. 25–82.

[20]Doris Bensimon and Sergio DellaPergola, *La population juive de France: socio-démographie et identité* (Jerusalem and Paris, 1984).

[21]Erik H. Cohen, *L'Etude et l'éducation juive en France ou l'avenir d'une communauté* (Paris, 1991).

[22]Steven Haberman, Barry A. Kosmin, and Caren Levy, "Mortality Patterns of British Jews 1975–79: Insights and Applications for the Size and Structure of British Jewry," *Journal of the Royal Statistical Society*, ser. A, 146, pt. 3, 1983, pp. 294–310.

[23]Marlena Schmool and Frances Cohen, *British Synagogue Membership in 1990* (London, 1991).

[24]Steven Haberman and Marlena Schmool, *Estimates of British Jewish Population 1984–88* (London, 1993).

TABLE 3. ESTIMATED JEWISH POPULATION DISTRIBUTION IN EUROPE, END 1992

Country	Total Population	Jewish Population	Jews per 1,000 Population	Accuracy Rating
Belgium	10,010,000	31,800	3.2	C 1987
Denmark	5,169,000	6,400	1.2	C 1990
France[a]	57,379,000	530,000	9.2	C 1990
Germany	80,606,000	50,000	0.6	C 1990
Greece	10,208,000	4,800	0.5	B 1990
Ireland	3,481,000	1,800	0.5	B 1990
Italy	57,826,000	31,000	0.5	B 1990
Luxembourg	380,000	600	1.6	B 1990
Netherlands	15,270,000	25,600	1.7	C 1990
Portugal	9,870,000	300	0.0	B 1986
Spain	39,153,000	12,000	0.3	D
United Kingdom	58,039,000	298,000	5.1	B 1991
Total European Community	347,391,000	992,300	2.9	
Austria	7,805,000	7,000	0.9	C 1990
Finland	5,020,000	1,300	0.3	B 1990
Gibraltar	31,000	600	19.4	C 1981
Norway	4,310,000	1,000	0.2	B 1987
Sweden	8,692,000	15,000	1.7	C 1990
Switzerland	6,862,000	19,000	2.8	C 1980
Other	771,000	100	0.1	D
Total other West Europe	33,491,000	44,000	1.3	
Belarus	10,300,000	46,600	4.5	B 1992
Estonia	1,600,000	3,400	2.1	A 1992
Latvia	2,600,000	13,500	5.2	B 1992
Lithuania	3,800,000	6,500	1.7	B 1992
Moldova	4,400,000	19,400	4.4	B 1992
Russia[b]	149,000,000	415,000	2.8	B 1992 X
Ukraine	51,900,000	276,000	5.3	B 1992
Total former USSR in Europe	223,600,000	780,400	3.5	

TABLE 3.—(Continued)

Country	Total Population	Jewish Population	Jews per 1,000 Population	Accuracy Rating
Bosnia-Herzegovina	4,000,000	300	0.1	D X
Bulgaria	8,926,000	1,900	0.2	C 1990
Croatia	4,400,000	1,400	0.3	D X
Czech Republic	10,300,000	3,800	0.4	D X
Hungary	10,493,000	56,000	5.3	D
Poland	38,518,000	3,600	0.1	C 1990
Romania	23,377,000	16,000	0.7	B 1988
Slovakia	5,300,000	3,800	0.7	D X
Slovenia	2,000,000	100	0.0	D X
Turkey[b]	59,577,000	19,500	0.3	C 1990
Yugoslavia[c]	9,800,000	1,700	0.2	C 1988 X
Total other East Europe and Balkans	181,991,000[d]	108,100	0.6	
Total	786,473,000	1,924,800	2.4	

a Including Monaco.
b Including Asian regions.
c Serbia and Montenegro.
d Including countries not listed separately.

estimate of 300,000 for 1991 and revised it downward to 298,000 for 1992.

In 1990, Germany was politically reunited. In the former (West) German Federal Republic, the 1987 population census reported 32,319 Jews. Immigration used to compensate for the surplus of deaths over births in this aging Jewish population. Estimates for the small Jewish population in the former (East) German Democratic Republic ranged between 500 and 2,000. While there is a lack of certainty about the number of recent immigrants from the former USSR, according to some reports as many as 20,000 have settled in unified Germany since the end of 1989. Jewish community records reported 27,711 affiliated Jews at the end of 1989, 28,468 in 1990, 33,692 in 1991, and 37,498 in 1992.[25] Allowing for some time lag between immigration and registering with the organized Jewish community, our estimate for unified Germany was 35,000 in 1989, 40,000 in 1990, 42,500 in 1991, and is now increased to 50,000 at the end of 1992, including the unaffiliated.

---

[25]Zentralwohlfartsstelle der Juden in Deutschland, *Vierteljahresmeldung über den Mitgliederstand* (Frankfurt, 1993).

Belgium, Italy, and the Netherlands each have Jewish populations ranging around 30,000. There is a tendency toward internal shrinkage of all these Jewries, but in some instances this is offset by immigration. In Belgium, the size of Jewish population is probably quite stable, owing to the comparatively strong Orthodox section in that community. In Italy, until 1984, Jews were legally bound to affiliate with the local Jewish communities, but then membership in these communities became voluntary. Although most Jews reaffiliated, the new looser legal framework may facilitate the ongoing attrition of the Jewish population.

Other EC member countries have smaller and, overall, slowly declining Jewish populations. An exception may be Spain, whose Jewish population is very tentatively estimated at 12,000.

Other Western Europe. Countries that are not EC members together account for a Jewish population of 44,000. Switzerland's Jews are estimated at below 20,000. Austria's permanent Jewish population is estimated at 7,000. While there is evidence of a negative balance of births and deaths, connected with great aging and frequent outmarriage, immigration may have offset the internal losses. The Jewish populations in Scandinavian countries are, on the whole, numerically rather stable.

Former USSR (European parts). Since 1989, the demographic situation of East European Jewry has been changing rapidly as a consequence of the dramatic geopolitical changes in the region. The economic and political crisis that culminated in the disintegration of the Soviet Union as a state in 1991 generated an upsurge in Jewish emigration. After rapidly reaching a peak in 1990, emigration continued, slightly attenuated, in 1991 and 1992. While mass emigration is an obvious factor in population decrease, the demography of East European Jewry has been characterized for years by very low levels of "effectively Jewish" fertility, frequent outmarriage, and heavy aging. As a result, the shrinking of Jewish population in that region must be comparatively rapid.

Data on nationalities (ethnic groups) from the Soviet Union's last official population census, carried out in January 1989, revealed a total of 1,450,500 Jews.[26] The figure confirmed the declining trend already apparent since the previous three censuses: 2,267,800 Jews in 1959, 2,150,700 in 1970, and 1,810,900 in 1979.

Our reservation about USSR Jewish population figures in previous AJYB volumes bears repeating: some underreporting is not impossible, but it cannot be quantified and should not be exaggerated. One should cautiously keep in mind the possible conflicting effects on census declarations of the prolonged existence of a totalitarian regime: on the one hand, stimulating a preference for other than Jewish nationalities in the various parts of the Soviet Union, especially in connection with mixed marriages; on the other hand, preserving a formal Jewish identification by coercion, through the mandatory registration of nationality on official documents such as passports. Viewed conceptually, the census figures represent the core Jewish

---

[26]Goskomstat SSSR, *Vestnik Statistiki* 10 (1990), pp. 69–71. This figure omits the Tats (Mountain Jews); see below.

population in the USSR. They actually constitute a good example of a large and empirically measured core Jewish population in the Diaspora, consisting of the aggregate of self-identifying Jews. The figures of successive censuses appear to be remarkably consistent with one another and with the known patterns of emigration and internal demographic evolution of the Jewish population in recent decades.[27]

A substantial amount of unpublished data was known to exist about the demographic characteristics and trends of Jews in the former USSR, but it was inaccessible. Systematic analysis of such material has now become possible and is producing important new insights into recent and current trends.[28] The new data confirm the prevalence of very low fertility and birthrates, high frequencies of outmarriage, a preference for non-Jewish nationalities among the children of outmarriages, aging, and a clear surplus of Jewish deaths over Jewish births. These trends are especially visible in the Slavic republics, which hold a large share of the total Jewish population.

The respective figures for the enlarged Jewish population—including all current Jews as well as any other persons of Jewish parentage and their non-Jewish household members—must be substantially higher in a societal context like that of the USSR, which has been characterized by high intermarriage rates for a considerable time. It is not yet possible to provide an actual estimate of this enlarged Jewish population for lack of appropriate data. Nor can any information about the ratio of Jews to non-Jews in an enlarged Jewish population in the USSR be derived from the statistics of immigrants to Israel. Due to the highly self-selective character of *aliyah*, non-Jews have constituted a relatively small minority of all new immigrants from the USSR.[29] It is obvious, though, that the broad provisions of Israel's Law

---

[27]U.O. Schmelz, "New Evidence on Basic Issues in the Demography of Soviet Jews," *Jewish Journal of Sociology* 16, no. 2, 1974, pp. 209–23; Mordechai Altshuler, *Soviet Jewry Since the Second World War: Population and Social Structure* (Westport, 1987).

[28]Viacheslav Konstantinov, "Jewish Population of the USSR on the Eve of the Great Exodus," *Jews and Jewish Topics in the Soviet Union and Eastern Europe* 3 (16), 1991, pp. 5–23; Mordechai Altshuler, "Socio-demographic Profile of Moscow Jews," ibid., pp. 24–40; Mark Tolts, "The Balance of Births and Deaths Among Soviet Jewry," *Jews and Jewish Topics in the Soviet Union and Eastern Europe* 2 (18), 1992, pp. 13–26; Leonid E. Darsky, "Fertility in the USSR; Basic Trends" (paper presented at European Population Conference, Paris, 1991); Mark Tolts, "Jewish Marriages in the USSR: A Demographic Analysis" (Moscow, 1991); Mark Tolts, "Trends in Soviet Jewish Demography Since the Second World War" (paper presented at conference, "From Revolution to Revolution: The Soviet Jews Under the Soviet Regime," Jerusalem, 1992); Mark Kupovetsky, "From Village Settlers to Urban Integration: Jews in the Soviet Union Between the Two World Wars," ibid.

[29]Israel's Ministry of Interior records the religion-nationality of each person, including new immigrants. Such attribution is made on the basis of documentary evidence supplied by the immigrants themselves and checked by competent authorities in Israel. According to data available from the Interior Ministry's Central Population Register, 90.3 percent of all new immigrants from the USSR during the period October 1989-August 1992 were recorded as Jewish. The annual trends clearly point to a growing proportion of non-Jews among the immigrants. See Sergio DellaPergola, "The Demographic Context of the Soviet Aliya," *Jews and Jewish Topics in the Soviet Union and Eastern Europe* 3 (16), 1991, pp. 41–56.

of Return (see above) apply to virtually the maximum emigration pool of self-declared Jews and close non-Jewish relatives. Any of the large figures attributed in recent years to the size of Soviet Jewry, insofar as they are based on demographic reasoning, do not relate to the core but to various measures of an enlarged Jewish population. The evidence also suggests that in the USSR core Jews constitute a smaller share of the total enlarged Jewish population than in some Western countries, such as the United States.

Just as the number of declared Jews evolved consistently between censuses, the number of persons of Jewish descent who preferred not to be identified as Jews was rather consistent too, at least until 1989. However, the recent political developments, and especially the current emigration urge, have probably led to greater readiness to declare a Jewish self-identification by persons who did not describe themselves as such in the 1989 census. In terms of demographic accounting, these "returnees" imply an actual net increment to the core Jewish population of the USSR, as well as to world Jewry.

With regard to updating the January 1989 census figure to the end of 1992 for each of the republics of the former USSR, Jewish emigration has played the major role among the intervening changes. An estimated 71,000, thereof about 62,000 declared Jews, left in 1989, as against 19,300 in 1988, 8,100 in 1987, and only 7,000 during the whole 1982–1986 period. In 1990, according to Soviet, Israeli, American, and other sources, an estimated 205,000 emigrated from the USSR, including 179,000 declared Jews, the balance being composed of non-Jewish family members. In 1991, 148,000 immigrants from the former USSR arrived in Israel, another 35,000 went to the United States, and possibly 12,000 went to other countries. We estimate that of these total 195,000 migrants, about 159,000 were Jewish. In 1992, 65,000 immigrated to Israel, another 45,000 went to the United States, and possibly up to 20,000 settled elsewhere. Of these 130,000, an estimated 96,000 were Jewish.[30] These apparently declining emigration figures should not be misconstrued: when compared with the similarly declining Jewish population figures for the former USSR, they actually demonstrate a remarkably stable desire to emigrate. At the same time, the heavy deficit of internal population dynamics continued and even intensified due to the great aging that is known to have prevailed for many decades. Aging in the communities of origin was exacerbated by the significantly younger age composition of the emigrants.[31]

---

[30]The figures reported here have been revised from our estimates in previous volumes of AJYB. See Sidney Heitman, "Soviet Emigration in 1990," *Berichte des Bundesinstitut für Ostwissenschaftliche und internationale Studien*, vol. 33, 1991.

[31]Age structures of the Jewish population in the Russian Federal Republic in 1970 and 1979 were reported in Goskomstat SSSR, *Itogi vsesoiuznoi perepisi naseleniia 1970 goda*, vol. 4, table 33 (Moscow, 1973); Goskomstat SSSR, *Itogi vsesoiuznoi perepisi naseleniia 1979 goda*, vol. 4, part 2, table 2 (Moscow, 1989); Goskomstat SSSR, *Itogi vsesoiuznoi perepisi naseleniia 1989 goda* (Moscow, 1991). Age structures of recent Jewish migrants from the USSR to the United States and to Israel appear, respectively, in HIAS, *Statistical Abstract*, vol. 30, no. 4 (New York, 1990), and unpublished data kindly communicated to the authors; Israel Central Bureau

On the strength of these considerations, our estimate of the core Jewish population in the USSR was reduced from the census figure of 1,450,500 at the end of 1988-beginning of 1989 to 1,370,000 at the end of 1989, to 1,157,000 at the end of 1990, and to 990,000 at the end of 1991.[32] The current update, beside taking into account changes during 1992, also corrects for the past omission of Tats, also known as Mountain Jews—a group mostly concentrated in the Caucasus area that enjoys full Jewish status and all the prerogatives granted by Israel's Law of Return. According to the 1989 census, there were 30,669 Tats in the USSR—thereof 19,420 in the Russian republic and 10,239 in Azerbaijan. These numbers, only slightly reduced in consideration of the demographic dynamics in the intervening years, have been integrated in our current estimates.

The Jewish population for the total of the former USSR was estimated at 890,000 at the end of 1992. Of these, 780,400 lived in the European republics and 109,600 in the Asian parts of the former USSR (see below). The pace of change of Jewish population in the different former republics has been significantly different because of variable propensities to emigrate, different rates of assimilation and natural decrease (or, in rare instances, increase), and some geographic redistribution across the different republics. The largest Jewish population in the former USSR's European parts remains in Russia (415,000, including a 19,000 upward revision to take into account the Tats). The Jewish population in Russia, though declining, is currently the fourth largest in the world. Jews in Ukraine, which in recent years has experienced large-scale emigration, are estimated at 276,000. A further 46,000 Jews are estimated to live in Belarus, 19,400 in the Moldovan Republic, and a combined total of 23,400 in the three Baltic states of Latvia, Lithuania, and Estonia.

Other East Europe and Balkans. The Jewish populations in Hungary and Romania and the small remnants in Bulgaria, the Czech and Slovak republics, Poland, and the former Yugoslavia are all reputed to be very overaged and to experience frequent outmarriage. In each of these countries, the recent political transformations have permitted greater autonomy of the organized Jewish communities and their registered membership, including the freedom to emigrate. Although some Jews or persons of Jewish origin have come out in the open after years of hiding their identity, the inevitable numerical decline of Jewish populations in Eastern Europe is reflected in reduced estimates for 1992.

The size of Hungarian Jewry—the largest in Eastern Europe outside the former USSR—is quite insufficiently known. Our estimate of 56,000 only attempts to reflect the declining trend that prevails there, too, according to the available indicators.

---

of Statistics, *Immigration to Israel 1991*, Special Series, no. 944 (Jerusalem, 1993); and Yoel Florsheim, "Immigration to Israel from the Soviet Union in 1990," *Jews and Jewish Topics in the Soviet Union and Eastern Europe* 2 (15), 1991, pp. 5–14.

[32]We greatly appreciate the collaboration of Dr. Mark Tolts, of the A. Harman Institute of Contemporary Jewry at the Hebrew University, in preparing these estimates. See Mark Tolts, "Recent Trends in the Jewish Population of the Former USSR (from the 1989 Census to the End of 1992)," unpublished report (Jerusalem, 1993).

Jewish emigration continued to flow from Romania. The January 1992 census of Romania indicated a Jewish population of 9,100. However, based on the detailed Jewish community records available there, our estimate for the end of 1992 was 16,000. Yugoslavia, torn apart by a devastating civil war and economic crisis, finally split into five separate republics. The overall core Jewish population, reduced through emigration—especially from Bosnia-Herzegovina—was estimated at 3,500 at the end of 1992. Of these, roughly 2,000 lived in the now reduced territory of Yugoslavia (Serbia with Montenegro), 1,400 in Croatia, and less than 100 each in Slovenia, Bosnia, and Macedonia. Czechoslovakia, too, split into two new states, the Czech Republic and Slovakia. The number of Jews in each was tentatively estimated at 3,800.

The Jewish population of Turkey, where a surplus of deaths over births has been reported for several years, is estimated at about 20,000.

ASIA

Israel. Israel accounts for 97 percent of all the nearly 4.4 million Jews in Asia, including the Asian republics of the former USSR, but excluding the Asian territories of the Russian Republic and Turkey (see table 4). By the end of 1992, Israeli Jews constituted nearly 33 percent of total world Jewry. Israel's Jewish population grew in 1992 by about 98,000, or 2.4 percent. This compared with growth rates of 6.2 percent in 1990 and 5 percent in 1991. Although the number of new immigrants declined from 199,500 in 1990 and 176,100 in 1991 to 77,100 in 1992, it was still the seventh highest immigration year in Israel's history. About 51 percent of Jewish population growth in 1992 was due to the net migration balance. The remaining 49 percent of Jewish population growth reflected natural increase, including some cases of immigrants from the former USSR who were previously listed as non-Jews being reregistered as Jews.[33]

Former USSR (Asian parts). The total Jewish population in the Asian republics of the former USSR was estimated at about 109,600 at the end of 1992. The fear of Muslim fundamentalism in Central Asia and the various ethnic conflicts in the Caucasus area caused concern and stimulated high emigration rates. Internal identificational and demographic processes were less a factor of attrition among these Jewish populations than was the case in the European republics of the former USSR. At the beginning of the 1990s, minimal rates of natural increase still existed among the more traditional sections of these Jewish communities, but the conditions were rapidly eroding this residual surplus.[34] Reflecting these trends, the largest commu-

---

[33]Israel Central Bureau of Statistics, *Statistical Abstract of Israel 1993* (Jerusalem, 1993). For a comprehensive review of sociodemographic changes in Israel, see U.O. Schmelz, Sergio DellaPergola, and Uri Avner, "Ethnic Differences Among Israeli Jews: A New Look," AJYB 1990, vol. 90, pp. 3–204; see also Sergio DellaPergola, "Demographic Changes in Israel in the Early 1990s," in *Israel's Social Services 1992–93*, ed. Y. Kop (Jerusalem, 1993), pp. 57–115.

[34]Tolts, "The Balance of Births and Deaths. . . ."

TABLE 4. ESTIMATED JEWISH POPULATION DISTRIBUTION IN ASIA, END 1992[a]

Country	Total Population	Jewish Population	Jews per 1,000 Population	Accuracy Rating
Israel	5,195,900[b]	4,242,500	816.5	A 1992
Armenia	3,500,000	300	0.1	B 1992
Azerbaijan	7,200,000	21,000	2.9	B 1992 X
Georgia	5,500,000	18,000	3.3	B 1992
Kazakhstan	17,200,000	14,500	0.8	B 1992
Kyrgyzstan	4,600,000	3,700	0.8	B 1992
Tajikistan	5,700,000	5,000	0.9	B 1992
Turkmenistan	4,000,000	1,900	0.5	B 1992
Uzbekistan	21,600,000	45,200	2.1	B 1992
Total former USSR in Asia[a]	69,300,000	109,600	1.8	
Hong Kong	5,845,000	1,000	0.2	D
India	896,567,000	4,500	0.0	C 1981
Iran	63,180,000	16,000	0.3	C 1986 X
Iraq	19,918,000	200	0.0	D
Japan	124,959,000	1,000	0.0	C 1988
Korea, South	44,508,000	100	0.0	D
Philippines	66,543,000	100	0.0	C 1988
Singapore	2,798,000	300	0.1	B 1990
Syria	13,762,000	1,200	0.1	C 1992
Thailand	56,868,000	200	0.0	C 1988
Yemen	12,977,000	1,600	0.1	B 1990
Other	1,918,506,100	300	0.0	D
Total other Asia	3,226,431,100	26,500	0.0	
Total	3,300,927,000	4,378,600	1.3	

a Not including Asian regions of Russia and Turkey.
b End 1992.

nity remained in Uzbekistan (45,200), followed by Azerbaijan (21,000)—revised upward by 10,000 to take into account the Tat Mountain Jews who had been omitted from previous estimates—Georgia (18,000), and Kazakhstan (14,500).

Other countries. It is difficult to estimate the Jewish population of Iran for any given date, but it continues to dwindle. Based on partial available estimates from the 1986 population census,[35] the estimate for 1992 was reduced to 16,000. In other Asian countries with small veteran communities—such as India, or several Muslim countries—the Jewish population tends to decline. The reduction was more notable in Syria, where for the first time in many years Jews were officially allowed to emigrate. Very small Jewish communities, partially of a transient character, exist in several countries of Southeast Asia.

AFRICA

Fewer than 115,000 Jews were estimated to remain in Africa at the end of 1992. The Republic of South Africa accounts for 87 percent of total Jews in that continent (see table 5). The last official population census, carried out in March 1991, did not provide a reliable new national figure of Jewish population size. The question on religion was not mandatory, and only about 66,000 people declared themselves as Jewish. In 1980, according to the previous official census, there were about 118,000 Jews among South Africa's white population.[36] Substantial Jewish emigration since then was only partially compensated for by Jewish immigration and return migration of former emigrants. An incipient negative balance of internal changes was producing some further attrition. The results of a Jewish-sponsored survey of the Jewish population in the five major South African urban centers, completed in 1991, confirm the ongoing demographic decline.[37] Based on the new evidence, the estimate for the end of 1992 has been revised to 100,000, substantially below our previous estimate of 114,000.

In recent years, the Jewish community of Ethiopia has been at the center of an international rescue effort. In the course of 1991, the overwhelming majority of Ethiopian Jews—about 20,000 people—were brought to Israel, most of them in a dramatic one-day airlift operation. (A few of these migrants were non-Jewish members of mixed households.) In connection with these events, it was assumed that the size of Ethiopian Jewry could be evaluated on a more accurate basis than previously, and the core Jewish population was estimated at 1,500 at the end of 1991. However, 3,650 immigrants from Ethiopia arrived in Israel in 1992, demonstrating that once again the number of Jews there had been underestimated. Based on the possibility that more Jews may appear requesting to emigrate to Israel, and the as yet unresolved status (and unknown numbers) of the Christian relatives of Ethiopian Jews, an estimate of 1,500 Jews is tentatively suggested for the end of 1992.

---

[35]Kindly provided by Dr. Mehdi Bozorghmehr, Von Grunebaum Center for Near Eastern Studies, University of California, Los Angeles.

[36]Sergio DellaPergola and Allie A. Dubb, "South African Jewry: A Sociodemographic Profile," AJYB 1988, vol. 88, pp. 59–140.

[37]The study was directed by Dr. Allie A. Dubb and supported by the Kaplan Centre for Judaic Studies, University of Cape Town.

TABLE 5. ESTIMATED JEWISH POPULATION DISTRIBUTION IN AFRICA, END 1992

Country	Total Population	Jewish Population	Jews per 1,000 Population	Accuracy Rating
Egypt	56,060,000	200	0.0	C 1988
Ethiopia	54,628,000	1,500	0.0	C 1992 X
Kenya	26,090,000	400	0.0	B 1990
Morocco	26,954,000	7,500	0.3	D
South Africa	40,774,000	100,000	2.5	C 1991 X
Tunisia	8,579,000	2,000	0.2	D
Zaire	41,166,000	400	0.0	C 1990
Zambia	8,885,000	300	0.0	C 1990
Zimbabwe	10,898,000	1,000	0.1	B 1990
Other	427,990,000	1,000	0.0	D
Total	702,024,000	114,300	0.2	

The remnants of Moroccan and Tunisian Jewry tend to shrink slowly through emigration, mostly to France and Canada. It should be pointed out, though, that some Jews have a foothold in Morocco or Tunisia and also in France or other Western countries, and their geographic attribution is therefore uncertain.

OCEANIA

The major country of Jewish residence in Oceania (Australasia) is Australia, where 95 percent of the estimated total of nearly 94,000 Jews live (see table 6). The April 1991 census of Australia, in which the question on religion is optional, enumerated 74,386 declared Jews.[38] This represented an increase of 5,303 (7.7 percent) over the figure reported in the 1986 census. In 1991, over 23 percent of the country's whole population either did not specify their religion or stated explicitly that they had none This large group must be assumed to contain persons who identify in other ways as Jews. However, a survey in Melbourne, Australia's largest Jewish community, revealed that less than 7 percent of the Jewish respondents had not identified as Jews in the census.[39] The Melbourne survey actually depicted a very

[38]Bill Rubinstein, "Census Total for Jews Up by 7.7 Percent; Big Gains in Smaller States," unpublished report (Geelong, Victoria, 1993).
[39]John Goldlust, *The Jews of Melbourne: A Report of the Findings of the Jewish Community Survey, 1991* (Melbourne, 1993).

TABLE 6. ESTIMATED JEWISH POPULATION DISTRIBUTION IN OCEANIA, END 1992

Country	Total Population	Jewish Population	Jews per 1,000 Population	Accuracy Rating
Australia	17,843,000	90,000	5.0	B 1991
New Zealand	3,487,000	4,500	1.3	C 1988
Other	6,617,000	100	0.0	D
Total	27,947,000	94,600	3.4	

stable community, even if one affected by growing acculturation. Australian Jewry has received migratory reinforcements during the last decade, especially from South Africa, the former USSR, and Israel. At the same time, there are demographic patterns with negative effects on Jewish population size, such as strong aging. Taking into account these various factors, we revised our estimate for 1992 to a figure of 90,000—substantially more than the official census returns, but less than would be obtained by adding the full proportion of those who did not report any religion in the census. The Jewish community in New Zealand is estimated at 4,500.

Dispersion and Concentration

Table 7 demonstrates the magnitude of Jewish dispersion. The 91 individual countries listed above as each having at least 100 Jews are scattered over all the continents. In 1992, more than half (57 out of 90 countries) had fewer than 5,000 Jews each. In relative terms, too, the Jews were thinly scattered nearly everywhere in the Diaspora. There is not a single Diaspora country where they amounted even to 25 per 1,000 (2.5 percent) of the total population. In most countries they constituted a far smaller fraction. Only three Diaspora countries had more than 10 per 1,000 (1 percent) Jews in their total population; and only 11 countries had more than 5 Jews per 1,000 (0.5 percent) of population. The respective 11 countries were, in descending order of the proportion, but regardless of the absolute number of their Jews: United States (21.8 per 1,000), Gibraltar (19.4), Canada (12.8), France (9.2), Uruguay (7.7), Argentina (6.4), Ukraine (5.3), Hungary (5.3), Latvia (5.2), United Kingdom (5.1), and Australia (5.0). The other major Diaspora Jewries, having lower proportions of Jews per 1,000 of total population, were Russia (2.8 per 1,000), South Africa (2.5), and Brazil (0.6).

In the State of Israel, by contrast, the Jewish majority amounted to 817 per 1,000 (81.7 percent) in 1992, compared to 819 per 1,000 (81.9 percent) in 1991—not including the Arab population of the administered areas.

TABLE 7. DISTRIBUTION OF THE WORLD'S JEWS, BY NUMBER AND PROPORTION (PER 1,000 POPULATION) IN EACH COUNTRY, END 1992

Number of Jews in Country	Jews per 1,000 Population					
	Total	0.0–0.9	1.0–4.9	5.0–9.9	10.0–24.9	25.0+
			Number of Countries			
Total	91[a]	57	22	8	3	1
100–900	26	21	4	—	1	—
1,000–4,900	25	23	2	—	—	—
5,000–9,900	7	4	3	—	—	—
10,000–49,900	20	7	11	2	—	—
50,000–99,900	3	1	—	2	—	—
100,000–999,900	8	1	2	4	1	—
1,000,000 or more	2	—	—	—	1	1
		Jewish Population Distribution (Absolute Numbers)				
Total	12,922,000[b]	383,800	819,000	1,498,300	5,976,600	4,242,500
100–900	10,000	7,800	1,600	—	600	—
1,000–4,900	58,900	51,000	7,900	—	—	—
5,000–9,900	43,900	26,000	17,900	—	—	—
10,000–49,900	462,900	149,000	276,600	37,300	—	—
50,000–99,900	196,000	50,000	—	146,000	—	—
100,000–999,900	2,286,000	100,000	515,000	1,315,000	356,000	—
1,000,000 or more	9,862,500	—	—	—	5,620,000	4,242,500
		Jewish Population Distribution (Percent of World's Jews)[c]				
Total	100.0[b]	3.0	6.3	11.6	46.3	32.8
100–900	0.1	0.1	0.0	—	0.0	—
1,000–4,900	0.5	0.4	0.1	—	—	—
5,000–9,900	0.3	0.2	0.1	—	—	—
10,000–49,900	3.6	1.2	2.1	0.3	—	—
50,000–99,900	1.5	0.4	—	1.1	—	—
100,000–999,900	17.7	0.8	4.0	10.2	2.8	—
1,000,000 or more	76.3	—	—	—	43.5	32.8

[a]Excluding countries with fewer than 100 Jews.
[b]Including countries with fewer than 100 Jews.
[c]Minor discrepancies due to rounding.

TABLE 8.   ELEVEN COUNTRIES WITH LARGEST JEWISH POPULATIONS, END 1992

| | | | % of Total Jewish Population | | | |
| | | Jewish | In the World | | In the Diaspora | |
Rank	Country	Population	%	Cumulative %	%	Cumulative %
1	United States	5,620,000	43.5	43.5	64.8	64.8
2	Israel	4,242,500	32.8	76.3	—	—
3	France	530,000	4.1	80.4	6.1	70.9
4	Russia	415,000	3.2	83.6	4.8	75.3
5	Canada	356,000	2.8	86.4	4.1	79.4
6	United Kingdom	298,000	2.3	88.7	3.4	82.8
7	Ukraine	276,000	2.1	90.8	3.2	86.0
8	Argentina	211,000	1.6	92.4	2.4	88.4
9	Brazil	100,000	0.8	93.2	1.2	89.6
10	South Africa	100,000	0.8	94.0	1.2	90.8
11	Australia	90,000	0.7	94.7	1.0	91.8

While Jews are widely dispersed, they are also concentrated to some extent (see table 8). In 1992, 94 percent of world Jewry lived in the ten countries with the largest Jewish populations; and over 76 percent lived in the two largest communities—the United States and Israel. Similarly, ten leading Diaspora countries together comprised about 92 percent of the Diaspora Jewish population; three countries (United States, France, and Russia) accounted for 75 percent, and the United States alone for about 65 percent of total Diaspora Jewry.

U.O. Schmelz
Sergio DellaPergola

Directories
Lists
Obituaries

National Jewish Organizations[1]

UNITED STATES

Organizations are listed according to functions as follows:

COMMUNITY RELATIONS

AMERICAN COUNCIL FOR JUDAISM (1943). PO Box 9009, Alexandria, VA 22304. (703)836–2546. Pres. Alan V. Stone; Exec. Dir. Allan C. Brownfeld. Seeks to advance the universal principles of a Judaism free of nationalism, and the national, civic, cultural, and social integration into American institutions of Americans of Jewish faith. *Issues of the American Council for Judaism; Special Interest Report.*

AMERICAN JEWISH ALTERNATIVES TO ZIONISM, INC. (1968). 347 Fifth Ave., Suite 900, NYC 10016. (212)213–9125. FAX: (212)213–9142. Pres. Elmer Berger; V.-Pres. Mrs. Arthur Gutman. Applies Jewish values of justice and humanity to the Arab-Israel conflict in the Middle East; rejects nationality attachment of Jews, particularly American Jews, to the State of Israel as self-segregating, inconsistent with American constitutional concepts of individual citizenship and separation of church and state, and as being a principal obstacle to Middle East peace. *Report.*

AMERICAN JEWISH COMMITTEE (1906). Institute of Human Relations, 165 E. 56 St., NYC 10022. (212)751–4000. FAX: (212)-750–0326. Pres. Alfred H. Moses; Exec. Dir. David A. Harris. Protects the rights and freedoms of Jews the world over; com-

[1]The information in this directory is based on replies to questionnaires circulated by the editors.

bats bigotry and anti-Semitism and promotes human rights for all; works for the security of Israel and deepened understanding between Americans and Israelis; advocates public policy positions rooted in American democratic values and the perspectives of the Jewish heritage; and enhances the creative vitality of the Jewish people. Includes Jacob and Hilda Blaustein Center for Human Relations, Project Interchange, William Petschek National Jewish Family Center, Jacob Blaustein Institute for the Advancement of Human Rights, Institute on American Jewish-Israeli Relations. AMERICAN JEWISH YEAR BOOK; *Commentary; AJC Journal.*

AMERICAN JEWISH CONGRESS (1918). Stephen Wise Congress House, 15 E. 84 St., NYC 10028. (212)879-4500. FAX: (212)-249-3672. Pres. David V. Kahn; Acting Exec. Dir. Phil Baum. Works to foster the creative survival of the Jewish people; to help Israel develop in peace, freedom, and security; to eliminate all forms of racial and religious bigotry; to advance civil rights, protect civil liberties, defend religious freedom, and safeguard the separation of church and state. *Congress Monthly; Judaism; Boycott Report; Inside Israel.*

ANTI-DEFAMATION LEAGUE OF B'NAI B'RITH (1913). 823 United Nations Plaza, NYC 10017. (212)490-2525. FAX: (212)-867-0779. Chmn. David H. Strassler; Dir. Abraham H. Foxman. Seeks to combat anti-Semitism and to secure justice and fair treatment for all citizens through law, education, and community relations. *ADL on the Frontline; Law Enforcement Bulletin; Dimensions: A Journal of Holocaust Studies; Hidden Child Newsletter; International Reports; Civil Rights Reports.*

ASSOCIATION OF JEWISH COMMUNITY RELATIONS WORKERS (1950). 7800 Northaven Road, Dallas, TX 75230. (214)-369-3313. FAX: (214)369-8943. Pres. Marlene Gorin. Aims to stimulate higher standards of professional practice in Jewish community relations; encourages research and training toward that end; conducts educational programs and seminars; aims to encourage cooperation between community relations workers and those working in other areas of Jewish communal service.

CENTER FOR JEWISH COMMUNITY STUDIES (1970). Temple University, Center City Campus, 1616 Walnut St., Suite 513, Philadelphia, PA 19103. (215)204-1459. FAX: (215)204-7784. Jerusalem office: Jerusalem Center for Public Affairs. Pres. Daniel J. Elazar. Worldwide policy-studies institute devoted to the study of Jewish community organization, political thought, and public affairs, past and present, in Israel and throughout the world. Publishes original articles, essays, and monographs; maintains library, archives, and reprint series. *Jerusalem Letter/Viewpoints; Survey of Arab Affairs; Jewish Political Studies Review.*

CENTER FOR RUSSIAN JEWRY WITH STUDENT STRUGGLE FOR SOVIET JEWRY (1964). 240 Cabrini Blvd., #5B, NYC 10033. (212)928-7451. FAX: (212)795-8867. Dir.-Founder Jacob Birnbaum; Acting Chmn. Dr. Ernest Bloch; Student Coord. Glenn Richter. Campaigns for the human rights of the Jews of the former USSR, with emphasis on emigration and Jewish identity; supports programs for needy Jews there and for newcomers in Israel and USA, stressing employment and Jewish education. As the originator of the grassroots movement for Soviet Jewry in the early 1960s, possesses unique archives.

COMMISSION ON SOCIAL ACTION OF REFORM JUDAISM (1953, joint instrumentality of the Union of American Hebrew Congregations and the Central Conference of American Rabbis). 838 Fifth Ave., NYC 10021. (212)249-0100. 2027 Massachusetts Ave., NW, Washington, DC 20036. Chmn. Evely Laser Shlensky; Dir. Rabbi Eric Yoffie; Codir. & Counsel Rabbi David Saperstein. Policy-making body that relates ethical and spiritual principles of Judaism to social-justice issues; implements resolutions through the Religious Action Center in Washington, DC, via advocacy, development of educational materials, and congregational programs. *Tsedek V'Shalom (social action newsletter); Chai Impact (legislative update).*

CONFERENCE OF PRESIDENTS OF MAJOR AMERICAN JEWISH ORGANIZATIONS (1955). 110 E. 59 St., NYC 10022. (212)-318-6111. FAX: (212)644-4135. Chmn. Lester Pollack. Exec. V.-Chmn. Malcolm Hoenlein. Seeks to strengthen the U.S.-Israel alliance and to protect and enhance the security and dignity of Jews abroad. Toward this end, the Conference of Presidents speaks and acts on the basis of consensus of its 49 member agencies on issues of national and international Jewish concern.

CONSULTATIVE COUNCIL OF JEWISH ORGANIZATIONS-CCJO (1946). 420 Lexington Ave., Suite 1733, NYC 10170. (212)808–5437. Pres.'s Ady Steg, Fred Tuckman, and Joseph Nuss; Sec.-Gen. Warren Green. A nongovernmental organization in consultative status with the UN, UNESCO, ILO, UNICEF, and the Council of Europe; cooperates and consults with, advises, and renders assistance to the Economic and Social Council of the UN on all problems relating to human rights and economic, social, cultural, educational, and related matters pertaining to Jews.

COORDINATING BOARD OF JEWISH ORGANIZATIONS (1947). 1640 Rhode Island Ave., NW, Washington, DC 20036. (202)-857–6545. Pres. Kent E. Schiner; Exec. V.-Pres. Dr. Sidney Clearfield; Dir. Internatl. Affairs Daniel S. Mariaschin; Dir. Internatl. Council Warren Eisenberg; Dir. UN Off. Harris Schoenberg. Coordinates the UN activities of B'nai B'rith and the British and South African Boards of Jewish Deputies.

COUNCIL OF JEWISH ORGANIZATIONS IN CIVIL SERVICE, INC. (1948). 45 E. 33 St., Rm. 604, NYC 10016. (212)689–2015. Pres. Louis Weiser. Supports merit system; encourages recruitment of Jewish youth to government service; member of Coalition to Free Soviet Jews, NY Jewish Community Relations Council, NY Metropolitan Coordinating Council on Jewish Poverty, Jewish Labor Committee, America-Israel Friendship League. *Council Digest.*

INSTITUTE FOR PUBLIC AFFAIRS (*see* Union of Orthodox Jewish Congregations of America)

INTERNATIONAL CONFERENCE OF JEWISH COMMUNAL SERVICE (*see* World Conference of Jewish Communal Service)

INTERNATIONAL LEAGUE FOR THE REPATRIATION OF RUSSIAN JEWS, INC. (1963). 2 Fountain Lane, Suite 2J, Scarsdale, NY 10583. (212)517–8271. Pres. Morris Brafman; Chmn. James H. Rapp. Helped to bring the situation of Soviet Jews to world attention; catalyst for advocacy efforts, educational projects, and programs on behalf of Russian Jews in the former USSR, Israel, and U.S.

JEWISH LABOR COMMITTEE (1934). Atran Center for Jewish Culture, 25 E. 21 St., NYC 10010. (212)477–0707. FAX: (212)-477–1918. Pres. Lenore Miller; Exec. Dir. Michael S. Perry. Serves as liaison between the Jewish community and the trade union movement; works with the U.S. and international labor movement to combat anti-Semitism and other forms of bigotry and to engender support for the State of Israel and Jews in and from the former Soviet Union; promotes effective teaching in American public schools about the Holocaust and Jewish resistance; strengthens support within the Jewish community for the social goals and programs of the labor movement; supports Yiddish-language and cultural institutions. *Jewish Labor Committee Review; Issues Alert; Alumni Newsletter.*

———, NATIONAL TRADE UNION COUNCIL FOR HUMAN RIGHTS (1956). Atran Center for Jewish Culture, 25 E. 21 St., NYC 10010. (212)477–0707. FAX: (212)477–1918. Chmn. Sol Hoffman; Exec. Dir. Michael S. Perry. Works with the American labor movement in advancing the struggle for social justice and equal opportunity and assists unions in every issue affecting human rights. Fights discrimination on all levels and helps to promote labor's broad social and economic goals.

JEWISH PEACE FELLOWSHIP (1941). Box 271, Nyack, NY 10960. (914)358–4601. FAX: (914)358–4924. Pres. Rabbi Philip Bentley; Sec. Naomi Goodman; Ed. Murray Polner. Unites those who believe that Jewish ideals and experience provide inspiration for a nonviolent philosophy and way of life; offers draft counseling, especially for conscientious objection based on Jewish "religious training and belief"; encourages Jewish community to become more knowledgeable, concerned, and active in regard to the war/peace problem. *Shalom/ Jewish Peace Letter.*

JEWISH WAR VETERANS OF THE UNITED STATES OF AMERICA (1896). 1811 R St., NW, Washington, DC 20009. (202)265–6280. FAX: (202)234–5662. Natl. Exec. Dir. Herb Rosenbleeth; Natl. Commander Edward D. Blatt. Seeks to foster true allegiance to the United States; to combat bigotry and prevent defamation of Jews; to encourage the doctrine of universal liberty, equal rights, and full justice for all; to cooperate with and support existing educational institutions and establish new ones; to foster the education of ex-servicemen, ex-servicewomen, and members in the ideals and principles of Americanism. *Jewish Veteran.*

——, NATIONAL MUSEUM OF AMERICAN JEWISH MILITARY HISTORY (1958). 1811 R St., NW, Washington, DC 20009. (202)-265–6280. FAX: (202)462–3192. Pres. Nathan M. Goldberg; Museum Dir./Curator Leslie M. Freudenheim; Asst. Dir./Archivist Sandor B. Cohen. Documents and preserves the contributions of Jewish Americans to the peace and freedom of the United States; educates the public concerning the courage, heroism, and sacrifices made by Jewish Americans who served in the armed forces; and works to combat anti-Semitism. *Museum News (quarterly newsletter).*

NATIONAL ASSOCIATION OF JEWISH LEGISLATORS (1976). 45 Thorndale Rd., Slingerlands, NY 12159. (518)455–2761. FAX: (518)455–2959. Exec. Dir. Pat Salkin; Pres. Assemblyman Byron Baer. Arranges visits to Israel for its members, has close ties with the Knesset; a Jewish legislative network on domestic issues; nonpartisan; issues newsletters from time to time.

NATIONAL CONFERENCE ON SOVIET JEWRY (formerly AMERICAN JEWISH CONFERENCE ON SOVIET JEWRY) (1964; reorg. 1971). 730 Broadway, 2nd fl., NYC 10003. (212)780–9500. FAX: (212)780–0888. 1640 Rhode Island Ave., NW, Suite 501, Washington, DC 20036. (202)898–2500. FAX: (202)898–0822. Chmn. Richard L. Wexler; Exec. Dir. Mark B. Levin. Coordinating agency for major national Jewish organizations and local community groups in the U.S., acting on behalf of Soviet Jewry through public education and social action; stimulates all segments of the community to maintain an interest in the problems of Soviet Jews by publishing reports and special pamphlets, sponsoring special programs and projects, organizing public meetings and forums. *Newswatch; annual report; action and program kits; Wrap-Up Leadership Report.*

——, SOVIET JEWRY RESEARCH BUREAU. Chmn. Richard L. Wexler. Organized by NCSJ to monitor emigration trends. Primary task is the accumulation, evaluation, and processing of information regarding Soviet Jews, especially those who apply for emigration.

NATIONAL JEWISH COALITION (1985). 415 2nd St., NE, Suite 100, Washington, DC 20002. (202)547–7701. FAX: (202)544–2434. Natl. Chmn. Cheryl Halpern; Hon. Chmn. Max M. Fisher, George Klein, Richard J. Fox, and Amb. Joseph Gildenhorn; Exec. Dir. Matt Brooks. Promotes involvement in Republican politics among its members; sensitizes Republican leaders to the concerns of the American Jewish community; promotes principles of free enterprise, a strong national defense, and an internationalist foreign policy. *NJC Bulletin.*

NATIONAL JEWISH COMMISSION ON LAW AND PUBLIC AFFAIRS (COLPA) (1965). 135 W. 50 St., 6th fl., NYC 10020. (212)-641–8992. FAX: (212)641–7186. Pres. Allen L. Rothenberg; Exec. Dir. Dennis Rapps. Voluntary association of attorneys whose purpose is to represent the observant Jewish community on legal, legislative, and public-affairs matters.

NATIONAL JEWISH COMMUNITY RELATIONS ADVISORY COUNCIL (1944). 443 Park Ave. S., 11th fl., NYC 10016. (212)-684–6950. FAX: (212)686–1353. Chmn. Lynn Lyss; Sec. Frederick Frank; Exec. V.-Chmn. Lawrence Rubin. National coordinating body for the field of Jewish community relations, comprising 13 national and 117 local Jewish community relations agencies. Promotes understanding of Israel and the Middle East; freedom for Soviet Jews; equal status for Jews and other groups in American society. Through the NJCRAC's work, its constituent organizations seek agreement on policies, strategies, and programs for effective utilization of their resources for common ends. *Joint Program Plan for Jewish Community Relations.*

NATIONAL JEWISH DEMOCRATIC COUNCIL (1990). 711 Second St., NE, #100, Washington, DC 20002. (202)544–7636. FAX: (202)544–7645. Chmn. Monte Friedkin; Sec. Esther R. Landa; Treas. Sheldon Cohen; Founding Chmn. Morton Mandel. An independent organization of Jewish Democrats committed to strengthening the Democratic party through its members' participation in the grassroots political process; to making the party sensitive to the views of American Jews; and to encouraging American Jewish support for the party. *Capital Communiqué.*

SHALOM CENTER (1983). 7318 Germantown Ave., Philadelphia, PA 19119. (215)247–9700. FAX: (215)247–9703. (Part of ALEPH Alliance for Jewish Renewal.) Exec. Dir. Arthur Waskow. National resource and organizing center for Jewish perspectives on dealing with global warming and nuclear and other environmental dangers. Assists local Jewish communities on environmental issues. "Eco-Shalom Corps" trains environmental organizers. Sponsors Sukkat Shalom, Eco-Kosher project, and Ira Silverman Memorial. Provides school curricula, sermon materials, legislative reports, liturgies, adult-education texts, and media for Jewish use. *New Menorah.*

STUDENT STRUGGLE FOR SOVIET JEWRY, INC. (*see* Center for Russian Jewry)

UNION OF COUNCILS (formerly the UNION OF COUNCILS FOR SOVIET JEWS) (1970). 1819 H St., NW, Suite 230, Washington, DC 20006. (202)775–9770. FAX: (202)-775–9776. Natl. Pres. Pamela B. Cohen; Natl. Dir. Micah H. Naftalin. Its 38 member councils and 100,000 members throughout the U.S. support and protect Soviet Jews by gathering and disseminating news on their condition and treatment; advocacy; publications and educational programs, including briefings and policy analyses. Matches U.S. synagogues to FSU Jewish communities in Yad L'Yad assistance program; operates five Human Rights Bureaus to monitor anti-Semitism and ethnic intolerance in FSU, advocate for refuseniks and political prisoners, and seek to advance democracy and rule of law. *Monitor (weekly digest of news and analysis from states of the FSU).*

WORLD CONFERENCE OF JEWISH COMMUNAL SERVICE (1966). 3084 State Highway 27, Suite 9, Kendall Park, NJ 08824–1657. (908)821–0282. FAX:(908)821–5335. Pres. Arthur Rotman; Sec.-Gen. Joel Ollander. Established by worldwide Jewish communal workers to strengthen their understanding of each other's programs and to communicate with colleagues in order to enrich the quality of their work. Conducts quadrennial international conferences in Jerusalem and periodic regional meetings. *Proceedings of international conferences; newsletters.*

WORLD JEWISH CONGRESS (1936; org. in U.S. 1939). 501 Madison Ave., 17th fl., NYC 10022. (212) 755–5770. FAX: (212)-755–5883. Pres. Edgar M. Bronfman; Cochmn. N. Amer. Branch Prof. Irwin Cotler (Montreal) and Evelyn Sommer; Sec.-Gen. Israel Singer; Exec. Dir. Elan Steinberg. Seeks to intensify bonds of world Jewry with Israel as central force in Jewish life; to strengthen solidarity among Jews everywhere and secure their rights, status, and interests as individuals and communities; to encourage development of Jewish social, religious, and cultural life throughout the world and coordinate efforts by Jewish communities and organizations to cope with any Jewish problem; to work for human rights generally. Represents its affiliated organizations—most representative bodies of Jewish communities in more than 80 countries and 35 national organizations in American section—at UN, OAS, UNESCO, Council of Europe, ILO, UNICEF, and other governmental, intergovernmental, and international authorities. Publications (including those by Institute of Jewish Affairs, London): *WJC Report; East European Jewish Affairs; Boletín Informativo OJI; Christian-Jewish Relations; Dateline: World Jewry; Patterns of Prejudice; Coloquio; Batfutsot; Gesher.*

CULTURAL

AMERICAN ACADEMY FOR JEWISH RESEARCH (1929). 3080 Broadway, NYC 10027. (212)678–8864. FAX: (212)678–8947. Pres. Arthur Hyman. Encourages Jewish learning and research; holds annual or semiannual meeting; awards grants for the publication of scholarly works. *Proceedings of the American Academy for Jewish Research; Texts and Studies; Monograph Series.*

AMERICAN BIBLICAL ENCYCLOPEDIA SOCIETY (1930). 24 W. Maple Ave., Monsey, NY 10952. (914)352–4609. Pres. Irving Fredman; Author-Ed. Rabbi M.M. Kasher. Fosters biblical-talmudical research; sponsors and publishes *Torah Shelemah* (Heb., 43 vols.), *Encyclopedia of Biblical Interpretation* (Eng., 9 vols.), *Divrei Menachem* (Heb., 4 vols.), and related publications. *Noam.*

AMERICAN GATHERING OF JEWISH HOLOCAUST SURVIVORS. 122 W. 30 St., NYC 10001. (212)239–4230. FAX: (212)279–2926. Pres. Benjamin Meed; Exec. Dir.

Arie Bucheister. Dedicated to recording the past and passing on a legacy of remembrance. Compiles the *National Registry of Jewish Holocaust Survivors*—to date, the records of more than 80,000 survivors and their families—housed at the U.S. Holocaust Memorial Museum in Washington, DC; holds an annual Yom Hashoah commemoration and occasional international gatherings; sponsors an intensive summer program for U.S. teachers in Poland and Israel to prepare them to teach about the Holocaust. *Together (newspaper).*

AMERICAN GUILD OF JUDAIC ART (1991). PO Box 1794, Murray Hill Station, NYC 10156–0609. (212)889–7581. FAX: (212)-779–9015. Pres. Michael Berkowicz. *Hiddur, a newsletter devoted to the Jewish visual arts; Guild Showcase, a marketing magazine supplement.*

AMERICAN JEWISH HISTORICAL SOCIETY (1892). 2 Thornton Rd., Waltham, MA 02154. (617)891–8110. FAX: (617)899–9208. Pres. Justin L. Wyner; Exec. Dir. Dr. Michael Feldberg. Collects, catalogues, publishes, and displays material on the history of the Jews in America; serves as an information center for inquiries on American Jewish history; maintains archives of original source material on American Jewish history; sponsors lectures and exhibitions; makes available historic Yiddish films and audiovisual material. *American Jewish History; Heritage.*

AMERICAN JEWISH PRESS ASSOCIATION (1943). Natl. Admin. Off.: 11312 Old Club Rd., Rockville, MD 20852–4537. (301)-881–4113. FAX: (301)816–2379. Exec. Dir. L. Malcolm Rodman; Pres. Harry Scharf. Seeks the advancement of Jewish journalism and the maintenance of a strong Jewish press in the U.S. and Canada; encourages the attainment of the highest editorial and business standards; sponsors workshops, services for members; sponsors annual competition for Simon Rockower awards for excellence in Jewish journalism. *Membership bulletin newsletter; Roster of Members.*

AMERICAN SEPHARDI FEDERATION (1973). 305 7th Ave., NYC 10001. (212)366–7223. FAX: (212)366–7263. Presidium Victor DeLoya, Murray Farash, Dr. Heskel Haddad, Leon Levy, Raymond Mallel, Aghajan Nassimi, Mehdi Nassimi, Bernard Ouziel, Jack Pesso; Exec. V.-Pres. Edward

Alcosser. Central umbrella organization for all Sephardic congregations, organizations, and agencies. Seeks to preserve and promote Sephardi culture, education, and traditions. Disseminates resource material on all aspects of Sephardic life. Strives to bring a Sephardic agenda and perspective to American Jewish life. *Sephardic Highlights Newsletter.*

AMERICAN SOCIETY FOR JEWISH MUSIC (1974). 170 W. 74 St., NYC 10023. (212)-874–4456. FAX: (212)874–8605. Pres. Jack Gottlieb; Co-V.-Pres. Michael Leavitt, Philip Miller; Sec. Hadassah Markson. Promotes the knowledge, appreciation, and development of Jewish music, past and present, for professional and lay audiences; seeks to raise the standards of composition and performance in Jewish music, to encourage research, and to sponsor performances of new and rarely heard works. *Musica Judaica Journal.*

ASSOCIATION OF JEWISH BOOK PUBLISHERS (1962). 838 Fifth Ave., NYC 10021. (212)-249–0100. Pres. Rabbi Elliot L. Stevens; Doris B. Gold, chair, cooperative advertising and exhibits. As a nonprofit group, provides a forum for discussion of mutual problems by publishers, authors, and other individuals and institutions concerned with books of Jewish interest. Provides national and international exhibit opportunities for Jewish books.

ASSOCIATION OF JEWISH GENEALOGICAL SOCIETIES (1988). 1485 Teaneck Rd., Teaneck, NJ 07666. (201)837–8300. FAX: (201)837–6272. Pres. Gary Mokotoff. Confederation of over 55 Jewish Genealogical Societies (JGS) in the U.S. and Canada. Encourages Jews to research their family history, promotes membership in the various JGSs, acts as representative of organized Jewish genealogy, implements projects of interest to persons researching their Jewish family history. Annual conference where members learn and exchange ideas. Each local JGS publishes its own newsletter.

ASSOCIATION OF JEWISH LIBRARIES (1965). c/o National Foundation for Jewish Culture, 330 Seventh Ave., 21st fl., NYC 10001. (212)678–8092. FAX: (212)678–8998. Pres. Ralph R. Simon; V.-Pres. Zachary Baker. Seeks to promote and improve services and professional standards in Jewish libraries; disseminates Jewish library information and guidance; promotes publication of literature in the field; encourages the establishment of Jewish libraries and collections of Judaica and the choice of Judaica librarianship as a profession; cocertifies Jewish libraries (with Jewish Book Council). *AJL Newsletter; Judaica Librarianship.*

BEIT HASHOAH–MUSEUM OF TOLERANCE OF THE SIMON WIESENTHAL CENTER (1993). 9786 W. Pico Blvd., Los Angeles, CA 90035. (310)553–8403. FAX: (310)-553–4521. Dean-founder Rabbi Marvin Hier; Dir. Dr. Gerald Margolis; Assoc. Dean Rabbi Abraham Cooper; Exec. Dir. Rabbi Meyer May. A unique experiential museum focusing on personal prejudice, group intolerance, struggle for civil rights, and 20th-century genocides, culminating in a major exhibition on the Holocaust. Archives, Multimedia Learning Center designed for individualized research, 6,700-square-foot temporary exhibit space, 324-seat theater, 150-seat auditorium, and outdoor memorial plaza. *Museum Update/ Commitment Magazine.*

B'NAI B'RITH KLUTZNICK NATIONAL JEWISH MUSEUM (1956). 1640 Rhode Island Ave., NW, Washington, DC 20036. (202)-857–6583. FAX: (202)857–0980. Dir. Ori Z. Soltes. A center of Jewish art and history in nation's capital, maintains temporary and permanent exhibition galleries, permanent collection of Jewish ceremonial and folk art, B'nai B'rith International reference archive, outdoor sculpture garden, and museum shop, as well as the American Jewish Sports Hall of Fame. Provides exhibitions, tours, educational programs, research assistance, and tourist information. *Semiannual newsletter; permanent collection catalogue; exhibition brochures.*

CENTER FOR HOLOCAUST STUDIES, DOCUMENTATION & RESEARCH (1974). Merged into A Living Memorial to the Holocaust–Museum of Jewish Heritage, Jan. 1991.

CENTRAL YIDDISH CULTURE ORGANIZATION (CYCO), INC. (1943). 25 E. 21 St., 3rd fl., NYC 10010. (212)505–8305. Mgr. Jacob Schneidman. Promotes, publishes, and distributes Yiddish books; publishes catalogues.

CONFERENCE ON JEWISH SOCIAL STUDIES, INC. (formerly CONFERENCE ON JEWISH RELATIONS, INC.) (1939). c/o Prof.

Mitchell Cohen, 515 W. 110 St., #11B, NYC 10025. Pres. Prof. Steven J. Zipperstein. *Jewish Social Studies.*

CONGREGATION BINA (1981). 600 W. End Ave., Suite 1-C, NYC 10024. (212)873–4261. Pres. Joseph Moses; Exec. V.-Pres. Moses Samson; Hon. Pres. Samuel M. Daniel; Secy. Gen. Elijah E. Jhirad. Serves the religious, cultural, charitable, and philanthropic needs of the Children of Israel who originated in India and now reside in the U.S. Works to foster and preserve the ancient traditions, customs, liturgy, music, and folklore of Indian Jewry and to maintain needed institutions. *Kol Bina.*

CONGRESS FOR JEWISH CULTURE (1948). 25 E. 21 St., NYC 10010. (212)505–8040. Co-pres.'s Prof. Yonia Fain, Dr. Barnett Zumoff; Exec. Dir. Michael Skakun. An umbrella group comprising 16 constituent organizations; perpetuates and enhances Jewish creative expression in the U.S. and abroad; fosters all aspects of Yiddish cultural life through the publication of the journal *Zukunft*, the conferring of literary awards, commemoration of the Holocaust and the martyrdom of the Soviet Jewish writers under Stalin, and a series of topical readings, scholarly conferences, symposiums, and concerts. *Zukunft.*

ELAINE KAUFMAN CULTURAL CENTER (1952). 129 W. 67 St., NYC 10023. (212)-362–8060. FAX: (212)874–7865. Chmn. Leonard Goodman; Pres. Victor Smukler; Exec. Dir. Lydia Kontos. Offers instruction in its Lucy Moses School for Music and Dance in music, dance, art, and theater to children and adults, combining Western culture with Jewish traditions. Presents frequent performances of Jewish and general music by leading artists and ensembles in its Merkin Concert Hall and Ann Goodman Recital Hall. The Birnbaum Music Library houses Jewish music scores and reference books. *Kaufman Cultural Center News; bimonthly concert calendars; catalogues and brochures.*

HEBREW CULTURE FOUNDATION (1955). 110 E. 59 St., NYC 10022. (212)339–6000. Chmn. Milton R. Konvitz; Sec. Herman L. Sainer. Sponsors the introduction and strengthening of Hebrew language and literature courses in institutions of higher learning in the United States.

HISTADRUTH IVRITH OF AMERICA (1916; reorg. 1922). 47 W. 34 St., Rm. 609, NYC

10001. (212)629–9443. Pres. Dr. David Sidorsky; Exec. V.-Pres. Dr. Aviva Barzel. Emphasizes the primacy of Hebrew in Jewish life, culture, and education; aims to disseminate knowledge of written and spoken Hebrew in N. America, thus building a cultural bridge between the State of Israel and Jewish communities throughout N. America. *Hadoar; Lamishpaha; Tov Lichtov.*

HOLOCAUST CENTER OF THE UNITED JEWISH FEDERATION OF GREATER PITTSBURGH (1980). 242 McKee Pl., Pittsburgh, PA 15213. (412)682–7111. Pres. Holocaust Comm. Jeffrey W. Letwin; Bd. Chmn. Stanley C. Ruskin; Dir. Linda F. Hurwitz. Develops programs and provides resources to further understanding of the Holocaust and its impact on civilization. Maintains a library, archive; provides speakers, educational materials; organizes community programs.

HOLOCAUST MEMORIAL RESOURCE & EDUCATION CENTER OF CENTRAL FLORIDA (1982). 851 N. Maitland Ave., Maitland, FL 32751. (407)628–0555. FAX: (407)-628–0555. Pres. Michael Nebel; Exec. V.-Pres. Tess Wise. An interfaith educational center devoted to teaching the lessons of the Holocaust. Houses permanent multimedia educational exhibit; maintains library of books, videotapes, films, and other visuals to serve the entire educational establishment; offers lectures, teacher training, and other activities. *Newsletter; Bibliography; "Holocaust—Lessons for Tomorrow. "*

INSTITUTE FOR RUSSIAN JEWRY, INC. (1990). PO Box 96, Flushing, NY 11367. (718)969–0911. Exec. Dir. Rosa Irgal; Sec. Azia Zverena. Disseminates knowledge of Judaism in Russian language, from historical and cultural perspectives; promotes knowledge of the religious and cultural heritage of Russian Jews through Russian folk and fine art exhibits, lecture series, music and dance workshops.

INTERNATIONAL JEWISH MEDIA ASSOCIATION (1987). U.S.: c/o St. Louis Jewish Light, 12 Millstone Campus Dr., St. Louis, MO 63146. (314)432–3353. FAX: (314)-432–0515. Israel: PO Box 92, Jerusalem 91920. 02–202–222. FAX: 02–513–642. Pres. Robert A. Cohn, Exec. Dir. Lisa Gann-Perkal (Israel); Staff Coord. Malcolm Rodman (Rockville, MD). A world-wide network of Jewish journalists in the Jewish and general media, which seeks to provide a forum for the exchange of materials and ideas, and to enhance the stature of Jewish media and journalists. *Presidents Bulletin; proceedings of international conferences on Jewish media.*

INTERNATIONAL NETWORK OF CHILDREN OF JEWISH HOLOCAUST SURVIVORS, INC. (1981). 3000 NE 145 St., N. Miami, FL 33181–3600. (305)940–5690. FAX: (305)-940–5691. Pres. Rositta E. Kenigsberg; V.-Pres. Jean Bloch Rosensaft, Marylin E. Kingston. Represents the shared views and interests of children of Holocaust survivors; aims to perpetuate the authentic memory of the Holocaust and prevent its recurrence; to strengthen and preserve the Jewish spiritual, ideological, and cultural heritage; to fight anti-Semitism and other forms of racial and ethnic hatred; to fight discrimination, persecution, and oppression anywhere in the world. International Study of Organized Persecution of Children.

JEWISH ACADEMY OF ARTS AND SCIENCES, INC. (1926). 888 Seventh Ave., Suite 403, NYC 10106. (212)757–1627. Hon. Pres. Prof. Abraham Katsh; Acting Pres. Prof. Milton Handler; V.- Pres. Joseph Handleman; V.-Chmn. Robert L. Sadoff, MD; Treas. Zvi Levavy. An honor society of Jews who have attained distinction in the arts, sciences, professions, and communal endeavors. Encourages the advancement of knowledge; stimulates scholarship, with particular reference to Jewish life and thought; recognition by election to membership and/or fellowship; publishes papers delivered at annual convocations.

JEWISH BOOK COUNCIL (1943). 15 E. 26 St., NYC 10010. (212)532–4949, ext. 297. Pres. Dr. Leonard Singer Gold; Ex. Dir. Carolyn Starman Hessel. Serves as clearinghouse for Jewish content literature; assists readers, writers, publishers, and those who market and sell product. Provides bibliographies, list of publishers, book stores, libraries, in cooperation with Association of Jewish Libraries. Sponsors National Jewish Book Awards, Jewish Book Month, Judaica Book and Crafts Marketplace, Library citations. *Jewish Book Annual; Jewish Book World.*

JEWISH HERITAGE PROJECT (1981). 150 Franklin St., #1W, NYC 10013. (212)

925–9067. Exec. Dir. Alan Adelson. Strives to bring to the broadest possible audience authentic works of literary and historical value relating to Jewish history and culture. Distributor of the film *Lodz Ghetto*, which it developed, as well as its companion volume *Lodz Ghetto: Inside a Community Under Siege.*

JEWISH MUSEUM (1904, under auspices of Jewish Theological Seminary of America). 1109 Fifth Ave., NYC 10128. (212)423–3200. FAX: (212)423–3232. Dir. Joan H. Rosenbaum; Bd. Chmn. E. Robert Goodkind. Newly expanded museum opened in June 1993, featuring permanent exhibition on the Jewish experience. Repository of the largest collection of Judaica—paintings, prints, photographs, sculpture, coins, medals, antiquities, textiles, and other decorative arts—in the Western Hemisphere. Includes the National Jewish Archive of Broadcasting. Tours, lectures, film showings, and concerts; special programs for children; cafe; shop. *Special exhibition catalogues; annual report.*

JEWISH PUBLICATION SOCIETY (1888). 1930 Chestnut St., Philadelphia, PA 19103. (215)564–5925. FAX: (215)564–6640. Pres. D. Walter Cohen; Exec. V.-Pres. Rabbi Michael A. Monson; Ed.-in-Chief Dr. Ellen Frankel; Dir. of Publishing Operations Jean Sue Libkind. Publishes and disseminates books of Jewish interest for adults and children; titles include TANAKH, religious studies and practices, life cycle, folklore, classics, art, history, belles-lettres. *The Bookmark; JPS Catalogue.*

JEWISH SPORTS CONGRESS (1992). PO Box 4549, Old Village Station, Great Neck, NY 11023. (516)482–5550. FAX: (516) 482–5583. Pres. David J. Kufeld; V.-Pres. Mike Cohen; Chmn. Marty Glickman. An independent, nondenominational organization that promotes and supports athletics and physical fitness within the international Jewish community. In recognition of the influential force of sports in contemporary society, the organization also seeks to harness this power for increased Jewish pride, enhanced Jewish identity, stronger Jewish unity, and improved interracial relations. *Jewish Sports & Fitness.*

JUDAH L. MAGNES MUSEUM–JEWISH MUSEUM OF THE WEST (1962). 2911 Russell St., Berkeley, CA 94705. (510)549–6950. FAX: (510)849–3650. Pres. Howard Fine;

Dir. Seymour Fromer. Collects, preserves, and makes available Jewish art, culture, history, and literature from throughout the world. Permanent collections of fine and ceremonial art, rare Judaica library, Western Jewish History Center (archives). The museum has changing exhibits, traveling exhibits, docent tours, lectures, numismatics series, poetry award, museum shop. *Magnes News; special exhibition catalogues; scholarly books.*

JUDAICA CAPTIONED FILM CENTER, INC. (1983). PO Box 21439, Baltimore, MD 21208–0439. Voice (after 4 PM) (410)655–4750; TDD (410)655–6767. Pres. Lois Lilienfeld Weiner. Developing a comprehensive library of captioned and subtitled films and tapes on Jewish subjects; distributes them to organizations serving the hearing-impaired, including mainstream classes and senior adult groups, on a free-loan, handling/shipping-charge-only basis. *Quarterly newsletter.*

LEAGUE FOR YIDDISH, INC. (1979). 200 W. 72 St., Suite 40, NYC 10023. (212)787–6675. Pres. Dr. Sadie Turak; Exec. Dir. Dr. Mordkhe Schaechter. Encourages the development and use of Yiddish as a living language; promotes its modernization and standardization; publisher of Yiddish textbooks and English-Yiddish dictionaries; most recent book publication: *Yiddish Two: An Intermediate and Advanced Textbook*, 1993. *Afn Shvel (quarterly).*

LEO BAECK INSTITUTE, INC. (1955). 129 E. 73 St., NYC 10021. (212)744–6400. FAX: (212)988–1305. Pres. Ismar Schorsch; Exec. Dir. Robert A. Jacobs. A library, archive, and research center for the history of German-speaking Jewry. Offers lectures, exhibits, faculty seminars; publishes a series of monographs, yearbooks, and journals. *LBI News; LBI Yearbook; LBI Memorial Lecture; LBI Library & Archives News.*

A LIVING MEMORIAL TO THE HOLOCAUST–MUSEUM OF JEWISH HERITAGE (1984). 342 Madison Ave., Suite 706, NYC 10173. (212)687–9141. FAX: (212)573–9847. Cochmn. George Klein, Hon. Robert M. Morgenthau, Peter Cohen, Sen. Manfred Ohrenstein; Museum Dir. David Altshuler. The museum will be New York's principal public memorial to the six million Jews murdered during the Holocaust. Scheduled to open in 1995, it will include permanent and temporary exhibition galleries, a computerized interactive learning center, a Memorial Hall, and education facilities. *Brochures; bimonthly newsletter.*

MAALOT–A SEMINARY FOR CANTORS AND JUDAISTS (1987). 15 W. Montgomery Ave., Suite 204, Rockville, MD 20850. (301)309–2310. FAX: (301)230–2009. Pres./Exec. Off. David Shneyer. An educational program established to train individuals in Jewish music, the liturgical arts, and the use, design, and application of Jewish customs and ceremonies. Offers classes, seminars, and an independent study program.

MARTYRS MEMORIAL & MUSEUM OF THE HOLOCAUST OF THE JEWISH FEDERATION COUNCIL OF GREATER LOS ANGELES (1963; reorg. 1978). 6505 Wilshire Blvd., Los Angeles, CA 90048. (213)651–3175. FAX: (213)852–1494. Chmn. Dr. Sam Goetz; Dir. Dr. Alex Grobman. A photo-narrative museum and resource center dedicated to Holocaust history, issues of genocide and prejudice, and curriculum development. *Pages (quarterly newsletter).*

MEMORIAL FOUNDATION FOR JEWISH CULTURE, INC. (1964). 15 E. 26 St., NYC 10010. (212)679–4074. Pres. the Right Hon., the Lord Jakobovits; Exec. V.-Pres. Jerry Hochbaum. Through the grants that it awards, encourages Jewish scholarship and Jewish education, supports communities that are struggling to maintain their Jewish identity, makes possible the training of Jewish men and women for professional careers in communal service in Jewishly deprived communities, and stimulates the documentation, commemoration, and teaching of the Holocaust.

NATIONAL FOUNDATION FOR JEWISH CULTURE (1960). 330 Seventh Ave., 21st fl., NYC 10001. (212)629–0500. FAX: (212)-629–0508. Pres. Tom L. Freudenheim; Exec. Dir. Richard A. Siegel. The leading Jewish organization devoted to promoting Jewish culture in the U.S. Administers the Council of American Jewish Museums, the Council of Archives and Research Libraries in Jewish Studies, and the Council of Jewish Theatres; supports Jewish scholarship through doctoral dissertation fellowships; provides funding to major Jewish cultural institutions through the Joint Cultural Appeal; organizes conferences, symposia, and festivals in the arts and humani-

ties; initiated the Jewish Endowment for the Arts and Humanities. *Jewish Cultural News.*

NATIONAL MUSEUM OF AMERICAN JEWISH MILITARY HISTORY *(see* Jewish War Veterans of the U.S.A.)

NATIONAL YIDDISH BOOK CENTER (1980). 48 Woodbridge St., South Hadley, MA 01075. (413)535–1303. FAX: (413)535–1007. Pres. Aaron Lansky; Development Dir. Michael Weisser. Collects and disseminates Yiddish books; conducts activities contributing to the revitalization of Yiddish culture in America. *Der Pakn-treger/The Book Peddler.*

ORTHODOX JEWISH ARCHIVES (1978). 84 William St., NYC 10038. (212)797–9000, ext. 73. FAX: (212)269–2843 Dir. Rabbi Moshe Kolodny. Founded by Agudath Israel of America; houses historical documents, photographs, periodicals, and other publications relating to the growth of Orthodox Jewry in the U.S. and related communities in Europe, Israel, and elsewhere. Particularly noteworthy are its holdings relating to rescue activities organized during the Holocaust and its traveling exhibits available to schools and other institutions.

RESEARCH FOUNDATION FOR JEWISH IMMIGRATION, INC. (1971). 570 Seventh Ave., NYC 10018. (212)921–3871. FAX: (212)-575–1918. Pres. Curt C. Silberman; Sec. and Coord. of Research Herbert A. Strauss; Archivist Dennis E. Rohrbaugh. Studies and records the history of the migration and acculturation of Central European German-speaking Jewish and non-Jewish Nazi persecutees in various resettlement countries worldwide, with special emphasis on the American experience. *International Biographical Dictionary of Central European Emigrés, 1933–1945; Jewish Immigrants of the Nazi Period in the USA.*

ST. LOUIS CENTER FOR HOLOCAUST STUDIES (1977). 12 Millstone Campus Dr., St. Louis, MO 63146. (314)432–0020. Chmn. Leo Wolf; Dir. Rabbi Robert Sternberg. Develops programs and provides resources and educational materials to further an understanding of the Holocaust and its impact on civilization. *Audio Visual and Curriculum Resources Guides.*

SEPHARDIC EDUCATIONAL CENTER (1979). 6505 Wilshire Blvd., Suite 403, Los Angeles, CA 90048. (213)653–7365. FAX: (213)653–9985. Pres. Dr. Jose A. Nessim; Exec. Dir. Dr. Michael M. Laskier. *Hamerkaz (quarterly bulletin).*

SEPHARDIC HOUSE (1978). 2112 Broadway, Suite 200A, NYC 10023. (212)496–2173. FAX: (212)496–2264. Hon. Pres. Rabbi Marc D. Angel; Exec. Dir. Dr. Janice E. Ovadiah. A cultural organization dedicated to fostering Sephardic history and culture; sponsors a wide variety of classes and public programs, film festivals, including summer program in Paris for high-school students; publication program disseminates materials of Sephardic value; outreach program to communities outside of the New York area; program bureau provides program ideas, speakers, and entertainers. *Sephardic House Newsletter.*

SIMON WIESENTHAL CENTER, Los Angeles, CA (*see* Yeshiva University *and* Beit Hashoah–Museum of Tolerance)

SKIRBALL MUSEUM, HEBREW UNION COLLEGE (1913; 1972 in Calif.). 3077 University Ave., Los Angeles, CA 90007. (213)-749–3424. FAX: (213)749–1192. Dir. Nancy Berman; Curators Barbara Gilbert, Grace Cohen Grossman; Admin. Peggy Kayser. Collects, preserves, researches, and exhibits art and artifacts made by or for Jews, or otherwise associated with Jews and Judaism. Provides opportunity to faculty and students to do research in the field of Jewish art. *Catalogues of exhibits and collections.*

SOCIETY FOR THE HISTORY OF CZECHOSLOVAK JEWS, INC. (1961). 87–08 Santiago St., Holliswood, NY 11423. (718)468–6844. Pres. and Ed. Lewis Weiner; Sec. Hana Borges. Studies the history of Czechoslovak Jews; collects material and disseminates information through the publication of books and pamphlets. *The Jews of Czechoslovakia (3 vols.); Review I–VI.*

SOCIETY OF FRIENDS OF THE TOURO SYNAGOGUE, NATIONAL HISTORICAL SHRINE, INC. (1948). 85 Touro St., Newport, RI 02840. (401)847–4794. Pres. Jacob Temkin; Coord. Kirsten L. Mann. Helps maintain Touro Synagogue as a national historic site, opening and interpreting it for visitors; promotes public awareness of its preeminent role in the tradition of American religious liberty; annually commemorates George Washington's letter of 1790 to the Hebrew Congregation of Newport. *Society Update.*

————, TOURO NATIONAL HERITAGE TRUST (1984). 85 Touro St., Newport, RI 02840. (401)847–0810. Pres. Bernard Bell; Exec. Dir. Kirsten L. Mann. Works to establish national education center within Touro compound; sponsors Touro Fellow through John Carter Brown Library; presents seminars and other educational programs; promotes knowledge of the early Jewish experience in this country within the climate of religions which brought it about.

SPERTUS MUSEUM, SPERTUS INSTITUTE OF JEWISH STUDIES (1968). 618 S. Michigan Ave., Chicago, IL 60605. (312)922–9012. FAX: (312)922–6406. Pres. Spertus Institute of Jewish Studies, Dr. Howard A. Sulkin; Museum Dir. Dr. Morris A. Fred. The largest, most comprehensive Judaic museum in the Midwest with 12,000 square feet of exhibit space and a permanent collection of some 3,000 works spanning 3,500 years of Jewish history. Also includes Holocaust memorial, gallery of contemporary art, changing special exhibitions, and children's artifact center, plus traveling exhibits for Jewish educators, life-cycle workshops, programs for seniors and the disabled, and community-generated art projects. *Newsletter; exhibition catalogues; educational pamphlets.*

UNITED STATES HOLOCAUST MEMORIAL MUSEUM (1980; opened Apr. 1993). 100 Raoul Wallenberg Place, SW, Washington, DC 20024. (202)488–0400. FAX: (202)-488–2690. Chmn. Miles Lerman; Exec. Dir. Jeshajahu Weinberg. Federally chartered and privately built, its mission is to teach about the Nazi persecution and murder of six million Jews and millions of others from 1933 to 1945 and to inspire visitors to contemplate their moral responsibilities as citizens of a democratic nation. Opened in April 1993 near the national Mall in Washington, DC, the museum's permanent exhibition tells the story of the Holocaust through authentic artifacts, videotaped oral testimonies, documentary film and historical photographs. Offers educational programs for students and adults, an interactive computerized learning center, and special exhibitions and community programs. *United States Holocaust Memorial Museum Update (bimonthly); Directory of Holocaust Institutions; Journal of Holocaust and Genocide*

Studies (quarterly); Days of Remembrance Guidebook (annual).

YESHIVA UNIVERSITY MUSEUM (1973). 2520 Amsterdam Ave., NYC 10033–3201. (212)960–5390. Dir. Sylvia A. Herskowitz. Collects, preserves, and interprets Jewish life and culture through changing exhibitions of ceremonial objects, paintings, rare books and documents, synagogue architecture, textiles, decorative arts, and photographs. Oral history archive. Special events, holiday workshops, live performances, lectures, etc. for adults and children. Guided tours and workshops are offered. *Seasonal calendars; special exhibition catalogues.*

YIDDISHER KULTUR FARBAND–YKUF (1937). 1133 Broadway, Rm. 1019, NYC 10010. (212)691–0708. Pres. and Ed. Itche Goldberg. Publishes a bimonthly magazine and books by contemporary and classical Jewish writers; conducts cultural forums; exhibits works by contemporary Jewish artists and materials of Jewish historical value; organizes reading circles. *Yiddishe Kultur.*

YIVO INSTITUTE FOR JEWISH RESEARCH, INC. (1925). 1048 Fifth Ave., NYC 10028. (212)535–6700. FAX: (212)734–1062. Chmn. Bruce Slovin; Exec. V.-Pres. Laurence H. Rubinstein; Resch. Dir. Allan Nadler. Engages in social and cultural research pertaining to East European Jewish life; maintains library and archives which provide a major international, national, and New York resource used by institutions, individual scholars, and the public; trains graduate students in Yiddish, East European, and American Jewish studies; offers continuing education classes in Yiddish language, exhibits, conferences, public programs; publishes books. *Yidishe Shprakh; YIVO Annual; YIVO Bleter; Yedies fun Yivo; Jewish Folklore and Ethnology Review.*

———, MAX WEINREICH CENTER FOR ADVANCED JEWISH STUDIES (1968). 1048 Fifth Ave., NYC 10028. (212)535–6700. FAX: (212)734–1062. Dean Allan Nadler. Provides advanced-level training in Yiddish language and literature, ethnography, folklore, linguistics, and history; offers guidance on dissertation or independent research; post-doctoral fellowships available.

YUGNTRUF–YOUTH FOR YIDDISH (1964). 200 W. 72 St., Suite 40, NYC 10023. (212)-787–6675. Cochmn. Dr. Adina Singer, Binyumen Schaechter; Editor David Braun. A worldwide, nonpolitical organization for high school and college students with a knowledge of, or interest in, Yiddish. Spreads the love and use of the Yiddish language; organizes artistic and social activities, including annual conference for young adults; sponsors Yiddish-speaking preschool for non-Orthodox children; disseminates new Yiddish teaching materials. *Yugntruf Journal.*

ISRAEL-RELATED

THE ABRAHAM FUND (1989). 477 Madison Ave., 8th fl., NYC 10022. (212)303–9421. FAX: (212)935–1834. Pres. Alan B. Slifka; Co-founder Dr. Eugene Weiner. Established solely to enhance and fund Jewish-Arab coexistence, to encourage the citizens of Israel to live and work together with mutual respect and in harmony. Supports programs run by both Jews and Arabs in a wide variety of fields, including health, social services, education, environment, culture, and women's rights. *Quarterly newsletter.*

ALYN–AMERICAN SOCIETY FOR HANDICAPPED CHILDREN IN ISRAEL (1934). 19 W. 44 St., NYC 10036. (212)869–8085. FAX: (212)768–0979. Pres. Caroline W. Halpern; Chmn. Simone P. Blum; Exec. Dir. Joan R. Mendelson. Supports the work of ALYN Hospital, rehabilitation center for severely orthopedically handicapped children, located in Jerusalem, whose aim is to prepare patients for independent living.

AMERICA-ISRAEL CULTURAL FOUNDATION, INC. (1939). 41 E. 42 St., Suite 608, NYC 10017. (212)557–1600. FAX: (212)-557–1611. Bd. Chmn. Isaac Stern; Pres. Vera Stern; Exec. Dir. Kathleen M. Hat. Supports and encourages the growth of cultural excellence in Israel through grants to cultural institutions; scholarships to gifted young artists and musicians. *Newsletter.*

AMERICA-ISRAEL FRIENDSHIP LEAGUE, INC. (1971). 134 E. 39 St., NYC 10016. (212)213–8630. FAX: (212)683–3475. Exec. V.-Pres. Ilana Artman. A nonsectarian, nonpartisan organization which seeks to broaden the base of support for Israel among Americans of all faiths and backgrounds. Activities include educational exchanges, tours of Israel for American leadership groups, symposia and public education activities, and the dissemination of printed information. *Newsletter.*

AMERICAN ASSOCIATES, BEN-GURION UNIVERSITY OF THE NEGEV (1973). 342 Madison Ave., NYC 10173. (212)687–7721. FAX: (212)370–0686. Pres. Harold L. Oshry; Exec. V.-Pres. Dr. Lee Katz. Bd. Chmn. Michael W. Sonnenfeldt. Serves as the university's publicity and fund-raising link to the U.S.; is committed to programs for the absorption of Soviet émigrés in the Negev, publicizing university activities and curricula, securing student scholarships, transferring contributions, and encouraging American interest in the university. *AABGU Reporter; BGU Bulletin; Negev; Overseas Study Program Catalog.*

AMERICAN COMMITTEE FOR SHAARE ZEDEK HOSPITAL IN JERUSALEM, INC. (1949). 49 W. 45 St., Suite 1100, NYC 10036. (212)354–8801. Pres. Charles H. Bendheim; Bd. Chmn. Ludwig Jesselson; Sr. Exec. V.-Pres. Morris Talansky. Raises funds for the various needs of the Shaare Zedek Medical Center, Jerusalem, such as equipment and medical supplies, nurses' training, and research; supports exchange program between Shaare Zedek Medical Center and Albert Einstein College of Medicine, NY. *Heartbeat Magazine.*

AMERICAN COMMITTEE FOR SHENKAR COLLEGE IN ISRAEL, INC. (1971). 855 Ave. of the Americas, NYC 10001. (212) 947–1597. FAX: (212)643–9887. Pres. H. Robert Miller; Exec. Dir. Charlotte Fainblatt. Raises funds for capital improvement, research and development projects, laboratory equipment, scholarships, lectureships, fellowships, and library/archives of fashion and textile design at Shenkar College in Israel, Israel's only fashion and textile technology college. Accredited by the Council of Higher Education, the college is the chief source of personnel for Israel's fashion and apparel industry. *Shenkar News.*

AMERICAN COMMITTEE FOR THE WEIZMANN INSTITUTE OF SCIENCE (1944). 51 Madison Ave., NYC 10010. (212)779–2500. FAX: (212)779–3209. Chmn. Sara Lee Schupf; Pres. S. Donald Sussman; Exec. V.-Pres. Bernard N. Samers. Through 14 regional offices in the U.S. raises funds, disseminates information, and does American purchasing for the Weiz-

mann Institute in Rehovot, Israel, a world-renowned center of scientific research and graduate study. The institute conducts research in disease, energy, the environment, and other areas; runs an international summer science program for gifted high-school students. *Rehovot; Interface; Research, Weizmann Now; annual report.*

AMERICAN FRIENDS OF ASSAF HAROFEH MEDICAL CENTER (1975). 110 E. 59 St., NYC 10022. (212)318–6125. FAX: (212)-826–8959. Pres. Martin Lifland; Chmn. Kenneth Kronen; Exec. Dir. Esther Sharon. Raises funds for Assaf Harofeh, Israel's third largest government hospital, serving a poor population of over 400,000 in the area between Tel Aviv and Jerusalem. The American Friends raises funds for medical equipment, medical training for immigrants, hospital expansion, school of nursing, and school of physiotherapy. *Newsletter.*

AMERICAN FRIENDS OF BAR-ILAN UNIVERSITY (1955). 91 Fifth Ave., Suite 200, NYC 10003. (212)337–1270. FAX: (212)337–1274. Chancellor Rabbi Emanuel Rackman; Chmn. Global Bd. of Trustees Aharon Meir; Pres. Amer. Bd. of Overseers Belda Lindenbaum; Exec. V.-Pres. Gen. Yehuda Halevy. Supports Bar-Ilan University, a traditionally oriented liberal arts and sciences institution, where all students must take Basic Jewish Studies courses as a requirement of graduation; located in Ramat-Gan, Israel, and chartered by the Board of Regents of the State of NY. *Update; Bar-Ilan News.*

AMERICAN FRIENDS OF BETH HATEFUTSOTH (1976). 110 E. 59 St., Suite 4099, NYC 10022. (212)339–6034. FAX: (212)-318–6176. Pres. Abraham Spiegel; V.-Pres. Sam E. Bloch; Exec. Dir. Gloria Golan. Supports the maintenance and development of Beth Hatefutsoth, the Nahum Goldmann Museum of the Jewish Diaspora in Tel Aviv, and its cultural and educational programs for youth and adults. Circulates its traveling exhibitions and provides various cultural programs to local Jewish communities. Includes Jewish genealogy center (DOROT); the center for Jewish music, and photodocumentation center. *Beth Hatefutsoth quarterly newsletter.*

AMERICAN FRIENDS OF HAIFA UNIVERSITY (1972). 488 Madison Ave., 10th fl., NYC 10021. (212)838–8069. FAX: (212)838–

3464. Pres. David I. Faust. Promotes, encourages, and aids higher and secondary education, research, and training in all branches of knowledge in Israel and elsewhere; aids in the maintenance and development of Haifa University; raises and allocates funds for the above purposes; provides scholarships; promotes exchanges of teachers and students. *Newsletter; Focus.*

AMERICAN FRIENDS OF TEL AVIV UNIVERSITY, INC. (1955). 360 Lexington Ave., NYC 10017. (212)687–5651. FAX: (212)-687–4085. Bd. Chmn. Melvin S. Taub; Pres. Robert J. Topchik; Exec. V.-Pres. Jules Love. Promotes higher education at Tel Aviv University, Israel's largest and most comprehensive institution of higher learning. Among its nine faculties are the Sackler School of Medicine with its fully accredited NY State English-language program, the Rubin Academy of Music, and 62 research institutes including the Moshe Dayan Center for Middle East & African Studies, the Jaffe Center for Strategic Studies, the Steinmetz Peace Studies Center, and the Brain Research Center. *Tel Aviv University News; Friends; FAX Flash.*

AMERICAN FRIENDS OF THE HEBREW UNIVERSITY (1925; inc. 1931). 11 E. 69 St., NYC 10021. (212)472–9800. FAX: (212)-744–2324. Pres. Barbara A. Mandel; Bd. Chmn. Harvey M. Krueger; Exec. V.-Pres. Daniel J. Mansoor. Fosters the growth, development, and maintenance of the Hebrew University of Jerusalem; collects funds and conducts programs of information throughout the U.S., highlighting the university's achievements and its significance. *Hebrew University News; Scopus magazine.*

AMERICAN FRIENDS OF THE ISRAEL MUSEUM (1972). 10 E. 40 St., Suite 1208, NYC 10016. (212)683–5190. FAX: (212)-683–3187. Pres. Maureen Cogan; Exec. Dir. Michele Cohn Tocci. Raises funds for special projects of the Israel Museum in Jerusalem; solicits works of art for exhibition and educational purposes. *Newsletter.*

AMERICAN FRIENDS OF THE SHALOM HARTMAN INSTITUTE (1976). 282 Grand Ave., Englewood, NJ 07631. (201)894–0566. FAX: (201)894–0377. Pres. Robert P. Kogod; Dir. Rabbi Donniel Hartman; Admin. Dorothy Minchin. Supports the Shalom Hartman Institute, Jerusalem, an institute of higher education and research center devoted to applying the teachings of classical Judaism to the issues of modern life. Founded in 1976 by David Hartman, the institute includes advanced research centers in philosophy, theology, political thought, education, ethics, and Halakhah; a Beit Midrash, teacher-training programs, Russian scholars program, an experimental high school, and programs for Diaspora lay leadership and Jewish communal professionals and educators.

AMERICAN FRIENDS OF THE TEL AVIV MUSEUM OF ART (1974). 133 E. 58 St., Suite 701, NYC 10022. (212)319–0555. FAX: (212)754–2987. Cochmn. David Genser, Hanno Mott; Exec. Dir. Hanita Davar. Raises funds for the Tel Aviv Museum of Art for special projects, art acquisitions, and exhibitions; seeks contributions of art to expand the museum's collection; encourages art loans and traveling exhibitions; creates an awareness of the museum in the USA; makes available exhibition catalogues, monthly calendars, and posters published by the museum. *Newsletter.*

AMERICAN FRIENDS/SARAH HERZOG MEMORIAL HOSPITAL–JERUSALEM (EZRATH NASHIM) (1895). 40 E. 34 St., Suite 907, NYC 10016. (212)725–8175. FAX: (212)-725–8176. Pres. Frederick L. Gorsetman; Exec. Dir. Lorrie M. Greif. Conducts research, education, and patient care at Sarah Herzog Memorial Hospital in Jerusalem, which includes a 290-bed hospital, comprehensive outpatient clinic, drug-abuse clinic, geriatric center, and psychiatric research center; Israel's only independent, nonprofit, voluntary geriatric and psychiatric hospital; affiliated with Hadassah Hospital, Hebrew University, Bar-Ilan University, and other major medical schools and facilities. *Friend to Friend; To Open the Gates of Healing.*

AMERICAN ISRAEL PUBLIC AFFAIRS COMMITTEE (AIPAC) (1954). 440 First St., NW, Washington, DC 20001. (202)639–5200. FAX: (202)347–4921. Pres. Steven Grossman; Exec. Dir. Neal M. Sher. Registered to lobby on behalf of legislation affecting U.S.-Israel relations; represents Americans who believe support for a secure Israel is in U.S. interest. Works for a strong U.S.-Israel relationship. *Near East Report; AIPAC Papers on U.S.-Israel Relations.*

AMERICAN-ISRAELI LIGHTHOUSE, INC. (1928; reorg. 1955). 30 E. 60 St., NYC 10022. (212)838–5322. Pres. Mrs. Leonard F. Dank; Sec. Frances Lentz. Provides education and rehabilitation for the blind and physically handicapped in Israel to effect their social and vocational integration into the seeing community; built and maintains Rehabilitation Center for the Blind (Migdal Or) in Haifa. *Tower.*

AMERICAN JEWISH LEAGUE FOR ISRAEL (1957). 130 E. 59 St., NYC 10022. (212)-371–1582. FAX: (212)371–3265. Pres. Dr. Martin L. Kalmanson. Seeks to unite all those who, notwithstanding differing philosophies of Jewish life, are committed to the historical ideals of Zionism; works independently of class, party, or religious affiliation for the welfare of Israel as a whole. Not identified with any political parties in Israel. Member of World Jewish Congress, World Zionist Organization, American Zionist Movement. *Newsletter.*

AMERICAN PHYSICIANS FELLOWSHIP FOR MEDICINE IN ISRAEL (1950). 2001 Beacon St., Brookline, MA 02146. (617)232–5382. Pres. Louis M. Sherwood, MD; Exec. Dir. Daniel C. Goldfarb. Helps Israel become a major medical center; secures fellowships for selected Israeli physicians and arranges lectureships in Israel by prominent American physicians; runs medical seminars in Israel; coordinates U.S. and Canadian medical and paramedical emergency volunteers to Israel; supports research and health-care projects in Israel. *APF News.*

AMERICAN RED MAGEN DAVID FOR ISRAEL, INC. (1940) (a.k.a. ARMDI & Red Magen David). 888 Seventh Ave., Suite 403, NYC 10106. (212)757–1627. FAX: (212)757–4662. Natl. Pres. Robert L. Sadoff, MD; Natl. Chmn. Louis Cantor; Exec. V.-Pres. Benjamin Saxe. An authorized tax-exempt organization; the sole support arm in the U.S. of Magen David Adom (MDA), Israel's equivalent to a Red Cross Society; raises funds for the MDA emergency medical, ambulance, blood, and disaster services for Israel's defense forces and civilian population. Helps to supply and equip ambulances, bloodmobiles, and cardiac rescue ambulances; 45 prehospital MDA Emergency Medical Clinics; and the MDA National Blood Service Center and MDA Fractionation Institute in Ramat Gan, Israel. *Lifeline.*

AMERICANS FOR A SAFE ISRAEL (1971). 147 E. 76 St., NYC 10021. (212)628–9400. FAX: (212)988–4065. Chmn. Herbert Zweibon. Seeks to educate Americans in Congress, the media, and the public in general about Israel's role as a strategic asset for the West; through meetings with legislators and the media, in press releases and publications, promotes the notion of Jewish rights to Judea and Samaria and the concept of "peace for peace" as an alternative to "territory for peace." *Outpost.*

AMERICANS FOR PEACE NOW (1984). 27 W. 20 St., 9th fl., NYC 10011. (212)645–6262. FAX: (212)645–7355. Copres. Linda Heller Kamm, Richard Gunther; Exec. Dir. Gary E. Rubin. Conducts educational programs and raises funds to support the Israeli peace movement, Shalom Achshav (Peace Now), and coordinates U.S. advocacy efforts through APN's Washington-based Center for Israeli Peace and Security. *National Newsletter.*

AMERICANS FOR PROGRESSIVE ISRAEL (1952). 224 W. 35 St., Suite 403, NYC 10001. (212)868–0386. Pres. Naftali Landesman. A socialist Zionist organization that calls for a just and durable peace between Israel and all its Arab neighbors, including the Palestinian people; works for the liberation of all Jews; seeks the democratization of Jewish communal and organizational life; promotes dignity of labor, social justice, and a deeper understanding of Jewish culture and heritage. Affiliate of American Zionist Federation and World Union of Mapam, with fraternal ties to Hashomer Hatzair and Kibbutz Artzi Federation of Israel. *Israel Horizons.*

AMERICAN SOCIETY FOR TECHNION–ISRAEL INSTITUTE OF TECHNOLOGY (1940). 810 Seventh Ave., 24th fl., NYC 10019. (212)262–6200. FAX: (212)262–6155. Pres. Ben Sosewitz; Chmn. Lewis M. Weston; Exec. V.-Pres. Melvyn H. Bloom. Supports the work of the Technion-Israel Institute of Technology in Haifa, which trains over 10,000 students in 19 faculties and a medical school, and conducts research across a broad spectrum of science and technology. *Technion USA.*

AMERICAN SOCIETY FOR YAD VASHEM (1981). 48 W. 37 St., NYC 10018. (212)-564–9606. FAX: (212)268–0529. Chmn. Eli Zborowski; Exec. Dir. Selma Schiffer. Development arm of Yad Vashem, Jerusalem, the central international authority created by the Knesset in 1953 for the purposes of commemoration and education in connection with the Holocaust. *Martyrdom and Resistance (newsletter).*

AMERICAN ZIONIST MOVEMENT (formerly AMERICAN ZIONIST FEDERATION) (1939; reorg. 1949, 1970, 1993). 110 E. 59 St., NYC 10022. (212)318–6100. FAX: (212)-935–3578. Pres. Seymour Reich; Exec. Dir. Karen J. Rubinstein. Umbrella organization for 22 American Zionist organizations and the voice of unified Zionism in the U.S. Conducts advocacy for Israel; strengthens Jewish identity; promotes the Israel experience; prepares the next generation of Zionist leadership. Regional offices in Chicago, Los Angeles, Detroit, South Florida. Groups in Atlanta, Philadelphia, Baltimore, Pittsburgh, Washington, DC. *The Zionist Advocate.*

AMERICAN ZIONIST YOUTH FOUNDATION, INC. (1963). 110 E. 59 St., NYC 10022. (212)339–6002 (Israel Programs) or (212)-339–6925,6 (Executive Offices). Chmn. Julius Berman; Exec. V.-Chmn. Don Adelman. Heightens Zionist awareness among Jewish youth through programs and services geared to high-school and college-age youngsters. Sponsors educational tours to Israel, study in leading institutions; sponsors field workers on campus and in summer camps; prepares and provides specialists who present and interpret the Israel experience for community centers and federations throughout the country. *Activist Newsletter; Guide to Education and Programming Material; Programs in Israel.*

AMIT WOMEN (formerly AMERICAN MIZRACHI WOMEN) (1925). 817 Broadway, NYC 10003. (212)477–4720. Pres. Norma Holzer; Exec. Dir. Marvin Leff. The State of Israel's official *reshet* (network) for religious secondary technological education; maintains innovative children's homes and youth villages in Israel in an environment of traditional Judaism; promotes cultural activities for the purpose of disseminating Zionist ideals and strengthening traditional Judaism in America. *AMIT Woman.*

AMPAL–AMERICAN ISRAEL CORPORATION (1942). 1177 Avenue of the Americas, NYC 10036. (212)782–2100. FAX: (212)-782–2114. Pres. Lawrence Lefkowitz; Bd. Chmn. Michael Arnon. Acquires interests in businesses located in the State of Israel or that are Israel-related. Interests include hotels and leisure-time, real estate, energy distribution, basic industry, and high technology and communications. *Annual report; quarterly reports.*

ARZA–ASSOCIATION OF REFORM ZIONISTS OF AMERICA (1977). 838 Fifth Ave., NYC 10021. (212)249–0100. FAX: (212)517–7968. Pres. Marcia L. Cayne; Exec. Dir. Rabbi Ammiel Hirsch. Individual Zionist membership organization devoted to achieving Jewish pluralism in Israel and strengthening the Israeli Reform movement. Chapter activities in the U.S. concentrate on these issues and on strengthening American public support for Israel. *ARZA Newsletter.*

BETAR ZIONIST YOUTH ORGANIZATION (1935). 218 E. 79 St., NYC 10021. (212)-650–1231. Central Shlicha Tova Vagami. Dir. Glenn Mones. Organizes youth groups across North America to teach Zionism, Jewish identity, and love of Israel; sponsors summer programs in Israel for Jewish youth ages 12–22; sponsors Tagar Zionist Student Activist Movement on college campuses.

BOYS TOWN JERUSALEM FOUNDATION OF AMERICA INC. (1948). 91 Fifth Ave., Suite 601, NYC 10003. (212)242–1118. FAX: (212)242–2190. Pres. Michael J. Scharf; Chmn. Josh S. Weston; V.-Chmn. Alexander S. Linchner; Exec. V.-Pres. Rabbi Ronald L. Gray. Raises funds for Boys Town Jerusalem, which was established in 1948 to offer a comprehensive academic, religious, and technical education to disadvantaged Israeli and immigrant boys from over 45 different countries, including Ethiopia, Russia, and Iran. Enrollment: over 1,400 students in jr. high school, academic and technical high school, and a college of applied engineering. *BTJ Newsbriefs; Your Town Magazine.*

CAMERA – COMMITTEE FOR ACCURACY IN MIDDLE EAST REPORTING IN AMERICA (1982). PO Box 428, Boston, MA 02258. (617)789–3672. FAX: (617)787–7853. Pres./ Exec. Dir. Andrea Levin. Monitors and responds to media distortion in order to promote better understanding of Middle East events; urges members to alert the media to errors, omissions, and distortions; unites all friends of Israel regardless of politics or religion to correct unbalanced or inaccurate coverage of Middle East. *CAM-*

ERA Media Report (quarterly); CAMERA on Campus; Action Alerts.

COALITION FOR ISRAEL, INC. (1989). POB 107, Knickerbocker Station, NYC 10002. (212)475–7128. FAX: (212)475–7128. Chmn. N.R. Greenfield; Pres. Howard B. Weber; Exec. Sec. Elliot M. Jager; Rabbinic Cabinet, Rabbi David Algaze. Publishes educational *"hasbara"* advertisements in the press regarding Jewish rights to the Land of Israel. Informally, coordinates activities of various "national camp" organizations.

COUNCIL FOR A BEAUTIFUL ISRAEL ENVIRONMENTAL EDUCATION FOUNDATION (1973). 350 Fifth Ave., 19th fl., NYC 10118. (212)947–5709. Pres. Dina A. Evan; Admin. Dir. Donna Lindemann. A support group for the Israeli body, whose activities include education, town planning, lobbying for legislation to protect and enhance the environment, preservation of historical sites, the improvement and beautification of industrial and commercial areas, and renovating bomb shelters into parks and playgrounds. *Yearly newsletter.*

EDUCATION FUND FOR ISRAELI CIVIL RIGHTS AND PEACE (1991). (212)447–6652. FAX: (212)447–7638. Chmn. Rabbi Douglas Krantz; Exec. Dir. Sara Zucker. A forum for addressing the issues of social justice and peace in Israel. Educates about issues related to democracy, human and civil rights, religious pluralism, and equality for women and ethnic minorities; promotes the resolution of Israel's conflict with the Palestinians on the basis of mutual recognition, self-determination, and peaceful coexistence. *Current Insight (bimonthly newsletter).*

EMUNAH WOMEN OF AMERICA (formerly HAPOEL HAMIZRACHI WOMEN'S ORGANIZATION) (1948). 7 Penn Plaza, NYC 10001. (212)564–9045. FAX: (212)643–9731. Pres. Sondra H. Fisch; Exec. Dir. Shirley Singer. Maintains and supports 200 educational and social-welfare institutions in Israel within a religious framework, including day-care centers, kindergartens, children's residential homes, vocational schools for the underprivileged, senior-citizen centers, a college complex, and Holocaust study center. Also involved in absorption of Soviet and Ethiopian immigrants (recognized by Israeli government as an official absorption agency). *Emunah Magazine; Lest We Forget.*

FEDERATED COUNCIL OF ISRAEL INSTITUTIONS–FCII (1940). 4702 15th Ave., Brooklyn, NY 11219. (718)972–5530. Bd. Chmn. Z. Shapiro; Exec. V.-Pres. Rabbi Julius Novack. Central fund-raising organization for over 100 affiliated institutions; handles and executes estates, wills, and bequests for the traditional institutions in Israel; clearinghouse for information on budget, size, functions, etc., of traditional educational, welfare, and philanthropic institutions in Israel, working cooperatively with the Israeli government and the overseas department of the Council of Jewish Federations. *Annual financial reports and statistics on affiliates.*

FRIENDS OF LABOR ISRAEL (1987). 27 W. 20 St., 9th fl., NYC 10011. FAX: (212)929–3459. Chmn. Rabbi Daniel Polish. American organization committed to a program of education in America and Israel on behalf of institutions, organizations, and projects in Israel designed to promote democracy, pluralism, social justice, and peace. FLI is an affinity group of the Israel Labor movement and represents the concerns of like-minded American Jews in Labor circles.

FRIENDS OF THE ISRAEL DEFENSE FORCES (1981). 21 W. 38 St., 5th fl., NYC 10018. (212)575–5030. FAX: (212)575–7815. Chmn. Marvin Josephson; Pres. Stephen Rubin. Supports the Agudah Lema'an Hahayal, Israel's Assoc. for the Well-Being of Soldiers, founded in the early 1940s, which provides social, recreational, and educational programs for soldiers, special services for the sick and wounded, and summer programs for widows and children of fallen soldiers. *Frontline (newsletter).*

FUND FOR HIGHER EDUCATION (1970). 1768 S. Wooster St., Los Angeles, CA 90035. (310)202–1879. Chmn. Amnon Barness; Chmn. Exec. Com. Max Candiotty. Raises funds and disseminates information in the interest of institutions of higher education in the U.S. and Israel. Over $18 million distributed to over 100 institutions of higher learning, including over $11 million in Israel and $6 million in the U.S. *In Response.*

GESHER FOUNDATION (1969). 421 Seventh Ave., #905, NYC 10001. (212) 564–0338. FAX: (212)967–2726. Pres. Matthew J. Maryles; Exec. V.-Pres. Hillel Wiener.

Seeks to bridge the gap between Jews of various backgrounds in Israel by stressing the interdependence of all Jews. Runs encounter seminars for Israeli youth; distributes curricular materials in public schools; offers Jewish identity classes for Russian youth, and a video series in Russian and English on famous Jewish personalities.

GIVAT HAVIVA EDUCATIONAL FOUNDATION, INC. (1966). 224 W. 35 St., Suite 403, NYC 10001. (212)868–0353; (800)385–3536. FAX: (212)868–0364. Chmn. Fred Howard; Exec. Dir. Steven Goldberg. Supports programs at the Givat Haviva Institute in Israel, which promote democratic coexistence between Jews and Arabs. Also hosts programs between Israelis and Palestinians to promote understanding and peace. In N. America, hosts "Children's Art for Peace" exhibit as well as public lectures by prominent Israeli speakers. *Givat Haviva News; special reports.*

GOLDA MEIR ASSOCIATION (1984). 110 E. 59 St., NYC 10022. (212)318–6197. FAX: (215)830–0351. Chmn. Abe Pollin; Pres. Robert C. Klutznick. Consultant, Robert I. Evans: 2300 Computer Ave., Bldg. G., Willow Grove, PA 19090. (215)830–0304. FAX: (215)830–0351. North American support group for the Israeli association, whose large-scale educational programs address the issues of democracy in Israel, Sephardi-Ashkenazi integration, religious pluralism, the peace process, and relations between Israeli Jews and Arabs. Its "Project Democracy" has been adapted to help new Soviet immigrants integrate into Israeli society by providing them an education in democratic ideals and principles. *Newsletter.*

HABONIM-DROR NORTH AMERICA (1935). 27 W. 20 St., 9th fl., NYC 10011. (212)-255–1796. FAX: (212)929–3459. Mazkir Tnua, Seth Brysk; Exec. Off. Dan Bobman. Fosters identification with progressive, cooperative living in Israel; stimulates study of Jewish and Zionist culture, history, and contemporary society; sponsors summer and year programs in Israel and on kibbutz, 6 summer camps in N. America modeled after kibbutzim, and *aliyah* frameworks. *Batnua–In Our Movement; Bimat Hamaapilim.*

HADASSAH, THE WOMEN'S ZIONIST ORGANIZATION OF AMERICA, INC. (1912). 50 W. 58 St., NYC 10019. (212)355–7900.

FAX: (212)303–8282. Pres. Deborah Kaplan; Exec. Dir. Beth Wohlgelernter. In America delivers factual information on the development and security of Israel to the American public; provides basic Jewish education as a background for intelligent and creative Jewish living; develops knowledgeable leadership for the American Jewish community; sponsors Young Judaea, largest Zionist youth movement in U.S.; operates six Zionist youth camps in this country; supports summer and all-year courses in Israel. Maintains in Israel Hadassah-Hebrew University Medical Center for healing, teaching, and research; Hadassah College of Technology; and Hadassah Career Counseling Institute. *Update; Headlines; Hadassah Magazine; Textures; Bat Kol; The American Scene; Communities; Connections; Vanguard; MedBriefs; Focus on Me.*

———, YOUNG JUDAEA (1909; reorg. 1967). 50 W. 58 St., NYC 10019. (212)355–7900. FAX: (212)247–9240 Natl. Dir. Doron Krakow; Coord. Hamagshimim (college level) Erika Marcus; Pres. of Sr. Judaea (high-school level) Polina Froymovich. Seeks to educate Jewish youth aged 9–22 toward Jewish and Zionist values, active commitment to and participation in the American and Israeli Jewish communities; maintains summer camps and year programs in Israel. *Hamagshimim Journal; Kol Hat'nua; The Young Judaean.*

HASHOMER HATZAIR, SOCIALIST ZIONIST YOUTH MOVEMENT (1923). 224 W. 35 St., Suite 403, NYC 10001. (212)868–0377. FAX: (212)868–0364. Pres. Avshalom Vilan; Natl. Sec. Adam Dromi; Dir. Itai Lavi. Seeks to educate Jewish youth to an understanding of Zionism as the national liberation movement of the Jewish people. Promotes *aliyah* to kibbutzim. Affiliated with AZYF and Kibbutz Artzi Federation. Espouses socialist-Zionist ideals of peace, justice, democracy, and brotherhood. *Young Guard.*

INTERNS FOR PEACE (NITZANEI SHALOM/ BARA'EM AS'SALAAM/BUDS OF PEACE) (1976). 165 E. 56 St., NYC 10022. (212)-319–4545. FAX: (212)319–4549. Internatl. Dir. Rabbi Bruce M. Cohen; Education Dir. Karen Wald Cohen. An independent, nonprofit, nonpolitical educational program training professional community peace workers. In Israel, initiated and operated jointly by Jews and Arabs; over 170 interns trained in 35 cities; over 70,000 Israeli citizens participating in joint programs in education, sports, culture, business, women's affairs, and community development. In USA/Russia, new ethnic projects. *IFP Reports Quarterly; Guidebooks for Ethnic Conflict Resolution.*

ISRAEL CANCER RESEARCH FUND (1975). 1290 Avenue of the Americas, NYC 10104. (212)969–9800. FAX: (212)969–9822. Pres. Dr. Yashar Hirshaut; Chmn. S. Donald Friedman. The largest single source of private funds for cancer research in Israel. Has a threefold mission: to encourage innovative cancer research by Israeli scientists; to harness Israel's vast intellectual and creative resources to establish a world-class center for cancer study; to broaden research opportunities within Israel to stop the exodus of talented Israeli cancer researchers. *Annual Report; Research Awards; "What/Where/Why"; Glossary; Towards a Cure; Newsletter.*

ISRAEL HISTADRUT FOUNDATION (1960). 276 Fifth Ave., Suite 901, NYC 10001. (212)683–5454. FAX: (212)213–9233. Pres. Marvin Sirota; Exec. V.-Pres. Alvin Smolin. A membership corporation providing philanthropic support to Histadrut, the federated association of working men and women in Israel. Helps the Histadrut build and maintain its network of social-service agencies, which is the largest in Israel and benefits over 85 percent of Israel's population.

ISRAEL POLICY FORUM (1994). 666 Fifth Ave., 21st fl., NYC 10103. (212)245–4227. FAX: (212)245–0517. Pres. Robert K. Lifton; Exec. V.-Pres. Jonathan Jacoby. A leadership institute committed to the belief that the best future for Israel lies in the vision promoted by the government of Israel's present policies. Works with major Jewish organizations to encourage programs and activities that educate about the positive aspects of these policies.

JEWISH INSTITUTE FOR NATIONAL SECURITY AFFAIRS (JINSA) (1976). 1717 K St., NW, Suite 300, Washington, DC 20006. (202)833–0020. FAX: (202)296–6452. Pres. Ted Dinerstein; Exec. Dir. Tom Neumann. A nonprofit, nonpartisan educational organization working within the American Jewish community to explain the link between American defense policy and the security of the State of Israel; and

within the national security establishment to explain the key role Israel plays in bolstering American interests. *Security Affairs.*

JEWISH NATIONAL FUND OF AMERICA (1901). 42 E. 69 St., NYC 10021. (212)-879–9300. FAX: (212)517–3293. Pres. Milton Shapiro; Exec. V.-Pres. Dr. Samuel I. Cohen. Exclusive fund-raising agency of the world Zionist movement for the afforestation, reclamation, and development of the land of Israel, including construction of roads, parks, and recreational areas, preparation of land for agriculture, new communities, and industrial facilities; helps emphasize the importance of Israel in schools and synagogues throughout the U.S. *JNF Almanac; Land and Life.*

JEWISH PEACE LOBBY (1989). 8604 Second Ave., Suite 317, Silver Spring, MD 20910. (301)589–8764. FAX: (301)589–2722. Pres. Jerome M. Segal. A legally registered lobby promoting changes in U.S. policy vis-à-vis the Israeli-Palestinian conflict. Supports Israel's right to peace within secure borders; a political settlement based on mutual recognition of the right of self-determination of both peoples; a two-state solution as the most likely means to a stable peace. *Washington Action Alerts.*

KEREN OR, INC. (1956). 350 Seventh Ave., Suite 200, NYC 10001–5103. (212)279–4070. FAX: (212)279–4043. Bd. Chmn. Dr. Edward L. Steinberg; Pres. Dr. Albert Hornblass; Exec. V.-Pres. Paul H. Goldenberg. Funds the Keren-Or Center for Multihandicapped Blind Children, at 3 Abba Hillel Silver St., Ramot, Jerusalem, housing and caring for 90 children, 1½ to 16 years of age. Provides long-term basic training, therapy, rehabilitative, and early childhood education to the optimum level of the individual; with major hospitals, is involved in research into causes of multihandicapped blind birth. *Insights Newsletter.*

LABOR ZIONIST ALLIANCE (formerly FARBAND LABOR ZIONIST ORDER; now uniting membership and branches of POALE ZION–UNITED LABOR ZIONIST ORGANIZATION OF AMERICA and AMERICAN HABONIM ASSOCIATION) (1913). 275 Seventh Ave., NYC 10001. (212)366–1194, (212)366–1387. FAX: (212)675–7685. Pres. Henry L. Feingold. Seeks to enhance Jewish life, culture, and education in U.S.;

aids in building State of Israel as a cooperative commonwealth and its Labor movement organized in the Histadrut; supports efforts toward a more democratic society throughout the world; furthers the democratization of the Jewish community in America and the welfare of Jews everywhere; works with labor and liberal forces in America. *Jewish Frontier; Yiddisher Kempfer.*

LIKUD USA (1925). 4 East 34 St., 4th fl., NYC 10016. (212)447-7887. FAX: (212)-447-7492. Chmn. George S. Meissner; Chmn. Young Leadership Div. Howard Barbanel. Educates the Jewish community and the American public about the views of Israel's Likud party; encourages support for a strong, secure State of Israel in all of its territory. *The Likud Newsletter.*

MEDICAL DEVELOPMENT FOR ISRAEL (1982). 130 E. 59 St., NYC 10022. (212)-759-3370. FAX: (212)759-0120. Bd. Chmn. H. Irwin Levy; Pres. Dr. Samuel C. Klagsbrun. Raises funds to help improve the quality of health care in Israel, its primary goal the construction of the Children's Medical Center of Israel, a 224-bed tertiary care facility for the entire region. *Brochures and newsletters.*

MERCAZ U.S.A. (1979). 155 Fifth Ave., NYC 10010. (212)533-7800. FAX: (212)-533-2601. Pres. Roy Clements, Exec. Dir. Renah L. Rabinowitz. The U.S. Zionist organization for Conservative/Masorti Judaism; works for religious pluralism in Israel, defending and promoting Conservative/Masorti institutions and individuals; fosters Zionist education and *aliyah* and develops young leadership. *Mercaz News & Views.*

NA'AMAT USA, THE WOMEN'S LABOR ZIONIST ORGANIZATION OF AMERICA, INC. (formerly PIONEER WOMEN/NA'A-MAT) (1925; reorg. 1985). 200 Madison Ave., 21st. fl., NYC 10016. (212)725-8010. FAX: (212)447-5187. Pres. Sylvia Lewis. Part of a world movement of working women and volunteers, NA'AMAT USA helps provide social, educational, and legal services for women, teenagers, and children in Israel. It also advocates legislation for women's rights and child welfare in the U.S., furthers Jewish education, and supports Habonim-Dror, the Labor Zionist youth movement. *NA'AMAT WOMAN magazine.*

NATIONAL COMMITTEE FOR LABOR ISRAEL (1923). 275 Seventh Ave., NYC 10001. (212)647-0300. FAX: (212)647-0308. Pres. Jay Mazur; Exec. Dir. Jerry Goodman; Chmn. Trade Union Council Morton Bahr. Conducts educational and communal activities in Jewish community and promotes relations and understanding between U.S. trade unions and Israel and Israel's Labor Federation-Histadrut. Brings together Jews, non-Jews, whites, blacks, and Hispanics to build support for Israel and the labor sector. Israel Histadrut Campaign raises funds for educational, health, social, and cultural projects. *NCLI Notebook; occasional background papers.*

NEW ISRAEL FUND (1979). 1625 K St., NW, Washington, DC 20006. (202)223-3333. FAX: (202)659-2789. New York office: 165 E. 56 St., NYC 10022. (212)302-0066. Pres. Herbert Teitelbaum; Exec. Dir. Norman S. Rosenberg. A partnership of Israelis and North Americans dedicated to strengthening democracy and advancing social justice in Israel. The Fund strengthens Israel's democratic fabric by providing funds and technical assistance to the independent, public-interest sector; cultivating a new generation of public-interest leaders; and educating citizens—both in Israel and abroad—to create a constituency for democracy. *Quarterly newsletter; annual report.*

PEC ISRAEL ECONOMIC CORPORATION (formerly PALESTINE ECONOMIC CORPORATION) (1926). 511 Fifth Ave., NYC 10017. (212)687-2400. Chmn. R. Recanati; Pres. Joseph Ciechanover; Exec. V.-Pres. James I. Edelson; Treas. William Gold. Primarily engaged in the business of organizing, acquiring interest in, financing, and participating in the management of companies located in the State of Israel or Israel-related. *Annual and quarterly reports.*

PEF ISRAEL ENDOWMENT FUNDS, INC. (1922). 41 E. 42 St., Suite 607, NYC 10017. (212)599-1260. Chmn. Sidney A. Luria; Pres. Abraham J. Kremer; Sec. Harvey Brecher. A totally volunteer organization that makes grants to educational, scientific, social, religious, health, and other philanthropic institutions in Israel. *Annual report.*

PIONEER WOMEN/NA'AMAT (*see* NA'AMAT USA)

POALE AGUDATH ISRAEL OF AMERICA, INC. (1948). 4405 13th Ave., Brooklyn,

NY 11219. (718)435–8228. Pres. Rabbi Fabian Schonfeld. Aims to educate American Jews to the values of Orthodoxy and *aliyah;* supports kibbutzim, trade schools, yeshivot, moshavim, kollelim, research centers, and children's homes in Israel. *PAI News; She'arim; Hamayan.*

———, WOMEN'S DIVISION OF (1948). Pres. Miriam Lubling; Presidium: Sarah Ivanisky, Tili Stark, Peppi Petzenbaum. Assists Poale Agudath Israel to build and support children's homes, kindergartens, and trade schools in Israel. *Yediot PAI.*

PROGRESSIVE ZIONIST CAUCUS (1982). 27 W. 20 St., 9th fl., NYC 10011. (212)675–1168. FAX: (212)929–3459. Dir. Jonathan Glick. A campus-based grassroots organization committed to a progressive Zionist agenda. Students organize local and regional educational, cultural, and political activities, such as speakers, films, *Kabbalot Shabbat,* and Arab-Jewish dialogue groups. The PZC Kvutzat Aliyah is a support framework for individuals interested in *aliyah* to a city or town. *baBayit.*

PRO ISRAEL (1990). 17 E. 45 St., Suite 603, NYC 10017. (212)867–0577. FAX: (212)-867–0615. Pres. Dr. Ernest Bloch; V.-Pres. Dr. Donald H. Miller. Educates the public about Israel and the Middle East through mailings, newsletters, and speakers; provides support for community development throughout the Land of Israel, particularly in Judea, Samaria, Gaza, and the Golan Heights; maintains a research and information center on Israel and the Middle East.

PROJECT NISHMA (1988). 1225 15 St., NW, Washington, DC 20005. (202)462–4268. FAX: (202)462–3892. Cochmn. Theodore R. Mann, Edward Sanders, Henry Rosovsky; Exec. Dir. Thomas R. Smerling. Conducts educational programs on Israeli security and the peace process; arranges military briefings for Jewish leaders; publishes articles by senior Israeli defense and foreign policy experts; analyzes Israeli and U.S. Jewish opinion and articulates pragmatic positions on peace and security. Sponsored by over 100 nationally active Jewish leaders from across the country.

RELIGIOUS ZIONISTS OF AMERICA. 25 W. 26 St., NYC 10010. (212)689–1414.

———, BNEI AKIVA OF NORTH AMERICA (1934). 25 W. 26 St., NYC 10010. (212)-889–5260. V.-Pres. Admin. Marc Haber;

Natl. Dir. Noah Slomowitz. The only religious Zionist youth movement in North America, serving over 10,000 young people from grade school through graduate school in 16 active regions across the United States and Canada, six summer camps, seven established summer, winter, and year programs in Israel. Stresses communal involvement, social activism, leadership training, and substantive programming to educate young people toward a commitment to Judaism and Israel. *Akivon; Hamvaser; Pinkas Lamadrich; Daf Rayonot; Ma'Ohalai Torah; Zraim.*

———, MIZRACHI-HAPOEL HAMIZRACHI (1909; merged 1957). 25 W. 26 St., NYC 10010. (212)689–1414. FAX: (212)779–3043. Pres. Rabbi Sol Roth; Exec. V.-Pres. Israel Friedman. Disseminates ideals of religious Zionism; conducts cultural work, educational program, public relations; raises funds for religious educational institutions in Israel, including *yeshivot hesder* and Bnei Akiva. *Newsletters; Kolenu.*

———, MIZRACHI PALESTINE FUND (1928). 25 W. 26 St., NYC 10010. Chmn. Joseph Wilon; Sec. Israel Friedman. Fundraising arm of Mizrachi movement.

———, NATIONAL COUNCIL FOR TORAH EDUCATION OF MIZRACHI-HAPOEL HAMIZRACHI (1939). 25 W. 26 St., NYC 10010. Pres. Rabbi Israel Schorr; Dir. Rabbi Meyer Golombek. Organizes and supervises yeshivot and Talmud Torahs; prepares and trains teachers; publishes textbooks and educational materials; organizes summer seminars for Hebrew educators in cooperation with Torah Department of Jewish Agency; conducts ulpan. *Hazarkor; Chemed.*

———, NOAM-MIZRACHI NEW LEADERSHIP COUNCIL (formerly NOAM-HAMISHMERET HATZEIRA) (1970). 25 W. 26 St., NYC 10010. (212)684–6091. Chmn. Rabbi Marc Schneier; V.-Chmn. Sheon Karol. Develops new religious Zionist leadership in the U.S. and Canada; presents young religious people with various alternatives for settling in Israel through *garinei aliyah* (core groups); meets the religious, educational, and social needs of Jewish young adults and young couples. *Forum.*

SOCIETY OF ISRAEL PHILATELISTS (1949). 24355 Tunbridge Lane, Beachwood, OH 44122. (216)292–3843. Pres. Samuel Resnick; Journal Ed. Dr. Oscar Stadtler. Promotes interest in, and knowledge of, all phases of Israel philately through sponsorship of chapters and research groups, maintenance of a philatelic library, and support of public and private exhibitions. *The Israel Philatelist; monographs; books.*

STATE OF ISRAEL BONDS (1951). 575 Lexington Ave., #600, NYC 10022. (212)644–2663. FAX: (212)644–3925. Bd. Chmn. & Internatl. Chmn. David B. Hermelin; Pres. & CEO Amb. Meir Rosenne. Seeks to provide Israel with large-scale investment funds, which are currently being allocated for immigrant absorption, through the sale of State of Israel securities worldwide.

THEODOR HERZL FOUNDATION (1954). 110 E. 59 St., NYC 10022. (212)339–6000. FAX: (212)318–6176. Chmn. Kalman Sultanik; Sec. Zelig Chinitz; Dir. of Publications Sam E. Bloch. Offers cultural activities, lectures, conferences, courses in modern Hebrew and Jewish subjects, Israel, Zionism, and Jewish history. *Midstream.*

———, HERZL PRESS. Chmn. Kalman Sultanik; Dir. of Publications Sam E. Bloch. Serves as "the Zionist Press of record," publishing books that are important for the light they shed on Zionist philosophy, Israeli history, contemporary Israel and the Diaspora and the relationship between them. They are important as contributions to Zionist letters and history. *Midstream.*

THEODOR HERZL INSTITUTE. 110 E. 59 St., NYC 10022. (212)339–6000. Chmn. Jacques Torczyner; Dir. Ida Reich. Program geared to review of contemporary problems on Jewish scene here and abroad, presentation of Jewish heritage values in light of Zionist experience of the ages, study of modern Israel, and Jewish social research with particular consideration of history and impact of Zionism. Lectures, forums, Encounter with Creativity; musicales, recitals, concerts; holiday celebrations; visual art programs, Nouveau Artist Introductions. *Annual Program Preview; Herzl Institute Bulletin.*

TSOMET (formerly TSOMET-TECHIYA USA) (1978). PO Box 501, NYC 10002. (212)475–7128. FAX: (212)475–7128. Acting Pres. Fredrica B. Tobin; Central Committee Members: Honey Rackman, Elliot Jager, Melvin D. Shay, Howard B. Weber. A member of the American Zionist Movement; supports the activities of the Israeli TSOMET party, which advocates Israeli control over the entire Land of Israel.

UNITED CHARITY INSTITUTIONS OF JERUSALEM, INC. (1903). 1467–48 St., Brooklyn, NY 11219. (718)633–8469. FAX: (718)633–8478. Chmn. Rabbi Charlop; Exec. Dir. Rabbi Pollak. Raises funds for the maintenance of schools, kitchens, clinics, and dispensaries in Israel; free loan foundations in Israel.

UNITED ISRAEL APPEAL, INC. (1925). 110 E. 59 St., NYC 10022. (212)339–6900. FAX: (212)754–4293. Chmn. Norman H. Lipoff; Exec. V.-Chmn. Jay Yoskowitz. Provides funds raised by UJA/Federation campaigns in the U.S. to aid the people of Israel through the programs of the Jewish Agency for Israel, UIA's operating agent. Serves as link between American Jewish community and Jewish Agency for Israel; assists in resettlement and absorption of refugees in Israel, and supervises flow and expenditure of funds for this purpose. *Annual report; newsletters; brochures.*

UNITED STATES COMMITTEE SPORTS FOR ISRAEL, INC. (1948). 1926 Arch St., Philadelphia, PA 19103. (215)561–6900. Pres. Robert E. Spivak; Exec. Dir. Barbara G. Lissy. Sponsors U.S. team for World Maccabiah Games in Israel every four years; seeks to enrich the lives of Jewish youth in the U.S., Israel, and the Diaspora through athletic, cultural, and educational programs; develops, promotes, and supports international, national, and regional athletic-based activities and facilities. *Maccabiah Newsletter; USCSFI Newsletter; commemorative Maccabiah Games journal; financial report.*

VOLUNTEERS FOR ISRAEL (1982). 330 W. 42 St., NYC 10036–6902. (212)643–4848. FAX: (212)643–4855. Pres. Rickey Cherner; Natl. Coord. Arthur W. Stern. Provides aid to Israel through volunteer work, building lasting relationships between Israelis and Americans. Affords persons aged 18 and over the opportunity to participate in various duties currently performed by overburdened Israelis on IDF bases and in other settings, enabling them to meet and work closely with Israelis and to gain an inside view of Israeli life and culture. *Quarterly newsletter; information documents.*

WOMEN'S LEAGUE FOR ISRAEL, INC. (1928). 160 E. 56 St., NYC 10022. (212)838–1997.

FAX: (212)888–5972. Pres. Trudy Miner; Exec. Dir. Dorothy Leffler. Promotes the welfare of young people in Israel; built and maintains homes in Jerusalem, Haifa, Tel Aviv; Natanya Vocational Training and Rehabilitation Center; and the National Library of Social Work. Also many facilities and programs on the campuses of the Hebrew University. *WLI Bulletin.*

WORLD CONFEDERATION OF UNITED ZIONISTS (1946; reorg. 1958). 130 E. 59 St., NYC 10022. (212)371–1452. FAX: (212)-371–3265. Copres. Bernice S. Tannenbaum, Kalman Sultanik, Melech Topiol. Promotes Zionist education, sponsors nonparty youth movements in the Diaspora, and strives for an Israel-oriented creative Jewish survival in the Diaspora. *Zionist Information Views (in English and Spanish).*

WORLD ZIONIST ORGANIZATION–AMERICAN SECTION (1971). 110 E. 59 St., NYC 10022. (212)339–6000. FAX: (212)826–8959. Chmn. Kalman Sultanik; Exec. V.-Chmn. Zelig Chinitz. As the American section of the overall Zionist body throughout the world, it operates primarily in the field of *aliyah* from the free countries, education in the Diaspora, youth and Hechalutz, organization and information, cultural institutions, publications; conducts a worldwide Hebrew cultural program including special seminars and pedagogic manuals; disperses information and assists in research projects concerning Israel; promotes, publishes, and distributes books, periodicals, and pamphlets concerning developments in Israel, Zionism, and Jewish history. *Midstream.*

———, DEPARTMENT OF EDUCATION AND CULTURE (1948). 110 E. 59 St., NYC 10022. (212)339–6001. FAX: (212)826–8959. Renders educational services to boards and schools: study programs, books, AV aids, instruction, teacher-in-training service. Judaic and Hebrew subjects. Annual National Bible Contest; Israel summer and winter programs for teachers and students.

———, NORTH AMERICAN ALIYAH MOVEMENT (1968). 110 E. 59 St., NYC 10022. (212)339–6060. FAX: (212)826–8959. Exec. Dir. Nellie Neeman. Promotes and facilitates *aliyah* and *klitah* from the U.S. and Canada to Israel; serves as a social framework for North American immigrants to Israel. *Aliyon; NAAM Newsletter; Coming Home.*

ZIONIST ORGANIZATION OF AMERICA (1897). ZOA House, 4 E. 34 St., NYC 10016. (212)481–1500. FAX: (212)481–1515. Pres. W. James Schiller; Exec. Dir. William H. Rothchild. Seeks to safeguard the integrity and independence of Israel, assists in its economic development, and fosters the unity of the Jewish people and the centrality of Israel in Jewish life in the spirit of General Zionism. In Israel, owns and maintains both the ZOA House in Tel Aviv, a cultural center, and the Kfar Silver Agricultural and Technical High School in Ashkelon, with a full-time enrollment of 900 students. *American Zionist Magazine; Zionist Information Service Weekly News Bulletin (ZINS); Public Affairs Action Guidelines; ZOA Insider Report for ZOA Leaders.*

OVERSEAS AID

AMERICAN FRIENDS OF THE ALLIANCE ISRAÉLITE UNIVERSELLE, INC. (1946). 420 Lexington Ave., Suite 1733, NYC 10170. (212)808–5437. FAX: (212)983–0094. Pres. Henriette Beilis; Exec. Dir. Warren Green. Participates in educational and human-rights activities of the AIU and supports the Alliance System of Jewish schools, teachers' colleges, and remedial programs in Israel, North Africa, the Middle East, Europe, and Canada. *Alliance Review.*

AMERICAN JEWISH JOINT DISTRIBUTION COMMITTEE, INC.–JDC (1914). 711 Third Ave., NYC 10017–4014. (212)687–6200. FAX: (212)370–5467. Pres. Hon. Milton A. Wolf; Exec. V.-Pres. Michael Schneider. Provides assistance to Jewish communities in Europe, Asia, Africa, and the Mideast, including welfare programs for Jews in need. Current concerns include rescue of Jews from areas of distress; Israel's social needs, and absorption efforts for Soviet and Ethiopian immigrants. Program expansions emphasize community development in the former Soviet Union and youth activities in Eastern Europe and nonsectarian development and disaster assistance. *Annual report; Fast Facts.*

AMERICAN JEWISH PHILANTHROPIC FUND (1955). 386 Park Ave. S., 10th fl., NYC 10016. (212)OR9–0010. Pres. Charles J. Tanenbaum. Provides resettlement assistance to Jewish refugees primarily through programs administered by the International Rescue Committee at its offices in Western Europe and the U.S.

AMERICAN ORT, INC.–ORGANIZATION FOR REHABILITATION THROUGH TRAINING (1924). 817 Broadway, NYC 10003. (212)-677–4400. FAX: (212)979–9545. Pres. Murray Koppelman; Exec. V.-Pres. Marshall M. Jacobson. Provides vocational/technical education to more than 250,000 students in 50 countries throughout the world. The largest ORT operation is in Israel, where 96,000 students attend 140 ORT schools and training centers. Expanded programs meet the needs of emigration of Jews from the Soviet Union: in Israel, special vocational training and job placement programs; in the U.S., special programs in New York, Chicago, and Los Angeles, with courses in English as a second language, bookkeeping, computer operations, and business math. Annual cost of program is approximately $187 million. *American ORT Federation Bulletin; American ORT Federation Yearbook.*

——, WOMEN'S AMERICAN ORT (1927). 315 Park Ave. S., NYC 10010. (212)505–7700. FAX: (212)674–3057. Pres. Sandy Isenstein; Exec. Dir. Tehila Elpern. Advances the programs and self-help ethos of ORT through membership, fund-raising, and educational activities. Supports 140 vocational schools, junior colleges, and technical training centers in Israel; helps meet the educational needs of Jewish communities in 30 countries; spearheads growing ORT-U.S. school operations in New York, Los Angeles, and Chicago, and associate programs in Miami and Atlanta. Domestic agenda espouses quality public education, combats anti-Semitism, champions women's rights, and promotes a national literacy campaign. *Women's American ORT Reporter; Women's American ORT Yearbook.*

CONFERENCE ON JEWISH MATERIAL CLAIMS AGAINST GERMANY, INC. (1951). 15 E. 26 St., Rm. 906, NYC 10010. (212)-696–4944. FAX: (212)679–2126. Pres. Dr. Israel Miller; Sec. and Exec. Dir. Saul Kagan. Monitors the implementation of restitution and indemnification programs of the German Federal Republic (FRG) arising from its agreements with West Germany and most recently with united Germany, especially with respect to property lost by Jewish Nazi victims on the territory of the former German Democratic Republic. Administers Hardship Fund for Jewish Nazi victims unable to file timely claims under original indemnification laws or who received minimal compensation. Also assists needy non-Jews who risked their lives to help Jewish survivors.

HIAS, INC. (HEBREW IMMIGRANT AID SOCIETY) (1880; reorg. 1954). 333 Seventh Ave., NYC 10001–5004. (212)967–4100. FAX: (212)967–4442. Pres. Martin Kesselhaut; Exec. V.-Pres. Martin A. Wenick. The international migration agency of the organized American Jewish community, assists in the rescue, protection, and movement of Jewish refugees and other Jewish migrants. HIAS also responds to the migration needs of other peoples at risk and represents and advocates on behalf of all these peoples, Jewish and other. *Annual report; Headlines and Highlights (monthly newsletter).*

INTERNATIONAL COALITION FOR THE REVIVAL OF THE JEWS OF YEMEN (ICROJOY) (1989). 24 Bennett Ave., Apt. 24B, NYC 10033. (212)781–4849 or (212)-923–1406. Chmn. Dr. Hayim Tawil; V.-Chmn. Shlomo Grafi; Sec. Lester Smerka. Seeks to enrich and assist the Jewish community of the Republic of Yemen.

JEWISH RESTITUTION SUCCESSOR ORGANIZATION (1947). 15 E. 26 St., Rm. 1355, NYC 10010. (212)696–4944. FAX: (212)-679–2126. Sec. and Exec. Dir. Saul Kagan. Acts to discover, claim, receive, and assist in the recovery of Jewish heirless or unclaimed property; to utilize such assets or to provide for their utilization for the relief, rehabilitation, and resettlement of surviving victims of Nazi persecution.

NORTH AMERICAN CONFERENCE ON ETHIOPIAN JEWRY (NACOEJ) (1982). 165 E. 56 St., NYC 10022. (212)752–6340. FAX: (212)980–5294. Pres. Neil Jacobs; Exec. Dir. Barbara Ribakove Gordon. Provides programming for Ethiopian Jews in Israel in the areas of education (preschool through college), vocational training, and cultural preservation. Informs American and other Jewish communities about the situation of Ethiopian Jews; works to increase involvement of world Jewish communities in assisting, visiting, and learning about Ethiopian Jews. *Lifeline (newsletter).*

RE'UTH WOMEN'S SOCIAL SERVICE, INC. (1937). 130 E. 59 St., NYC 10022. (212)-

836–1570. FAX: (212)836–1114. Pres. Rosa Strygler; Chmn. Ursula Merkin. Maintains in Israel subsidized housing for self-reliant elderly; old-age homes for more dependent elderly; Lichtenstadter Hospital for chronically ill and young accident victims not accepted by other hospitals; subsidized meals; Golden Age clubs. *Annual dinner journal.*

THANKS TO SCANDINAVIA, INC. (1963). 745 Fifth Ave., Rm. 603, NYC 10151. (212)-486–8600. FAX: (212)486–5735. Natl. Chmn. Victor Borge; Pres. Richard Netter; Exec. Dir. Judith S. Goldstein. Provides scholarships and fellowships at American universities and medical centers to students and doctors from Denmark, Finland, Norway, and Sweden in appreciation of the rescue of Jews from the Holocaust. Informs current and future generations of Americans and Scandinavians of these singular examples of humanity and bravery; funds books about this chapter of history. *Annual report.*

UNITED JEWISH APPEAL, INC. (1939). 99 Park Ave., Suite 300, NYC 10016. (212)-818–9100. FAX: (212)818–9509. Natl. Chmn. Richard Pearlstone; Pres. Joel D. Tauber; Exec. V.-Pres. Rabbi Brian L. Lurie. The annual UJA/Federation Campaign is the primary instrument for the support of humanitarian programs and social services for Jews at home and abroad. In Israel, through the Jewish Agency, campaign funds help absorb, educate, and settle new immigrants, build villages and farms in rural areas, support innovative programs for troubled and disadvantaged youth, and promote the revitalization of distressed neighborhoods. The Operation Exodus Campaign provides funds for the settlement of Soviet and Ethiopian Jews in Israel. UJA/Federation funds also provide for the well-being of Jews and Jewish communities in more than 40 other countries around the world through the American Jewish Joint Distribution Committee.

RELIGIOUS AND EDUCATIONAL ORGANIZATIONS

AGUDATH ISRAEL OF AMERICA (1922). 84 William St., NYC 10038. (212)797–9000. Pres. Rabbi Moshe Sherer; Exec. V.-Pres. Rabbi Shmuel Bloom; Exec. Dir. Rabbi Boruch B. Borchardt. Mobilizes Orthodox Jews to cope with Jewish problems in the spirit of the Torah; speaks out on contem-

porary issues from an Orthodox viewpoint; sponsors a broad range of projects aimed at enhancing religious living, education, children's welfare, protection of Jewish religious rights, outreach to the assimilated and to arrivals from the former Soviet Union, and social services. *Jewish Observer; Dos Yiddishe Vort; Coalition.*

——, AGUDAH WOMEN OF AMERICA–N'SHEI AGUDATH ISRAEL (1940). 84 William St., NYC 10038. (212)363–8940. Presidium Aliza Grund, Rose Isbee; Exec. V.-Pres. Rita Siff. Organizes Jewish women for philanthropic work in the U.S. and Israel and for intensive Torah education.

——, BOYS' DIVISION–PIRCHEI AGUDATH ISRAEL (1925). 84 William St., NYC 10038 (212)797–9000. Natl. Dir. Rabbi Joshua Silbermintz; Natl. Coord. Rabbi Avraham Perl. Educates Orthodox Jewish children in Torah; encourages sense of communal responsibility. Branches sponsor weekly youth groups and Jewish welfare projects. National Mishnah contests, rallies, and conventions foster unity on a national level. *Leaders Guides.*

——, GIRLS' DIVISION–BNOS AGUDATH ISRAEL (1921). 84 William St., NYC 10038. (212)797–9000. Natl. Dirs. Devorah Streicher and Leah Zagelbaum. Sponsors regular weekly programs on the local level and unites girls from throughout the Torah world with extensive regional and national activities. *Newsletters.*

——, YOUNG MEN'S DIVISION–ZEIREI AGUDATH ISRAEL (1921). 84 William St., NYC 10038. (212)797–9000. Dir. Rabbi Labish Becker. Educates youth to see Torah as source of guidance for all issues facing Jews as individuals and as a people. Inculcates a spirit of activism through projects in religious, Torah-educational, and community-welfare fields. *Am Hatorah; Daf Chizuk; Ohr Hakollel.*

AGUDATH ISRAEL WORLD ORGANIZATION (1912). 84 William St., NYC 10038. (212)-797–9000. Chmn. Rabbi Moshe Sherer, Rabbi Yehudah Meir Abramowitz. Represents the interests of Orthodox Jewry on the national and international scenes. Sponsors projects to strengthen Torah life worldwide.

ALEPH: ALLIANCE FOR JEWISH RENEWAL (1963; reorg. 1993). 7318 Germantown

Ave., Philadelphia, PA 19119–1720. (215)-247–9700. FAX: (215)247–9703. Cochmn. Barbara Breitman, Ann Weiss; Exec. Dir. Susan Saxe. A multifaceted international organization serving the movement for Jewish renewal, formed out of a merger of P'nai Or Religious Fellowship and the Shalom Center. Activities include creation and dissemination of publications, liturgy, curricula, audio and video tapes; a country retreat center; lay and professional leadership training; spiritual activism on social and environmental issues; and a network of local Jewish renewal communities. *New Menorah (quarterly journal); Pumbedissa (newsletter forum for rabbis and rabbinical students).*

AMERICAN ASSOCIATION OF RABBIS (1978). 350 Fifth Ave., Suite 3304, NYC 10118. (212)244–3350. Pres. Rabbi Harold Lerner; Exec. Dir. Rabbi David L. Dunn. An organization of rabbis serving in pulpits, in areas of education, and in social work. *Quarterly bulletin; monthly newsletter; membership directory.*

AMISHAV USA (1993). 1211 Ballard St., Silver Spring, MD 20910. (301)681–5679. FAX: (301)681–5679. Pres. Jack Zeller; V.-Pres. Bob Lande. Engages in outreach to marginal Jewish communities around the world who wish to return to their Jewish roots. Current projects include the formal conversion of Shinlung-Menashe tribesmen in India currently practicing Judaism, and supplying materials and rabbis for conversos/marranos in Mexico and Brazil. *Newsletter.*

ASSOCIATION FOR JEWISH STUDIES (1969). Widener Library M., Harvard University, Cambridge, MA 02138. Pres. Herbert H. Paper; Exec. Sec. Charles Berlin. Seeks to promote, maintain, and improve the teaching of Jewish studies in colleges and universities by sponsoring meetings and conferences, publishing a newsletter and other scholarly materials, aiding in the placement of teachers, coordinating research, and cooperating with other scholarly organizations. *AJS Review; Newsletter.*

ASSOCIATION FOR THE SOCIAL SCIENTIFIC STUDY OF JEWRY (1971). University of Connecticut, Dept. of Sociology, Center for Judaic Studies, Storrs, CT 06269–2068. (203)486–2271. FAX: (203)486–6356. Pres. Arnold Dashefsky; V.-Pres. Sherry Israel; Journal Ed. J. Alan Winter; Newsletter Ed. Gail Glickman. Arranges academic sessions and facilitates communication among social scientists studying Jewry through meetings, newsletter, and related materials. *Contemporary Jewry; ASSJ Newsletter.*

ASSOCIATION OF HILLEL/JEWISH CAMPUS PROFESSIONALS (1949). c/o B'nai B'rith Hillel Foundation, U. of Rochester, Interfaith Chapel, Wilson Blvd., Rochester, NY 14627. (716)275–5981. FAX: (716)442–4279. Pres. Rabbi Paul Saiger. Seeks to promote professional relationships and exchanges of experience, develop personnel standards and qualifications, safeguard integrity of Hillel profession; represents and advocates before National Hillel Staff, National Hillel Commission, B'nai B'rith International, Council of Jewish Federations. *Handbook for Hillel Professionals; Guide to Hillel Personnel Practices.*

ASSOCIATION OF ORTHODOX JEWISH SCIENTISTS (1948). 3 W. 16 St., NYC 10011. (212)229–2340. FAX: (212)229–2319. Pres. Allen J. Bennett, MD; Bd. Chmn. Neil Maron, PhD; Exec. Dir. Joel Schwartz. Seeks to contribute to the development of science within the framework of Orthodox Jewish tradition; to obtain and disseminate information relating to the interaction between the Jewish traditional way of life and scientific developments—on both an ideological and practical level; to assist in the solution of problems pertaining to Orthodox Jews engaged in scientific teaching or research. Two main conventions are held each year. *Intercom; Proceedings; Halacha Bulletin; newsletter.*

B'NAI B'RITH HILLEL FOUNDATIONS, INC. (1923). 1640 Rhode Island Ave., NW, Washington, DC 20036. (202)857–6560. FAX: (202)857–6693. Chmn. B'nai B'rith Hillel Comm. David L. Bittker; Internatl. Dir. Richard M. Joel. Provides cultural, social, community-service, educational, and religious activities for Jewish college students of all backgrounds. Maintains a presence on over 450 campuses in the U.S., Canada, and overseas. Sponsors national leaders assembly, forum on public policy, endowment in ethics and the campus, institute for student leadership, national Jewish law students network. *Campus Connection; Mekorot; Igeret; The Hillel Guide to Jewish Life on Campus: A Directory of Resources for Jewish College Students.*

B'NAI B'RITH YOUTH ORGANIZATION (1924). 1640 Rhode Island Ave., NW, Washington, DC 20036. (202)857–6633. FAX: (212)857–1099. Chmn. Youth Comm. Dennis Glick; Dir. Sam Fisher. Helps Jewish teenagers achieve self-fulfillment and make a maximum contribution to the Jewish community and their country's culture; helps members acquire a greater knowledge and appreciation of Jewish religion and culture. *Shofar; Monday Morning; BBYO Parents' Line; Hakol; Kesher; The Connector.*

CANTORS ASSEMBLY (1947). 3080 Broadway, NYC 10027. (212)678–8834. FAX: (212)662–8989. Pres. Stephen J. Stein; Exec. V.-Pres. Samuel Rosenbaum. Seeks to unite all cantors who adhere to traditional Judaism and who serve as full-time cantors in bona fide congregations to conserve and promote the musical traditions of the Jews and to elevate the status of the cantorial profession. *Annual Proceedings; Journal of Synagogue Music.*

CENTER FOR CHRISTIAN-JEWISH UNDERSTANDING (1992). 5151 Park Ave., Fairfield, CT 06432. (203)365–7592. FAX: (203)365–7512. Bd. Chmn. Russ Berrie; Dir. Rabbi Jack Bemporad; Admin. Rabbi Joseph H. Ehrenkranz. An educational and research division of Sacred Heart University; brings together clergy, laity, scholars, theologians, and educators with the purpose of promoting interreligious research, education, and dialogue, with particular focus on current religious thinking within Christianity and Judaism. *Highlights (tri-annual newsletter).*

CENTRAL CONFERENCE OF AMERICAN RABBIS (1889). 192 Lexington Ave., NYC 10016. (212)684–4990. FAX: (212)689–6419. Pres. Rabbi Sheldon Zimmerman; Exec. V.-Pres. Rabbi Joseph B. Glaser. Seeks to conserve and promote Judaism and to disseminate its teachings in a liberal spirit. The CCAR Press provides liturgy and prayerbooks to the worldwide Reform Jewish community. *CCAR Journal: A Reform Jewish Quarterly; CCAR Yearbook.*

CLAL–NATIONAL JEWISH CENTER FOR LEARNING AND LEADERSHIP (1974). 99 Park Ave., Suite C-300, NYC 10016–1599. (212)867–8888. FAX: (212)867–8853. Pres. Rabbi Irving Greenberg; Chmn. Shoshana S. Cardin. Dedicated to preparing Jewish leaders to respond to the challenges of a new era in Jewish history; challenges which include the freedom to accept or reject one's Jewish heritage, the liberty to choose from an abundance of Jewish values and life-styles, and the exercise of Jewish power after the Holocaust and the rebirth of the State of Israel. *Newsletter; Sh'ma; annual calendar.*

COALITION FOR THE ADVANCEMENT OF JEWISH EDUCATION (CAJE) (1976). 261 W. 35 St., #12A, NYC 10001. (212)268–4210. FAX: (212)268–4214. Chmn. Rabbi Michael A. Weinberg; Exec. Dir. Dr. Eliot G. Spack. Brings together Jews from all ideologies who are involved in every facet of Jewish education and are committed to transmitting the Jewish heritage. Sponsors annual Conference on Alternatives in Jewish Education and Curriculum Bank; publishes a wide variety of publications; organizes shared-interest networks; offers mini grants for special projects. *Bikurim; timely curricular publications; CAJE Jewish Education News.*

CONGRESS OF SECULAR JEWISH ORGANIZATIONS (1970). 1130 S. Michigan Ave., #2101, Chicago, IL 60605. (312)922–0386. FAX: (312)263–3634. Cochmn. Jack Rosenfeld, Larry Schofer; Exec. Dir. Gerry Revzin. An umbrella organization of schools and adult clubs; facilitates exchange curricula and educational programs for children and adults stressing our Jewish historical and cultural heritage and the continuity of the Jewish people. *Newsletter; Holiday Celebration Book.*

COUNCIL FOR INITIATIVES IN JEWISH EDUCATION (1991). PO Box 94553, Cleveland, OH 44101. (216)391–1852. FAX: (216)-391–5430. Bd. Chmn. Morton Mandel; Exec. Dir. Alan D. Hoffmann; Sr. Educ. Officer Barry W. Holtz. Created by the Commission on Jewish Education in N. America to implement its recommendations. Aims to revitalize Jewish education through systemic reform—to build the profession of Jewish education, mobilize support of community leadership for Jewish education, develop a research agenda for Jewish education, and help secure funding for that research.

COUNCIL FOR JEWISH EDUCATION (1926). 730 Broadway, 2nd fl., NYC 10003. (212)-529–2000. FAX: (212)529–2009. Pres. Solomon Goldman; Consultant Philip Gorodetzer. Fellowship of Jewish education professionals—administrators and supervisors and teachers in Hebrew high schools and Jewish teachers colleges—of all ideological groupings; conducts annual national and regional conferences; represents the Jewish education profession before the Jewish community; cosponsors, with the Jewish Education Service of North America, a personnel committee and other projects; cooperates with Jewish Agency Department of Education and Culture in promoting Hebrew culture and studies; conducts lectureship at Hebrew University. *Jewish Education.*

FEDERATION OF JEWISH MEN'S CLUBS (1929). 475 Riverside Dr., Rm. 244, NYC 10115. (212)749–8100. FAX: (212)316–4271. Internatl. Pres. Allen Wm. Brown; Exec. Dir. Rabbi Charles E. Simon; Dir. Operations Dr. Joel Sperber. Promotes principles of Conservative Judaism; develops family-education and leadership-training programs; offers the Art of Jewish Living series and Yom Hashoah Home Commemoration; sponsors Hebrew literacy adult-education program; presents awards for service to American Jewry. *Torchlight.*

FEDERATION OF RECONSTRUCTIONIST CONGREGATIONS AND HAVUROT (1954). Church Rd. and Greenwood Ave., Wyncote, PA 19095. (215)887–1988. FAX: (215)887–5348. Pres. Valerie Kaplan; Exec. Dir. Rabbi Mordechai Liebling. Services affiliated congregations and havurot educationally and administratively; fosters the establishment of new Reconstructionist congregations and fellowship groups. Runs the Reconstructionist Press and provides programmatic materials. Maintains regional offices in New York, Los Angeles, and Chicago. *The Reconstructionist; Reconstructionism TODAY.*

———, RECONSTRUCTIONIST RABBINICAL ASSOCIATION (1974). Church Rd. and Greenwood Ave., Wyncote, PA 19095. (215)576–5210. FAX: (215)576–6143. Pres. Rabbi Ron Aigen; Dir. Yael Shuman. Professional organization for graduates of the Reconstructionist Rabbinical College and other rabbis who identify with Reconstructionist Judaism; cooperates with Federation of Reconstructionist Congregations and Havurot in furthering Reconstructionism in N. America. *Newsletters; position papers.*

———, RECONSTRUCTIONIST RABBINICAL COLLEGE (*see* p. 533)

INSTITUTE FOR COMPUTERS IN JEWISH LIFE (1978). 7074 N. Western Ave., Chicago, IL 60645. (312)262–9200. FAX: (312)262–9298. Pres. Thomas Klutznick; Exec. V.-Pres. Dr. Irving J. Rosenbaum. Explores, develops, and disseminates applications of computer technology to appropriate areas of Jewish life, with special emphasis on Jewish education; creates educational software for use in Jewish schools; provides consulting service and assistance for national Jewish organizations, seminaries, and synagogues. *Monitor.*

JEWISH CHAUTAUQUA SOCIETY, INC. (sponsored by NATIONAL FEDERATION OF TEMPLE BROTHERHOODS) (1893). 838 Fifth Ave., NYC 10021. (212)570–0707 or (800)765–6200. FAX: (212)570–0960. Pres. Roger B. Jacobs; Chancellor/1st V.-Pres. Kenneth Keenan; Office Mgr. Dora Lee. Works to promote interfaith understanding by sponsoring accredited college courses and one-day lectures on Judaic topics, providing book grants to educational institutions, producing educational videotapes on interfaith topics, and convening interfaith institutes. Also supports extracurricular intergroup programming on college campuses in cooperation with Hillel and is a founding sponsor of the National Black/Jewish Relations Center at Dillard University. *Brotherhood.*

JEWISH EDUCATION IN MEDIA (1978). PO Box 180, Riverdale Sta., NYC 10471. (212)362–7633; (203)968–2225. Pres. Bernard Samers; Exec. Dir. Rabbi Mark S. Golub. Devoted to producing radio, television, film, video-cassette, and audio-cassette programming for a popular Jewish audience, in order to inform, entertain, and inspire a greater sense of Jewish identity and Jewish commitment. "L'Chayim," JEM's weekly half-hour program, airs on WOR Radio in New York and in radio and television syndication; it features outstanding figures in the Jewish world addressing issues and events of importance to the Jewish community.

JEWISH EDUCATION SERVICE OF NORTH AMERICA (JESNA) (1981). 730 Broadway, NYC 10003–9540. (212)529–2000. FAX: (212)529–2009. Pres. Billie Gold; Exec. V.-Pres. Dr. Jonathan S. Woocher. The advocacy, planning, coordinating, and service agency for Jewish education of the federated system in North America. Works with federations, central agencies for Jewish education, and other local, national, and international institutions, and undertakes activities in the areas of research, program and human-resource development, information and resource dissemination, consultation, conferences and publications. *Agenda: Jewish Education; TRENDS; information research reports and bulletins; JESNA Update.*

JEWISH TEACHERS ASSOCIATION–MORIM (1931). 45 E. 33 St., Suite 604, NYC 10016. (212)684–0556. Pres. Phyllis L. Pullman; V.-Pres. Joseph Varon; Sec. Helen Parnes; Treas. Mildred Safar. Protects teachers from abuse of seniority rights; fights the encroachment of anti-Semitism in education; provides legal counsel to protect teachers from discrimination; offers scholarships to qualified students; encourages teachers to assume active roles in Jewish communal and religious affairs. *Morim JTA Newsletter.*

MACHNE ISRAEL, INC. (1940). 770 Eastern Pkwy., Brooklyn, NY 11213. (718)774–4000. FAX: (718)774–2718. Pres. Menachem M. Schneerson (Lubavitcher Rebbe); Dir., Treas. M.A. Hodakov; Sec. Nissan Mindel. The Lubavitcher movement's organ dedicated to the social, spiritual, and material welfare of Jews throughout the world.

MERKOS L'INYONEI CHINUCH, INC. (THE CENTRAL ORGANIZATION FOR JEWISH EDUCATION) (1940). 770 Eastern Pkwy., Brooklyn, NY 11213. (718)493–9250. Pres. Menachem M. Schneerson (Lubavitcher Rebbe); Dir., Treas. M.A. Hodakov; Sec. Nissan Mindel. The educational arm of the Lubavitcher movement. Seeks to promote Jewish education among Jews, regardless of their background, in the spirit of Torah-true Judaism; to establish contact with alienated Jewish youth; to stimulate concern and active interest in Jewish education on all levels; and to promote religious observance as a daily experience among all Jews. Maintains worldwide network of regional offices, schools, summer camps, and Chabad-Lubavitch Houses; publishes Jewish educational literature in numerous languages and monthly journal in five languages. *Conversaciones con la juventud; Conversations avec les jeunes; Schmuessen mit Kinder un Yugent; Sihot la-No-ar; Talks and Tales.*

NATIONAL COMMITTEE FOR FURTHERANCE OF JEWISH EDUCATION (1941). 824 Eastern Pkwy., Brooklyn, NY 11213. (718)735–0200. FAX: (718)735–4455. Pres. Milton E. Kramer; Bd. Chmn. Rabbi Shea Hecht; Chmn. Exec. Com. Rabbi Sholem Ber Hecht. Seeks to disseminate the ideals of Torah-true education among the youth of America; provides education and compassionate care for the poor, sick, and needy in U.S. and Israel; provides aid to Iranian Jewish youth; sponsors camps; Operation Survival, War on Drugs; Yeshivas Kol Yaakov Yehuda Hadar HaTorah, Machon Chana Women's College, and Mesivta Ohr Torah; Ivy League Torah Study Program; maintains schools in Brooklyn and Queens, family and vocational counseling services; early intervention, after-school, and preschool programs. *Panorama; Passover Handbook; Seder Guide; Cultbusters; Intermarriage; Brimstone & Fire.*

NATIONAL COUNCIL OF YOUNG ISRAEL (1924). 3 W. 16 St., NYC 10011. (212)929–1525. Pres. Chaim Kaminetzky; Exec. Dir. Rabbi Pesach Lerner. Maintains a program of spiritual, cultural, social, and communal activity aimed at the advancement and perpetuation of traditional, Torah-true Judaism; seeks to instill in American youth an understanding and appreciation of the ethical and spiritual values of Judaism. Sponsors kosher dining clubs and fraternity houses and an Israel program. *Viewpoint; Divrei Torah Bulletin.*

———, AMERICAN FRIENDS OF YOUNG ISRAEL IN ISRAEL–YISRAEL HATZA'IR (1926). 3 W. 16 St., NYC 10011. (212)929–1525. FAX: (212)727–9526. Pres. Meir Mishkoff; Dir. Rabbi Elias Lauer. Promotes Young Israel synagogues and youth work in Israel; works to help absorb Russian and Ethiopian immigrants.

———, MESILAH–INSTITUTE FOR JEWISH STUDIES (1947). 3 W. 16 St., NYC 10011. (212)929–1525. Pres. Chaim Kaminetzky; Exec. Dir. Rabbi Pesach Lerner. Introduces students to Jewish learning and knowledge; helps form adult branch schools; aids Young Israel synagogues in their adult education programs. *Bulletin.*

———, YOUNG ISRAEL COLLEGIATES AND YOUNG ADULTS (1951; reorg. 1982). 3 W. 16 St., NYC 10011. (212)929–1525. Chmn. Kenneth Block; Dir. Richard Stareshefsky. Organizes and operates kosher dining clubs on college and university campuses; provides information and counseling on *kashrut* observance at colleges; gives college-age youth understanding and appreciation of Judaism and information on issues important to Jewish community; arranges seminars and meetings, weekends and trips.

————, YOUNG ISRAEL YOUTH (reorg. 1968). 3 W. 16 St., NYC 10011. (212)929–1525. Dir. Richard Stareshefsky. Fosters a program of spiritual, cultural, social, and communal activities for the advancement and perpetuation of traditional Torah-true Judaism; strives to instill an understanding and appreciation of high ethical and spiritual values and to demonstrate compatibility of ancient faith of Israel with good Americanism. Operates Achva East summer program for 8th graders, Achva West summer program for 9th graders, and Achva Israel summer program for 10th graders. *Monthly newsletter.*

NATIONAL HAVURAH COMMITTEE (1979). 7318 Germantown Ave., Philadelphia, PA 19119–1720. (215)248–9760. FAX: (215)-247–9703. Chmn. Steven Lewis. A center for Jewish renewal devoted to spreading Jewish ideas, ethics, and religious practices through *havurot*, participatory and inclusive religious mini-communities. Maintains a directory of N. American *havurot* and sponsors a weeklong summer institute, regional weekend retreats, a teacher's bureau, and a D'var Torah newspaper column. *Havurah! (newsletter).*

NATIONAL JEWISH CENTER FOR LEARNING AND LEADERSHIP (*see* CLAL)

NATIONAL JEWISH COMMITTEE ON SCOUTING (Boy Scouts of America) (1926). 1325 West Walnut Hill Lane, PO Box 152079, Irving, TX 75015–2079. (214)580–2119. FAX: (214)580–7870. Chmn. Shelly Weil; Dir. Donald L. Townsend. Assists Jewish institutions in meeting their needs and concerns through use of the resources of scouting. Works through local Jewish committees on scouting to establish Tiger Cub groups (1st grade), Cub Scout packs, Boy Scout troops, and coed Explorer posts in synagogues, Jewish community centers, day schools, and other Jewish organizations wishing to draw Jewish youth. Support materials and resources on request. *Hatsofe (quarterly).*

NATIONAL JEWISH GIRL SCOUT COMMITTEE (1972). Synagogue Council of America, 327 Lexington Ave., NYC 10016. (212)686–8670. FAX: (212)686–8673. Chmn. Rabbi Herbert W. Bomzer; Field Chmn. Adele Wasko. Under the auspices of the Synagogue Council of America, serves to further Jewish education by promoting Jewish award programs, encouraging religious services, promoting cultural exchanges with the Israel Boy and Girl Scouts Federation, and extending membership in the Jewish community by assisting councils in organizing Girl Scout troops and local Jewish Girl Scout committees. *Newsletter.*

NATIONAL JEWISH HOSPITALITY COMMITTEE (1973; reorg. 1993). PO Box 15832, Philadelphia, PA 19103. (215)546–8293. Pres. Rabbi Allen S. Maller; Exec. Dir. Steven S. Jacobs. Assists persons interested in Judaism—for intermarriage, conversion, general information, or to respond to missionaries. *Special reports.*

OZAR HATORAH, INC. (1946). 1 E. 33 St., NYC 10016. (212)696–1212. Pres. Joseph Shalom; Sec. Sam Sutton. An international educational network which builds Sephardic communities worldwide through Jewish education.

P'EYLIM–AMERICAN YESHIVA STUDENT UNION (1951). 805 Kings Highway, Brooklyn, NY 11223. (718)382–0113. Pres. Jacob Y. Weisberg; Exec. V.-Pres. Avraham Hirsch. Aids and sponsors pioneer work by American graduate teachers and rabbis in new villages and towns in Israel; does religious, organizational, and educational work and counseling among new immigrant youth; maintains summer camps for poor immigrant youth in Israel; belongs to worldwide P'eylim movement which has groups in Argentina, Brazil, Canada, England, Belgium, the Netherlands, Switzerland, France, and Israel; engages in relief and educational work among North African immigrants in France and Canada, assisting them to relocate and reestablish a strong Jewish community life. *P'eylim Reporter; News from P'eylim; N'shei P'eylim News.*

RABBINICAL ALLIANCE OF AMERICA (IGUD HARABONIM) (1942). 3 W. 16 St., 4th fl., NYC 10011. (212)242–6420. FAX: (212)-255–8313. Pres. Rabbi Abraham B. Hecht; Admin. Judge of Beth Din (Rabbinical

Court) Rabbi Herschel Kurzrock. Seeks to promulgate the cause of Torah-true Judaism through an organized rabbinate that is consistently Orthodox; seeks to elevate the position of Orthodox rabbis nationally and to defend the welfare of Jews the world over. Also has Beth Din Rabbinical Court for Jewish divorces, litigation, marriage counseling, and family problems. *Perspective; Nahalim; Torah Message of the Week; Registry.*

RABBINICAL ASSEMBLY (1900). 3080 Broadway, NYC 10027. (212)678–8060. Pres. Rabbi Alan Silverstein; Exec. V.-Pres. Rabbi Joel H. Meyers. Seeks to promote Conservative Judaism and to foster the spirit of fellowship and cooperation among rabbis and other Jewish scholars; cooperates with the Jewish Theological Seminary of America and the United Synagogue of Conservative Judaism. *Conservative Judaism; Proceedings of the Rabbinical Assembly; Rabbinical Assembly Newsletter.*

RABBINICAL COUNCIL OF AMERICA, INC. (1923; reorg. 1935). 305 Seventh Ave., NYC 10001. Pres. Rabbi Moshe Gorlelik; V.-Pres. Rabbi Marc D. Angel. Promotes Orthodox Judaism in the community; supports institutions for study of Torah; stimulates creation of new traditional agencies. *Hadorom; Record; Sermon Manual; Tradition.*

RESEARCH INSTITUTE OF RELIGIOUS JEWRY, INC. (1941; reorg. 1964). 471 W. End Ave., NYC 10024. (212)222–6839. Pres. Rabbi Oswald Besser; Hon. Sec. Marcus Retter. Engages in research and publishes studies concerning the situation of religious Jewry and its history in various countries.

SHOMREI ADAMAH/KEEPERS OF THE EARTH (1988). 5500 Wissahickon Ave., #804C, Philadelphia, PA 19144. (215)-844–8150. Pres./Dir. Ellen Bernstein. A research, development, and education institute involved with nature and environmental issues from a Jewish perspective. Provides liturgical, educational, and other materials to members, including ecologically oriented services, sermons, and children's activities for school, camp, and home, as well as guides for study and action. Works with congregations and groups across North America on "greening" their communities. *Kol Hallanot/Voice of the Trees (newspaper).*

SOCIETY FOR HUMANISTIC JUDAISM (1969). 28611 W. Twelve Mile Rd., Farmington Hills, MI 48334. (810)478–7610. FAX: (810)477–9014. Pres. Rosalyn Hill; Exec. Dir. Miriam Jerris; Asst. Dir. M. Bonnie Cousens. Serves as a voice for Jews who value their Jewish identity and who seek an alternative to conventional Judaism, who reject supernatural authority and affirm the right of individuals to be the masters of their own lives. Publishes educational and ceremonial materials; organizes congregations and groups. *Humanistic Judaism* (quarterly journal); *Humanorah* (quarterly newsletter).

SYNAGOGUE COUNCIL OF AMERICA (1926). 327 Lexington Ave., NYC 10016. (212)-686–8670. FAX: (212)686–8673. Pres. Rabbi Haskel Lookstein; Bd. Chmn. Myron Pomerantz; Exec. V.-Pres. Rabbi Shel Schiffman. Represents congregational and rabbinic organizations of Conservative, Orthodox, and Reform Jewry; acts as "one voice" for religious Jewry. *SCA News; special reports.*

TORAH SCHOOLS FOR ISRAEL–CHINUCH ATZMAI (1953). 40 Exchange Pl., NYC 10005. (212)248–6200. FAX: (212)248–6202. Pres. Rabbi Abraham Pam; Exec. Dir. Rabbi Henach Cohen. Conducts information programs for the American Jewish community on activities of the independent Torah schools educational network in Israel; coordinates role of American members of international board of governors; funds special programs of Mercaz Hachinuch Ha-Atzmai B'Eretz Yisroel.

TORAH UMESORAH–NATIONAL SOCIETY FOR HEBREW DAY SCHOOLS (1944). 160 Broadway, NYC 10038. (212)227–1000. Pres. Sheldon Beren; Bd. Chmn. David Singer; Exec. V.-Pres. Rabbi Joshua Fishman. Establishes Hebrew day schools in U.S. and Canada and provides a full gamut of services, including placement and curriculum guidance, teacher-training on campuses of major yeshivahs, an annual intensive teacher institute in July, and regional seminars and workshops. Parent Enrichment Program established in 1991 provides enhanced educational experience for students from less Jewishly educated and marginally affiliated homes through parent education programs, curriculum, training of parent-ed. coordinators, and a monthly magazine, *The Jewish Parent*

Connection. Publishes textbooks; runs Shabbatonim, extracurricular activities. National PTA groups; national and regional teacher conventions. *Olomeinu–Our World; Parshah Sheets.*

———, NATIONAL ASSOCIATION OF HEBREW DAY SCHOOL ADMINISTRATORS (1960). 1114 Ave. J, Brooklyn, NY 11230. (718)258–7767. Pres. David H. Schwartz. Coordinates the work of the fiscal directors of Hebrew day schools throughout the country. *NAHDSA Review.*

———, NATIONAL ASSOCIATION OF HEBREW DAY SCHOOL PARENT-TEACHER ASSOCIATIONS (1948). 160 Broadway, NYC 10038. (212)227–1000. Natl. PTA Coord. Bernice Brand. Acts as a clearinghouse and service agency to PTAs of Hebrew day schools; organizes parent education courses and sets up programs for individual PTAs. *Fundraising with a Flair; Monthly Sidrah Series Program; PTA with a Purpose for the Hebrew Day School.*

———, NATIONAL CONFERENCE OF YESHIVA PRINCIPALS (1956). 160 Broadway, NYC 10038. (212)227–1000. Pres. Rabbi Baruch M. Hilsenrath; Bd. Chmn. Rabbi Dov Leibenstein; Exec. V.-Pres. Rabbi A. Moshe Possick. Professional organization of elementary and secondary yeshivah/day-school principals providing yeshivah/day schools with school evaluation and guidance, teacher and principal conferences—including a Mid-Winter Curriculum Conference and a National Educators Convention. *Directory of Elementary Schools and High Schools.*

———, NATIONAL LAY LEADERSHIP COMMITTEE (LLC) (1991). Chmn. Barry Ray; Dir. Rabbi Nate Segal. Provides a lay leaders' executive report-professional journal; national lay leadership convention; national policy setting committees.

———, NATIONAL YESHIVA TEACHERS BOARD OF LICENSE (1953). 160 Broadway, NYC 10038. (212)227–1000. Exec. V.-Pres. & Dir. Rabbi Joshua Fishman. Issues licenses to qualified instructors for all grades of the Hebrew day school and the general field of Torah education.

UNION FOR TRADITIONAL JUDAISM (1984). 241 Cedar Lane, Teaneck, NJ 07666. (201)801–0707. FAX: (201)801–0449. Pres. Burton G. Greenblatt; Exec. V.-Pres. Rabbi Ronald D. Price. Through innova-

tive outreach programs, seeks to bring the greatest possible number of Jews closer to an open-minded observant Jewish lifestyle. Activities include the Kashrut Initiative, Operation Pesah, the Panel of Halakhic Inquiry, Speakers Bureau, adult and youth conferences, and congregational services. Includes, since 1992, the MORASHAH rabbinic fellowship. *Hagahelet (quarterly newsletter); Cornerstone (journal); Tomeikh Kahalakhah (Jewish legal responsa).*

UNION OF AMERICAN HEBREW CONGREGATIONS (1873). 838 Fifth Ave., NYC 10021–7064. (212)249–0100. FAX: (212)734–2857. Pres. Rabbi Alexander M. Schindler; Bd. Chmn. Melvin Merians; Sr. V.-Pres. Rabbi Daniel B. Syme; V.-Pres. Rabbi Eric H. Yoffie. Serves as the central congregational body of Reform Judaism in the Western Hemisphere; serves its approximately 850 affiliated temples and membership with religious, educational, cultural, and administrative programs. *Reform Judaism.*

———, AMERICAN CONFERENCE OF CANTORS (1953). 170 W. 74 St., NYC 10023. (212)874–4762. FAX: (212)874–3527. Pres. Vicki L. Axe; Exec. V.-Pres. Howard M. Stahl; Dir. of Placement Richard Botton; Admin. Asst. Karyn Turner. Members receive investiture and commissioning as cantors at recognized seminaries, i.e., Hebrew Union College–Jewish Institute of Religion, School of Sacred Music, or Jewish Theological Seminary, as well as full certification through HUC-JIR-SSM. Through the Joint Cantorial Placement Commission, the ACC serves Reform congregations seeking cantors and music directors. Dedicated to creative Judaism, preserving the best of the past, and encouraging new and vital approaches to religious ritual, music, and ceremonies. *Koleinu.*

———, COMMISSION ON JEWISH EDUCATION OF THE UNION OF AMERICAN HEBREW CONGREGATIONS, CENTRAL CONFERENCE OF AMERICAN RABBIS, AND NATIONAL ASSOCIATION OF TEMPLE EDUCATORS (1923). 838 Fifth Ave., NYC 10021. (212)249–0100. Chmn. Rabbi Robert Orkand; V.-Chmn. Robert E. Tornberg, Joe Kleiman; Dir. Seymour Rossel. Long-range planning and policy development for congregational programs of lifelong education; network projects with affiliates and associate groups including:

special-needs education, Reform Jewish outreach, and Reform Day Schools; activities administered by the UAHC Department for Education. *Compass Magazine.*

———, COMMISSION ON SOCIAL ACTION OF REFORM JUDAISM (*see* p. 494)

———, COMMISSION ON SYNAGOGUE MANAGEMENT (UAHC-CCAR) (1962). 838 Fifth Ave., NYC 10021. (212)249–0100. FAX: (212)734–2857. Chmn. Paul Vanek; Dir. Joseph C. Bernstein. Assists congregations in management, finance, building maintenance, design, construction, and art aspects of synagogues; maintains the Synagogue Architectural Library.

———, NATIONAL ASSOCIATION OF TEMPLE ADMINISTRATORS (NATA) (1941). c/o Wilshire Boulevard Temple, 3663 Wilshire Blvd., Los Angeles, CA 90010. (213)-388–2401. FAX: (213)388–2595. Pres. Steven Breuer. Prepares and disseminates administrative information and procedures to member synagogues of UAHC; provides training of professional synagogue executives; formulates and establishes professional standards for the synagogue executive; provides placement services. *NATA Journal; Temple Management Manual.*

———, NATIONAL ASSOCIATION OF TEMPLE EDUCATORS (NATE) (1955). 707 Summerly Dr., Nashville, TN 37209–4253. (615)352–6800. FAX: (615)352–7800. Pres. Roberta Louis Goodman; Exec. V.-Pres. Richard M. Morin. Represents the temple educator within the general body of Reform Judaism; fosters the full-time profession of the temple educator; encourages the growth and development of Jewish religious education consistent with the aims of Reform Judaism; stimulates communal interest in and responsibility for Jewish religious education. *NATE NEWS; Compass.*

———, NATIONAL FEDERATION OF TEMPLE BROTHERHOODS (1923). 838 Fifth Ave., NYC 10021. (212)570–0707. Pres. Roger B. Jacobs; 1st V.-Pres./JCS Chancellor Kenneth Keenan; Program Dir. Dora Lee. Dedicated to enhancing the world through the ideal of brotherhood, NFTB and its 300 affiliated clubs are actively involved in education, social action, youth activities, and other programs that contribute to temple and community life. Supports the Jewish Chautauqua Society,

an interfaith educational project. *Brotherhood.*

———, WOMEN OF REFORM JUDAISM–NATIONAL FEDERATION OF TEMPLE SISTERHOODS (1913). 838 Fifth Ave., NYC 10021–7064. (212)249–0100. FAX: (212)-861–0831. Pres. Judith O. Rosenkranz; Exec. Dir. Ellen Y. Rosenberg. Serves more than 600 sisterhoods of Reform Judaism; promotes interreligious understanding and social justice; awards scholarships and grants to rabbinic students; provides braille and large-type Judaic materials for Jewish blind; supports projects for Israel, Soviet Jewry, and the aging; is an affiliate of UAHC and the women's agency of Reform Judaism; works in behalf of the Hebrew Union College–Jewish Institute of Religion; cooperates with World Union for Progressive Judaism. *Notes for Now; Art Calendar.*

———, YOUTH DIVISION AND NORTH AMERICAN FEDERATION OF TEMPLE YOUTH (1939). PO Box 443, Bowen Rd., Warwick, NY 10990. (914)987–6300. FAX: (914)986–7185. Dir. Rabbi Allan L. Smith; Pres. Jeff Berger. Seeks to train Reform Jewish youth in the values of the synagogue and their application to daily life through service to the community and congregation; runs department of summer camps and national leadership-training institute; arranges overseas academic tours, work-study programs, international student-exchange programs, and college-student programs in the U.S. and Israel, including accredited study programs in Israel. *Ani V'Atah; The Jewish Connection.*

UNION OF ORTHODOX JEWISH CONGREGATIONS OF AMERICA (1898). 333 Seventh Ave., NYC 10001. (212)563–4000. Pres. Sheldon Rudoff; Exec. V.-Pres. Rabbi Pinchas Stolper. Serves as the national central body of Orthodox synagogues; sponsors Institute for Public Affairs; National Conference of Synagogue Youth; LAVE— Learning and Values Experiences; Israel Center in Jerusalem; *aliyah* department; national OU *kashrut* supervision and certification service; Marriage Commission; "Taste of Torah" radio program; provides educational, religious, and organizational programs, events, and guidance to synagogues and groups; represents the Orthodox Jewish community to governmental and civic bodies and the general Jewish community. *Jewish Action magazine; OU*

Kosher Directory; OU Passover Directory; OU News Reporter; Synagogue Spotlight; Our Way magazine; Yachad magazine; Luach Limud Torah Diary Home Study Program.

————, INSTITUTE FOR PUBLIC AFFAIRS (1989). 333 Seventh Ave., NYC 10001. (212)563-4000. FAX: (212)564-9058. Pres. Sheldon Rudoff; Chmn. Mandell Ganchrow; Exec. Dir. Betty Ehrenberg. Serves as the policy analysis, advocacy, mobilization, and programming department responsible for representing Orthodox/traditional American Jewry. *IPA Currents (quarterly newsletter); Briefing (monthly updates).*

————, NATIONAL CONFERENCE OF SYNAGOGUE YOUTH (1954). 333 Seventh Ave., NYC 10001. (212)563-4000. Dir. Rabbi Raphael Butler. Central body for youth groups of Orthodox congregations; provides educational guidance, Torah study groups, community service, programs consultation, Torah library, Torah fund scholarships, Ben Zakkai Honor Society, Friends of NCSY; weeklong seminars, Israel Summer Seminar for teens and Camp NCSY East, Teen Torah Center. Divisions include Senior NCSY in 14 regions and 400 chapters, Junior NCSY for preteens, Our Way for the Jewish deaf, Yachad for the developmentally disabled, Israel Center in Jerusalem, and NCSY in Israel. *Keeping Posted with NCSY; Face the Nation–President's Newsletter; Oreich Yomeinu–Education Newsletter; Mitsvah of the Month.*

————, WOMEN'S BRANCH (1923). 156 Fifth Ave., NYC 10010. (212)929-8857. Pres. Sophie Ebert. Seeks to spread the understanding and practice of Orthodox Judaism and to unite all Orthodox women and their synagogal organizations; services affiliates with educational and programming materials, leadership, and organizational guidance, and has an NGO representative at the UN. Supplies candelabra for Jewish patients in hospitals and nursing homes; supports Stern and Touro College scholarship funds and Jewish braille publications. *Hachodesh; Hakol.*

UNION OF ORTHODOX RABBIS OF THE UNITED STATES AND CANADA (1902). 235 E. Broadway, NYC 10002. (212)964-6337. Dir. Rabbi Hersh M. Ginsberg. Seeks to foster and promote Torah-true Ju-

daism in the U.S. and Canada; assists in the establishment and maintenance of yeshivot in the U.S.; maintains committee on marriage and divorce and aids individuals with marital difficulties; disseminates knowledge of traditional Jewish rites and practices and publishes regulations on synagogal structure; maintains rabbinical court for resolving individual and communal conflicts. *HaPardes.*

UNION OF SEPHARDIC CONGREGATIONS, INC. (1929). 8 W. 70 St., NYC 10023. (212)873-0300. FAX: (212)724-6165. Pres. Rabbi Marc D. Angel; Bd. Chmn. Alvin Deutsch. Promotes the religious interests of Sephardic Jews; prints and distributes Sephardic prayer books. *Annual International Directory of Sephardic Congregations.*

UNITED LUBAVITCHER YESHIVOTH (1940). 841–853 Ocean Pkwy., Brooklyn, NY 11230. (718)859-7600. Supports and organizes Jewish day schools and rabbinical seminaries in the U.S. and abroad.

UNITED SYNAGOGUE OF CONSERVATIVE JUDAISM (1913). 155 Fifth Ave., NYC 10010–6802. (212)533-7800. FAX: (212)353-9439. Pres. Alan Ades; Exec. V.-Pres./CEO Rabbi Jerome M. Epstein. International organization of 800 Conservative congregations. Maintains 12 departments and 20 regional offices to assist its affiliates with religious, educational, youth, community, and administrative programming and guidance; aims to enhance the cause of Conservative Judaism, further religious observance, encourage establishment of Jewish religious schools, draw youth closer to Jewish tradition. Extensive Israel programs. *United Synagogue Review; Art/Engagement Calendar; Program Suggestions; Directory & Resource Guide; Book Service Catalogue of Publications.*

————, COMMISSION ON JEWISH EDUCATION (1930). 155 Fifth Ave., NYC 10010. (212)533-7800. FAX: (212)353-9439. Cochmn. Dr. Jack Porter, Rabbi Marim Charry; Dir. Rabbi Robert Abramson. Develops educational policy for the United Synagogue of Conservative Judaism and sets the educational direction for Conservative congregations, their schools, and the Solomon Schechter Day Schools. Seeks to enhance the educational effectiveness of congregations through the publication of materials and in-service programs. *Tov*

L'Horot; Your Child; Dapim; Shiboley Schechter; Advisories.

———, COMMITTEE ON SOCIAL ACTION AND PUBLIC POLICY (1958). 155 Fifth Ave., NYC 10010. (212)533–7800. FAX: (212)353–9439. Cochmn. Scott Kaplan, Marc Gary. Develops and implements positions and programs on issues of social action and public policy for the United Synagogue of Conservative Judaism; represents these positions to other Jewish and civic organizations, the media, and government; and provides guidance, both informational and programmatic, to its affiliated congregations in these areas.

———, JEWISH EDUCATORS ASSEMBLY (1951). 106–06 Queens Blvd., Forest Hills, NY 11375–9452. (718)268–9452. FAX: (718)520–4369. Pres. Dr. Michael H. Halzel; Exec. Dir. Bernard Dov Troy. Promotes the vitality of the Conservative movement by encouraging professional growth and development, maintaining professional standards, acting as an advocate for Jewish education, and supporting educators' well- being. Services offered: annual convention, placement service, career services, research grants, and personal benefits. *V'Aleh Ha-Chadashot newsletter.*

———, KADIMA (formerly PRE-USY; reorg. 1968). 155 Fifth Ave., NYC 10010–6802. (212)533–7800. Dir. Ari Goldberg. Involves Jewish preteens in a meaningful religious, educational, and social environment; fosters a sense of identity and commitment to the Jewish community and the Conservative movement; conducts synagogue-based chapter programs and regional Kadima days and weekends. *Mitzvah of the Month; Kadima Kesher; Chagim; Advisors Aid; Games; quarterly Kadima magazine.*

———, NORTH AMERICAN ASSOCIATION OF SYNAGOGUE EXECUTIVES (1948). c/o Beth Shalom Congregation, 94 Wornall Rd., Kansas City, MO 64114. (816)361–2990. FAX: (816)361–4495. Pres. Lawrence Trope; Hon. Pres. Rhoda F. Myers. Aids congregations affiliated with the United Synagogue of America to further the aims of Conservative Judaism through more effective administration (Program for Assistance by Liaisons to Synagogues—PALS); advances professional standards and promotes new methods in administration; cooperates in United Synagogue

placement services and administrative surveys. *NAASE Connections Newsletter; NAASE Journal.*

———, UNITED SYNAGOGUE YOUTH OF (1951). 155 Fifth Ave., NYC 10010. (212)-533–7800. FAX: (212)353–9439. Pres. Shira Kaplan. Exec. Dir. Jules A. Gutin. Seeks to strengthen identification with Conservative Judaism, based on the personality development, needs, and interests of the adolescent, in a mitzvah framework. *Achshav; Tikun Olam; A.J. Heschel Honor Society Newsletter; SATO Newsletter; USY Alumni Assn. Newsletter; USY Program Bank; Hakesher Newsletter for Advisors.*

VAAD MISHMERETH STAM (1976). 4902 16th Ave., Brooklyn, NY 11204. (718)-438–4963. FAX: (718)854–5948. Pres. Rabbi David L. Greenfeld. A nonprofit consumer-protection agency dedicated to preserving and protecting the halakhic integrity of Torah scrolls, tefillin, phylacteries, and *mezuzoth.* Publishes material for laymen and scholars in the field of scribal arts; makes presentations and conducts examination campaigns in schools and synagogues; created an optical software system to detect possible textual errors in *stam.* Offices in Israel, Strasbourg, Chicago, London, Manchester, Montreal, and Zurich. Publishes *Guide to Mezuzah* and *Encyclopedia of the Secret Aleph Beth. The Jewish Quill.*

WOMEN'S LEAGUE FOR CONSERVATIVE JUDAISM (1918). 48 E. 74 St., NYC 10021. (212)628–1600. Pres. Audrey Citak; Exec. Dir. Bernice Balter. Parent body of Conservative (Masorti) women's synagogue groups in U.S., Canada, Puerto Rico, Mexico, and Israel; provides programs and resources in Jewish education, social action, Israel affairs, American and Canadian public affairs, leadership training, community service programs for persons with disabilities, conferences on world affairs, study institutes, publicity techniques; publishes books of Jewish interest; contributes to support of Jewish Theological Seminary of America. *Women's League Outlook magazine; Ba'Olam newsletter.*

WORLD COUNCIL OF SYNAGOGUES (1957). 155 Fifth Ave., NYC 10010. (212)533–7693. Pres. Dr. Henry Sender; Rabbi of Council, Rabbi Benjamin Z. Kreitman; Bd. Chmn. Rabbi Marc Liebhaber. International representative of Conservative organizations and congregations; promotes the growth and development of the Conservative movement in Israel and throughout the world; supports educational institutions overseas; holds biennial international conventions; represents the world Conservative movement on the Executive of the World Zionist Organization. *World Spectrum.*

WORLD UNION FOR PROGRESSIVE JUDAISM, LTD. (1926). 838 Fifth Ave., NYC 10021. (212)249–0100. FAX: (212)517–3940. Pres. Donald Day; Exec. Dir. Rabbi Richard G. Hirsch; N. Amer. Dir. Martin Strelzer; Dir. Internatl. Relations & Development Rabbi Clifford Kulwin. International umbrella organization of Liberal Judaism; promotes and coordinates efforts of Liberal congregations throughout the world; starts new congregations, recruits rabbis and rabbinical students for all countries; organizes international conferences of Liberal Jews. *Rodnik; News Updates.*

SCHOOLS, INSTITUTIONS

ACADEMY FOR JEWISH RELIGION (1955). 15 W. 86 St., NYC 10024. (212)875–0540. FAX: (212)875–0541. Chmn. Presidential Council Rabbi Manuel Gold; Exec. Dean Rabbi Shohama Wiener. The only rabbinic and cantorial seminary in the U.S. at which students explore the full range of Jewish spiritual learning and practice. Graduates serve in Conservative, Reform, Reconstructionist, and Orthodox congregations, chaplaincies, and educational institutions. Programs include rabbinic and cantorial studies in NYC and on/off-campus nonmatriculated studies.

ANNENBERG INSTITUTE (formerly DROPSIE COLLEGE FOR HEBREW AND COGNATE LEARNING) (1907; reorg. 1986). 420 Walnut St., Philadelphia, PA 19106. (215)-238–1290. FAX: (215)238–1540. Assoc. Dir. David M. Goldenberg. A center for advanced research in Judaic and Near Eastern studies at the postdoctoral level. *Jewish Quarterly Review.*

BALTIMORE HEBREW UNIVERSITY (1919). 5800 Park Heights Ave., Baltimore, MD 21215. (410)578–6900. FAX: (410)578–6940. Pres. Dr. Norma Fields Furst; Bd. Chmn. Beverly Penn. Offers PhD, MA, and BA programs in Jewish studies, Jewish education, biblical and Near Eastern archaeology, philosophy, literature, history, Hebrew language and literature; School of Continuing Education; Joseph Meyerhoff Library; community lectures, film series, seminars. *The Scribe (annual newsletter).*

———, BALTIMORE INSTITUTE FOR JEWISH COMMUNAL SERVICE. 101 W. Mt. Royal Ave., Baltimore, MD 21201–5781. Dir. Debra S. Weinberg; Dean Robert O. Freedman. Trains Jewish communal professionals; offers joint degree program: MA in Jewish studies from BHU; MSW from U. of Maryland; MA in policy sciences from UMBC.

———, BERNARD MANEKIN SCHOOL OF UNDERGRADUATE STUDIES. Dean Judy Meltzer. BA program; interinstitutional program with Johns Hopkins University; interdisciplinary concentrations: contemporary Middle East, American Jewish culture, and the humanities; Russian/English program for New Americans.

———, LEONARD AND HELEN R. STULMAN SCHOOL OF CONTINUING EDUCATION. Dean Judy Meltzer. Noncredit program open to the community, offering a variety of courses, trips, and events covering a range of Jewish subjects.

———, PEGGY MEYERHOFF PEARLSTONE SCHOOL OF GRADUATE STUDIES. Dean Robert O. Freedman. PhD and MA programs; MA and MSW with University of Maryland School of Social Work and Community Planning in federation, community organization, center, and family services; MA and MEd in Jewish education and double MA in journalism with Towson State University; MA program in community relations with University of Maryland Graduate School.

BRAMSON ORT TECHNICAL INSTITUTE (1977). 69–30 Austin St., Forest Hills, NY 11375. (718)261–5800. Dir. Dr. Seymour B. Foreman; Dean of Academic Services Barry Glotzer. A two-year Jewish technical college offering certificates and associate degrees in high technology and business fields, including computer, electronics technology, business management, and ophthalmic technology. Houses the Center for Computers in Jewish Education. Extension sites in Manhattan and Brooklyn.

BRANDEIS-BARDIN INSTITUTE (1941). 1101 Peppertree Lane, Brandeis, CA 93064. (805)582–4450, (818)348–7201. FAX: (805)526–1398. Pres. Judge Joseph Wapner; Exec. V.-Pres. Dr. Alvin Mars. A

Jewish pluralistic, nondenominational educational institution providing programs for people of all ages: BCI (Brandeis Collegiate Institute), a summer leadership program for college-age adults from around the world; Camp Alonim, a summer Jewish experience for children 8–16; Gan Alonim Day Camp for children in kindergarten to 6th grade; House of the Book weekend retreats for adults, with leading contemporary Jewish scholars-in-residence; Jewish music concerts; Family Days, Family Weekends, Grandparents Weekends, Elderhostel, and a variety of Young Adult programs. *Monthly Updates; BBI Newsletter; BCI Alumni News.*

BRANDEIS UNIVERSITY (1948). 415 South St., Waltham, MA 02254. (617)736–2000. Bd. Chmn. Louis Perlmutter; Pres. Jehuda Reinharz. Founded under Jewish sponsorship as a nonsectarian institution offering to all the highest quality undergraduate and graduate education. The Lown School is the center for all programs of teaching and research in the areas of Judaic studies, ancient Near Eastern studies, and Islamic and modern Middle Eastern studies. The school includes the Department of Near Eastern and Judaic Studies, which offers academic programs in the major areas of its concern; the Hornstein Program in Jewish Communal Service, a professional training program; the Cohen Center for Modern Jewish Studies, which conducts research and teaching in contemporary Jewish studies, primarily in the field of American Jewish studies, and the Tauber Institute for the study of European Jewry. *Various newsletters, scholarly publications.*

CLEVELAND COLLEGE OF JEWISH STUDIES (1964). 26500 Shaker Blvd., Beachwood, OH 44122. (216)464–4050. Pres. David S. Ariel; Dean Lifsa Schachter. Provides courses in all areas of Judaic and Hebrew studies to adults and college-age students; offers continuing education for Jewish educators and administrators; serves as a center for Jewish life and culture; expands the availability of courses in Judaic studies by exchanging faculty, students, and credits with neighboring academic institutions; grants bachelor's and master's degrees.

DROPSIE COLLEGE FOR HEBREW AND COGNATE LEARNING (*see* Annenberg Institute)

FEINBERG GRADUATE SCHOOL OF THE WEIZMANN INSTITUTE OF SCIENCE (1958). 51 Madison Ave., NYC 10010. (212)779–2500. FAX: (212)779–3209. Chmn. Melvin Schwartz; Pres. Robert Asher; Dean Prof. Benjamin Geiger. Situated on the Weizmann campus in Rehovot, Israel, provides the school's faculty and research facilities. Accredited by the Council for Higher Education of Israel and the NY State Board of Regents for the study of natural sciences, leading to MSc and PhD degrees.

GRATZ COLLEGE (1895). Old York Rd. and Melrose Ave., Melrose Park, PA 19126. (215)635–7300. FAX: (215)635–7320. Bd. Chmn. Steven Fisher; Pres. Dr. Gary S. Schiff. Offers a wide variety of undergraduate and graduate degrees and continuing education programs in Judaic, Hebraic, and Middle Eastern studies. Grants BA and MA in Jewish studies, MA in Jewish education, MA in Jewish music, MA in Jewish liberal studies, certificates in Jewish communal service, Jewish education, Israel studies, Jewish librarianship (joint graduate program with Drexel U.), and other credentials. Joint graduate program in Jewish communal service with the U. of Pennsylvania. High-school-level programs are offered by the affiliated Jewish Community High School of Gratz College. *Various newsletters, annual academic bulletin, and scholarly publications.*

HEBREW COLLEGE (1921). 43 Hawes St., Brookline, MA 02146. (617)232–8710. Pres. Dr. David M. Gordis; Bd. Chmn. Theodore H. Teplow. New England's only accredited college of Judaic studies offering bachelor's/master's degrees in Jewish studies and Jewish education and bachelor's in Hebrew literature. Two-year training institutes for afternoon-school directors, teachers, Jewish music professionals, and early childhood educators also available. Operates overnight Hebrew-speaking Camp Yavneh, Northwood, N.H.; Ulpan conversational language program; Prozdor High School; 100,000-volume library; continuing education courses; arts and film festivals on Jewish themes. Accredited by New England Assoc. Schools and Colleges. *Hebrew College Today.*

HEBREW SEMINARY FOR THE DEAF (1992). 4435 Oakton, Skokie, IL 60076. (708)677–3330. FAX: (708)674–0327. Pres. Rabbi Douglas Goldhamer; Bd. Cochmn. Rabbi William Frankel, Alan Crane. Trains deaf and hearing men and women to become rabbis and teachers for Jewish deaf communities across America. All classes in the 5-year program are interpreted in Sign Language. Rabbis teaching in the seminary are Reform, Conservative, and Reconstructionist.

HEBREW THEOLOGICAL COLLEGE (1922). 7135 N. Carpenter Rd., Skokie, IL 60077. (312)267-9800. Acting Pres. Rabbi Dr. Jerold Isenberg. An institution of higher Jewish learning which includes a graduate school; school of liberal arts and sciences; division of advanced Hebrew studies; Fasman Yeshiva High School; Anne M. Blitstein Teachers Institute for Women. *Or Shmuel; Torah Journal; Likutei P'shatim; Turrets of Silver.*

HEBREW UNION COLLEGE–JEWISH INSTITUTE OF RELIGION (1875). 3101 Clifton Ave., Cincinnati, OH 45220. (513)221-1875. FAX: (513)221-2810. Pres. Alfred Gottschalk; Exec. V.-Pres. Uri D. Herscher; V.-Pres. Academic Affairs Samuel Greengus; V.-Pres. Paul M. Steinberg; V.-Pres. John S. Borden; Chmn. Bd. Govs. Stanley P. Gold. Academic centers: 3101 Clifton Ave., Cincinnati, OH 45220 (1875), Dean Kenneth Ehrlich; 1 W. 4 St., NYC 10012 (1922), Dean Norman J. Cohen; 3077 University Ave., Los Angeles, CA 90007 (1954), Dean Lee Bycel; 13 King David St., Jerusalem, Israel 94101 (1963), Dean Michael L. Klein. Prepares students for Reform rabbinate, cantorate, religious-school teaching and administration, community service, academic careers; promotes Jewish studies; maintains libraries, archives, and museums; offers master's and doctoral degrees; engages in archaeological excavations; publishes scholarly works through Hebrew Union College Press. *American Jewish Archives; Bibliographica Judaica; HUC-JIR Catalogue; Hebrew Union College Annual; Studies in Bibliography and Booklore; The Chronicle.*

——, AMERICAN JEWISH ARCHIVES (1947). 3101 Clifton Ave., Cincinnati, OH 45220. (513)221-1875. FAX: (513)221-7812. Dir. Jacob R. Marcus; Admin. Dir. Abraham Peck. Promotes the study and preservation of the Western Hemisphere Jewish experience through research, publications, collection of important source materials, and a vigorous public-outreach program. *American Jewish Archives; monographs, publications, and pamphlets.*

——, AMERICAN JEWISH PERIODICAL CENTER (1957). 3101 Clifton Ave., Cincinnati, OH 45220. (513)221-1875. Dir. Jacob R. Marcus; Codir. Herbert C. Zafren. Maintains microfilms of all American Jewish periodicals 1823–1925, selected periodicals since 1925. *Jewish Periodicals and Newspapers on Microfilm (1957); First Supplement (1960); Augmented Edition (1984).*

——, EDGAR F. MAGNIN SCHOOL OF GRADUATE STUDIES (1956). 3077 University Ave., Los Angeles, CA 90007. (213)-749-3424. FAX: (213)747-6128. Dir. Stanley Chyet. Supervises programs leading to PhD (education), DHS, DHL, and MA degrees; participates in cooperative PhD programs with the University of Southern California.

——, GRADUATE STUDIES PROGRAM. 1 West 4 St. NYC 10012. (212)674-5300. FAX: (212)533-1029. V.-Pres. and Dean of Faculty Paul M. Steinberg; Dean Norman Cohen; Dir. Kerry M. Olitzky. Offers the DHL (doctor of Hebrew letters) degree in a variety of fields; the MAJS (master of arts in Judaic studies), a multidisciplinary degree; and is the only Jewish seminary to offer the DMin (doctor of ministry) degree in pastoral care and counseling.

——, IRWIN DANIELS SCHOOL OF JEWISH COMMUNAL SERVICE (1968). 3077 University Ave., Los Angeles, CA 90007. (213)749-3424. FAX: (213)747-6128. Dir. H. Jack Mayer; Dir. of Field Ed. Marla Eglash Abraham. Offers certificate and master's degree to those employed in Jewish communal services, or preparing for such work; offers joint MA in Jewish education and communal service with Rhea Hirsch School; offers dual degrees with the School of Social Work, the School of Public Administration, the Annenberg School for Communication, and the School of Gerontology of the University of S. California and with other institutions. Single master's degrees can be completed in 15 months and certificates are awarded for the completion of two full-time summer sessions.

——, JEROME H. LOUCHHEIM SCHOOL OF JUDAIC STUDIES (1969). 3077 University Ave., Los Angeles, CA 90007. (213)749-3424. FAX: (213)747-6128. Dir. David Ellenson. Offers programs leading to MA, BS, BA, and AA degrees; offers courses as part of the undergraduate program of the University of S. California.

————, NELSON GLUECK SCHOOL OF BIBLICAL ARCHAEOLOGY (1963). 13 King David St., Jerusalem, Israel 94101. (972)-2-203333. FAX: (972)2-251478. Dir. Avraham Biran. Offers graduate-level research programs in Bible and archaeology. Summer excavations are carried out by scholars and students. University credit may be earned by participants in excavations. Consortium of colleges, universities, and seminaries is affiliated with the school.

————, RHEA HIRSCH SCHOOL OF EDUCATION (1967). 3077 University Ave., Los Angeles, CA 90007. (213)749-3424. FAX: (213)747-6128. Dir. Sara Lee. Offers PhD and MA programs in Jewish and Hebrew education; conducts joint degree programs with University of S. California; offers courses for Jewish teachers, librarians, and early educators on a nonmatriculating basis; conducts summer institutes for professional Jewish educators.

————, SCHOOL OF EDUCATION (1947). 1 W. 4 St., NYC 10012. (212)674-5300. FAX: (212)533-0129. V.-Pres. and Dean of Faculty Paul M. Steinberg; Dean Norman J. Cohen; Dir. Kerry M. Olitzky. Trains teachers and principals for Reform religious schools; offers MA degree with specialization in religious education.

————, SCHOOL OF GRADUATE STUDIES (1949). 3101 Clifton Ave., Cincinnati, OH 45220 (513)221-1875. FAX: (513)221-0321. Dir. Alan Cooper. Offers programs leading to MA and PhD degrees; offers program leading to DHL degree for rabbinic graduates of the college.

————, SCHOOL OF JEWISH STUDIES (1963). 13 King David St., Jerusalem, Israel, 94101. (972)2-203333. FAX: (972)2-251-478. Dean Michael L. Klein; Assoc. Dean Rabbi Shaul R. Feinberg. Offers first year of graduate rabbinic, cantorial, and Jewish education studies (required) for American students; program leading to ordination for Israeli rabbinic students; undergraduate one-year work/study program on a kibbutz and in Jerusalem in cooperation with Union of American Hebrew Congregations; public outreach programs (lectures, courses, concerts, exhibits).

————, SCHOOL OF SACRED MUSIC (1947). 1 W. 4 St., NYC 10012. (212)674-5300.

FAX: (212)533-0129. Dir. Israel Goldstein. Trains cantors for congregations; offers MSM degree. Sacred Music Press.

————, SKIRBALL MUSEUM (see p. 503)

HERZLIAH-JEWISH TEACHERS SEMINARY (1967). Division of Touro College. 844 Ave. of the Americas, NYC 10001. (212)-447-0700. Pres. Bernard Lander; Dir. Jacob Katzman.

————, GRADUATE SCHOOL OF JEWISH STUDIES (1981). 160 Lexington Ave., NYC 10016. (212)213-2230. Pres. Bernard Lander; Dean Michael A. Shmidman. Offers courses leading to an MA in Jewish studies, with concentrations in Jewish history or Jewish education. Students may complete part of their program in Israel, through MA courses offered by Touro faculty at Touro's Jerusalem center.

————, JEWISH PEOPLE'S UNIVERSITY OF THE AIR. (212)447-0700. Dir./Producer Jacob Katzman. The educational outreach arm of Touro College, it produces and disseminates Jewish educational and cultural programming for radio broadcast and on audiocassettes.

INSTITUTE OF TRADITIONAL JUDAISM (1990). 241 Cedar Lane, Teaneck, NJ 07666. (201)801-9898. FAX: (201)801-0449. Rector (Reish Metivta) Rabbi David Weiss Halivni; Dean Rabbi Ronald D. Price. A nondenominational halakhic rabbinical school dedicated to genuine faith combined with intellectual honesty and the love of Israel. Graduates receive "yoreh yoreh" smikhah.

JEWISH THEOLOGICAL SEMINARY OF AMERICA (1886; reorg. 1902). 3080 Broadway, NYC 10027-4649. (212)678-8000. FAX: (212)678-8947. Chancellor Dr. Ismar Schorsch; Bd. Chmn. Gershon Kekst. Operates undergraduate and graduate programs in Judaic studies; professional schools for training Conservative rabbis and cantors; Melton Research Center for Jewish Education; the Jewish Museum; and such youth programs as the Ramah Camps and the Prozdor high-school division. Produces network television programs in cooperation with interfaith broadcasting commission. Academic Bulletin; Masoret; The Melton Journal.

————, ALBERT A. LIST COLLEGE OF JEWISH STUDIES (formerly SEMINARY COLLEGE OF JEWISH STUDIES-TEACHERS IN-

STITUTE) (1909). 3080 Broadway, NYC 10027. (212)678–8826. Dean Dr. Shuly Rubin Schwartz. Offers complete undergraduate program in Judaica leading to BA degree; conducts joint programs with Columbia University and Barnard College enabling students to receive two BA degrees.

———, CANTORS INSTITUTE AND SEMINARY COLLEGE OF JEWISH MUSIC (1952). 3080 Broadway, NYC 10027. (212)678–8038. Dean Rabbi Morton M. Leifman. Trains cantors, music teachers, and choral directors for congregations. Offers fulltime programs in sacred music leading to degrees of MSM and DSM, and diploma of *Hazzan.*

———, DEPARTMENT OF RADIO AND TELEVISION (1944). 3080 Broadway, NYC 10027. (212)678–8020. Produces radio and TV programs expressing the Jewish tradition in its broadest sense, including hourlong documentaries on NBC and ABC. Distributes cassettes of programs at minimum charge.

———, GRADUATE SCHOOL (formerly INSTITUTE FOR ADVANCED STUDY IN THE HUMANITIES) (1968). 3080 Broadway, NYC 10027. (212)678–8024. Dean Dr. Stephen P. Garfinkel. Programs leading to MA, MPhil, DHL, and PhD degrees in Jewish studies, Bible, Jewish education, history, literature, ancient Judaism, philosophy, rabbinics, and medieval Jewish studies; dual degree with Columbia University School of Social Work.

———, JEWISH MUSEUM (*see* p. 501)

———, LIBRARY OF THE JEWISH THEOLOGICAL SEMINARY. 3080 Broadway, NYC 10027. (212)678–8075. FAX: (212)678–8998. Librarian Dr. Mayer E. Rabinowitz. Contains one of the largest collections of Hebraica and Judaica in the world, including manuscripts, incunabula, rare books, and Cairo Geniza material. The 270,000-volume collection is housed in a state-of-the-art building and is open to the public. *New Acquisitions List; Friends of the Library Newsletter.*

———, LOUIS FINKELSTEIN INSTITUTE FOR RELIGIOUS AND SOCIAL STUDIES (1938). 3080 Broadway, NYC 10027. (212)678–8815. A scholarly and scientific fellowship of clergy and other religious teachers who desire authoritative information regarding some of the basic issues now confronting spiritually minded individuals.

———, MELTON RESEARCH CENTER FOR JEWISH EDUCATION (1960). 3080 Broadway, NYC 10027. (212)678–8031. Dirs. Dr. Eduardo Rauch, Dr. Barry W. Holtz. Develops new curricula and materials for Jewish education; prepares educators through seminars and in-service programs; maintains consultant and supervisory relationships with a limited number of pilot schools; develops and implements research initiatives; sponsors "renewal" retreats for teachers and principals. *The Melton Journal.*

———, NATIONAL RAMAH COMMISSION (1951). 3080 Broadway, NYC 10027. (212)678–8881. FAX: (212)749–8251. Pres. Dr. Saul Shapiro; Natl. Dir. Sheldon Dorph. Sponsors 7 overnight Conservative Jewish camps in U.S. and Canada, emphasizing Jewish education, living, and culture; offers opportunities for qualified college students and older to serve as counselors, administrators, specialists, etc., and programs for children with special needs (Tikvah program); offers special programs in U.S. and Israel, including National Ramah Staff Training Institute, Ramah Israel Seminar, Ulpan Ramah Plus, and Tichon Ramah Yerushalayim. Family and synagogue tours to Israel and summer day camp in Israel for Americans.

———, PROZDOR (1951). 3080 Broadway, NYC 10027. (212)678–8824. Principal Rabbi Judd Kruger Levingston. The highschool department of JTS, it provides a supplementary Jewish education for students who attend both Jewish and secular daytime schools. Classes in classical Jewish studies, with emphasis on Hebrew language, meet one evening a week and Sundays.

———, RABBINICAL SCHOOL (1886). 3080 Broadway, NYC 10027. (212)678–8816. Offers a program of graduate and professional studies leading to the degree of Master of Arts and ordination; includes one year of study in Jerusalem and an extensive field-work program.

———, SAUL LIEBERMAN INSTITUTE OF JEWISH RESEARCH (1985). 3080 Broadway, NYC 10027. (212)678–8994. Engaged in preparing for publication a series of scholarly editions of selected chapters of the Talmud. The following projects support and help disseminate the research:

Talmud Text Database; Bibliography of Talmudic Literature; Catalogue of Geniza Fragments; Teachers Training and Curriculum Development in Oral Law for Secondary Schools.

———, SCHOCKEN INSTITUTE FOR JEWISH RESEARCH (1961). 6 Balfour St., Jerusalem, Israel 92102. (972)2–631288. Dir. Shmuel Glick. Comprises the Schocken collection of rare books and manuscripts and a research institute dedicated to the exploration of Hebrew religious poetry (*piyyut*). *Schocken Institute Yearbook (P'raqim).*

———, UNIVERSITY OF JUDAISM (1947). 15600 Mulholland Dr., Los Angeles, CA 90077. (310)476–9777. FAX: (310)471–1278. Pres. Rabbi Robert D. Wexler; V.P. of Academic Affairs Dr. Hanan Alexander; Dean of Students Mary Raz. The undergraduate school, Lee College of Arts and Sciences, is an accredited liberal arts college offering a core curriculum of Jewish and Western studies, with majors including psychology, business, literature, political science, and Jewish studies. Accredited graduate programs in nonprofit business management (MBA), Jewish education, and Jewish studies, plus a preparatory program for the Conservative rabbinate. Two institutes for research and program development, the Wilstein Institute for Jewish Policy Studies and the Whizin Center for the Jewish Future. A broad range of continuing-education courses, cultural-arts programs, and a variety of outreach services for West Coast Jewish communities. *Direction Magazine (bi-yearly); Bulletin of General Information.*

MESIVTA YESHIVA RABBI CHAIM BERLIN RABBINICAL ACADEMY (1905). 1605 Coney Island Ave., Brooklyn, NY 11230. (718)377–0777. Exec. Dir. Y. Mayer Lasker. Maintains fully accredited elementary and high schools; collegiate and postgraduate school for advanced Jewish studies, both in America and Israel; Camp Morris, a summer study retreat; Prof. Nathan Isaacs Memorial Library; Gur Aryeh Publications.

NER ISRAEL RABBINICAL COLLEGE (1933). 400 Mt. Wilson Lane, Baltimore, MD 21208. (410)484–7200. FAX: (410)484–3060. Rabbi Yaakov S. Weinberg, Rosh Hayeshiva; Pres. Rabbi Herman N. Neuberger. Trains rabbis and educators for Jewish communities in America and worldwide. Offers bachelor's, master's, and doctoral degrees in talmudic law, as well as teacher's diploma. College has four divisions: Mechina High School, Rabbinical College, Teachers Training Institute, Graduate School. Maintains an active community-service division. Operates special programs for Iranian and Russian Jewish students. *Ner Israel Update; Alumni Bulletin; Ohr Hanair Talmudic Journal; Iranian B'nei Torah Bulletin.*

RABBINICAL COLLEGE OF TELSHE, INC. (1941). 28400 Euclid Ave., Wickliffe, OH 44092. (216)943–5300. Pres. Rabbi Mordecai Gifter; V.-Pres. Rabbi Abba Zalka Gewirtz. College for higher Jewish learning specializing in talmudic studies and rabbinics; maintains a preparatory academy including a secular high school, postgraduate department, teacher-training school, and teachers' seminary for women. *Pri Etz Chaim; Peer Mordechai; Alumni Bulletin.*

RECONSTRUCTIONIST RABBINICAL COLLEGE (1968). Church Rd. and Greenwood Ave., Wyncote, PA 19095. (215)576–0800. FAX: (215)576–6143. Pres. David Teutsch; Bd. Chmn. Jacques G. Pomeranz; Genl. Chmn. Aaron Ziegelman. Coeducational. Trains rabbis for all areas of Jewish communal life: synagogues, academic and educational positions, Hillel centers, federation agencies; confers title of rabbi and grants degrees of Master and Doctor of Hebrew Letters. *RRC Report.*

SPERTUS INSTITUTE OF JEWISH STUDIES (1924). 618 S. Michigan Ave., Chicago, IL 60605. (312)922–9012. FAX: (312)922–6406. Pres. Howard A. Sulkin; Bd. Chmn. Eric Joss; V.-Pres. for Academic Affairs Byron L. Sherwin; Dir. Spertus Museum Morris A. Fred; Dir. Asher Library Michael Terry. An accredited institution of higher learning offering doctor of Jewish studies degree, five master's degree programs in Jewish studies, Jewish education, Jewish communal service, and human-services administration, plus an extensive program of continuing education. Major resources of the college encompass Spertus Museum, Asher Library, Chicago Jewish Archives, and Spertus College of Judaica Press.

———, SPERTUS MUSEUM (*see* p. 503)

TOURO COLLEGE (1970). Executive Offices: Empire State Bldg., 350 Fifth Ave., Suite

5122, NYC 10018. (212)643–0700. FAX: (212)643–0759. Pres. Bernard Lander; Bd. Chmn. Max Karl. Chartered by NY State Board of Regents as a nonprofit four-year college with business, Judaic studies, health sciences, and liberal arts programs leading to BA, BS, and MA degrees; emphasizes relevance of Jewish heritage to general culture of Western civilization. Also offers JD degree and a biomedical program leading to the MD degree from Technion–Israel Institute of Technology, Haifa.

———, BARRY Z. LEVINE SCHOOL OF HEALTH SCIENCES AND CENTER FOR BIOMEDICAL EDUCATION (1970). 135 Common Rd., Bldg. #10, Dix Hills, NY 11746. (516)673–3200. Dean Dr. Joseph Weisberg. Along with the Manhattan campus, offers 5 programs: 5-year program leading to MA from Touro and MD from Faculty of Medicine of Technion–Israel Institute of Technology, Haifa; BS/MA—physical therapy and occupational therapy programs; BS—physician assistant and health-information management programs.

———, COLLEGE OF LIBERAL ARTS AND SCIENCES. 27–33 W. 23 St., NYC 10010. (212)463–0400. FAX: (212)627–9144. Exec. Dean Stanley Boylan. Offers comprehensive Jewish studies along with studies in the arts, sciences, humanities, and preprofessional studies in health sciences, law, accounting, business, computer science, education, and finance. Women's Division, 160 Lexington Ave., NYC 10016. (212)213–2230. FAX: (212)683–3281. Dean Sara E. Freifeld.

———, GRADUATE SCHOOL OF JEWISH STUDIES (1981). 160 Lexington Ave., NYC 10016. (212)213–2230. FAX: (212)-683–3281. Pres. Bernard Lander; Dean Michael A. Shmidman. Offers courses leading to an MA in Jewish studies, with concentrations in Jewish history or Jewish education. Students may complete part of their program in Israel, through MA courses offered by Touro faculty at Touro's Jerusalem center.

———, INSTITUTE OF JEWISH LAW. (516)-421–2244. Based at Fuchsberg Law Center, serves as a center and clearinghouse for study and teaching of Jewish law. Coedits *Dinei Israel* (Jewish Law Journal) with Tel Aviv University Law School.

———, JACOB D. FUCHSBERG LAW CENTER (1980). Long Island Campus, 300 Nassau Rd., Huntington, NY 11743. (516)421–2244. Dean Howard A. Glickstein. Offers studies leading to JD degree.

———, JEWISH PEOPLE'S UNIVERSITY OF THE AIR. (1979). 844 Sixth Ave., NYC 10001. (212)447–0700, Ext. 589. Producer/Dir. Jacob Katzman. Produces and disseminates courses in Jewish subject matter for radio broadcasting and on audiocassettes. Printed course outlines for all courses and discussion; leader's guides for some.

———, MOSCOW BRANCH. 35 Arbat St., 121002 Moscow, Russia. 248–38–21. Offers BS program in business and BA program in Jewish studies.

———, SCHOOL OF GENERAL STUDIES. 240 E. 123 St., NYC 10021. (212)722–1575. Dean Stephen Adolphus. Offers educational opportunities to minority groups and older people; courses in the arts, sciences, humanities, and special programs of career studies.

———, TOURO COLLEGE FLATBUSH CENTER (1929). 1277 E. 14 St., Brooklyn, NY 11230. (718)253–7538. Dean Robert Goldschmidt. A division of the College of Liberal Arts and Sciences; options offered in accounting and business, education, mathematics, political science, psychology, and speech. Classes are given on weeknights and during the day on Sunday.

———, TOURO COLLEGE ISRAEL CENTER. 23 Rehov Shivtei Yisrael, Jerusalem. 2–894–086/088. Assoc. Dean Carmi Horowitz; Resident Dir. Chana Sosevsky. Offers undergraduate courses in business, computer science, and education. Houses the MA degreee program in Jewish studies. The Touro Year Abroad Option for American students is coordinated from this center.

WEST COAST TALMUDICAL SEMINARY (Yeshiva Ohr Elchonon Chabad) (1953). 7215 Waring Ave., Los Angeles, CA 90046. (213)937–3763. Dean Rabbi Ezra Schochet. Provides facilities for intensive Torah education as well as Orthodox rabbinical training on the West Coast; conducts an accredited college preparatory high school combined with a full program of Torah-talmudic training and a graduate talmudical division on the college level. *Torah Quiz; Kobetz Migdal Ohr.*

YESHIVA UNIVERSITY (1886). Main Campus, 500 W. 185 St., NYC 10033-3201. (212)960-5400. FAX: (212)960-0055. Pres. Dr. Norman Lamm; Chmn. Bd. of Trustees David S. Gottesman. In its second century, the nation's oldest and largest independent university founded under Jewish auspices, with a broad range of undergraduate, graduate, and professional schools, a network of affiliates, a widespread program of research and community outreach, publications, and a museum. Curricula lead to bachelor's, master's, doctoral, and professional degrees. Undergraduate schools provide general studies curricula supplemented by courses in Jewish learning; graduate schools prepare for careers in medicine, law, social work, Jewish education, psychology, Jewish studies, and other fields. It has six undergraduate schools, seven graduate and professional schools, and three affiliates. *Alumni Review/Inside.*

Yeshiva University has four campuses in Manhattan and the Bronx: Main Campus, 500 W. 185 St., NYC 10033-3201; Midtown Center, 245 Lexington Ave., NYC 10016-4699; Brookdale Center, 55 Fifth Ave., NYC 10003-4391; Jack and Pearl Resnick Campus, Eastchester Rd. & Morris Pk. Ave., Bronx, NY 10461-1602.

Undergraduate schools for men at Main Campus (212)960-5400: Yeshiva College (Bd. Chmn. Jay Schottenstein; Dean Dr. Norman S. Rosenfeld) provides liberal arts and sciences curricula; grants BA degree. Isaac Breuer College of Hebraic Studies (Dean Dr. Michael D. Shmidman) awards Hebrew teacher's diploma, AA, BA, and BS. James Striar School of General Jewish Studies (Dean Dr. Michael D. Shmidman) grants AA degree. Yeshiva Program/Mazer School of Talmudic Studies (Dean Rabbi Zevulun Charlop) offers advanced course of study in Talmudic texts and commentaries.

Undergraduate school for women at Midtown Center (212)340-7700: Stern College for Women (Bd. Chmn. David Yagoda; Dean Dr. Karen Bacon) offers liberal arts and sciences curricula supplemented by Jewish studies programs; awards BA, AA, and Hebrew teacher's diploma.

Syms School of Business at Main Campus and Midtown Center (Bd. Chmn. Josh S. Weston; Dean Dr. Harold Nierenberg) offers undergraduate business curricula in conjunction with study at Yeshiva College or Stern College; grants BS degree.

Sponsors one high school for boys (Manhattan) and one for girls (Queens).

———, ALBERT EINSTEIN COLLEGE OF MEDICINE (1955). Eastchester Rd. & Morris Pk. Ave., Bronx, NY 10461-1602. (718)430-2000. Pres. Dr. Norman Lamm; Chmn. Bd. of Overseers Burton P. Resnick; Dean Dr. Dominick P. Purpura. Prepares physicians and conducts research in the health sciences; awards MD degree; includes Sue Golding Graduate Division of Medical Sciences (Dir. Dr. Michael D. Brenowitz), which grants PhD degree. Einstein College's clinical facilities, affiliates, and resources encompass Jack D. Weiler Hospital of Albert Einstein College of Medicine, Montefiore Medical Center, Bronx Municipal Hospital Center, and the Rose F. Kennedy Center for Research in Mental Retardation and Human Development. *Einstein; AECOM Today; Einstein Quarterly Journal of Biology and Medicine.*

———, ALUMNI OFFICE, 500 W. 185 St., NYC 10033-3201. (212)960-5373. Dir. Toby Hilsenrad Weiss. Seeks to foster a close allegiance of alumni to their alma mater by maintaining ties with all alumni and servicing the following associations: Yeshiva College Alumni (Pres. Zev S. Berman); Stern College for Women Alumnae (Pres. Jan Schechter); Sy Syms School of Business Alumni (Pres. Martin Lifshutz); Albert Einstein College of Medicine Alumni (Pres. Dr. Michael S. Frank); Ferkauf Graduate School of Psychology Alumni (Pres. Dr. Abraham Givner); Wurzweiler School of Social Work Alumni (Pres. Ilene Stein Himber); Rabbinic Alumni (Pres. Rabbi Bernard Rosensweig); Benjamin N. Cardozo School of Law Alumni (Cochmn. Karel Turner, Joan Ehrlich White). *Alumni Review/Inside; AECOM Alumni News; Jewish Social Work Forum.*

———, BELFER INSTITUTE FOR ADVANCED BIOMEDICAL STUDIES (1978). Eastchester Rd. & Morris Pk. Ave., Bronx, NY 10461-1602. (718)430-2801. Dir. Dr. Chester M. Edelmann, Jr. Integrates and coordinates the Medical College's postdoctoral research and training-grant programs in the basic and clinical biomedical sciences. Awards certificate as Research Fellow or Research Associate on completion of training.

——, BENJAMIN N. CARDOZO SCHOOL OF LAW (1976). 55 Fifth Ave., NYC 10003–4391. (212)790–0200. Pres. Dr. Norman Lamm; Bd. Chmn. Earle I. Mack; Dean Dr. Frank J. Macchiarola. Provides innovative courses of study within a traditional legal framework; program includes judicial internships; grants Juris Doctor (JD) degree. Programs and services include institute for advanced legal studies; center for ethics in the practice of law; legal services clinic; institute of Jewish law; international law and human-rights programs; center on corporate governance; program in communications law, conflict-resolution program, and other special programs; center for professional development; international summer institutes on law, trade, and social change. *Cardozo Studies in Law and Literature; Cardozo Law Review; Cardozo Arts and Entertainment Law Journal; Cardozo Women's Law Journal; New Europe Law Review; Cardozo Law Forum.*

——, BERNARD REVEL GRADUATE SCHOOL (1935). 500 W. 185 St., NYC 10033–3201. (212)960–5253. Pres. Dr. Norman Lamm; Bd. Chmn. Irwin Shapiro; Dean Dr. Arthur Hyman. Offers graduate programs in Bible, talmudic studies, Jewish history, and Jewish philosophy; confers MA and PhD degrees. Harry Fischel School for Higher Jewish Studies offers the Revel program during the summer.

——, DAVID J. AZRIELI GRADUATE INSTITUTE OF JEWISH EDUCATION AND ADMINISTRATION (1945). 245 Lexington Ave., NYC 10016–4699. (212)340–7705. Dir. Dr. Yitzchak S. Handel. Offers MS degree in Jewish elementary and secondary education; specialist's certificate and EdD in administration and supervision of Jewish education. Block Education Program, initiated under a grant from the Jewish Agency's L.A. Pincus Fund for the Diaspora, provides summer course work to complement year-round field instruction in local communities.

——, FERKAUF GRADUATE SCHOOL OF PSYCHOLOGY (1957). Eastchester Rd. & Morris Pk. Ave., Bronx, NY 10461–1602. (718)430–4201. Dean Dr. Barbara G. Melamed. Offers MA in general psychology; PsyD in clinical and school psychology; and PhD in school, developmental, and health psychology.

——, (affiliate) RABBI ISAAC ELCHANAN THEOLOGICAL SEMINARY (1896). 2540 Amsterdam Ave., NYC 10033–9986. (212)960–5344. Chmn. Bd. of Trustees Judah Feinerman; V.-Pres. for Administration & Professional Education Rabbi Robert S. Hirt; Dean Rabbi Zevulun Charlop. Grants *semikhah* (ordination) and the degrees of Master of Religious Education, Master of Hebrew Literature, Doctor of Religious Education, and Doctor of Hebrew Literature.

Kollelim include Marcos and Adina Katz Kollel (Institute for Advanced Research in Rabbinics) (Dir. Rabbi Hershel Schachter); Kollel l'Horaah (Yadin Yadin) and External Yadin Yadin (Dir. Rabbi J. David Bleich); Caroline and Joseph S. Gruss Kollel Elyon (Postgraduate Kollel Program) (Dir. Rabbi Aharon Kahn); Caroline and Joseph S. Gruss Institute in Jerusalem (Dir. Rabbi Aharon Lichtenstein); Chaver Program (Dir. Rabbi J. David Bleich).

The service arm of the seminary, Max Stern Division of Communal Services (Dir. Rabbi Robert S. Hirt), provides personal and professional service to the rabbinate and related fields, as well as educational, consultative, organizational, and placement services to congregations, schools, and communal organizations around the world; coordinates a broad spectrum of outreach programs.

Other seminary programs are Jacob E. Safra Institute of Sephardic Studies and the Institute of Yemenite Studies; Maybaum Sephardic Fellowship Program; Dr. Joseph and Rachel Ades Sephardic Outreach Program; Sephardic Community Program; Stone-Sapirstein Center for Jewish Education; National Commission on Torah Education.

PHILIP AND SARAH BELZ SCHOOL OF JEWISH MUSIC (1954). 560 W. 185 St., NYC 10033–3201. (212)960–5353. Dir. Cantor Bernard Beer. Provides professional training of cantors and courses in Jewish liturgical music; maintains a specialized library and conducts outreach; awards Associate Cantor's certificate and Cantorial diploma.

——, (affiliate) YESHIVA OF LOS ANGELES (1977). 9760 W. Pico Blvd., Los Angeles, CA 90035–4701. (213)553–4478. Dean Rabbi Marvin Hier; Bd. Chmn. Samuel Belzberg; Dir. Academic Programs Rabbi Sholom Tendler. Provides Jewish studies program for beginners. Affiliates are high schools, Jewish Studies Institute for Adult Education, and Simon Wiesenthal Center. SIMON WIESENTHAL CENTER (1977). 9760 W. Pico Blvd., Los Angeles, CA 90035–4701. (310)553–9036. FAX: (310)-553–8007. Dean-Founder Rabbi Marvin Hier; Assoc. Dean Rabbi Abraham Cooper; Dir. Dr. Gerald Margolis; Exec. Dir. Rabbi Meyer May. Regional offices in New York, Chicago, Miami, Jerusalem, Paris, Toronto. The largest institution of its kind in N. America dedicated to the study of the Holocaust, its contemporary implications, and related human-rights issues through education and awareness. Incorporates the Beit Hashoah-Museum of Tolerance, library, media, archives, "Testimony to the Truth" oral histories, educational outreach, research department, Jewish Studies Institute (in cooperation with Yeshiva of Los Angeles), international social action, "Page One" (syndicated weekly radio news magazine presenting contemporary Jewish issues). *Response Magazine.*

——, WOMEN'S ORGANIZATION (1928). 500 W. 185 St., NYC 10033–3201. (212)-960–0855. Pres. Dinah Pinczower. Supports Yeshiva University's national scholarship program for students training in education, community service, law, medicine, and other professions, and its development program. *YUWO News Briefs.*

——, WURZWEILER SCHOOL OF SOCIAL WORK (1957). 500 W. 185 St., NYC 10033–3201. (212)960–0800. Pres. Norman Lamm; Chmn. Bd. of Govs. Herbert H. Schiff; Dean Dr. Sheldon R. Gelman. Offers graduate programs in social work; grants MSW and DSW degrees and certificate in Jewish communal service. MSW programs are: Concurrent Plan, 2-year, full-time track, combining classroom study and supervised field instruction; Plan for Employed Persons (PEP), for people working in social agencies; Block Education Plan (Dir. Dr. Adele Weiner), which combines summer course work with regular-year field placement in local agencies; Clergy Plan, training in counseling for clergy of all denominations; Center for Professional Training in the Care of the Elderly. *Jewish Social Work Forum.*

——, YESHIVA UNIVERSITY MUSEUM (see p. 504)

YESHIVATH TORAH VODAATH AND MESIVTA RABBINICAL SEMINARY (1918).

425 E. 9 St., Brooklyn, NY 11218. (718)-941–8000. Bd. Chmn. Chaim Leshkowitz. Offers Hebrew and secular education from elementary level through rabbinical ordination and postgraduate work; maintains a teachers institute and community-service bureau; maintains a dormitory and a non-profit camp program for boys. *Chronicle; Mesivta Vanguard; Thought of the Week; Torah Vodaath News; Ha'Mesifta.*

——, ALUMNI ASSOCIATION (1941). 425 E. 9 St., Brooklyn, NY 11218. (718)941–8000. Pres. Marcus Saffer; Bd. Chmn. George Weinberg. Promotes social and cultural ties between the alumni and the schools through fund-raising; offers vocational guidance to students; operates Camp Torah Vodaath; sponsors research fellowship program for boys. *Annual Journal; Hamesivta Torah periodical.*

SOCIAL, MUTUAL BENEFIT

ALPHA EPSILON PI FRATERNITY (1913). 8815 Wesleyan Rd., Indianapolis, IN 46268–1171. (317)876–1913. FAX: (317)-876–1057. Internatl. Pres. Marc P. Katz; Exec. V.-Pres. Sidney N. Dunn. International Jewish fraternity active on over 100 campuses in the U.S. and Canada; encourages Jewish students to remain loyal to their heritage and to assume leadership roles in the community; active in behalf of Soviet Jewry, the State of Israel, the United States Holocaust Memorial Museum, and other Jewish causes. *The Lion of Alpha Epsilon Pi (quarterly magazine).*

AMERICAN ASSOCIATION OF RUSSIAN JEWS, INC. (1989). 45 E. 33 St., Suite B2, New York, NY 10016. (212)779–0383, (516)-937–3819. FAX: (212)251–0569. Pres. Leonid Stonov; V.-Pres. Inna Arolovich. National mutual assistance and refugee-advocacy organization, uniting Jews who immigrated to the U.S. from the former Soviet Union. Has chapters in four states, Anti-Fascist/Anti-Racist chapter, and Council of Refuseniks. Assists newcomers in their resettlement and vocational and cultural adjustment; fosters their Jewish identity and involvement in civic and social affairs; fights anti-Semitism and violation of human rights in the FSU and the U.S.; informs U.S. government and general public about the situation of Jews in the FSU and the Russian-Jewish community in the U.S. *Chronicle of Anti-Semitic Incidents and Inciting of Ethnic Hatred in the For-*

mer Soviet Union (in English, semiannually); Information Bulletin (in Russian, bimonthly).

AMERICAN FEDERATION OF JEWS FROM CENTRAL EUROPE, INC. (1938). 570 Seventh Ave., NYC 10018. (212)921–3871. FAX: (212)575–1918. Pres. Robert L. Lehman; Bd. Chmn. Curt C. Silberman; Exec. Asst. Katherine Rosenthal. Seeks to safeguard the rights and interests of American Jews of German-speaking Central European descent, especially in reference to restitution and indemnification; through its affiliate Research Foundation for Jewish Immigration sponsors research and publications on the history, immigration, and acculturation of Central European émigrés in the U.S. and worldwide; through its affiliate Jewish Philanthropic Fund of 1933 supports social programs for needy Nazi victims in the U.S.; undertakes cultural activities, annual conferences, publications; member, Council of Jews from Germany, London.

AMERICAN VETERANS OF ISRAEL (1949). 136 E. 39 St., NYC 10016. Pres. Simon Spiegelman; Sec. Sidney Rabinovich. Maintains contact with American and Canadian volunteers who served in Aliyah Bet and/or Israel's War of Independence; promotes Israel's welfare; holds memorial services at grave of Col. David Marcus; is affiliated with World Mahal. *Newsletter.*

ASSOCIATION OF YUGOSLAV JEWS IN THE UNITED STATES, INC. (1941). 130 E. 59 St., Suite 1202, NYC 10022. (212)371–6891. Pres. Mary Levine; Exec. Off. Emanuel Salom; Treas./V.-Pres. Mirko Goldschmidt. Assists all Jews originally from Yugoslavia; raises funds for Israeli agencies and institutions. *Bulletin.*

BNAI ZION–THE AMERICAN FRATERNAL ZIONIST ORGANIZATION (1908). 136 E. 39 St., NYC 10016. (212)725–1211. FAX: (212)684–6327. Pres. Rabbi Reuben M. Katz; Exec. V.-Pres. Mel Parness. Fosters principles of Americanism, fraternalism, and Zionism; offers life insurance and other benefits to its members. The Bnai Zion Foundation supports various humanitarian projects in Israel and the USA, chiefly the Bnai Zion Medical Center in Haifa and homes for retarded children—Maon Bnai Zion in Rosh Ha'ayin and the Herman Z. Quittman Center in Jerusalem. In the U.S. sponsors program of awards for excellence in Hebrew for high school and college students. Chapters all over U.S. and a New Leadership division in Greater NY area. *Bnai Zion Voice; Bnai Zion Foundation Newsletter.*

BRITH ABRAHAM (1859; reorg. 1887). 136 E. 39 St., NYC 10016. (212)725–1211. Grand Master Robert Freeman. Protects Jewish rights and combats anti-Semitism; supports Soviet and Ethiopian emigration and the safety and dignity of Jews worldwide; helps to support Bnai Zion Medical Center in Haifa and other Israeli institutions; aids and supports various programs and projects in the U.S.: Hebrew Excellence Program—Gold Medal presentation in high schools and colleges; Camp Loyaltown; Brith Abraham and Bnai Zion Foundations. *Voice.*

BRITH SHOLOM (1905). 3939 Conshohocken Ave., Philadelphia, PA 19131. (215)878–5696. Pres. Reuben Rochvarg; Exec. Dir. Albert Liss. Fraternal organization devoted to community welfare, protection of rights of Jewish people, and activities which foster Jewish identity and provide support for Israel; sponsors Brith Sholom House for senior citizens in Philadelphia and Brith Sholom Beit Halochem in Haifa, a rehabilitation center for Israel's permanently war-wounded. *Brith Sholom Presents; monthly news bulletin.*

CENTRAL SEPHARDIC JEWISH COMMUNITY OF AMERICA WOMEN'S DIVISION, INC. (1941). 8 W. 70 St., NYC 10023. (212)787–2850. Pres. Mrs. A. Lopes Cardozo; Treas. Laura Capelluto; Sec. Esther Shear. Promotes Sephardic culture by awarding scholarships to qualified needy students in New York and Israel; raises funds for hospital and religious institutions in U.S. and Israel.

FREE SONS OF ISRAEL (1849). 250 Fifth Ave., Suite 201, NYC 10001. (212)725–3690. FAX: (212)725–5874. Grand Master Charles Mackoff; Grand Sec. Rudolph Gordon. Oldest Jewish fraternal-benefit order in U.S. Supports the State of Israel; fights anti-Semitism; helps Soviet Jewry. Maintains scholarship fund for members and children of members; insurance fund and credit union; social functions. *Free Sons Reporter.*

JEWISH LABOR BUND (Directed by WORLD COORDINATING COMMITTEE OF THE BUND) (1897; reorg. 1947). 25 E. 21 St., NYC 10010. (212)475–0059. Exec. Sec.

Benjamin Nadel. Coordinates activities of Bund organizations throughout the world and represents them in the Socialist International; spreads the ideas of socialism as formulated by the Jewish Labor Bund; publishes books and periodicals on world problems, Jewish life, socialist theory and policy, and on the history, activities, and ideology of the Jewish Labor Bund. *Unser Tsait* (U.S.); *Lebns-Fragn* (Israel); *Unser Gedank* (Australia); *Unser Shtimme* (France).

SEPHARDIC JEWISH BROTHERHOOD OF AMERICA, INC. (1915). 97–45 Queens Blvd., Rm. 610, Rego Park, NY 11374. (718)459–1600. Pres. Bernard Ouziel; Sec. Michael Cohen. A benevolent fraternal organization seeking to promote the industrial, social, educational, and religious welfare of its members. *Sephardic Brother.*

THE WORKMEN'S CIRCLE/ARBETER RING (1900). 45 E. 33 St., NYC 10016. (212)889–6800. FAX: (212)532–7518. Exec. Dir. Robert A. Kaplan. Fosters Jewish identity and participation in Jewish life among its members through Jewish, especially Yiddish, culture and education, friendship, mutual aid, and the pursuit of social and economic justice. Offices are located throughout the U.S. and Canada. Member services include: Jewish cultural seminars, concerts, theater, Jewish schools, children's camp and adult resort, fraternal and singles activities, a Jewish Book Center, public affairs/social action, health insurance plans, medical/dental/legal services, life insurance plans, cemetery/funeral benefits, social services, geriatric homes and centers, and travel services.

SOCIAL WELFARE

AMC CANCER RESEARCH CENTER (formerly JEWISH CONSUMPTIVES' RELIEF SOCIETY, 1904; incorporated as AMERICAN MEDICAL CENTER AT DENVER, 1954). 1600 Pierce St., Denver, CO 80214. (303)233–6501. Dir. Dr. Douglass C. Torney; Pres./CEO Bob R. Baker. A nationally recognized leader in the fight against cancer; employs a three-pronged, interdisciplinary approach that combines laboratory, clinical, and community cancer-control research to advance the prevention, early detection, diagnosis, and treatment of the disease. *Quarterly report.*

AMCHA FOR TSEDAKAH (1990). 7700 Wisconsin Ave., Suite 500-A, Bethesda, MD 20814. (301) 652–7846. FAX: (301) 657–4180. Pres. Rabbi Bruce E. Kahn. Solicits and distributes contributions to Jewish charitable organizations in the U.S. and Israel; accredits organizations which serve an important *tsedakah* purpose, demonstrate efficiency and fiscal integrity, and also support pluralism. Contributors are encouraged to earmark contributions for specific organizations; all contributions to General Fund are forwarded to the charitable institutions, as operating expenses are covered by a separate fund.

AMERICAN JEWISH CORRECTIONAL CHAPLAINS ASSOCIATION, INC. (formerly NATIONAL COUNCIL OF JEWISH PRISON CHAPLAINS) (1937). 10 E. 73 St., NYC 10021–4194. (212)879–8415. FAX: (212)-772–3977. (Cooperates with the New York Board of Rabbis.) Pres. Rabbi Irving Koslowe; Exec. Off. Rabbi Moses A. Birnbaum. Supports spiritual, moral, and social services for Jewish men and women in corrections; stimulates support of correctional chaplaincy; provides spiritual and professional fellowship for Jewish correctional chaplains; promotes sound standards for correctional chaplaincy; schedules workshops and research to aid chaplains in counseling and with religious services for Jewish inmates. Constituent, American Correctional Chaplains Association. *Chaplains Manual.*

AMERICAN JEWISH SOCIETY FOR SERVICE, INC. (1950). 15 E. 26 St., Rm. 1029, NYC 10010. (212)683–6178. Pres. Arthur Lifson; Exec. Dir. Elly Saltzman. Conducts voluntary work-service camps each summer to enable high-school juniors and seniors to perform humanitarian service.

AMERICAN JEWISH WORLD SERVICE (1985). 15 W. 26 St., 9th fl., NYC 10010. (212)683–1161. FAX: (212)683–5187. Chmn. Larry Buttenwieser; Exec. Dir. Andrew Griffel. Provides assistance on nonsectarian basis to relieve hunger, poverty, and suffering in Africa, Asia, and Latin America. Funds international economic development and education projects and disaster relief; promotes awareness of these issues in the American Jewish community and sends volunteers overseas through newly established Jewish Volunteer Corps.

ASSOCIATION OF JEWISH CENTER PROFESSIONALS (1918). 15 E. 26 St., NYC 10010–1579. (212)532–4949. FAX: (212)481–

4174. Pres. Michael Witkes; Exec. Dir. Marilyn Altman. Seeks to enhance the standards, techniques, practices, scope, and public understanding of Jewish Community Center and kindred agency work. *Kesher.*

ASSOCIATION OF JEWISH COMMUNITY ORGANIZATION PERSONNEL (AJCOP) (1969). 1750 Euclid Ave., Cleveland, OH 44115. (216)566–9200. FAX: (216)861–1230. Pres. Peter Wells. Exec. Dir. Howard R. Berger. An organization of professionals engaged in areas of fund-raising, endowments, budgeting, social planning, financing, administration, and coordination of services. Objectives are to develop and enhance professional practices in Jewish communal work; to maintain and improve standards, practices, scope, and public understanding of the field of community organization, as practiced through local federations, national agencies, other organizations, settings, and private practitioners.

ASSOCIATION OF JEWISH FAMILY AND CHILDREN'S AGENCIES (1972). 3086 State Highway 27, Suite 11, PO Box 248, Kendall Park, NJ 08824–0248. (800)634–7346. FAX: (908)821–0493. Pres. George Wolly; Exec. V.-Pres. Bert J. Goldberg. The national service organization for Jewish family and children's agencies in Canada and the U.S. Reinforces member agencies in their efforts to sustain and enhance the quality of Jewish family and communal life. Operates the Elder Support Network for the National Jewish Community. *Bulletin (bimonthly); Directory; Professional Opportunities Bulletin; Resettlement Bulletin (quarterly).*

BARON DE HIRSCH FUND (1891). 130 E. 59 St., NYC 10022. (212)836–1358. Pres. Arthur D. Sporn; Mng. Dir. Lauren Katzowitz. Aids Jewish immigrants in the U.S. and Israel by giving grants to agencies active in educational and vocational fields; has limited program for study tours in U.S. by Israeli agriculturists.

B'NAI B'RITH (1843). 1640 Rhode Island Ave., NW, Washington, DC 20036. (202)-857–6600. FAX: (202)857–1099. Pres. Kent E. Schiner; Exec. V.-Pres. Dr. Sidney Clearfield. International Jewish organization, with affiliates in 51 countries. Offers programs designed to ensure the preservation of Jewry and Judaism: Jewish educa-

tion, community volunteer service, expansion of human rights, assistance to Israel, housing for the elderly, leadership training, rights of Soviet Jews and Jews of other countries to emigrate and study their heritage. *International Jewish Monthly.*

———, ANTI-DEFAMATION LEAGUE OF (see p. 494)

———, HILLEL FOUNDATIONS, INC. (see p. 518)

———, KLUTZNICK MUSEUM (see p. 499)

———, YOUTH ORGANIZATION (see p. 519)

B'NAI B'RITH WOMEN (1897). 1828 L St., NW, Suite 250, Washington, DC 20036. (202)857–1370. FAX: (202)857–1380. Pres. Susan Bruck; Exec. Dir. Elaine K. Binder. Supports Jewish women in their families, in their communities, and in society. Offers programs that contribute to preservation of Jewish life and values; supports treatment of emotionally disturbed children in BBW Residential Treatment Center in Israel; advocates for Israel and for family issues. *Women's World.*

CITY OF HOPE NATIONAL MEDICAL CENTER AND BECKMAN RESEARCH INSTITUTE (1913). 1500 E. Duarte Rd., Duarte, CA 91010. (818)359–8111. Pres. and Chief Exec. Off. Dr. Sanford M. Shapero; Bd. Chmn. Richard Ziman. Offers care to those with cancer and major diseases, medical consultation service for second opinions, and pilot research programs in genetics, immunology, and the basic life process. *City News; City of Hope Cancer Center Report.*

CONFERENCE OF JEWISH COMMUNAL SERVICE (see Jewish Communal Service Association of N. America)

COUNCIL OF JEWISH FEDERATIONS, INC. (1932). 730 Broadway, NYC 10003. (212)-475–5000. FAX: (212)529–5842. Pres. Maynard I. Wishner; Exec. V.-Pres. Martin Kraar. Provides national and regional services to more than 200 associated federations embracing 800 communities in the U.S. and Canada, aiding in fund-raising, community organization, health and welfare planning, personnel recruitment, and public relations; operates CJF satellite network linking 75 federations throughout North America for conferences, seminars, training, and board meetings (network available for use by other not-for-profit agencies). *Directory of Jewish Federations, Welfare Funds and Community Councils; Directory of Jewish Health and Welfare Agencies (biennial); What's New in Federations; Newsbriefs; annual report.*

INTERNATIONAL ASSOCIATION OF JEWISH VOCATIONAL SERVICES (formerly JEWISH OCCUPATIONAL COUNCIL) (1939). 1845 Walnut St., Suite 608, Phildelphia, PA 19103. (215)854–0233. FAX: (215)854–0212. Bd. Pres. Norman Zilber; Exec. Dir. Dr. Marvin S. Kivitz; Asst. Dir. Shira E. Goldman. Liaison and coordinating body for 26 vocational and family service agencies in the U.S., Israel, and Canada that provide a broad range of counseling, training, job-placement, and rehabilitation services to the Jewish and general community. These services are available to the public as well as many refugee populations.

INTERNATIONAL COUNCIL ON JEWISH SOCIAL AND WELFARE SERVICES (1961). c/o American Jewish Joint Distribution Committee, 711 Third Ave., NYC 10017. (NY liaison office with UN headquarters.) (212)687–6200. Chmn. David Cope-Thompson; Exec. Sec. Cheryl Mariner. Provides for exchange of views and information among member agencies on problems of Jewish social and welfare services, including medical care, old age, welfare, child care, rehabilitation, technical assistance, vocational training, agricultural and other resettlement, economic assistance, refugees, migration, integration and related problems, representation of views to governments and international organizations. Members: six national and international organizations.

JEWISH BRAILLE INSTITUTE OF AMERICA, INC. (1931). 110 E. 30 St., NYC 10016. (212)889–2525. FAX: (212)689–3692. Pres. Dr. Jane Evans; Exec. V.-Pres. Gerald M. Kass. Provides Judaic materials in braille, talking books, and large print for blind, visually impaired, and reading-disabled; offers counseling for full integration into the life of the Jewish community. International program serves clients in more than 40 communities. Comprehensive braille and talking-book library on Judaic topics; many titles in large print. *Jewish Braille Review; JBI Voice; Likutim, Hebrew-language magazine on blindness issues.*

JEWISH COMMUNAL SERVICE ASSOCIATION OF N. AMERICA (1899; formerly CONFERENCE OF JEWISH COMMUNAL SERVICE). 3084 State Hwy. 27, Suite 9, Kendall Park, NJ 08824–1657. (908)821–1871. FAX: (908)821–5335. Pres. Ernest M. Kahn; Exec. Dir. Joel Ollander. Serves as forum for all professional philosophies in community service, for testing new experiences, proposing new ideas, and questioning or reaffirming old concepts; umbrella organization for seven major Jewish communal service groups. Concerned with advancement of professional personnel practices and standards. *Concurrents; Journal of Jewish Communal Service.*

JEWISH COMMUNITY CENTERS ASSOCIATION OF NORTH AMERICA (formerly JWB) (1917). 15 E. 26 St., NYC 10010–1579. (212)532–4949. FAX: (212)481–4174. Pres. Lester Pollack; Exec. V.-Pres. Arthur Rotman. Central leadership agency for 275 Jewish community centers, YM-YWHAs, and camps in the U.S. and Canada, serving over one million Jews. Provides a variety of consulting services and staff training programs to members, including informal Jewish educational and cultural experiences in Israel. U.S. government-accredited agency for the religious, Jewish educational, and recreational needs of Jewish military personnel, their families, and hospitalized VA patients through JWB Jewish Chaplains Council. *Circle; Briefing; Personnel Reporter.*

———, JWB JEWISH CHAPLAINS COUNCIL (formerly COMMISSION ON JEWISH CHAPLAINCY) (1940). 15 E. 26 St., NYC 10010–1579. Chmn. Rabbi Frank W. Waldorf; Dir. Rabbi David Lapp. Recruits, endorses, and serves Jewish military and Veterans Administration chaplains on behalf of the American Jewish community and the major rabbinic bodies; trains and assists Jewish lay leaders where there are no chaplains, for service to Jewish military personnel, their families, and hospitalized veterans. *CHAPLINES newsletter.*

JEWISH CONCILIATION BOARD OF AMERICA, INC. (A Division of the JEWISH BOARD OF FAMILY AND CHILDREN'S SERVICES) (1920). 120 W. 57 St., NYC 10019. (212)582–9100. FAX: (212)245–2096. Pres. Seymour R. Askin, Jr.; Exec. V.-Pres. Dr. Alan B. Siskind. Offers dispute-resolution services to families, individuals, and organizations. Social-work, rabbinic, and legal expertise are available for family and divorce mediation and arbitration. Fee—sliding scale.

JEWISH FAMILY AND CHILDREN'S PROFESSIONALS ASSOCIATION (1965). c/o NYANA, 17 Battery Pl., NYC 10004. (212)425-2900. FAX:(212)514-6938. Pres. Mark Handelman. Brings together Jewish caseworkers and related professionals in Jewish family, children's, and health services. Seeks to improve personnel standards, further Jewish continuity and identity, and strengthen Jewish family life; provides forums for professional discussion at national conference of Jewish communal service and regional meetings; takes action on social-policy issues. *Newsletter.*

JEWISH FUND FOR JUSTICE (1984). 920 Broadway, Suite 605, NYC 10010. (212)-677-7080. Bd. Chmn. Lawrence S. Levine; Exec. Dir. Marlene Provizer. A national grant-making foundation supporting efforts to combat the root causes of poverty in the U.S. Provides diverse opportunities for individual, family, and synagogue involvement through memorial, youth endowment, and synagogue challenge funds; works cooperatively with other denominational funders and philanthropies promoting social and economic justice. *Annual Report.*

JWB (*see* Jewish Community Centers Association of North America)

LEVI HOSPITAL (sponsored by B'nai B'rith) (1914). 300 Prospect Ave., Hot Springs, AR 71902. (501)624-1281. FAX: (501)-622-3500. Pres. Steven Kirsch; Admin. Patrick G. McCabe. Offers arthritis treatment, stroke rehabilitation, orthopedic rehabilitation, Levi Life Center, a hospice program, and Team Rehabilitation Center, a joint venture of Levi Hospital and St. Josephs Regional Health Center. Services provided: outpatient rehab, speech therapy, hard therapy, occupational therapy, work hardening, sports medicine. *Quarterly newsletter.*

MAZON: A JEWISH RESPONSE TO HUNGER (1985). 2940 Westwood Blvd., Suite 7, Los Angeles, CA 90064. (310)470-7769. FAX: (310)470-6736. Bd. Chmn. Rabbi Mark Loeb; Exec. Dir. Irving Cramer; Associate Dir./Grants Dir. Susan Cramer. Raises funds by asking American Jews to contribute a suggested amount of 3 percent of the cost of life-cycle celebrations as well as through annual Passover and Yom Kippur appeals. Funds are granted to nonprofit organizations in the U.S. and abroad that work to alleviate hunger, malnutrition, and poverty. 1993 grants totaled $1.65 million. *Mazon Newsletter.*

NATIONAL ASSOCIATION OF JEWISH CHAPLAINS (1988). PO Box 7921, San Francisco, CA 94120. (415)885-7786. FAX: (415)885-7439. Pres. Rabbi Jeffrey M. Silberman. A professional organization for people functioning as Jewish chaplains in hospitals, nursing homes, geriatric, psychiatric, correctional, and military facilities. Provides collegial support, continuing education, professional certification, and resources for the Jewish community on issues of pastoral and spiritual care. *Journal of Pastoral Care* (cosponsor).

NATIONAL ASSOCIATION OF JEWISH FAMILY, CHILDREN'S AND HEALTH PROFESSIONALS (*see* Association of Jewish Family and Children's Agency Professionals)

NATIONAL COUNCIL OF JEWISH PRISON CHAPLAINS, INC. (*see* American Jewish Correctional Chaplains Association, Inc.)

NATIONAL COUNCIL OF JEWISH WOMEN (1893). 53 W. 23 St., NYC 10010. (212)-645-4048. Pres. Susan Katz; Exec. Dir. Iris Gross. Furthers human welfare through program of community service, education, advocacy for children and youth, aging, women's issues, constitutional rights, Jewish life and Israel. Promotes education for the disadvantaged in Israel through the NCJW Research Institute for Innovation in Education at Hebrew University, Jerusalem. Promotes welfare of children in U.S. through Center for the Child. *NCJW Journal; Washington Newsletter.*

NATIONAL INSTITUTE FOR JEWISH HOSPICE (1985). 8723 Alden Drive, Suite 652, Los Angeles, CA 90048. 1-800-446-4448; (213)HOSPICE (Calif. only). Pres. Rabbi Maurice Lamm; Exec. Dir. Levana Lev. Serves as a national Jewish hospice resource center. Through conferences, research, publications, referrals, and counseling services offers guidance, training, and information to patients, family members, clergy of all faiths, professional caregivers, and volunteers who work with the Jewish terminally ill. *Jewish Hospice Times.*

NATIONAL JEWISH CENTER FOR IMMUNOLOGY AND RESPIRATORY MEDICINE (formerly NATIONAL JEWISH HOSPITAL/NATIONAL ASTHMA CENTER) (1899). 1400 Jackson St., Denver, CO 80206. (800)222-LUNG. Pres. & CEO Lynn M. Taussig, MD; Bd. Chmn. Joseph Davis. Seeks to discover and disseminate knowledge that will prevent the occurrence of respiratory, allergic, and immunologic disorders and to develop improved clinical programs for those already afflicted. *New Direction (quarterly); Lung Line Letter (quarterly); Medical Scientific Update.*

NATIONAL JEWISH CHILDREN'S LEUKEMIA FOUNDATION (1990). 1310 48 St., Brooklyn, NY 11219. (718)853–0510. FAX: (718)435–0335. Pres./Founder Tzvi Shor; Dev. Allen Fuchs. Dedicated to saving the lives of children; educates the public on the importance of being a bone marrow donor and conducts bone marrow blood drives.

NORTH AMERICAN ASSOCIATION OF JEWISH HOMES AND HOUSING FOR THE AGING (1960). 10830 North Central Expressway, Suite 150, Dallas, TX 75231-1022. (214)696–9838. FAX: (214)360–0753. Pres. Sheldon Blumenthal; Pres.-Elect. Elliot Palevsky; Exec. V.-Pres. Dr. Herbert Shore. Represents a community of not-for-profit charitable homes and housing for the Jewish aging; promotes excellence in performance and quality of service through fostering communication and education and encouraging advocacy for the aging; conducts annual conferences and institutes. *Perspectives (newsletter); Directory; Membership Handbook; From the Home & Housing Front (house organ).*

UNITED ORDER TRUE SISTERS, INC. (UOTS) (1846). 212 Fifth Ave., NYC 10010. (212)679–6790. Pres. Lenore Bloch; Exec. Admin. Dorothy B. Giuriceo. Charitable, community service, especially home supplies etc., for indigent cancer victims; supports camps for children with cancer. *Echo.*

PROFESSIONAL ASSOCIATIONS*

AMERICAN ASSOCIATION OF RABBIS (Religious, Educational)

AMERICAN CONFERENCE OF CANTORS, UNION OF AMERICAN HEBREW CONGREGATIONS (Religious, Educational)

AMERICAN JEWISH CORRECTIONAL CHAPLAINS ASSOCIATION, INC. (Social Welfare)

AMERICAN JEWISH PRESS ASSOCIATION (Cultural)

AMERICAN JEWISH PUBLIC RELATIONS SOCIETY (1957). 234 Fifth Ave., NYC 10001. (212)697–5895. Pres. Henry R. Hecker; Treas. Hyman Brickman. Advances professional status of workers in the public-relations field in Jewish communal service; upholds a professional code of ethics and standards; serves as a clearinghouse for employment opportunities; exchanges professional information and ideas; presents awards for excellence in professional attainments, including the Maggid Award for outstanding achievement that enhances Jewish life. *AJPRS Newsletter; AJPRS Directory.*

ASSOCIATION OF HILLEL/JEWISH CAMPUS PROFESSIONALS (Religious, Educational)

ASSOCIATION OF JEWISH CENTER PROFESSIONALS (Social Welfare)

ASSOCIATION OF JEWISH COMMUNITY ORGANIZATION PERSONNEL (Social Welfare)

ASSOCIATION OF JEWISH COMMUNITY RELATIONS WORKERS (Community Relations)

CANTORS ASSEMBLY (Religious, Educational)

CENTRAL CONFERENCE OF AMERICAN RABBIS (Religious, Educational)

COUNCIL OF JEWISH ORGANIZATIONS IN CIVIL SERVICE (Community Relations)

INTERNATIONAL JEWISH MEDIA ASSOCIATION (Cultural)

JEWISH CHAPLAINS COUNCIL, JWB (Social Welfare)

JEWISH COMMUNAL SERVICE ASSOCIATION OF N. AMERICA (Social Welfare)

JEWISH EDUCATORS ASSEMBLY, UNITED SYNAGOGUE OF AMERICA (Religious, Educational)

JEWISH TEACHERS ASSOCIATION–MORIM (Religious, Educational)

NATIONAL ASSOCIATION OF HEBREW DAY SCHOOL ADMINISTRATORS, TORAH UMESORAH (Religious, Educational)

---

*For fuller listing see under categories in parentheses.

NATIONAL ASSOCIATION OF JEWISH CHAP-LAINS (Social Welfare)

NATIONAL ASSOCIATION OF TEMPLE AD-MINISTRATORS, UNION OF AMERICAN HEBREW CONGREGATIONS (Religious, Educational)

NATIONAL ASSOCIATION OF TEMPLE EDUCATORS, UNION OF AMERICAN HE-BREW CONGREGATIONS (Religious, Educational)

NATIONAL CONFERENCE OF YESHIVA PRIN-CIPALS, TORAH UMESORAH (Religious, Educational)

NORTH AMERICAN ASSOCIATION OF SYNA-GOGUE EXECUTIVES, UNITED SYNA-GOGUE OF CONSERVATIVE JUDAISM (Religious, Educational)

RABBINICAL ALLIANCE OF AMERICA (Religious, Educational)

RABBINICAL ASSEMBLY (Religious, Educational)

RABBINICAL COUNCIL OF AMERICA (Religious, Educational)

RECONSTRUCTIONIST RABBINICAL ASSOCI-ATION (Religious, Educational)

UNION OF ORTHODOX RABBIS OF THE U.S. AND CANADA (Religious, Educational)

WORLD CONFERENCE OF JEWISH COMMU-NAL SERVICE (Community Relations)

WOMEN'S ORGANIZATIONS*

AMIT WOMEN (Israel-Related)

B'NAI B'RITH WOMEN (Social Welfare)

BRANDEIS UNIVERSITY NATIONAL WOMEN'S COMMITTEE (1948). PO Box 9110, Waltham, MA 02254–9110. (617)-736–4160. FAX: (617)736–4183. Pres. Belle Jurkowitz. Provides financial support for the Brandeis Libraries and works to enhance the image of Brandeis, a Jewish-sponsored, nonsectarian university. Offers its members opportunity for intellectual pursuit, continuing education, community service, social interaction, personal enrich-ment, and leadership development. Open to all, regardless of race, religion, national-ity, or gender. *Imprint.*

EMUNAH WOMEN OF AMERICA (Israel-Related)

HADASSAH, THE WOMEN'S ZIONIST ORGA-NIZATION OF AMERICA (Israel-Related)

NA'AMAT USA, THE WOMEN'S LABOR ZIONIST ORGANIZATION OF AMERICA (Is-rael-Related)

NATIONAL COUNCIL OF JEWISH WOMEN (Social Welfare)

NATIONAL FEDERATION OF TEMPLE SIS-TERHOODS, UNION OF AMERICAN HE-BREW CONGREGATIONS (Religious, Edu-cational)

UOTS (Social Welfare)

WOMEN'S AMERICAN ORT, AMERICAN ORT FEDERATION (Overseas Aid)

WOMEN'S BRANCH OF THE UNION OF OR-THODOX JEWISH CONGREGATIONS OF AMERICA (Religious, Educational)

WOMEN'S DIVISION OF POALE AGUDATH ISRAEL OF AMERICA (Israel-Related)

WOMEN'S LEAGUE FOR CONSERVATIVE JU-DAISM (Religious, Educational)

WOMEN'S LEAGUE FOR ISRAEL, INC. (Israel-Related)

WOMEN'S ORGANIZATION, YESHIVA UNI-VERSITY (Religious, Educational)

YOUTH AND STUDENT ORGANIZATIONS*

AGUDATH ISRAEL OF AMERICA (Religious, Educational)

AMERICAN ZIONIST YOUTH FOUNDATION (Israel-Related)

B'NAI B'RITH HILLEL FOUNDATIONS (Reli-gious, Educational)

B'NAI B'RITH YOUTH ORGANIZATION (Reli-gious, Educational)

BNEI AKIVA OF NORTH AMERICA, RELI-GIOUS ZIONISTS OF AMERICA (Israel-Related)

HABONIM-DROR NORTH AMERICA (Israel-Related)

HASHOMER HATZAIR, SOCIALIST ZIONIST YOUTH MOVEMENT (Israel-Related)

KADIMA, UNITED SYNAGOGUE OF CON-SERVATIVE JUDAISM (Religious, Educa-tional)

---

*For fuller listing see under categories in parentheses.

NATIONAL CONFERENCE OF SYNAGOGUE YOUTH, UNION OF ORTHODOX JEWISH CONGREGATIONS OF AMERICA (Religious, Educational)

NATIONAL JEWISH COMMITTEE ON SCOUTING (Religious, Educational)

NATIONAL JEWISH GIRL SCOUT COMMITTEE (Religious, Educational)

NOAM-MIZRACHI NEW LEADERSHIP COUNCIL, RELIGIOUS ZIONISTS OF AMERICA (Israel-Related)

NORTH AMERICAN FEDERATION OF TEMPLE YOUTH, UNION OF AMERICAN HEBREW CONGREGATIONS (Religious, Educational)

NORTH AMERICAN JEWISH STUDENTS APPEAL (1971). 165 Pidgeon Hill Rd., Huntington Station, NY 11746–9998. (516)385–8771. FAX: (516)385–8772. Pres. Robin Fox; Chmn. Dr. S. Hal Horwitz; Exec. Dir. Brenda Gevertz. Serves as central fund-raising mechanism for six national, independent Jewish student organizations; ensures accountability of public Jewish communal funds used by these agencies; advises and assists Jewish organizations in determining student project feasibility and impact; fosters development of Jewish student leadership in the Jewish community. Beneficiaries include local and regional Jewish student projects; current constituents include Jewish Student Press Service, Student Struggle for Soviet Jewry, *Response Magazine,* Yugntruf Youth for Yiddish, Progressive Zionist Caucus, Project Orchim for outreach on campus, Lights in Action, and the Beneficiary Grants Program.

STUDENT STRUGGLE FOR SOVIET JEWRY— *see* CENTER FOR RUSSIAN JEWRY (Community Relations)

YOUNG JUDAEA/HASHACHAR, HADASSAH (Israel-Related)

YUGNTRUF–YOUTH FOR YIDDISH (Cultural)

CANADA

B'NAI BRITH CANADA (1875). 15 Hove St., Downsview, ONT M3H 4Y8. (416)633–6224. FAX: (416)630–2159. Pres. Brian Morris; Exec. V.-Pres. Frank Dimant. Canadian Jewry's senior organization; makes representations to all levels of government on matters of Jewish concern; promotes humanitarian causes and educational programs, community volunteer projects, adult Jewish education, and leadership development; dedicated to human rights. *Covenant Newspaper.*

———, INSTITUTE FOR INTERNATIONAL AFFAIRS (1987). 15 Hove St., Downsview, ONT M3H 4Y8. (416)633–6224. FAX: (416)630–2159. Pres. Brian Morris; Natl. Dir. Paul Marcus. Identifies and protests the abuse of human rights throughout the world. Monitors the condition of Jewish communities worldwide and advocates on their behalf when they experience serious violations of their human rights. *Institute Report.*

———, LEAGUE FOR HUMAN RIGHTS (1970). 15 Hove St., Downsview, ONT M3H 4Y8. (416)633–6227. FAX: (416)-630–2159. Natl. Chmn. Prof. Stephen Scheinberg; Natl. Dir. Dr. Karen Mock. A national volunteer association dedicated to combating racism and bigotry. Objectives include human rights for all Canadians, improved inter-community relations, and the elimination of racial discrimination and anti-Semitism. Conducts educational programs, engages in community action, and provides legal advice and action. Canadian distributor of ADL material. *Review of Anti-Semitism; Annual Audit of Anti-Semitic Incidents; Holocaust and Hope, Educators' Newsletter; Combatting Hate: Guidelines for Community Action.*

CANADIAN ASSOCIATION FOR LABOR ISRAEL (HISTADRUT) (1944). 7005 Kildare Rd., Suite 14, Cote St. Luc, PQ H4W 1C1. (514)484–9430. FAX: (514)487–6727. Pres. Harry J.F. Bloomfield. Conducts fund-raising and educational activities on behalf of Histadrut, Kupat Holim, and Amal schools in Israel.

CANADIAN FRIENDS OF THE ALLIANCE ISRAÉLITE UNIVERSELLE (1958). PO Box 578, Victoria Station, Montreal, PQ H3Z 2Y6. (514)481–3552. Pres. Joseph Nuss. Supports the educational work of the Alliance.

CANADIAN FRIENDS OF THE HEBREW UNIVERSITY (1944). 3080 Yonge St., Suite 5024, Toronto, ONT M4N 3P4. (416)485–8000. FAX: (416)485–8565. Pres. J. Stephen Lipper; Exec. Dir. Yoel Nesson. Represents the Hebrew University of Jerusalem in Canada; serves as fund-raising arm for the university in Canada; accepts Canadians for study at the university;

sponsors educational programs. *Dateline Jerusalem.*

CANADIAN JEWISH CONGRESS (1919; reorg. 1934). 1590 Dr. Penfield Ave., Montreal, PQ H3G 1C5. (514)931–7531. FAX: (514)931–0548. Pres. Irving Abella; Exec. V.-Pres. Alan Rose. The official voice of Canadian Jewish communities at home and abroad; acts on all matters affecting the status, rights, concerns and welfare of Canadian Jewry; internationally active on behalf of Soviet Jewry, Jews in Arab lands, Holocaust remembrance and restitution; largest Jewish archives in Canada. *National Small Communities Newsletter; Intercom; National Archives Newsletter; regional newsletters.*

CANADIAN ORT ORGANIZATION (Organization of Rehabilitation Through Training) (1942). 5165 Sherbrooke St. W., Suite 208, Montreal, PQ H4A 1T6. (514)481–2787. Pres. Dr. Mel Schwartz; Exec. Dir. Mac Silver. Carries on fund-raising projects in support of the worldwide vocational-training-school network of ORT. *ORT Reporter.*

———, WOMEN'S CANADIAN ORT (1948). 3101 Bathurst St., Suite 604, Toronto, ONT M6A 2A6. (416)787–0339. Pres. Edie Glazer; Exec. Dir. Diane Uslaner. Chapters in 11 Canadian cities raise funds for ORT's nonprofit global network of schools, where Jewish students learn a wide range of marketable skills, including the most advanced high-tech professions. *Focus Magazine.*

CANADIAN YOUNG JUDAEA (1917). 788 Marlee Ave., Suite 205, Toronto, ONT M6B 3K1. (416)781–5156. FAX: (416)-787–3100. Eastern Region Shaliach Gadi Anavi; Natl. Exec. Dir. Risa Epstein-Gamliel; Natl. Shaliach Shmuel Levkowitz. Strives to attract Jewish youth to Zionism, with goal of *aliyah;* educates youth about Jewish history and Zionism; prepares them to provide leadership in Young Judaea camps in Canada and Israel and to be concerned Jews. *The Judaean.*

CANADIAN ZIONIST FEDERATION (1967). 5250 Decarie Blvd., Suite 550, Montreal, PQ H3X 2H9. (514)486–9526. FAX: (514)483–6392. Pres. Kurt Rothschild. Umbrella organization of distinct constituent member Zionist organizations in Canada; carries on major activities in all areas of Jewish life through its departments of education and culture, *aliyah,* youth and students, public affairs, and small Jewish communities, for the purpose of strengthening the State of Israel and the Canadian Jewish community. *Canadian Zionist.*

———, BUREAU OF EDUCATION AND CULTURE (1972). Pres. Kurt Rothschild. Provides counseling by pedagogic experts, inservice teacher-training courses and seminars in Canada and Israel; national pedagogic council and research center; distributes educational material and teaching aids; conducts annual Bible contest and Hebrew-language courses for adults; awards scholarships to Canadian high-school graduates studying for one year in Israel.

FRIENDS OF PIONEERING ISRAEL (1950s). 1111 Finch Ave. W., Suite 154, Downsview, ONT M3J 2E5. (416)736–1339. FAX: (416)736–1405. Pres. Joseph Podemsky. Acts as a voice of Socialist and Zionist points of view within the Jewish community and a focal point for progressive Zionist elements in Canada; Canadian representative of Mapam; affiliated with Hashomer-Hatzair and the Givat Haviva Education Foundation.

HADASSAH–WIZO ORGANIZATION OF CANADA (1917). 1310 Greene Ave., Suite 900, Montreal, PQ H3Z 2B8. (514)937–9431. FAX: (514)933–6483. Pres. Judy Mandleman; Exec. V.-Pres. Lily Frank. Largest women's volunteer Zionist organization in Canada; located in 43 Canadian cities; dedicated to advancing the quality of life of the women and children in Israel through financial assistance and support of its many projects, day-care centers, schools, institutions, and hospitals. In Canada, the organization promotes Canadian ideals of democracy and is a stalwart advocate of women's issues. *Orah Magazine.*

HASHOMER HATZAIR (1913). 1111 Finch Ave. W., #154, Downsview, Ontario M3J 2E5. (416)736–1339. FAX: (416)736–1405. Pres. Tuvia Liberman; Exec. Off. Mintzy Clement. Zionist youth movement associated with the Kibbutz Artzi Federation in Israel. Educational activities emphasize Jewish culture and identity as well as the kibbutz lifestyle and values; runs summer camps as well as programs in Israel. *Ken Kronicle.*

JEWISH IMMIGRANT AID SERVICES OF CANADA (JIAS) (1919). 5151 Cote Ste. Catherine Rd., Suite 220, Montreal, PQ H3W 1M6. (514)342-9351. FAX: (514)342-8452. Pres. Carolyn Steinman; Exec. Dir. Joel Moss. Serves as a national agency for immigration and immigrant welfare.

JEWISH NATIONAL FUND OF CANADA (KEREN KAYEMETH LE'ISRAEL, INC.) (1901). 1980 Sherbrooke St. W., Suite 500, Montreal, PQ H3H 1E8. (514)934-0313. FAX: (514)934-0382. Pres. Sidney Halpern; Exec. V.-Pres. Avner Regev. Fundraising organization affiliated with the World Zionist Organization; involved in afforestation, soil reclamation, and development of the land of Israel, including the construction of roads and preparation of sites for new settlements; provides educational materials and programs to Jewish schools across Canada.

LABOUR ZIONIST ALLIANCE OF CANADA (1909). 272 Codsell Ave., Downsview, Ont. M3H 3X2. (416)630-9444. FAX: (416)636-5248. Pres. Josef Krystal; City Committee Chmn.: Toronto-Julius Sokoloff, Montreal-Harry Froimovitch. Associated with the World Labor Zionist movement and allied with the Israel Labor party. Provides recreational and cultural programs, mutual aid, and fraternal care to enhance the social welfare of its membership; actively promotes Zionist education, cultural projects, and forums on aspects of Jewish and Canadian concern.

MIZRACHI ORGANIZATION OF CANADA (1941). 3101 Bathurst St., #503, Toronto, ONT M6A 2A6. (416)789-7576. FAX: (416)789-7733. Pres. Jack Kahn; Exec. V.-Pres. Rabbi Menachem Gopin. Promotes religious Zionism, aimed at making Israel a state based on Torah; maintains Bnei Akiva, a summer camp, adult educa-

tion program, and touring department; supports Mizrachi-Hapoel Hamizrachi and other religious Zionist institutions in Israel which strengthen traditional Judaism. *Mizrachi Newsletter; Or Hamizrach Torah Quarterly.*

NATIONAL COUNCIL OF JEWISH WOMEN OF CANADA (1897). 1588 Main St., Winnipeg, MAN R2V 1Y3. (204)339-9700. Pres. Sharon Wolchock. Dedicated to furthering human welfare in Jewish and non-Jewish communities, locally, nationally, and internationally; provides essential services and stimulates and educates the individual and the community through an integrated program of education, service, and social action.

NATIONAL JOINT COMMUNITY RELATIONS COMMITTEE OF CANADIAN JEWISH CONGRESS (1936). 4600 Bathurst St., Willowdale, ONT M2R 3V2. (416)635-2883. FAX: (416)635-1408. Natl. Dir. Bernie M. Farber (ext. 186); Assoc. Dir. Steven H. Shulman (ext. 175); Chmn. Hal Joffe. Seeks to safeguard the status, rights, and welfare of Jews in Canada; to combat anti-Semitism, and promote understanding and goodwill among all ethnic and religious groups.

STATE OF ISRAEL BONDS (CANADA-ISRAEL SECURITIES, LTD.) (1953). 3101 Bathurst St., Suite 400, Toronto, ONT M6A 2A6. (416)789-3351. FAX: (416)789-9436. Pres. Myer Samuels; Bd. Chmn. Alex E. Grossman. An international securities organization offering interest-bearing instruments issued by the government of Israel. Invests in every aspect of Israel's economy, including agriculture, commerce and industry. Israel Bonds are RRSP approved.

Jewish Federations, Welfare Funds, Community Councils

UNITED STATES

ALABAMA

BIRMINGHAM

BIRMINGHAM JEWISH FEDERATION (1936; reorg. 1971); PO Box 130219 (35213); (205)-879–0416. FAX: (205)879–0466. Pres. Judy Abrams; Exec. Dir. Richard Friedman.

MOBILE

MOBILE JEWISH WELFARE FUND, INC. (inc. 1966); One Office Park, Suite 219 (36609); (205)343–7197. Pres. Elliot Maisel.

MONTGOMERY

JEWISH FEDERATION OF MONTGOMERY, INC. (1930); PO Box 20058 (36120); (205)-277–5820. Pres. Dr. David Franco; Exec. Dir. Beverly Lipton.

ARIZONA

PHOENIX

JEWISH FEDERATION OF GREATER PHOE-NIX (1940); 32 W. Coolidge, Suite 200 (85013); (602)274–1800. FAX: (602)266–7875. Pres. Leonard Miller; Exec. Dir. Har-old Morgan.

TUCSON

JEWISH FEDERATION OF SOUTHERN ARI-ZONA (1946); 3822 East River Rd. (85718); (602)577–9393. FAX: (602)577–0734. Pres. Richard Fink; Exec. V.-Pres. Richard Fruchter.

ARKANSAS

LITTLE ROCK

JEWISH FEDERATION OF ARKANSAS (1911); 2821 Kavanaugh Blvd., Garden Level (72205); (501)663–3571. FAX: (501)663–7286. Pres. Elaine Weiss; Exec. Dir. Harvey David Luber.

CALIFORNIA

EAST BAY

JEWISH FEDERATION OF THE GREATER EAST BAY (1917); 401 Grand Ave., Oakland (94610); (510)839–2900. Pres. Mort Fried-kin; Exec. V.-Pres. Ami Nahshon.

LONG BEACH

JEWISH FEDERATION OF GREATER LONG BEACH AND W. ORANGE COUNTY (1937; inc. 1946); 3801 E. Willow St. (90815); (213)-426–7601. FAX: (213)424–3915. Pres. Ar-thur Miller; Exec. Dir. Sandi Goldstein.

LOS ANGELES

JEWISH FEDERATION COUNCIL OF GREATER LOS ANGELES (1912; reorg. 1959); 6505 Wilshire Blvd. (90048); (213)852–1234. FAX: (213)655–4458. Pres. Irwin Field; Exec. V.-Pres. John Fishel.

ORANGE COUNTY

JEWISH FEDERATION OF ORANGE COUNTY (1964; inc. 1965); 1385 Warner Ave., Suite A,

---

This directory is based on information supplied by the Council of Jewish Federations.

Tustin (92680–6442); (714)259–0655. FAX: (714)259–1635. Pres. Blossom Siegel; Exec. Dir. Edward Cushman.

PALM SPRINGS

JEWISH FEDERATION OF PALM SPRINGS (1971); 255 El Cielo N., Suite 430 (92262); (619)325–7281. Pres. Henry Frank; Exec. Dir. Irving Ginsberg.

SACRAMENTO

JEWISH FEDERATION OF SACRAMENTO (1948); PO Box 254589 (95865); (916)486–0906. FAX: (916)486–0816. Pres. Lynn Dean; Exec. Dir. Ted Feldman.

SAN DIEGO

UNITED JEWISH FEDERATION OF SAN DIEGO COUNTY (1936); 4797 Mercury St. (92111–2102); (619)571–3444. FAX: (619)-571–0701. Pres. Rebecca Newman; Exec. V.-Pres. Stephen M. Abramson.

SAN FRANCISCO

JEWISH COMMUNITY FEDERATION OF SAN FRANCISCO, THE PENINSULA, MARIN, AND SONOMA COUNTIES (1910; reorg. 1955); 121 Steuart St. (94105); (415)777–0411. FAX: (415)495–6635. Pres. Douglas Heller; Exec. Dir. Wayne Feinstein.

SAN JOSE

JEWISH FEDERATION OF GREATER SAN JOSE (incl. Santa Clara County except Palo Alto and Los Altos) (1930; reorg. 1950); 14855 Oka Rd., Los Gatos (95030); (408)-358–3033. FAX: (408)356–0733. Pres. Robert Krandel; Exec. Dir. Paul Ellenbogen.

SANTA BARBARA

SANTA BARBARA JEWISH FEDERATION (1974); 104 W. Anapamu, Suite A. Mailing Address: PO Box 90110, Santa Barbara (93190); (805)963–0244. FAX: (805)569–5052. Pres. Cynthia Luria; Exec. Dir. Barbara Zonen.

COLORADO

DENVER

ALLIED JEWISH FEDERATION OF COLORADO (1936); 300 S. Dahlia St. (80222); (303)321–3399. FAX: (303)322–8328. Pres. Robyn Loup; Exec. V.-Pres. Steve Gelfand.

CONNECTICUT

BRIDGEPORT

JEWISH FEDERATION OF GREATER BRIDGEPORT, INC. (1936; reorg. 1981); 4200 Park Ave. (06604); (203)372–6504. FAX: (203)-374–0770. Pres. Kurt Hersher; Interim Exec. Dir. Susan Bauchner.

DANBURY

JEWISH FEDERATION OF GREATER DANBURY (1945); 105 Newtown Rd. (06810); (203)792–6353. Pres. Dr. Martin Vigdor; Exec. Dir. Lauren Bernard.

EASTERN CONNECTICUT

JEWISH FEDERATION OF EASTERN CONNECTICUT, INC. (1950; inc. 1970); 28 Channing St., PO Box 1468, New London (06320); (203)442–8062. FAX: (203)443–4175. Pres. Helen Glick; Exec. Dir. Jerome E. Fischer.

GREENWICH

GREENWICH JEWISH FEDERATION (1956); 600 W. Putnam Ave. (06830); (203)622–1434. FAX: (203)622–1237. Pres. Steven Levy; Exec. Dir. Michael Marcus.

HARTFORD

JEWISH FEDERATION OF GREATER HARTFORD (1945); 333 Bloomfield Ave., W. Hartford (06117); (203)232–4483. FAX: (203)-232–5221. Pres. Marvin Catler; Exec. Dir. Cindy Chazan.

NEW HAVEN

JEWISH FEDERATION OF GREATER NEW HAVEN (1928); 360 Amity Rd., Woodbridge (06525); (203)387–2424. FAX: (203)387–1818. Pres. Dr. Alvin Greenberg; Exec. Dir. Jay Rubin.

NORWALK

(See Westport)

STAMFORD

UNITED JEWISH FEDERATION (inc. 1973); 1035 Newfield Ave., PO Box 3038 (06905); (203)321–1373. FAX: (203)322–3277. Pres. Candace Caplin; Exec. Dir. Sheila L. Romanowitz.

WATERBURY

JEWISH FEDERATION OF GREATER WATERBURY, INC. (1938); 73 Main St. South, Box F (06798); (203)263–5121. FAX: (203)263–5143. Pres. Dr. Michael Blumenthal; Exec. Dir. Robert Zwang.

WESTPORT–WESTON–WILTON–NORWALK

UNITED JEWISH APPEAL/FEDERATION OF WESTPORT-WESTON-WILTON-NORWALK (inc. 1980); 431 Post Road East, Suite 22, Westport (06880); (203)266–8197. FAX:

(203)226–5051. Pres. Lois Block; Exec. Dir. Robert Kessler.

DELAWARE

WILMINGTON

JEWISH FEDERATION OF DELAWARE, INC. (1934); 101 Garden of Eden Rd. (19803); (302)478–6200. FAX: (302)478–5374. Pres. Toni Young; Exec. Dir. Judy Wortman.

DISTRICT OF COLUMBIA

WASHINGTON

UNITED JEWISH APPEAL–FEDERATION OF GREATER WASHINGTON, INC. (1935); 6101 Montrose Rd., Rockville, MD 20852; (301)-230–7200. FAX: (301)230–7272. Pres. Phyllis Margolius; Exec. V.-Pres. Ted B. Farber.

FLORIDA

BREVARD COUNTY

JEWISH FEDERATION OF BREVARD; 108-A Barton Ave., Rockledge (32955); (407)636–1824. FAX: (407)636–0614. Pres. Dr. Steven Podnos; Exec. Dir. Robert E. Swire.

COLLIER COUNTY

JEWISH FEDERATION OF COLLIER COUNTY (1974); 1250 Tamiami Trail North, Suite 304C, Naples (33940); (813) 263–4205. Pres. Jerry Flagel; Exec. Dir. Craig Frankel.

DAYTONA BEACH

(See Volusia & Flagler Counties)

FT. LAUDERDALE

JEWISH FEDERATION OF GREATER FT. LAUDERDALE (1968); 8358 W. Oakland Park Blvd. (33351); (305)748–8400. FAX: (305)748–6332. Pres. Paul R. Lehrer; Exec. Dir. Kenneth B. Bierman.

JACKSONVILLE

JACKSONVILLE JEWISH FEDERATION (1935); 8505 San Jose Blvd. (32217); (904)-448–5000. FAX: (904)448–5715. Pres. Richard L. Sisisky; Exec. V.-Pres. Alan Margolies.

LEE COUNTY

JEWISH FEDERATION OF LEE COUNTY (1974); 6315 Presidential Court, Suite A, Ft. Myers (33919–3568); (813)481–4449. FAX: (813)275–9114. Pres. Jonathan Frantz; Exec. Dir. Helene Kramer.

MIAMI

GREATER MIAMI JEWISH FEDERATION, INC. (1938); 4200 Biscayne Blvd. (33137); (305)576–4000. FAX: (305)573–2176. Pres. Nedra Oren; Exec. V.-Pres. Jacob Solomon.

ORLANDO

JEWISH FEDERATION OF GREATER ORLANDO (1949); 851 N. Maitland Ave., PO Box 941508, Maitland (32794–1508); (407)-645–5933. FAX: (407)645–1172. Pres. Robert Yarmuth; Exec. Dir. Howard Stone.

PALM BEACH COUNTY

JEWISH FEDERATION OF PALM BEACH COUNTY, INC. (1962); 4601 Community Dr., W. Palm Beach (33417–2760); (407)478–0700. FAX: (407)478–9696. Pres. Alan H. Miller. Exec. Dir. Jeffrey L. Klein.

PINELLAS COUNTY

JEWISH FEDERATION OF PINELLAS COUNTY, INC. (incl. Clearwater and St. Petersburg) (1950; reincorp. 1974); 301 S. Jupiter Ave., Clearwater (34615); (813) 446–1033. FAX: (813)461–0700. Pres. Jim Soble; Exec. Dir. Robert F. Tropp.

SARASOTA

SARASOTA-MANATEE JEWISH FEDERATION (1959); 580 S. McIntosh Rd. (34232); (813)-371–4546. FAX: (813)378–2947. Pres. Ian Black; Exec. Dir. Norman Olshansky.

SOUTH BROWARD

JEWISH FEDERATION OF SOUTH BROWARD, INC. (1943); 2719 Hollywood Blvd., Hollywood (33020); (305)921–8810. FAX: (305)-921–6491. Pres. Dr. Peter Livingston; Exec. Dir. Gary N. Rubin.

SOUTH PALM BEACH COUNTY

SOUTH PALM BEACH COUNTY JEWISH FEDERATION (inc. 1979); 9901 Donna Klein Blvd., Boca Raton (33428–1788); (407) 852–3100. FAX: (407)852–3150. Pres. Richard L. Okonow; Exec. Dir. Michael Ostroff; Interim Exec. V.-Pres. Spencer H. Gellert.

TAMPA

TAMPA JEWISH FEDERATION (1941); 6617 Gunn Highway, Suite 118 (33625); (813)960–1840. FAX: (813)265–8450. Pres. Jack Roth; Interim Exec. V.-Pres. Merv Lemerman.

VOLUSIA & FLAGLER COUNTIES

JEWISH FEDERATION OF VOLUSIA & FLAGLER COUNTIES, INC.; 733 South Nova Rd., Ormond Beach (32174); (904)672–0294. FAX: (904)673–1316. Pres. Ron Sherman; Exec. Dir. Maxine Kronick.

GEORGIA

ATLANTA

ATLANTA JEWISH FEDERATION, INC. (1905; reorg. 1967); 1753 Peachtree Rd. NE

(30309); (404)873–1661. FAX: (404)874–7043. Pres. David N. Minkin; Exec. Dir. David I. Sarnat.

AUGUSTA

AUGUSTA JEWISH FEDERATION (1937); PO Box 15443 (30909); (706)736–1818. FAX: (706)667–8081. Pres. Sam Budenstein; Exec. Dir. Michael Pousman.

COLUMBUS

JEWISH WELFARE FEDERATION OF COLUMBUS, INC. (1941); PO Box 6313 (31907); (404)568–6668. Pres. Murray Solomon; Sec. Irene Rainbow.

SAVANNAH

SAVANNAH JEWISH FEDERATION (1943); PO Box 23527 (31403); (912)355–8111. FAX: (912)355–8116. Pres. Dr. Michael Zoller; Exec. Dir. Jeff Feld.

HAWAII

HONOLULU

JEWISH FEDERATION OF HAWAII (1956); 444 Hobron Lane, PH 4A (96815); (808)941–2424. FAX: (808)941–5372. Pres. Dr. George Plechety; Exec. Dir. Rabbi Melvin Libman.

ILLINOIS

CHAMPAIGN-URBANA

CHAMPAIGN-URBANA JEWISH FEDERATION (1929); 503 E. John St., Champaign (61820); (217)367–9872. Pres. Lynn Wachtel; Exec. Dir. Janie Yairi.

CHICAGO

JEWISH FEDERATION OF METROPOLITAN CHICAGO (1900); 1 S. Franklin St. (60606–4694); (312)346–6700. FAX: (312)855–2474. Pres. Edward A. Fox; Exec. V.-Pres. Steven B. Nasatir.

ELGIN

ELGIN AREA JEWISH WELFARE CHEST (1938); 330 Division St. (60120); (312)741–5656. Pres. Dr. Albert Simon; Treas. Robert C. Levine.

PEORIA

JEWISH FEDERATION OF PEORIA (1933; inc. 1947); 5901 N. Prospect Rd., Suite 203, Town Hall Bldg., Junction City (61614); (309)689–0063. Pres. Raymond Huff; Exec. Dir. Eunice Galsky.

QUAD CITIES

JEWISH FEDERATION OF QUAD CITIES (incl. Rock Island, Moline, Davenport, Bettendorf) (1938; comb. 1973); 209 18 St., Rock Island (61201); (309)793–1300. Pres. David Andich; Exec. Dir. Ida Kramer.

ROCKFORD

JEWISH FEDERATION OF GREATER ROCKFORD (1937); 1500 Parkview Ave. (61107); (815)399–5497. Pres. Goldie Pekarsky; Exec. Dir. Tony Toback.

SOUTHERN ILLINOIS

JEWISH FEDERATION OF SOUTHERN ILLINOIS, SOUTHEASTERN MISSOURI AND WESTERN KENTUCKY (1941); 6464 W. Main, Suite 7A, Belleville (62223); (618)398–6100. FAX: (618)398–0539. Pres. Elizabeth Linkon; Exec. Dir. Steve Low.

SPRINGFIELD

SPRINGFIELD JEWISH FEDERATION (1941); 730 E. Vine St. (62703); (217)528–3446. Pres. Luda Smikun; Exec. Dir. Gloria Schwartz.

INDIANA

EVANSVILLE

EVANSVILLE JEWISH COMMUNITY COUNCIL, INC. (1936; inc. 1964); PO Box 5026 (47716); (812)477–7050. Pres. Gary M. Smith; Exec. Sec. Ernest W. Adler.

FORT WAYNE

FORT WAYNE JEWISH FEDERATION (1921); 227 E. Washington Blvd. (46802–3121); (219)422–8566. FAX: (219)422–8567. Pres. Frances Stein; Exec. Dir. Vivian Lansky.

INDIANAPOLIS

JEWISH FEDERATION OF GREATER INDIANAPOLIS, INC. (1905); 615 N. Alabama St., Suite 412 (46204–1430); (317)637–2473. FAX: (317)637–2477. Pres. Estelle Nelson; Exec. V.-Pres. Harry Nadler.

LAFAYETTE

FEDERATED JEWISH CHARITIES (1924); PO Box 708 (47902); (317)742–9081. FAX: (317)742–4379. Pres. Arnold Cohen; Finan. Sec. Louis Pearlman, Jr.

MICHIGAN CITY

MICHIGAN CITY UNITED JEWISH WELFARE FUND; 2800 S. Franklin St. (46360); (219)-874–4477. Chrmn. Iris Ourach.

NORTHWEST INDIANA

THE JEWISH FEDERATION, INC. (1941; reorg. 1959); 2939 Jewett St., Highland (46322); (219)972–2250. FAX: (219)972–4779. Pres. Dr. Jay Karol; Exec. Dir. Marty Erann.

ST. JOSEPH VALLEY

JEWISH FEDERATION OF ST. JOSEPH VALLEY (1946); 105 Jefferson Centre, Suite 804, South Bend (46601); (219)233–1164. FAX: (219)288–4103. Pres. Dr. Harvey Weingarten; Interim Exec. V.-Pres. Marilyn Gardner.

IOWA

DES MOINES

JEWISH FEDERATION OF GREATER DES MOINES (1914); 910 Polk Blvd. (50312); (515)277–6321. FAX: (515)277–4069. Pres. Larry Engman; Exec. Dir. Elaine Steinger.

SIOUX CITY

JEWISH FEDERATION (1921); 525 14th St. (51105); (712)258–0618. Pres. Paul Kaiman; Exec. Dir. Doris Rosenthal.

KANSAS

WICHITA

MID-KANSAS JEWISH FEDERATION, INC. (1935); 400 N. Woodlawn, Suite 8 (67208); (316)686–4741. Pres. Nancy Zamow; Exec. Dir. Beverly Jacobson.

KENTUCKY

LEXINGTON

CENTRAL KENTUCKY JEWISH FEDERATION (1976); 340 Romany Rd. (40502); (606)268–0672. Pres. Elizabeth Goldman; Exec. Dir. Howard Ross.

LOUISVILLE

JEWISH COMMUNITY FEDERATION OF LOUISVILLE, INC. (1934); 3630 Dutchman's Lane (40205); (502)451–8840. FAX: (502)-458–0702. Pres. Edward B. Weinberg; Exec. Dir. Dr. Alan S. Engel.

LOUISIANA

ALEXANDRIA

THE JEWISH WELFARE FEDERATION AND COMMUNITY COUNCIL OF CENTRAL LOUISIANA (1938); 1227 Southhampton (71303); (318)445–4785. Pres. Alvin Mykoff; Sec.-Treas. Judy Task.

BATON ROUGE

JEWISH FEDERATION OF GREATER BATON ROUGE (1971); 5647 Galeria, Suite D (70816); PO Box 80827 (70898); (504) 291–5895. FAX: (504)291–2138. Pres. Dale Maas; Exec. Dir. Louis Goldman.

NEW ORLEANS

JEWISH FEDERATION OF GREATER NEW ORLEANS (1913; reorg. 1977); 1539 Jackson Ave. (70130); (504)525–0673. FAX: (504)-568–9290. Pres. Jerome Hanaw; Exec. Dir. Eli Sikora.

SHREVEPORT

SHREVEPORT JEWISH FEDERATION (1941; inc. 1967); 2032 Line Ave. (71104); (318)-221–4129. Pres. Henry Brenner; Exec. Dir. Monty Pomm.

MAINE

LEWISTON-AUBURN

LEWISTON-AUBURN JEWISH FEDERATION (1947); 74 Bradman St., Auburn (04210); (207)786–4201. Pres. Scott Nussinow.

PORTLAND

JEWISH FEDERATION COMMUNITY COUNCIL OF SOUTHERN MAINE (1942); 57 Ashmont St. (04103); (207)773–7254. FAX: (207)772–2234. Pres. Stephen Schwartz; Exec. Dir. Meyer Bodoff.

MARYLAND

BALTIMORE

THE ASSOCIATED: JEWISH COMMUNITY FEDERATION OF BALTIMORE (1920; reorg. 1969); 101 W. Mt. Royal Ave. (21201); (301) 727–4828. FAX: (301)783–8991. Chmn. Richard M. Lansburgh; Pres. Darrell D. Friedman.

MASSACHUSETTS

BERKSHIRE COUNTY

JEWISH FEDERATION OF THE BERKSHIRES (1940); 235 East St., Pittsfield (01201); (413)-442–4360. FAX: (413)443–6070. Pres. C. Jeffrey Cook; Exec. Dir. Robert N. Kerbel.

BOSTON

COMBINED JEWISH PHILANTHROPIES OF GREATER BOSTON, INC. (1895; inc. 1961); One Lincoln Plaza (02111); (617)330–9500. FAX: (617)330–5197. Chmn. Michael J. Bohnen; Exec. V.-Pres. Barry Shrage.

CAPE COD

JEWISH FEDERATION OF CAPE COD; 396 Main St., PO Box 2568, Hyannis (02601); (508)778–5588. Pres. Linda G. Kipnes.

FRAMINGHAM (Merged with Boston)

LEOMINSTER

LEOMINSTER JEWISH COMMUNITY COUNCIL, INC. (1939); 268 Washington St. (01453); (617)534–6121. Pres. Dr. Milton Kline; Sec.-Treas. Howard J. Rome.

MERRIMACK VALLEY

MERRIMACK VALLEY JEWISH FEDERATION (Serves Lowell, Lawrence, Andover, Haverhill, Newburyport, and 22 surrounding communities) (1988); 805 Turnpike St., N. Andover (01845); (508)688–0466. FAX: (508)688–1097. Chmn. Jeffrey D. Queen; Interim Exec. Dir. Edward Finkel.

NEW BEDFORD

JEWISH FEDERATION OF GREATER NEW BEDFORD, INC. (1938; inc. 1954); 467 Hawthorn St., N. Dartmouth (02747); (508)997–7471. FAX: (508)997–7730. Pres. Kenneth Lipman; Exec. Dir. Wil Herrup.

NORTH SHORE

JEWISH FEDERATION OF THE NORTH SHORE, INC. (1938); 4 Community Rd., Marblehead (01945); (617)598–1810. FAX: (617)639–1284. Pres. Edward Braun; Exec. Dir. Neil A. Cooper.

SPRINGFIELD

JEWISH FEDERATION OF GREATER SPRINGFIELD, INC. (1925); 1160 Dickinson St. (01108); (413)737–4313. FAX: (413)737–4348. Pres. Kenneth Abrahams; Exec. Dir. Joel Weiss.

WORCESTER

WORCESTER JEWISH FEDERATION, INC. (1947; inc. 1957); 633 Salisbury St. (01609); (508)756–1543. FAX: (508)798–0962. Pres. Dr. Mark O. Cutler; Exec. Dir. Michael L. Minkin.

MICHIGAN

ANN ARBOR

JEWISH FEDERATION OF WASHTENAW COUNTY/UNITED JEWISH APPEAL (1986); 2939 Birch Hollow Dr. (48108); (313)677–0100. Pres. Carol S. Smokler; Exec. Dir. Nancy N. Margolis.

DETROIT

JEWISH FEDERATION OF METROPOLITAN DETROIT (1899); 6735 Telegraph Rd., Suite 30, PO Box 2030, Bloomfield Hills (48303–2030); (810)642–4260. FAX: (810)642–4985 (executive offices); (810)642–4941 (all other departments). Pres. David K. Page; Exec. V.-Pres. Robert P. Aronson.

FLINT

FLINT JEWISH FEDERATION (1936); 619 Wallenberg St. (48502); (810)767–5922. FAX: (810)767–9024. Pres. Diane Lindholm; Exec. Dir. David Nussbaum.

GRAND RAPIDS

JEWISH COMMUNITY FUND OF GRAND RAPIDS (1930); 2609 Berwyck SE (49506); (616)956–9365. FAX: (616)956–9365#1. Pres. Morton M. Finkelstein; Admin. Dir. Judy Joseph.

MINNESOTA

DULUTH–SUPERIOR

TWIN PORTS JEWISH FEDERATION & COMMUNITY COUNCIL (1937); 1602 E. Second St. (55812); (218)724–8857. Pres. Jack Seiler; Sec. Admin. Gloria Vitullo.

MINNEAPOLIS

MINNEAPOLIS FEDERATION FOR JEWISH SERVICE (1929; inc. 1930); 5901 S. Cedar Lake Rd., P.O. Box 16437 (55416); (612)-593–2600. FAX: (612)593–2544. Pres. Robert Barrows; Exec. Dir. Max L. Kleinman.

ST. PAUL

UNITED JEWISH FUND AND COUNCIL (1935); 790 S. Cleveland, Suite 201 (55116); (612)690–1707. FAX: (612)690–0228. Pres. Barry Glaser; Exec. Dir. Samuel Asher.

MISSISSIPPI

JACKSON

JACKSON JEWISH WELFARE FUND, INC. (1945); 5315 Old Canton Rd. (39211–4625); (601)956–6215. Pres. Erik Hearon; V.-Pres. Marcy Cohen.

MISSOURI

KANSAS CITY

JEWISH FEDERATION OF GREATER KANSAS CITY (1933); 5801 W. 115th St., Overland Park, KS 66211–1824; (913)469–1340. FAX: (913)451–9358. Pres. Robert C. Levy; Exec. Dir. A. Robert Gast.

ST. JOSEPH

UNITED JEWISH FUND OF ST. JOSEPH (1915); c/o Mrs. Chapnick, 2710 N. 39 Terr. (64506); (816)232–7043. Pres. Mrs. Judy Chapnick; Exec. Sec. Mrs. Beryl Shapiro.

ST. LOUIS

JEWISH FEDERATION OF ST. LOUIS (incl. St. Louis County) (1901); 12 Millstone Campus Dr. (63146); (314)432–0020. FAX: (314)-432–1277. Pres. Michael N. Newmark; Exec. Dir. Barry Rosenberg.

NEBRASKA

LINCOLN

LINCOLN JEWISH WELFARE FEDERATION, INC. (1931; inc. 1961); PO Box 67218

(68506); (402)488–9562. Pres. Steven Seglin; Exec. Dir. Karen Sommer.

OMAHA

JEWISH FEDERATION OF OMAHA (1903); 333 S. 132nd St. (68154–2198); (402)334–8200. FAX: (402)334–1330. Pres. Jerry Slusky; Exec. Dir. Howard Bloom.

NEVADA

LAS VEGAS

JEWISH FEDERATION OF LAS VEGAS (1973); 3909 S. Maryland Parkway, Suite 400 (89119); (702)732–0556. FAX: (702)732–3228. Pres. Allan Boruszak, M.D.; Exec. Dir. Ronni Epstein.

NEW HAMPSHIRE

MANCHESTER

JEWISH FEDERATION OF GREATER MANCHESTER (1974); 698 Beech St. (03104); (603)627–7679. FAX: (603) 627–7963. Pres. Beth Ann Salzman; Exec. Dir. Mark Silverberg.

NEW JERSEY

ATLANTIC AND CAPE MAY COUNTIES

JEWISH FEDERATION OF ATLANTIC AND CAPE MAY COUNTIES (1924); 505–507 Tilton Rd., Northfield (08225); (609)646–7077. FAX: (609)646–8053. Pres. David Schultz; Exec. Dir. Bernard Cohen.

BERGEN COUNTY

UNITED JEWISH COMMUNITY OF BERGEN COUNTY (inc. 1978); 111 Kinderkamack Rd., PO Box 4176, N. Hackensack Station, River Edge (07661); (201)488–6800. FAX: (201)-488–1507. Pres. Charles J. Rothschild, Jr.; Exec. V.-Pres. James Young.

CENTRAL NEW JERSEY

JEWISH FEDERATION OF CENTRAL NEW JERSEY (1940; merged 1973); 843 St. Georges Ave., Roselle (07203); (908)298–8200. FAX: (980)298–8220. Pres. Gerald Cantor; Exec. V.-Pres. Stanley Stone.

CLIFTON–PASSAIC

JEWISH FEDERATION OF GREATER CLIFTON-PASSAIC (1933); 199 Scoles Ave., Clifton (07012). (201)777–7031. FAX: (201)777–6701. Pres. Joseph Bukiet; Exec. Dir. Yosef Y. Muskin.

CUMBERLAND COUNTY

JEWISH FEDERATION OF CUMBERLAND COUNTY (inc. 1971); 629 Wood St., Suite 204, Vineland (08360); (609)696–4445. Pres. Leonard Wasserman; Exec. Dir. Leon Silver.

ENGLEWOOD

(Merged with Bergen County)

MERCER COUNTY

JEWISH FEDERATION OF MERCER COUNTY (1929; reorg. 1982); 999 Lower Ferry Rd., Trenton (08628); (609)883–5000. FAX: (609)883–2563. Pres. Arthur M. Edelman; Exec. Dir. Danny Goldberg.

METROWEST NEW JERSEY

UNITED JEWISH FEDERATION OF METROWEST (1923); 901 Route 10, Whippany (07981–1156); (201)884–4800. FAX: (201)-884–7361. Pres. Stanly Strauss; Exec. V.-Pres. Howard E. Charish.

MIDDLESEX COUNTY

JEWISH FEDERATION OF GREATER MIDDLESEX COUNTY (org. 1948; reorg. 1985); 100 Metroplex Dr., Suite 101, Edison (08817); (201)985–1234. FAX: (201)985–3295. Pres. Ron Grayzel; Exec. V.-Pres. Michael Shapiro.

MONMOUTH COUNTY

JEWISH FEDERATION OF GREATER MONMOUTH COUNTY (1971); 100 Grant Ave., PO Box 210, Deal (07723–0210); (908)531–6200–1. FAX: (908)531–9518. Pres. William A. Schwartz; Exec. Dir. Bonnie Komito.

MORRIS–SUSSEX COUNTY

(Merged with MetroWest New Jersey)

NORTH JERSEY

JEWISH FEDERATION OF NORTH JERSEY (1933); One Pike Dr., Wayne (07470–2498); (201)595–0555. FAX: (201)595–1532. Pres. Peter M. Kolben; Exec. Dir. Barry Rosenberg.

NORTHERN MIDDLESEX COUNTY

(See Middlesex County)

OCEAN COUNTY

OCEAN COUNTY JEWISH FEDERATION (1977); 301 Madison Ave., Lakewood (08701); (908)363–0530. FAX: (908)363–2097. Pres. Richard Gaines; Exec. Dir. Stephanie Ackerman.

PRINCETON

PRINCETON AREA UJA–FEDERATION; 15 Roszel Rd., Princeton (08540); (609)243–9440. Pres. Iris G. Brener; Exec. Dir. Jerilyn Zimmerman.

RARITAN VALLEY

(See Middlesex County)

SOMERSET COUNTY

JEWISH FEDERATION OF SOMERSET, HUNTERDON & WARREN COUNTIES (1960); 1011 Rt. 22 West, PO Box 6455, Bridgewater (08807); (908)725–6994. FAX: (908)725–9753. Pres. Len Knauer; Exec. Dir. Alan J. Nydick.

SOUTHERN NEW JERSEY

JEWISH FEDERATION OF SOUTHERN NEW JERSEY (incl. Camden, Burlington, and Gloucester counties) (1922); 2393 W. Marlton Pike, Cherry Hill (08002); (609)665–6100. FAX: (609)665–0074. Pres. Harvey N. Shapiro, Esq.; Exec. V.-Pres. Stuart Alperin.

NEW MEXICO

ALBUQUERQUE

JEWISH FEDERATION OF GREATER ALBUQUERQUE, INC. (1938); 8205 Spain, NE (97109); (505)821–3214. FAX: (505)821–3355. Pres. Miriam Efroymson; Exec. Dir. Andrew Lipman.

NEW YORK

ALBANY

(Merged with Schenectady; see Northeastern New York)

BROOME COUNTY

JEWISH FEDERATION OF BROOME COUNTY (1937; inc. 1958); 500 Clubhouse Rd., Vestal (13850); (607)724–2332. FAX: (607)724–2311. Pres. Michael Wright; Exec. Dir. Victoria Rouff.

BUFFALO

JEWISH FEDERATION OF GREATER BUFFALO, INC. (1903); 787 Delaware Ave. (14209); (716)886–7750. FAX: (716)886–1367. Pres. Nathan Benderson; Exec. Dir. Harry Kosansky.

DUTCHESS COUNTY

JEWISH FEDERATION OF DUTCHESS COUNTY; 110 S. Grand Ave., Poughkeepsie (12603); (914)471–9811. Pres. Martin Charwat; Exec. Dir. Endre Sarkany.

ELMIRA

ELMIRA-CORNING JEWISH FEDERATION (1942); Grandview Ave. Ext., PO Box 3087 (14905); (607)734–8122. FAX: (607)734–8123. Pres. Andrew Rothstein; Exec. Dir. Frank Kramerman.

NEW YORK

UJA–FEDERATION OF JEWISH PHILANTHROPIES OF NEW YORK, INC. (incl. Greater NY; Westchester, Nassau, and Suffolk counties) (Fed. org. 1917; UJA 1939; merged 1986); 130 E. 59th St. (10022); (212)980–1000. FAX: (212)888–7538. Pres. Alan S. Jaffe; Chmn. Irwin Hochberg; Exec. V.-Pres. Stephen D. Solender.

NIAGARA FALLS

JEWISH FEDERATION OF NIAGARA FALLS, NY, INC. (1935); Temple Beth Israel, Rm. #5, College & Madison Aves. (14305); (716)284–4575. Pres. Howard Kushner.

NORTHEASTERN NEW YORK

UNITED JEWISH FEDERATION OF NORTHEASTERN NEW YORK (1986); Latham Circle Mall, 800 New Loudon Rd., Latham (12110); (518)783–7800. FAX: (518)783–1557. Pres. Kenneth Segel; Exec. Dir. Norman J. Schimelman.

ORANGE COUNTY

JEWISH FEDERATION OF GREATER ORANGE COUNTY (1977); 360 Powell Ave., Newburgh (12550); (914)562–7860. Pres. Dr. William Cieplinski; Exec. Dir. Shari Seiner.

ROCHESTER

JEWISH COMMUNITY FEDERATION OF ROCHESTER, NY, INC. (1939); 441 East Ave. (14607); (716)461–0490. FAX: (716)461–0912. Pres. Rochelle Gutkin; Exec. Dir. Lawrence W. Fine.

ROCKLAND COUNTY

UNITED JEWISH COMMUNITY OF ROCKLAND COUNTY (1985); 240 W. Nyack Rd., W. Nyack (10994–1711); (914)627–3700. FAX: (914)627–7881. Pres. Ronald Langus; Exec. Dir. Neal Potash.

SCHENECTADY

(Merged with Albany; see Northeastern New York)

SYRACUSE

SYRACUSE JEWISH FEDERATION, INC. (1918); 101 Smith St., PO Box 510, DeWitt (13214–0510); (315)445–0161. FAX: (315)-445–1559. Pres. Edward Zachary; Exec. V.-Pres. Barry Silverberg.

TROY

(Merged with Albany-Schenectady; see Northeastern New York)

ULSTER COUNTY

JEWISH FEDERATION OF ULSTER COUNTY (1951); 159 Green Street, Kingston (12401); (914)338–8131. Pres. Steve Nachimson; Exec. Dir. Bonnie Meadow.

UTICA

JEWISH FEDERATION OF UTICA, NY, INC. (1933; inc. 1950); 2310 Oneida St. (13501); (315)733–2343. Pres. Michael Cominsky; Exec. Dir. Haim Morag.

NORTH CAROLINA

ASHEVILLE

WESTERN NORTH CAROLINA JEWISH FEDERATION (1935); 236 Charlotte St. (28801); (704)253–0701. FAX: (704)251–9144. Pres. Stan Greenberg; Exec. Dir. Marlene Breger-Joyce.

CHARLOTTE

THE JEWISH FEDERATION OF GREATER CHARLOTTE (1938); 5007 Providence Rd. (28226); (704)366–5007. FAX: (704)365–4507. Pres. Shelton Gorelick; Exec. Dir. Daniel Z. Lepow.

DURHAM–CHAPEL HILL

DURHAM–CHAPEL HILL JEWISH FEDERATION & COMMUNITY COUNCIL (1979); 210 W. Cameron Ave., P.O. Box 989, Chapel Hill (27514); (919)929–6717. Pres. Patricia Z. Fischer; Exec. Dir. Linda E. Ritt Kupfer.

GREENSBORO

GREENSBORO JEWISH FEDERATION (1940); 713-A N. Greene St. (27401); (919)272–3189. FAX: (919)272–0214. Pres. Sara Lee Sapterstein; Exec. Dir. Marilyn Forman-Chandler.

WAKE COUNTY

WAKE COUNTY JEWISH FEDERATION, INC. (1987); 3900 Merton Dr., Suite 108, Raleigh (27609); (919)781–5459. FAX: (919)787–0666. Pres. Allan From; Exec. Dir. Tobie Kramer.

OHIO

AKRON

AKRON JEWISH COMMUNITY FEDERATION (1935); 750 White Pond Dr. (44320); (216)869–CHAI. FAX: (216)867–8498. Pres. Judge Marvin Shapiro; Exec. Dir. Michael Wise.

CANTON

CANTON JEWISH COMMUNITY FEDERATION (1935; reorg. 1955); 2631 Harvard Ave., NW (44709); (216)452–6444. FAX: (216)-452–4487. Pres. Dr. Ronald Gelb; Exec. Dir. Neil Berro.

CINCINNATI

JEWISH FEDERATION OF CINCINNATI (1896; reorg. 1967); 1811 Losantiville, Suite 320 (45237); (513) 351–3800. FAX: (513)351–3863. Pres. Mel Fischer; Exec. V.-Pres. Aubrey Herman.

CLEVELAND

JEWISH COMMUNITY FEDERATION OF CLEVELAND (1903); 1750 Euclid Ave. (44115); (216)566–9200. FAX: (216)861–1230. Pres. Bennett Yanowitz; Exec. Dir. Stephen H. Hoffman.

COLUMBUS

COLUMBUS JEWISH FEDERATION (1926); 1175 College Ave. (43209); (614)237–7686. FAX: (614)237–2221. Pres. Edwin M. Ellman; Exec. Dir. Mitchel Orlik.

DAYTON

JEWISH FEDERATION OF GREATER DAYTON (1910); 4501 Denlinger Rd. (45426); (513)854–4150. FAX: (513)854–2850. Pres. Ralph E. Heyman; Exec. V.-Pres. Peter H. Wells.

STEUBENVILLE

JEWISH COMMUNITY COUNCIL (1938); 300 Lovers Lane (43952); (614)264–5514. Pres. Morris Denmark; Exec. Sec. Jennie Bernstein.

TOLEDO

JEWISH FEDERATION OF GREATER TOLEDO (1907; reorg. 1960); 6505 Sylvania Ave., Sylvania (43560); (419)885–4461. FAX: (419)885–3207. Pres. Michael Berebitsky; Exec. Dir. Steven J. Edelstein.

YOUNGSTOWN

YOUNGSTOWN AREA JEWISH FEDERATION (1935); PO Box 449, 505 Gypsy Lane (44501); (216)746–3251. FAX: (216)746–7926. Pres. Samuel A. Roth; Exec. V.-Pres. Sam Kooperman.

OKLAHOMA

OKLAHOMA CITY

JEWISH FEDERATION OF GREATER OKLAHOMA CITY (1941); 2800 Quail Plaza Dr. (73120). (405)752–7307. FAX: (405)752–7309. Pres. Louis Price; Exec. Dir. Edie S. Roodman.

TULSA

JEWISH FEDERATION OF TULSA (1938); 2021 E. 71st St. (74136); (918)495–1100.

FAX: (918)495–1220. Pres. Steven Zeligson; Exec. Dir. David Bernstein.

OREGON

PORTLAND
JEWISH FEDERATION OF PORTLAND (incl. state of Oregon and adjacent Washington communities) (1920; reorg. 1956); 6651 SW Capitol Highway (97219); (503)245–6219. FAX: (503)245–6603. Pres. Elizabeth Menashe; Exec. Dir. Charles Schiffman.

PENNSYLVANIA

ALTOONA
FEDERATION OF JEWISH PHILANTHROPIES (1920; reorg. 1940; inc. 1944); 1308 17th St. (16601); (814)944–4072. Pres. William Wallen.

BUCKS COUNTY
(See Jewish Federation of Mercer County, New Jersey)

ERIE
JEWISH COMMUNITY COUNCIL OF ERIE (1946); 1322 G. Daniel Baldwin Bldg., 1001 State St. (16501); (814)455–4474. FAX: (814)455–4475. Pres. Judi S. Hines.

HARRISBURG
UNITED JEWISH COMMUNITY OF GREATER HARRISBURG (1941); 100 Vaughn St. (17110); (717)236–9555. FAX: (717)236–8104. Pres. Allan Noddle; Exec. Dir. Jordan Harburger.

JOHNSTOWN
UNITED JEWISH FEDERATION OF JOHNSTOWN (1938); c/o Beth Sholom Temple, 700 Indiana St. (15905); (814)539–6440 (office), (814)539–9891 (home). Pres. Isadore Suchman.

LEHIGH VALLEY
JEWISH FEDERATION OF THE LEHIGH VALLEY (serving Allentown, Bethlehem and Easton) (1948); 702 North 22nd St. (18104); (215)821–5500. FAX: (215)821–8946. Pres. Jeanette Eichenwald; Exec. Dir. Stuart Mellan.

PHILADELPHIA
JEWISH FEDERATION OF GREATER PHILADELPHIA (includes Bucks, Chester, Delaware, Montgomery, and Philadelphia counties) (1901; reorg. 1956); 226 S. 16th St. (19102); (215)893–5600. FAX: (215)546–0349. Pres. Alan Casnoff; Exec. V.-Pres. Don Cooper.

PITTSBURGH
UNITED JEWISH FEDERATION OF GREATER PITTSBURGH (1912; reorg. 1955); 234 McKee Pl. (15213); (412)681–8000. FAX: (412)681–3980. Pres. Stanley C. Ruskin; Exec. V.-Pres. Howard M. Rieger.

READING
JEWISH FEDERATION OF READING, PA., INC. (1935; reorg. 1972); 1700 City Line St. (19604); (610)921–2766. FAX: (610)929–0886. Pres. Neal Jacobs; Exec. Dir. Daniel Tannenbaum.

SCRANTON
SCRANTON-LACKAWANNA JEWISH FEDERATION (incl. Lackawanna County) (1945); 601 Jefferson Ave. (18510); (717)961–2300. FAX: (717)346–6147. Pres. David M. Epstein, Esq.; Exec. Dir. Seymour Brotman.

RHODE ISLAND

PROVIDENCE
JEWISH FEDERATION OF RHODE ISLAND (1945); 130 Sessions St. (02906); (401)421–4111. FAX: (401)331–7961. Pres. Harris N. Rosen; Exec. V.-Pres. Steve A. Rakitt.

SOUTH CAROLINA

CHARLESTON
CHARLESTON JEWISH FEDERATION (1949); 1645 Raoul Wallenberg Blvd., PO Box 31298 (29407); (803)571–6565. FAX: (803)556–6206. Pres. Jerry Zucker; Exec. Dir. Michael Abidor.

COLUMBIA
COLUMBIA JEWISH FEDERATION (1960); 4540 Trenholm Rd., PO Box 6968 (29260); (803)787–0580. FAX: (803)787–0475. Pres. Alan Kahn; Exec. Dir. Steven Terner.

GREENVILLE
FEDERATED JEWISH CHARITIES OF GREENVILLE, INC.; PO Box 17615 (29606); (803)-244–1261. Pres. Dr. Steven J. Gold.

SOUTH DAKOTA

SIOUX FALLS
JEWISH WELFARE FUND (1938); National Reserve Bldg., 513 S. Main Ave. (57102); (605)336–2880. Pres. Laurence Bierman; Exec. Sec. Louis R. Hurwitz.

TENNESSEE

CHATTANOOGA
THE JEWISH COMMUNITY FEDERATION OF GREATER CHATTANOOGA (1931); 5326

Lynnland Terrace, PO Box 8947 (37411); (615)894–1317. FAX: (615)894–1319. Pres. Pris Siskin; Exec. Dir. Louis B. Solomon.

KNOXVILLE

KNOXVILLE JEWISH FEDERATION (1939); 6800 Deane Hill Dr., PO Box 10882 (37939–0882); (615)693–5837. Pres. Ianne Kopel; Exec. Dir. Conrad J. Koller.

MEMPHIS

MEMPHIS JEWISH FEDERATION (incl. Shelby County) (1935); 6560 Poplar Ave. (38138–3614); (901)767–7100. FAX: (901)-767–7128. Pres. Diane Mendelson; Exec. Dir. Gary Siepser.

NASHVILLE

JEWISH FEDERATION OF NASHVILLE & MIDDLE TENNESSEE (1936); 801 Percy Warner Blvd. (37205); (615)356–3242. FAX: (615)352–0056. Pres. Sandy Cohen; Exec. Dir. Ruth Tanner.

TEXAS

AUSTIN

JEWISH FEDERATION OF AUSTIN (1939; reorg. 1956); 11713 Jollyville Rd. (78759); (512)331–1144. FAX: (512)331–7059. Pres. Marilyn Stahl; Exec. Dir. Wayne Silverman.

DALLAS

JEWISH FEDERATION OF GREATER DALLAS (1911); 7800 Northaven Rd., Suite A (75230); (214)369–3313. FAX: (214)369–8943. Pres. Stan Rabin; Exec. Dir. Avrum I. Cohen.

EL PASO

JEWISH FEDERATION OF EL PASO, INC. (incl. surrounding communities) (1937); 405 Wallenberg Dr., PO Box 12097 (79913–0097); (915)584–4437. FAX: (915)584–0243. Pres. Norman Gordon; Exec. Dir. Mark Alan Zober.

FORT WORTH

JEWISH FEDERATION OF FORT WORTH AND TARRANT COUNTY (1936); 6801 Dan Danciger Rd. (76133); (817)292–3081. FAX: (817)292–3214. Pres. Elliott Garsek; Exec. Dir. Naomi Etzkin.

GALVESTON

GALVESTON COUNTY JEWISH WELFARE ASSOCIATION (1936); PO Box 146 (77553); (409)763–5241. Pres. Ben Gelman.

HOUSTON

JEWISH FEDERATION OF GREATER HOUSTON (1936); 5603 S. Braeswood Blvd.

(77096–3999); (713)729–7000. FAX: (713)-721–6232. Pres. Arthur Schechter; Exec. Dir. Hans Mayer.

SAN ANTONIO

JEWISH FEDERATION OF SAN ANTONIO (incl. Bexar County) (1922); 8434 Ahern Dr. (78216); (210)341–8234. FAX: (210)341–2842. Pres. J. David Oppenheimer; Exec. Dir. Stan Ramati.

WACO

JEWISH FEDERATION OF WACO AND CENTRAL TEXAS (1949); PO Box 8031 (76714–8031); (817)776–3740. Pres. Mike Stupak; Exec. Sec. Martha Bauer.

UTAH

SALT LAKE CITY

UNITED JEWISH FEDERATION OF UTAH (1936); 2416 E. 1700 South (84108); (801)-581–0098. FAX: (801) 581–1334. Pres. Nano B. Podolsky; Exec. Dir. Roberta Grunauer.

VIRGINIA

RICHMOND

JEWISH COMMUNITY FEDERATION OF RICHMOND (1935); 5403 Monument Ave., PO Box 17128 (23226); (804)288–0045. FAX: (804)282–7507. Pres. Cathy Plotkin; Exec. Dir. David Nussbaum.

TIDEWATER

UNITED JEWISH FEDERATION OF TIDEWATER (incl. Norfolk, Portsmouth, and Virginia Beach) (1937); 7300 Newport Ave., PO Box 9776, Norfolk (23505); (804)489–8040. FAX: (804)489–8230. Pres. Art Sandler; Exec. V.-Pres. Mark Goldstein.

VIRGINIA PENINSULA

UNITED JEWISH COMMUNITY OF THE VIRGINIA PENINSULA, INC. (1942); 2700 Spring Road, Newport News (23606); (804)930–1422; FAX: (804)872–9532. Pres. Elizabeth David; Exec. Dir. Barbara T. Gordon.

WASHINGTON

SEATTLE

JEWISH FEDERATION OF GREATER SEATTLE (incl. King County, Everett, and Bremerton) (1926); 2031 Third Ave. (98121); (206)443–5400. FAX: (206)443–0303. Pres. Irwin L. Treiger; Exec. Dir. Michael Novick.

WEST VIRGINIA

CHARLESTON

FEDERATED JEWISH CHARITIES OF CHARLESTON, INC. (1937); PO Box 1613

(25326); (304)346–7500. Pres. Carl Lehman; Exec. Sec. William H. Thalheimer.

WISCONSIN

KENOSHA

KENOSHA JEWISH WELFARE FUND (1938); 7503 3rd Ave. (53143); (414)654–2189. Pres. Edward Chulew; Sec.-Treas. Steven Barasch.

MADISON

MADISON JEWISH COMMUNITY COUNCIL, INC. (1940); 310 N. Midvale Blvd., Suite 325 (53705); (608)231–3426. Pres. Evelyn W. Minkoff; Exec. Dir. Steven H. Morrison.

MILWAUKEE

MILWAUKEE JEWISH FEDERATION, INC. (1902); 1360 N. Prospect Ave. (53202); (414)-271–8338. Pres. Gerald Stein; Exec. Dir. Richard H. Meyer.

CANADA

ALBERTA

CALGARY

CALGARY JEWISH COMMUNITY COUNCIL (1962); 1607 90th Ave. SW (T2V 4V7); (403)-253–8600. FAX: (403)253–7915. Pres. Cheryl Shore; Exec. Dir. Drew J. Staffenberg.

EDMONTON

JEWISH FEDERATION OF EDMONTON (1954; reorg. 1982); 7200 156th St. (T5R 1X3); (403)487–5120. FAX: (403)481–3463. Pres. Michael Goldstein; Exec. Dir. Sidney Indig.

BRITISH COLUMBIA

VANCOUVER

JEWISH FEDERATION OF GREATER VANCOUVER (1932; reorg. 1987); 950 W. 41st Ave., Suite 200 (V5Z 2N7); (604)257–5100. FAX: (604)257–5110. Pres. Ted Zacks; Exec. Dir. Drew Staffenberg.

MANITOBA

WINNIPEG

WINNIPEG JEWISH COMMUNITY COUNCIL (1938; reorg. 1973); 370 Hargrave St. (R3B 2K1); (204)943–0406. FAX: (204)956–0609. Pres. Donald N. Aronovitch; Exec. Dir. Robert Freedman.

ONTARIO

HAMILTON

JEWISH FEDERATION OF HAMILTON, WENTWORTH & AREA (1932; merged 1971); PO Box 7258, 1030 Lower Lion Club Rd.,

Ancaster (L9G 3N6); (905)648–0605. FAX: (905)648–8388. Pres. David Steinberg; Exec. Dir. Patricia Tolkin Eppel.

LONDON

LONDON JEWISH FEDERATION (1932); 536 Huron St. (N5Y 4J5); (519)673–3310. FAX: (519)673–1161. Pres. Robert Siskind; Exec. Dir. Gerald Enchin.

OTTAWA

JEWISH COMMUNITY COUNCIL OF OTTAWA (1934); 151 Chapel St. (K1N 7Y2); (613)-232–7306. FAX: (613)563–4593. Pres. Dr. Eli Rabin.

TORONTO

JEWISH FEDERATION OF GREATER TORONTO (1917); 4600 Bathurst St., Willowdale (M2R 3V2); (416)635–2883. FAX: (416)635–1408. Pres. Charles S. Diamond; Exec. Dir. Allan Reitzes.

WINDSOR

JEWISH COMMUNITY FEDERATION (1938); 1641 Ouellette Ave. (N8X 1R9); (519)973–1772. FAX: (519)973–1774. Pres. Ted Hochberg; Exec. Dir. Allen Juris.

QUEBEC

MONTREAL

FEDERATION CJA (formerly Allied Jewish Community Services) (1965); 5151 Cote Ste. Catherine Rd. (H3W 1M6); (514)735–3541. FAX: (514)735–8972. Pres. Lester Lazarus; Exec. Dir. Steven Drysdale.

Jewish Periodicals[1]

UNITED STATES

ALABAMA

SOUTHERN SHOFAR (1990). PO Box 130052, Birmingham, 35213. (205) 870–9255. FAX: (205)870–9255. Lawrence M. Brook. Monthly.

ARIZONA

ARIZONA JEWISH POST (1946). 3812 East River Rd., Tucson, 85718. (602)529–1500. FAX: (602)577–0734. Sandra R. Heiman. Fortnightly. Jewish Federation of Southern Arizona.

JEWISH NEWS OF GREATER PHOENIX (1948). PO Box 26590, Phoenix, 85068. (602)870–9470. FAX: (602)870–0426. Pub. Flo Eckstein, Mng. Ed. Leni Reiss. Weekly.

CALIFORNIA

B'NAI B'RITH MESSENGER (1897). PO Box 35915, Los Angeles, 90035. (310)659–2952. Rabbi Yale Butler. Weekly.

HADSHOT L.A. (1988). 13535 Ventura Blvd., Suite 200, Sherman Oaks, 91423. (818)-783–3090. Meir Doron. Weekly. Hebrew.

HERITAGE-SOUTHWEST JEWISH PRESS (1914). 2130 S. Vermont Ave., Los Angeles, 90007. (213) 737–2122. Dan Brin. Weekly. (Also SAN DIEGO JEWISH HERITAGE, weekly; ORANGE COUNTY JEWISH HERITAGE, weekly; CENTRAL CALIFORNIA JEWISH HERITAGE, monthly.) Heritage Group.

JEWISH BULLETIN OF NORTHERN CALIFORNIA (1946). 88 First St., Suite 300, San Francisco, 94105. (415)957–9340. FAX: (415)957–0266. Marc S. Klein. Weekly. San Francisco Jewish Community Publications, Inc.

JEWISH JOURNAL OF GREATER LOS ANGELES (1986). 3660 Wilshire Blvd., Suite 204, Los Angeles, 90010. (213)738–7778. FAX: (213)386–9501. Gene Lichtenstein. Weekly.

JEWISH NEWS (1973). 11071 Ventura Blvd., Studio City, 91604. (818)786–4000. FAX: (818)760–4648. Phil Blazer. Monthly.

JEWISH SOCIAL STUDIES: HISTORY, CULTURE, AND SOCIETY (1939). c/o Program in Jewish Studies, Building 70, Stanford University, Stanford, 94305–2165. (415)-723–7589. Steven J. Zipperstein, Aron Rodrigue. Three times a year. Conference on Jewish Social Studies, Inc.

JEWISH SPECTATOR (1935). 4391 Park Milano, Calabasas, 91302. (818)591–7481. FAX: (818)591–7267. Robert Bleiweiss. Quarterly. American Friends of Center for Jewish Living and Values.

NORTHERN CALIFORNIA JEWISH BULLETIN See JEWISH BULLETIN OF NORTHERN CALIFORNIA

JEWISH STAR (1956). 109 Minna St., Suite 323, San Francisco, 94108. (415)834–1192. FAX: (415)834–0989. Nevon Stuckey. Quarterly.

SAN DIEGO JEWISH TIMES (1979). 2592 Fletcher Pkwy., El Cajon, 92020. (619)-463–5515. Carol Rosenberg. Biweekly.

WESTERN STATES JEWISH HISTORY (1968). 3111 Kelton Ave., Los Angeles, 90034. (310)475–1415. FAX: (310)475–2996. Prof. William M. Kramer. Quarterly. Western States Jewish History Association.

---

[1]The information in this directory is based on replies to questionnaires circulated by the editors. For organization bulletins, see the directory of Jewish organizations.

COLORADO

INTERMOUNTAIN JEWISH NEWS (1913). 1275 Sherman St., Suite 214, Denver, 80203-2299. (303)861-2234. FAX: (303)-832-6942. Exec. Ed. Rabbi Hillel Goldberg; Ed./Pub. Miriam Goldberg. Weekly.

CONNECTICUT

CONNECTICUT JEWISH LEDGER; HARTFORD JEWISH LEDGER; NEW HAVEN JEWISH LEDGER; BRIDGEPORT JEWISH LEDGER; STAMFORD JEWISH LEDGER (1929). 740 N. Main St., W. Hartford, 06117. (203)231-2424. FAX: (203)231-2428. Jonathan S. Tobin. Weekly. Jewish Media Group, Inc.

CONTEMPORARY JEWRY (1974, under the name JEWISH SOCIOLOGY AND SOCIAL RESEARCH). Dept. of Sociology, Box 5302, Connecticut College, New London, 06320. J. Alan Winter. Annually. Association for the Social Scientific Study of Jewry.

JEWISH LEADER. 28 Channing St., PO Box 1468, New London, 06320. (203) 442-7395. FAX: (203) 442-8062. Mgr. Sidney Schiller. Biweekly. Jewish Federation of Eastern Connecticut.

MITZVAH CONNECTION. PO Box 948, Avon, 06001. (203)675-7763. C. Dianne Zweig. Annually.

DELAWARE

JEWISH VOICE. 101 Garden of Eden Rd., Wilmington, 19803-1579. (302) 478-6200. FAX: (302) 478-5374. Daniel Weintraub. Biweekly (monthly July/Aug.). Jewish Federation of Delaware.

DISTRICT OF COLUMBIA

B'NAI B'RITH INTERNATIONAL JEWISH MONTHLY (1886, under the name MENORAH). 1640 Rhode Island Ave., NW, Washington, 20036. (202)857-6645. Jeff Rubin. Eight times a year. B'nai B'rith.

CAPITAL COMMUNIQUÉ (1991). 711 Second St., NE, Suite 100, Washington, 20002. (202)544-7636. FAX: (202)544-7645. Pat Lewis. Monthly. National Jewish Democratic Council.

JEWISH VETERAN (1896). 1811 R St., NW, Washington, 20009. (202)265-6280. FAX: (202)234-5662. Albert Schlossberg. Five times a year. Jewish War Veterans of the U.S.A.

MOMENT (1975). 3000 Connecticut Ave., NW, Suite 300, Washington, 20008. (202)-387-8888. FAX: (202)483-3423. Hershel Shanks. Bimonthly. Jewish Educational Ventures, Inc.

MONITOR (1990). 1819 H Street, NW, Suite 230, Washington, 20006. (202)775-9770. FAX: (202)775-9776. Kelly Anne Gallagher (Washington), Steven Sassaman (San Francisco). Weekly. Union of Councils for Soviet Jews.

NEAR EAST REPORT (1957). 440 First St., NW, Suite 607, Washington, 20001. (202)-639-5300. Dr. Raphael Danziger. Weekly. Near East Research, Inc.

SECURITY AFFAIRS (1978). 1717 K St., NW, Suite 300, Washington, 20006. (202)833-0020. FAX: (202)296-6452. Jim Colbert. Monthly. Jewish Institute for National Security Affairs.

WASHINGTON JEWISH WEEK. See under MARYLAND

FLORIDA

BROWARD JEWISH WORLD (1986). 3550 Biscayne Blvd., 3rd fl., Miami, 33137-3845. (305)576-9500. FAX: (305)573-9551. Bertram Korn, Jr. Weekly. Jewish Media Group, Inc.

THE CHRONICLE (1971). 580 S. McIntosh Rd., Sarasota, 34232. (813)371-4546. FAX: (813)378-2947. Barry Millman. Fortnightly. Sarasota-Manatee Jewish Federation.

HERITAGE FLORIDA JEWISH NEWS (1976). PO Box 300742, Fern Park, 32730. (407) 834-8787 or 834-8277. FAX: (407)831-0507. Pub. Jeffrey Gaeser; Assoc. Ed. Vivian Gallimore. Weekly.

JEWISH COMMUNITY ADVOCATE OF SOUTH BROWARD (1986). 2719 Hollywood Blvd., Hollywood, 33020. (305)922-8603. FAX: (305)922-8604. Amy Jacobson Boxer. Biweekly.

JEWISH JOURNAL (PALM BEACH-BROWARD-DADE) (1977). 601 Fairway Dr., Deerfield Beach, 33441. (305)698-6397. FAX: (305)429-1207. Andrew Polin. Weekly. South Florida Newspaper Network.

JEWISH PRESS OF PINELLAS COUNTY (CLEARWATER-ST. PETERSBURG) (1985). 301 Jupiter Ave. S., Clearwater, 34615-6561. (813)535-4400. FAX: (813)530-3039. Karen Wolfson Dawkins. Biweekly. Jewish Press Group of Tampa Bay (FL), Inc.

JEWISH PRESS OF TAMPA (1987). 2808 Horatio St., Tampa, 33609. (813)871–2332. FAX: (813)530–3039. Karen Wolfson Dawkins. Biweekly. Jewish Press Group of Tampa Bay (FL), Inc.

MIAMI JEWISH TRIBUNE (1986). 3550 Biscayne Blvd., 3rd fl., Miami, 33137–3845. (305)576–9500. FAX: (305)573–9551. Bertram Korn, Jr. Weekly. Jewish Media Group, Inc.

NATIONAL JEWISH ADVOCATE (1924; formerly SOUTHERN JEWISH WEEKLY). 8301 Cypress Plaza Dr., Suite 124, Jacksonville, 32256. (904)281–0888. FAX: (904)281–0922. Lester N. Garripee. Semimonthly. First Coast Media Group.

PALM BEACH JEWISH WORLD (1982). 3550 Biscayne Blvd., 3rd fl., Miami, 33137–3845. (305)576–9500. FAX: (305)573–9551. Bertram Korn, Jr. Weekly. Jewish Media Group, Inc.

GEORGIA

ATLANTA JEWISH TIMES (1925; formerly SOUTHERN ISRAELITE). 1575 Northside Dr., NW, Atlanta, 30318. (404)352–2400. FAX: (404)355–9388. Mng. Ed. Neil Rubin; Sr. Ed. Vida Goldgar. Weekly.

JEWISH CIVIC PRESS (1972). 3500 Piedmont Rd., Suite 612, Atlanta, 30305. (404)231–2194. Abner L. Tritt. Monthly.

ILLINOIS

CHICAGO JEWISH STAR (1991). PO Box 268, Skokie, 60076–0268. (708)674–7827. FAX: (708)674–0014. Ed. Douglas Wertheimer; Assoc. Ed. Gila Wertheimer. Fortnightly.

CHICAGO JUF NEWS (1972). One S. Franklin St., Rm. 706, Chicago, 60606. (312)-444–2853. FAX: (312)855–2470. Joseph Aaron. Monthly. Jewish United Fund/Jewish Federation of Metropolitan Chicago.

JEWISH COMMUNITY NEWS (1941). 6464 W. Main, Suite 7A, Belleville, 62223. (618)-398–6100. Steve Low. Every other month. Jewish Federation of Southern Illinois.

THE SENTINEL (1911). 150 N. Michigan Ave., Chicago, 60601. (312)407–0060. FAX: (312)407–0096. J.I. Fishbein. Weekly.

INDIANA

ILLIANA NEWS (1976). 2939 Jewett St., Highland, 46322. (219)972–2250. FAX: (219)972–4779. Monthly (except July/Aug.). Jewish Federation, Inc./Northwest Indiana.

INDIANA JEWISH POST AND OPINION (1935). PO Box 449097, 2120 N. Meridian St., Indianapolis, 46202. (317)927–7800. FAX: (317)927–7807. Ed Stattman. Weekly.

NATIONAL JEWISH POST AND OPINION (1932). 2120 N. Meridian St., Indianapolis, 46202. (317)927–7800. FAX: (317)927–7807. Gabriel Cohen. Weekly.

KANSAS

KANSAS CITY JEWISH CHRONICLE. See under MISSOURI

KENTUCKY

COMMUNITY (1975). 3630 Dutchman's Lane, Louisville, 40205–3200. (502) 451–8840. FAX: (502) 458–0702. Shiela Wallace. Biweekly. Jewish Community Federation of Louisville.

KENTUCKY JEWISH POST AND OPINION (1931). 1551 Bardstown Rd., Louisville, 40205. (502)459–1914. Julie D. Segal. Weekly.

LOUISIANA

COMMUNITY. See JEWISH VOICE

JEWISH CIVIC PRESS (1965). 924 Valmont St., New Orleans, 70115. (504)895–8784. Abner Tritt. Monthly.

JEWISH VOICE (1989). 924 Valmont St., New Orleans, 70115. (504)895–8784. FAX: (504)895–8784. Ed. Roberta Brunstetter; Pub. Abner Tritt. Semiweekly. Jewish Federation of Greater New Orleans.

MARYLAND

BALTIMORE JEWISH TIMES (1919). 2104 N. Charles St., Baltimore, 21218. (410)752–3504. FAX: (410)752–2375. Michael Davis. Weekly.

MODERN JUDAISM (1980). Johns Hopkins University Press, 2715 N. Charles St., Baltimore, 21218–4319. (410)516–6987. FAX: (410)516–6968. (Editorial address: 92 Riverside Dr., Binghamton, NY 13905.) Steven Katz. Three times a year.

PROOFTEXTS: A JOURNAL OF JEWISH LITERARY HISTORY (1980). Johns Hopkins University Press, 2715 N. Charles St., Baltimore, 21218–4319. (410)516–6987. FAX: (410)516–6968. Editorial address (for contributors): NEJS Dept., Brandeis U., Waltham, MA 02254. Alan Mintz, David G. Roskies. Three times a year.

WASHINGTON JEWISH WEEK (1930, as the NATIONAL JEWISH LEDGER). 12300 Twinbrook Pkwy., Suite 250, Rockville, 20852. (301)230–2222. FAX: (301)881–6362. Eric Rozenman. Weekly.

MASSACHUSETTS

AMERICAN JEWISH HISTORY (1893). Two Thornton Rd., Waltham, 02154. (617)891–8110. FAX: (617)899–9208. Marc Lee Raphael. Quarterly. American Jewish Historical Society.

BOSTON JEWISH TIMES (1945). 169 Norfolk Ave., Boston, 02119. (617)442–9680. Sten Lukin. Fortnightly.

JEWISH ADVOCATE (1902). 15 School St., Boston, 02108. (617)367–9100. FAX: (617)-367–9310. Robert Israel. Weekly.

JEWISH CHRONICLE (1927). 131 Lincoln St., Worcester, 01605. (508)752–3400. FAX: (508)752–9057. Sondra Shapiro. Biweekly.

JEWISH WEEKLY NEWS (1945). PO Box 1569, Springfield, 01101. (413)739–4771. FAX: (413)739–7099. Kenneth G. White. Weekly.

JOURNAL OF THE NORTH SHORE JEWISH COMMUNITY (1976). 201 Washington St., PO Box 555, Salem, 01970. (508)745–4111. FAX: (508)745–5333. Bette W. Keva. Biweekly. Russian section. North Shore Jewish Press Ltd.

METROWEST JEWISH REPORTER (1970). 76 Salem End Rd., Framingham, 01701. (508)879–3300. FAX: (508)879–5856. Marcia T. Rivin. Monthly. Combined Jewish Philanthropies of Greater Boston.

DER PAKN-TREGER/THE BOOK PEDDLER (1980). 48 Woodbridge St., S. Hadley, 01075. (413)535–1303. FAX: (413)535–1007. Mng. Ed. Karen Bagnini. Semiannually. Yiddish. National Yiddish Book Center.

MICHIGAN

DETROIT JEWISH NEWS (1942). 27676 Franklin Rd., Southfield, 48034. (313)354–6060. FAX: (313)354–6069. Phil Jacobs. Weekly.

HUMANISTIC JUDAISM (1968). 28611 W. Twelve Mile Rd., Farmington Hills, 48334. (810)478–7610. FAX: (810)477–9014. M. Bonnie Cousens, Ruth D. Feld-

man. Quarterly. Society for Humanistic Judaism.

MINNESOTA

AMERICAN JEWISH WORLD (1912). 4509 Minnetonka Blvd., Minneapolis, 55416. (612)920–7000. FAX: (612)920–6205. Marshall Hoffman. Weekly.

MISSOURI

KANSAS CITY JEWISH CHRONICLE (1920). 7373 W. 107 St., Suite 250, Overland Park, KS 66212. (913)648–4620. FAX: (913)381–9889. Barbara Bayer. Weekly. Sun Publications.

ST. LOUIS JEWISH LIGHT (1947; reorg. 1963). 12 Millstone Campus Dr., St. Louis, 63146. (314)432–3353. FAX: (314)432–0515. Robert A. Cohn. Weekly. St. Louis Jewish Light.

NEBRASKA

JEWISH PRESS (1920). 333 S. 132 St., Omaha, 68154. (402)334–8200. FAX: (402)334–5422. Morris Maline. Weekly. Jewish Federation of Omaha.

NEVADA

JEWISH REPORTER (1976). 3909 S. Maryland Pkwy., Las Vegas, 89119–7520. (702)732–0556. FAX: (702)732–3228. Katherine E. Scott. Twice a month. HBC Publications.

LAS VEGAS ISRAELITE (1965). PO Box 14096, Las Vegas, 89114. (702)876–1255. FAX: (702)364–1009. Michael Tell. Biweekly.

NEW JERSEY

AVOTAYNU (1985). 1485 Teaneck Rd., Teaneck, 07666. (201)837–8300. FAX: (201)-837–6272. Sallyann Amdur Sack. Quarterly.

JEWISH COMMUNITY NEWS. 199 Scoles Ave., Clifton, 07012. (201) 777–8313. FAX: (201) 777–6701. Edith Sobel. Biweekly. Jewish Federation of North Jersey and Jewish Federation of Greater Clifton-Passaic.

JEWISH COMMUNITY VOICE (1941). 2393 W. Marlton Pike, Cherry Hill, 08002. (609)-665–6100. FAX: (609)665–0074. Harriet Kessler. Biweekly. Jewish Federation of Southern NJ.

JEWISH HORIZON (1981). 812 Central Ave., Westfield, 07090. (908)654–0077. FAX: (908)654–4567. Fran Gold. Weekly.

JEWISH RECORD (Atlantic City area) (1939). 1525 S. Main St., Pleasantville, 08232. (609)383–0999. Martin Korik. Weekly.

JEWISH STANDARD (1931). 1086 Teaneck Rd., Teaneck, 07666. (201)837–8818. FAX: (201)833–4959. Rebecca Kaplan Boroson. Weekly.

JEWISH STAR (1975). 100 Metroplex Dr., Edison, 08817. (908)985–1234. FAX: (908)-985–3295. Marlene A. Heller. Bimonthly. Jewish Federation of Greater Middlesex County.

JEWISH VOICE (1971). 100 Grant Ave., Deal Park, 07723. (908)531–6200. FAX: (908)-531–9518. Suzanne G. Michel. Monthly. Jewish Federation of Greater Monmouth County.

JEWISH VOICE & OPINION (1987). 73 Dana Place, Englewood, 07631. (201) 569–2845. FAX: (201)569–1739. Susan L. Rosenbluth. Monthly.

JOURNAL OF JEWISH COMMUNAL SERVICE (1899). 3084 State Hwy. 27, Suite 9, Kendall Pk., 08824–1657. (908)821–1871. FAX: (908)821–5335. Gail Naron Chalew. Quarterly. Jewish Communal Service Association of North America.

JUDAICA NEWS (1989). PO Box 1130, Fair Lawn, 07410. (201)796–6151. FAX: (201)-796–6545. Terry Cohn. Quarterly.

METROWEST JEWISH NEWS (1947). 901 Route 10, Whippany, 07981–1157. (201)-887–3900. FAX: (201)887–5999. David Twersky. Weekly. United Jewish Federation of MetroWest.

NEW MEXICO

THE LINK (1971). 8205 Spain NE, Suite 107, Albuquerque, 87109. (505)821–3214. FAX: (505)821–3351. Rebeca Zimmermann. Monthly. Jewish Federation of Greater Albuquerque.

NEW YORK

AFN SHVEL (1941). 200 W. 72 St., Suite 40, NYC, 10023. (212)787–6675. Mordkhe Schaechter. Quarterly. Yiddish. League for Yiddish, Inc.

AGENDA: JEWISH EDUCATION (1949; formerly PEDAGOGIC REPORTER). JESNA, 730 Broadway, NYC, 10003. (212)529–2000. FAX: (212)529–2009. Rabbi Arthur Vernon. Twice a year. Jewish Education Service of North America, Inc.

ALGEMEINER JOURNAL (1972). 211 63 St., Brooklyn, 11220. (718)492–6420. FAX: (718)492–6571. Gershon Jacobson. Weekly. Yiddish-English.

AMERICAN JEWISH YEAR BOOK (1899). 165 E. 56 St., NYC, 10022. (212)751–4000. FAX: (212)751–4017. David Singer, Ruth R. Seldin. Annually. American Jewish Committee.

AMERICAN ZIONIST (1910). 4 E. 34 St., NYC, 10016. (212)481–1500. FAX: (212)-481–1515. Paul Flacks. Quarterly. Zionist Organization of America.

AMIT WOMAN (1925). 817 Broadway, NYC, 10003. (212)477–4720. FAX: (212)353–2312. Micheline Ratzersdorfer. Four times a year. AMIT Women (formerly American Mizrachi Women).

AUFBAU (1934). 2121 Broadway, NYC, 10023. (212)873–7400. FAX: (212)496–5736. Ed. Henry Marx; Mng. Ed. Herman Pichler. Fortnightly. German. New World Club, Inc.

BUFFALO JEWISH REVIEW (1918). 15 E. Mohawk St., Buffalo, 14203. (716)854–2192. FAX: (716)854–2198. Harlan C. Abbey. Weekly. Kahaal Nahalot Israel.

THE CALL (1933). 45 E. 33 St., NYC, 10016. (212)889–6800, ext. 210. FAX: (212)532–7518. Diane H. Merlin. Bimonthly. The Workmen's Circle/Arbeter Ring.

CCAR JOURNAL: A REFORM JEWISH QUARTERLY (formerly JOURNAL OF REFORM JUDAISM) (1953). 192 Lexington Ave., NYC, 10016. (212)684–4990. FAX: (212)689–1649. Ed. Henry Bamberger; Mng. Ed. Elliot Stevens. Quarterly. Central Conference of American Rabbis.

CIRCLE (1943). 15 E. 26 St., NYC, 10010–1579. (212)532–4949. FAX: (212)481–4174. Dr. Shirley Frank. Quarterly. Jewish Community Centers Association of North America (formerly JWB).

COMMENTARY (1945). 165 E. 56 St., NYC, 10022. (212)751–4000. FAX: (212)751–1174. Norman Podhoretz, Neal Kozodoy. Monthly. American Jewish Committee.

CONGRESS MONTHLY (1933). 15 E. 84 St., NYC, 10028. (212)879–4500. Maier Deshell. Seven times a year. American Jewish Congress.

CONSERVATIVE JUDAISM (1945). 3080 Broadway, NYC, 10027. (212)678–8049.

FAX: (212)749–9166. Rabbi Benjamin Edidin Scolnic. Quarterly. Rabbinical Assembly.

FORVERTS (YIDDISH FORWARD) (1897). 45 E. 33 St., NYC, 10016. (212)889–8200. FAX: (212)684–3949. Mordechai Strigler. Weekly. Yiddish. Forward Association, Inc.

FORWARD (1897). 45 E. 33 St., NYC, 10016. (212)889–8200. FAX: (212)447–6406. Seth Lipsky. Weekly. Forward Publishing Company, Inc.

HADAROM (1957). 275 Seventh Ave., NYC, 10001. (212)807–7888. Rabbi Gedalia Dov Schwartz. Annually. Hebrew. Rabbinical Council of America.

HADASSAH MAGAZINE (1914). 50 W. 58 St., NYC, 10019. (212)333–5946. FAX: (212)-333–5967. Alan M. Tigay. Monthly (except for combined issues of June–July and Aug.–Sept.). Hadassah, the Women's Zionist Organization of America.

HADOAR (1921). 47 W. 34 St., Rm. 609, NYC, 10001. (212)629–9443. FAX: (212)-629–9472. Ed. Shlomo Shamir; Lit. Ed. Dr. Yael Feldman. Biweekly. Hebrew. Hadoar Association, Inc., Organ of the Histadruth of America.

HAMACHNE HACHAREIDI (1980). PO Box 216, Brooklyn, 11218. (718)438–1263. FAX: (718)438–1263. Rabbi Yisroel Eichler. Weekly. Khal Machzikei Hadas.

ISRAEL HORIZONS (1952). 224 W. 35 St., Rm. 403, NYC, 10001. (212)868–0386. Ralph Seliger. Quarterly. Americans for Progressive Israel.

ISRAEL QUALITY (1976). 350 Fifth Ave., Suite 1919, NYC, 10118. (212)971–0310. Beth Belkin. Quarterly. Government of Israel Trade Center and American-Israel Chamber of Commerce and Industry.

JBI VOICE (1978). 110 E. 30 St., NYC, 10016. (212)889–2525. FAX: (212)689–3692. Dr. Jacob Freid. Ten times a year (audiocassettes). Jewish Braille Institute of America, Inc.

JEWISH ACTION MAGAZINE (1950). 333 Seventh Ave., 18th fl., NYC, 10008. (212)563–4000, ext. 147. Charlotte Friedland. Quarterly. Union of Orthodox Jewish Congregations of America.

JEWISH BOOK ANNUAL (1942). 15 E. 26 St., NYC, 10010. (212)532–4949. Jacob Kabakoff. English-Hebrew-Yiddish. Jewish Book Council.

JEWISH BOOK WORLD (1945). 15 E. 26 St., NYC, 10010. (212)532–4949. Amy Gottlieb. Quarterly. Jewish Book Council.

JEWISH BRAILLE REVIEW (1931). 110 E. 30 St., NYC, 10016. (212)889–2525. Jacob Freid. 10 times a year. English braille. Jewish Braille Institute of America, Inc.

JEWISH CURRENTS (1946). 22 E. 17 St., Suite 601, NYC, 10003–1919. (212)924–5740. Morris U. Schappes. Monthly (July/Aug. combined). Association for Promotion of Jewish Secularism, Inc.

JEWISH EDUCATION (1929). 730 Broadway, NYC, 10003. (212)529–2000. FAX: (212)-529–2009. Dr. Alvin I. Schiff. Three times a year. Council for Jewish Education.

JEWISH FRONTIER (1934). 275 Seventh Ave., 17th fl., NYC, 10001. (212)229–2280. FAX: (212)675–7685. Nahum Guttman. Bimonthly. Labor Zionist Letters, Inc.

JEWISH JOURNAL (1969). 210 E. Sunrise Hwy., Suite 304, Valley Stream, NY 11581. (516)561–6900. FAX: (516)561–6971. Harold Singer. Weekly.

JEWISH LEDGER (1924). 2535 Brighton-Henrietta Town Line Rd., Rochester, 14623. (716)427–2434. FAX: (716)427–8521. Barbara Morgenstern. Weekly.

JEWISH OBSERVER (1963). 84 William St., NYC, 10038. (212)797–9000. FAX: (212)-269–2843. Rabbi Nisson Wolpin. Monthly (except July and Aug.). Agudath Israel of America.

JEWISH OBSERVER (1978). PO Box 510, DeWitt, 13214. (315)445–0161. FAX: (315)-445–1559. Mollie Leitzes Collins. Biweekly. Syracuse Jewish Federation, Inc.

JEWISH PARENT CONNECTION. 160 Broadway, 4th fl., NYC, 10038. (212)227–1000. FAX: (212)406–6934. Prod. Mgr. Rachel F. Wolff. Monthly except for June, July, August and October. Torah Umesorah-National Society for Hebrew Day Schools.

JEWISH POST OF NY (1974). 130 W. 29 St., 10th fl., NYC, 10001. (212)967–7313. FAX: (212)967–8321. Henry J. Levy. Monthly.

JEWISH PRESS (1950). 338 Third Ave., Brooklyn, 11215. (718)330–1100. FAX: (718)935–1215. Rabbi Sholom Klass. Weekly.

JEWISH SPORTS & FITNESS (1992). PO Box 4549, Old Village Station, Great Neck, 11023. (516)482–5550. FAX: (516)482–5583. David J. Kufeld. Quarterly. The Jewish Sports Congress.

JEWISH TELEGRAPHIC AGENCY COMMUNITY NEWS REPORTER (1962). 330 Seventh Ave., 11th fl., NYC, 10001–5010. (212)643–1890. FAX: (212)643–8498. Mark Joffe, Rifka Rosenwein. Weekly.

JEWISH TELEGRAPHIC AGENCY DAILY NEWS BULLETIN (1917). 330 Seventh Ave., 11th fl., NYC, 10001–5010. (212)-643–1890. FAX: (212)643–8498. Mark Joffe, Rifka Rosenwein. Daily.

JEWISH TELEGRAPHIC AGENCY WEEKLY NEWS DIGEST (1933). 330 Seventh Ave., 11th fl., NYC, 10001–5010. (212)643–1890. FAX: (212)643–8498. Mark Joffe, Rifka Rosenwein. Weekly.

JEWISH WEEK (1876; reorg. 1970). 1501 Broadway, NYC, 10036–5503. (212)921–7822. FAX: (212)921–8420. Gary Rosenblatt. Weekly.

JEWISH WORLD (1965). 1104 Central Ave., Albany, 12205. (518)459–8455. FAX: (518)-459–5289. Laurie J. Clevenson. Weekly.

JOURNAL OF REFORM JUDAISM. See CCAR JOURNAL

JUDAISM (1952). 15 E. 84 St., NYC, 10028. (212)879–4500. FAX: (212)249–3672. Dr. Ruth B. Waxman. Quarterly. American Jewish Congress.

KASHRUS FAXLETTER (1980). PO Box 204, Brooklyn, 11204. (718)336–8544. FAX: (718)336–8550. Rabbi Yosef Wikler. Monthly. Yeshiva Birkas Reuven.

KASHRUS MAGAZINE (1980). PO Box 204, Brooklyn, 11204. (718)336–8544. FAX: (718)336–8550. Rabbi Yosef Wikler. Five times a year. Yeshiva Birkas Reuven.

KOL HAT'NUA (VOICE OF THE MOVEMENT) (1975). c/o Young Judea, 50 W. 58 St., NYC, 10019. (212)303–4576. FAX: (212)-303–4572. Andrew Harris. Three times a year. Hadassah Zionist Youth Commission–Young Judaea.

KULTUR UN LEBN–CULTURE AND LIFE (1967). 45 E. 33 St., NYC, 10016. (212)-889–6800. Joseph Mlotek. Three times a year. Yiddish. The Workmen's Circle.

LAMISHPAHA (1963). 47 W. 34 St., Rm. 609, NYC, 10001–3012. (212)629–9443. FAX:

(212)629–9472. Dr. Vered Cohen-Raphaeli. Illustrated. Monthly (except July and Aug.). Hebrew. Histadruth Ivrith of America.

LIKUTIM (1981). 110 E. 30 St., NYC, 10016. (212)889–2525. Joanne Jahr. Two to four times a year (audiocassettes). Hebrew. Jewish Braille Institute of America, Inc.

LILITH–THE INDEPENDENT JEWISH WOMEN'S MAGAZINE (1976). 250 W. 57 St., #2432, NYC, 10107. (212)757–0818. Susan Weidman Schneider. Quarterly.

LONG ISLAND JEWISH WORLD (1971). 115 Middle Neck Rd., Great Neck, 11021. (516)829–4000. FAX: (516)829–4776. Jerome W. Lippman. Weekly.

MANHATTAN JEWISH SENTINEL (1993). 21 W. 39 St., NYC, 10018. (212)764–6835. FAX: (212)764–0752. Andrew Polin. Weekly.

MARTYRDOM AND RESISTANCE (1974). 48 W. 37 St., 9th fl., NYC, 10018–4708. (212)-564–1865. FAX: (212)268–0529. Eli Zborowski. Bimonthly. International Society for Yad Vashem.

MELTON JOURNAL (1982). 3080 Broadway, NYC, 10027. (212)678–8031. Eduardo Rauch, Barry W. Holtz. Biannually. Melton Research Center for Jewish Education.

MIDSTREAM (1954). 110 E. 59 St., NYC, 10022. (212)339–6040. FAX: (212)318–6176. Joel Carmichael. Nine times a year. Theodor Herzl Foundation, Inc.

MODERN JEWISH STUDIES ANNUAL (1977). Queens College, NSF 350, 65–30 Kissena Blvd., Flushing, 11367. (718)997–3622. Joseph C. Landis. Annually. American Association of Professors of Yiddish.

NA'AMAT WOMAN (1926). 200 Madison Ave., Suite 2120, NYC, 10016. (212)725–8010. Judith A. Sokoloff. Five times a year. English-Yiddish-Hebrew. NA'AMAT USA, the Women's Labor Zionist Organization of America.

OLAM HADASH (1960). 110 E. 59 St., #4100, NYC, 10022. (212)339–6020. FAX: (212)318–6176. Bina Ofek–Israel; Irene S. Wolk–U.S. Monthly. Hebrew. Hebrew Publications for Israel.

OLOMEINU–OUR WORLD (1945). 5723 18th Ave., Brooklyn, 11204. (718)259–1223. FAX: (718)259–1795. Rabbi Yaakov Fruchter, Rabbi Nosson Scherman.

Monthly. English-Hebrew. Torah Umesorah–National Society for Hebrew Day Schools.

PASSOVER DIRECTORY (1923). 333 Seventh Ave., NYC, 10001. (212)563–4000. FAX: (212)564–9058. Shelley Scharf. Annually. Union of Orthodox Jewish Congregations of America.

PEDAGOGIC REPORTER. *See* AGENDA: JEWISH EDUCATION

PROCEEDINGS OF THE AMERICAN ACADEMY FOR JEWISH RESEARCH (1920). 3080 Broadway, NYC, 10027. (212)678–8864. FAX: (212)678–8947. Dr. Nahum Sarna. Annually. English-Hebrew-French-Arabic-Persian-Greek. American Academy for Jewish Research.

RCA RECORD (1953). 275 Seventh Ave. NYC, 10001. (212)807–7888. FAX: (212)-727–8452. Rabbi Mark Dratch. Quarterly. Rabbinical Council of America.

REFORM JUDAISM (1972; formerly DIMENSIONS IN AMERICAN JUDAISM). 838 Fifth Ave., NYC, 10021. (212)249–0100. Aron Hirt-Manheimer. Quarterly. Union of American Hebrew Congregations.

THE REPORTER (1972). 500 Clubhouse Rd., Vestal, 13850. (607)724–2360. FAX: (607)-724–2311. Marc S. Goldberg. Weekly. Jewish Federation of Broome County, Inc.

THE REPORTER (1966; formerly WOMEN'S AMERICAN ORT REPORTER). 315 Park Ave. S., NYC, 10010. (212)505–7700. FAX: (212)674–3057. Dana B. Asher. Quarterly. Women's American ORT, Inc.

RESPONSE (1967). 27 W. 20 St., 9th fl., NYC, 10011–3707. (212)675–1168. FAX: (212)-929–3459. Yigal Schleifer, Adam Margolis. Quarterly. Response Magazine Inc.

SH'MA (1970). c/o CLAL, 99 Park Ave., Suite S-300, NYC, 10016. (212)867–8888. FAX: (212)867–8853. Sr. Eds. Eugene B. Borowitz, Irving Greenberg, Harold M. Schulweis; Ed. Nina Beth Cardin. Biweekly (except June, July, Aug.). CLAL–The National Jewish Center for Learning and Leadership.

SULLIVAN/ULSTER JEWISH STAR (1991). PO Box 776 (2793 Route 209 South), Wurtsboro, 12790. (914)888–4680. FAX: (914)888–2209. Edith Schapiro. Monthly. Jewish Focus, Inc.

SYNAGOGUE LIGHT AND KOSHER LIFE (1933). 47 Beekman St., NYC, 10038. (212)227–7800. Rabbi Meyer Hager. Quarterly. The Kosher Food Institute.

TIKKUN: A BIMONTHLY JEWISH CRITIQUE OF POLITICS, CULTURE & SOCIETY (1986). 251 W. 100 St., NYC, 10025. (212)864–4110. FAX: (212)864–4137. Michael Lerner. Bimonthly. Institute for Labor & Mental Health.

TRADITION (1958). 275 Seventh Ave., NYC, 10001. (212)807–7888. Rabbi Emanuel Feldman. Quarterly. Rabbinical Council of America.

TRENDS (1982). 730 Broadway, NYC, 10003. (212)529–2000. FAX: (212)529–2009. Leora W. Isaacs. Irregularly. Jewish Education Service of North America, Inc.

UNITED SYNAGOGUE REVIEW (1943). 155 Fifth Ave., NYC, 10010. (212)533–7800. FAX: (212)353–9439. Lois Goldrich. Biannually. United Synagogue of Conservative Judaism.

UNSER TSAIT (1941). 25 E. 21 St., 3rd fl., NYC, 10010. (212)475–0055. Mitchell Lokiec. Monthly. Yiddish. Jewish Labor Bund.

VOICE OF THE DUTCHESS JEWISH COMMUNITY (1990). 110 Grand Ave., Poughkeepsie, 12603. (914)471–9811. Dena Hirsh. Monthly. Jewish Federation of Dutchess County, Inc.

WOMEN'S LEAGUE OUTLOOK (1930). 48 E. 74 St., NYC, 10021. (212)628–1600. FAX: (212)772–3507. Janis Sherman Popp. Quarterly. Women's League for Conservative Judaism.

WORKMEN'S CIRCLE CALL. *See* THE CALL

YEARBOOK OF THE CENTRAL CONFERENCE OF AMERICAN RABBIS (1890). 192 Lexington Ave., NYC, 10016. (212)684–4990. FAX: (212)689–1649. Rabbi Elliot L. Stevens. Annually. Central Conference of American Rabbis.

YIDDISH (1973). Queens College, NSF 350, 65–30 Kissena Blvd., Flushing, 11367. (718)997–3622. Joseph C. Landis. Quarterly. Queens College Press.

DI YIDDISHE HEIM (1958). 770 Eastern Pkwy., Brooklyn, 11213. (718)493–9250. Rachel Altein. Quarterly. English-Yiddish. Neshei Ub'nos Chabad-Lubavitch Women's Organization.

YIDDISHE KULTUR (1938). 1133 Broadway, Rm. 1019, NYC, 10010. (212)243–1304. Itche Goldberg. Bimonthly. Yiddish. Yiddisher Kultur Farband, Inc.—YKUF.

YIDDISHE SHPRAKH (1941). 1048 Fifth Ave., NYC, 10028. (212)231–7905. Dr. Mordkhe Schaechter. Irregularly. Yiddish. YIVO Institute for Jewish Research, Inc.

DOS YIDDISHE VORT (1953). 84 William St., NYC, 10038. (212)797–9000. Joseph Friedenson. Monthly. Yiddish. Agudath Israel of America.

YIDDISHER KEMFER (1900). 275 Seventh Ave., NYC, 10001. (212)675–7808. FAX: (212) 675–7685. Mordechai Strigler. Fortnightly. Yiddish. Labor Zionist Letters.

DER YIDDISHER VEG (1981). 1274 49th St., Suite 1974, Brooklyn, 11219. (718)435–9474. FAX: (718)438–1263. Meir Dov Grosz. Weekly. Yiddish. Archives of Chasidai Belz.

YIVO ANNUAL (1946). 1048 Fifth Ave., NYC, 10028. (212)535–6700. FAX: (212)-734–1062. Deborah Dash Moore. Annually. YIVO Institute for Jewish Research, Inc.

YIVO BLETER (1931). 1048 Fifth Ave., NYC, 10028. (212)535–6700. David E. Fishman. Biannually. Yiddish. YIVO Institute for Jewish Research, Inc.

YOUNG ISRAEL VIEWPOINT (1952). 3 W. 16 St., NYC, 10011. (212)929–1525. FAX: (212)727–9526. Tovah Holzer. Quarterly. National Council of Young Israel.

YOUNG JUDAEAN (1910). 50 W. 58 St., NYC, 10019. (212)303–4577. FAX: (212)-303–4572. Claudia Herman. Three times a year between Sept. and June. Hadassah Zionist Youth Commission.

YUGNTRUF: YIDDISH YOUTH MAGAZINE (1964). 200 W. 72 St., Suite 40, NYC, 10023. (212)787–6675. FAX: (212)769–2820. David S. Braun. Three times a year. Yiddish. Yugntruf Youth for Yiddish.

ZUKUNFT (THE FUTURE) (1892). 25 E. 21 St., NYC, 10010. (212)505–8040. Yonia Fain. Bimonthly. Yiddish. Congress for Jewish Culture.

NORTH CAROLINA

AMERICAN JEWISH TIMES OUTLOOK (1934; reorg. 1950). PO Box 33218, Charlotte, 28233–3218. (704)372–3296. FAX : (704)-377–9237. Geri Zhiss. Monthly. The Blumenthal Foundation.

CHARLOTTE JEWISH NEWS (1978). 5007 Providence Rd., Charlotte, 28226. (704) 366–5007, ext. 268. FAX: (704) 365–4507. Rita Mond. Monthly (except July). Jewish Federation of Greater Charlotte.

OHIO

AKRON JEWISH NEWS (1929). 750 White Pond Drive, Akron, 44320. (216)869–2424. FAX: (216)867–8498. Toby Liberman. Fortnightly. Akron Jewish Community Federation.

AMERICAN ISRAELITE (1854). 906 Main St., Rm. 508, Cincinnati, 45202. (513)621–3145. FAX: (513)621–3744. Phyllis R. Singer. Weekly.

AMERICAN JEWISH ARCHIVES (1948). 3101 Clifton Ave., Cincinnati, 45220. (513)221–1875. Jacob R. Marcus, Abraham J. Peck. Semiannually. American Jewish Archives of Hebrew Union College–Jewish Institute of Religion.

CLEVELAND JEWISH NEWS (1964). 3645 Warrensville Center Rd., Suite 230, Cleveland, 44122. (216)991–8300. FAX: (216)-991–9556. Cynthia Dettelbach. Weekly. Cleveland Jewish News Publication Co.

DAYTON JEWISH CHRONICLE (1961). 6929 N. Main St., Dayton, 45415. (513)278–0783. Leslie Cohen Zukowsky. Weekly.

INDEX TO JEWISH PERIODICALS (1963). PO Box 18570, Cleveland Hts., 44118. (216)-381–4846. Lenore Pfeffer Koppel. Annually.

JEWISH JOURNAL (1987). PO Box 449, Youngstown, 44501. (216)744–7902. FAX: (216)746–7926. Sherry Weinblatt. Biweekly (except July/Aug.). Youngstown Area Jewish Federation.

OHIO JEWISH CHRONICLE (1922). 2862 Johnstown Rd., Columbus, 43219. (614)-337–2055. FAX: (614)337–2059. Judith Franklin. Weekly.

STARK JEWISH NEWS (1920). 2631 Harvard Ave. NW, Canton, 44709. (216)452–6444. FAX: (216)452–4487. Adele Gelb. Monthly. Canton Jewish Community Federation.

STUDIES IN BIBLIOGRAPHY AND BOOKLORE (1953). 3101 Clifton Ave., Cincinnati, 45220. (513)221–1875. FAX: (513)221–0519. Herbert C. Zafren. Irregularly. English-Hebrew-German. Library of Hebrew Union College–Jewish Institute of Religion.

TOLEDO JEWISH NEWS (1951). 6505 Sylvania Ave., Sylvania, 43560. (419)885–4461. FAX: (419)885–3207. Laurie Cohen. Monthly. Jewish Federation of Greater Toledo.

OKLAHOMA

TULSA JEWISH REVIEW (1930). 2021 E. 71 St., Tulsa, 74136. (918)495–1100. FAX: (918)495–1220. Ed Ulrich. Monthly. Jewish Federation of Tulsa.

OREGON

JEWISH REVIEW (1959). 6800 SW Beaverton-Hillsdale Hwy., Suite C, Portland, 97210. (503) 292–4913. FAX: (503)292–8965. Paul Haist. Fortnightly. Jewish Federation of Portland.

PENNSYLVANIA

COMMUNITY REVIEW (1925). 100 Vaughn St., Harrisburg, 17110. (717)236–9555. FAX: (717)236–8104. Carol L. Cohen. Fortnightly. United Jewish Community of Greater Harrisburg.

JEWISH CHRONICLE OF PITTSBURGH (1962). 5600 Baum Blvd., Pittsburgh, 15206. (412)687–1000. FAX: (412)687–5119. Joel Roteman. Weekly. Pittsburgh Jewish Publication and Education Foundation.

JEWISH EXPONENT (1887). 226 S. 16 St., Philadelphia, 19102. (215)893–5700. FAX: (215)546–3957. Albert Erlick. Weekly. Jewish Federation of Greater Philadelphia.

JEWISH POST (1988). 301 Oxford Valley Rd., Yardley, 19067. (215)321–3443. FAX: (215)321–7245. Brenda Lesley Segal. Bimonthly.

JEWISH QUARTERLY REVIEW (1910). 420 Walnut St., Philadelphia, 19106. (215)238–1290. FAX: (215)238–1540. Leon Nemoy, David M. Goldenberg. Quarterly. Center for Judaic Studies, University of Pennsylvania.

JEWISH TIMES (1976). 103A Tomlinson Rd., Huntingdon Valley, 19006. (215)938–1177. FAX: (215)938–0692. Matthew Schuman. Weekly. Jewish Federation of Greater Philadelphia.

NEW MENORAH (1978). 7318 Germantown Ave., Philadelphia, 19119–1793. (215)-242–4074. FAX: (215)247–9703. Dr. Arthur Waskow. Quarterly. ALEPH: Alliance for Jewish Renewal.

RECONSTRUCTIONISM TODAY (1993). Church Rd. and Greenwood Ave., Wyncote, 19095. (215)887–1988. FAX: (215)-877–5348. Larry Bush. Quarterly. Federation of Reconstructionist Congregations and Havurot.

RECONSTRUCTIONIST (1934). Church Rd. and Greenwood Ave., Wyncote, 19095. (215)887–1988. FAX: (215)887–5348. Dr. Herbert Levine. Annually. Federation of Reconstructionist Congregations and Havurot.

RHODE ISLAND

JEWISH VOICE. 130 Sessions St., Providence, 02906. (401)421–4111. FAX: (401)331–7961. Jane S. Sprague. Monthly. Jewish Federation of Rhode Island.

RHODE ISLAND JEWISH HISTORICAL NOTES (1954). 130 Sessions St., Providence, 02906. (401)331–1360. Judith Weiss Cohen. Annually. Rhode Island Jewish Historical Association.

SOUTH CAROLINA

CHARLESTON JEWISH JOURNAL. 1645 Wallenberg Blvd., Charleston, 29407. (803)-571–6565. FAX: (803)556–7304. Eileen F. Chepenik. Monthly. Charleston Jewish Federation.

TENNESSEE

HEBREW WATCHMAN (1925). 4646 Poplar Ave., Suite 232, Memphis, 38117. (901)-763–2215. Herman I. Goldberger. Weekly.

OBSERVER (1934). 801 Percy Warner Blvd., Nashville, 37205. (615)356–3242. FAX: (615)352–0056. Judith A. Saks. Biweekly (except July). Jewish Federation of Nashville.

SHOFAR. PO Box 8947, Chattanooga, 37414. (615)894–1317. FAX: (615)894–1319. Marlene Solomon. Monthly. Jewish Community Federation of Greater Chattanooga.

TEXAS

JEWISH HERALD-VOICE (1908). PO Box 153, Houston, 77001–0153. (713)630–0391. FAX: (713)630–0404. Jeanne Samuels. Weekly.

JEWISH JOURNAL OF SAN ANTONIO (1973). 8434 Ahern, San Antonio, 78216. (210)-341–8234. FAX: (210)341–2842. Layney

Cohen Berkus. Monthly (11 issues). Jewish Federation of San Antonio. TEXAS JEWISH POST (1947). 3120 S. Expressway, Fort Worth, 76110. (817)927–2831. FAX: (817)429–0840. 11333 N. Central Expressway, Dallas, 75243. (214)-692–7283. FAX: (214)692–7285. Jimmy Wisch. Weekly.

VIRGINIA

RENEWAL MAGAZINE (1984). 7300 Newport Ave., Norfolk, 23505. (804)489–8040. FAX: (804)489–8230. Reba Karp. Quarterly. United Jewish Federation of Tidewater.

UJF VIRGINIA NEWS (1959). 7300 Newport Ave., Norfolk, 23505. (804)489–8040. FAX: (804) 489–8230. Reba Karp. 21 issues yearly. United Jewish Federation of Tidewater.

WASHINGTON

JEWISH TRANSCRIPT (1924). 2031 Third Ave., Suite 200, Seattle, 98121. (206)441–4553. FAX: (206)441–2736. Craig Degginger. Fortnightly. Jewish Federation of Greater Seattle.

WISCONSIN

WISCONSIN JEWISH CHRONICLE (1921). 1360 N. Prospect Ave., Milwaukee, 53202. (414)271–2992. FAX: (414)271–0487. Andrew Muchin. Weekly. Milwaukee Jewish Federation.

INDEXES

INDEX TO JEWISH PERIODICALS (1963). PO Box 18570, Cleveland Hts., OH 44118. (216)381–4846. FAX: (216)381–4321. Lenore Pfeffer Koppel. Annually.

NEWS SYNDICATES

JEWISH TELEGRAPHIC AGENCY, INC. (1917). 330 Seventh Ave., 11th fl., NYC., 10001–5010. (212)643–1890. FAX: (212)-643–8498. Mark Joffe, Rifka Rosenwein. Daily.

CANADA

CANADIAN JEWISH HERALD (1977). 17 Anselme Lavigne, Dollard des Ormeaux, PQ H9A 1N3. (514)684–7667. Dan Nimrod. FAX: (514)737–7636. Irregularly. Dawn Publishing Co., Ltd.

CANADIAN JEWISH NEWS (1971). 10 Gateway Blvd., #420, Don Mills, ONT M3C 3A1. (416)422–2331. FAX: (416)422–3790 (Adv.); (416)424–1886 (Ed.). Patricia Rucker. Weekly. English and French.

CANADIAN JEWISH OUTLOOK (1963). 6184 Ash St., #3, Vancouver, BC V5Z 3G9. (604)324–5101. FAX: (604)325–2470. Henry M. Rosenthal. Monthly. Canadian Jewish Outlook Society.

CANADIAN ZIONIST (1934). 5250 Decarie Blvd., Suite 550, Montreal, PQ H3X 2H9. (514)486–9526. FAX: (514)483–6392. Five times a year. English, Hebrew, French. Canadian Zionist Federation.

DIALOGUE (1988). 1590 Dr. Penfield Ave., Montreal, PQ H3G 1C5. (514)931–7531. FAX: (514)931–3281. Rebecca Rosenberg. Semiannually. French-English. Canadian Jewish Congress, Quebec Region.

JEWISH POST & NEWS (1987). 117 Hutchings St., Winnipeg, MAN R2X 2V4. (204)694–3332. Matt Bellan. Weekly.

JEWISH STANDARD (1930). 77 Mowat Ave., Suite 016, Toronto, ONT M6K 3E3. (416)-537–2696. FAX: (416)789–3872. Julius Hayman. Fortnightly.

JEWISH WESTERN BULLETIN (1930). 3268 Heather St., Vancouver, BC V5Z 3K5. (604)879–6575. FAX: (604)879–6573. Samuel Kaplan. Weekly.

JOURNAL OF PSYCHOLOGY AND JUDAISM (1976). 1747 Featherston Dr., Ottawa, ONT K1H 6P4. (613)731–9119. Reuven P. Bulka. Quarterly. Center for the Study of Psychology and Judaism.

OTTAWA JEWISH BULLETIN (1954). 151 Chapel St., Ottawa, ONT K1N 7Y2. (613)-789–7306. FAX: (613)789–4593. Myra Aronson. Biweekly. Jewish Community Council of Ottawa.

WINDSOR JEWISH FEDERATION (1942). 1641 Ouellette Ave., Windsor, ONT N8X 1K9. (519)973–1772. FAX: (519)973–1774. Dr. Allen Juris. Quarterly. Windsor Jewish Federation.

Obituaries: United States[1]

ABEL, SHERRY GOLDMAN, editor; b. Chicago, Ill., (?), 1904; d. NYC, May 28, 1992. Educ.: U. Chicago. Writer, Universal Jewish Encyclopedia, 1942–43; ed.: Overseas News Agency, 1943–44; Schocken Books (free-lance), 1947–50; ed. asst., *Commentary* magazine, 1950–51; asst. ed., 1951–1959; mng. ed., 1960–63.

ADLER, STELLA, actress, teacher; b. NYC, Feb. 10, 1902; d. Los Angeles, Calif., Dec. 21, 1992. Mem. leading Yiddish theatrical family in the golden age of Yiddish theater, she (and her brother Luther) successfully bridged the Yiddish and English worlds. Made stage debut at age 4 in her father Jacob Adler's Yiddish Art Company; learned Stanislavsky acting techniques at the Amer. Laboratory Theatre Sch. in the 1920s; mem. Lee Strasberg's Group Theatre, 1930s; acted in Hollywood films and Broadway productions and directed a number of plays; in 1949 founded acting school that became the Stella Adler Conservatory of Acting, where she taught her interpretation of "method" acting to Marlon Brando, Warren Beatty, Robert DeNiro, and many others, into the late 1980s. Au: *Stella Adler on Acting*.

APPLEMAN, NATHAN, business exec., philanthropist; b. Marietta, Ohio, May 30, 1904; d. Palm Beach, Fla., Nov. 26, 1992. Educ.: Wharton School–U. Penna. Pres., Central Petroleum Co., 1933 on. Bd. mem.: Fed. Jewish Philanthropies of N.Y.; Montefiore Hosp.; Baron de Hirsch Fund; Palm Beach, Fla. United Way, Civic Assn.,

Hospice Bd., Preservation Fund; adv. bd. mem. St. Mary's Hosp., Palm Beach. Hon. v.p., mem. bd. govs., bd. trustees, and natl. affairs comm., Amer. Jewish Com., which named the Nathan Appleman Inst. for the Advancement of Christian-Jewish Understanding in his honor.

ASIMOV, ISAAC, writer, scientist; b. Soviet Union, Jan. 2, 1920; d. NYC, Apr. 6, 1992; in U.S. since 1923. Educ.: Columbia U. (BA, MA, PhD). Taught biochemistry, Boston U. School of Medicine, 1948–58. Sold first science fiction-story at age 18; first book, *Pebble in the Sky*, a science-fiction novel, published 1950. Subsequently published nearly 500 books, from children's works to college texts to expository texts on science for lay readers, to works on Bible, Shakespeare, history, and humor. Noteworthy works include: *I, Robot* (1950); *Foundation* trilogy (1951–53); *The Gods Themselves* (1972); *Murder at the A.B.A.* (1976); *Foundation's Edge* (1982); 2 vols. of an autobiog.: *In Memory Yet Green* (1979) and *In Joy Still Felt* (1980); *The Genetic Code* (1963); *Asimov's Guide to the Bible* (1968); and *Asimov's New Guide to Science* (1984). Recipient: 5 Hugo Awards; several awards from the Science Fiction Writers of Amer.; Amer. Chemical Soc. Award; Amer. Assoc. for the Advancement of Science–Westinghouse Science Writing Award.

AYALTI, HANAN J. (CHONEL KLENBORT), author; b. Soposkien, Russia, (?), 1911; d. NYC, Jan. 21, 1992; in U.S. since 1946.

---

[1]Including American Jews who died between January 1 and December 31, 1992.

Moved to Palestine, 1929, then to Paris and, during WWII, to Uruguay. Some of his Yiddish stories and novels were serialized in the *Forward*; his stories appeared in *Commentary*, *Midstream*, and other pubs. Ed.: *Yiddish Proverbs*; au.: *The Hotel That Doesn't Exist*, *No Escape from Brooklyn*, and *Father and Son*.

BEE (BIRZOWSKI), NOAH, political cartoonist, graphic artist; b. Warsaw, Poland, Sept. 25, 1916; d. Bethesda, Md., Oct. 4, 1992; in U.S. since 1943. Lived in Palestine, 1933–43; joined Irgun and later Haganah; drew political cartoons and caricatures for Hebrew dailies and *Palestine Post*. Illustrator, art dir., McGraw-Hill Publications, 1943–76; political cartoonist, Jewish Telegraphic Agency, 1959–92; designer of new Jewish National Fund blue box after estab. of Israel and of Israel's first currency. Au.: three collections of cartoons: *In Spite of Everything*, *The Impossible Takes a Little Longer*, and *Israel at 40–Years of Triumph, Trials and Errors*.

BERKOVITS, ELIEZER, rabbi, theologian; b. Oradea (Nagyvarad), Transylvania, (?), 1908; d. Jerusalem, Israel, Aug. 20, 1992; in U.S. since 1950. Educ.: Hilsdesheimer Rabbinical Sem. (ord.). Rabbi: Berlin, Ger., 1934–39; Leeds, Eng., 1940–46; Sydney, Aust., 1946–1950; Boston, Mass., 1950–58. Prof., philosophy, Hebrew Theological Coll. (Skokie Yeshivah), Chicago, 1958–1973, when he retired and moved to Jerusalem. Wrote extensively about the tensions between secular Jewish nationalism and Jewish religious tradition and the theological implications of the Holocaust, among other issues. Au.: *Was ist der Talmud* (1938); *Towards a Historic Judaism* (1943); *Between Yesterday and Tomorrow* (1945), a collection of sermons; *Judaism: Fossil or Ferment* (1956); *God, Man and History* (1959); *Jewish Critique of the Philosophy of Martin Buber* (1962); *Faith After the Holocaust* (1973); *Major Themes in Modern Philosophies of Judaism* (1974); *Crisis and Faith* (1975); *With God in Hell: Judaism in the Ghettos and Deathcamps* (1979); *Not in Heaven: The Nature and Function of Halakha* (1983); *The Jewish Woman in Time and Torah* (1990); and numerous articles.

BLOCK, JOSEPH L., business exec., civic leader; b. Chicago, Ill., Oct. 6, 1902; d. Chicago, Ill., Nov. 17, 1992. Joined Inland Steel Co., which his grandfather had helped found and which his father headed (1919–1940), in 1922 as a trainee; during WWII, served as dollar-a-year exec. of the steel div. of the War Production Bd. Held various positions at Inland Steel, 1927–71, incl. pres., 1953–59; CEO, chmn., 1959–1967; chmn. exec. com., 1967–71, hon. dir. thereafter. Pres., Jewish Fed. of Chicago, 1947–50, dir. 1931–52. Dir., hon. v.p., Amer. Iron and Steel Inst.; pres., Chicago Community Fund, 1961–63, dir. 1951–77; dir.: Chicago Bd. of Trade, Commonwealth Edison Co., 1st Natl. Bank, Chicago. Mem.: President's Adv. Com. on Labor-Mgmt. Policy, 1961–66; Adv. Comm. on Labor Mgmt. Policy for Ill. Pub. Employees; Ill. Bd. Higher Educ.; mem. and chmn., welfare services com., Cook County Dept. Public Aid; chmn., dir., Natl. Merit Scholarship Corp.; hon. trustee, Museum of Science and Industry, and other activities. Recipient: numerous awards, incl. silver plaque, Natl. Conf. Christians and Jews, Chicago Press Club Man of the Year, Catholic Council on Working Life Award; hon. degrees from St. Josephs Coll., Bradley U., Roosevelt Coll., Northwestern U., U. Illinois, and others.

BLOOM, ALLAN, professor; b. Indianapolis, Ind., Sept. 14, 1930; d. Chicago, Ill., Oct. 7, 1992. Educ.: U. Chicago (BA, MA, PhD), U. Paris, Heidelberg U. Reader, U. Paris, 1954–55; lect., U. Chicago, 1955–60; visiting asst. prof., poli. sci., Yale U., 1962–63; asst. and assoc. prof., govt., Cornell U., 1963–70; prof., poli. sci., U. Toronto, 1970–79; prof., poli. phil. and codir., Olin Center for Inquiry into the Theory and Practice of Democracy, U. Chicago, 1979 on. Author of scholarly works and transl. of Plato's *Republic* and Jean-Jacques Rousseau's *Emile*; his *The Closing of the American Mind: How Higher Education Has Failed Democracy and Impoverished the Souls of Today's Students* (1987), a conservative critique of Amer. universities and intellectual life, became a best-seller. Au. (in addition to the above): *Shakespeare's Politics* (1964); *Giants and Dwarfs* (essays, 1990); *Love and Friendship* (1993); ed.: *Confronting the Constitution* (1990).

BOHNEN, ELI A., rabbi; b. Toronto, Canada, Sept. 16, 1909; d. Providence, R.I., Dec. 1, 1992; in U.S. since 1931. Educ.: U. Toronto; Jewish Theol. Sem. of Amer. (ord., DHL). Chaplain, U.S. Army,

WWII; entered Dachau concentration camp with the 42nd Infantry (Rainbow Div.) and worked with DPs after the war. Rabbi: Cong. Adath Jeshurun, Philadelphia, Pa., 1935–39; Temple Emanu-El, Buffalo, N.Y., 1939–48; Temple Emanu-El, Providence, R.I., 1948–74. Pres., Rabbinical Assembly, 1966–68; chmn. its Com. on Law and Standards, Joint Placement Comm., and Ethics Com.; pres., R.I. Bd. of Rabbis; dir.: Jewish Fed. of R.I., United Fund, Council Community Services, Jewish Community Center, Providence Hebrew Day School; chmn.: Israel Bond campaign; State of R.I. Special Com. on Jurisprudence of the Future. Recipient: Bronze Star and Commendation Ribbon; Natl. Bronze Brotherhood Award, Natl. Conf. Christians and Jews; hon. degrees from JTS, U. Rhode Island, Brown U., and Roger Williams Coll., and other honors.

BUTTENWIESER, BENJAMIN J., banker, civic leader; b. NYC, Oct. 22, 1900; d. NYC, Dec. 31, 1991. Educ.: Columbia U. Served U.S. Navy, WWII. Associated with Kuhn, Loeb & Co. beginning 1918, genl. partner, 1932–49, limited partner, 1952–77. Mem. natl. bank code com., Natl. Recovery Act, 1933; asst. to U.S. High Comm. for Germany, 1949–52; dir.: Revlon Inc., Benrus Watch Co., Tishman Realty and Construction, Venus Pen & Pencil Co., and other cos.; gov., Investment Bankers Assoc.; trustee: Fed. of Jewish Philanthropies, 1938–40; Lenox Hill Hosp., Columbia U., Fisk U., N.Y. Philharmonic, and other insts.

CARNOVSKY, MORRIS, actor; b. St. Louis, Mo., Sept. 5, 1897; d. Easton, Conn., Aug. 12, 1992. Educ.: Washington U. (Phi Beta Kappa). First professional appearances in Boston repertory theater; New York debut in 1922 in Provincetown Playhouse's production of Sholem Asch's God of Vengeance; mem. New York Theatre Guild, 1920s; cofounder of politically oriented Group Theater, 1930s; in Los Angeles, 1940s, became a leading mem. of Actors' Lab and performed in movies, incl. Edge of Darkness and Rhapsody in Blue; blacklisted by Hollywood in early 1950s, after House Un-American Activities Com. charged him with Communist activity; returned to N.Y.; had featured role in off-Broadway production of The World of Sholem Aleichem, 1953–55; joined American Shakespeare Festival in Stratford,

Conn., in 1956, where he remained for 21 years, giving his most acclaimed performances as Shylock in The Merchant of Venice and the title role in King Lear. In later years, took on directing and teaching assignments, incl. adj. prof. at Brandeis U. Elected to Theatre Hall of Fame, 1979.

COHEN, SAUL Z., attorney, philanthropist; b. Rochester, N.Y., May 5, 1926; d. NYC, Jan. 23, 1992. Educ.: U. Rochester; Harvard U. (LLB). Atty., ABC, 1952–54; mem. Kaye, Scholer, Fierman, Hays & Handler, NYC, 1954–84, partner, 1959–84; partner, 61 Assoc., investments, 1984 on. Trustee, Sarah Lawrence Coll. Pres., Jewish Bd. Family and Children's Svc., 1977–81, v.-chmn. 1981–83, chmn. exec. com. 1983–86; v.p., UJA-Fed. of Greater NY, 1988 on, chmn. its capital campaign and governance com. and mem. various coms. Founder, with his wife, and bd. mem., S.H. and Helen R. Scheuer Family Found.

COOPERMAN, HASYE, poet, professor; b. NYC, Feb. 2, 1906; d. NYC, Apr. 8, 1992. Educ.: Hunter Coll., Columbia U. (MA, PhD). Lect., Amer., Yiddish, and compar. lit., New School for Social Research, NYC, for over 40 years; teacher of radio courses on Yiddish lit., Jewish People's U. of the Air. Mem.: Poetry Soc. of Amer., James Joyce Soc. of Amer. Au.: The Chase (poems), Men Walk the Earth, The Aesthetics of Stéphane Mallarmé, The Making of a Woman, and articles and poems in various pubs. Recipient: Natl. Award for Poetry, Amer. Lit. Assoc.

DALVEN, RAE, professor, translator; b. Preveza, Greece, Apr. 25, 1904; d. NYC, July 30, 1992; in U.S. since 1909. Educ.: Hunter Coll., NYU (PhD). Prof., Eng. lit., and dept. chmn., Ladycliff Coll., Highland Falls, N.Y. Transl. of modern Greek poets and historian of the Jews in Greece, esp. the community of pre-Sephardic Romaniotes in Ioannina. Pres., Amer. Soc. of Sephardic Studies and ed. its journal, Sephardic Scholar; bd. mem., Amer. Friends of the Jewish Museum in Greece. Transl.: Modern Greek Poetry, Complete Poems of Cavafy, The Fourth Dimension (Yannis Ritsos), and others. Au.: The Jews of Ioannina (1990); A Season in Hell, a play about Rimbaud and Verlaine; and Our Kind of People, an autobiographical play.

DIAMOND, JOSEPH, educator, communal worker; b. Ukraine, Nov. 1, 1905; d. Miami, Fla., May 25, 1992; in U.S. since (?). Educ.: Clark U., Boston Hebrew Coll.; Dropsie Coll. (PhD). Principal: Ivriah Schl., Worcester, Mass., 1926–31 and 1935–39; Phila. Hebrew Schl., 1931–35; natl. dir., League for Labor Palestine, 1939–41; educ. dir., Minneapolis, Minn., Talmud Torah, 1941–44; exec. dir.: Rochester, N.Y. Jewish Educ. Assoc., 1944–49 (where he founded Hillel Day School); Bureau of Jewish Educ., Toronto, Can., 1949–69 (where he founded Midrasha L'morim and co-founded United Syn. Day Sch.). Pres., Natl. Council for Jewish Educ., 1961–63.

DIMONT, MAX I., author, lecturer; b. Helsinki, Finland, Aug. 12, 1912; d. St. Louis, Mo., Mar. 25, 1992; in U.S. since 1929. Educ.: High school, Finland. Served U.S. Army Intell., WWII. Ed., house organ, and dir. employee relations, Edison Bros. Stores, 1945–76. Au.: *Jews, God and History* (1963; sold over 1.5 million copies in over 16 editions in at least 6 langs.); *The Indestructible Jews* (1970); *The Jews in America* (1978); *The Amazing Adventures of the Jewish People* (1984); *Appointment in Jerusalem: A Search for the Historical Jesus* (1991).

DINNERSTEIN, DOROTHY; professor; b. NYC, (?), 1923; d. Englewood, N.J., Dec. 17, 1992. Educ.: Brooklyn Coll., New School for Social Research (PhD). Faculty mem., psych., Brooklyn Coll., Bryn Mawr, Swarthmore, Bank St. Coll.; prof., psych., Rutgers U.–Newark, 1961–89. Au: *The Mermaid and the Minotaur*, regarded as a classic in women's studies, and numerous articles in psych. journals.

FORMAN, SIDNEY, professor; b. Brooklyn, N.Y., Mar. 17, 1915; d. Spring Valley, N.Y., Sept. 7, 1992. Educ.: CCNY, Columbia U. (PhD). Served U.S. Army, WWII. Archivist and library dir., U.S. Military Acad. (West Point), 1946–62; prof. of educ. and librarian, Teacher's Coll., Columbia U., 1962–77. Au.: *West Point: A History of the United States Military Academy* (1950).

FRIEDMAN, HAROLD, business executive, communal worker; b. Brooklyn, N.Y., Mar. 14, 1911; d. NYC, Feb. 28, 1992. Educ.: St. John's Coll., NYU. Stockbrokerage exec.: Sutro Bros. & Co., 1928–62, where he started as a teenager; Edward

Viner Co., 1962–67; Abraham & Co., 1967–74; Neuberger & Berman, 1972–89. Bd. mem.: UJA-Fed. of N.Y., several times chmn. its Wall St. div.; pres. and bd. mem.: HIAS, American ORT; bd. mem.: World ORT Union, Joint Distribution Com., Park Ave. Syn.; chmn., Overseas Services Com., Council of Jewish Feds. and Welfare Funds. Mem.: N.Y. Soc. CPAs; Amer. Inst. CPAs.

FRIEDMAN, RALPH, business executive, communal worker; b. NYC, Jan. 11, 1904; d. NYC, July 21, 1992. Educ.: School of Commerce, NYU. Sr. genl. partner, Friedman & Co.; mem. N.Y. Stock Exchange, 1932–48; chmn.: Metropolitan Body Co. (truck bodies) and Standard Milling Co. (flour and grain); dir. in charge of N. Amer. operations, Bank Leumi L'Israel, 1963–79; dir., Bank Leumi Trust of N.Y., 1968–79. Chmn., exec. bd., Amer. J. Com., 1964–66, chmn. its foreign affairs com., and initiator of discussions with Catholic Church leaders that led to establishment in 1962 of a program in interreligious studies at Pro Deo Univ. in Rome. Dir. or trustee: Conf. on Jewish Material Claims Against Germany; Montefiore Hosp., Hillside Hosp., Menninger Found., Yale U. School of Forestry and Environmental Studies. Mem.: Amer. Geog. Soc. and other conservation and scientific groups.

FRIEDMAN, THEODORE, rabbi; b. Stamford, Conn., Jan. 5, 1908; d. Jerusalem, Israel, Dec. 18, 1992. Educ.: CCNY; Columbia U. (MA, PhD); Jewish Theol. Sem. of Amer. (ord.). Rabbi: Temple Beth El, Woodcliff, N.J., 1931–41; Temple Beth David, Buffalo, N.Y., 1941–43; Jackson Heights Jewish Center, NYC, 1943–54; Cong. Beth El, Maplewood and the Oranges, N.J., 1954–70, when he retired and moved to Jerusalem. Pres., Rabbinical Assembly, 1962–64, and chmn. its Com. on Law and Standards; visiting prof., homiletics, JTS; visiting prof., Seminario Rabbinico Latino Americano in Buenos Aires, Argentina; mng. ed., *Judaism*, 1953–61; an ed. of *Encyclopedia Judaica*. In Israel: mem. exec., World Zionist Org.; mem. law com., Rabbinical Assembly Israel Region. Au.: a study of *Sefer Hachida*; over 200 articles and essays in English, Hebrew, and Spanish; co-ed., *Jewish Life in America*.

FROST, SHIMON, educator; b. Warsaw, Poland, Jan. 4, 1924; d. Jerusalem, Israel, Dec. 17, 1992; in U.S. since 1949. Educ.:

Sorbonne (MA); Teacher's Coll., Columbia U. (EdD). Principal, Hebrew schools: Burlington, Vt., 1953–58; Malverne, N.Y., 1958–63; exec. dir., Jewish Educators Assembly, 1961–63; headmaster, Brandeis School, Lawrence, N.Y., 1963–77; exec. v.-pres., Amer. Assoc. for Jewish Educ. (later JESNA), 1977–84, when he moved to Jerusalem; assoc. prof., Hebrew U., 1985–92, and David Yellin Teachers Coll., 1990–92. Pres., Jewish Educators Assembly; off. or dir.: Solomon Schechter Day School Assoc., United Syn. Comm. on Jewish Educ., Gordonia Assoc. and Korczak Assoc., Israel. Au.: numerous articles and chapters in books, in English, Hebrew, and Polish, on Jewish education and on Janusz Korczak, incl. the introd. to a Hebrew-Arabic collection of Korczak's writings (1991). Recipient: hon. doctorate, JTS.

GASTER, THEODOR HERZL, professor; b. London, Eng., July 21, 1906; d. Philadelphia, Pa., Feb. 3, 1992; in U.S. since 1939. Educ.: U. London (BA, classics; MA, archaeology; DLit.); Columbia U. (PhD). Curator, Near Eastern antiquities, Wellcome Mus., London, 1928–32, 1936–38; chief, Hebraic section, Library of Congress, 1944–48; prof., religion, Dropsie Coll., 1944–59; prof., ancient civilizations and religion, Fairleigh Dickinson U., 1959–66; prof., religion, Barnard Coll., 1966–72; visiting prof.: Yale, 1972–74; CCNY, 1974–75; lect.: NYU, Columbia U., U. Florida. Mem.: Amer. Oriental Soc., Archaeol. Inst. of Amer., Soc. for Bibl. Exegesis, Soc. for Old Testament Study, N.Y. Oriental Club; bd. mem., YIVO. Contrib.: *Encycl. Britannica, Interpreters Dicty. of the Bible, Standard Dicty. of Folklore, Mythology and Legend*. Au.: *The Dead Sea Scriptures in English Translation, Oldest Stories in the World, Festivals of the Jewish Year, The New Golden Bough; Thespis: Ritual Myth and Drama in the Ancient Near East; Myth, Legend and Custom in the Old Testament, The Holy and the Profane: Evolution of Jewish Folkways*, and other works. Recipient: 2 Guggenheim fellowships and 2 Fulbright professorships; hon. degrees from U. Vt., Kenyon Coll.

GORDIS, ROBERT, rabbi, scholar; b. Brooklyn, N.Y., Feb. 6, 1908; d. NYC, Jan. 3, 1992. Educ.: City Coll. N.Y.; Dropsie Coll. (PhD); Jewish Theol. Sem. of Amer. (ord., DD). Teacher: Hebrew Teachers Training Schl. for Girls, 1926–28; Yeshiva Coll., 1929–30. Rabbi: Temple Beth El, Rockaway Park, N.Y., 1931–68, where he established the first Conservative day school. At JTS: teacher, Coll. of Jewish Studies, 1931; lect., rabbinical schl., 1937–40; prof., biblical exegesis, 1940–60; Sem. prof., 1961–69; prof. Bible and phil. of relig., 1974–81. Adj. prof., religion, Columbia U., 1948–57; vis. prof., Union Theol. Sem., 1953–54; consult. and assoc., Center for Study Democratic Insts., Santa Barbara, Calif., 1960–79; prof., religion, Temple U., 1967–74; vis. prof., Hebrew U., 1970. Chmn.: Comm. on the Philosophy of Conservative Judaism, 1985–87; joint prayerbook comm. of Rabbinical Assembly and United Syn.; pres.: Rabbinical Assembly, Synagogue Council of Amer., Jewish Book Council; mem. exec. com., Natl. Hillel Comm. Assoc. ed., Bible, *Universal Jewish Encyclopedia*; mem. bd. eds. *Judaism*, 1942–68, and ed. 1969–1990. Au.: many articles in scholarly and popular journals; over 20 books, incl. *The Wisdom of Ecclesiastes* (1945); *Koheleth: The Man and His World* (1951); *The Song of Songs* (1954); *The Book of God and Man: A Study of Job* (1965); *Poets, Prophets and Sages: Essays in Biblical Interpretation* (1970); *Understanding Conservative Judaism* (1978); *Love and Sex–A Modern Jewish Perspective* (1978); and *The Dynamics of Jewish Law* (1991). Recipient: Fellow, Amer. Acad. for Jewish Research; Guggenheim fellowship; Natl. Jewish Book Award, 1979.

GRUENEWALD, MAX, rabbi, scholar; b. Koenighuette, Upper Silesia, Dec. 4, 1899; d. Millburn, N.J., Dec. 28, 1992; in U. S. since 1939. Educ.: U. Breslau (PhD), Jewish Theol. Sem. of Breslau (ord.). Rabbi: Liberal Syn. of Mannheim, Ger., 1925–38, and pres., Mannheim Jewish community; researcher, Jewish Theol. Sem. of Amer., 1939–1943; rabbi, Cong. B'nai Israel, Millburn, N.J., 1944–70. Cofounder, Leo Baeck Insts. of London, N.Y., and Jerusalem; internatl. pres. 1974–91; pres, LBI of N.Y., 1956 on. Pres., Amer. Fed. of Jews from Central Europe, 1952–62, which he co-founded in 1942; copres., Wurzweiler Found., 1954–85. Mem.: Rabbinical Assembly. Au.: *Here, There and Above* and articles in various journals. Recipient: hon. doctorates, Bar-Ilan U., JTS.

HAUSMAN, SAMUEL, business executive, communal worker; b. Bolechow, Austria,

Nov. 14, 1897; d. NYC, Aug. 13, 1992; in U.S. since 1907. Textile manuf.; pres., Weldon Mills; dir., chmn., Belding Hemingway; chmn., Belding Hausman Fabrics; Va Dying; dir. L.I. Lighting. An early fundraiser for the Amer. Palestine Com.; cofounder, UJA of Greater N.Y. and its hon. bd. chmn.; v.pres. natl. UJA; v.pres. and trustee, Fed. of Jewish Philanthropies, N.Y.; exec. v.pres., Beth Israel Medical Center; active in behalf of Hebrew U., Weizmann Inst., Technion, Soviet Jewry, Yeshiva U. Mem.: N.Y. State Comm. Against Discrimination, N.Y. State Manpower Adv. Council; trustee, SUNY.

KAGANOFF, NATHAN M., librarian, editor; b. Gaisin, Russia, Apr. 8, 1926; d. Boston, Mass., Feb. 4, 1992; in U.S. since 1932. Educ.: Northwestern U., Hebrew Theol. Coll. (ord.), Amer. U. (PhD, Amer. hist.). Chaplain, U.S. Army, WWII. Hebrew and Yiddish cataloguer, specialist in Judaica, Lib. of Congress, 1950–62; libr., Amer. Jewish Hist. Soc., 1962–68, libr.-ed. 1969 on; ed., *American Jewish History*, 1969–90. Pres., Research. Div., Assoc. of Jewish Libs., 1968–72; mem., Council of Archives and Research Libs. in Jewish Studies. Exhibition consult.: AJHS headquarters, various Jewish museums, hist. socs., and orgs. (incl. Diaspora Museum in Israel, Jewish Museum in NYC, and Smithsonian Inst. Traveling Exhibits). Au.: *Guide to America–Holy Land Studies*, 3 vols.; semi-annual "Judaica Americana" bibliogs. in *American Jewish History*; annual listing of Hebrew books printed in U.S. in *Jewish Book Annual*; articles in various periodicals and books. Ed.: *Turn to the South* (1979); *Solidarity and Kinship: Essays on American Zionism* (1980); *The Sang Collection of American Judaica* (1984); *Haym Salomon Papers*.

KAUFMAN, IRVING R., lawyer, judge; b. NYC, June 24, 1910; d. NYC, Feb. 1, 1992. Educ.: Fordham U. (LLB). Special asst., U.S. Atty., S. Dist. N.Y., 1935; Asst. U.S. Atty., 1936–40; private law practice, 1940–49; on special assignment in 1947 with Justice Dept., set up section to oversee lobbying; appointed judge: U.S. Dist. Court, S. Dist. N.Y., 1949; U.S. Court of Appeals, 2nd Circuit, 1961, chief judge, 1973–80, retired 1987 but remained on the bench. Although best known to the public as the judge who sentenced convicted spies Julius and Ethel Rosenberg to death in

1951, his long career was notable for landmark decisions in 1st Amendment, antitrust, and civil-rights cases, incl. the 1st desegregation order of a school in the North and decisions expanding freedom of the press. Chmn., President's Comm. on Organized Crime, mid-1980s; mem. exec. com., U.S. Judicial Conf., 1975–80, and mem. or chmn. various coms., 1966–83; trustee, Mt. Sinai Med. Center, Med. School, and Hosp., NYC. Recipient: Presidential Medal of Freedom, 1987; fellow, Inst. Jud. Admin.; and many awards from profl. assocs.

KIRSCHENBAUM, WALTER L., journalist, communal worker; b. NYC, Oct. 28, 1919; d. NYC, July 11, 1992. Educ.: NYU. Served U.S. Army, WWII. Public rel. contact, UJA, 1939–41; research dir., Amer. Jewish Cong., 1941–43, 1946–47; exec. dir., Bronx County div., Liberal party, 1947–51; public rel. dir., Jewish Labor Com., 1951–62; asst. comm.: NYC License Dept., 1962–66, Finance Dept., 1966–78; radio producer: Barry Gray show, 1952–62, Victor Riesel show, 1963–83; press officer, 1981 World Gathering of Jewish Holocaust Survivors. Associated with Workmen's Circle for more than 40 years, as ed. of its pubs., dir. public affairs, and other capacities. Mem.: exec. bd., Workmen's Circle; N.Y. Press Club, admin. com., Jewish Labor Com.; Community Bd. #3; UJA/FJP; Workers Defense League, Social Democrats USA, Overseas Press Club, Exec. Council, Lower East Side Neighborhood Assoc.; bd. dirs. Jewish Daily Forward/WEVD. Founder, 1989, Com. for the Revitalization of Yiddish and Yiddish Culture in the Soviet Union.

LERNER, MAX, author, professor; b. Minsk, Russia, Dec. 20, 1902; d. NYC, June 5, 1992; in U.S. since 1907. Educ.: Yale U., Washington U., Robert Brookings Grad. Sch. Econ. and Govt., Washington (PhD). Faculty mem., Sarah Lawrence Coll. and Wellesley Summer Inst., 1932–35; prof.: poli. sci., Williams Coll., 1938–43; Amer. civilization, Brandeis U., 1949–73, and chmn. Grad. Sch. Arts and Sciences, 1954–56. Ed.: *The Nation*, 1936–38; edit. dir., *PM* (short-lived left-of-center N.Y. daily), 1943–48; columnist, *New York Post* and L. A. Times Syndicate. Au.: *Ideas Are Weapons* (1939); *Ideas for the Ice Age: Studies in a Revolutionary Era* (1941); *It Is Later Than You Think* (1938, rev. ed. 1943); *The*

Mind and Faith of Justice Holmes (1943); *Actions and Passions* (1949); *America as a Civilization* (1957, rev. ed. 1987); *The Unfinished Country* (1958); *Book of American Symbols* (1960); *Wrestling with the Angel* (1990); and other works.

LONDON, PERRY, professor; b. Omaha, Neb., June 18, 1931; d. New Brunswick, N.J., June 19, 1992. Educ.: Yeshiva Coll., Columbia U. (PhD). Served U.S. Army Medical Svc., 1954–59. Asst. and assoc. prof., psych., U. Ill., 1959–63; assoc. prof. and prof., U. So. Calif., 1963–84; prof. and dean, Rutgers U. Grad. Sch. of Applied and Prof. Psych., 1988 on; faculty, Bell Labs, 1975–85; visiting prof.: Stanford U., Hebrew U.–Jerusalem, Tel Aviv U., Harvard Grad. Sch. Educ. Consult.: World Chair, United Israel Appeal, Jerusalem; Harvard U. Health Svcs.; Mass. Genl. Hosp.; Israel Air Force Aerospace Med. Center; Natl. Inst. of Alcoholism, Drug Abuse, and Mental Health; and others. Research interests incl. hypnosis, psychotherapy integration, altruistic behavior of Holocaust rescuers, and Jewish identity. Au.: over 150 articles and books, incl. *The Modes and Morals of Psychotherapy* (1964, rev. ed. 1986); *Behavior Control* (1969); *Beginning Psychology* (1975).

MAEIR, DAVID M., physician, hospital admin.; b. NYC, June 7, 1926; d. Jerusalem, Israel, Dec. 14, 1992. Educ.: Yeshiva U., U. Ottawa (MD). Served U.S. Air Force, 1954–56. Asst. in pathology, U. Rochester Medical Schl., 1956–58; instr., asst. prof., assoc. prof., Albert Einstein Coll. of Medicine, 1958–67; dir. genl. and chief physician, Shaare Zedek Medical Center, Jerusalem, 1968–82. Mem.: bd. govs., Bar-Ilan U.; bd. dirs., Jerusalem Trust for Aged; ed. bd., *Israel Journal of Medicine & Law* and *Assia, Journal of Medicine and Halacha*; Jerusalem City Councillor, 1978–83. Au.: scientific articles, articles on medical ethics, medicine and Halakhah, and hereditary diseases.

MEYER, ISIDORE S., rabbi, librarian; b. New London, Conn., Nov. 19, 1903; d. NYC, Sept. 8, 1992. Educ.: CCNY, Columbia U. (MA), Jewish Theol. Sem. of Amer. (ord.). Rabbi: Jewish Center, Bayshore, L.I., N.Y., 1937–43; Cong. Sons of Israel, Palisades Park, N.J., 1944–48. Librarian, Amer. Jewish Historical Soc., 1940–62; ed., *American Jewish History*, 1940–68;

coord., Jewish Hist. Comm.'s Civil War Centennial, 1960–65. Au.: *The Hebrew Exercises of Governor William Bradford* (1973) and many essays and studies. Ed.: *The Early History of Zionism in America* (1958); *The American Jew in the Civil War* (1962); co-ed.: *The Writing of American Jewish History* (1960); *Lee Max Friedman Collection: Letters of the Franks Family 1733–48* (1968). Recipient: hon. doctorate, JTS; 1st AJHS Lee M. Friedman Award.

MILSTEIN, NATHAN, violinist; b. Odessa, Russia, Dec. 31, 1903; d. London, Eng., Dec. 21, 1992; in U.S. since 1929. Began studying violin at age 4; debuted at age 10; gained admittance to St. Petersburg Conservatory (which limited entry of Jews) at age 12; left for Paris in 1926, where his career was launched as one of the world's great violinists; made U.S. debut in 1929; became U.S. citizen in 1942. A preeminent exponent of the 19th-cent. Romantic repertoire and interpreter of Bach, who was admired for making technique look and sound easy. Recipient: Kennedy Center Honors, 1987.

MOWSHOWITZ, ISRAEL, rabbi, communal worker; b. Olinka, Poland, July 11, 1914; d. NYC, June 30, 1992; in U.S. since 1929. Educ.: Yeshiva. U. (BA, ord.), Duke U. (MA, PhD). Rabbi: Beth El Cong., Durham, N.C., 1937–43; Beth Israel Cong., Omaha, Neb., 1943–49; Hillcrest Jewish Center, Flushing, N.Y., 1949–83. Asst. to N.Y. Gov. Mario Cuomo for community affairs, 1980s; founder and hon. pres., Internatl. Syn. (Kennedy Airport); pres., N.Y. Bd. of Rabbis; mem. natl. comm. and chmn., interreligious affairs com., ADL; mem. bd. dirs.: HIAS, Jewish Community Services of L.I., Greater N.Y. UJA, Fed. Jewish Philanthropies. Au.: *To Serve in Faithfulness, Fires to Warm Us, A Rabbi's Rovings*. Recipient: City of N.Y. Medallion; Federation Tzedek Award, ADL Torch of Liberty, hon. doctorates from Yeshiva U. and St. John's U., and many other honors.

ORLINSKY, HARRY M., professor; b. Owen Sound, Ont., Canada, Mar. 17, 1908; d. Baltimore, Md., Mar. 21, 1992; in U.S. since 1931. Educ.: U. Toronto, Dropsie Coll. (PhD). Fellow: Amer. Schools of Oriental Research and Hebrew U., Jerusalem, 1935–36; Johns Hopkins U., 1937–43; staff mem., Hebrew U. excavation at Ramat Gan, 1936. Prof., Bible and Jewish hist.,

Baltimore Hebrew Coll., 1936–44; prof., Bible, Hebrew Union Coll.–Jewish Inst. Religion, 1943–91; visiting prof.: Brandeis U., Hebrew U., Union Theol. Sem. N.Y. Pres.: Soc. Bibl. Lit., Amer. Friends of Isr. Exploration Soc. (1951–79), Internatl. Org. Septuagint and Cognate Studies (1969–75), Amer. Acad. for Jewish Research, Internatl. Org. for Masoretic Studies (1972–92). Mem., Soc. Scholars of Johns Hopkins U.; trustee, Amer. Schools for Oriental Research. Only Jewish mem. of coms. that produced 1952 Revised Standard Version of the Bible (for Protestant churches) and 1990 New Revised Standard Version. Ed.-in-chief, Jewish Publication Soc. transl. of *The Torah*, 1963; ed., *Israel Exploration Journal Reader*, 2 vols. (1982); cotransl.: *Rashi's Commentary on The Pentateuch: A Linear Translation*, 5 vols. (1949–50). Au: many works on the Bible and Dead Sea Scrolls, incl. *Ancient Israel* (1954, 2d ed. 1960); *Understanding the Bible Through History and Archaeology* (1969); and *Essays in Biblical and Jewish Culture and Bible Translation* (1973). Recipient: Fellow, Amer. Acad. for Jewish Research; Guggenheim fellowship; Centennial Award for Biblical Scholarship; HUC-JIR Dr. Bernard Heller Prize.

PARETZKY, PHILIP S., rabbi, professor; b. (?), Poland, Apr. 17, 1917; d. NYC, Oct. 4, 1992; in U.S. since ca. 1935. Educ.: Yeshivas Chofetz Chaim of Radin, Poland; Semikhah: Grodno, Warsaw, Yeshiva U.; Columbia U. (MA, Semitics), Fordham U. (LLB). Founding rabbi, Young Israel of Tremont, Bronx, N.Y., 1938–64; prof., Talmud (rosh yeshivah), and examiner of rabbinical candidates, Rabbi Isaac Elchanan Theol. Sem., Yeshiva U., 1963 on. Mem.: Rabbinical Council of Amer., Union of Orthodox Rabbis of USA and Canada. Au.: articles on Halakhah and law in various journals.

PICON, MOLLY, actress, singer; b. NYC, June 1, 1898; d. Lancaster, Pa., Apr. 6, 1992. First appeared on stage at age 5, in an amateur show; at age 15 joined a Yiddish-Engl. repertory co., playing Topsy in *Uncle Tom's Cabin*, then toured in vaudeville; around 1919 joined Yiddish troupe of Jacob Kalich, who became her husband, manager, and au. of many of her starring vehicles, incl. *Yankele* (1923), *Abi Gezunt* (1949), and *Mazel Tov Molly* (1950). With her mischievous eyes (*ganayvishe oygen*)

and vivacious delivery, was the darling of the Yiddish stage. Made worldwide vaudeville and concert tours in 1930s, performing in many langs., and starring in two Polish-made Yiddish films: *Yiddel Mitn Fiddel* and *Mamale*. First Engl.-speaking starring role in *Morning Star*, 1940; most notable success on Broadway in *Milk and Honey*, 1961–62. Appeared in Engl. theater and films in '60s and '70s, the latter incl. *Come Blow Your Horn* and *For Pete's Sake*. Returned to Yiddish stage in 1959 in *The Kosher Widow*. Au.: autobiog., *Molly!* (1960).

RAUH, JOSEPH L., JR., lawyer, political activist; b. Cincinnati, Ohio, Jan. 3, 1911; d. Washington, D.C., Sept. 3, 1992. Educ.: Harvard U. (BS, JD). Served US Army, WWII. Law secy. to Justices Cardozo and Frankfurter, U.S. Supreme Court, 1936–39; counsel, various govt. agencies, incl. Dept. of Labor, FCC, and Lend-Lease Admin., 1939–42; deputy U.S. housing expediter, 1946; private law practice, 1946 on. Mem. Democratic Central Com. and chmn., 1964–67; a founder in 1946 of Amers. for Democratic Action, and natl. chmn., 1955–57; mem. and genl. counsel, Leadership Conf. on Civil Rights; mem.: UAHC social action com., Amer. Jewish Congress, Temple Sinai of D.C. Strong supporter of NAACP, a leading champion of civil rights, civil liberties, and other liberal causes; in 1950s defended Lillian Hellman and Arthur Miller against charges of leftist subversion. Recipient: Disting. Service Star; Legion of Merit; Brandeis U. fellow; U. Penna. Law School hon. fellow; Franklin D. Roosevelt Four Freedoms Award; Hubert H. Humphrey Civil Rights Award; and many other honors.

ROSENFELD, ALVIN Z., journalist; b. St. Louis, Mo., June 8, 1919; d. Washington, D.C., Oct. 10, 1992. Educ.: Washington U., Columbia U. School of Journalism. Israel corresp. for *New York Post*, late 1940s, early 1950s; covered 1956 Sinai campaign for *N.Y. Herald Tribune* and Eichmann trial for that paper and NBC News; as NBC corresp., was severely wounded in Cyprus in 1964; NBC bureau chief, Madrid, 1965; returned to Jerusalem as NBC bureau chief in 1967, a few days before outbreak of Six Day War, when he was the only Western reporter to enter the Old City of Jerusalem with Israeli forces. Posted to Washington in 1971 as NBC State Dept.

corresp.; returned to Israel as special corresp. in 1973, covering Yom Kippur War for *Washington Post*. Dir., off. of public affairs, Smithsonian Inst., 1978–86; vicedir. for admin., U.S. Holocaust Memorial Museum, in its planning phase, 1986 on.

SELIKOFF, IRVING J., physician, researcher; b. Brooklyn, N.Y., Jan. 15, 1915; d. Ridgewood, N.J., May 20, 1992. Educ.: Columbia U.; U. Melbourne, Australia (MD). Affiliated with Mt. Sinai Hosp., NYC, and later its medical school, from 1941 until his death. A pioneer in environmental and occupational medicine, his proof of the health hazards of asbestos led to passage of worker safeguards and limits on its use. Consult.: World Health Org., Natl. Cancer Inst., and various agencies, businesses, and unions. Mem. National Cancer Soc. adv. bd.; Inst. Medicine, Natl. Acad. of Sciences; pres., Soc. for Occupational and Environmental Health; pres. and mem. bd. govs., N.Y. Acad. of Sciences; pres.: Collegium Ramazzini; N.Y. Acad. of Medicine; Amer. Thoracic Soc. Coau.: *Asbestos and Disease* (1978), *Health Hazards of Asbestos Exposure* (1979), ed. of other works, and au. numerous scientific articles. Recipient: Lasker Award in Medicine; Amer. Cancer Soc. Research Award; fellow: Amer. Public Health Assn., Amer. Coll. Chest Physicians; and other honors.

SHAPIRO, ALEXANDER M., rabbi; b. Brooklyn, N.Y., Nov. 29, 1929; d. Philadelphia, Pa., Dec. 10, 1992. Educ.: Brooklyn Coll., NYU (MA, history), Dropsie U. (PhD), Jewish Theol. Sem. of Amer. (ord.). Chaplain, U.S. Army, 1955–57. Dir., youth activities, Philadelphia, 1957–59; rabbi: Temple Beth Tikvah, Erdenheim, Pa., 1959–69; Germantown Jewish Center, Philadelphia, 1969–70; Cong. Oheb Shalom, S. Orange, N.J., 1972 until his death. Instr.: Temple U., 1968–70; U. of the Negev, David Yellin Teachers Sem., and Hebrew U., all in Israel, 1970–72. Pres., Rabbinical Assembly, 1985–87, the period in which women were admitted to membership, for which he had been an outspoken advocate. Also active in behalf of civil rights and Soviet Jewry. Au.: articles in *Tziyon*, *Encyclopedia Judaica*, *Conservative Judaism*, *Journal of Ecumenical Studies*, *United Synagogue Review*, and *Dictionary of the Middle Ages*; ed., *Festschrift* in honor of Dr. Louis Newman, *Lilmod Ul'lamed*.

SILBERT, THEODORE H., banker, communal worker; b. Boston, Mass., July 5, 1904; d. NYC, May 26, 1992. In 1933, with a borrowed stake of $1,000., founded Standard Capital Corp., which ultimately became Sterling Bancorp, parent co. of Sterling Natl. Bank. Bd. chmn. and CEO, Sterling Bancorp; chmn. bd. Sterling Natl. Bank and Trust Co. Trustee: Brandeis U., Bard Coll., Park Ave. Syn., NYC. Bd. mem.: UJA-Federation of N.Y., Jewish Theol. Sem. of Amer., Bronx Lebanon Hosp., Brookdale Center on Aging, Hebrew Free Loan Soc.; chmn.: Soc. of Founders, Einstein Coll. of Medicine; Jewish Assoc. for Services to the Aged; hon. v. chmn., ADL natl. comm.; also active in behalf of Israel Bonds, the Educ. Found. at the Fashion Inst. of Technology, Amer. Cancer Soc., and other causes.

SKLARE, MARSHALL, professor; b. Chicago, Ill., Oct. 21, 1921; d. Newton, Mass., Mar. 1, 1992. Educ.: Northwestern U., Chicago Coll. Jewish Studies, U. Chicago, Columbia U. (PhD). Dir., div. scientific research, Amer. Jewish Com., 1953–66; prof., soc., Wurzweiler and Ferkauf Schools, Yeshiva U., 1966–70; prof., contemporary Jewish studies and soc., Brandeis U., 1969–90; dir., Cohen Center for Modern Jewish Studies, 1980–86, and chmn. Near East and Judaic studies dept., 1982–83. Mem.: Assoc. for Jewish Studies (sec.-treas. 1979–83); Assoc. for the Sociol. Study of Jewry (pres. 1976–78); Amer. Jewish Hist. Soc. (library com., acad. council); edit. bd. mem.: *Contemporary Jewry*, *Modern Judaism*, *American Jewish History*. Consult., Memorial Found. for Jewish Culture; fellow, Center for Jewish Community Studies. Regarded as the "father of American Jewish sociology," he directed ground-breaking research in the '50s and '60s, including "The Riverton Study: How Jews Look at Themselves and Their Neighbors," and "The Lakeville Studies" (coauthor, vol. 1, with Joseph Greenblum, *Jewish Identity on the Suburban Frontier: A Study of Group Survival in the Open Society*, and, with Greenblum and Benjamin B. Ringer, *Not Quite at Home: How an American Jewish Community Lives with Itself and Its Neighbors*). Au. (in addition to the above): *Conservative Judaism: An American Religious Movement* (1955); *America's Jews* (1971); and many essays and articles. Ed.: *The Jews: Social Patterns of an American Group*

(1958); *Understanding American Jewry* (1982); *American Jews: A Reader* (1983). Recipient: sr. fellow, Natl. Endowment for the Humanities; fellow, Amer. Acad. for Jewish Research.

STARR, HARRY, attorney, foundation president; b. Vitebsk, Russia, (?), 1900; d. Gloversville, N.Y., July 25, 1992; in U.S. since 1906. Educ.: Harvard Coll., Harvard Law School. Upon graduation in 1924 became legal adv. to glove manuf. Lucius Littauer—both from Gloversville, both Harvard alumni, both interested in Jewish causes. Instrumental in organizing the Lucius N. Littauer Found. in 1929, which has helped fund Jewish studies depts. and Judaica book collections at Harvard and over 40 other colleges and universities. Served as its secy. 1929–44, pres. 1944–85, chmn. 1985–91, and hon. chmn. thereafter. Mem.: Harvard U. Overseers Com. for dept. of Middle Eastern civilizations; bd. mem.: Nathan Littauer Hosp. (Gloversville), N.Y. Fed. of Jewish Philanthropies, Amer. Jewish Hist. Soc., Beth Israel Hosp. (NYC), Dropsie Coll., Jewish Pub. Soc., Jewish Book Council, Amer. Jewish Com., Amer. Friends of Hebrew U., Touro Coll., and other orgs. Recipient: Harvard U. Medal.

STAVIS, MORTON (STAVISKY), attorney; b. NYC, May 27, 1915; d. Laguna Beach, Calif., Dec. 17, 1992. Educ.: CCNY, Columbia U. Law School. Lawyer, Social Security Bd., Washington, D.C., and asst. to Sen. Robert F. Wagner, 1930s–early '40s; private law practice from 1943 on: lead negotiator for workers in 1949 Singer Co. strike; in 1960s, natl. coord. of 168 lawyers collecting evidence of exclusion of black voters in Mississippi congr. races; counsel to Martin Luther King, Jr., William M. Kunstler, and Philip and Daniel Berrigan. Cofounder and pres. since 1976, Center for Constitutional Rights; bd. mem., Givat Haviva Educ. Found.

STERN, NORTON B., optometrist, historian; b. St. Paul, Minn., June 10, 1920; d. (?), Calif., Mar. 15, 1992. Educ.: Santa Monica City Coll., UCLA, Coll. of Jewish Studies, L.A. Coll. of Optometry. Private practice in optometry, 1946- (?). Founder-ed., *Western States Jewish Historical Quarterly*, 1968 on. Instr., Western Jewish hist., UCLA extension courses; research assoc., L.A. County Museum. Bd. mem.: Bay Cities Jewish Community Council, Santa Monica Community Chest; secy., Crescent Bay B'nai B'rith; v.-chmn., Santa Monica Landmarks Comm.; pres., bd. mem. Santa Monica Jewish Family Svc. Au. or coau.: a number of works, incl. *California Jewish History: A Descriptive Biography*, *Baja California: Jewish Refuge and Homeland*, and many articles on California and Western Jewish hist.

TANENBAUM, MARC H., rabbi, communal worker; b. Baltimore, Md., Oct. 13, 1925; d. NYC, July 3, 1992. Educ.: Yeshiva U., Jewish Theol. Sem. of Amer. (ord.). Rabbi: Northeast Hebrew Cong., Washington, D.C., 1951–52; Jewish Center of Mahopacs, 1952–54; ed. and pub. rel. consult. for various publishers, columnist, 1950s; writer, *Time* magazine, 1951–53; exec. dir., Synagogue Council of Amer., 1954–60; dir. interreligious affairs, Amer. Jewish Com., 1961–83, and its dir. internatl. affairs, 1983–89. A pioneer in the field of Christian-Jewish relations; official observer (and the only rabbi) at the Second Vatican Council, 1960–65; a founder and leading mem. of the joint liaison com. of the Vatican Secretariat on Catholic-Jewish Relations and the Internatl. Jewish Com. on Interreligious Consultations (IJCIC) (elected its chmn. in 1987); cochmn., 1st internatl. colloquium on Judaism and Christianity, Harvard Divinity Schl., 1966; invited by W. German govt. to consult on revisions to Oberammergau Passion Play, 1978, and on abolishing the statute of limitations on Nazi war criminals, 1979; one of ten religious leaders invited by Pres. Carter to discuss the state of the nation, 1979; in early '80s, del. of Internatl. Rescue Com. to investigate plight of Vietnamese boat people; 1st Jewish leader to address World Council of Churches, 1983; served on White House comms. on children, the elderly, and the Holocaust. Cofounder: Natl. Interreligious Task Force on Soviet Jewry, Amer. Jewish World Service, People for the American Way; bd. mem. numerous insts., incl. Internatl. Rescue Com., Covenant House. Syndicated radio commentator, 1965–92, and weekly columnist, Jewish Telegraphic Agency, 1980–92. Au.: many articles, monographs, and symposium papers, published in such vols. as *Vatican II; An Interfaith Appraisal*, *Torah and Gospel*, and *Encyclopedia Judaica*; co-ed. or coau. a number of works, incl. *Jewish-Christian Dialogues*; *Speaking of God*

Today: Jews and Lutherans in Conversation; and *Twenty Years of Jewish-Catholic Relations*. Recipient: numerous honors, incl. 15 hon. degrees; Internatl. Interfaith Achievement Award, Conf. of Christians and Jews; Interfaith Medallion, Internatl. Council of Christians and Jews; Religion in American Life Award; selected one of ten most respected religious leaders in nationwide *Christian Century* poll, 1978.

WARBURG, EDWARD M.M., communal and civic worker, patron of the arts; b. White Plains, N.Y., June 5, 1908; d. Norwalk, Conn., Sept. 21, 1992. Educ.: Harvard Coll. Served U.S. Army, WWII. Instr., art, Bryn Mawr Coll., 1931–33; staff mem., Museum of Modern Art, 1933–34. Cofounder (with Lincoln Kirstein), George Balanchine's American Ballet (forerunner of N.Y. City Ballet), 1933; an early supporter and collector of modern art, helped to found the Museum of Modern Art and served as trustee, 1932–58; v.-dir. for public affairs, Metropolitan Museum of Art, 1971–74, and hon. trustee, 1983 to his death. Mem. N.Y. State Bd. of Regents, 1958–75; cochmn., Amer. Jewish Joint Distribution Com. 1939–41, chmn. 1941–65; chmn., natl. UJA, 1951–54; 1st pres., UJA of Greater N.Y., 1967; founding trustee, Jewish Assoc. for Services to the Aged; bd. mem.: Inst. for Internatl. Educ., Hebrew U.–Jerusalem, HIAS, Amer.-Israel Cultural Found.; chmn., Amer. Patrons of the Israel Museum. Recipient: Bronze Star and decorations from Belgium and Italy for work with displaced persons; UJA's Herbert Lehman Award.

WEISS, THEODORE, attorney, legislator; b. Gava, Hungary, Sept. 17, 1927; d. NYC, Sept. 14, 1992; in U.S. since 1938. Educ.: Syracuse U. (BA, LLB). Served U.S. Army, 1946–47. Asst. dist. atty., N.Y. County, 1955–59. A reform Dem., served on N.Y. City Council, 1962–77; mem., U.S. House of Reps. from Manhattan's Upper West Side, 1977 until his death. Known as one of Congr.'s most liberal mems., served on various coms., incl. Banking, Finance and Urban Affairs; Foreign Affairs and Govt. Operations; and the Select Com. on Children, Youth and Families. Chmn., Congr. Arts Caucus and mem., Congr. Coalition for Soviet Jewry; mem.: Stephen S. Wise Free Syn., World Fed. Hungarian Jews; Emanuel Found. for Hungarian Culture and its Internatl. Tribute Com. for Holocaust Victims; mem. adv. bd., N. Amer. Conf. on Ethiopian Jewry.

Calendars

SUMMARY JEWISH CALENDAR, 5754–5758 (Sept. 1993–Aug. 1998)

HOLIDAY	5754			5755			5756			5757			5758		
	1993			1994			1995			1996			1997		
Rosh Ha-shanah, 1st day	Th	Sept.	16	T	Sept.	6	M	Sept.	25	Sa	Sept.	14	Th	Oct.	2
Rosh Ha-shanah, 2nd day	F	Sept.	17	W	Sept.	7	T	Sept.	26	S	Sept.	15	F	Oct.	3
Fast of Gedaliah	S	Sept.	19	Th	Sept.	8	W	Sept.	27	M	Sept.	16	S	Oct.	5
Yom Kippur	Sa	Sept.	25	Th	Sept.	15	W	Oct.	4	M	Sept.	23	Sa	Oct.	11
Sukkot, 1st day	Th	Sept.	30	T	Sept.	20	M	Oct.	9	Sa	Sept.	28	Th	Oct.	16
Sukkot, 2nd day	F	Oct.	1	W	Sept.	21	T	Oct.	10	S	Sept.	29	F	Oct.	17
Hosha'na' Rabbah	W	Oct.	6	M	Sept.	26	S	Oct.	15	F	Oct.	4	W	Oct.	22
Shemini 'Azeret	Th	Oct.	7	T	Sept.	27	M	Oct.	16	Sa	Oct.	5	Th	Oct.	23
Simhat Torah	F	Oct.	8	W	Sept.	28	T	Oct.	17	S	Oct.	6	F	Oct.	24
New Moon, Heshwan, 1st day	F	Oct.	15	W	Oct.	5	T	Oct.	24	S	Oct.	13	F	Oct.	31
New Moon, Heshwan, 2nd day	Sa	Oct.	16	Th	Oct.	6	W	Oct.	25	M	Oct.	14	Sa	Nov.	1
New Moon, Kislew, 1st day	S	Nov.	14	F	Nov.	4	Th	Nov.	23	T	Nov.	12	S	Nov.	30
New Moon, Kislew, 2nd day	M	Nov.	15				F	Nov.	24						
Hanukkah, 1st day	Th	Dec.	9	M	Nov.	28	M	Dec.	18	F	Dec.	6	W	Dec.	24
New Moon, Ṭevet, 1st day	T	Dec.	14	Sa	Dec.	3	Sa	Dec.	23	W	Dec.	11	M	Dec.	29
New Moon, Ṭevet, 2nd day	W	Dec.	15	S	Dec.	4	S	Dec.	24				T	Dec.	30
								1996						1998	
Fast of 10th of Ṭevet	F	Dec.	24	T	Dec.	13	T	Jan.	2	F	Dec.	20	Th	Jan.	8

	1994	1995	1996	1997	1998
New Moon, Shevat	Th Jan. 13	M Jan. 2	M Jan. 22	Th Jan. 9	W Jan. 28
Hamishshah-'asar bi-Shevat	Th Jan. 27	M Jan. 16	M Feb. 5	Th Jan. 23	W Feb. 11
New Moon, Adar I, 1st day	F Feb. 11	T Jan. 31	T Feb. 20	F Feb. 7	Th Feb. 26
New Moon, Adar I, 2nd day	Sa Feb. 12	W Feb. 1	W Feb. 21	Sa Feb. 8	F Feb. 27
New Moon, Adar II, 1st day		Th Mar. 2		S Mar. 9	
New Moon, Adar II, 2nd day		F Mar. 3		M Mar. 10	
Fast of Esther	Th Feb. 24	W Mar. 15	M Mar. 4	Th Mar. 20	W Mar. 11
Purim	F Feb. 25	Th Mar. 16	T Mar. 5	S Mar. 23	Th Mar. 12
Shushan Purim	Sa Feb. 26	F Mar. 17	W Mar. 6	M Mar. 24	F Mar. 13
New Moon, Nisan	S Mar. 13	Sa Apr. 1	Th Mar. 21	T Apr. 8	Sa Mar. 28
Passover, 1st day	S Mar. 27	Sa Apr. 15	Th Apr. 4	T Apr. 22	Sa Apr. 11
Passover, 2nd day	M Mar. 28	S Apr. 16	F Apr. 5	W Apr. 23	S Apr. 12
Passover, 7th day	Sa Apr. 2	F Apr. 21	W Apr. 10	M Apr. 28	F Apr. 17
Passover, 8th day	S Apr. 3	Sa Apr. 22	Th Apr. 11	T Apr. 29	Sa Apr. 18
Holocaust Memorial Day	F Apr. 8*	Th Apr. 27	T Apr. 16	W May 4	Th Apr. 23
New Moon, Iyar, 1st day	M Apr. 11	S Apr. 30	F Apr. 19	W May 7	S Apr. 26
New Moon, Iyar, 2nd day	T Apr. 12	M May 1	Sa Apr. 20	Th May 8	M Apr. 27
Israel Independence Day	Sa Apr. 16†	F May 5*	W Apr. 24	M May 12	F May 1*
Lag Ba-'omer	F Apr. 29	Th May 18	T May 7	S May 25	Th May 14
Jerusalem Day	M May 9	S May 28	F May 17*	W June 4	S May 24
New Moon, Siwan	W May 11	T May 30	S May 19	F June 6	T May 26
Shavu'ot, 1st day	M May 16	S June 4	F May 24	W June 11	S May 31
Shavu'ot, 2nd day	T May 17	M June 5	Sa May 25	Th June 12	M June 1
New Moon, Tammuz, 1st day	F June 10	W June 28	M June 17	Sa July 5	W June 24
New Moon, Tammuz, 2nd day		Th June 29	T June 18	S July 6	Th June 25
Fast of 17th of Tammuz	S June 26	S July 16	Th July 4	T July 22	S July 12
New Moon, Av	Sa July 9	F July 28	W July 17	M Aug. 4	F July 24
Fast of 9th of Av	S July 17	S Aug. 6	Th July 25	T Aug. 12	S Aug. 2
New Moon, Elul, 1st day	S Aug. 7	Sa Aug. 26	Th Aug. 15	T Sept. 2	Sa Aug. 22
New Moon, Elul, 2nd day	M Aug. 8	S Aug. 27	F Aug. 16	W Sept. 3	S Aug. 23

*Observed Thursday, a day earlier, to avoid conflict with the Sabbath.
†Observed Thursday, two days earlier, to avoid conflict with the Sabbath.

CONDENSED MONTHLY CALENDAR
(1993–1996)

1992, Dec. 25–Jan. 22, 1993] ṬEVET (29 DAYS) [5753

Civil Date	Day of the Week	Jewish Date	SABBATHS, FESTIVALS, FASTS	PENTATEUCHAL READING	PROPHETICAL READING
Dec. 25	F	Ṭevet 1	New Moon; Hanukkah, sixth day	Num. 28:1–15 Num. 7:42–47	
26	Sa	2	Mi-kez; Hanukkah, seventh day	Gen. 41:1–44:17 Num. 7:48–53	Zechariah 2:14–4:7
27	S	3	Hanukkah, eighth day	Num. 7:54–8:4	
Jan. 2	Sa	9	Wa-yiggash	Gen. 44:18–47:27	Ezekiel 37:15–28
3	S	10	Fast of 10th of Ṭevet	Exod. 32:11–14 Exod. 34:1–10 (morning and afternoon)	Isaiah 55:6–56:8 (afternoon only)
9	Sa	16	Wa-yeḥi	Gen. 47:28–50:26	I Kings 2:1–12
16	Sa	23	Shemot	Exod. 1:1–6:1	Isaiah 27:6–28:13 29:22–23 *Jeremiah 1:1–2:3*

Italics are fo
Sephardi Minhag

1993, Jan. 23–Feb. 21]   SHEVAṬ (30 DAYS)   [5753

Civil Date	Day of the Week	Jewish Date	SABBATHS, FESTIVALS, FASTS	PENTATEUCHAL READING	PROPHETICAL READING
Jan. 23	Sa	Shevaṭ 1	Wa-'era'; New Moon	Exod. 6:2–9:35 Num. 28:9–15	Isaiah 66:1–24
30	Sa	8	Bo'	Exod. 10:1–13:16	Jeremiah 46:13–28
Feb. 6	Sa	15	Be-shallah (Shabbat Shirah); Hamishshah-'asar bi-Shevaṭ	Exod. 13:17–17:16	Judges 4:4–5:31 *Judges 5:1–31*
13	Sa	22	Yitro	Exod. 18:1–20:23	Isaiah 6:1–7:6; 9:5–6 *Isaiah 6:1–13*
20	Sa	29	Mishpaṭim (Shabbat Sheḳalim)	Exod. 21:1–24:18 Exod. 30:11–16	II Kings 12:1–17 *II Kings 11:17–12:17* *I Sam. 20:18, 42*
21	S	30	New Moon, first day	Num. 28:1–15	

Italics are for Sephardi Minhag.

1993, Feb. 22–Mar. 22]   ADAR (29 DAYS)   [5753

Civil Date	Day of the Week	Jewish Date	SABBATHS, FESTIVALS, FASTS	PENTATEUCHAL READING	PROPHETICAL READING
Feb. 22	M	Adar 1	New Moon, second day	Num. 28:1–15	
27	Sa	6	Terumah	Exod. 25:1–27:19	I Kings 5:26–6:13
Mar. 4	Th	11	Fast of Esther	Exod. 32:11–14 Exod. 34:1–10 (morning and afternoon)	Isaiah 55:6–56:8 (afternoon only)
6	Sa	13	Tezawweh (Shabbat Zakhor)	Exod. 27:20–30:10 Deut. 25:17–19	I Samuel 15:2–34 *I Samuel 15:1–34*
7	S	14	Purim	Exod. 17:8–16	Book of Esther (night before and in the morning)
8	M	15	Shushan Purim		
13	Sa	20	Ki tissa' (Shabbat Parah)	Exod. 30:11–34:35 Num. 19:1–22	Ezekiel 36:16–38 *Ezekiel 36:16–36*
20	Sa	27	Wa-yakhel, Pekude (Shabbat Ha-hodesh)	Exod. 35:1–40:38 Exod. 12:1–20	Ezekiel 45:16–46:18 *Ezekiel 45:18–46:15*

*Italics are
Sephardi Minh*

1993, Mar. 23–Apr. 21]   NISAN (30 DAYS)   [5753

Civil Date	Day of the Week	Jewish Date	SABBATHS, FESTIVALS, FASTS	PENTATEUCHAL READING	PROPHETICAL READING
Mar. 23	T	Nisan 1	New Moon	Num. 28:1–15	
27	Sa	5	Wa-yiḳra'	Levit. 1:1–5:26	Isaiah 43:21–44:24
Apr. 3	Sa	12	Ẓaw (Shabbat Ha-gadol)	Levit. 6:1–8:36	Malachi 3:4–24
5	M	14	Fast of Firstborn		
6	T	15	Passover, first day	Exod. 12:21–51 Num. 28:16–25	Joshua 5:2–6:1, 27
7	W	16	Passover, second day	Levit. 22:26–23:44 Num. 28:16–25	II Kings 23:1–9, 21–25
8	Th	17	Ḥol Ha-moʻed, first day	Exod. 13:1–16 Num. 28:19–25	
9	F	18	Ḥol Ha-moʻed, second day	Exod. 22:24–23:19 Num. 28:19–25	
10	Sa	19	Ḥol Ha-moʻed, third day	Exod. 33:12–34:26 Num. 28:19–25	Ezekiel 37:1–14
11	S	20	Ḥol Ha-moʻed, fourth day	Num. 9:1–14 Num. 28:19–25	
12	M	21	Passover, seventh day	Exod. 13:17–15:26 Num. 28:19–25	II Samuel 22:1–51
13	T	22	Passover, eighth day	Deut. 15:19–16:17 Num. 28:19–25	Isaiah 10:32–12:6
17	Sa	26	Shemini	Levit. 9:1–11:47	II Samuel 6:1–7:17 *II Samuel 6:1–19*
18	S	27	Holocaust Memorial Day		
21	W	30	New Moon, first day	Num. 28:1–15	

Italics are for Sephardi Minhag.

1993, Apr. 22–May 20] IYAR (29 DAYS) [5753

Civil Date	Day of the Week	Jewish Date	SABBATHS, FESTIVALS, FASTS	PENTATEUCHAL READING	PROPHETICAL READING
Apr. 22	Th	Iyar 1	New Moon, second day	Num. 28:1–15	
24	Sa	3	Tazria', Mezora'	Levit. 12:1–15:33	II Kings 7:3–20
26	M	5	Israel Independence Day		
May 1	Sa	10	Aḥare mot, Ķedoshim	Levit. 16:1–20:27	Amos 9:7–15 *Ezekiel 20:2–20*
8	Sa	17	Emor	Levit. 21:1–24:23	Ezekiel 44:15–31
9	S	18	Lag Ba-'omer		
15	Sa	24	Be-har, Be-ḥukkotai	Levit. 25:1–27:34	Jeremiah 16:19–17:14
19	W	28	Jerusalem Day		

Italics are for Sephardi Minhag.

1993, May 21–June 19]   SIWAN (30 DAYS)   [5753

Civil Date	Day of the Week	Jewish Date	SABBATHS, FESTIVALS, FASTS	PENTATEUCHAL READING	PROPHETICAL READING
May 21	F	Siwan 1	New Moon	Num. 28:1–15	
22	Sa	2	Be-midbar	Num. 1:1–4:20	Hosea 2:1–22
26	W	6	Shavu'ot, first day	Exod. 19:1–20:23 Num. 28:26–31	Ezekiel 1:1–28 3:12
27	Th	7	Shavu'ot, second day	Deut. 15:19–16:17 Num. 28:26–31	Habbakuk 3:1–19 *Habbakuk 2:20–3:19*
29	Sa	9	Naso'	Num. 4:21–7:89	Judges 13:2–25
June 5	Sa	16	Be-ha'alotekha	Num. 8:1–12:16	Zechariah 2:14–4:7
12	Sa	23	Shelaḥ lekha	Num. 13:1–15:41	Joshua 2:1–24
19	Sa	30	Ḳoraḥ; New Moon, first day	Num. 16:1–18:32 Num. 28:9–15	Isaiah 66:1–24 *Isaiah 66:1–24* *I Samuel 20:18, 42*

Italics are for Sephardi Minhag.

1993, June 20–July 18]   TAMMUZ (29 DAYS)   [5753

Civil Date	Day of the Week	Jewish Date	SABBATHS, FESTIVALS, FASTS	PENTATEUCHAL READING	PROPHETICAL READING
June 20	S	Tammuz 1	New Moon, second day	Num. 28:1–15	
26	Sa	7	Ḥukkat	Num. 19:1–22:1	Judges 11:1–33
July 3	Sa	14	Balak	Num. 22:2–25:9	Micah 5:6–6:8
6	T	17	Fast of 17th of Tammuz	Exod. 32:11–14 Exod. 34:1–10 (morning and afternoon)	Isaiah 55:6–56:8 (afternoon only)
10	Sa	21	Pineḥas	Num. 25:10–30:1	I Kings 18:46–19:21
17	Sa	28	Maṭṭot, Mas'e	Num. 30:2–36:13	Jeremiah 2:4–28 3:4 *Jeremiah 2:4–28 4:1–2*

Italics are f
Sephardi Minha

1993, July 19–Aug. 17] AV (30 DAYS) [5753

Civil Date	Day of the Week	Jewish Date	SABBATHS, FESTIVALS, FASTS	PENTATEUCHAL READING	PROPHETICAL READING
July 19	M	Av 1	New Moon	Num. 28:1–15	
24	Sa	6	Devarim (Shabbat Ḥazon)	Deut. 1:1–3:22	Isaiah 1:1–27
27	T	9	Fast of 9th of Av	Morning: Deut. 4:25–40 Afternoon: Exod. 32:11–14 Exod. 34:1–10	(Lamentations is read the night before) Jeremiah 8:13–9:23 (morning) Isaiah 55:6–56:8 (afternoon)
31	Sa	13	Wa-ethannan (Shabbat Naḥamu)	Deut. 3:23–7:11	Isaiah 40:1–26
Aug. 7	Sa	20	'Eḳev	Deut. 7:12–11:25	Isaiah 49:14–51:3
14	Sa	27	Re'eh	Deut. 11:26–16:17	Isaiah 54:11–55:5
17	T	30	New Moon, first day	Num. 28:1–15	

1993, Aug. 18–Sept. 15]   ELUL (29 DAYS)   [5753

Civil Date	Day of the Week	Jewish Date	SABBATHS, FESTIVALS, FASTS	PENTATEUCHAL READING	PROPHETICAL READING
Aug. 18	W	Elul 1	New Moon, second day	Num. 28:1–15	
21	Sa	4	Shofeṭim	Deut. 16:18–21:9	Isaiah 51:12–52:12
28	Sa	11	Ki teze'	Deut. 21:10–25:19	Isaiah 54:1–10
Sept. 4	Sa	18	Ki tavo'	Deut. 26:1–29:8	Isaiah 60:1–22
11	Sa	25	Nizzavim, Wa-yelekh	Deut. 29:9–31:30	Isaiah 61:10–63:9

Civil Date	Day of the Week	Jewish Date	SABBATHS, FESTIVALS, FASTS	PENTATEUCHAL READING	PROPHETICAL READING
Sep. 16	Th	Tishri 1	Rosh Ha-shanah, first day	Gen. 21:1–34 Num. 29:1–6	1 Samuel 1:1–2:10
17	F	2	Rosh Ha-shanah, second day	Gen. 22:1–24 Num. 29:1–6	Jeremiah 31:2–20
18	Sa	3	Ha'azinu (Shabbat Shuvah)	Deut. 32:1–52	Hosea 14:2–10 Micah 7:18–20 Joel 2:15–27 *Hosea 14:2–10* *Micah 7:18–20*
19	S	4	Fast of Gedaliah	Exod. 32:11–14 Exod. 34:1–10 (morning and afternoon)	Isaiah 55:6–56:8 (afternoon only)
25	Sa	10	Yom Kippur	Morning: Levit. 16:1–34 Num. 29:7–11 Afternoon: Levit. 18:1–30	Isaiah 57:14–58:14 Jonah 1:1–4:11 Micah 7:18–20
30	Th	15	Sukkot, first day	Levit. 22:26–23:44 Num. 29:12–16	Zechariah 14:1–21
Oct. 1	F	16	Sukkot, second day	Levit. 22:26–23:44 Num. 29:12–16	I Kings 8:2–21
2	Sa	17	Ḥol Ha-mo'ed, first day	Exod. 33:12–34:26 Num. 29:17–22	Ezekiel 38:18–39:16
3–5	S–T	18–20	Ḥol Ha-mo'ed, second to fourth days	S Num. 29:20–28 M Num. 29:23–31 T Num. 29:26–34	
6	W	21	Hosha'na' Rabbah	Num. 29:26–34	
7	Th	22	Shemini 'Aẓeret	Deut. 14:22–16:17 Num. 29:35–30:1	I Kings 8:54–66
8	F	23	Simḥat Torah	Deut. 33:1–34:12 Gen. 1:1–2:3 Num. 29:35–30:1	Joshua 1:1–18 *Joshua 1:1–9*
9	Sa	24	Be-re'shit	Gen. 1:1–6:8	Isaiah 42:5–43:10 *Isaiah 42:5–21*
15	F	30	New Moon, first day	Num. 28:1–15	

*Italics are for
Sephardi Minhag.*

1993, Oct. 16–Nov. 14]   ḤESHWAN (30 DAYS)   [5754

Civil Date	Day of the Week	Jewish Date	SABBATHS, FESTIVALS, FASTS	PENTATEUCHAL READING	PROPHETICAL READING
Oct. 16	Sa	Heshwan 1	Noaḥ; New Moon, second day	Gen. 6:9–11:32 Num. 28:9–15	Isaiah 66:1–24
23	Sa	8	Lekh lekha	Gen. 12:1–17:27	Isaiah 40:27–41:16
30	Sa	15	Wa-yera'	Gen. 18:1–22:24	II Kings 4:1–37 *II Kings 4:1–23*
Nov. 6	Sa	22	Ḥayye Sarah	Gen. 23:1–25:18	I Kings 1:1–31
13	Sa	29	Toledot	Gen. 25:19–28:9	I Samuel 20:18–42
14	S	30	New Moon, first day	Num. 28:1–15	

*Italics are for
Sephardi Minhag.*

1993, Nov. 15–Dec. 14]   KISLEW (30 DAYS)   [5754

Civil Date	Day of the Week	Jewish Date	SABBATHS, FESTIVALS, FASTS	PENTATEUCHAL READING	PROPHETICAL READING
Nov. 15	M	Kislew 1	New Moon, second day	Num. 28:1–15	
20	Sa	6	Wa-yeze'	Gen. 28:10–32:3	Hosea 12:13–14:10 *Hosea 11:7–12:12*
27	Sa	13	Wa-yishlah	Gen. 32:4–36:43	Hosea 11:7–12:12 *Obadiah 1:1–21*
Dec. 4	Sa	20	Wa-yeshev	Gen. 37:1–40:23	Amos 2:6–3:8
9–10	Th–F	25–26	Hanukkah, first, second days	Th Num. 7:1–17 F Num. 7:18–29	
11	Sa	27	Mi-kez; Hanukkah, third day	Gen. 41:1–44:17 Num. 7:24–29	Zechariah 2:14–4:7
12–13	S–M	28–29	Hanukkah, fourth, fifth days	S Num. 7:30–41 M Num. 7:36–47	
14	T	30	New Moon, first day; Hanukkah, sixth day	Num. 7:42–47 Num. 28:1–15	

Italics are for Sephardi Minhag.

1993, Dec. 15–Jan. 12, 1994] ṬEVET (29 DAYS) [5754

Civil Date	Day of the Week	Jewish Date	SABBATHS, FESTIVALS, FASTS	PENTATEUCHAL READING	PROPHETICAL READING
Dec. 15	W	Ṭevet 1	New Moon, second day; Hanukkah, seventh day	Num. 28:1–15 Num. 7:48–53	
16	Th	2	Hanukkah, eighth day	Num. 7:54–8:4	
18	Sa	4	Wa-yiggash	Gen. 44:18–47:27	Ezekiel 37:15–28
24	F	10	Fast of 10th of Ṭevet	Exod. 32:11–14 Exod. 34:1–10 (morning and afternoon)	Isaiah 55:6–56:8 (afternoon only)
25	Sa	11	Wa-yeḥi	Gen. 47:28–50:26	I Kings 2:1–12
Jan. 1	Sa	18	Shemot	Exod. 1:1–6:1	Isaiah 27:6–28:13 29:22–23 *Jeremiah 1:1–2:3*
8	Sa	25	Wa-'era'	Exod. 6:2–9:35	Ezekiel 28:25–29:21

Italics are fo
Sephardi Minhag

1994, Jan. 13–Feb. 11]   SHEVAṬ (30 DAYS)   [5754

Civil Date	Day of the Week	Jewish Date	SABBATHS, FESTIVALS, FASTS	PENTATEUCHAL READING	PROPHETICAL READING
Jan. 13	Th	Shevaṭ 1	New Moon	Num. 28:1–15	
15	Sa	3	Bo'	Exod. 10:1–13:16	Jeremiah 46:13–28
22	Sa	10	Be-shallaḥ (Shabbat Shirah)	Exod. 13:17–17:16	Judges 4:4–5:31 *Judges 5:1–31*
27	Th	15	Ḥamishshah-'asar bi-Shevaṭ		
29	Sa	17	Yitro	Exod. 18:1–20:23	Isaiah 6:1–7:6; 9:5–6 *Isaiah 6:1–13*
Feb. 5	Sa	24	Mishpaṭim	Exod. 21:1–24:18	Jeremiah 34:8–22 33:25–26
11	F	30	New Moon, first day	Num. 28:1–15	

Italics are for Sephardi Minhag.

1994, Feb. 12–Mar. 12]   ADAR (29 DAYS)   [5754

Civil Date	Day of the Week	Jewish Date	SABBATHS, FESTIVALS, FASTS	PENTATEUCHAL READING	PROPHETICAL READING
Feb. 12	Sa	Adar 1	Terumah; New Moon, second day (Shabbat Shekalim)	Exod. 25:1–27:19 Num. 28:9–15 Exod. 30:11–16	II Kings 12:1–17 *II Kings 11:17–12:17*
19	Sa	8	Tezawweh (Shabbat Zakhor)	Exod. 27:20–30:10 Deut. 25:17–19	I Samuel 15:2–34 *I Samuel 15:1–34*
24	Th	13	Fast of Esther	Exod. 32:11–14 34:1–10 (morning and afternoon)	Isaiah 55:6–56:8 (afternoon only)
25	F	14	Purim	Exod. 17:8–16	Book of Esther (night before and in the morning)
26	Sa	15	Ki tissa'; Shushan Purim	Exod. 30:11–34:35	I Kings 18:1–39 *I Kings 18:20–39*
Mar. 5	Sa	22	Wa-yakhel (Shabbat Parah)	Exod. 35:1–38:20 Num. 19:1–22	Ezekiel 36:16–38 *Ezekiel 36:16–36*
12	Sa	29	Pekude (Shabbat Ha-hodesh)	Exod. 38:21–40:38 Exod. 12:1–20	Ezekiel 45:16–46:18 *Ezekiel 45:18–46:15 I Samuel 20:18, 42*

Italics are for Sephardi Minhag.

1994, Mar. 13–Apr. 11]   NISAN (30 DAYS)   [5754

Civil Date	Day of the Week	Jewish Date	SABBATHS, FESTIVALS, FASTS	PENTATEUCHAL READING	PROPHETICAL READING
Mar. 13	S	Nisan 1	New Moon	Num. 28:1–15	
19	Sa	7	Wa-yiḵra'	Levit. 1:1–5:26	Isaiah 43:21–44:24
24	Th	12	Fast of Firstborn		
26	Sa	14	Zaw (Shabbat Ha-gadol)	Levit. 6:1–8:36	Malachi 3:4–24
27	S	15	Passover, first day	Exod. 12:21–51 Num. 28:16–25	Joshua 5:2–6:1, 27
28	M	16	Passover, second day	Levit. 22:26–23:44 Num. 28:16–25	II Kings 23:1–9, 21–25
29	T	17	Ḥol Ha-mo‘ed, first day	Exod. 13:1–16 Num. 28:19–25	
30	W	18	Ḥol Ha-mo‘ed, second day	Exod. 22:24–23:19 Num. 28:19–25	
31	Th	19	Ḥol Ha-mo‘ed, third day	Exod. 34:1–26 Num. 28:19–25	
Apr. 1	F	20	Ḥol Ha-mo‘ed, fourth day	Num. 9:1–14 28:19–25	
2	Sa	21	Passover, seventh day	Exod. 13:17–15:26 Num. 28:19–25	II Samuel 22:1–51
3	S	22	Passover, eighth day	Deut. 15:19–16:17 Num. 28:19–25	Isaiah 10:32–12:6
8	F	27	Holocaust Memorial Day*		
9	Sa	28	Shemini	Levit. 9:1–11:47	II Samuel 6:1–7:17 *II Samuel 6:1–19*
11	M	30	New Moon, first day	Num. 28:1–15	

*Observed April 7, to avoid conflict with the Sabbath.

Italics are for Sephardi Minhag.

1994, Apr. 12–May 10]   IYAR (29 DAYS)   [5754

Civil Date	Day of the Week	Jewish Date	SABBATHS, FESTIVALS, FASTS	PENTATEUCHAL READING	PROPHETICAL READING
Apr. 12	T	Iyar 1	New Moon, second day	Num. 28:1–15	
16	Sa	5	Tazria', Mezora'; Israel Independence Day*	Levit. 12:1–15:33	II Kings 7:3–20
23	Sa	12	Aḥare mot, Ḳedoshim	Levit. 16:1–20:27	Amos 9:7–15 *Ezekiel 20:2–20*
29	F	18	Lag Ba-o'mer		
30	Sa	19	Emor	Levit. 21:1–24:23	Ezekiel 44:15–31
May 7	Sa	26	Be-har, Be-ḥukkotai	Levit. 25:1–27:34	Jeremiah 16:19–17:14
9	M	28	Jerusalem Day		

*Observed Apr. 14, to avoid conflict with the Sabbath.

Italics are for Sephardi Minhag.

1994, May 11–June 9]　　　SIWAN (30 DAYS)　　　[5754

Civil Date	Day of the Week	Jewish Date	SABBATHS, FESTIVALS, FASTS	PENTATEUCHAL READING	PROPHETICAL READING
May 11	W	Siwan 1	New Moon	Num. 28:1–15	
14	Sa	4	Be-midbar	Num. 1:1–4:20	Hosea 2:1–22
16	M	6	Shavu'ot, first day	Exod. 19:1–20:23 Num. 28:26–31	Ezekiel 1:1–28 3:12
17	T	7	Shavu'ot, second day	Deut. 15:19–16:17 Num. 28:26–31	Habbakuk 3:1–19 *Habbakuk 2:20–3:19*
21	Sa	11	Naso'	Num. 4:21–7:89	Judges 13:2–25
28	Sa	18	Be-ha'alotekha	Num. 8:1–12:16	Zechariah 2:14–4:7
June 4	Sa	25	Shelah lekha	Num. 13:1–15:41	Joshua 2:1–24
9	Th	30	New Moon, first day	Num. 28:1–15	

*Italics are for
Sephardi Minhag.*

1994, June 10–July 8]   TAMMUZ (29 DAYS)   [5754

Civil Date	Day of the Week	Jewish Date	SABBATHS, FESTIVALS, FASTS	PENTATEUCHAL READING	PROPHETICAL READING
June 10	F	Tammuz 1	New Moon, second day	Num. 28:1–15	
11	Sa	2	Korah	Num. 16:1–18:32	I Samuel 11:14–12:22
18	Sa	9	Hukkat	Num. 19:1–22:1	Judges 11:1–33
25	Sa	16	Balak	Num. 22:2–25:9	Micah 5:6–6:8
26	S	17	Fast of 17th of Tammuz	Exod. 32:11–14 34:1–10 (morning and afternoon)	Isaiah 55:6–56:8 (afternoon only)
July 2	Sa	23	Pinehas	Num. 25:10–30:1	Jeremiah 1:1–2:3

1994, July 9–Aug. 7]   AV (30 DAYS)   [5754

Civil Date	Day of the Week	Jewish Date	SABBATHS, FESTIVALS, FASTS	PENTATEUCHAL READING	PROPHETICAL READING
July 9	Sa	Av 1	Maṭṭot, Mas'e; New Moon	Num. 30:2–36:13 Num. 28:9–15	Jeremiah 2:4–28 3:4 *Jeremiah 2:4–28 4:1–2 Isaiah 66:1, 23*
16	Sa	8	Devarim (Shabbat Ḥazon)	Deut. 1:1–3:22	Isaiah 1:1–27
17	S	9	Fast of 9th of Av	Morning: Deut. 4:25–40 Afternoon: Exod. 32:11–14 34:1–10	(Lamentations is read the night before) Jeremiah 8:13–9:23 (morning) Isaiah 55:6:56–8 (afternoon)
23	Sa	15	Wa-etḥannan (Shabbat Naḥamu)	Deut. 3:23–7:11	Isaiah 40:1–26
30	Sa	22	'Eḳev	Deut. 7:12–11:25	Isaiah 49:14–51:3
Aug. 6	Sa	29	Re'eh	Deut. 11:26–16:17	Isaiah 54:11–55:5 *Isaiah 54:11–55:5 I Samuel 20:18, 42*
7	S	30	New Moon, first day	Num. 28:1–15	

Italics are for Sephardi Minhag.

1994, Aug. 8–Sept. 5]   ELUL (29 DAYS)   [5754

Civil Date	Day of the Week	Jewish Date	SABBATHS, FESTIVALS, FASTS	PENTATEUCHAL READING	PROPHETICAL READING
Aug. 8	M	Elul 1	New Moon, second day	Num. 28:1–15	
13	Sa	6	Shofetim	Deut. 16:18–21:9	Isaiah 51:12–52:12
20	Sa	13	Ki teze'	Deut. 21:10–25:19	Isaiah 54:1–10
27	Sa	20	Ki tavo'	Deut. 26:1–29:8	Isaiah 60:1–22
Sept. 3	Sa	27	Nizzavim	Deut. 29:9–30:20	Isaiah 61:10–63:9

Civil Date	Day of the Week	Jewish Date	SABBATHS, FESTIVALS, FASTS	PENTATEUCHAL READING	PROPHETICAL READING
Sept. 6	T	Tishri 1	Rosh Ha-shanah, first day	Gen. 21:1–34 Num. 29:1–6	I Samuel 1:1–2:10
7	W	2	Rosh Ha-shana, second day	Gen. 22:1–24 Num. 29:1–6	Jeremiah 31:2–20
8	Th	3	Fast of Gedaliah	Exod. 32:11–14 34:1–10 (morning and afternoon)	Isaiah 55:6–56:8 (afternoon only)
10	Sa	5	Wa-yelekh (Shabbat Shuvah)	Deut. 31:1–30	Hosea 14:2–10 Micah 7:18–20 Joel 2:15–27 *Hosea 14:2–10* *Micah 7:18–20*
15	Th	10	Yom Kippur	Morning: Levit. 16:1–34 Num. 29:7–11 Afternoon: Levit. 18:1–30	Isaiah 57:14–58:14 Jonah 1:1–4:11 Micah 7:18–20
17	Sa	12	Ha'azinu	Deut. 32:1–52	II Samuel 22:1–51
20	T	15	Sukkot, first day	Levit. 22:26–23:44 Num. 29:12–16	Zechariah 14:1–21
21	W	16	Sukkot, second day	Levit. 22:26–23:44 Num. 29:12–16	I Kings 8:2–21
22–25	Th-S	17–20	Ḥol Ha-mo'ed	Th Num. 29:17–25 F Num. 29:20–28 Sa Exod. 33:12– 34:26 Num. 29:23–28 S Num. 29:26–34	Ezekiel 38:18–39:16
26	M	21	Hosha'na' Rabbah	Num. 29:26–34	
27	T	22	Shemini 'Azeret	Deut. 14:22–16:17 Num. 29:35–30:1	I Kings 8:54–66
28	W	23	Simḥat Torah	Deut. 33:1–34:12 Gen. 1:1–2:3 Num. 29:35–30:1	Joshua 1:1–18 *Joshua 1:1–9*
Oct. 1	Sa	26	Be-re'shit	Gen. 1:1–6:8	Isaiah 42:5–43:10 *Isaiah 42:5–21*
5	W	30	New Moon, first day	Num. 28:1–15	

Italics are for
Sephardi Minhag.

1994, Oct. 6–Nov. 3]   ḤESHWAN (29 DAYS)   [5755

Civil Date	Day of the Week	Jewish Date	SABBATHS, FESTIVALS, FASTS	PENTATEUCHAL READING	PROPHETICAL READING
Oct. 6	Th	Heshwan 1	New Moon, second day	Num. 28:1–15	
8	Sa	3	Noaḥ	Gen. 6:9–11:32	Isaiah 54:1–55:5 *Isaiah 54:1–10*
15	Sa	10	Lekh lekha	Gen. 12:1–17:27	Isaiah 40:27–41:16
22	Sa	17	Wa-yera'	Gen. 18:1–22:24	II Kings 4:1–37 *II Kings 4:1–23*
29	Sa	24	Ḥayye Sarah	Gen. 23:1–25:18	I Kings 1:1–31

Italics are for
Sephardi Minhag.

1994, Nov. 4–Dec. 3] KISLEW (30 DAYS) [5755

Civil Date	Day of the Week	Jewish Date	SABBATHS, FESTIVALS, FASTS	PENTATEUCHAL READING	PROPHETICAL READING
Nov. 4	F	Kislew 1	New Moon	Num. 28:1–15	
5	Sa	2	Toledot	Gen. 25:19–28:9	Malachi 1:1–2:7
12	Sa	9	Wa-yeze'	Gen. 28:10–32:3	Hosea 12:13–14:10 *Hosea 11:7–12:12*
19	Sa	16	Wa-yishlah	Gen. 32:4–36:43	Hosea 11:7–12:12 *Obadiah 1:1–21*
26	Sa	23	Wa-yeshev	Gen. 37:1–40:23	Amos 2:6–3:8
Nov. 28– Dec. 2	M–F	25–29	Hanukkah, first to fifth days	M Num. 7:1–17 T Num. 7:18–29 W Num. 7:24–35 Th Num. 7:30–41 F Num. 7:36–47	
3	Sa	30	Mi-kez; New Moon, first day; Hanukkah, sixth day	Gen. 41:1–44:17 Num. 28:9–15 Num. 7:42–47	Zechariah 2:14–4:7

*Italics are for
Sephardi Minhag.*

1994, Dec. 4–Jan. 1, 1995]   ṬEVET (29 DAYS)   [5755

Civil Date	Day of the Week	Jewish Date	SABBATHS, FESTIVALS, FASTS	PENTATEUCHAL READING	PROPHETICAL READING
Dec. 4	S	Ṭevet 1	New Moon, second day; Ḥanukkah, seventh day	Num. 28:1–15 Num. 7:48–53	
5	M	2	Ḥanukkah, eighth day	Num. 7:54–8:4	
10	Sa	7	Wa-yiggash	Gen. 44:18–47:27	Ezekiel 37:15–28
13	T	10	Fast of 10th of Ṭevet	Exod. 32:11–14 Exod. 34:1–10 (morning and afternoon)	Isaiah 55:6–56:8 (afternoon only)
17	Sa	14	Wa-yeḥi	Gen. 47:28–50:26	I Kings 2:1–12
24	Sa	21	Shemot	Exod. 1:1–6:1	Isaiah 27:6–28:13 29:22–23 *Jeremiah 1:1–2:3*
31	Sa	28	Wa-'era'	Exod. 6:2–9:35	Ezekiel 28:25–29:21

*Italics are for
Sephardi Minhag.*

1995, Jan. 2–Jan. 31]　　　SHEVAṬ (30 DAYS)　　　[5755

Civil Date	Day of the Week	Jewish Date	SABBATHS, FESTIVALS, FASTS	PENTATEUCHAL READING	PROPHETICAL READING
Jan. 2	M	Shevaṭ 1	New Moon	Num. 28:1–15	
7	Sa	6	Bo'	Exod. 10:1–13:16	Jeremiah 46:13–28
14	Sa	13	Be-shallaḥ (Shabbat Shirah)	Exod. 13:17–17:16	Judges 4:4–5:31 *Judges 5:1–31*
16	M	15	Hamishshah-'asar bi-Shevaṭ		
21	Sa	20	Yitro	Exod. 18:1–20:23	Isaiah 6:1–7:6; 9:5–6 *Isaiah 6:1–13*
28	Sa	27	Mishpaṭim	Exod. 21:1–24:18	Jeremiah 34:8–22 33:25–26
31	T	30	New Moon, first day	Num. 28:1–15	

Italics are for Sephardi Minhag.

1995, Feb. 1–Mar. 2]   ADAR I (30 DAYS)   [5755

Civil Date	Day of the Week	Jewish Date	SABBATHS, FESTIVALS, FASTS	PENTATEUCHAL READING	PROPHETICAL READING
Feb. 1	W	Adar I 1	New Moon, second day	Num. 28:1–15	
4	Sa	4	Terumah	Exod. 25:1–27:19	I Kings 5:26–6:13
11	Sa	11	Tezawweh	Exod. 27:20–30:10	Ezekiel 43:10–27
18	Sa	18	Ki tissa'	Exod. 30:11–34:35	I Kings 18:1–39 *I Kings 18:20–39*
25	Sa	25	Wa-yakhel (Shabbat Shekalim)	Exod. 35:1–38:20 Exod. 30:11–16	II Kings 12:1–17 *II Kings 11:17–12:17*
Mar. 2	Th	30	New Moon, first day	Num. 28:1–15	

Italics are for Sephardi Minhag.

1995, Mar. 3–Mar. 31] ADAR II (29 DAYS) [5755

Civil Date	Day of the Week	Jewish Date	SABBATHS, FESTIVALS, FASTS	PENTATEUCHAL READING	PROPHETICAL READING
Mar. 3	F	Adar II 1	New Moon, second day	Num. 28:1–15	
4	Sa	2	Pekude	Exod. 38:21–40:38	I Kings 7:51–8:21 *I Kings 7:40–50*
11	Sa	9	Wa-yikra' (Shabbat Zakhor)	Levit. 1:1–5:26 Deut. 25:17–19	I Samuel 15:2–34 *I Samuel 15:1–34*
15	W	13	Fast of Esther	Exod. 32:11–14 Exod. 34:1–10 (morning and afternoon)	Isaiah 55:6–56:8 (afternoon only)
16	Th	14	Purim	Exod. 17:8–16	Book of Esther (night before and in the morning)
17	F	15	Shushan Purim		
18	Sa	16	Zaw	Levit 6:1–8:36	Jeremiah 7:21–8:3 9:22–23
25	Sa	23	Shemini (Shabbat Parah)	Levit 9:1–11:47 Num. 19:1–22	Ezekiel 36:16–38 *Ezekiel 36:16–36*

Italics are for Sephardi Minhag.

1995, April 1–April 30]   NISAN (30 DAYS)   [5755

Civil Date	Day of the Week	Jewish Date	SABBATHS, FESTIVALS, FASTS	PENTATEUCHAL READING	PROPHETICAL READING
Apr. 1	Sa	Nisan 1	Tazria'; New Moon (Shabbat Ha-hodesh)	Levit 12:1–13:59 Num. 28:9–15 Exod. 12:1–20	Ezekiel 45:16–46:18 *Ezekiel 45:18–46:15* *Isaiah 66:1, 23*
8	Sa	8	Mezora' (Shabbat Ha-gadol)	Levit 14:1–15:33	Malachi 3:4–24
14	F	14	Fast of Firstborn		
15	Sa	15	Passover, first day	Exod. 12:21–51 Num. 28:16–25	Joshua 5:2–6:1, 27
16	S	16	Passover, second day	Levit 22:26–23:44 Num. 28:16–25	II Kings 23:1–9, 21–25
17	M	17	Hol Ha-mo'ed, first day	Exod. 13:1–16 Num. 28:19–25	
18	T	18	Hol Ha-mo'ed, second day	Exod. 22:24–23:19 Num. 28:19–25	
19	W	19	Hol Ha-mo'ed, third day	Exod. 34:1–26 Num. 28:19–25	
20	Th	20	Hol Ha-mo'ed, fourth day	Num. 9:1–14 Num. 28:19–25	
21	F	21	Passover, seventh day	Exod. 13:17–15:26 Num. 28:19–25	II Samuel 22:1–51
22	Sa	22	Passover, eighth day	Deut. 15:19–16:17 Num. 28:19–25	Isaiah 10:32–12:6
27	Th	27	Holocaust Memorial Day		
29	Sa	29	Ahare mot	Levit. 16:1–18:30	I Samuel 20:18–42
30	S	30	New Moon, first day	Num. 28:1–15	

Italics are for
Sephardi Minhag.

1995, May 1–May 29] IYAR (29 DAYS) [5755

Civil Date	Day of the Week	Jewish Date	SABBATHS, FESTIVALS, FASTS	PENTATEUCHAL READING	PROPHETICAL READING
May 1	M	Iyar 1	New Moon, second day	Num. 28:1–15	
5	F	5	Israel Independence Day*		
6	Sa	6	Ḳedoshim	Levit. 19:1–20:27	Amos 9:7–15 *Ezekiel 20:2–20*
13	Sa	13	Emor	Levit. 21:1–24:23	Ezekiel 44:15–31
18	Th	18	Lag Ba-'omer		
20	Sa	20	Be-har	Levit. 25:1–26:2	Jeremiah 32:6–27
27	Sa	27	Be-ḥukkotai	Levit. 26:3–27:34	Jeremiah 16:19–17:14
28	S	28	Jerusalem Day		

*Observed April 7, to avoid conflict with the Sabbath.

Italics are for Sephardi Minhag.

1995, May 30–June 28]   SIWAN (30 DAYS)   [5755

Civil Date	Day of the Week	Jewish Date	SABBATHS, FESTIVALS, FASTS	PENTATEUCHAL READING	PROPHETICAL READING
May 30	T	Siwan 1	New Moon	Num. 28:1–15	
June 3	Sa	5	Be-midbar	Num. 1:1–4:20	Hosea 2:1–22
4	S	6	Shavu'ot, first day	Exod. 19:1–20:23 Num. 28:26–31	Ezekiel 1:1–28 3:12
5	M	7	Shavu'ot, second day	Deut. 15:19–16:17 Num. 28:26–31	Habbakuk 3:1–19 *Habbakuk 2:20–3:19*
10	Sa	12	Naso'	Num. 4:21–7:89	Judges 13:2–25
17	Sa	19	Be-ha'alotekha	Num. 8:1–12:16	Zechariah 2:14–4:7
24	Sa	26	Shelaḥ lekha	Num. 13:1–15:41	Joshua 2:1–24
28	W	30	New Moon, first day	Num. 28:1–15	

Italics are for
Sephardi Minhag.

1995, June 29–July 27] TAMMUZ (29 DAYS) [5755

Civil Date	Day of the Week	Jewish Date	SABBATHS, FESTIVALS, FASTS	PENTATEUCHAL READING	PROPHETICAL READING
June 29	Th	Tammuz 1	New Moon, second day	Num. 28:1–15	
July 1	Sa	3	Korah	Num. 16:1–18:32	I Samuel 11:14–12:22
8	Sa	10	Hukkat	Num. 19:1–22:1	Judges 11:1–33
15	Sa	17	Balak	Num. 22:2–25:9	Micah 5:6–6:8
16	S	18	Fast of 17th of Tammuz	Exod. 32:11–14 34:1–10 (morning and afternoon)	Isaiah 55:6–56:8 (afternoon only)
22	Sa	24	Pinehas	Num. 25:10–30:1	Jeremiah 1:1–2:3

1995, July 28–Aug. 26]   AV (30 DAYS)   [5755

Civil Date	Day of the Week	Jewish Date	SABBATHS, FESTIVALS, FASTS	PENTATEUCHAL READING	PROPHETICAL READING
July 28	F	Av 1	New Moon	Num. 28:1–15	
29	Sa	2	Maṭṭot, Mas'e	Num. 30:2–36:13	Jeremiah 2:4–28 3:4 *Jeremiah 2:4–28 4:1–2*
Aug. 5	Sa	9	Devarim (Shabbat Ḥazon)	Deut. 1:1–3:22	Isaiah 1:1–27
6	S	10	Fast of 9th of Av	Morning: Deut. 4:25–40 Afternoon: Exod. 32:11–4 34:1–10	(Lamentations is read the night before) Jeremiah 8:13–9:23 (morning) Isaiah 55:6–56:8 (afternoon)
12	Sa	16	Wa-ethannan (Shabbat Naḥamu)	Deut. 3:23–7:11	Isaiah 40:1–26
19	Sa	23	'Ekev	Deut. 7:12–11:25	Isaiah 49:14–51:3
26	Sa	30	Re'eh; New Moon, first day	Deut. 11:26–16:17 Num. 28:9–15	Isaiah 66:1–24 I Samuel 20:18,42

Italics are for Sephardi Minhag.

1995, Aug. 27–Sept. 24]   ELUL (29 DAYS)   [5755

Civil Date	Day of the Week	Jewish Date	SABBATHS, FESTIVALS, FASTS	PENTATEUCHAL READING	PROPHETICAL READING
Aug. 27	S	Elul 1	New Moon, second day	Num. 28:1–15	
Sept. 2	Sa	7	Shofeṭim	Deut. 16:18–21:9	Isaiah 51:12–52:12
9	Sa	14	Ki teze'	Deut. 21:10–25:19	Isaiah 54:1–55:5
16	Sa	21	Ki tavo'	Deut. 26:1–29:8	Isaiah 60:1–22
23	Sa	28	Niẓẓavim	Deut. 29:9–30:20	Isaiah 61:10–63:9

Civil Date	Day of the Week	Jewish Date	SABBATHS, FESTIVALS, FASTS	PENTATEUCHAL READING	PROPHETICAL READING
Sept. 25	M	Tishri 1	Rosh Ha-shanah, first day	Gen. 21:1–34 Num. 29:1–6	I Samuel 1:1–2:10
26	T	2	Rosh Ha-shanah, second day	Gen. 22:1–24 Num. 29:1–6	Jeremiah 31:2–20
27	W	3	Fast of Gedaliah	Exod. 32:11–14 34:1–10 (morning and afternoon)	Isaiah 55:6–56:8 (afternoon only)
30	Sa	6	Wa-yelekh (Shabbat Shuvah)	Deut. 31:1–30	Hosea 14:2–10 Micah 7:18–20 Joel 2:15–27 *Hosea 14:2–10* *Micah 7:18–20*
Oct. 4	W	10	Yom Kippur	Morning: Levit. 16:1–34 Num. 29:7–11 Afternoon: Levit. 18:1–30	Isaiah 57:14–58:14 Jonah 1:1–4:11 Micah 7:18–20
7	Sa	13	Ha'azinu	Deut. 32:1–52	II Samuel 22:1–51
9	M	15	Sukkot, first day	Levit. 22:26–23:44 Num. 29:12–16	Zechariah 14:1–21
10	T	16	Sukkot, second day	Levit. 22:26–23:44 Num. 29:12–16	I Kings 8:2–21
11–14	W–Sa	17–20	Ḥol Ha-mo'ed	W Num. 29:17–25 Th Num. 29:20–28 F Num. 29:23–31 Sa Exod. 33:12– 34:26 Num. 29:26–34	Ezekiel 38:18–39:16
15	S	21	Hosha'na'Rabbah	Num. 29:26–34	
16	M	22	Shemini 'Aẓeret	Deut. 14:22–16:17 Num. 29:35–30:1	I Kings 8:54–66
17	T	23	Simḥat Torah	Deut. 33:1–34:12 Gen. 1:1–2:3 Num. 29:35–30:1	Joshua 1:1–18 *Joshua 1:1–9*
21	Sa	27	Be-re'shit	Gen. 1:1–6:8	Isaiah 42:5–43:10 *Isaiah 42:5–21*
24	T	30	New Moon, first day	Num. 28:1–15	

Italics are for
Sephardi Minhag.

1995, Oct. 25–Nov. 23]   ḤESHWAN (30 DAYS)   [5756

Civil Date	Day of the Week	Jewish Date	SABBATHS, FESTIVALS, FASTS	PENTATEUCHAL READING	PROPHETICAL READING
Oct. 25	W	Ḥeshwan 1	New Moon, second day	Num. 28:1–15	
28	Sa	4	Noaḥ	Gen. 6:9–11:32	Isaiah 54:1–55:5 *Isaiah 54:1–10*
Nov. 4	Sa	11	Lekh lekha	Gen. 12:1–17:27	Isaiah 40:27–41:16
11	Sa	18	Wa-yera'	Gen. 18:1–22:24	II Kings 4:1–37 *II Kings 4:1–23*
18	Sa	25	Ḥayye Sarah	Gen. 23:1–25:18	I Kings 1:1–31
23	Th	30	New Moon, first day	Num. 28:1–15	

*Italics are for
Sephardi Minhag.*

1995, Nov. 24–Dec. 23]   KISLEW (30 DAYS)   [5756

Civil Date	Day of the Week	Jewish Date	SABBATHS, FESTIVALS, FASTS	PENTATEUCHAL READING	PROPHETICAL READING
Nov. 24	F	Kislew 1	New Moon, second day	Num. 28:1–15	
25	Sa	2	Toledot	Gen. 25:19–28:9	Malachi 1:1–2:7
Dec. 2	Sa	9	Wa-yeze'	Gen. 28:10–32:3	Hosea 12:13–14:10 *Hosea 11:7–12:12*
9	Sa	16	Wa-yishlah	Gen. 32:4–36:43	Hosea 11:7–12:12 *Obadiah 1:1–21*
16	Sa	23	Wa-yeshev	Gen. 37:1–40:23	Amos 2:6–3:8
18	M–F	25–29	Hanukkah, first to fifth days	M Num. 7:1–17 T Num. 7:18–29 W Num. 7:24–35 Th Num. 7:30–41 F Num. 7:36–47	
23	Sa	30	Mi-kez; New Moon, first day; Hanukkah, sixth day	Gen. 41:1–44:17 Num. 28:9–15 Num. 7:42–47	Zechariah 2:14–4:7

Italics are for Sephardi Minhag.

1995, Dec. 24–Jan. 21, 1996] ṬEVET (29 DAYS) [5756

Civil Date	Day of the Week	Jewish Date	SABBATHS, FESTIVALS, FASTS	PENTATEUCHAL READING	PROPHETICAL READING
Dec. 24	S	Ṭevet 1	New Moon, second day; Hanukkah, seventh day	Num. 28:1–15 Num. 7:48–53	
25	M	2	Hanukkah, eighth day	Num. 7:54–8:4	
30	Sa	7	Wa-yiggash	Gen. 44:18–47:27	Ezekiel 37:15–28
Jan. 2	T	10	Fast of 10th of Ṭevet	Exod. 32:11–14 Exod. 34:1–10 (morning and afternoon)	Isaiah 55:6–56:8 (afternoon only)
6	Sa	14	Wa-yeḥi	Gen. 47:28–50:26	I Kings 2:1–12
13	Sa	21	Shemot	Exod. 1:1–6:1	Isaiah 27:6–28:13 29:22–23 *Jeremiah 1:1–2:3*
20	Sa	28	Wa-'era'	Exod. 6:2–9:35	Ezekiel 28:25–29:21

Italics are for Sephardi Minhag.

SELECTED ARTICLES OF INTEREST IN RECENT VOLUMES OF THE AMERICAN JEWISH YEAR BOOK

624

OBITUARIES

Leo Baeck	By Max Gruenewald 59:478–82
Salo W. Baron	By Lloyd P. Gartner 91:544–554
Jacob Blaustein	By John Slawson 72:547–57
Martin Buber	By Seymour Siegel 67:37–43
Abraham Cahan	By Mendel Osherowitch 53:527–29
Albert Einstein	By Jacob Bronowski 58:480–85
Louis Finkelstein	By Abraham J. Karp 93:527–34
Felix Frankfurter	By Paul A. Freund 67:31–36
Louis Ginzberg	By Louis Finkelstein 56:573–79
Jacob Glatstein	By Shmuel Lapin 73:611–17
Sidney Goldmann	By Milton R. Konvitz 85:401–03
Hayim Greenberg	By Marie Syrkin 56:589–94
Abraham Joshua Heschel	By Fritz A. Rothschild 74:533–44
Horace Meyer Kallen	By Milton R. Konvitz 75:55–80
Mordecai Kaplan	By Ludwig Nadelmann 85:404–11
Herbert H. Lehman	By Louis Finkelstein 66:3–20
Judah L. Magnes	By James Marshall 51:512–15
Alexander Marx	By Abraham S. Halkin 56:580–88
Reinhold Niebuhr	By Seymour Siegel 73:605–10
Joseph Proskauer	By David Sher 73:618–28
Maurice Samuel	By Milton H. Hindus 74:545–53
Isaac Bashevis Singer	By Hillel Halkin 93:535-38
John Slawson	By Murray Friedman 91:555–558
Leo Strauss	By Ralph Lerner 76:91–97
Max Weinreich	By Lucy S. Dawidowicz 70:59–68
Chaim Weizmann	By Harry Sacher 55:462–69
Stephen S. Wise	By Philip S. Bernstein 51:515–18
Harry Austryn Wolfson	By Isadore Twersky 76:99–111

Index